THE PAPERS OF

WOODROW WILSON

VOLUME 12
1900-1902

SPONSORED BY THE WOODROW WILSON
FOUNDATION
AND PRINCETON UNIVERSITY

THE PAPERS OF

WOODROW
WILSON

ARTHUR S. LINK, *EDITOR*

JOHN WELLS DAVIDSON, DAVID W. HIRST, AND

JOHN E. LITTLE, *ASSOCIATE EDITORS*

JEAN MACLACHLAN, *CONTRIBUTING EDITOR*

M. HALSEY THOMAS, *CONSULTING EDITOR*

Volume 12 · 1900-1902

PRINCETON, NEW JERSEY

PRINCETON UNIVERSITY PRESS

1972

Printed in the United States of America
by Princeton University Press
Princeton, New Jersey

INTRODUCTION

THE opening of this volume finds Wilson deep in work on articles for the series in *Harper's Magazine*, "Colonies and Nation," which he revised and published as *A History of the American People* in 1902. Correspondence with the publisher chronicles nearly every stage of his work, while his letters to scholars and to the illustrator, Howard Pyle, yield considerable evidence of his methods of work and his attention to detail. While growing in maturity as an historian, Wilson for the first time thinks broadly about American historical writing and what further work needs to be done. All the while, his increasing eminence in the profession is reflected in an invitation from President Gilman to succeed Herbert Baxter Adams as Professor of American and Institutional History at The John Hopkins University, and by an invitation to contribute to the "American Nation Series" now being planned for Harper and Brothers by Albert Bushnell Hart of Harvard University.

The documents in this volume also disclose a man come to national stature in affairs, affirming America's civilizing mission as a great power while ardently defending the right of anti-imperialists who disagreed with him to speak and be heard. They show a leader of the faculty and a teacher idolized by students, and they shed much light, as earlier volumes have done, upon life in Princeton and the Wilson household.

The climax of this volume is a series of letters and documents which reveal in startling and complete detail the eruption of a crisis in the presidential leadership of Princeton University during the spring of 1902. The long-simmering discontent with President Patton's do-nothing, reactionary policies breaks out in full-scale rebellion among a group of faculty members and trustees. Wilson is at once drawn into the plans to take control of the university out of Patton's hands. Documents from the Wilson Papers, the Papers of Cyrus H. McCormick, a leader of the anti-Patton trustees, and other sources enable us to follow developments from day to day to their unexpected dénouement, Patton's resignation and Wilson's election as thirteenth President of Princeton University.

This volume marks the end of the seminal period of Wilson's boyhood, education, and career as a teacher and scholar. It also signals the beginning of the next important stage, the presidency of Princeton, just as he was entering those "richly contemplative years" when he planned to write his long-projected magnum opus, "The Philosophy of Politics."

Volume 13 will consist of a cumulative table of contents and comprehensive index of the first twelve volumes of *The Papers of Woodrow Wilson*. It obviously cannot be completed until the page proofs of Volume 12 are in hand. Volumes 14 and 15, which are now in production, may well appear before Volume 13, but the latter will not be long delayed.

Readers are again reminded that *The Papers of Woodrow Wilson* is a continuing series; that persons, institutions, and events that figure prominently in earlier volumes are not re-identified in subsequent ones; and that the Index to each volume gives cross references to fullest earlier identifications.

We are grateful to Mrs. Bryant Putney of Princeton University Press for continued help in copyediting; to Miss Marjorie Sirlouis and Colonel James B. Rothnie, U.S.A., Ret., for deciphering Wilson's shorthand; to Professor Lewis L. Gould of the University of Texas at Austin for very generous help in finding Wilson letters in various collections at the Dallas Historical Society and the University of Texas at Austin; and to Professor David S. Patterson of Rice University for information about discussions between various peace workers and President Wilson.

THE EDITORS

Princeton, New Jersey
January 11, 1972

CONTENTS

Introduction, vii
Illustrations, xix
Abbreviations and Symbols, xxi

The Papers, September 17, 1900–July 4, 1902

Announcement of Wilson's Plans for a European Trip in 1901-1902, 51; Cancellation of the Trip, 104
Article by Robert Bridges, "President Woodrow Wilson," New York *Review of Reviews*, 468
Class Report in Professor Herbert Baxter Adams's Course, "History of Politics," at The Johns Hopkins University, Nov. 19, 1884, 480
Conferral of a Litt.D. Degree upon Wilson at the Yale Bicentennial, 193
Editorial Note
    The Crisis in Presidential Leadership at Princeton, 289
Inscription to Wilson by Andrew Fleming West, 402
Interview with Wilson About His Views on State Laws to Suppress Anarchy, 187
Letters from James Waddel Alexander to Cyrus Hall McCormick, 321, 354
Letters from Cornelius Cuyler Cuyler to Cyrus Hall McCormick, 316, 318, 323, 329, 371, 372, 378, 394, 473
Letters from Henry Burchard Fine to David Benton Jones, 364, 373
Letter from A. S. Hammond to David Benton Jones, 366
Letter from Bayard Henry to Cyrus Hall McCormick, 379
Letter from Jenny Davidson Hibben to Ellen Axson Wilson, 407
Letter from Thomas Alexander Hoyt to Ellen Axson Wilson, 444
Letters from David Benton Jones to Cyrus Hall McCormick, 303, 363, 366, 373, 376, 380, 384
Letters from David Benton Jones to Francis Landey Patton, 377, 388
Letter from David Benton Jones to Moses Taylor Pyne, 386
Letter from Cyrus Hall McCormick to James Waddel Alexander, 344
Letter from Cyrus Hall McCormick to Grover Cleveland, 315
Letters from Cyrus Hall McCormick to Cornelius Cuyler Cuyler, 316, 319, 377, 383, 397, 478
Letter from Cyrus Hall McCormick to Bayard Henry, 383
Letters from Cyrus Hall McCormick to David Benton Jones, 297, 305, 340
Letters from Cyrus Hall McCormick to Simon John McPherson, 346, 368, 372
Letters from Cyrus Hall McCormick to Francis Landey Patton, 308, 343, 349, 367, 395
Letters from Cyrus Hall McCormick to Moses Taylor Pyne, 349, 367, 374, 395
Letters from Simon John McPherson to Cyrus Hall McCormick, 324, 347, 368
Letter from an Old-Fashioned Democrat to the Editor of the *Indianapolis News*, 356
Letter from Francis Landey Patton to James Waddel Alexander, 319

Letters from Francis Landey Patton to David Benton Jones, 388 (2)
Letters from Francis Landey Patton to Cyrus Hall McCormick, 327, 356, 395
Letter from Annie Bliss Perry to Ellen Axson Wilson, 405
Letter from Moses Taylor Pyne to David Benton Jones, 386
Letters from Moses Taylor Pyne to Cyrus Hall McCormick, 355, 381, 479
Letter from Frederick A. Steuert to Cornelius Cuyler Cuyler, 355, 383
Letter from Frederick A. Steuert to Bayard Henry, 344
Letters from Frederick A. Steuert to David Benton Jones, 355, 359
Letter from Frederick A. Steuert to Cyrus Hall McCormick, 371
Letter from Stephen van Rensselaer Trowbridge to John Norris Miller, 155
Letter from William Royal Wilder to Robert Randolph Henderson, 412
Letter from Ellen Axson Wilson to Florence Stevens Hoyt, 463
Letter from Ellen Axson Wilson to Thomas L. Snow, 146
Letters from Wilson to
    Andrew Varick Stout Anthony, 439
    Thomas Randolph Ball, 266
    Daniel Moreau Barringer, 434, 456
    Sarah Baxter Bird, 66, 437
    Charles Bradley, 51, 58
    Robert Bridges, 65, 139, 206, 239, 294, 436, 462, 467, 478
    Nicholas Murray Butler, 436
    Edward Perkins Clark, 427
    Lucian Howard Cocke, 70
    Varnum Lansing Collins, 196, 208
    Josephine Hunt Cutter, 192 (2)
    Richard Heath Dabney, 92
    Cleveland Hoadley Dodge, 434
    Laura Bowman Elder, 355
    Edward Graham Elliott, 3, 73, 119, 159, 162, 195, 381
    Richard Theodore Ely, 264, 434
    David Fentress, 457
    James Gayley, 467
    John Franklin Genung, 143
    Joseph Bensen Gilder, 264
    Richard Watson Gilder, 38, 48, 67, 84, 86, 427
    Basil Lanneau Gildersleeve, 271
    Daniel Coit Gilman, 110, 174
    Edward Herrick Griffin, 347
    William Gardner Hale, 90
    Joseph Henry Harper, 233
    William Rainey Harper, 111
    Harper and Brothers, 134
    Albert Bushnell Hart, 231
    George Brinton McClellan Harvey, 232
    Azel Washburn Hazen, 137
    Robert Randolph Henderson, 144, 433
    Miss Hillard, 21
    Edward Washburn Hopkins, 434
    Houghton, Mifflin and Company, 113, 138

Rebecca Caroline Webb Hoyt, 204
Eleanor Varnum Mitchell Hutton, 460
Laurence Hutton, 92, 101, 460
Edward Ingle, 102, 163, 171, 440
Mrs. Alexander F. Jameson, 206
John Franklin Jameson, 427
Robert Underwood Johnson, 158, 444
David Benton Jones, 298
Thomas Davies Jones, 326
Alexander James Kerr, 433
Charles Williston McAlpin, 160, 161, 380
Cyrus Hall McCormick, 133, 146, 234, 302, 314, 322, 330
Isaac Wayne MacVeagh, 453
William Nelson, 143
Thomas Nelson Page, 230, 428
Walter Hines Page, 435
Bliss Perry, 3
President and Board of Trustees of Princeton University, 27
Howard Pyle, 31, 39, 97, 103, 117
Rector of the University of Halle, 30
Edith Gittings Reid, 82, 196, 198, 272, 283, 397
Richard Austin Rice, 157
Noah Cornwell Rogers, 203
Theodore Roosevelt, 172
Thomas L. Snow, 370
Edward Otis Stanley, 440
Frederick A. Steuert, 346
Burton Egbert Stevenson, 113
Charles Andrew Talcott, 205
Charles Franklin Thwing, 467
Frederick Jackson Turner, 239, 436
Lyon Gardiner Tyler, 68
Unidentified Person, 189
Henry van Dyke, 195
Beverly Randolph Wellford, Jr., 457
Harriet Woodrow Welles, 462
Barrett Wendell, 428
Ellen Axson Wilson, 74, 80, 118, 120, 122, 125, 126, 128, 390
James Wilson Woodrow, 172
James Woodrow, 88
Letters to Wilson from
  Henry Mills Alden, 5, 22, 23, 27, 37, 40, 41, 49, 60, 69, 85, 90, 91, 94, 112, 134
  Samuel Alexander, 455
  Andrew Varick Stout Anthony, 439
  Stockton Axson, 117
  Daniel Moreau Barringer, 430, 451
  A. Elizabeth Wilson Begges, 414
  Sarah Baxter Bird, 59
  John Albert Blair, 271
  Max Boucard, 81
  Clarence Valentine Boyer, 459

Charles Bradley, 50
Alexander Scott Bullitt, 405
John Alexander Campbell, 227
Jesse Benedict Carter, 466
Lucian Howard Cocke, 69
Frank Moore Colby, 87
Varnum Lansing Collins, 194
Jabez Lamar Monroe Curry, 448
Cornelius Cuyler Cuyler, 323
Frederick Morgan Davenport, 442
Alfred Lewis Dennis, Jr., 403
George Hutcheson Denny, 306
Samuel Bayard Dod, 457
Cleveland Hoadley Dodge, 66
William Earl Dodge, 58
Franklin Woolman D'Olier, 452
Edith Duer, 409
William Archibald Dunning, 403
Edward Graham Elliott, 31, 85, 109, 134, 160, 369, 431
Richard Theodore Ely, 402
Robert Erskine Ely, 293
Robert Ewing, 424
David Fentress, 438
John Franklin Fort, 454
Abel McIver Fraser, 404
William Goodell Frost, 308
James Gayley, 458
Richard Watson Gilder, 48
Basil Lanneau Gildersleeve, 271
Daniel Coit Gilman, 108, 112, 447
Harold Godwin, 404
Elgin Ralston Lovell Gould, 430
William Gardner Hale, 79
Abram Woodruff Halsey, 193
Joseph Henry Harper, 230
Harper and Brothers, 142, 146, 155, 206, 207, 234, 267, 284, 307, 313
Abram Winegardner Harris, 443
Albert Bushnell Hart, 229, 404
George Brinton McClellan Harvey, 230, 234
Azel Washburn Hazen, 132, 413
Daniel Collamore Heath, 419
Job Elmer Hedges, 114
Robert Randolph Henderson, 431
John Bell Henneman, 425
Bayard Henry, 382, 393
Jenny Davidson Hibben, 76, 163, 394
John Grier Hibben, 35, 77
Franklin William Hooper, 301
Walter Ewing Hope, 266
Houghton, Mifflin and Company, 265
Annie Wilson Howe, 130, 147

George Howe III, 25, 149
James Alfred Hoyt, 425
Laurence Hutton, 101, 407
Edward Ingle, 94, 164
William Burhans Isham, Jr., 407
Thomas Armstrong Jacobs, 438
Adrian Hoffman Joline, 409
David Benton Jones, 288, 294, 304, 310, 312, 317, 321
Thomas Davies Jones, 322
Frank Hathaway Kemper, 409
William Blake Kennedy, 24, 32
Orin Grant Libby, 102, 446
Edgar Odell Lovett, 402
Mary Gresham Machen, 465
William Francis Magie, 448
Charles Williston McAlpin, 159, 370, 375, 378
Alfred James Pollock McClure, 410
John James McCook, 437
Cyrus Hall McCormick, 133, 144, 228, 297, 305, 315, 339
Charles Wolf McFee, 413
Charles Howard McIlwain, 452
St. Clair McKelway, 449
John Bach McMaster, 284
Charles White Merrill, 174, 190, 200
Elmer Truesdale Merrill, 414
James Cowden Meyers, 411
Hugh Gordon Miller, 306
John Norris Miller, 96, 107, 154
Franklin Murphy, 454
David Murray, 445
William Nelson, 141
Charles Richard Nisbet, 432
Frank Mason North, 408
Walter Hines Page, 88
Francis Landey Patton, 26, 97, 376, 461
John H. Pearson, 415
William Battle Phillips, 442
Bowdre Phinizy, 416
Francis Southmayd Phraner, 411
George Walter Prothero, 313, 443
Howard Pyle, 29, 38, 39, 95, 103, 115
Moses Taylor Pyne, 441
Percy Rivington Pyne, 445
Edith Gittings Reid, 81, 197, 199, 453
Legh Wilbur Reid, 412
Ira Remsen, 447
James Ford Rhodes, 465
Richard Austin Rice, 156
William Henry Roberts, 446
Charles H. Robinson, 71
Henry Edward Rood, 60
Theodore Roosevelt, 164, 454

Albert Shaw, 416
Charles Howard Shinn, 437
Thomas L. Snow, 49, 73
James Sprunt, 72, 419
Edward Otis Stanley, 426
William G. Starr, 305
Bernard Christian Steiner, 412
Frederick A. Steuert, 344, 345
George Black Stewart, 435
Alois P. Swoboda, 190
Charles Andrew Talcott, 408
James Monroe Taylor, 294
Augustus Thomas, Francis Hopkinson Smith, and Robert Under-
    wood Johnson, 93
Nancy Saunders Toy, 458
Frederick Jackson Turner, 473
Henry van Dyke, 408
Louis Clark Vanuxem, 416
James Edward Webb, 106
Harriet Woodrow Welles, 417
Beverley Randolph Wellford, Jr., 433
William Royal Wilder, 441
Jesse Lynch Williams, 456
Joseph Ruggles Wilson, 52, 91
Ellen Axson Wilson, 75, 78, 118, 119, 121, 123, 125, 127, 129,
    131, 392
Joseph R. Wilson, Jr., 105
Caleb Thomas Winchester, 314
George Parker Winship, 65
Helen Sill Woodrow, 418
James Woodrow, 417
James Wilson Woodrow, 104, 171
Edward Augustus Woods, 157, 189
Lawrence Crane Woods, 420
Memorandum on Leadership, 365
News Item About the Princeton Historical Association, 4
News Item About Wilson as President Gilman's Possible Successor
    at the Johns Hopkins, 35
News Item About Wilson's Appointment to a Committee of New
    Brunswick Presbytery, 328
News Item About Wilson's Appointment to the New Jersey State
    Commission to Secure Uniformity of Laws, 173
Preface by Léon Duguit to the French Edition of *The State*, 241
Princeton Alumni Meetings and Addresses
    Notes for a Talk to the Alumni of St. Louis, Mo., 200; Report, 202
    Report of an Annual Banquet of the Alumni Association of North-
        eastern Pennsylvania, Wilkes-Barre, Pa., 231
    Notes for a Talk, "The University and the Country,—the Age," to
        the Alumni of Union County, N.J., 301; Report, 312
    Notes for an After-Dinner Talk, "The Ideal Princeton Student," to
        the Princeton Club of Trenton, N.J., 325; Report, 325
    Report of a Speech to the Princeton Club of Chicago, Ill., 348

Report of a Speech at an Annual Alumni Luncheon at Princeton University, 420

Princeton University: Documentary and Course Material

Minutes of the Princeton University Faculty, 23, 155, 185, 191, 205, 207, 230, 235, 256, 286, 307, 326 (2), 329, 331

News Items About Wilson's Absence from Classes, 44, 80; Resumption of Classes, 51

Minutes of the Board of Trustees of Princeton University, 156, 192, 287, 398, 413

Memorandum on the Formation of a Faculty-Trustee Committee, 300, 310

Memorandum on Proposed Changes in the Curriculum, 391

Princeton University: Meetings and Addresses

Notes for an Address to the American Whig and Cliosophic Societies, 23; Report, 24

Citation by Wilson for an Honorary Degree, 28

Announcement of a Talk to the Philadelphian Society, 33; Notes for the Talk, "The Principle of Rectitude," 33; Report, 34

Report of a Speech at a *Daily Princetonian* Banquet, 99

News Items About a Princeton-Yale Debate, 100, 115

News Item About a Whig Hall Smoker, 108

Report of a Lecture, "Alexis de Tocqueville," to the Monday Night Club, 111

Memorandum on Wilson's Introduction of Grover Cleveland at Alexander Hall, 114; Report of Cleveland's Stafford Little Lectures on the Venezuelan Boundary Dispute, 116

Announcement of an Address to the 1904 Class Prayer Meeting, 132

News Item About a Princeton-Harvard Debate, 132

Announcement of a Banquet of the University Press Club, 138; Notes for a Talk, "The College Man in Journalism," 139

Report of an Address, "Gladstone," to the Philadelphian Society, 139

Report of an Annual Banquet of the *Nassau Literary Magazine*, 140

Report of the 154th Commencement Exercises, 158

Remarks at a University Convocation on the Assassination of President McKinley, 185

Notes for a Religious Talk to the Philadelphian Society, 273; Report, 273

Notes for an After-Dinner Talk at a *Daily Princetonian* Board Banquet, 285; Report, 285

Announcement of a Vesper Service to Be Conducted by Wilson, 286; Notes for His Chapel Talk, 286

Report of a Hall Smoker, 303

Report of a Princeton-Harvard Debate, 311

Report of a Lecture, "Sir Henry Maine," to the Monday Night Club, 330

Report of a Speech at a *Nassau Literary Magazine* Banquet, 368

Report of the 155th Commencement Exercises, 422

Public Lectures and Addresses

Notes for an Address, "Americanism," at the New-Century Club, Wilmington, Del., 41; Report, 42

Notes for a Lecture, "Self-Government," to the Women's Club, Waterbury, Conn., 44; Report, 46

Report of a Speech to the New England Society in the City of New York, N.Y., 52

Announcement of Future Lecture Engagements, 67

Announcement of a Series of Lectures to the American Society for the Extension of University Teaching in Philadelphia, 71

Report of an Address, "Americanism," at the Lawrenceville, N.J., School, 98

Notes for a Speech to the St. Nicholas Society, New York, N.Y., 124

Announcement of a Lecture, "Patriotism," to the Lyceum Association, Greenville, S. C., 203; Report, 204

Address, "The Ideals of America," Commemorating the 125th Anniversity of the Battle of Trenton, N.J., 208; Presentation to Wilson of a Testimonial Pitcher, 463

Report of a Lecture, "What It Means to Be an American," in Reading, Pa., 238

Report of a Speech, "Patriotism," to the Woman's Club, Worcester, Mass., 258

Report of a Lecture, "What It means to Be an American," to the Peninsula Twentieth Century Club, Fort Monroe, Va., 265

Report of a Speech at a Lincoln's Birthday Dinner of the Lincoln Association of Jersey City, N.J., 267

Presentation Address to Retiring President Daniel Coit Gilman at the Inauguration of Ira Remsen as President of The Johns Hopkins University, 274; Reports of the Inauguration Ceremonies, 278, 280

Notes for a Talk to the Alumni of the University of Virginia in New York, N.Y., 328

Notes for an Address, "The Man and the Man of Letters," at Lake Forest College, Chicago, Ill., 348

Announcement of Wilson's Arrival in Indianapolis, Ind., to Address the Contemporary Club, 349; Report of His Address, "What It Means to Be an American," 351

Report of an Address, "The Teaching of Patriotism in the Schools," at the Benjamin Harrison School, Indianapolis, Ind., 350

Report of a Founder's Day Address, "Americanism," at Vassar College, Poughkeepsie, N.Y., 359

Report of Remarks at a Meeting of the Village Improvement Society of Princeton, N.J., 384

Report of an Address, "Religion and Patriotism," at the Northfield, Mass., Student Conference, 474

Table of Contents for a Collection of Essays, 84

Telegrams

Cornelius Cuyler Cuyler to Cyrus Hall McCormick, 370, 372

David Benton Jones to Cyrus Hall McCormick, 343 (2)

Cyrus Hall McCormick to Cornelius Cuyler Cuyler, 319, 371

Cyrus Hall McCormick to David Benton Jones, 340

Cyrus Hall McCormick to Wilson, 345

Harriet Hammond McCormick to Wilson, 141

Moses Taylor Pyne to Cyrus Hall McCormick, 397

Testimonial by Wilson to Professor Francis Henry Smith of the University of Virginia, 287
Writings
"Democracy and Efficiency," 6
"Editor's Study" (An Historical Commentary and Critique), 60
Introduction to *The Autobiography of Benjamin Franklin*, 164
"The Real Idea of Democracy," 175
"The Significance of American History," 179

ILLUSTRATIONS

Following page 162

Wilson at the time of his election as President of Princeton
Princeton University Library

President Patton in 1902
Princeton University Archives

Grover Cleveland
Princeton University Library

James Waddel Alexander
Princeton University Library

Cyrus Hall McCormick
State Historical Society of Wisconsin

David Benton Jones
Princeton University Library

Moses Taylor Pyne
Princeton University Archives

Cornelius Cuyler Cuyler
Princeton University Archives

Henry van Dyke
Princeton University Archives

William Francis Magie
Princeton University Archives

Stockton Axson
Princeton University Archives

John Huston Finley
Princeton University Archives

A recently discovered photograph of Ellen Louise Axson as a young girl
Library of Congress

Edith Gittings Reid
Library of Congress

TEXT ILLUSTRATIONS

The shorthand draft of one section of Wilson's essay, "Democracy and Efficiency," which he pasted on cards for easy copying, 21

A page of the manuscript of Chapter II of "A History of the American People," showing Wilson's emendations and additions to the "Harper's" article, 135

The final page of Wilson's own typescript of "A History of the American People," 429

ABBREVIATIONS

ALI	autograph letter initialed
ALS	autograph letter(s) signed
att(s).	attached, attachment(s)
CCL	carbon copy of letter
EAW	Ellen Axson Wilson
enc(s).	enclosed, enclosure(s)
env.	envelope
hw	handwriting, handwritten
L	letter
PL	printed letter
S	signed
sh	shorthand
T	typed
TCL	typed copy of letter
TLS	typed letter signed
WW	Woodrow Wilson
WWhw	Woodrow Wilson handwriting, handwritten
WWsh	Woodrow Wilson shorthand
WWT	Woodrow Wilson typed
WWTLS	Woodrow Wilson typed letter signed

ABBREVIATIONS FOR COLLECTIONS AND LIBRARIES

Following the National Union Catalog of the Library of Congress

CtY	Yale University Library
DLC	Library of Congress
FTU	University of Tampa Library
ICU	University of Chicago Library
MdBJ	The Johns Hopkins University Library
MdHi	Maryland Historical Society, Baltimore
MH	Harvard University Library
NcD	Duke University Library
NjHi	New Jersey Historical Society, Newark
NjP	Princeton University Library
NN	New York Public Library
NNC	Columbia University Library
PHi	Historical Society of Pennsylvania, Philadelphia
PPiUS	United States Steel Corporation Archives, Pittsburgh
RSB Coll., DCL	Ray Stannard Baker Collection of Wilsoniana, Library of Congress
UA, NjP	University Archives, Princeton University Library
ViU	University of Virginia Library
ViW	College of William and Mary Library
WC, NjP	Woodrow Wilson Collection, Princeton University
WHi	State Historical Society of Wisconsin, Madison
WP, DLC	Woodrow Wilson Papers, Library of Congress
WU	University of Wisconsin Library

[Sept. 26, 1900]	publication date of a published writing; also date of document when date is not part of text
[*Oct. 1, 1900*]	latest composition date of a published writing
[[Oct. 20, 1900]]	delivery date of a speech if publication date differs

THE PAPERS OF
WOODROW WILSON

VOLUME 12
1900-1902

THE PAPERS OF
WOODROW WILSON

To Edward Graham Elliott

Princeton, New Jersey,
17 September, 1900.

My dear Mr. Elliott,

Your letter of the sixth reached me this morning.[1] The reasons you give for going first to Berlin, instead of to Heidelberg, seem excellent; and there is no sufficient reason why you should not take the places in the order named.[2] The sequence is of no particular significance; and you can judge much better than I could at this distance.

My sister[3] writes me very entertaining and delightful details of your experiences in Hasserode.[4] I wish I could look in upon your circle and enjoy some of it.

I write this in haste to catch the next steamer.

With regards and best wishes,

Sincerely Yours,   Woodrow Wilson

WWTLS (WC, NjP).

[1] It is missing.

[2] Elliott had just gone to Germany to obtain a Ph.D. in political science and jurisprudence. Wilson not only had agreed to advise him on his program of study abroad but also had arranged for financial support for him from a wealthy Princeton alumnus, John Lambert Cadwalader of New York. There was an understanding among Wilson, President Patton, and Elliott that the latter would return to Princeton after receiving his degree to assist Wilson in his courses. See J. L. Cadwalader to WW, July 9, 1900, n. 1, Vol. 11, and the correspondence between Wilson and Elliott subsequent to that date, also in *ibid*.

[3] Annie Wilson (Mrs. George) Howe, Jr., who had accompanied her son George to Germany, where he was studying for the Ph.D. in classics at the University of Halle.

[4] Her letter is missing.

Two Letters to Bliss Perry

My dear Perry,   Princeton, New Jersey, 17 September, 1900.

We reached home on Saturday night;[1] and this is to say that, since getting to my desk dutiful thoughts have returned to me again, and that I mean to devote the next two weeks of writing time to "Democracy and Efficiency."[2] I think, therefore, that I can promise to send it to you not much if at all later than October first; in which case I shall feel like a good boy, restored to the good graces of his own conscience.

We have been deeply distressed to hear of Mrs. Perry's and the childrens' illness. Pray write us that they are getting well and strong. It seems a strange Princeton without you all.[3]

With warmest regards from us all,

Cordially and faithfully Yours,   Woodrow Wilson

WWTLS (B. Perry Papers, MH).

  [1] From Judd Haven, Muskoka district, Ontario, where the Wilsons had spent their summer vacation.

  [2] It is printed at Oct. 1, 1900.

  [3] The Perrys were now living at 4 Mercer Circle in Cambridge, Mass. Perry had recently resigned his professorship of English at Princeton to devote full time to his work as editor of the *Atlantic Monthly*.

My dear Perry,   Princeton, 18 Sept., 1900.

Thank you most heartily for letting me know that my article[1] has really been of use to you: it was thoughtful of you to think of telling me. I did not know that my last paragraph had a "bluggy" sound,—and am glad to have been set right with Mr. MacVeagh![2] Too bad he can't elucidate Louisiana for you![3] Hurrah for Mercer Circle, and for the delightful newcomers there!

As ever   Yours,   Woodrow Wilson

ALS (B. Perry Papers, MH).

  [1] "The Reconstruction of the Southern States," printed at March 2, 1900, Vol. 11.

  [2] This reference is mysterious. "Mr. MacVeagh" was Isaac Wayne MacVeagh (1833-1917), a prominent Pennsylvania politician, whom President Hayes sent to Louisiana in 1877 as head of a commission to settle an election dispute and arrange for the withdrawal of federal troops from New Orleans.

  [3] Wilson's article was to be the lead in a series on Reconstruction in the *Atlantic Monthly* in 1901. About this series, see WW to EAW, Feb. 25, 1900, n. 2., Vol. 11.

A News Report

[Sept. 26, 1900]

PRINCETON HISTORICAL ASSOCIATION.

Just before Commencement a number of friends of the University, who are interested both in the University Library and in local history, held a meeting to consider the advisability of forming a club or society for the purpose of publishing historical material relating to Princeton and New Jersey. A club was formed, under the name of the Princeton Historical Association, which will publish matter of a historical nature, especially documents and sources; and will develop the University Library collections for historical study and encourage research particularly with reference to Princeton and New Jersey.[1]

Mr. Taylor Pyne, Esq., was elected president of the association, and Dr. Ernest C. Richardson, the University Librarian, was made secretary.

It was decided to hold a meeting in October for complete organization, and Messrs. Henry W. Green, Francis B. Lee and V. L. Collins[2] were appointed a committee to submit plan and rules for work. A committee on publication, consisting of Gen. Wm. S. Stryker, William Nelson, Esq., Prof. Woodrow Wilson, and Junius S. Morgan, Esq.,[3] was also appointed at this meeting.

Others interested in the organization are, Messrs. William R. Weeks, Charles Scribner, George A. Armour, and John W. Garrett.[4]

It is expected that the first publication of the association, the Journal of Philip V. Fithian, mentioned in yesterday's issue of the *Daily Princetonian*, will be published in November.[5]

Printed in the *Daily Princetonian*, Sept. 26, 1900.

[1] The Princeton Historical Association was active at least until 1907.

[2] Henry Woodhull Green, Princeton, 1891, lawyer of Trenton and member of the Princeton University Board of Trustees; Francis Bazley Lee, lawyer and amateur historian of Trenton; and Varnum Lansing Collins, Princeton, 1892, Reference Librarian at Princeton University.

[3] William Scudder Stryker, Princeton, 1858, of Trenton, Adjutant General of New Jersey and President of the New Jersey Historical Society; William Nelson, lawyer of Paterson, N.J., prolific author and editor of the *New Jersey Archives*; and Junius Spencer Morgan, Princeton, 1888, Associate Librarian of Princeton University.

[4] William Raymond Weeks, corporation lawyer of New York and amateur historian; Charles Scribner, Princeton, 1875, publisher of New York; George Allison Armour, Princeton, 1877, a gentleman of leisure who resided in Princeton; and John Work Garrett, Princeton, 1895, at this time a partner in the banking firm of Robert Garrett & Sons of Baltimore.

[5] John Rogers Williams (ed.), *Philip Vickers Fithian: Journal and Letters, 1767-1774* (Princeton, N.J.: The University Library, 1900). In later years the Association published Fred Lewis Pattee (ed.), *The Poems of Philip Freneau, Poet of the American Revolution* (3 vols., Princeton, N.J.: The University Library, 1902-1907), and Varnum Lansing Collins (ed.), *A Brief Narrative of the Ravages of the British and Hessians at Princeton in 1776-77* (Princeton, N.J.: The University Library, 1906).

From Henry Mills Alden

My dear Mr Wilson,   New York City Sept. 26. 1900

We have just received the 4th part of the History[1]—for which payment will be sent promptly.

I have adopted your suggestion for title: *Colonies & Nation*: A Short History of the People of the United States. Mr [Howard] Pyle has made a Heading for the 1st Part, which will open the

January No. We have succeeded very well with the illustrations for that part & hope to do better with the second.

I have not yet taken my holiday, reserving it for the late autumn. I am very glad to hear that you have had a restful & invigorating outing.

With friendly regard   Yours always   H. M. Alden

ALS (WP, DLC).
¹ The fourth installment of Wilson's "Colonies and Nation," a series which was to be published in *Harper's Magazine* beginning in January 1901. For a discussion of this enterprise and its culmination, see the Editorial Note, "Wilson's History of the American People," Vol. 11.

A Political Essay

[*c. Oct. 1, 1900*]

DEMOCRACY AND EFFICIENCY.

It is no longer possible to mistake the reaction against democracy. The nineteenth century was above all others a century of democracy; and yet the world is no more convinced of the benefits of democracy as a form of government at its end than it was at its beginning. The history of closeted Switzerland has not been accepted as proving the stability of democratic institutions; the history of the United States has not been accepted as establishing their tendency to make governments just and liberal and pure. Their eccentric influence in France, their disastrous and revolutionary operation in South America, their power to intoxicate and their powerlessness to reform,—except where the states which use them have had in their training and environment what Switzerland or the colonies and commonwealths sprung from England have had, to strengthen and steady them,—have generally been deemed to offset every triumph or success they can boast. When we praise democracy, we are still put to our proofs; when we excuse its errors, we are understood to have admitted its failure.

There need be in this, however, no serious discouragement for us, whose democratic institutions have in all large things succeeded. It means nothing more than that the world is at last ready to accept the moral long ago drawn for it by de Tocqueville. He predicted the stability of the government of the United States, not because of its intrinsic excellence, but because of its suitability to the particular social, economic, and political conditions of the people and the country for whose use and administration it had been framed; because of the deliberation and sober sagacity with which it had been devised and set up; because it could reckon upon a sufficient "variety of information and excellence of discretion" on the part of the people who were to live under it to insure its intelligent operation; because he observed a certain uniformity of civilization to obtain throughout the country, and saw its affairs steadied by their fortunate separation from European politics; because he found a sober, religious habit of thought among our people, and a clear sense of right. Democracy was with us, he perceived, already a thing of principle and custom and nature, and our institutions admirably expressed our training and experience. No other people could expect to succeed by the same means, unless those means equally suited their character and stage of development. Democracy, like every other form of government, depended for its success upon qualities and conditions which it did not itself create, but only obeyed.

Many excellent suggestions, valid and applicable everywhere, we have given the world, with regard to the spirit in which government should be conducted. No doubt class privilege has been forever discredited because of our example. We have taught the world the principle of the general welfare as the object and end of government, rather than the prosperity of any class or section of the nation, or the preferment of any private or petty interest. We have made the law appear to all men an instrument wherewith to secure equality of rights and a protection which shall be without respect of persons. There can be no misgivings about the currency or the permanency of the *principles* of right which we have exalted. But we have not equally commended the forms or the organization of the government under which we live.

A federal union of diverse commonwealths we have indeed made to seem both practicable and efficient as a means of organizing government on a great scale, while preserving at the same time the utmost possible latitude and independence in local self-government. Germany, Canada, Australia, Switzerland herself, have built and strengthened their constitutions in large part upon our model. It would be hard to exaggerate the shock which has been given to old theories, or the impetus which has been given to hopeful experiment, in the field of political action, by our conspicuous successes as constitution-makers and reformers. But those successes have not been unlimited. We have not escaped the laws of error that government is heir to. It is said that riots and disorders are more frequent amongst us than in any other country of the same degree of civilization; justice is not always done in our courts; our institutions do not prevent, they do not seem even to moderate, contests between capital and labor; our laws of property are no more equitable, our laws of marriage no more moralizing, than those of undemocratic nations, our contemporaries; our cities are perhaps worse governed than any in Europe outside the Turkish Empire and Spain; crime defies or evades the law amongst us as amongst other peoples, less favored in matters of freedom and privilege; we have no monopoly either of happiness or of enlightened social order. As we grow older, we grow also perplexed and awkward in the doing of justice and in the perfecting and safeguarding of liberty. It is character and good principle, after all, which are to save us, if we are to escape disaster.

That moral is the justification of what we have attempted. It is for this that we love democracy: for the emphasis it puts on character; for its tendency to exalt the purposes of the average man to some high level of endeavor; for its just principle of common assent in matters in which all are concerned; for its ideals of duty and its sense of brotherhood. Its forms and institutions are meant to be subservient to these things. Democracy is merely the most radical form of "constitutional" government. A "constitutional" government is one in which there is a definite understanding as to the sphere and powers of government; one in which individual liberty is defined and guaranteed by specific safeguards, in which the authority and the functions of those who rule are limited and determined by unmistakable custom or explicit fundamental law. It is a government in which these understandings are kept up, alike in the making and in the execution of laws, by frequent conferences between those who govern and those who are governed. This is the purpose of representation: stated conference and a cordial agreement between those who govern and those who are governed. The process of the understanding is discussion,—public and continuous, and conducted by those who stand in the midst of affairs, at the official centre and seat of management, where affairs can be looked into and disposed with full knowledge and authority; those intrusted with government being present in person, the people by deputy.

Representative government has had its long life and excellent development, not in order that common opinion, the opinion of the street, might prevail, but in order that the best opinion, the opinion generated by the best possible methods of general counsel, might rule in affairs; in order that some sober and best opinion might be created, by thoughtful and responsible discussion conducted by men intimately informed concerning the public weal, and officially commissioned to look to its safeguarding and advancement,—by discussion in parliaments, discussion face to face between authoritative critics and responsible ministers of state.

This is the central object to which we have devoted our acknowledged genius for practical politics. During the first half century of our national life we seemed to have succeeded in an extraordinary degree in approaching our ideal, in organizing a nation for counsel and coöperation, and in moving forward with cordial unison and with confident and buoyant step toward the accomplishment of tasks and duties upon which all were agreed. Our later life has disclosed serious flaws, has even seemed ominous of pitiful failure, in some of the things we most prided ourselves upon having managed well: notably, in pure and efficient local government, in the successful organization of great cities, and in well-considered schemes of administration. The boss—a man elected by no votes, preferred by no open process of choice, occupying no office of responsibility—makes himself a veritable tyrant amongst us, and seems to cheat us of self-government; parties appear to hamper the movements of opinion rather than to give them form and means of expression; multitudinous voices of agitation, an infinite play of forces at cross-purpose, confuse us; and there seems to be no common counsel or definite union for action, after all.

We keep heart the while because still sure of our principles and of our ideals: the common weal, a common and cordial understanding in matters of government, secure private rights and yet concerted public action, a strong government and yet liberty also. We know what we have to do; what we have missed and mean to find; what we have lost and mean to recover; what we still strive after and mean to achieve. Democracy is a principle with us, not a mere form of government. What we have blundered at is its new applications and details, its successful combination with efficiency and purity in governmental action. We tell ourselves that our partial failure in these things has been due to our absorption in the tasks of material growth; that our practical genius has spent itself upon wealth and the organization of industry. But it is to be suspected that there are other elements in the singular fact. We have supposed that there could be one way of efficiency for democratic governments, and another for monarchical. We have declined to provide ourselves with a professional civil service, because we deemed it undemocratic; we have made shift to do without a trained diplomatic and consular service, because we thought the training given by other governments to their foreign agents unnecessary in the case of affairs so simple and unsophisticated as the foreign relations of a democracy in politics and trade,—transactions so frank, so open, so straightforward, interests so free from all touch of chicane or indirection; we have hesitated to put our presidents or governors or mayors into direct and responsible relations of leadership with our legislatures and councils in the making of laws and ordinances, because such a connection between lawmakers and executive officers seemed inconsistent with the theory of checks and balances whose realization in practice we understood Montesquieu to have proved essential to the maintenance of a free government. Our theory, in short, has paid as little heed to efficiency as our practice. It has been a theory of non-professionalism in public affairs; and in many great matters of public action non-professionalism is non-efficiency.

"If only we had our old leisure for domestic affairs, we should devise a way of our own to be efficient, consonant with our principles, characteristic of our genius for organization," we have heard men say. "How fatal it may prove to us that our attention has been called off from a task but half done to the tasks of the world, for which we have neither inclination nor proper training nor suitable organization,—from which, until now, we were so happily free! We shall now be forever barred from perfection, our own perfection, at home!" But may it not be that the future will put another face upon the matter, and show us our advantage where least we thought it to lie? May it not be that the way to perfection lies along these new paths of struggle, of discipline, and of achievement? What will the reaction of new duty be? What self-revelations will it afford; what lessons of unified will, of simplified method, of clarified purpose; what disclosures of the fundamental principles of right action, the efficient means of just achievement, if we but keep our ideals and our character?

At any rate, it is clear that we could not have held off. The affairs of the world stand in such a case, the principles for which we have battled the long decades through are now put in such jeopardy amidst the contests of nations, the future of mankind faces so great a peril of reactionary revolution, that our own private business must take its chances along with the greater business of the world at large. We dare not stand neutral. All mankind deem us the representatives of the moderate and sensible discipline which makes free men good citizens, of enlightened systems of law and a temperate justice, of the best experience in the reasonable methods and principles of self-government, of public force made consistent with individual liberty; and we shall not realize these ideals at home, if we suffer them to be hopelessly discredited amongst the peoples who have yet to see liberty and the peaceable days of order and comfortable progress. We should lose heart ourselves, did we suffer the world to lose faith in us as the champions of these things.

There is no masking or concealing the new order of the world. It is not the world of the eighteenth century, nor yet of the nineteenth. A new era has come upon us like a sudden vision of things unprophesied, and for which no polity has been prepared. Here is straightway a new frontage for the nations,—this frontage toward the Orient. Our almost accidental possession of the Philippines has put us in the very presence of the forces which must make the politics of the twentieth century radically unlike the politics of the nineteenth; but we must have taken cognizance of them and dealt with them in any event. They concern us as nearly as they concern any other nation in the world. They concern all nations, for they shall determine the future of the race. Fortunately, they have not disclosed themselves before we were ready. I do not mean that our thought was prepared for them; I do not mean that our domestic affairs were in such shape as to seem fairly well ordered, so that we might in good conscience turn from them as from things finished and complete, and divert our energies to tasks beyond our borders. I mean that this change in the order of the world came, so far as we are concerned, at the natural point in our national development. The matter is worth looking into.

There has been a certain singular unity in our national task, hitherto; and these new duties now thrust upon us will not break that unity. They will perpetuate it, rather, and make it complete, if we keep but our integrity and our old-time purpose true. Until 1890 the United States had always a frontier; looked always to a region beyond, unoccupied, unappropriated, an outlet for its energy, a new place of settlement and of achievement for its people. For nearly three hundred years their growth had followed a single law,—the law of expansion into new territory. Themselves through all their history a frontier, the English colonies in America grew into a nation whose life poured still with strong tide along the old channel. Over the mountains on to the long slopes that descended to the Mississippi, across the great river into the plains, up the plains to the crowning heights of the Rockies, beyond the Rockies to the Pacific, slowly moved the frontier nation. England sought colonies at the ends of the earth to set her energy free and give vent to her enterprise; we, a like people in every impulse of mastery and achievement, had our own vast continent and were satisfied. There was always space and adventure enough and to spare, to satisfy the feet of our young men.

The great process put us to the making of states; kept the wholesome blood of sober and strenuous and systematic work warm within us; perpetuated in us the spirit of initiative and of practical expediency which had made of the colonies vigorous and heady states; created in us that national feeling which finally put sectionalism from the field and altered the very character of the government; gave us the question of the extension of slavery, brought on the Civil War, and decided it by the weight of the West. From coast to coast across the great continent our institutions have spread, until the western sea has witnessed the application upon a great scale of what was begun upon a small scale on the shores of the Atlantic, and the drama has been played almost to its last act,—the drama of institutional construction on the vast scale of a continent. The whole European world, which gave us our materials, has been moralized and liberalized by the striking and stupendous spectacle.

No other modern nation has been schooled as we have been in big undertakings and the mastery of novel difficulties. We have become confirmed in energy, in resourcefulness, in practical proficiency, in self-confidence. We have become confirmed, also, so far as our character is concerned, in the habit of acting under an odd mixture of selfish and altruistic motives. Having ourselves a population fit to be free, making good its freedom in every sort of unhampered enterprise, determining its own destiny unguided and unbidden, moving as it pleased within wide boundaries, using institutions, not dominated by them, we have sympathized with freedom everywhere; have deemed it niggardly to deny an equal degree of freedom to any race or community that desired it; have pressed handsome principles of equity in international dealings; have rejoiced to believe that our principles might some day make every government a servant, not a master, of its people. Ease and prosperity have made us wish the whole world to be as happy and well to do as ourselves; and we have supposed that institutions and principles like our own were the simple prescription for making them so. And yet, when issues of our own interest arose, we have not been unselfish. We have shown ourselves kin to all the world, when it came to pushing an advantage. Our action against Spain in the Floridas, and against Mexico on the coasts of the Pacific; our attitude toward first the Spaniards, and then the French, with regard to the control of the Mississippi; the unpitying force with which we thrust the Indians to the wall wherever they stood in our way, have suited our professions of peacefulness and justice and liberality no better than the aggressions of other nations that were strong and not to be gainsaid. Even Mr. Jefferson, philanthropist and champion of peaceable and modest government though he was, exemplified this double temper of the people he ruled. "Peace is our passion," he had declared; but the passion abated when he saw the mouth of the Mississippi about to pass into the hands of France. Though he had loved France and hated England, he did not hesitate then what language to hold. "There is on the globe," he wrote to Mr. Livingston at Paris, "one single spot the possessor of which is our natural and habitual enemy. The day that France takes possession of New Orleans seals the union of two nations, who, in conjunction, can maintain exclusive possession of the sea. From that moment we must marry ourselves to the British fleet and nation." Our interests must march forward, altruists though we are; other nations must see to it that they stand off, and do not seek to stay us.

It is only just now, however, that we have awakened to our real relationship to the rest of mankind. Absorbed in our own development, we had fallen into a singular ignorance of the rest of the world. The isolation in which we lived was quite without parallel in modern history. Our only near neighbor of any consequence was like ourselves in every essential particular. The life of Canada has been unlike ours only in matters which have turned out in the long run to be matters of detail; only because she has had direct political connection with the mother country, and because she has had to work out the problem of forming a real union of life and sentiment between alien strains of French and English blood in her population. The contrast grows less and less between the two sides of the friendly border. And so we have looked upon nothing but our own ways of living, and have been formed in isolation. This has made us—not provincial, exactly: upon so big and various a continent there could not be the single pattern of thought and manners and purpose to be found cloistered in a secluded province. But if *provincial* be not the proper word, it suggests the actual fact. We have, like provincials, too habitually confined our view to the range of our own experiences. We have acquired a false self-confidence, a false self-sufficiency, because we have heeded no successes or failures but our own.

There could be no better illustration of this than the constant reargument, *de novo*, of the money question among us, and the easy currency to be obtained, at every juncture of financial crisis, for the most childish errors with regard to the well-known laws of value and exchange. No nation not isolated like ourselves in

thought and experience could possibly think itself able to estab-
lish a value of its own for gold and silver, by legislation which
paid no regard either to the commercial operations or to the laws
of coinage and exchange which obtained outside its own borders.
That a great political party should be able to win men of un-
doubted cultivation and practical sense to the support of a platform which embodied palpable and thrice-proven errors in such
matters, and that, too, at a great election following close upon
protracted, earnest, frank, and universal discussion, and should
poll but little less than half the votes of the nation, is startling
proof enough that we have learned to think, for the most part,
only in terms of our own separate life and independent action,
and have come to think ourselves a divided portion of mankind,
masters and makers of our own laws of trade.

We have been equally deceived in matters in which we might
more reasonably have deemed ourselves accredited experts. Misled by our own splendid initial advantage in the matter of self-
government, we have suffered ourselves to misunderstand
self-government itself, when the question was whether it could
be put into practice amidst conditions totally unlike those with
which, and with which alone, we have been familiar. The people
of the United States have never known anything but self-government since the colonies were founded. They have forgotten the
discipline which preceded the founding of the colonies, the long
drill in order and in obedience to law, the long subjection to kings
and to parliaments which were not in fact of the people's choosing. They have forgotten how many generations were once in
tutelage in order that the generations which discovered and
settled the coasts of America might be mature and free. No
thoughtful student of history or observer of affairs needs to be
told the necessary conditions precedent to self-government: the
slow growth of the sense of law; the equally slow growth of the
sense of community and of fellowship in every general interest;
the habit of organization, the habit of discipline and obedience
to those intrusted with authority, the self-restraint of give and
take; the allegiance to ideals, the consciousness of mutual obligation; the patience and intelligence which are content with a
slow and universal growth. These things have all been present
in abundant measure in our own national life; but we have not
deemed them singular, and have assumed that they were within
reach of all others as well, and at as little cost of conscious effort.

Our own form of self-government is, in fact, by no means
the one necessary and inevitable form. England is the oldest

home of self-government in the modern world; our own principles
and practices of self-government were derived from her; she has
served as the model and inspiring example of self-government
for every country in Europe throughout a century of democratic
reform. And yet England did not have what we should call local
self-government until 1888, outside her boroughs. Until 1888,
influential country gentlemen, appointed justices of the peace
by the crown upon the nomination of the Lord Chancellor, were
the governing officers of her counties. Practically every important
matter of local administration was in their hands, and yet the
people of the counties had absolutely no voice in their selection.
Things had stood so for more than four hundred years. Professor
Rudolph Gneist, the great German student of English institutions,
in expounding English ideas of self-government as he found
them exemplified in the actual organization of local administration, declared that the word *government* was quite as emphatic
in the compound as the word *self*. The people of the counties
were not self-directed in affairs: they were governed by crown
officials. The policy of the crown was indeed moderated and
guided in all things by the influence of a representative parliament; the justices received no salaries; were men resident in
the counties for which they were commissioned, identified with
them in life and interest, landlords and neighbors among the
men whose public affairs they administered. They had nothing
to gain by oppression, much to gain by the real advancement of
prosperity and good feeling within their jurisdictions: they were
in a very excellent and substantial sense representative men.
But they were not elected representatives; their rule was not
democratic either in form or in principle. Such was the local
self-government of England during some of the most notable and
honorable periods of her history.

Our own, meanwhile, though conceived in the same atmosphere and spirit, had been set up upon a very different pattern,
suitable to a different order of society. The appointment of officials was discredited amongst us; election everywhere took its
place. We made no hierarchy of officials. We made laws,—laws
for the selectmen, laws for the sheriff, laws for the county commissioners, laws for the district attorney, laws for each official
from bailiff to governor,—and bade the courts see to their enforcement; but we did not subordinate one officer to another. No man
was commanded from the capital, as if he were a servant of
officials rather than of the people. Authority was put into commission and distributed piecemeal; nowhere gathered or organ-

ized into a single commanding force. Oversight and concentration were omitted from the system. Federal administration, it is true, we constituted upon a different principle,—the principle of appointment and of responsibility to the President; but we did not, when that new departure was made, expect the patronage of the President to be large, or look to see the body of federal officials play any very important or intimate part in our life as a people. The rule was to be, as before, the dispersion of authority. We printed the SELF large and the *government* small in almost every administrative arrangement we made; and that is still our attitude and preference.

We have found that even among ourselves such arrangements are not universally convenient or serviceable. They give us untrained officials, and an expert civil service is almost unknown amongst us. They give us petty officials, petty men of no ambition, without hope or fitness for advancement. They give us so many elective offices that even the most conscientious voters have neither the time nor the opportunity to inform themselves with regard to every candidate on their ballots, and must vote for a great many men of whom they know nothing. They give us, consequently, the local machine and the local boss; and where population crowds, interests compete, work moves strenuously and at haste, life is many-sided and without unity, and voters of every blood and environment and social derivation mix and stare at one another at the same voting places, government miscarries, is confused, irresponsible, unintelligent, wasteful. Methods of electoral choice and administrative organization, which served us admirably well while the nation was homogeneous and rural, serve us oftentimes ill enough now that the nation is heterogeneous and crowded into cities.

It is of the utmost importance that we should see the unmistakable truth of this matter and act upon it with all candor. It is not a question of the excellence of self-government: it is a question of the method of self-government, and of choosing which word of the compound we shall emphasize in any given case. It is a matter of separating the essentials from the non-essentials, the principle of self-government from its accidental forms. Democracy is unquestionably the most wholesome and livable kind of government the world has yet tried. It supplies as no other system could the frank and universal criticism, the free play of individual thought, the open conduct of public affairs, the spirit and pride of community and of coöperation, which make governments just and public-spirited. But the question of efficiency is the same for it as for any other kind of polity; and if only it have the principle of representation at the centre of its arrangements, where counsel is held and policy determined and law made, it can afford to put into its administrative organization any kind of businesslike power or official authority and any kind of discipline as if of a profession that it may think most likely to serve it. This we shall see, and this we shall do.

It is the more imperative that we should see and do it promptly, because it is our present and immediate task to extend self-government to Porto Rico and the Philippines, if they be fit to receive it,—so soon as they can be made fit. If there is to be preparation, we must know of what kind it should be, and how it ought to be conducted. Although we have forgot our own preparatory discipline in that kind, these new tasks will undoubtedly teach us that some discipline—it may be prolonged and tedious—must precede self-government and prepare the way for it; that one kind of self-government is suitable for one sort of community, one stage of development, another for another; that there is no universal form or method either of preparation or of practice in the matter; that character and the moralizing effect of law are conditions precedent, obscure and difficult, but absolutely indispensable. An examination of our own affairs will teach us these things; an examination of the affairs of the peoples we have undertaken to govern will confirm us in the understanding of them.

We shall see now more clearly than ever before that we lack in our domestic arrangements, above all things else, concentration, both in political leadership and in administrative organization; for the lack will be painfully emphasized, and will embarrass us sadly in the career we have now set out upon. Authority has been as much dispersed and distributed in the making of law and the choice of policy, under the forms we have used hitherto, as it has been in administrative action. We have been governed in all things by mass meetings. Committees of Congress, as various in their make-up as the body itself, sometimes guided by the real leaders of party, oftener guided by men whom the country at large neither knew nor looked to for leadership, have determined our national policy, piece by piece, and the pieces have seldom been woven together into any single or consistent pattern of statesmanship. There has been no leadership except the private leadership of party managers, no integration of the public business except such as was effected by the compromises and votes of party caucuses. Such methods will serve very awkwardly, if at all, for action in international affairs or in the government of distant dependencies. In such matters leadership must be single, open, responsible, and of the whole. Leadership and expert organization have become imperative, and our practical sense, never daunted hitherto, must be applied to the task of developing them at once and with a will.

We did not of deliberate choice undertake these new tasks which shall transform us. All the world knows the surprising circumstances which thrust them upon us. Sooner or later, nevertheless, they would have become inevitable. If they had not come upon us in this way, they would have come in another. They came upon us, as it was, though unexpected, with a strange opportuneness, as if part of a great preconceived plan for changing the world. Every man now knows that the world is to be changed,—changed according to an ordering of Providence hardly so much as foreshadowed until it came; except, it may be, to a few Europeans who were burrowing and plotting and dreaming in the mysterious East. The whole world had already become a single vicinage; each part had become neighbor to all the rest. No nation could live any longer to itself, the tasks and the duties of neighborhood being what they were. Whether we had had a material foothold there or not, it would have been the duty of the United States to play a part, and a leading part at that, in the opening and transformation of the East. We might not have seen our duty, had the Philippines not fallen to us by the willful fortune of war; but it would have been our duty, nevertheless, to play the part we now see ourselves obliged to play. The East is to be opened and transformed, whether we will or no; the standards of the West are to be imposed upon it; nations and peoples which have stood still the centuries through are to be quickened, and made part of the universal world of commerce and of ideas which has so steadily been a-making by the advance of European power from age to age. It is our peculiar duty, as it is also England's, to moderate the process in the interests of liberty: to impart to the peoples thus driven out upon the road of change, so far as we have opportunity or can make it, our own principles of self-help; teach them order and self-control in the midst of change; impart to them, if it be possible by contact and sympathy and example, the drill and habit of law and obedience which we long ago got out of the strenuous processes of English history; secure for them, when we may, the free intercourse and the natural development which shall make them at least equal members of the family of nations. In China, of course, our part will be indirect, but in the Philippines it will be direct;

and there in particular must the moral of our polity be set up and vindicated.

This we shall do, not by giving them out of hand our codes of political morality or our methods of political action, the generous gifts of complete individual liberty or the full-fangled institutions of American self-government,—a purple garment for their nakedness,—for these things are not blessings, but a curse, to undeveloped peoples, still in the childhood of their political growth; but by giving them, in the spirit of service, a government and rule which shall moralize them by being itself moral, elevate and steady them by being itself pure and steadfast, inducting them into the rudiments of justice and freedom. In other words, it is the aid of our character they need, and not the premature aid of our institutions. Our institutions must come after the ground of character and habit has been made ready for them; as effect, not cause, in the order of political growth. It is thus that we shall ourselves recognize the fact, at last patent to all the world, that the service of democracy has been the development of ideals rather than the origination of practical methods of administration of universal validity, or any absolute qualification of the ultimate conceptions of sovereignty and the indispensable disciplinary operation of law. We must aid their character and elevate their ideals, and then see what these will bring forth, generating after their kind. As the panacea for oppressive taxation lies in honesty and economy rather than in this, that, or the other method of collection, in reasonable assessment rather than in a particular machinery of administration, so the remedy for oppressive government in general is, not a constitution, but justice and enlightenment. One set of guarantees will be effective under one set of circumstances, another under another.

The best guarantee of good government we can give the Filipinos is, that we shall be sensitive to the opinion of the world; that we shall be sensitive in what we do to our own standards, so often boasted of and proclaimed, and shall wish above all things else to live up to the character we have established, the standards we have professed. When they accept the compulsions of that character and accept those standards, they will be entitled to partnership with us, and shall have it. They shall, meanwhile, teach us, as we shall teach them. We shall teach them order as a condition precedent to liberty, self-control as a condition precedent to self-government; they shall teach us the true assessment of institutions,—that their only invaluable content is motive and character. We shall no doubt learn that democracy and efficiency go together by no novel rule. Democracy is not so much a form of government as a set of principles. Other forms of government may be equally efficient; many forms of government are more efficient,—know better ways of integrating and purifying administration than we have yet learned, more successful methods of imparting drill and order to restless and undeveloped peoples than we are likely to hit upon of ourselves, a more telling way of getting and a more effectual way of keeping leadership in a world of competitive policies, doubtful concerts, and international rivalries. We must learn what we can, and yet scrupulously square everything that we do with the high principles we brought into the world: that justice may be done to the lowly no less than to the great; that government may serve its people, not make itself their master,—may in its service heed both the wishes and the needs of those who obey it; that authority may be for leadership, not for aggrandizement; that the people may be the state.

The reactions which such experiments in the universal validity of principle and method are likely to bring about in respect of our own domestic institutions cannot be calculated or forecast. Old principles applied in a new field may show old applications to have been clumsy and ill considered. We may ourselves get responsible leadership instead of government by mass meeting; a trained and thoroughly organized administrative service instead of administration by men privately nominated and blindly elected; a new notion of terms of office and of standards of policy. If we but keep our ideals clear, our principles steadfast, we need not fear the change.   *Woodrow Wilson.*[1]

Printed in the *Atlantic Monthly*, LXXXVII (March 1901), 289-99.

[1] Wilson's letter to Bliss Perry of September 17, 1900, discloses that he began work on "Democracy and Efficiency" soon after mailing this letter to his friend. The manuscript remains relating to this essay in the Wilson Papers in the Library of Congress enable us to see fairly clearly how he went about writing it. He set down his first thoughts in shorthand in the pocket notebook described at June 18, 1899, Volume 11; then he wrote out a brief outline in longhand. Next Wilson wrote a draft of "Democracy and Efficiency" in shorthand, which he then cut into sections and pasted on cards with topical headings for easy rearrangement. To this draft he later added three new sections in shorthand. Either immediately before or after completing the shorthand draft, Wilson prepared a new—and full—outline consisting of the twenty-five topical headings that were written on the cards on which he had pasted his shorthand sections. At this point, Wilson began to transcribe his shorthand draft on his typewriter, following that draft closely and adding only some transitional sentences and a brief insertion in the text. The typed version does not seem to have survived, but two first pages which he discarded remain in his papers. On one of these pages he added the phrase that became "The whole world had already become a single vicinage . . . ," ascribing it to President Patton.

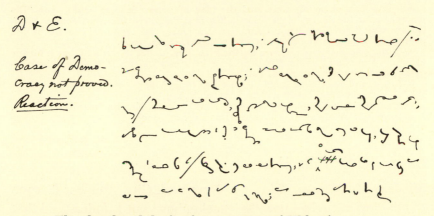

The shorthand draft of one section of Wilson's essay,
"Democracy and Efficiency," which he pasted
on cards for easy copying

To Miss Hillard[1]

My dear Miss Hillard,   Princeton, 2 Oct., 1900

The second invitation is always more flattering than the first,[2] particularly when it follows close on the heels of the first, and I hope very much that I shall be able to be on your list.

My chief embarrassment is as to subject. I am more absorbed than ever in literary work,—and shall be working during the winter, alas, under contract,—so that, unless I *read* a lecture,— which I always prefer not to do, even though I can express myself better in that form,—I am practically shut in to subjects already thought out, but which *sound* very didactic: "Liberty,"[3] "Self-Government,"[4] "Nationality."[5]

If any one of these would do (by the way, my *written* lectures are on "Leaders of Men"[6] and "Democracy"[7]), I could come December 12, February 20, or March 13,—with a strong *preference* for the first named date.[8]

With warm regard and appreciation,
         Sincerely Yours,   Woodrow Wilson

Terms, one hundred dollars and expenses.

ALS (WC, NjP).

[1] As later documents reveal, Miss Hillard lived in Wilmington, Del., and was probably secretary or program chairman of the New Century Club of that city, before which Wilson had spoken several times. She is not listed in the Wilmington city directories of this period or mentioned in the standard local history.

[2] Her first invitation is missing.

[3] The fullest report of this address, which Wilson usually entitled "Political Liberty," is printed at Dec. 20, 1894, Vol. 9.

4 Wilson had obviously conceived the idea of a new lecture based upon "Democracy and Efficiency," just printed. He first delivered his new lecture, "Self-Government," at Waterbury, Conn., on December 12, 1900. Notes for it are printed at Dec. 12, 1900, and a news report at Dec. 13, 1900.

5 Wilson had given this lecture for the first time, under the title "What It Means to Be an American," at the Hill School on February 22, 1900. See the announcement printed at Feb. 20, 1900, Vol. 11.

6 "Leaders of Men" is printed at June 17, 1890, Vol. 6.

7 "Democracy" is printed at Dec. 5, 1891, Vol. 7.

8 As it turned out, Wilson spoke to the New Century Club on December 6, 1900. A news report of his address is printed at Dec. 7, 1900.

From Henry Mills Alden

My dear Mr Wilson   New York City   October 8. 1900

I don't personally know Dr Quackenbos,[1] but I understand that [he] is in good standing with the medical profession. I don't think there is any "quack" about him except in his name. He is, I think, sincere as well as enthusiastic in the lines taken in his magazine articles about hypnotism.[2] How much real importance is to be attached to such speculations & practices—*that* is another matter &, of course, every thoughtful man has opinions of his own concerning it. The power of the human imagination is wonderful & sometimes works miracles.[3]

We will send you proofs of the illustrations for your History. We are just beginning the make up of the January number & your article leads.

By the way I have undertaken to do the *Editor's Study* (which is revived in our December No.) & I shall have in the January *Study* something to say about American History & Historians *apropos* of the beginning of this work of yours. I shall welcome any suggestions you can give me that are of importance from your own point of view in this connection. I should not quote these but make them my own.[4]

With friendly regard   Yours faithfully   H. M. Alden

ALS (WP, DLC).

1 John Duncan Quackenbos (1848-1926), A.B., Columbia, 1868; M.D., 1871. Lecturer and author of books and articles on a variety of subjects, in 1900 he was engaged in medical practice in New York with a specialty in diseases of the nervous system. He also ran a summer sanatorium at Lake Sunapee, New Hampshire.

2 John D. Quackenbos, "The Moral Value of Hypnotic Suggestion," *Harper's Magazine*, c (Feb. 1900), 466-73, and "Educational Uses of Hypnotism," *ibid.*, cI (July 1900), 264-68. Harper and Brothers also published Quackenbos's *Hypnotism in Mental and Moral Culture* in 1900.

3 No evidence indicates that Wilson ever consulted Dr. Quackenbos.

4 Wilson's reply is missing; however, see the historical commentary and critique printed at Jan. 1, 1901.

From the Minutes of the Princeton University Faculty

5 5′ P.M. Wednesday, Oct. 10th, 1900.

. . . Professors Brackett, Woodrow Wilson and Fine were elected by ballot a Committee to appear before and confer with the Trustees if required.[1]

"Minutes of the Faculty, 1894-1902," bound minute book (UA, NjP).
[1] They did not confer with the trustees at their meeting on Oct. 19, 1900.

From Henry Mills Alden

My dear Mr. Wilson: New York City   October 11, 1900.

You are very kind in your prompt and most satisfactory response to my request. We will send you finished proofs of the cuts for each part of your History. I hope you will—in this connection—keep in view the possibility of a more costly edition of the History with more abundant illustrations, like that published by the HARPER's of Green's Short History in four volumes, royal octavo.   Yours cordially,   H. M. Alden

TLS (WP, DLC).

Notes for an Address to the American Whig and Cliosophic Societies

Rally for the Halls, 12 October, 1900.

Our theme and plea is, that both you and the University should have an audible and telling Voice in the world.

Besides many other things obvious upon the surface (companionship, amusement, access to sources of information which touch the world at large) the Halls will give you these two things:

(1) The power of expression,
(2) The power of association.

Both these are powers of *coördination*.

The power of expression, however, is something more than a power of coördination. It is also a power of lucidity, of clarification, of effective phrase, and of imaginative release.

In both aspects it is as necessary in scholarship as in debate or in literary art.

In literary work (that is, in the release of everything that is *individual* in you) it is the art of interpretation, the art of beauty, the art of power over the blood and over the sensibilities that compel to action or to thought.

The power of association is both a pleasure and an indispensable means of influence. It is also a power which enlarges and illuminates and makes various.

WWT and WWhw MS. (WP, DLC).

A News Report

[Oct. 13, 1900]

HALL MASS MEETING.

The annual Mass Meeting in the interests of Whig and Clio Halls was held at seven o'clock last evening in Murray Hall. President Patton presided; Professor Woodrow Wilson represented Whig Hall, and Professor Andrew F. West, Clio Hall. Professor Wilson spoke of the purpose of the Halls and the value of a Hall training. He said in part:

There are some things which the Halls do which underlie every other course of training in the University. Scholarship is by no means a dead thing, yet to-day it possesses little of its possible power, simply because men are unable to give telling utterance to the things they have learned. There are two important parts of a liberal education which a Hall training will give, the power of expression and the power of association. It is the purpose of the Halls to unite men in order to unite ideas, and in uniting ideas they discover the best method of uniting men. Those who pursue the training which the Halls offer, are not only developing their powers, but also individuality. . . .

Printed in the *Daily Princetonian*, Oct. 13, 1900; one editorial heading omitted.

From William Blake Kennedy

Dear Uncle Woodrow: Newport, Ark. Oct 14th 1900

Last Sunday I spent my time in Batesville and while talking to Woodrow[1] he requested that I write to you in his behalf. He said he didn't answer your much appreciated letter because of his aversion to telling you the truth in regard to his condition. He knows himself, how he is[,] but he hates to tell anyone whom he thinks interested in him.

To be plain, and tell what will not surprise you much, he is in a very serious condition. Or I do not know that I can say this of Woodrow, when I know his mind as I do, and feel so sure of his soul's safety. But so far as life goes, his chances each day, diminish. He is now in bed most of the time and I don't think, can last thro the winter, if he goes thro this year. Since he has been at home, he has worried continually about not having work, and this has made his condition more serious. He now has decided symptoms which indicate impoverishment of blood in the brain, which is most pitiful in one as bright as he is! He cannot think consecutively on anything, without feeling as if his head were being stopped up. He is a total wreck in fact.

I write the above somewhat detailed, statement of his case, in order that you may know how he is, as we, who see him, know. This because I believe you are interested in him.

He speaks often and with much affection of you and Princeton. As to my own feeling, I cannot express the thanks I feel for your kindness to him.

Feeling as I do that he is to last but a short while longer,[2] I am thankful to you for giving him what none of us could— Something to think over with pleasure during his hours of weakness and confinement.

If you can spare time and think of anything interesting to him I would be glad if you would write him, but he can't answer you. Doesn't write any. The doctors say nothing can cure, and only cheer can, help him.

He speaks of our aunt and cousins too, please give them a message from him and me of regard and affection.

Again I thank you uncle Woodrow. I hope I may someday be of a different, but equally appreciable service to you or yours.

Your Nephew   Will B. Kennedy

ALS (WP, DLC).
    [1] His brother, Wilson Woodrow Kennedy, who had withdrawn from Princeton during the spring term of 1900 on account of ill health.
    [2] He died on November 8, 1900, as W. B. Kennedy to WW, Nov. 9, 1900, reports.

From George Howe III

Dear Uncle Woodrow,   Halle a/S.   Oct. 15/1900

Only a note written hastily in hopes of catching the next steamer. I have met with an unforeseen difficulty in the matter of matriculation. I brought with me only my Princeton diploma, Professor Carter[1] having told me that that would be enough. I presented it today—the opening day—and they accepted it, but demanded a paper accounting for my time since graduation. I told them I had none, told them what I had done in the last three years, but they insisted upon having something to show for it—said I could not matriculate until I had such a paper. It seems foolish, but I suppose it is for the police. I thought of writing to Mrs. Moulton[2] but feared that a carelessly written note from her would not sound *official* enough. Mother suggested that a note from you as Professor in Princeton stating where I had been and what I had done since graduation would answer the purpose. I asked a German student about it and he said the same. Would it be too much trouble to do this for me? There is a mere chance that I shall not need it because a German friend of mine is going to try to have it arranged for me. At the same time, the Recktor advised me to write to America at once in order to have a reply before matriculation days end—3 weeks

I cannot write much more now but will let you know very soon about what I am studying and what progress I am making. I have had a good many discouragements but will come thro' all right in the end, I believe. I have certainly been taught how little I know. So far I have put all my time on German and can manage now to carry on a very halting conversation and to understand far more than I can say. I can read quite easily. I have done nothing yet in Latin & Greek but begin tomorrow translating into German, if possible.

Mother has probably told you how we are situated here. The facilities for learning the language could not be better, and we are not without some comforts. We have been very fortunate, all things considered. Our being together so much of course keeps us back a trifle in German, but we are willing to make the sacrifice in order to save ourselves from the horrible loneliness of it all. Eddie[3] and I have worked together, but I really believe we shall both do better now that he has gone to Berlin. He left today.

I am very sorry indeed that we had no chance to tell you goodbye. I had counted on it. Please give my love to all & keep a great deal from

Your devoted nephew,   George Howe.

You understand just what I want, do you not? A mere statement of what I have done & where I have been & my respectable standing. Thank you in advance.[4]

ALS (WP, DLC).
    [1] Jesse Benedict Carter, Assistant Professor of Latin at Princeton, who had taken the Ph.D. at Halle.
    [2] Catharine Lewis (Mrs. Arthur Julian) Moulton of 27 West 39th St., New York. George Howe had tutored her son, Arthur J. Moulton, from 1898 to 1900.
    [3] Edward Graham Elliott.
    [4] See WW to the Rector of the University of Halle, Oct. 28, 1900.

From Francis Landey Patton

Dear Professor Wilson: [Princeton, N.J.] October 15, 1900.

I believe you are one of the gentlemen intrusted with the grave responsibility of naming the American "immortals."[1] I therefore take the liberty of enclosing this letter from the postmaster of Alton, Illinois,[2] who thinks that Mr. [Elijah Parish]

Lovejoy is a very suitable candidate for a place in the Hall of Fame. Please do as your own judgment will indicate.[3]

I am,   Very faithfully yours,   Francis L. Patton

TLS (Patton Letterpress Books, UA, NjP).

[1] Patton referred to Wilson's connection with the Hall of Fame of Great Americans of New York University. About this matter, see the news report printed at April 28, 1900, Vol. 11.

[2] Wilbur T. Norton.

[3] Lovejoy has never been elected to the Hall of Fame. His name was not even formally submitted to be voted upon until the election of 1950, when he received no votes.

From Henry Mills Alden

Dear Mr. Wilson: New York City   October 16, 1900.

I have received your note of October 12th concerning Part II of your History, and find that through a clerical error, uncorrected, rough proofs were sent you. By this time you probably have received corrected proofs of Part I, accompanied by the manuscript, which I hope you will return at your early convenience. Hereafter I will endeavor to send you galley proofs somewhat earlier than in the present case.

I am exceedingly sorry that you had any annoyance with the rough proofs of Part II, and am glad that you informed me regarding the matter.   Sincerely yours,   H. M. Alden

TLS (WP, DLC).

To the President and Board of Trustees
of Princeton University

GENTLEMEN: [Princeton, N.J., c. Oct. 19, 1900]

After ten years of practically uninterrupted service in the University, it is my earnest desire to spend a year abroad in travel and study. My chief object is to prepare myself for what I shall hope to make the principal literary work of my life: a series of studies in political organization and development for which my historical writings have been meant to supply me with closely scrutinized materials.[1] My plan would be, not formal study in a university, but observation and travel in countries whose institutions I most wish to see at first hand. The plan involves more expense than ordinary plans of study, and yet I feel that it is indispensable.

I therefore make bold to ask that you will do me the very great favour of granting me leave of absence for the academic year 1901-1902 with full salary.

I feel the freer to ask this at this time because, now that I have an able colleague in the Department[2] which I have hitherto filled alone, I shall not by my absence be leaving a whole Department neglected even for the time being. The time is most opportune for me because I hope during the present winter to complete a considerable piece of historical work upon which I have been long engaged, and so clear the way for the immediate undertaking, upon my return, of the task for which I have all along been seeking to prepare myself, and for which my year of leave would be a final step of preparation.

Should I be disappointed in my expectation of finishing the task I am now engaged upon by Spring, I may have to beg this favour for the academic year 1902-1903, instead of the year 1901-1902. But it is my present confident hope to be able to free myself for the trip by the Spring; and I venture to bring my request before you at this early date in order that, should you generously grant it, I may have abundant time within which to make the many arrangements which will be necessary for what I wish to do.[3]

With sincere respect, WOODROW WILSON.

WWTCL (WP, DLC).
[1] That is, his projected magnum opus, "The Philosophy of Politics," about which see the Editorial Note, "Wilson's First Treatise on Democratic Government," Vol. 5.
[2] The new Professor of Politics, John Huston Finley.
[3] As future documents in this volume will show, Wilson was unable to go abroad on account of the illness of his father.

A Citation for an Honorary Degree[1]

[[Oct. 20, 1900]]

MR. PRESIDENT—I take pleasure in presenting for the degree of Doctor of Laws the Hon. John Hay, Secretary of State, whose achievements in statesmanship and diplomacy command the attention of the world, and whom we are glad to honor as also poet, historian and critic. He has understood and safeguarded the honor and interests of the United States; he has confirmed our happy alliance of sentiment and purpose with Great Britain; he has promoted that concert of nations which is the best security for the peace of the world; and in the midst of affairs he has illustrated the tact, the elevation, and the chastened eloquence of the man of letters.[2]

Printed in the *Princeton University Bulletin*, XII (Nov. 1900), 12.
[1] The LL.D. degree, awarded to John Hay at ceremonies held in Alexander Hall on October 20, 1900, to commemorate the 154th anniversary of the signing of the

first charter of the College of New Jersey. Hay made a brief speech in accepting his degree. The principal address of the day was delivered by the Rev. Dr. Henry Yates Satterlee, Protestant Episcopal Bishop of Washington, who spoke on "The Ethics of American Civilization in Its National and Political Aspects."
2 There is a WWhw draft of this citation dated Oct. 20, 1900, in WP, DLC.

From Howard Pyle

Dear Professor Wilson: Wilmington, Del., Oct. 23rd, 1900.

I am about undertaking the three drawings for Part Third of your History of the United States. I notice that you have five subjects marked as follows:

    I. Surrender of the New Netherlands.

   II. Ships taking their cargo in Albermarle Sound.

 III. Nathaneal Bacon demanding his commission in the House of Burgesses.

     or

    Bacon come for tis [his] commission at the head of his troops.

 IV. Drummond and Berkeley.

  V. A Virginia Vestry Meeting after the Restoration.

I remember in our work upon the History of the Life of Washington you specified your subjects and I upon my part after carefully reading the manuscript was allowed to give my ideas concerning them from the standpoint of an illustrator.

After reading the Third Part, it seems to me that I would somewhat amend my choice of subjects as follows:

Instead of having a picture of the surrender of the New Netherlands (an equivalent subject of which we have), I would make an illustration of some theme of the Indian War, such as the death of King Philip, or perhaps, of a more popular subject, of a farmer plowing his clearing and an Indian watching him in ambush—or some such typical subject of the war of civilization and savagery for the possession of the Continent.

I am almost sure you will like some such subject as this because it will illuminate your History with a point not so generally used by historical illustrators.

I am going to make a picture of the ships taking on cargo at Albermarle Sound.

In regard to the two Bacon pictures, I feel that while both of them are very dramatic from a literary standpoint, they may not be so easy to make clear in an illustration where the words must necessarily be omitted. It seems to me that a much better illustration would be the burning of Jamestown with Bacon's tatterdemalion army marching through the wide Colonial street or road.

In short, the three subjects I should select would be as follows:

I. A picture of Indian life.

II. Vessels loading at Albermarle Sound.

III. The burning of Jamestown.

If you approve of these, will you kindly telegraph me so that I may lose no time in going on with them?

I am almost sure that you will agree with me in thinking them the best points for illustration.

It seems extremely pleasant to be writing to you again in collaboration of such interesting work. I wish I could see more of you and that the mere acquaintanceship which I now have might become riper. Do you ever come to Philadelphia or Wilmington? I remember you being here once to deliver a lecture and I was absent that day and only had time to see you late in the evening and to shake hands with you.[1]

Believe me to be,   Faithfully yours   Howard Pyle

TLS (WP, DLC).
[1] On one of the occasions when Wilson spoke before the New Century Club of Wilmington, Del., on Feb. 4, Oct. 21, Nov. 4, and Nov. 18, 1897.

To the Rector of the University of Halle[1]

Princeton University,

Sir,   Princeton, New Jersey, 28 October, 1900.

This is to certify that Mr. George Howe, who graduated from this University in 1897, has since that time been engaged as a private tutor. For the first year he travelled, as private tutor, with the son of Mr. James W. Alexander, a prominent business man of the City of New York.[2] During the two remaining years he was employed as private tutor in the family of a Mrs. Moulton, of the same City. He was, during all the three years, in a general way under my direction and advice. I can, therefore, speak of his occupations with authority. He has throughout enjoyed the respect and admiration of all who have known or dealt with him, both as a man and as a student. He can be most highly commended to your consideration; and any favours you may be able to show him will be highly appreciated here.

Very respectfully Yours,   Woodrow Wilson
Professor of Jurisprudence, Princeton University.

WWTLS (WP, DLC).
[1] Richard Pischel (1849-1908), a Sanskrit scholar who had been at Halle

since 1885 and who had assumed the office of Rector on July 12, 1900. He
became Professor of Sanskrit at the University of Berlin in 1902.
  2 See George Howe III to WW, Aug. 29, 1897, Vol. 10.

To Howard Pyle

My dear Mr. Pyle,   Princeton, New Jersey, 31 October, 1900.

I was delighted when Mr. Alden wrote me that you had consented to take part in illustrating my history; not only because
you are easily the first of illustrators, but also because we are
once more brought into correspondence. It was exceedingly
pleasant to see your name on an envelope again; and, had I not
been desperately busy the day your letter came, I would have
replied by mail as well as by telegraph at once.

I do not go to Philadelphia often, I am sorry to say; but am a
great stay-at-home. I am to speak in Wilmington some time this
winter, though, before the Woman's Club. The exact date has not
yet been fixed upon. When it is decided on I will write and find
out whether by coming down a little early in the day I can get a
chance to see you.

With much regard, and renewed expressions of satisfaction at
being once more associated with you in work,
                         Sincerely Yours,   Woodrow Wilson

WWTLS (de Coppet Coll., NjP).

From Edward Graham Elliott

                                    Berlin Behren St. 57 III
Dear Prof. Wilson;   Nov. 3rd 1900.

I have been in Berlin now nearly three weeks and have begun
to form some idea of what a German Univ. is like. The first week
I spent in matriculating, about which I had no trouble, and in
getting an abode; the latter was most difficult but after a week's
search I found a place with which I am so far much pleased. I
am boarding in a family consisting of the father, who is engaged
in the electrical business, the mother, daughter aged 14 and son,
aged 9. I am the only boarder and have good opportunities to
learn German. Further I am not far from the Univ. and have a
pleasant room. So much for my temporal welfare: the second and
third weeks I have spent in behalf of my mental improvement.

At first I went to as many lectures as possible, both to get
accustomed to the sound of the language and to find out which
men I could understand best, for I thought it would be time

thrown away to take men who spoke so indistinctly I couldn't understand a word. After two weeks of such investigation I have chosen the following courses—Einführung in d. Rechtswissenschaft—3 hrs. Römische Rechtsgeschichte—4 hrs[.] Both these courses are given by Prof. Oertonan,[1] a young man and one of the "ausserordentliche Professoren," but very interesting, and seems quite popular; further I can understand him better than any of the others. Allgemeines und deutsches Staatsrecht—4 hrs. by Prof. Gierke,[2] one of the "ordentliche Professoren" and perhaps the oldest man I'm hearing; I think his course will be good—Völkerrecht und Politik—4 hrs. by Prof. Hübler,[3] another of the 'ordentliche,' one of the most popular men here, but he speaks rather indistinctly[.] Politik—2 hrs—by Prof. Hintze,[4] 'ausserordentlicher': and also a public course of one hour by Hintze—Geschichte der neueren politischen und sozialen Theorien.

These then are my courses, and while as yet I can't understand all that is said by a good deal, still I think it will not be long before I can understand and I think I shall be much pleased here.

I find several Princeton men studying here this winter—McElroy, McMillan from the Seminary, Robinson '98 and Kellogg '99.[5] The two last are studying physics.

With very kindest regards to Mrs. Wilson, believe me,

Most sincerely   Edward G. Elliott.

ALS (WP, DLC) with WWhw notation on env.: "Ans."
[1] Paul Ernst Wilhelm Oertmann (1865-1938).
[2] Otto Friedrich von Gierke (1841-1921).
[3] Bernhard Hübler (1835-1912).
[4] Otto Hintze (1861-1940).
[5] Robert McNutt McElroy '96; Kerr Duncan Macmillan, B.D., Princeton Theological Seminary, 1897, Instructor in Old Testament, 1897-1900; Philip Ely Robinson '98; and Oliver Dimon Kellogg '99.

From William Blake Kennedy

Dear Uncle Woodrow: Newport, Ark., Nov 9th 1900

This line to you will prove more satisfactory, no doubt, than a telegram to tell you of Woodrow's death. He went to rest,—an expression especially applicable in his case,—about 4 o'clock yesterday morning. I thought of telegraphing you, but knew you could not come in time if you were able to get away,—and—a message of that kind is so cold—and—generally unsatisfactory. As it is I may say, He was conscious to the last,—and simply ceased to breathe.

Of course, I need hardly add, this death touches me more than any of my experience,—and more than any that could have come.

But, knowing that it was only a question of short or long suffering—and,—at best, a lingering death, I almost, yes in fact, tho
it bereaves me,—am thankful. He's better now than ever and so
different from the last 2 months.

He received your letter and asked that it be answered, with
request that you write again. I am sure it gave him immeasurable
pleasure,—and for this,—and all your kindness to him, I thank
you. His attachment for you was marked, and he always spoke of
you with only pleasure.

I also thank you for your heart-full letter to me,—and your
messages of regard from Aunt and cousins. Please express my
affectionate regard for them—and consider me sincerely—
                    Your affectionate nephew   Will B K.

ALS (WP, DLC) with WWhw notation on env.: "Ans. 13 Nov. 1900."

An Announcement

[Nov. 15, 1900]
ADDRESS BY PROF. WOODROW WILSON TO-NIGHT.

The regular Thursday evening meeting [of the Philadelphian
Society][1] will be addressed by Professor Woodrow Wilson this
evening at 6.40 o'clock, in Murray Hall. Prof. Wilson is so well-
known to the students, that the mere announcement that he is
to speak this evening is sufficient for the upper classmen. All
members of the Freshman class and especially those who have
not had the pleasure of hearing him, are urged to attend the
meeting.

Printed in the *Daily Princetonian*, Nov. 15, 1900.
  [1] About this organization, see n. 1 to the news item printed at Nov. 1, 1890,
Vol. 7.

Notes for a Religious Talk

Philadelphian Society, 15 November, 1900

The Principle of Rectitude   Read Eccl. XI., 4 to XII., 7 & XII., 13, 14.

The object of a University, chastened and disciplined force,—and
    the beauty and glory of life which that yields. And this not alone
    in the intellectual life.
In my day I have seen the University grow from a body of pupils
    into a community, in some degree self-governed and self-dis-
    ciplined. Shall that growth continue?
A qu. of Christian principle. None but a Christian body can realize
    the full ideal of a University[.] A society like the Philadelphian
    an organized part of its spiritual power.

"Fear God and keep his commandments: for this is the whole
   duty of man"
   (1) In youth, while the blood is warm, and the ardour quick
   (2) Without regard to clouds and wind XI., 4.

WWhw MS. (WP, DLC).

A News Report of a Religious Talk

[Nov. 16, 1900]

PROFESSOR WILSON ADDRESSES THE
PHILADELPHIAN SOCIETY.

Professor Woodrow Wilson addressed the regular weekly meeting of the Philadelphian Society last evening in Murray Hall, taking as his subject "The Principles of Rectitude." After a few
introductory remarks in which he spoke of the important place
which courage and perseverance occupy in the affairs of men,
Professor Wilson said: There is nothing so desirable for the
accomplishment of anything in life as a motive power which is
thoroughly complete in all of its departments, a force which is
perfectly rounded and developed. This is true in nature, where
nothing is more marvelous than the perfect poise of the hawk
as he soars with never a movement of his wings, and it is as
true in life as in nature. It is the football team which has its
team work more nearly perfect which wins, other things being
equal, and it is this team work, this perfect distribution of force
which is responsible for the world's greatest achievements. It is
also the possession of this perfect adjustment of all the faculties
which marks the difference between the man who has had the
benefits of university training and the man who has not. The
problem then becomes, in what way can the various standards
and purposes of university life be so moulded together and inter-
woven as to form one compact powerful force? And this is the
formula by which the college man may solve it; he must realize
that the one great object of his existence is to create a chastened
and disciplined force. In doing so, however, the mere power of
bulky force must be avoided, the brute strength which is weak
without the true spirit, for it is the spirit which chastens and
disciplines. There is nothing which gives force to life like self-
discipline and there is no way in which this can be fostered more
surely than by living up to the resolution to "Fear God and keep
his Commandments," for that is the whole duty of man.

Printed in the *Daily Princetonian*, Nov. 16, 1900.

A News Item

[Nov. 24, 1900]

President Gilman, of Johns Hopkins University, has resigned after a service of a quarter of a century.[1] Among the names suggested as his possible successor, Professor Woodrow Wilson is prominently mentioned. How he would regard the position if chosen to it is not known, but it is to be sincerely hoped that he will remain in Princeton in the instructor's chair.

Printed in the *Princeton Press*, Nov. 24, 1900.

[1] Daniel Coit Gilman, on November 20, 1900, announced his decision to relinquish the presidency of The Johns Hopkins University. The *New York Times*, Nov. 21, 1900, noted in its report of the announcement that Woodrow Wilson of Princeton, Professors Ira Remsen and Herbert Baxter Adams of the Johns Hopkins, and Albert Shaw, editor of the New York *Review of Reviews* had been "mentioned as successors to Dr. Gilman." Gilman's resignation took effect on September 1, 1901. Remsen was his successor.

From John Grier Hibben

My dear Woodrow,   Strassburg Nov 25/1900

We felt very rich in receiving your letter, & the day following one from Mrs. Wilson. It brought you very near to us & we rejoiced in all you had to tell us both of Princeton news and of the assurances of your affection and friendship. I wish that you could see the excitement which is occasioned in the Hibben household whenever a mail from America arrives. We are always disappointed when we do not find a letter from you. Mrs. Wilson told us of the struggle with Dr. Patton in reference to the graduate school & of his overthrow.[1] We were most interested in her account of it, & I hope you will not forget all the details of the story before we see you again.

I was sorry to hear that you have really made your plans to be abroad next year, that is sorry on our account & yet I can not but rejoice with you that you are to have a year of complete change & freedom from your routine work in Princeton.

So many changes have occurred in Princeton since we left last summer that we shall hardly know the place again. Just think of it, to be confronted with nine or ten new babies, & all the pleasant remarks we shall have to make to the many fathers & mothers. We were disturbed to hear of the unbroken line of foot-ball defeats. It has been certainly a most disastrous year.[2]

It is very strange to hear of only one kind of sport here among the students, that of duelling. It is their only form of exercise, & their one kind of recreation. Our system of athletics may have its disadvantages as some would insist, but it has a large preponderance of advantage as can be clearly seen by way of contrast with the conditions of student life here. There is however on all sides a great earnestness in study, and real hunger & thirst after knowledge, which would meet with your most hearty approval. . . .

We have two weeks for the Christmas vacation & we are planning to go to Florence, stopping a day or two at Lucerne on our way down, & going to Venice on the return journey.

Jenny[3] is very much absorbed in her French & German lessons which she is taking on alternate days. She is making progress very rapidly. Beth[4] is very happy in her school & in the little friends she has made among the German children. We are very sorry that we are so far away from Mrs. Howe & her family. It would [be] such a pleasure to meet them again. I am glad they are so well pleased with all their new surroundings.

I had a letter some time ago from Mrs. Burt of Philadelphia[5] asking me to look after grandson, Strouthers Burt of the present Freshman class.[6] If you have a chance to speak to him, I am sure Mrs. Burt will appreciate it. She seemed to be quite anxious about his getting a right start in his college career. I wrote to her that I would ask you to interest yourself in him. You know his Uncle, Fred Burt[7] was a classmate of mine & my most intimate friend.

Jenny & Beth join me in love to you all.
Affectionately Yours   John Grier Hibben.

ALS (WP, DLC).
    1 The Princeton faculty, led by Andrew Fleming West and others, including Wilson and Hibben, had been pressing strongly since 1896 for the establishment of a full-fledged Graduate School. As Hibben's letter indicates, President Patton had been notably unenthusiastic about, if not outright opposed to, the project. (For a brief history of events concerning the proposed Graduate School between 1896 and 1900, see n. 1 to the memorial to the Princeton trustees printed at Dec. 2, 1896, Vol. 10.)
    The faculty resumed their pressure on June 6, 1900, by adopting a resolution calling the attention of the Board of Trustees to "the importance of establishing a Graduate College in liberal studies as of the highest concern for the welfare of our Graduate work and for the reputation of Princeton as a University." Reminding the trustees that this matter had been brought before them shortly after the Sesquicentennial Celebration in 1896, the faculty concluded by stating: "In our opinion the reasons for establishing the Graduate College are as urgent as ever. We therefore respectfully ask leave to present the matter again in this minute hoping that the Board may be able to take early and decisive action."
    President Patton embodied the faculty resolution in his report to the Board of Trustees on June 11, 1900, and added a significant comment and recommendation of his own: "Inasmuch as there are matters of serious importance in reference to the graduate department which need consideration, and differences of opinion respecting the wisest mode of procedure exist in the Faculty, I recommend that a Special Committee of this Board be appointed to confer with a similar committee of the Faculty to consider the whole question and to report at the next meeting of the Trustees." Accepting Patton's recommendation, the trustees appointed Moses Taylor Pyne, George Black Stewart, Simon John Mc-

Pherson, Charles Beatty Alexander, and Patton to serve on the trustees' special committee. At the faculty meeting on October 10, 1900, Patton appointed Dean Winans and Professors West, Magie, Harper, and Macloskie as a "Committee of the Graduate Department" to meet with the trustees' committee.

Hibben's letter can only mean that even at this late date Patton continued to oppose establishment of a Graduate School. The President's "overthrow" occurred on October 19, 1900, when the trustees finally took decisive action. The special committee reported that they had conferred with the faculty committee and had concluded that "the best way to organize and develop the [Graduate] Department with the highest economy and efficiency is to appoint a responsible chief executive officer thereof." The special committee further recommended that such a chief executive officer be appointed and that a new special committee be named to determine his title, duties, and mode of appointment and removal. The Board of Trustees approved the report and asked the special committee already in existence to undertake the recommended study and propose a plan.

The special committee reported a "Plan of Organization of the Graduate School" to the trustees at their meeting on December 13, 1900. It established a Graduate School of Princeton University to be headed by a Dean to be elected by the trustees and hold office during their pleasure. In addition, the Dean would be advised by a faculty committee appointed by him. However, the Dean was specifically required to consult with the President on "all matters of importance" and to submit "all proposed measures" to the President and trustees for their approval. The trustees approved this plan and implemented it by amending the University by-laws in order to put it into effect. Later at the same meeting, the trustees elected West as the first Dean of the Graduate School.

The above discussion is based upon "Minutes of the Faculty, 1894-1902" and "Minutes of the Trustees of Princeton University, Dec. 1898-Mar. 1901" (bound minute books in UA, NjP), entries at the dates mentioned in this note.

[2] The Princeton football team had done well in October and early November, winning eight games in a row against outclassed teams from smaller colleges. But disaster struck at the end of the season when Princeton lost its last three games: Princeton 0, Cornell 12; Princeton 5, Columbia 6; and, worst of all, Princeton 5, Yale 29.

[3] His wife, Jenny Davidson Hibben.

[4] The Hibbens' daughter, Elizabeth Grier Hibben.

[5] Jane Anna Brooke (Mrs. Nathaniel) Burt.

[6] Maxwell Struthers Burt, a special student in 1900-1901. He received his A.B. from Princeton in 1904.

[7] Alfred Farmer Burt '82, who had died in 1893.

From Henry Mills Alden

Dear Mr. Wilson: New York City   November 27, 1900.

I have received Part IV of "Colonies and Nation," with memorandum of illustrations for that part and beg to thank you again for your promptness. Payment therefor will be sent you in the usual course.

With cordial regards, I remain

Sincerely yours,   H. M. Alden

TLS (WP, DLC).

To Richard Watson Gilder

My dear Mr. Gilder,   Princeton, 29 Nov., 1900.

You have perhaps noticed that *Harpers* is to have running through next year a history of the United States by one Woodrow Wilson. Mr. Wilson is anxious to have you know that this is *not* the history whose MSS you read last winter, but, except for the introductory chapter, an entirely different work.[1] It is, indeed, none other than the history which came

Facsimile of first page of WWhwL (Woodrow Wilson File, Presidential Series, NN).

[1] For Wilson's and Gilder's earlier discussions about this manuscript, see the Editorial Note, "Wilson's History of the American People," Vol. 11.

From Howard Pyle

Dear Professor Wilson: Wilmington, Del., Nov. 30th, 1900.

For the illustration of the Fourth Part of the Short History of the United States I have received the four following general subjects from Mr Penfield.[1] Presumably they were suggested by yourself.

    I. Seth Sothel on trial in the Albermarle Assembly.
       Or,
       Seth Sothel seizing the gover[n]ment of South Carolina.
    II. Slaughter induced to sign Leisler's death warrant.
       Or,
       Reburial of Leisler.
    III. Captain Phips raising the Spanish galleon.
    IV. Blair and Andros.

So far there has been nothing typical of the settlement of Pennsylvania. I would suggest in this respect that possibly it might be well to change the third subject (which though very picturesque is hardly historical) so as to make of it a picture of a cave home in the early Quaker settlement of Pennsylvania. There are several accounts of how these caves were made, and I think I could make an image of it so as to let the reader see pretty clearly what they looked like.

Do you approve of this change, and if so will you kindly let me know?   Faithfully yours   Howard Pyle

TLS (WP, DLC).

[1] Edward Penfield, art editor of *Harper's Magazine*, *Harper's Weekly*, and *Harper's Bazar*.

To Howard Pyle

My dear Mr. Pyle,   Princeton, New Jersey, 1 December, 1900.

I am very loath to give up Phips and the Treasure Ship. There is so little that is romantic in our national story that I greatly value these too infrequent touches of the picturesque. I should not mind losing Seth Sothel or Slaughter half so much as losing Capt. Phips. Why not substitute the cave home for one of them? I should quite like that, both for variety and for real intrinsic interest.

I am surprised to hear you say that the Phips incident is "hardly historical." The details are not known, but the raising of the ship is perfectly historical, and was the basis of all Phips's later prominence and success. See the little sketch of Phips, for example, in *Vol. VI. of Sparks's "American Biography."*[1]

I find (have only just now found for certain) that the date fixed for my lecture before the New Century Club in Wilmington is December sixth, next Thursday. I am to stay at Mr. Job Jackson's.[2] If you are to be at home the next morning, will you not let me know at what time I may call on you? A lecture rather does me up; but the next morning I will be fit to enjoy myself again.

With much regard,

In haste,   Faithfully Yours,   Woodrow Wilson

WWTLS (de Coppet Coll., NjP).

[1] Francis Bowen, "Life of Sir William Phips," in Jared Sparks (ed.), *Library of American Biography* (25 vols., Boston and London, 1834-48), 1st Series, VII, 1-102.

[2] Job H. Jackson, president of Jackson and Sharpe Co., who lived at 510 Adams St., Wilmington, Del.

From Howard Pyle

Dear Professor Wilson: [Wilmington, Del.] Dec. 3rd. 1900.

Of course I shall be most delighted to see you, say at my studio the day after you lecture here in Wilmington[.] I am only sorry that we are not to have the pleasure of entertaining you. I shall probably see you the night of the lecture.

In regard to the picture of Phips raising the Spanish treasure I shall of course[,] with a great deal of pleasure, follow your wishes in the matter. I will use the picture of the Pennsylvania cave dwelling instead of the subject of Seth Sothel seizing the Government of Carolina.

I did not mean to question of the historic accuracy of the story of lifting the Spanish treasure, I only meant that it was a personal history rather than a national history and was, perhaps, not so pertinent to your book.

Believe me to be, faithfully yours,   [Howard Pyle]

CCL (de Coppet Coll., NjP).

Two Letters from Henry Mills Alden

Dear Mr. Wilson: New York City December 4, 1900.

In your list of illustrations for Part IV of "Colonies and Nation" you have included a signature of La Salle in Volume IV of Winsor's History, page 244. The Art Department reports that this signature cannot be found in the place mentioned, and, therefore, unless you send us another reference we will have to omit it.[1]

In the same list of illustrations you mention a portrait of Sir Thomas Dongan as appearing in the Memorial History of New York City,[2] Volume I, page 399. The Memorial does contain what is alleged to be a portrait of Sir Thomas Dongan, and a footnote mentions that the original is in the New York Historical Society. Inquiry of the Society reveals the fact that the portrait referred to is of a gentleman and his wife which was found in the old Dongan mansion on Staten Island. But the Society also states that as Sir Thomas Dongan was never married, this is not a portrait of him. So positive is the Society in regard to the matter that they have declined to allow us to make a photograph to be used as a supposed portrait of Sir Thomas Dongan. The Society adds that so far as it has knowledge, there is no portrait in existence of Sir Thomas Dongan.

In the same list of illustrations for Part IV you mention a portrait of William Penn at the age of 52. This portrait is published in Bryant & Gay's History,[3] as you mention, but the Art Department is unable to trace it further than that, and as we cannot find the original of it, it would not be wise, in my opinion, to make a copy of this if it can be avoided. Therefore, if you have no objections I should like to substitute for this portrait of Penn at 52 another portrait of Penn at the age of 22, painted in 1666, which is in the Histori[c]al Society of Pennsylvania. I think this portrait of Penn as a young man would have unusual interest for our readers, because it is not familiar.

Would you please let me know about these three matters at your very earliest convenience?

Yours sincerely,   H. M. Alden

[1] The Art Department was right. A picture of La Salle appears in Justin Winsor (ed.), *Narrative and Critical History of America* (8 vols., Boston and

New York, 1884-89), IV, 244, but La Salle's signature is not printed in the volume.

[2] James Grant Wilson (ed.), *The Memorial History of the City of New-York* (4 vols., New York, 1892-93).

[3] William Cullen Bryant and Sydney Howard Gay, *A Popular History of the United States* . . . (4 vols., New York, 1876-81).

Dear Mr. Wilson: New York City December 5, 1900.

In your list of illustrations for Part IV of "Colonies and Nation" you mention the Seal of the Massachusetts Province, and refer to page 93, Volume 5, Winsor. Upon looking up this reference the Art Department finds that the Seal on the page mentioned by you is the Great Seal of Massachusetts used in the time of George I. In Volume 5 of the Records of Massachusetts on the cover and on the title page is a Seal of the Massachusetts Province which was used in the last quarter of the Seventeenth Century. Please let us know at once which one of these to use.

Sincerely yours,   H. M. Alden

TLS (WP, DLC).

Notes for an Address on Americanism

[Dec. 6, 1900]

All the world just now intensely conscious of the existence and the power of America.

A time of self-consciousness, too. We do not have to prove that we are the chief nation of the world: we admit it!

And yet it is the self-consciousness, not of youth, but of manhood. We are conscious of a new turn in the plot,—a dramatic situation, with all the world for audience,—and not a sympathetic audience, either.

"Americanism" is a fact, and needs analysis.

The difficulty of analyzing national character.

Certain of our traits as Americans evident enough:

Alertness, inquisitiveness, unconventionality, readiness for change, eagerness for the newest things and the most convenient.

The foreigner feels in us a lack of form, a lack of respect for things long established, a lack of reserve, a certain crudeness and immaturity as of men who do their work and their thinking on the run.

Our characteristics have been born of our life and our tasks. We have had a century of beginnings, and are only now about to have a century of finishings, in which we must turn about and examine What we have done: perfect it, test it, amend it, complete it.

A century our dramatic unit:

A century of colonization

A century of war, to oust the French and gain independence

A century of nation-making

A century of ————?

Our century of nation-making has bred in us the gifts and the strength of initiative,—has made us
    Builders,—building strong, but with elasticity, to take the strains off.
    Constitutional lawyers, by the same token.
    Fit for frontiers,—for rough and unsensitive work. Every man ready to use his own hands, and to be labourer or boss. Close to practical work.
    With sound and steadfast hearts.
    Confident of the validity of Liberty, but not too confident of its necessary or final form.
    With principles, still held with bigotry. But learners ever.
    With ideals, but without sentimentality.
    Ready for anything except the impossible.
    Mindful of the past and of human nature.
        There is now ay [an] American past,—of which the lesson is the same as that brought by the experience of every race: that Wisdom and Right are of old, and do not alter with environment.
    There is no special American human nature.
Education must foster ideals
    Effect adjustments and modulations
    Drive out
        Ignorance,
        Provincialism
        Noxious error.

Compare notes on Hill School Address, "What It Means To Be An American."[1]

WWT MS. (WP, DLC); Wilson's list of deliveries of this address omitted.
[1] They are missing.

A Newspaper Report of an Address on Americanism in Wilmington, Delaware

[Dec. 7, 1900]

LECTURE AT NEW-CENTURY CLUB.

An admirable address was delivered at the club last evening by Prof. Woodrow Wilson on "Americanism," a theme, he said, not profitable to discuss some time ago when it was a thing admired only in the home market and there was no evidence that the Old World wanted it, but now that the United States sets the pace for the nations it is necessary to examine it, and make it acceptable in the world's market by making it excellent and suitable for leadership in the world. It is baffling to get a look at our national character, especially as we own no mirror that we can get far enough away from for a fair idea of our national stature, and we do not like the pictures made of us elsewhere. The foreigner sees in Americanism an undue aggressiveness and crudeness, a deplorable inquisitiveness, insufficient respect for established order and disregard for the small conventionalities. He feels that we thrust our opinion where it is not desired and do our thinking on the run without stopping to perfect it, and he wishes we would grow up and get some mellowing experiences and adopt the little amenities of life. We render foreigners uneasy as a youngster does a roomful of elderly people, and especially his own mother. So we make England uncomfortable; she does not understand us; she recognizes most of the words we use, but not the way we put them together; she cannot account for our unlikeness to her in view of our likeness.

If we are to be statesmanlike, self-poised, and know the errand on which we have started we must assess our qualities and get rid of the undesirable; perfect ourselves in those that make for power and know what sort of power we wish to possess; examine the brand of those we are carrying into the field of international politics and asking the world to admire.

Some night the world will come to the threshold of a new century, but, as far as our national life is concerned, we have passed the threshold. We stepped into the arena of the world since the Spanish war and entered a new century. The last was one of beginnings all the way through. We pushed our border across the United States, but we left great spaces skipped and we've been filling them up on the same process. We beat a track across the prairie, finishing nothing, putting up shells of boards, instead of houses to hand down to our children; we sped on our way and did not stop to finish, and we have much to apologize for and explain to those who desire to study our institutions. Fancy any one making a scientific study of the government of New York City. Yet we are not more corrupt than other nations, but we have not finished our government any more than we have finished anything else; we have just hastily knocked things together. To perfect and complete them must be our work in the next century. That will be a more thorough test of our Americanism, to learn whether we have the patience to make a perfect instrument. We have not made our implements to last, for we will make new and better ones next year. In England one can read the whole history of bicycles on the road, for nobody has given up the one he first bought; he would not think of doing so till the old one was worn out. Here we would be as ashamed of riding a wheel a year or two old as of wearing an old-fashioned coat. This eagerness for newness and change is largely a pushing for something better, but we must get over that for we will not have the superabundance of material much longer. We must use our inventive faculty to perfect the old things.

The buoyancy and force of this century of beginning have given us force and splendid self-confidence and made men always ready for the frontier, to be ditch-diggers or State builders; it takes quick thinking and immediate action when things are being made out of nothing. We have a quick-wittedness in adjusting ourselves to new conditions that will make the new century tell a different story. We have gained an outlook, have seen the bigness of the world and the widening circle of our prosperity and influence and are not afraid of what we will find over the big curve. We must have ideals without sentimentality; principles without bigotry. Our inheritance of liberty, and drill in its principles, far antedates Magna Charta. The form of liberty which we now embody, are we to say this is the same form it must have for the undisciplined Filipinos? To us it means fixed, stable order and power of self-government. I do not believe they can be made ready for such for three or four generations. You cannot make people over by substituting one flag for another. Our flag is a thrilling sight in a foreign country but it cannot create character in races that have never lived under it. We must not expect the impossible but insist on education preceding power.

A. S.

Printed in the Wilmington,. Del., *Every Evening*, Dec. 7, 1900.

A News Item

[Dec. 11, 1900]
UNIVERSITY NOTICES. . . .
JURISPRUDENCE AND POLITICS.

Professor Woodrow Wilson is still unable to meet his classes, on account of an inflamed throat, which makes it imprudent for him to speak.

Printed in the *Daily Princetonian*, Dec. 11, 1900.

Notes for a Lecture

Waterbury, 12 Dec., 1900.
Self-Government.

Liberty is *institutional*: and *self-government* is *its embodiment*.
"I sh. suspend my congratulations on the new liberty of France, until I was informed how it had been combined with government;

with public force; with the discipline and obedience of armies; with the collection of an effective and well distributed revenue; with morality and religion; with the solidity of property; with peace and order; with social and civil manners."—*Burke*.[1]

Historically, national self-government is *English, and* the combination of local with national.

And yet this was *not popular government until the nineteenth century*. Justices of the Peace till '88; an *unpopular* House of Commons till '85 ('84). (Municipal Corporations Act, 1835).

At no time has self-government *meant*, in England, the *popular origination of institutions*.

In America, Self-Government has meant *self-originated organization*. But *everywhere else*, and amongst us by training, it has meant the habitual *accommodation of government*,—government possessed of an originative force and authority almost wholly its own,—*to the purposes and interests of the nation by* the processes which produce *Constitutional Government*:

Which we know, and can follow and define.

These processes have meant that, at each stage of national development, *the effective part of the nation has dealt with and controlled the Government* in the name of the whole; until, in our case (but in our case for a long time *alone*) the whole had become fit to act for itself, by popular representation.

(Free *brothers* upon the field of Agincourt with King Harry)

This is what Burke meant by combining Liberty with government. *Liberty is not itself government*: is not necessarily compatible with government. Postulates of the combination: A *sense of discipline: Self-control.*

The one invariable feature of Self-Government, underlying diversity of form, is a more than persuasive, an imperative *lay voice in affairs.*

It *involves*, ∴ , (1) *Publicity* of governmental action and freedom of opinion, and
(2) Full license of concerted public *agitation*.

It is best *supported and advanced* where there are
(1) A clear experimental *understanding of Rights*
(2) Sufficiently *equal social and economic conditions* to breed community of feeling.
(3) *Education* and *experience* in affairs.
(4) A polity likely to produce (a) a habit and spirit of *civic duty*, and managing talents
(b) *leading characters*

11 Dec., 1900[2]

WWhw MS. (WP, DLC).
[1] Edmund Burke, *Reflections on the Revolution in France*, in *The Works of the Right Honorable Edmund Burke*, 5th edn. (12 vols., Boston, 1877), III, 241-42.
[2] Wilson's composition date.

A Newspaper Report of a Lecture in
Waterbury, Connecticut

[Dec. 13, 1900]

WOODROW WILSON.

The Lecture of the Distinguished Professor
at Leavenworth Hall on "Self-Government."

Prof Woodrow Wilson of Princeton at Leavenworth hall delivered his lecture on "Self-Government" in the Women's club course before a large and fascinated audience last evening. Prof Wilson was introduced by A.R. Kimball[1] with a reference to the new place in popular esteem which is coming to be filled by the men of thought and leading [learning], the presidents and professors of our colleges. The lecture itself was a new one which had never been delivered before. The lecturer spoke entirely without notes and, as the charm lay largely in the felicity and strength of phrase, no report that is not stenographic can give the effect. Even that would miss a presence, manner and diction, that are almost perfect.

Prof Wilson began by pointing out that it is one thing to understand for ourselves what self-government is and quite another to explain it to somebody else. We propose to give self-government to various races that have come under our control. The fact that they do not know quite what we expect to give to them, and therefore we must make self-government in some way clear to them, has brought home to ourselves appreciation of the fact that we were not entirely clear in our own minds in what essentials self-government consists, familiar as we are with it concretely. The first popular notion of it was that self-government was a synonym for liberty, and that you could have no liberty under a government of force, that is, with a standing army. For this reason Jefferson and Madison, at the very time when they were extending our territory through the Louisiana purchase and the Florida seizure, cut down our standing army and practically paralyzed our navy by sending the ships out of commission. Hence, there was nothing to fight England with except shutting our doors to her, and war had to be made by a series of embargo acts. Self-government, then, was not the doing away with governing; it was simply setting the limits to governing at which the supreme power must stop. At this point Prof Wilson announced his text, a passage from Burke on the French revolution, in which Burke refused to recognize the new French regime as one that made for liberty, until he was sure it was a regime under which law, order and individual rights were protected.

Prof Wilson next discussed the popular idea that self-government was something that could be created, that government itself was something that could be made, unmade or re-made. He pointed out that our form of self-government was really an inheritance from the experience of England reaching back for centuries, although its special application to our own conditions was worked out by ourselves. The popular notion that self-government consists in electing somebody to some office was falsified by the fact that England, in this sense, did not have self-government until 1884; nor did it have local self-government until 1888. In 1884 the ballot was extended to pretty much everybody and in 1888 people had gained locally the control of their own affairs. Before 1888 pretty much everything locally was managed by magistrates, who were country gentlemen appointed by the crown and received no salaries. What a magistrate could do or could not do was something so anomalous and undefined that the only way one could get at a magistrate's duties was to arrange them alphabetically, bringing together a very queer assortment, as, under D, dog licenses and drainage. Self-government was really established in England when the barons bargained with King John at Runnymede and the Great Charter was adopted. The barons promised that they would be the king's faithful lieges if he did not overstep certain and definite limits of power, and in this bargain they acted as the representatives of the nation, since they represented its other classes no less than their own.

Self-government in other words is the government of self-control, control of the people by the superior power represented in the government, and the control of the government within the limits prescribed by the people. Under self-government no man can be deprived of life, liberty or property "without due process of law." This last qualifying phrase is one which continental advocates of a theoretical liberty can not understand. But it is in the poise between liberty to the individual and control by the government under a system of laws which constitutes self-government. It is therefore attached to no particular form. Its guarantee lies in publicity, in the people knowing what the policy of government is to be and therefore being free from fear of encroachment on popular rights.

It was in respect of this that Prof Wilson criticized our policy hitherto in the Philippines. It had been too much a policy of secrecy which was irritating and which was inconsistent with self-government.[2] He also warned his hearers not to feel that the forms of government there must be like our forms at home; that the institution of self-government in the Philippines meant the imposition of an American form of government upon them. He pleaded also for patience with those to whom was entrusted the responsibility of the inaugurating a departure, of the necessity for faith in them so long as they were known as faith-keeping men. Incidentally and humorously he touched upon the absurdity of expecting direction from the voice of the people. The average man remains only the average man though he be magnified to hundreds of thousands of voters. The real governing force comes from the few men of insight and power who initiate and control the policies of government.

Printed in the Waterbury, Conn., *American*, Dec. 13, 1900.
    [1] Arthur Reed Kimball, Associate Editor of the Waterbury *American*.
    [2] On this point, the *Waterbury Republican*, Dec. 13, 1900, reported as follows: "He spoke frankly what he thought concerning the Filipinos, blaming Gen Otis for not taking the people into his confidence and disclosing and explaining the plans of the United States regarding their future. He stated that if that had been done many regretable things which have since happened would have been avoided."
    Elwell Stephen Otis, Major General of the United States Army, had served as commanding general of United States forces in the Philippines and as military governor of the Islands from August 29, 1898, to May 5, 1900. In these capacities, he had been responsible for putting down the insurrection of Filipino nationalists under Emilio Aguinaldo.

From Richard Watson Gilder

My dear Professor Wilson: New York   December 13, 1900.
    I heartily appreciate your kind explanation.
    Meantime I am wondering what has become of the longer history.[1] Are you still to write that? I understood that you would consult with The Century Co. about *that* before it was arranged for, but perhaps circumstances have made that impossible. I wish circumstances had been in our favor this time, all along the line, but it can't be helped. I am sure you will make a delightful book.
                                Yours sincerely,   R. W. Gilder

TLS (WP, DLC).
    [1] That is, Wilson's "Short History of the United States," about which see the Editorial Note, "Wilson's 'Short History of the United States,'" Vol. 8.

To Richard Watson Gilder

My dear Mr. Gilder,   Princeton, 14 Dec., 1900
    Your note of yesterday has just been handed me.
    I find historical writing takes greater and greater hold on my

thought and imagination, and it is going to be desperately hard to drop it. But, when this present job is finished, I expect to take a year off in Europe, to break the current; and there is no telling when I shall return to the larger History, now locked safely away to mellow. You shall know if I take it up again.

Meanwhile I am to turn (closet) politician, and tell the world what history really means in the terms of institutions and practical affairs (ahem!)[1] May the world attend, and not smile!

With warm regard,

Sincerely Yours,   Woodrow Wilson

ALS (in possession of Andrew L. Brown).
[1] Here Wilson was referring to his projected "The Philosophy of Politics."

From Henry Mills Alden

Dear Mr. Wilson: New York City December 14, 1900.

Again I am under obligations to you for your promptness in returning the proofs which were sent to you by special delivery.

The map of New Amsterdam and Vicinity, 1666, which you say you do not recognize, is the one which appears in our copy of Winsor's History, in volume 4, page 440, as called for in the list of illustrations you furnished us. Of course we followed the list exactly, that accounts for this particular map having been reproduced.   Sincerely yours,   H. M. Alden

TLS (WP, DLC).

From Thomas L. Snow

The Bluff[,] Judd-Haven
My dear Prof. Wilson,   Muskoka, Ontario Dec 14th 1900

Last mail brought to me yr. long letter, embodying a highly generous offer for my brother's property.[1] Whether or no he will decline to sell in the face of such tremendous inducement, the fact remains that he may never again expect to receive such an offer and this I have taken pains to illustrate for him in a letter, which, *together with yours*, I despatch to him by tomorrow's mail.

In compliance with yr. request an introduction to my brother Cecil is herein enclosed, and I shall be more than pleased if future correspondence between you and him results in "The Bluff" property being partially bounded by yours.[2]

Will you let Mrs. Wilson and the family know that our Xmas greetings to them are proportionate to the impressions which they left behind at The Bluff last summer, and which for fear of seeming extravagant, we will leave for them to surmise.

Thanking you for the cordial sentiments expressed in yr. letter, Believe me   Very faithfully yours,   Thos L Snow.

ALS (WP, DLC). Enc.: Thomas L. Snow to Cecil Snow, Dec. 14th, 1900, ALS (WP, DLC).

¹ It included a small island in Lake Rosseau, together with some adjacent mainland. In May 1902, Wilson purchased additional acreage from Thomas L. Snow (see T. L. Snow to WW, May 17, 1902), giving him a total of approximately one hundred acres. There is a map of Wilson's property and the surrounding area enclosed in T. L. Snow to WW, Sept. 13, 1904, ALS (WP, DLC).

² Wilson did in fact purchase most of Cecil Snow's property a short time later, as T. L. Snow to WW, Jan. 12, 1904, discloses.

From Charles Bradley[1]

Dear Sir,   Newark, New Jersey Dec. 16, 1900

My attention was recently called, by my son—a student at Harvard—to your book "Congressional Government," used I believe, in the regular course at that Institution, in which he said there were opinions regarding the appointment of Mr. Justice [Joseph P.] Bradley (my Father) to the Supreme Court, somewhat derogatory to his independence of judgment in the famous Legal Tender decision of 1870.[2]

I have since purchased the book and read your "Introductory" as well as the article entitled the "Session" in Vol: CXI. pp. 48 et seq. of the Not'h. American Review, and regret to observe that you have fallen into the same error that others have done as to the date of that decision.

On page 38 of your book you state, "In December 1869, the Sup. Ct. decided against the constitutionality of Congress's pet Legal Tender Acts; and in the following March a vacancy on the bench opportunely occurring, and a new justiceship having been created to meet the emergency &c &c &c"

These statements are so absolutely refuted in a paper written by Senator Geo. F. Hoar of Mass., that I take the liberty of sending you one,[3] believing that after reading it, you as a fair-minded man, will be glad to correct in some equally public way, the erroneous impression to be gathered from your book—especially as it is used by *young* students.

As to the Article in the Nth. Amn. Review, it is so obviously partisan that I do not care to discuss it—except to say that I have in my possession the answer to the question at the bottom of page 50, "What occurred when the Court retired for consultation" &c. in a "statement" prepared by Justice [Samuel Freeman] Miller and signed by the majority of the Court, stating in detail the occurrences of that consultation & the true inside history of the whole controversy *in the Court*. This Statement has never been published, but certain publicists & distinguished gentlemen have seen it, and it would give me great pleasure to submit to you if you desire it.

Pardon my thus addressing you, but whenever & wherever I see this mistake as to an *historical* fact, in which I take naturally a personal interest, I undertake to correct it & I trust after reading Sen. Hoar's paper, you will say that *he* has succeeded.

Very Respectfully   Charles Bradley

ALS (Wilson Library, DLC).
¹ Associated with P. Ballantine & Sons, brewers of Newark, Bradley was the son of Joseph P. Bradley, Associate Justice of the United States Supreme Court, 1870-92.
² He referred to a passage in *Congressional Government* (Boston and New York, 1885), p. 38, which reads as follows: "In December, 1869, the Supreme Court decided against the constitutionality of Congress's pet Legal Tender Acts; and in the following March a vacancy on the bench opportunely occurring, and a new justiceship having been created to meet the emergency, the Senate gave the President to understand that no nominee unfavorable to the debated acts would be confirmed, two justices of the predominant party's way of thinking were appointed, the hostile majority of the court was outvoted, and the obnoxious decision reversed." In support of his statement Wilson cited the article by Henry Adams in the *North American Review* mentioned later in Bradley's letter. Though Wilson mentioned no names, Joseph P. Bradley was one of the two men appointed to the Supreme Court in 1870.
³ George F. Hoar, *The Charge against President Grant and Attorney General Hoar of Packing the Supreme Court of the United States, to Secure the Reversal of the Legal Tender Decision, by the Appointment of Judges Bradley and Strong, Refuted* (Worcester, Mass., 1896). A copy of this pamphlet is in the Wilson Library, DLC.

Two Announcements

[Dec. 17, 1900]

Professor Woodrow Wilson will go abroad next June, travelling in Europe during the academic year 1901-1902.

UNIVERSITY NOTICES. . . .

Professor Woodrow Wilson will meet his classes as usual this week.

Printed in the *Daily Princetonian*, Dec. 17, 1900.

To Charles Bradley

My dear Sir,   Princeton, New Jersey, 20 December, 1900.

I very much appreciate your letter of the sixteenth. I have for some time been convinced of the unfair imputations of the passage to which you refer in my "Congressional Government";

but I have never had an opportunity of revising the text since its publication. It has many times been reprinted; but no change has been made in any part of it since its original appearance. Stereotyped plates are regarded by publishers as a very rigid finality; the change necessary in that passage would be very considerable; and I have never had the chance to make it. I very much hope that before very long I shall be allowed to revise at least that part.

Thanking you again for thus taking it for granted that I wished to know and speak the truth,

Very sincerely Yours,   Woodrow Wilson

WWTLS (NjHi).

From Joseph Ruggles Wilson

109 North 5th St., Wilmington, N. C.,[1]

My dearest son,   December 22/.00

Please allow me to trouble you again to mail to me the coupon due Jan. 1, 1901 on Augusta City Bond.

I have been quite ill but under good doctoring I am I believe in statu quo.

Love to all.   Your affc.   Father

ALS (WP, DLC).
[1] Dr. Wilson was making an extended visit in Wilmington and staying with Mrs. Frederick J. Robinson, daughter-in-law of his old friend, Charles H. Robinson.

An After-Dinner Speech to the New England Society in the City of New York[1]

[[Dec. 22, 1900]]

Mr. Dodge,[2] Ladies and Gentlemen: I cannot but regard it as a whimsical fortune that a Scotch-Irishman should be brought here to pay tribute to the New England Society. The Scotch-Irishman is not fond of paying anything except his just debts, and there is always a certain risk in letting him speak his real mind. Mr. Dodge himself has given you some intimation of the risk he knows he is incurring by intimating to you—he was thinking of the Irish in me, I hope, rather than of the Scotch—that if I spoke long enough it would be a desecration of the Sabbath.

And yet I believe, gentlemen, that nothing gives one strong race so much satisfaction as to pay its respects to another strong race. We came later to this continent than you did, but we had the better opportunity for observing your characters and the cut of your jibs. We saw how important was the task which you had half completed. We saw how necessary it was that certain other elements should be added which you had not contributed, and so we are here, gentlemen, and we don't mind talking about it. We, like you, are beginning to form societies to annex the universe; we, like you, are beginning to elect memorialists who shall record how every line of strength in the history of the world is a line colored by Scotch-Irish blood. There is a great deal in that. [Laughter and applause.] I believe that it is necessary that races of different characters should exchange their ideas as well as their compliments, and that we should understand just what our relative parts are to be in the great game that we are to play upon this continent. The Puritan was—as Dr. Hadley[3] has said— intensely human; but you will remember that he apologized to God as many as three times a day for the fact [laughter], and that it was an imperative part of his creed that he should root out diligently, in season and out of season, the pestiferous elements of the flesh that were in him. [Laughter.] Now, I have no objection to the hatred that Dr. Hadley referred to. I believe in a certain degree of intolerance. It is an eminently comfortable indulgence. I believe that intolerance can express itself, if not exactly as a dear old President of Princeton expressed it, at any rate, in more parliamentary form. I refer to that occasion when he brought all the strong flavor of his Scotch-Presbyterianism to a meeting of the Evangelical alliance—one of the early gatherings of that interesting association—when Dr. Huntington arose and proposed that they adopt the Apostles' Creed as a platform upon which all could stand. "Tut! tut!" said Dr. McCosh in an undertone, to a neighbor, "I'll not descend into hell with the Episcopalians." [Laughter.] There is in this, gentlemen, the flavor and the definiteness which go with the Scotch character.

I believe that if you will look into it you will find that you are worshipping your ancestors at a safe distance. Dr. Hadley said that we had met this evening to celebrate your *descent* from those Fathers [laughter], and the old phrase came into my mind: *Facilis descensus*. It is not very much to your credit that you have descended; it will be to your credit if you ascend to the standards which they established. I sometimes recall when I think of the shock and the change which the Puritan principles underwent when they came to the City of New York [laughter], the story, half-pathetic and half-amusing, which is told of an old lady who, unaccustomed to travel, boarded a train some-

where in the neighborhood of New Haven, coming in this direction, and nervously asked the brakeman if that train stopped at
Forty-second Street. "Well, ma'am, if it don't, you'll get the
dumbdest bumping you ever got!" Now, I have sometimes thought
that the New England principles, when they stopped at Forty-
second Street, got the "dumbdest bumping" they ever got. [Laugh-
ter and applause.]

And yet, seriously, gentlemen, there is a great deal which you
have preserved besides your handsome persons. You have preserved what I may be allowed to call, in rhetorical phrase, a great
deal of the old structural iron, though you have changed a good
deal about the exterior of the building and have employed new
and French architects. I ask you to consider with me just what
contribution it was that the Puritans seem to have made to the
civilization of this country. Of course I can tell you. [Laughter.]
That contribution is worth considering, because, having been
obliged to read many of the historians of this country, and having
found that most of them were also celebrating their descent from
the Pilgrim Fathers, I have read in their pages, and for a long
time believed, that the history of this country was the expansion
of New England. If it was the expansion of New England, it
spread thin. [Laughter.] And having been born, as I was born,
in the valley of Virginia, where they do not accept that view,
except as heretical, I was led in my maturer years to question
its validity. I did not see reason to believe that all the elements
of this country came out of what was, after all, the not very
productive soil of New England, because when I looked at the
character of those Puritan men they seemed to me to stand for
one single principle—a very splendid principle, I allow you, but,
nevertheless, the single principle of discipline, of order, of polity.
It was for the discipline that pulls in harness; it was for subjection to authority; it was for crucifixion of the things which did
not comport with a fixed and rigid creed that they strove. These
men stood for the discipline of life. They did not stand for the
quick pulses which have operated in some of the most momentous things that have taken place on this continent, but they
stood for those lessons of duty which they read out of a Bible,
interpreted in the light of a Calvinistic creed, cut in a definite
pattern, not allowing elasticity of interpretation; which forced
men to settle in different parts of New England, because, if they
differed with each other, they had to go and live somewhere else
[laughter]; they could not continue to live with each other. The
churches of Massachuetts did indeed pay their tribute of respect,
and very generously, to Mr. Thomas Hooker, but Mr. Hooker

found it more convenient to live at Hartford, and he lived at Hartford, because he did not like the doctrine of Mr. Cotton; because he did not like the doctrine of Mr. Wilson—a very respectable name; because he did not feel that there was just the sort of room for his doctrine in Newtown that there might be in the new places on the Connecticut. There is a sense in which the development of America is represented by the movement of people out of Massachusetts into that wild Cave of Adullam in Rhode Island, whither all who were heretical, all who were discontented, all who were ungovernable, betook themselves, and where they combined to form that fine, effervescent mixture which is more like the rest of the country than the plain, unmixed material of the places of older settlements. Those men who struggled South through the Narragansett country, through the cold, forbidding woods, and made their new homes on the delightful prospects along the Bay of Narragansett—who made those places destined to have the distinction of containing the most fashionable summer resort in the United States—they represented that expulsive power of New England which certainly has been one of the causes of the growth of this country. [Applause.] There is an application here for an old theme of Dr. Chalmers,[4] who preached one of the greatest of his sermons on the subject: "The Expulsive Power of a New Affection."[5] These men got an affection for new things, and they found that only old things would be permitted in the places where they were living, and so they had to seek homes elsewhere.

So when the race to which I belong landed on this continent and made its way in its principal migrations through the State of Pennsylvania and down through the Cumberland Valley and the valley of the Shenandoah and into the country of the Southwest; and then crossed the mountains and was among the first to face the French on the Ohio, and, going with the vanguard of the whole movement, deployed at last upon the plains that led to the Great Valley of the Mississippi, it saw the thing which it remained for another principle than that of discipline to do—the principle of aspiration, the principle of daring, the principle of unrest, the principle of mere adventure, which made the level lines of the prairie seem finer and more inviting than the uplifted lines of the mountain; that made it seem as if the world were bigger on the plains, and as if the feet of young men were the feet of leaders. And this was a place where all those new things should be tried and all those ungoverned adventures should be made which filled this continent with an abounding life. For there is something, gentlemen, of this balance in our lives be-

tween the discipline of restraint, the discipline of the old re-
minders of moral principle, and that uplifting power of an
unregulated ambition. I believe that there is a sense, if you
will permit me to say so in all soberness, in which there is a contrast between the New England spirit and the national spirit.
You contributed something without which the national spirit
would have simply set the world on fire, without being able to
confine its power in piston rods to drive the heart of machines to
make furnaces hold the abounding heat. You contributed the
restraint—that mechanical combination, that poise, that power
of union, which is the spirit of discipline. But there was besides
a national spirit which, if it had not received this restraint, would
have broken all bonds. The spirit of progression is this spirit of
aspiration which has led us into new conditions and to face a
new destiny. [Applause.]

I pray that sober principle may ever be whispered at our ear,
that we may be ever critical of our motives, that we may ever
be self-examining men with regard to our lives and conduct; but
I also pray that that fine discipline of the heart may but precede
the expansion of power; that that fine elevation and expansion
of nature which ventures everything may go with us to the ends
of the earth, so be it we go to the ends of the earth carrying
conscience and the principles that make for good conduct. I
believe that it is necessary that when we get reformers upon our
platforms we should see that their function is properly spelled.
[Applause.] Most of our reformers are retro-reformers. They want
to hale us back to an old chrysalis which we have broken; they
want us to resume a shape which we have outgrown; they want
us to take back the outward form of principles which they think
cannot live in a new habiliment, or prosper under new forms and
conditions. It is not the forms of our lives; it is the principles of
our lives that count. I can quote Scripture for this [laughter],
though not Scripture which, I am afraid, would be regarded as
exactly orthodox in Princeton. There was an old darkey preacher
who said, "The Lord said unto Moses, Come fo'th; and he came
fifth, and lost the race." [Great laughter.] Now, I think we ought
to come forth, and not to come fifth and lose the race; and if
we sufficiently obey this fine, expansive impulse in us we shall
not make it necessary that we should forget the fine old discipline
of ancient doctrine; we shall not forget to have some sense of
duty, something of a faith, some reverence for the laws ourselves
have made.

I believe that the principal menace of a democracy is that the
disciplinary power of the common thought should overwhelm

the individual instinct of man's originative power, and that that individuality should be a little rubbed off and lost. I should wish to hear every man dare speak his thoughts. I should wish to have every man use a boldness, which I should also wish to see in the nation. I pray that the time may never come when we are not ready to do new things, when we are not ready to acknowledge that the age has changed. I suppose you have all heard Mr. Joseph Jefferson tell the story about the little boy who was to be taken by his mother to hear the play of "Rip Van Winkle." His mother fell ill and could not take him, but rather than disappoint him she turned the ticket over to his aunt and asked her to take the lad. "But," she said, "you must remember that he never has been to the theatre before, and you must explain things to him, as he cannot understand it." But the aunt, being less solicitous than the mother, forgot all about the boy until the curtain went down on the young "Rip Van Winkle" and was about to rise on the old "Rip Van Winkle," when it occurred to the aunt to say to the boy, "You know, Johnny, twenty years have gone by since the curtain went down." He said, "Where's my mamma?" [Laughter.] Now, that is the attitude of a great many people whom I very sincerely respect. You say to them, "Twenty years have gone by since we fought Spain," and they say, "Where are our papas?" [Laughter.] They go to consult a generation that did not know anything about it. They even take liberties with the Father of his Country. Now Washington was a Virginian, and, perhaps, since I am a Virginian, I may be allowed to interpret Washington. [Laughter.] We all know each other down there. [Applause.] When you reflect that Washington wrote his Farewell Address to something over three million people, to whom he was, if his letters are to be believed, very willing to say good-bye [laughter], and if you will understand that Address to have meant, as it would seem to have meant: "I want you to discipline yourselves and stay still and be good boys until you grow up, until you are big enough to stand the competition of foreign countries, until you are big enough to go abroad in the world," I think you will have put the proper interpretation on it. "Wait," he said, "until you need not be afraid of foreign influence, and then you shall be ready to take your part in the field of the world." I do not accept the interpretation of Washington's Farewell Address that those people who have but seen the curtain go down accept. [Laughter and applause.]

Now, gentlemen, will you follow the Scotch-Irish across the continent and into the farther seas of the Pacific? Will you follow the Star of Empire with those men who will follow anything which they think will drop profit or amusement? [Laughter.] Are you ready, are we ready, to go shoulder to shoulder, forgetting our differences of origin, forgetting our fatal descent, forgetting all the things which might restrain us, not going with faces averted over shoulder, but going with faces to the front, faces that will scorn to face a shame but will dare to face a glory? [Applause.]

Printed in *Ninety-Fifth Anniversary Celebration of the New England Society in the City of New York* . . . (New York, n.d.), pp. 39-46.
  [1] Delivered in the grand ballroom of the Waldorf-Astoria Hotel on December 22, 1900.
  [2] William Earl Dodge (the second generation of the name), president of Phelps, Dodge & Company, wholesale metal merchants of New York. He was the father of Cleveland Hoadley Dodge and William Earl Dodge (deceased), Wilson's classmates at Princeton.
  [3] President Arthur Twining Hadley of Yale, who had spoken just before Wilson, on "Forefathers' Day." Other speakers at the dinner were St. Clair McKelway, Senator Albert J. Beveridge, Lieutenant General Nelson A. Miles, and Rear Admiral Albert S. Barker.
  [4] Thomas Chalmers (1780-1847), Scottish minister, theologian, and prolific author, first Moderator of the Free Church of Scotland, noted for his homiletical ability and his interest in the relation of Christianity to social and economic problems.
  [5] Wilson had probably read "The Expulsive Power of a New Affection" in *The Select Works of Thomas Chalmers, D.D., LL.D.* (4 vols., New York, 1848), IV, 271-78. The sermon, with an introduction by John Angus MacVannel, was reprinted in the autumn of 1901 by Crowell & Co. of New York. Wilson referred to it many times later.

From William Earl Dodge

My dear Professor Wilson: New York.   December 24th, 1900.

Yesterday afternoon I called at Mr. [C. C.] Cuyler's, hoping to find you. I had no opportunity on Saturday evening to thank you as I wanted to, for the very brilliant and charming address, which you gave us at the New England Society festival. It was a great delight to all who were present, and warmly appreciated by all of our officers.

With sincere regard, and best wishes for the Christmas season, I am,   Very cordially yours,   W. E. Dodge

TLS (WP, DLC).

To Charles Bradley

My dear Sir,   Princeton, New Jersey, 26 December, 1900.

In reply to your very kind and courteous note of the twenty-third,[1] I would say that I shall be quite willing to have you publish such part of my recent letter to you as you may deem suitable in the connection you speak of.[2] I had never, by the way, regarded the view expressed in my "Congressional Government" as in any way bringing personal discredit on your eminent father. It never seemed to me the case of a bargain. I had supposed simply that his views were known, not that he was asked what they were as a condition precedent to his appointment.

Very truly Yours,   Woodrow Wilson

WWTLS (NjHi).
　[1] It is missing.
　[2] At this time, Bradley was compiling the volume that appeared a year later as Charles Bradley (ed.), *Miscellaneous Writings of the Late Hon. Joseph P. Bradley* (Newark, N.J., 1901). In a brief biographical sketch of his father, Charles Bradley, in a footnote on page 7, cited Wilson's remarks in *Congressional Government* as one example of the "unjust imputations" cast upon Justice Bradley "by many writers." Bradley reproduced Wilson's letter to him of December 20, 1900, in full on page 8.

From Sarah Baxter Bird

22 Mount Vernon Place. [Baltimore] Dec 26/oo

The picture is charming! The *art* aspect is beautiful & I thank you so much for the remembrance. Dear little Jessie! How the childish face has changed & while still a child, it is *so* spirituelle. My love to them all, the three Graces & a *lot* for the sweet Mother & for the dear Father.

I have been troubled about my old friend "Tom" Hoyt.[1] He was to have preached for us one Sunday & to have been my guest while here, but his illness prevented. The gentleman who filled his place, told my son,[2] that while the Dr was not alarmingly ill, he was considered very sick. Tell Ellen if she knows aught of his condition, please to write & let me know. I am sincerely fond of him, my dear true old friend.

I subscribed to Harper this year, because I saw you were to have an article in it & have all enjoyed that since. You are to appear again, n'est-ce pas? . . .

I wish I could see you two dear ones. Can't you come over for a little visit soon? Think of it, & write me "yes."

Your sincerely attached friend   S. C. B.

You can *almost* name your own time. Say it. All send love.

ALI (WP, DLC).
　[1] Mrs. Wilson's uncle, the Rev. Dr. Thomas Alexander Hoyt of Philadelphia.
　[2] Wilson Edgeworth Bird of Baltimore.

From Henry Mills Alden

Dear Mr. Wilson: New York City December 27, 1900

I have received Part VII of "Colonies and Nation," and have had voucher made out in payment for same, which will reach you in due course.

With all good wishes of the season,

Sincerely yours,   H. M. Alden

TLS (WP, DLC).

From Henry Edward Rood[1]

Dear Mr. Wilson: New York City December 29, 1900.

In your list of illustrations for Part V of "Colonies and Nation" you call for a facsimile page of the New York Weekly Journal. What Number of that newspaper do you wish reproduced—the first Number dated November 5th, or the second Number dated November 12th, which contains an article on the freedom of the press? We have already had a plate made of the first Number of the New York Weekly Journal, and it is barely possible that we will be unable to get a plate made of the Number containing the freedom of the press, in time for Part V. But if you desire to have the freedom of the press Number reproduced every endeavor will be made to meet your wishes.

With best wishes for a happy New Year,

Sincerely yours,   H. E. Rood

For Mr. Alden, and in his absence.

TLS (WP, DLC).
[1] Assistant Editor of *Harper's Magazine*.

An Historical Commentary and Critique[1]

[January 1901]

EDITOR'S STUDY.

. . . Truth is really stranger than fiction. True history is therefore more interesting than any other writing. Bald facts are not the truth; they will not serve for so much as the mere warp of its

[1] In reply to H. M. Alden to WW, Oct. 8, 1900, Wilson sent the editor of *Harper's Magazine* a critique of American history and historians, along with a commentary on his own forthcoming work, receipt of which Alden acknowledged on October 11. Wilson's manuscript is missing. However, internal evidence—particularly style, phraseology, and points made—indicates that the following document is Wilson's text, only slightly revised and rephrased by Alden.

texture. Every great fact of history as aggressively as the Theban Sphinx propounds its riddle concerning itself, not only as to Whence and Why, but as to What it is. Accuracy is not illumination; and no logic furnishes a key to interpretation, for there is no philosophy of history distinct from that of our human nature. Some of the writing known as fiction—like a few of Harrison Ainsworth's novels—more vividly and clearly tells the truth than any annalist. Imagination of a high order seems essential to the fidelity of portrayal. The historian must be an artist and his interpretation creative—a vital speculation. The impenetrable mask under which the event first appears to us is withdrawn and the living alchemy disclosed. Next to poetry the best history should be the highest form of literature. The ideal has never been fully realized, but all great historians have had a conception of the dignity and magnitude of their office. Thucydides, the earliest of them, breathed that air which was the inspiration of Phidias and Sophocles, and boldly claimed for his work that, like theirs, it was something everlasting. Gibbon and Macaulay show signs of this lofty claim and aspiration, not so apparent in the easy and graceful narrative of the genial Hume.

Giving ample credit to the erudition and versatility of Freeman and to the vividly dramatic power of Froude, yet it is true that for a real history of her national development England waited for Green, who was the first English historian willing to sacrifice all else to the one simple purpose of writing a history of the English people, and whose accomplishment of this ideal had a literary and artistic value which gave it distinction and general acceptance.

It is no disparagement to the able writers of United States history to say that none of them thus far has met or attempted to meet the requirements which Green deemed essential to the realization of his ideal. Bancroft gave fifty years of his life to his elaborate work, closing with the adoption of the Constitution, but neither in structure nor in style can it be called satisfactory. Hildreth, covering a later period, is to the student what good dry wine is to the epicure, but his history is wholly political. Henry Adams, covering much of the same period as Hildreth, gives a fuller view, and is so picturesque and brilliant that, for merely intellectual satisfaction, we regret the limitations of his canvas, and wish that he might in the same vein write a complete history of the United States. No one better than Parkman could have written the story of the conflict between the French and the English for the dominion of this continent. McMaster has undertaken a history of the people of the United States which is most interesting, and grows better with each new volume; but the plan he set out with necessarily limits its value as history in the largest sense. Winsor has embodied in a true and skilful narrative his most valuable collection of material concerning the discovery and early history of America. Rhodes impartially and with graphic portraiture tells the story of the conflict between freedom and slavery. John Fiske has given the most philosophical interpretation of our history; whatever he touches he illuminates; to the thoughtful reader he is explicit and satisfactory, and he effectively does what he attempts—which is not a direct narrative wherein the philosophy is wholly implicit and the illumination incidental. None of the historians we have mentioned has attempted to give in large lines and on a plan similar to Green's a comprehensive history of the United States.

Such an undertaking has been ventured by Professor Woodrow Wilson, and the first instalment of his "Colonies and Nation: A Short History of the People of the United States," is presented in this number of the Magazine. The purpose rather than the plan suggests a comparison with Green's work. The ideal is the same, though the method must be different. The history of the United States has a unity which belongs to that of no other modern nation. There is no break in it like that which Freeman points out dividing the England before from the England after Edward the First. For a century and a half—its longer period—our history is properly English, as racially and radically it must be to the end; moreover, our colonial determined the lines of our national development, institutionally. But the conditions of our growth, and especially of our national growth, have been peculiar, and have made for us critical moments quite distinct from those punctuating English history. It is only now that, in the crucial conflict of Christendom, we stand before the world in policy as well as in race alongside of England.[2] Napoleon in the Louisiana cession anticipated our perpetual antagonism to that nation; and the chief enemies of England have, from the Revolution, been the friends of the United States.

It is interesting, when a historical work is undertaken like that of Professor Wilson, to note the author's own views concerning the writing of history.

Mr. Charles Francis Adams, who is president of the Massachusetts Historical Society, said, in a recent address before the Historical Society of Wisconsin, that the three elements which enter into the make-up of the ideal historian are training, judg-

[2] Here Wilson seems to have been referring to the growing naval and imperialistic rivalry between Great Britain and Germany.

ment, and the literary sense, and laid stress upon the necessity for such a historian to be in close touch with the generation he addresses: "The true historian—he who most sympathetically as well as correctly reads to the present the lessons to be derived from the past—I hold to be the only latter-day prophet."[3]

This is in accord with Freeman's view that "past politics is present history," and following this conception we shall doubtless have in every generation new histories of the United States reading new lessons from the past, adapted to new audiences and new conditions. The lessons will have value, but is the office of the historian primarily didactical? Listen to Professor Wilson in his essay on this subject, published (in a volume entitled *Mere Literature*) a few years ago:

"The truth of history is a very complex and very occult matter. It consists of things which are invisible as well as of things that are visible. It is full of secret motives and of a chance interplay of trivial and yet determining circumstances; it is shot through with transient passions, and broken athwart here and there by what seem cruel accidents; it cannot all be reduced to statistics or newspaper items or official recorded statements. And so it turns out, when the actual test of experiment is made, that the historian must have something more than a good conscience, must be something more than a good man. He must have an eye to see the truth; and nothing but a very catholic imagination will serve to illuminate his matter for him: nothing less than keen and steady insight will make even illumination yield him the truth of what he looks upon. Even when he has seen the truth only half his work is done, and that not the more difficult half. He must then make others see it just as he does; only when he has done that has he told the truth. What an art of penetrative phrase and just selection must he have to take others into the light in which he stands! . . . It is his purpose, or should be, to give a true impression of his theme as a whole—to show it, not lying upon his page in an open and dispersed analysis, but set close as an intimate synthesis, every line, every stroke, every bulk even, omitted which does not enter of very necessity into a single and unified image of the truth. Standing sure, a man of science as well as an artist, he must take and use all of his equipment for the sake of his art—not to display his materials, but to subordinate and transform them in his effort to make, by

[3] Charles Francis Adams, *The Sifted Grain and the Grain Sifters: An Address at the Dedication of the Building of the State Historical Society of Wisconsin at Madison, October 19, 1900* (Cambridge, Mass., 1900), p. 40. This paragraph referring to Adams's address was obviously inserted by Alden.

touch and cunning of hand and tool, the perfect image of what he sees, the very truth of his seer's vision of the world. The true historian works always for the whole impression, the truth with unmarred proportions, unexaggerated parts, undistorted visage."

Professor Wilson instances Green as an exceptional example of one "who saw the truth and had the art and mastery to make others see it as he did in all its breadth and multiplicity"; but he complains of this great master of narrative as lacking variety: "His method, whatever the topic, is ever the same. His sentences, his paragraphs, his chapters, are pitched one and all in the same key. It is a very fine and moving key, . . . but some themes it will not serve." His book "is full of a certain sort of variety, but it is only a variety of a great plan's detail, not the variety of English life. It has none of the irregularity of the actual experiences of men and communities. It explains, but does not contain, their variety. The matter should rule the plan, not the plan the matter."

Professor Wilson insists that the historian should not from his present point of view look backward upon the material he handles. "A nineteenth-century plan laid like a standard and measure upon a seventeenth-century narrative will infallibly twist it and make it false."[4] He thinks comment, deliberate and formal comment, by the historian is, from the point of view of his own day, futile and impertinent. In other words, the thing is not a matter of didactics, but a matter of art, of reproduction. The only present-day element to be admitted is the mind of the audience—and this only so far as necessary to insure the production of the illusion of reality for present-day minds. Speaking for himself, in regard to his present undertaking, he would say: "I am writing a history of the people of the United States—a short history, but upon a plan which allows the writer more freedom than that of a work designed for a text-book. It is my intention to give a true picture, with a just perspective. I am trying to produce explanatory narrative, the explanation being not so much express and formal as carried in the colors and grouping of the narrative itself, and being an explanation made (or rather implied) as much as may be from the point of view of the times described."[5]

Printed in *Harper's Magazine*, cii (Jan. 1901), 322-24.

[4] All the quotations in this and the preceding paragraph are also from "The Truth of the Matter."

[5] Here, of course, Alden is quoting directly from Wilson's commentary.

From George Parker Winship[1]

My dear Mr. Wilson,   Providence 2 January 1901

When you make a book out of your "Colonies and Nation" *please* don't tell about Coronado "threading the cañons of the Colorado . . . to the Missouri." He went to the Missouri, but the other is neither fact nor geographically possible fiction, & the "river cliffs" were not where Coronado found the pueblo peoples. Even the man who "life-saved" the enchanted Mesa knows enough to know better than that.[2]

I am on behalf of my good friend Vazquez Coronado,
                    Sincerely yours   George Parker Winship.

ALS (WP, DLC).

[1] Librarian of the John Carter Brown Library, Providence, R.I., and prolific bibliographer.

[2] Winship was referring to a paragraph on Coronado in "Colonies and Nation," *Harper's Magazine*, CII (Jan. 1901), 179-80. He had written extensively on the Coronado expedition and was to publish a translation of the extant narratives of the expedition in 1904. Wilson drastically revised the paragraph that Winship criticized in his *History of the American People* (5 vols., New York and London, 1902), I, 16.

To Robert Bridges

My dear Bobby,   Princeton, 3 Jan'y, 1901

I enjoyed the poem *very* much. It is done with delightful delicacy and skill and keeps the flavour of the original with singular success.[1] The Christmas greeting I enjoyed no less. By the way, the poem on old age in the *Scribner* was by yourself, *nicht wahr*?[2]

We missed you all through the evening at Billy's.[3] One of the things I *go* for is to see you. But C. C. [Cuyler] tells me you made a perfect *tear* at the Williams [College] dinner, and that's much on the other side of the a/c.

                    Affectionately Yours,   Woodrow Wilson

ALS (WC, NjP).

[1] As a Christmas present, Bridges had sent to Wilson and other friends a printed pamphlet containing his own season's greetings in poetical form; "Le Bonheur de ce monde," a sonnet by Christophe Plantin (c. 1514-89), the celebrated French printer and typographer; and his own translation of Plantin's poem. A copy of the pamphlet is in the Wilson Papers, Library of Congress.

[2] Robert Bridges, "A Prayer of Old Age," *Scribner's Magazine*, XXIX (Jan. 1901), 28-29. Wilson's query is mysterious, since Bridges' name appears just below the title of the poem. Perhaps it had been omitted inadvertently in early printings of this issue.

[3] That is, the annual Isham dinner in New York. About these celebrated affairs, see WW to EAW, May 6, 1886, n. 1, Vol. 5.

From Cleveland Hoadley Dodge

My Dear "Tommie,"　　　　　　　　New York. Jany. 3, 1901.

I did not have a chance after the New England dinner to tell you how pleased and delighted I was with your speech. Everybody was crazy about it, and I heard many a man say that it was the best speech they had had for years at the New England dinners. You certainly got your revenge on Yale for the Catastrophe of Nov. 18th.

You remember that last year I wrote to you[1] about the Students' Conference at Northfield.[2] The men who have the Conference in charge do not propose to give up trying to get you there. Of course I do not know what your plans are, but I sincerely hope you can arrange to go to Northfield next July. I know you would be intensely interested in the meeting, and you would have a wonderful opportunity of reaching and impressing the most representative meeting of students which ever comes together in this country.

I know how terribly burdened you are with work, and how many irons you have in the fire, and I would not ask you to sacrifice your time and energy unless I was permitted to make up, in some way, for what you would lose by undertaking this service. I send you Mr. Mott's letter,[3] which explains itself, and I sincerely hope that you will be able to accept his invitation.[4]

Congratulating you again on your splendid work at the New England dinner, and wishing you a very Happy New Year, believe me,　　　　　　　　Yours faithfully,　C H Dodge

TLS (WP, DLC).

[1] Dodge's letter is missing.

[2] A series of annual summer evangelical conferences for college students in Northfield, Mass., founded in 1886 by the most famous American evangelist of the late nineteenth century, Dwight Lyman Moody. The Dodge family supported Moody's work for many years. John R. Mott, mentioned below, was a leader of the Northfield conferences at this time, as well as General Secretary of the World's Student Christian Federation and Associate General Secretary of the Y.M.C.A.'s International Committee.

[3] It is missing.

[4] Wilson was unable to accept the invitation to speak at Northfield in July 1901 but did speak there a year later. The text of his speech, "Religion and Patriotism," is printed at July 4, 1902.

To Sarah Baxter Bird

My very dear Mrs. Bird,　　　　　　　Princeton, 5 Jan'y, 1901.

I slave so at my desk every morning, over that slow-growing "Colonies and Nation," that will never get done, that positively I've no wits left for anything else. This business of *weaving* a narrative, close knit, takes all the life out of me (would that a corresponding amount would get into the narrative!) and I am *ashamed* to write letters to any body who knows a good letter from a poor one!

Would that I *could* come down to Baltimore for refreshment at No. 22; but no such luck. As the Father of His Country used to say, I am tied by the leg: and the thong is this same history for *Harpers*, which goes inexorably on, a number a month, whether the poor devils who write for it have any breathing time or not. When this job is over, we hope to go to Europe, children and all, for fifteen months and forget all about it!

Dr. Hoyt, we learn, is getting on towards recovery very nicely indeed. At least, so we heard before vacation.

We are so glad you liked the picture

With love from all of us,

Your devoted friend,   Woodrow Wilson

ALS (photostat in L. W. Smith Coll., Morristown National Historical Park).

An Announcement

[Jan. 5, 1901]

LECTURES BY PROFESSOR WILSON.

In addition to the course of lectures which Professor Woodrow Wilson will deliver in Philadelphia before the American Society for the Extension of University Teaching during January and February, on "Leaders of Political Thought,"[1] is a lecture before the Scotch-Irish Society of Philadelphia, which he will delivered [deliver] on February 21.[2] On Washington's Birthday, Professor Wilson will deliver the annual address to the Lawrenceville School. His subject will be "What it means to be an American."[3]

Printed in the *Daily Princetonian*, Jan. 5, 1901.
[1] See the news item printed at Jan. 12, 1901.
[2] Wilson addressed the annual meeting of the Pennsylvania Scotch-Irish Society in Philadelphia on February 21, 1901. The only news account of this affair—a brief report in the Philadelphia *Public Ledger*, Feb. 22, 1901—noted merely that Wilson was among the speakers.
[3] See the news report of this address printed at Feb. 27, 1901.

To Richard Watson Gilder

My dear Mr. Gilder,   Princeton, 6 Jan'y, 1901

I've put off answering your letter of Dec. 18, with its question as to what I was going to do with that other book (may the gods graciously bring it into comely being) in which I am "to tell the world what history really means in the terms of institutions and practical affairs"(!), not because I forgot either it or my manners; but simply because I did not know how to answer the question.

I do not want to determine just yet even the form of the book; only its main conceptions are of moment to me now. I shall not begin actually to construct it until after my mental *wanderjahr* (1891-'2) [1901-1902] in Europe, which shall serve to give me my offing and perspective, as I intend it. In the meantime, I do not wish to tell even myself too definitely what it is to be. It has been forming itself in my mind these twenty years and more,— ever since I was an undergraduate; but the testing and coördination and actual organization of the stuff that is to go into it must not be attempted quite yet, in this didactic, academic air, where I am an accepted teacher and speak too much unchecked, uncontradicted. I must air myself and it, for a little, in the contentious air of the large world, where books count for less than sagacity, insight, and hard sense.

I do not wish just now, therefore, to think of publishers,— except as friends,—or of the business side of the book, lest I should somehow get a particular audience or market into my imagination. Straight thinking, frank, disengaged, must go into the whole conception of the book; and *then*, when it is done, we shall see who will think it a thing worth publishing,—and how it will be best to publish it.

You see, therefore, why I have not known what to say in answer to your question, and why, at last I have made this long explanation.

It is very gratifying to have you interested.

With sincere regard,

Faithfully Yours,   Woodrow Wilson

ALS (MWiW-C).

To Lyon Gardiner Tyler

My dear Dr. Tyler,   Princeton, New Jersey, 8 January, 1901.

Your letter reached me this morning.[1] Mr. [Grover] Cleveland is away from home, on a hunting trip in the South; and I do not know when he will return.

Even if he were here, I should do you no service by talking with him about the celebration you have in mind. I have it from his own lips that he specially dislikes to be "sounded," and likes every invitation to come direct, to be judged on its own merits. He thinks the latter method subtly complimentary, because based upon the assumption that, if the thing proposed is worth doing, and he can do it, he will not decline.

Possibly, since the papers are so apt to chronicle his movements, you might yourself meet him somewhere on his way North, and lay your plans before him in conversation. But in any case the direct invitation is the best.

Very truly Yours,   Woodrow Wilson

WWTLS (Tyler Family Papers, ViW).
¹ It is missing.

From Henry Mills Alden

Dear Mr. Wilson: New York City   January 8, 1901.

It is necessary for me to guard against using too many illustrations for the "Colonies and Nation" in the MAGAZINE, and therefore I am returning to you a copy of your list of illustrations for Part VI with the request that you would kindly indicate those which could be best spared.

As you will notice there are some fifty subjects mentioned, and I am sure that I could not spare the space to use them all, although of course they will all be made for use in book publication later. But I would be greatly obliged if you would kindly indicate on the margin which are of first, second and third importance. You see I desire to use every endeavor to meet your wishes in regard to the MAGAZINE publication, and think you would probably prefer to make the selection, as indeed I would prefer to have you.   Sincerely yours,   H. M. Alden

TLS (WP, DLC) with WWhw notation on first page of letter: "Ans. 1/9/'01."

From Lucian Howard Cocke¹

My dear Wilson: Roanoke, Va.   Jan. 9th., 1901.

You know there is a vacancy in the office of President of Washington & Lee University, by reason of the death of Mr. Wm. L. Wilson. I am a member of the Board, and the question of a successor in office has been receiving the most solicitous consideration. In conversation with individual members of the Board, not infrequently the question has been propounded "How about Woodrow Wilson?", and without having consulted with any of my colleagues, I have deemed it proper to take advantage of our University acquaintance to write to you for the purpose of ascertaining whether or not it would be agreeable for you to consider the question of taking up educational work in Virginia.

The Rector of the University has called a meeting of the Board for next Tuesday, the 15th. I am satisfied that no definite action will be taken at that time with reference to filling the vacancy, but that the Board will meet for the purpose of exchanging views and perhaps settling a definite temporary policy until the position is filled.

If you think you can consider a suggestion with reference to taking up the work at Washington & Lee, I would be very glad to make an intimation to the Board that such arrangement is possible. Of course, it would not be expected that any intimation would be made concerning this matter until there has been a full conference in which you will be put in possession of all the facts in connection with the Institution. Its general history, I am sure, is already well known to myself [yourself].

To myself, personally, as well as to hundreds of your friends in Virginia, it would be exceedingly agreeable for you to be associated with the higher educational work in the State.

Most cordially yours,   Lucian H. Cocke.

TLS (WP, DLC).
1 Lawyer of Roanoke and fellow-student with Wilson at the University of Virginia.

To Lucian Howard Cocke

My dear Cocke,   Princeton, New Jersey, 10 January, 1901.

You may be sure that I appreciate more deeply than I can say the compliment you pay me in wishing to consider my name in connection with the presidency of Washington and Lee. You may rest assured, too, that I would meet you half way in the matter, did I feel at liberty to take such a position at present. I know a great deal about Washington and Lee, and everything that I know would incline me to regard a call to its presidency as a great opportunity opened to me.

But the fact is, that I am under obligations here which I do not feel at liberty to turn away from or disregard. The Princeton people have so bound me to the place by every kindness and favour and honour and have on several recent occasions made such a point of my staying here that I should really be ashamed to leave, as if I had not found my interests sufficiently advanced by them, or were weary of their service. It is a point of delicacy which I should not know how to meet.[1]

Let me thank you again for what your letter contains. Let me be of service to you in any other way I can; and believe me

Cordially and Faithfully Yours,   Woodrow Wilson

WWTLS (ViU).
¹ For one of the reasons why Wilson felt bound to Princeton, see the agreement printed as an Enclosure with C. C. Cuyler to WW, May 16, 1898, Vol. 10.

From Charles H. Robinson¹

My dear Sir,   Wilmington, N. C., Jan. 11, 1901

I think it best to write you about the condition of your Father, although he has all the time objected to anything being said to disturb you. He has had frequently, periods of sickness usually taking the form of a chill or rather rigors, the Dr says, and each one leaves him weaker and very feeble and night before last it seemed probable he might not rally. Last night he was better and the Dr thought he might be up this morning, but he had a restless night, and I will know before I mail this, how he is. He has a man nurse with him, and all the attention necessary. He spent Christmas day with us, and was very bright and enjoyable. I do not want to alarm you, but I am sure you will want to know how it is with the good old Father. I am afraid he will not be here very long. He is more comfortable this P M, but the Dr thinks you had better be informed as to his condition.
                    Yours truly   C. H. Robinson

ALS (WP, DLC).
¹ Partner in the naval stores firm of Robinson & King of Wilmington, N.C., Robinson had been a close friend of Dr. Joseph Ruggles Wilson since his pastorate in that city.

A News Item

[Jan. 12, 1901]

Under the auspices of the American Society for the Extension of University Teaching, Prof. Woodrow Wilson began on Jan. 9, in Philadelphia, a series of six lectures on Great Leaders of Political Thought.¹ The lectures are scheduled for each Wednesday afternoon from Jan. 9 to Feb. 13, at four o'clock, in Witherspoon Hall, the subjects being (1) Aristotle, the Father of Political Science; (2) Machiavelli, the Politician of the Renaissance; (3) Montesquieu, the French Political Seer; (4) Burke, the Interpreter of English Liberty; (5) Tocqueville, the student of Democracy, and (6) Walter Bagehot, the Literary Politician.

Printed in the *Princeton Alumni Weekly*, 1 (Jan. 12, 1901), 414-15.
¹ See J. M. Nolen to WW, June 12, 1900, n. 2, Vol 11. About this series, see the Editorial Note, "Wilson's Lectures on Great Leaders of Political Thought," Vol. 9.

From James Sprunt[1]

My dear Doctor: Wilmington, N.C., January 12th, 1901.

You have probably been informed of your good father's recent severe illness which on Wednesday last caused his friends apprehension of greater danger as the rigor which continued from 8 in the morning until noon was hard to overcome. He rallied from this attack and is now much better but the morphine which he has taken and a stupid reference to the nature of his illness in the morning paper,[2] which his nurse unfortunately permitted him to read[,] depressed him exceedingly today. I remained with him long enough to cheer him into better spirits and the physician says that he will recover from this attack; he fears however that a recurrence of this rigor would terminate fatally. It was currently reported through some misunderstanding of a newspaper writer in Atlanta that you would lecture in that city and proceed to New Orleans to-day or to-morrow; I therefore telegraphed you to Atlanta and also to New Orleans care of Dr. Alderman,[3] to assure you of your father's improvement and suggested that you stop over here on your return. Since then we have ascertained from your letters to your father that you were to lecture in Philadelphia and that you have engagements for the whole month. Your father desires me to say that you are not to have any apprehension regarding him as he is growing better steadily and that his illness is not to interfere in any way with your engagements, and should it become necessary for you to see him you will be advised in due time. You may rely upon my telegraphing you in case of any recurrence of your good father's trouble which I do not apprehend at present, and should you come to Wilmington at any time I wish to assure you that I would feel greatly honoured to have you for my guest.

With kindest wishes,

Yours very truly,   James Sprunt

TLS (WP, DLC).
  [1] Prominent merchant, philanthropist, and local historian of Wilmington.
  [2] It was an item in the *Wilmington Messenger*, Jan. 12, 1901, which ran as follows: "The Messenger is pained to note that the Rev. Joseph R. Wilson lies quite sick and very much enfeebled at the residence of Mrs. F. J. Robinson, on North Fifth street. His friends are very anxious about him and fear the worst. Dr. Wilson is greatly beloved by our people and they will learn with deep sorrow of his serious condition."
  [3] Edwin Anderson Alderman, President of Tulane University.

From Thomas L. Snow

"The Bluff" [Judd Haven, Muskoka, Ont.]

My Dear Profr. Wilson   Jan 12/01.

Gregory Allen and I did our accurate best the other morning to test Mr. Galbraith's location of your southern boundary. Our result showed him to be not far wrong,—not more than about 52 links (11 yds. 1 ft.) further to the north than our showing.

If our measurement can be sustained as correct, it at least throws on to yr. side all that is desirable of that imposing front of rock on the summit of the ridge: but does not take in the pretty point of rock to the East of the shanty.

Mr. Galbraith impressed upon us, distinctly, that in devoting but two days work to the survey at that time he could not undertake to give a result that he would be willing to stand by in a court of law:—that, with the expenditure of another day, he would undertake to accurately test the conclusion of his first survey: and, that when the ice was good this finishing touch could be accomplished more expeditiously, and, even more accurately than at another time.

Undoubtedly, the government map is absurdly incorrect, and, in my idea so utterly misleading as to justify some very pointed enquiries and remarks in the direction of the Crown Lands Dept. in Toronto.

Please do not hesitate to ask me for any further particulars, which, it may be in my power to give

Believe me   Very faithfully yours   Thos. L. Snow.

ALS (WP, DLC).

To Edward Graham Elliott

My dear Elliott,   Princeton, New Jersey, 15 January, 1901.

I am sure that you have not attributed my long silence to negligence, indifference, or even forgetfulness, but to the real cause. I have approved of each step you have taken, so far as reported, have felt that tacit assent was enough, and have been so busy that every thing not absolutely necessary has had to wait upon the tasks that were imperative.

I am publishing an all-the-year serial in *Harpers* ("A Short History of the People of the United States") and every hour I take from that increases the risk that the presses will catch up with me. Moreover, the Trustees have granted me leave of absence for next year, and I am working under a forced draught to get everything out of the way so as to be free to leave early in June, and make the vacation as big as possible, with two summers in it. I shall of course come to your side of the water, look you up sooner or later, and come back at the same time you do, so that we may begin our new deal together. Perhaps you have heard all this from George.

I trust you are enjoying your work and that it is proving to be of the kind you were seeking. Nothing happens here. Everything goes quietly its appointed way. No doubt you take the *Alumni Weekly*[1] and know as much as we do of the general news of the University, and there really is no special news.

This is only a note of greeting. I merely want to let you know that I am thinking of you and so to say keeping conscious of you from month to month. Every one here speaks most cordially of you, and looks forward with satisfaction to your return. May all good fortune attend you.

Mrs. Wilson joins me in warm regards.

Faithfully Yours,   Woodrow Wilson

WWTLS (WC, NjP).
   [1] Successor to the *Alumni Princetonian*, the *Princeton Alumni Weekly* began publication on April 7, 1900, under the editorship of Jesse Lynch Williams '92. With an executive committee consisting of M. Taylor Pyne, James W. Alexander, Charles Scribner, Robert Bridges, C. C. Cuyler, and Frank Presbrey, the *Princeton Alumni Weekly* was to serve as "a news-sheet addressed to the alumni" of the university.

To Ellen Axson Wilson[1]

My precious one,   Wilmington [N. C.], 18 Jan'y, 1901

   You already know, by my telegram,[2] the delightful news that met me when I reached here. Dear father is really *very* much better, *looks* as well as I could wish, though he is, of course, still quite weak. I have decided to stay, nevertheless,—chiefly on his account, partly on my own. I should be so worn out that Monday and Tuesday would quite *do* for me. Not that I am *too* tired now. I am very tired, as always after travel and excitement (and all day yesterday, as I rode through the drizzling rain, I was of course in the painful state of suspense which is a *form* of excitement); but not enough to hurt. I spent last evening and this morning with dear Father. He is very bright and thoroughly himself. I have not seen his doctor yet, and shall not know what to think until I hear what he has to say; but, if I may judge for myself, he is nearly all right again, and quite "out of the woods." The Sprunts[3] are entertaining me quite royally, in a house[4] which is really one of the most spacious and elegant I was ever in. Mr.

Sprunt is, you know, a patron of the muse of History[5] (I've forgotten her name, as usual[,] Clio, isn't it?) and has interesting things to show and to tell me; and he is, moreover, a cultivated and conversible man. Mrs. Sprunt is,—just the usual thing for such surroundings,—though perhaps a little better than the usual, after all.

I can't tell you my thoughts about you and my sweet home. My devotion to you, my darling, becomes a deeper and deeper passion with me every day of my life. My love becomes more and more consciously the comfort and stay of everything good in me. You are all the world to me, and I am

Your own   Woodrow

Father asks after you all with the deepest emotion, and sends every message of affection.

I am perfectly well.

ALS (WC, NjP). Enc.: clipping from the *Wilmington*, N.C., *Messenger*, Jan. 18, 1901, with heading, "Prof. Woodrow Wilson."

[1] As this letter intimates, Wilson had left at once for Wilmington after receiving a telegram from James Sprunt on January 16 saying that his father was worse. Sprunt's telegram is missing.

[2] It is missing.

[3] James and Luola Murchison Sprunt.

[4] Their town house at 400 South Front St., Wilmington, N.C.

[5] By this time James Sprunt had published two books of local history and lore as well as many historical and biographical articles. In 1900 he had also established a fund at the University of North Carolina for the publication of the "James Sprunt Historical Monographs."

From Ellen Axson Wilson

My own darling,   Princeton, Jan. 17 [18], 1901

Your telegram came this morning and was a great relief;— I wonder if that means that you will be back tomorrow night!

I sent on yesterday,—by *express* since it came that way,—the Harper proofs. Today came the proof of the speech[1] with the request that it be read & returned at once. So I read it, found it all right and am now sending it back. That leaves me only the old proof to forward you for dear Father's entertainment. There are no other letters of importance,—I answered those you spoke of.

There is of course no news in this short time, except indeed that yesterday it was thought Mrs. Young[2] might not live through the day. I have not heard this morning.[3]

I ran over to Mrs. Murrays[4] to see the [Bliss] Perry's for a few moments after my return from Phila. I found them looking very well and it was certainly good to see them. Mrs. Armour,[5] as I predicted, did not want me without you! The Finlays[6] are to be there—am glad for them to meet the Perrys.

How I did *hate* to go out last night! I could scarcely force myself to the point. But I enjoyed it fairly well after I got there. Stockton went after all; he is much better and thinks now it was only vaccination. We are all perfectly well & everything goes smoothly. I am looking forward to the club meeting this afternoon,[7] where I will see a little more of Mrs. Perry. The children are to have company for luncheon,—such is the sum total of our doings so far.

How glad I shall be to get a letter from my darling tomorrow and to know more in detail how he is and how he found things in Wilmington! Is it quite out of the question, notwithstanding his improvement, for him to be brought here? Do give him from us all tenderest love. Dear Father! How I wish I were there! Oh how I want to see,—to be with my darling! I love you, Woodrow, dearest, beyond all words. In every heart-throb I am as always—

Your little wife,   Eileen.

ALS (WC, NjP).
    [1] That is, of his after-dinner speech to the New England Society in the City of New York, printed at Dec. 22, 1900.
    [2] Augusta Mixer (Mrs. Charles Augustus) Young, of 16 Prospect Ave.
    [3] She died on January 18, 1901.
    [4] Julia Richards Haughton (Mrs. James Ormsbee) Murray, of Library Place.
    [5] Harriette Foote (Mrs. George Allison) Armour, of "Allison House" at 83 Stockton St.
    [6] Professor and Mrs. John Huston Finley.
    [7] The Present Day Club of Princeton, a woman's organization founded in 1898.

From Jenny Davidson Hibben, with Enclosure

My dear Mr. Wilson,   Rome—January 18. 1901

Our time in Italy is almost over—and on this 31st we sail from Naples—on the Kaiserin Maria Theresia, and by February 15th I hope we shall be in Princeton! Jack & I so often think of you & Mrs. Wilson—now that we are in Italy—for there is so much that is beyond words that is lovely & so much also of discomfort in the dreary unheated houses, & we wonder how Mrs. Wilson will ever endure it! And yet with such treasures of art, & such a lovely land of beauty she will want to stay here for months!! We have a long list of pensions & hotels to tell you about, & perhaps our discomfort, and also our delightful places may help you. I never dreamed of such a beautiful land—and every day is a delight to us. We never tire of exploring Rome—and when the day is over we have found a comfortable little English tea room, with an open wood fire, & there Jack & Beth & I go—and talk over our day. We have met many delightful people, and some who have made me long to annihilate them! It never hurts me to see disagreeable English or German people, but when our own countrymen are vulgar, it is hard to see it.

Beth is quite well again, & rosy, but she longs again for her dear little friends & a fine *play*,—she has been quite a perfect little traveller. Jack knows Rome thoroughly for he was here several weeks, years ago—& he is the best of guides. He looks very well too, but like both Beth & myself he is ready to turn his face toward home, & end our wandering life, lovely as it is.

With love for you & Mrs. Wilson & all good wishes for you for the New Year—

Believe me,

Ever your friend   Jenny Davidson Hibben

E N C L O S U R E

From John Grier Hibben

My dear Woodrow,   Rome Jan. 18th, 1901

I am going to put in a note with Jenny's letter. It is hard to write at length now that we are almost within hailing distance of you. There is so much to say that it is better to reserve all until we meet face to face. Your last letter[1] reached us a few days ago, giving us great pleasure. I can not begin to tell you how glad I shall be to see you again, and once more to enjoy the companionship which I prize so highly, and have so constantly missed during the time of our separation. Not a day passes without our speaking of Mrs. Wilson & yourself in this land of absorbing interest. Italy has proved to be a perfect climax to the many delightful experiences of the past months. The home stretch will seem very tedious I am afraid, & we will count the days with impatience until we are with our own again. You quite whet my curiosity with your promised tales about Baldwin.[2] I hope that they will equal the one which I have been saving for you concerning the same remarkable individual. Mine is a choice bit relating to his Oxford residence.[3] I have also a most entertaining story about Dr. Patton & his break at Aberdeen.[4] Now I hope you are properly curious & ready for revelations. We hope to reach New York on Feb 10th, & I shall probably reach Princeton the following day, if all goes well. With warmest love for you, Mrs. Wilson & all the children,

Your affectionate friend   John Grier Hibben

ALS (WP, DLC).

    [1] It is missing.
    [2] James Mark Baldwin, Stuart Professor of Psychology at Princeton.
    [3] That is, when Baldwin had been in Oxford in 1900 to receive the honorary degree of D.Sc. from Oxford University, the first honorary degree in science ever conferred by that university.
    [4] The Editors have been unable to discover any information about this incident.

From Ellen Axson Wilson

My own darling,   Princeton Jan. 19, 1901

To my great disappointment there is no letter from you this morning. So I am left in entire doubt as to your plans; I sent the notice of course to the Princetonian[1] according to directions, yet I cannot but hope a little to see you tonight, since you found Father so much better. I doubt whether this will reach you in any event, but will send a few lines on the chance.

We are having something of a blizzard today, that is, it is not snowing *now* but a tremendous windstorm is whirling the snow that fell yesterday. A branch from the dying pine was broken off an hour ago. And—isn't it provoking?—the telephone has refused to work either yesterday or today!—just when we needed it most. Mrs. Cleveland, who brought me home from the Club, says hers is in the same condition.

Isn't it a pity that the Perry's should have such weather for their visit? I meant to go to the [Samuel Ross] Winans this morning but had to give it up; will drive to the tea this afternoon. Mr. and Mrs. [John Howell] Westcott are both in bed with the grip, but the tea is to go on, the other women receiving. The Perry's will remain over Sunday at the Winans. They *must* leave Monday morning, so our dinner is off. Isn't the Armour dinner ill-fated, first we fail, and now the Westcotts.

Mrs. Young died yesterday afternoon. The body is to be taken to Hanover.

We had great fun at the Club yesterday; we elected nineteen men,—nine of them unanimously. There were ten present. Not a Southerner was elected! Was not that narrow-minded? Lee & Stonewall had each four votes, Calhoun, *one*[,] *mine*[,] Clay, three (though Webster had all ten,) Poe, four.

We are all perfectly well, and send love beyond words to dear Father & you. I *love* you dear,—how tenderly how passionately even you do not know.   Your own   Eileen

No important mail except the proofs of your essay.[2]

ALS (WC, NjP).

1 It is printed at Jan. 21, 1901.
2 "Democracy and Efficiency," printed at Oct. 1, 1900.

From William Gardner Hale[1]

The University of Chicago

My dear Professor Wilson: January 19th, 1901.

I made a canvass of the Faculty of the University of Chicago before the election, and incidentally learned that there was a good deal of dissatisfaction with McKinley's policy, even among those who were going to vote for him. After the election I asked Professor Freund,[2] who was one of these men, to ascertain exactly what the feeling was among McKinley's supporters. He sent out a letter, of which the enclosed is a copy, to everybody except those who I knew were going to vote against McKinley. The result is,— or was at last accounts,—thirty-six in favor of McKinley's policy, and twenty-six in favor of giving the Philippines that which we have promised to give to Cuba. If to the twenty-six the number of those who voted for Bryan is added, and of those who voted for the Prohibition candidate, or who refused to vote at all because of dissatisfaction, it becomes clear that there is a considerable majority in our Faculty against McKinley's policy.

I should have liked to have these figures made known immediately, meanwhile asking people in other universities if they would not take up the same task. Freund, however, in whose hands of course the matter now is, thinks it better not to publish the facts for a single university, but to wait until they can be had from several universities.

Will you not, as a national service, undertake to get the facts for Princeton?

I wrote to Professor Ladd[3] at Yale. You probably know how strongly he feels. He has found some one at Yale to do the work. For Columbia, I have written to Professor Burgess, and, for Harvard, to Professor MacVane.[4]

Of course it is for the one who sends out the letter to determine what the form of inquiry shall be. In a general way, it seems desirable that it should be similar in the various universities. Moreover, the line of least resistance lies in assuming that the Philippines should be treated like Cuba. I myself, on the whole, think that it would be better to find out how many of those who did not vote for McKinley, but who had a vote, were opposed to his policy. I, as I implied above, know approximately the facts here in Chicago, and they make a very considerable majority in the Faculty against McKinley's method. If, without reference to my opinion, you think this the better form of inquiry, it would be best to make it in this way, and I will then attempt to get a readjustment in the other places.

Professor Freund is ready, if desired, to put the whole material finally together, and I will see that it gets into the hands of the Associated Press.

Very sincerely yours,   W. G. Hale

If you think a franker expression of opinion would be got through the promise that only results, not names, should be published, the letter of inquiry might be so drawn.

TLS (WP, DLC). Enc.: Ernst Freund to "Dear Sir," Nov. 17, 1900, TCL (WP, DLC).
    1 Professor of Latin and Head of the Department of Latin at the University of Chicago.
    2 Ernst Freund, Associate Professor of Jurisprudence and Public Law at the University of Chicago.
    3 The Rev. Dr. George Trumbull Ladd, Clark Professor of Moral Philosophy and Metaphysics, Yale University.
    4 John William Burgess, Professor of Political Science and Constitutional Law and Dean of the Faculty of Political Science at Columbia University; and Silas Marcus MacVane, McLean Professor of Ancient and Modern History, Harvard University.

An Announcement

[Jan. 21, 1901]

UNIVERSITY NOTICES.
JURISPRUDENCE AND POLITICS.

Professor Woodrow Wilson has been summoned South to the bedside of his father, who is very ill, and the classes in Jurisprudence and Politics will not meet this week.

Printed in the *Daily Princetonian*, Jan. 21, 1901.

To Ellen Axson Wilson

My precious Sweetheart,   Wilmington [N.C.], 21 Jan'y, 1901

It's astonishing that I should have had no time to write; but that is the literal fact, as you will understand when I tell you how my days have been filled—with father—with meals—with friends, of whom I find a delightful number here. *I* am well; dear Father is doing excellently; I am a good deal easier about him; and I am off to-night (Monday). I reach Phila. to-morrow (Tuesday) morning at about half after ten and shall stay there rather than face the embarrassment of *not* lecturing in Princeton that afternoon,—and meet you there at Wanamaker's as appointed, doing some heavy resting, as well as a little studying, in the meantime. If for any reason you can't come, send me word at the Hotel Lafayette.

I am now sitting with dear Father, who sends you the tenderest love, whenever he speaks of you.

My love for you passes all words,—and my longing.

Your own   Woodrow

ALS (WP, DLC).

From Max Boucard

Cher Monsieur,   Paris le 21 Janvier 1901.

Je vous ai écrit, il y a déjà quelques semaines, pour vous demander l'autorisation de faire traduire en français votre si bel ouvrage *"The State."*[1]

N'ayant pas reçu de réponse, j'ai du mal mettre l'adresse, et je viens de nouveau, vous demander cette autorisation.[2]

Vous avez déjà été tellement gracieux avec nous que je ne sais comment vous remercier et je vous prie de croire à notre véritable reconnaissance.

Veuillez agréer, Cher Monsieur, l'expression de mes sentiments les plus distingués.

Boucard

ALS (WP, DLC).
  [1] Wilson probably never received this letter; in any event, it is missing.
  [2] Wilson did indeed authorize Boucard to proceed with the translation and publication of *The State*. For bibliographical information concerning the publication of the French edition, see the location-description note following Léon Duguit's Preface to this edition printed at Jan. 24, 1902.

From Edith Gittings Reid

My dear Mr Wilson   [Baltimore] Jan 25th 1901

I had hoped to see you & thank you for the charming photograph of Jessie—but things went awry & I had to stay at home & must send you my thanks in this poor fashion. The little lassie is charming and the photograph would be a pleasure from an artistic point of view even if the affection were not waiting for your dear child.

I must add a word of thanks for the great delight your article in the Harpers—& the one in the Atlantic [—][1] have given me. How proud I am of you *really*—and how thankful that you can never be done up into calendars, or day books, or tracts by your admiring friends.

Don't forget me off there in Europe. Give my love to Mrs Wilson and believe me

ever faithfully your friend   Edith G. Reid

ALS (WP, DLC).
    [1] That is, the first installment of "Colonies and Nation" in *Harper's Magazine*, CII (Jan. 1901), 173-203, and "The Reconstruction of the Southern States," printed at March 2, 1900, Vol. 11, which had just appeared in the *Atlantic Monthly*, LXXXVII (Jan. 1901), 1-15.

To Edith Gittings Reid

My dear Friend,   Princeton, 27 Jan'y, 1901

Yesterday was a lucky, happy day for me. The postman, instead of bringing me business letters, brought me nothing but letters from friends, and I saw your handwriting again with a real delight. Since some perversity of fortune seems to deprive me even of such occasional glimpses of you as I might reasonably hope for, I wish my conscience could forget how selfish and essentially unreasonable it would be for me to propose a scheme of regular correspondence,—so that my pleasures might seem less haphazard and I might have always the zest of expectation to go before them! A conscience is a great nuisance! To know what you want and not be able to get your own consent to ask for it! To know that your friends have something very much better and more important to do than to attend to your pleasure! These are the things which strengthen character, no doubt; but they are also the things which make life look a sort of bluish-grey. I *could* urge an unusual argument for indulging me in this case. Your letters, though never so short, always contain a delicious flavour of *your self*; and it would be an invaluable thing to a literary fellow, seriously bent upon acquiring a real mastery in his art, to have abundant, various, and ever fresh material for studying that most illusive, and yet most central, question of the craft: how individuality is expressed. But of course I shall urge nothing of the kind,—nothing at all.

I need not tell you that there is a special bit of heartening for me in the sentence in which you speak your approval of the opening chapters of my History. This, you know, is neither the *full* history of the country I used to discuss with you (that was begun, and was written down to about 1688, on about treble the scale of this) nor the short sketch that I began for use as a school text-book.[1] The text-book was cut off almost at its birth by the upset in the Harpers' business; and the longer history has been (quite indefinitely) postponed for this middle-sized creature which is no doubt of a more serviceable stature than either of the others. The particular features I wanted to make prominent in the writing began, I found, to be a good deal obscured,—and that inevitably, so far as I can see,—at any rate for a fellow of my degree of skill,—in the use of the larger scale. As for the unfortunate school history,—that is another story, too involved and tedious and vexatious to be set down by a good natured chronicler.

The trip to Europe seems just now to be receding rather than drawing near. My dear father's health has within the last few weeks shown rather serious signs of breaking, and unless he shows some remarkable improvement within the next month or two we shall give the trip up for the present. He is in the South. I made a flying trip to see him last week. He is excellently well taken care of by a host of devoted friends where he is; is much better now than he was when his attacks first came on; and will return to us again when the winter relaxes; but I could not put the ocean between us unless matters mend materially. And so we may not go, after all. As for forgetting you when we do go, that were easier said than done. Some people attend to that matter themselves and avoid all risk of carelessness or shallowness on the part of their friends by taking pains to be of such a quality that, once known, they *can't* be forgotten. They somehow manage it so that when once they have consented to be another's friend, "sure enough," as the children say, it makes that other's life once for all different and more delightful, and he does not forget unless he "scorns delight" and lives *oblivious* days.

I was keenly disappointed at missing Mr. Reid when he was here. It was peculiarly ill luck. I hurried around to van Dyke's as soon as I knew of it and could escape or curtail engagements, but it was too late. He had gone. Could he be dared to try it again? And his wife?

Mrs. Wilson sends warm love both to yourself and to Mrs. Gittings;[2] I send mine to Mrs. Gittings, and our warmest regards to Mr. Reid; and am in all things

Your devoted friend, Woodrow Wilson

ALS (WC, NjP).

[1] For descriptions of these works, see the Editorial Notes, "Wilson's 'Short History of the United States,'" Vol. 8, and "Wilson's History of the United States for Schools," Vol. 10.

[2] Mrs. Reid's mother, Mary E. (Mrs. James) Gittings, who lived with her.

A Table of Contents for a Collection of Essays

[c. Jan. 28, 1901]

I. On Being Human
II. When a Man Comes to Himself
III. Leaders of Men
IV. Burke and the French Revolution
V. A Wit and a Seer
VI. A Lawyer with a Style
VII. Princeton in the Nation's Service
VIII. Mr. Cleveland as President
IX. Democracy.
　　The Making of the Union

WWhw MS. (WP, DLC).

To Richard Watson Gilder

My dear Mr. Gilder,　　　Princeton, New Jersey, 28 January, 1901.

The translated journal you describe sounds most interesting and al[l]uring.[1] I don't know of anything that would attract me more in that kind; but the simple truth is, that I hardly have time to shave, that young printer's devil at Harpers being hot foot on my trail. I dare not dally by the way.

By the way, I am not too busy to think at odd moments: and I have been thinking for some time past that I must get out another volume of essays. Do you think that you are going to have room this year for my essay on Burke in your safe? (Room in the *Magazine*, I mean,—not in the safe!)[2] I cannot spare it from the modest little volume contemplated.

That was an amusing blunder in dates you caught me in; but it does not embarrass me. I am not an historian: I am only a writer of history, and these little faults must be overlooked in a fellow who merely tries to tell the story, and is not infallible on dates.

With warm regard,

Sincerely Yours,　　Woodrow Wilson

WWTLS (Berg Coll., NN).
　[1] Gilder's letter asking Wilson to edit this document is missing.
　[2] Gilder finally published "Edmund Burke and the French Revolution" in the *Century Magazine*, LXII (Sept. 1901), 784-92. It is printed in this series at Feb. 23, 1898, Vol. 10.

From Henry Mills Alden

Dear Mr. Wilson: New York City   January 28, 1901.

I am glad to receive Part VIII of "Colonies and Nation" which came this morning, and will write you in a day or two in regard to the illustrated editions of John Fiske's Illustrated Histories.[1]

Voucher in payment of Part VIII will be sent in the usual course.   Sincerely yours,   H. M. Alden

TLS (WP, DLC).

[1] In the late 1890's, John Fiske's publisher, Houghton, Mifflin and Co., began reissuing many of his historical works in new editions elaborately illustrated with plates, facsimiles, maps, and so on. The books which had been so published by this time were *The American Revolution* (2 vols., Boston and New York, 1896); *The Beginnings of New England* (Boston and New York, 1898); *The Critical Period of American History, 1783-1789* (Boston and New York, 1898); and *Old Virginia and Her Neighbours* (2 vols., Boston and New York, 1900). Wilson soon made arrangements with Houghton, Mifflin to purchase all of these volumes. See WW to Houghton, Mifflin and Co., March 26, 1901.

From Edward Graham Elliott

My dear Professor Wilson,   Berlin, Jan. 30th, 1901.

Your letter of the 15th reached me on yesterday and was most heartily welcomed. I did not suppose you had forgotten me, but a visible reminder was most pleasant. I was in Dresden a few days during the holidays and saw Mrs. Howe, Annie, Miss Flinn[1] and George—we had a reunion that was delightful.

I learned from them of your plans for next year and how you were living in dread of the printers, so I was not surprised that I did not hear from you. I hope the printers won't catch you and that you will be able to leave as you anticipate. I shall look forward with eagerness to the time when you shall reach Germany, and it will indeed be a great pleasure to see you here.

My plans for the next semester are, as you know, to go to H[eidelberg]. and hear Jellinek:[2] he is more often quoted and referred to by the men I'm now hearing than any other living writer, so I'm quite anxious to make his acquaintance in the flesh. The most interesting man I am now hearing is Schmoller[3] in a course entitled "Preussische Verfassungs—Verwaltung—und Rechtsgeschichte von 1640 bis Gegenwart," four hours a week. I only began to hear him since Christmas; he speaks in a dialect that is a little difficult to understand, so it would have done me little good to have heard him sooner.

Now that I can understand the lectures with some ease, I am hearing more than those I wrote you in November—Wagner,[4] four hours in Political Economy and Kohler,[5] four hours in the

Philosophy of Law—a pretty full schedule of lectures. But I am trying to get as much as possible into the next last six weeks of the semester, for I feel I have been so handicapped heretofore and have lost so much through my lack of German—in fact the greater part of my time thus far has been devoted to German till now I can understand what is said and read with some ease, so that I hope my progress from now on will be more rapid.

I find too that what I learned under you has not all left me. Many of the things I hear bear a not altogether strange aspect. I regret I don't remember it all—it would have been of such assistance. I am enjoying my work very much and I truly believe it is the one above all others most congenial to my tastes. It is just what I wanted to do.

I know how precious your time is, so I feel sure you will not let me or my affairs interfere—nor shall I assign any other reason than this, if I do not hear from you—and I shall keep you informed as to my movements—but I am always very glad to hear from you; the general tone of your letters is always a fresh incentive.

Please give my very kindest regards to Mrs. Wilson.

Yours most sincerely,   Edward G. Elliott.

ALS (WP, DLC).

[1] Jean A. Flinn, daughter of the Rev. Dr. John William Flinn, Professor of Philosophy and Chaplain at South Carolina College. She was living with Mrs. Howe in Dresden while studying music there.

[2] Georg Jellinek (1851-1911), the distinguished political scientist and jurist of Heidelberg.

[3] Gustav Friedrich von Schmoller (1838-1917), economist and Professor at the University of Berlin.

[4] Adolf Heinrich Gotthilf Wagner (1835-1917), economist and Professor at Berlin.

[5] Josef Kohler (1849-1919), specialist in legal history and Professor at Berlin.

To Richard Watson Gilder

My dear Mr. Gilder,   Princeton, New Jersey, 1 February, 1901.

Of course I will drop in and lunch with you some day. I do not know just when I shall be in New York, having no special engagement there yet awhile; but no doubt some occasion will turn up.

There will be no occasion to withdraw the Burke. My plan of getting out a volume of essays in the autumn has nothing imperative about it.[1] I only meant that, if you could do so without too much forcing your plans, I should be glad to have it appear in season for me to compile the volume before the Christmas time. But such things can wait when necessary.

Yes I do like Morley's Burke. It seems to me far and away the best, least artificial, most wholesome, sanest, least affected thing he ever did. I believe I have read practically everything he ever wrote, and that seems to me the least spoiled by any fault. There is so delightfully little self-consciousness in it, for one thing. He has grown frightfully self-conscious of late. Would that there were some special providence to guard literary men who succeed against that worst of all taints!

With much regard,

Sincerely Yours,   Woodrow Wilson

WWTLS (R.W. Gilder Papers, NN).
1 For reasons unknown, Wilson never published this collection of essays.

From Frank Moore Colby[1]

Dear Sir: New York, Feb. 1, 1901.

We are resetting the International Cyclopaedia[2] and require a very thorough revision of all its departments. Would you care to cooperate with us in any way in the preparation of the articles in Early American History down to 1783? This period comprises about 36 pages of 1,000 words each. The rates which we pay are $10.00 a page for new matter and $5.00 for revision, the relative proportion to be determined upon the examination of the department by the specialist. As to the time for delivering the copy we have arranged generally to have the work completed by the end of next summer, but in this case as we are late in assigning the department we should be willing to postpone the final date to November 1st, 1901. The editors of the new edition are President Gilman of Johns Hopkins, Professor Peck of Columbia,[3] and myself. I will give you further details if I hear from you favorably and will also send the clippings of the articles themselves in order that you may see what sort of work would be required.[4]

Yours sincerely,   F. M. Colby

TLS (WP, DLC).
1 Journalist and editor of encyclopedias, Colby had recently resigned a professorship of economics at New York University to devote himself to writing and editorial work. At this time he was an editorial writer for the New York *Commercial Advertiser* and co-editor of the *New International Encyclopaedia* (17 vols., New York, 1902-1904).
2 The *International Cyclopaedia*, first published in fifteen volumes by Dodd, Mead and Co. of New York in 1887, had undergone periodic revisions in the 1890's.
3 Harry Thurston Peck, Professor of the Latin Language and Literature at Columbia University.
4 Wilson did not contribute to the *New International Encyclopaedia*.

From Walter Hines Page

My dear Mr. Wilson: New York   February 4th, 1901

I thank you very heartily for your encouraging good word about my honest and innocent little paragraph on the dumbness of American scholarship.[1] The dickens of it all is that you can't reform these fellows by preaching. One of these days when I get time I am going to do a really valuable piece of work. I have had it in mind for twenty years, and it grows upon me. I am going to take a beautiful home in the country somewhere where I can have an outdoor life and physical exercise, and consequently can be in the best physical condition for twelve months. I am going to admit to my household seven men of learning, and I am going to undertake for three hundred and sixty-five consecutive days to teach them to write the English language. I will not take boys, but grown men, men who have read English literature and are ready and willing to begin the elementary study of historical English syntax. Such a book is the only one I should use. Then I should require them to write four hours a day; No[.] 1 should be required the next day to rewrite the writing of No. 2, and No. 2 of No. 3, and so on. At the end of the year I should have killed them or made them, the Lord knows which. I shall give my whole time to this work. If I succeed, as I know I shall, I shall volunteer to deliver at every principal institution in the country a free lecture explaining how men may be taught to write. Of course the whole organized pack of English professors will bay at me and prove that I am an ignoramus—as I am—but that will be only a part of the fun.

It may interest you to know that I advertised the other day for an editor for a position that will lead to better pay than a college professorship; I advertised, of course, for an educated man. It may interest you to know that I received one letter which began thus:

"Am a grad. of Princeton."

Always heartily yours,   Walter H. Page

TLS (WP, DLC).
  1 [Walter Hines Page] "Dumb and Formless Scholarship," *World's Work*, 1 (Feb. 1901), 350-53. Wilson's letter is missing.

To James Woodrow

                                    Princeton, New Jersey,
My dear Uncle James,   4 February, 1901.

Your note enclosing a letter to Wilson Howe[1] came this morning, and I at once forwarded the letter. I am by no means sure of his address. He was about to change it the last time I heard from him. I thought it safe, however, to send the letter to his last address, in the confidence that it would be forwarded to him. It will, at worst, come back to you.

Yes, we spent five really delightful weeks on the Muskoka lakes in Ontario last summer, and came back much refreshed. The goods [good] effects are by no means worn off yet. We were so much charmed, indeed, that, land there being singularly cheap and the cost of building in that region of lumber still more in contrast with prices anywhere else where summers would be well spent, we have bought a little island, with some mainland adjacent, and mean as soon as possible to build there.

It was my intention to take Ellen and the children abroad this summer and spend fifteen months over there, our Trustees having very generously granted me the leave of absence at full salary. But the uncertain state of dear Father's health has made it seem our duty to change our plans. I was sharply alarmed about him week before last. He is in Wilmington, among his old people, and a letter came from one of the elders describing a recent illness of his in such a way as to take me down there at once. He was four times in somewhat rapid succession stricken with a sort of rigour which kept him for as much as an hour unconscious and which caused him to turn a sort of yellowish green colour. The doctor thought it due to an obstruction in the gall bladder. He rallied from the series of attacks with singular vigour and recuperative power, but of course it has made it seem to me necessary not to leave him at present,—not, at any rate, to put the ocean between us, with dear sister[2] already out of reach.

I wonder what this sending of money to Wilson means? It renders me very uneasy. Certainly dear sister cannot spare six hundred dollars to any one. She is living with painful economy now.

Ellen joins me in the warmest love to you all. I do hope that your health is good now, and that Aunt Felie[3] is well.

With warmest love,

Your affectionate nephew,   Woodrow Wilson

WWTLS (in possession of James Woodrow).
    [1] Wilson's nephew, James Wilson Howe, whose address and occupation at this time are unknown to the Editors. Dr. Woodrow's note is missing.
    [2] Annie Wilson Howe.
    [3] Felexiana Shepherd Baker (Mrs. James) Woodrow.

From Henry Mills Alden

Dear Mr. Wilson: New York City February 6, 1901.

I am not surprised that you find it difficult to complete your history in the twelve papers assigned for it; and I appreciate the value not only of the text of what may run over that limit but of the illustrations which Magazine publication would justify. We are satisfied that you should formally conclude the regular series with the end of Reconstruction. But we hold ourselves in readiness to consider independent articles reaching beyond that period, with a view to our use of them in our MAGAZINE, with illustration before the appearance of the book. You will readily understand that we shall wish to give these additional papers a place if possible.[1]

With cordial regard,   Yours sincerely,   H. M. Alden

TLS (WP, DLC).
  [1] In fact, Wilson did not get to the end of Reconstruction in the magazine series, and *Harper's Magazine* did not print anything beyond the agreed-upon twelve articles. See the Editorial Note, "Wilson's History of the American People," Vol. 11.

To William Gardner Hale

                                      Princeton, New Jersey,
My dear Professor Hale,   7 February, 1901.

I beg that you will not think that I am so rude as even to imply a criticism of yourself when I say that such an inquiry anent the last election as you ask me to institute among my colleagues here seems to me unwise. I may be wholly mistaken, but it seems to me that, after performing in every way that is open to them their individual duty as citizens and voters, it is best for college professors, as such, to appear as little as possible in politics. More than that, I do not think their attitude towards affairs typical or normal: and do not see, therefore, how such results as you intend publishing would be helpful to the country.

Pardon if these views are distasteful. I have thought the matter over very carefully and can come to no other conclusion.

With sincere regard,
                  Faithfully Yours,   Woodrow Wilson

TCL (RSB Coll., DLC).

From Joseph Ruggles Wilson

My precious Son,   Wilmington, N. Carolina, Feb. 13/01

I thank you for the letter received on yesterday. It of course startled me a little to learn that you have purchased an island in Canada, on which you expect to build soon. No doubt you are right in making this bold venture, and I wish you all success in this as in everything else which you attempt for the betterment of your current life. How I should like to feel able to share this Canada venture with you—to look forward to a summer to be spent with you all on your island home!

It does me good to know that your own health and that of your household continues excellent. Also it is cheering to learn that No. 11 is reached in the Magazine series, for your mind will be freed from some of its anxiety with the end in such near view. My own health improves, I think, from day to day. The weather is so open, and thus so constantly wetting all things, as to forbid my taking much exercise, which is a considerable drawback.

The folk here talk rapturously about your recent visit to W., and I can never forget its blessed influence upon me.

Please write when you are in the mood. Meanwhile be assured— for your dear self and all—of my stedfast love.

                    Your affc.   Father.

The *photograph* was rec'd—thanks.

ALS (WP, DLC) with WWhw names on verso of env.

From Henry Mills Alden

Dear Mr. Wilson: New York City February 14, 1901.

From a recent letter of yours we understand the difficulty you find of bringing a complete history of the United States within the twelve parts originally assigned, and that the best you can probably do within that compass is to come down to the end of Reconstruction. Some trespass on next year's space seems to be inevitable in order to secure completeness,—and we have accordingly offered to consider additional matter independently of our original agreement.

We also have encountered a difficulty. In order to illustrate the history as fully as we desire the monthly instalments are made to occupy two sheets in each Number of the MAGAZINE. I find that, even so, I am omitting illustrations that I would like to give. To give me more freedom of selection I am dividing the Fifth

Part (for May) into two instalments,—and I propose to make such divisions hereafter—regarding, of course, natural periods for conclusions of the several parts. The division may not always be into halves. Sometimes two-thirds of a part may be included, the remainder running over. In the case of the Fifth Part there is a natural division, about midway (after the Negro Plot.)

Apart from the undue curtailment of illustrations for serial use (it being understood that your suggestions for pictures are to be as fully as possible met for the book) I have a difficulty, owing to so long instalments of the history, in my make-up of the several Numbers of the MAGAZINE, in securing a sufficient variety.

The longer period given to serial publication on my proposed plan will enable us to give more time to the procuring of suitable material for illustration.

I trust that my plan will commend itself to you.

With cordial regard,   Yours faithfully,   H. M. Alden

TLS (WP, DLC).

To Laurence Hutton

My dear Mr. Hutton,   Princeton, 14 Feb'y, 1901

I was so sorry to miss your lecture last evening.[1] I was myself condemned to lecture in Philadelphia yesterday afternoon,[2] and did not get back till half past eight. I am glad to see by the *Princetonian* that you had a fine audience, and I hope you took no harm from the savage night.

                    Cordially Yours,   Woodrow Wilson

ALS (WC, NjP).
[1] Hutton delivered a series of five lectures on "Literary Reminiscences of Oxford" in University Hall on February 13, 18, 20, and 27, and March 1, 1901. They were published as *Literary Landmarks of Oxford* (London and New York, 1903).
[2] Wilson gave the last of his University Extension lectures—on Walter Bagehot—in Witherspoon Hall in Philadelphia on February 13. See the news item printed at Jan. 12, 1901.

To Richard Heath Dabney

O Thou Very Ass,   Princeton, New Jersey, 14 February, 1901

Truly this is an event[1] which even an Illimitable Idiot can realize to be of the deepest and most delightful significance! I cry Hurrah! with all my heart. Your overflow of high spirits in your letter[2] has done me more good than any draught I have taken in many a long day. I don't wonder you are happy,—and you communicate your happiness to your friends, who bless you for the pleasure of it all.

This is indeed the best thing that could have happened, and we congratulate you with all our hearts. I was just starting for Philadelphia, to give an afternoon lecture, when you[r] letter came. I read it on the train, and it put a fine *glow* into my thoughts for the rest of the day. Mrs. Wilson joins me in warmest congratulations to you both,—to all *three* of you, and unites with me in all cordial messages of warmest friendship,—and I am, as ever,

Faithfully and affectionately Yrs.,   Woodrow Wilson

Hurrah for the 670+![3]

ALS (in possession of Virginius Dabney).
 [1] The birth of a son, Virginius, to the Dabneys on February 8, 1901.
 [2] This letter is missing.
 [3] The enrollment at the University of Virginia.

From Augustus Thomas, Francis Hopkinson Smith, and Robert Underwood Johnson[1]

Dear Sir: New York, February 18, 1901.

At the annual meeting of the Institute of Arts and Letters[2] in January it was determined to give a private dinner of the members for the purpose of installing the new officers, and for informal consideration of the future activities of the Institute.

The dinner will be given on Tuesday, March 12, at eight o'clock, at the rooms of the Aldine Association, 111 Fifth Avenue, New York, the cost to each member, without wine, being two dollars and a half. As this is the first dinner of the Institute it is desired that there shall be a large attendance. As soon as convenient, will you kindly inform Mr. Johnson, of the dinner committee, whether it is your intention to be present on this occasion, inclosing check to his order in case of acceptance?

Faithfully yours,   Augustus Thomas, F. Hopkinson Smith,
Robert Underwood Johnson
33 East 17th Street, New York
Committee on Dinner

PL (WP, DLC). Enc.: printed list of the officers and members of the National Institute of Arts and Letters.
 [1] Thomas was a playwright who specialized in light comedy and melodrama; Smith, an engineer, artist, and author of many books of travel and fiction; and Johnson, Associate Editor of the *Century Magazine*.
 [2] About the organization of the National Institute of Arts and Letters and Wilson's membership in it, see F. S. Root to WW, May 27, 1898, Vol. 10, and the notes to that document.

From Henry Mills Alden

Dear Mr. Wilson: New York City February 20, 1901.

I will be glad to see you any Wednesday between 9:30 and 12 A.M. or between 2 and 3.30 P.M., to confer with you about plans for the division of your History.

I assume that you are willing that the May instalment (which is now ready for the press) should conclude with the Negro Plot. The first sentence of the June instalment would need a slight modification. Always sincerely yours, H. M. Alden

TLS (WP, DLC).

From Edward Ingle[1]

Dear Dr. Wilson: Baltimore, Feb. 21st, 1901.

I have found much pleasure in reading your current work in Harper's Monthly. My interest in you, which has been maintained for fifteen or sixteen years, has led me to call your attention to certain facts suggested by your statements on page 365 of the Feb. issue of the magazine regarding Captain Richard Ingle. You say "Richard Ingle, who was little better than an impudent buccaneer." You give 1644 as the date of his foray in Maryland, and add "It was close upon two years before he was driven out, and by that time he had stripped the people and the place of everything he could conveniently send away and sell."

In 1883, with the aid of original documents then made available, I was able to embody in a paper much material bearing upon the career of Captain Richard Ingle in Maryland, which had been overlooked or disregarded by earlier writers. The paper was read before the Maryland Historical Society on May 12th, 1884 and was printed as No. 19 of the Peabody Fund Publication.[2] If you have opportunity to read the paper you will find that Ingle, who had been trading for several years between England and America, and who had visited Maryland as early as 1642, returned to the province in February, 1645. He was in command of the "Reformation," one of the eight vessels commissioned in 1644 by Parliament for the "supply and defence and relief of the planters" in the plantations of the Chesapeake. Ingle had been given letters of marque, at that time a means of securing a naval force. When he reached St. Mary's the province of Maryland was in a decidedly unsettled condition, reflecting the unrest in the mother country. There is no doubt that Ingle gave material aid to those of the people in the province who were opposing the Government there adhering to Charles 1st. There is evidence that he availed himself of the opportunity to settle certain business affairs. But the charges that he stripped the people and the place are based upon exceedingly flimsy testimony. There is no evidence, as far as I have learned, that Ingle was driven out of the province, though for fourteen months the province was without a settled Government. Ingle was certainly in London in February, 1646, less than a year after the affair at St. Mary's, and had probably reached England before the on-set of winter. Later in that same year the election of Captain Edward Hill as Governor of Maryland, revealed the presence there of members of the Council.

Ingle was subsequently in the service of the English Commonwealth in England.

I am sorry that I have no copy of my paper to send you; you may probably find it in the Princeton Library. Since I wrote it other facts have come to me modifying to some extent my views of the Ingle episode, but modifying them in Ingle's favor. By the way, as far as I know, Richard Ingle was not of my family. The trouble with that period of Maryland history is that it has been written largely by persons under the influence of the Calvert cult. There has been so much juggling of statements and even manipulation of records, that it is exceedingly difficult to discover the facts of Maryland between 1640 and 1660. I believe, though, that you will modify your opinion of Richard Ingle after you have read my little paper which bears the marks, to be sure, of immaturity.   Sincerely yours,   Edward Ingle.

TLS (WP, DLC).
[1] A fellow-student of Wilson's at the Johns Hopkins, Ingle at this time was a free-lance journalist and an editor of the *Manufacturers' Record* of Baltimore.
[2] Edward Ingle, *Captain Richard Ingle, The Maryland "Pirate and Rebel,"* 1642-1653, Maryland Historical Society, Fund Publication No. 19 (Baltimore, 1884).

From Howard Pyle

Dear Professor Wilson: Wilmington, Del., Feb. 21st. 1901.

I will, in a few days, be prepared to make the illustrations for your seventh historical paper dealing with the Revolution. I would like to make some amendments to your list of illustrations so as to embody the following scheme:

The first illustration, to represent some of the earlier triumphs of Washington[,] such, for instance, as the battle of Trenton or the battle of Princeton.

Second; to illustrate the gloomier period of the Revolution; such, for instance, as the retreat from Brandywine—or some instance of the encampment at Valley Forge (preferably the former subject.)

Third; to represent the final triumph, either with the Siege of Yorktown, or the successful charge of the Americans upon the earthworks at that place, or the meeting of Washington and Cornwallis.

If you approve of this plan of illustration, I would like to have the liberty of final selection of the individual subjects from a picture maker's standpoint.

Harper's will probably assign the other subjects to some other artist.   very truly yours,   Howard Pyle

TLS (WP, DLC).

From John Norris Miller[1]

My dear Prof. Wilson,   New York City [c. Feb. 22, 1901]

I must ask you to pardon my seeming neglect in not writing you, concerning the work of the Committee,[2] on which I have the honor to be associated with you. Through sickness and work, I have been forced to delay matters a little; and I had thought to be able to be in Princeton today for a short talk with you but owing to the death of an uncle here, I was forced to abandon my trip.

However I have not been as negligent as affairs seem to appear, for I have called on Mr. Hedges twice and this morning we agreed on the following plan of operation. I labor under the supposition that you are quite well informed of the resolution passed last June by the senate and of the work that lies before us. The purport of the resolution was the abrogation of the treaty, six months from the ratification of the same at Clio and an invitation to co-operate with us in drawing up a new treaty, which shall permit of individual campaigning within certain well-defined limits; the said limits to act as a bar to organized campaigning, which seemed to have necessitated the passage of the treaty just abrogated.

I shall immediately write to a senior member of Halls, Mr. Hawkins,[3] and ask him to secure a copy of the treaty, which may assist us in our work of framing the new one; Mr. Hedges will this week draw up a formal notification to Clio of the abrogation of the old treaty and with it an invitation to co-operation. This we will forward to you for your affirmance and signature. This done we will arrange for a meeting at Princeton and push rapidly forward the work.

I am sorry that such an important proceeding should have been so delayed but it was owing to the carelessness of the sec. of the senate.

I would like your valuable advice on the above. With very kindest regards, I am   Very Cordially   J. Norris Miller

ALS (WP, DLC) with WWhw notations on env.: "(Hall treaty)" and "Ans. 4 March, 1901."

[1] Princeton, 1900, at this time a first-year student in the Columbia University Law School.

[2] Miller, Wilson, and Job Elmer Hedges '84 had been appointed a committee by the Senate of the American Whig Society to arrange for the abrogation of the existing treaty with the Cliosophic Society governing recruiting for the halls and for the negotiation of a new *modus vivendi*. Hedges was Deputy Attorney General of New York and also maintained a private law office at 141 Broadway.

[3] Gaylord Roscoe Hawkins, B.S., Princeton, 1901.

To Howard Pyle

My dear Mr. Pyle   Princeton, New Jersey, 22 February, 1901.

By all means make the selection of illustrations for No. VII. in accordance with the scheme you suggest. You know a great deal better than I do what will lend itself to picture-making, and, since this is the No. which, alone perhaps, lends itself to the carrying out of a scheme of illustration, I hope that you will make the sort of selection you propose. Sometimes I have a very strong preference as to subjects; but not in this case of the scenes of the actual Revolution itself

With warm regard,

Sincerely Yours,   Woodrow Wilson

WWTLS (de Coppet Coll., NjP).

Two Letters from Francis Landey Patton

My dear Professor Wilson: [Princeton, N.J.] February 25, 1901.

It is a matter of deep regret to me that I am unable to accept the invitation of President Venable to attend the commencement of the University of North Carolina in June; but you know how full my hands are always at that season of the year. The relation which Princeton sustains to the University of North Carolina is such that I feel it quite natural that the authorities of that university should wish to have Princeton represented on this important occasion,[1] and I appreciate very cordially the courtesy that is implied in their invitation. President Venable tells me that he has written you expressing the desire that you will represent Princeton at their commencement. May I venture to express the very earnest hope that the way will be clear for you to render both the University of North Carolina and Princeton University the service of being present and taking part in the exercises referred to in President Venable's invitation.

    I am,   Very sincerely yours,   Francis L. Patton

   1 President Francis Preston Venable had probably asked Patton to speak at the main exercises of the University of North Carolina's annual commencement on June 5, 1901, on the historic relations between that institution and Princeton.

My dear Professor Wilson: [Princeton, N.J.] February 26, 1901.

I have just received your letter and beg to repeat my expression of regret that you are unable to attend the commencement of the University of North Carolina, but I quite understand how difficult it would be for you to do so.

I am sorry to learn that your father's health continues so uncertain, and am sorry that you have been obliged to defer your contemplated vacation.

I read with great interest your first article in Harper's, and congratulate you on the bright promise of success with which the series opens. I anticipate great pleasure in reading the articles month by month.

               Very sincerely yours,   Francis L. Patton

TLS (Patton Letterpress Books, UA, NjP).

A News Report of an Address on Americanism at the Lawrenceville School

                                     [Feb. 27, 1901]

PROFESSOR WOODROW WILSON'S ADDRESS

It was decided last year that the patriotic address of the year should be alternatively on Lincoln's and Washington's Birthday. This year the 22nd was honored by a notable address by Prof. Woodrow Wilson, himself one of the foremost Americans of the day. His subject was one on which he is well qualified to speak.— What it means to be an American.

He began by emphasizing the fact that any person or nation who hoped to win any goal in life must first learn what that goal is toward which he is striving. He then went on to say that America is no ordinary country as is shown by the fact that it was the first nation to make its own character, a character which was not deceitful and which handled things in a straightforward, blunt way. There was no fear of rough work or frontier dangers in the founders of the American nation. Every man of this nation seems to be a born debater and to have had the rules of public meetings instilled into him from very childhold [childhood]. Prof. Wilson, with reference to the Philippines, said that since we now hold the islands we can not hope to settle affairs at once as the natives are still too inexperienced to undertake to carry on a government so intricate as that with which we govern ourselves.

The American government or any other institution can not be any better or any worse than the men who are leaders in it, therefore every citizen should strive to make himself better in every way possible and so improve his country and prevent the nation from sinking rather than rising in civilization.

Printed in the Lawrenceville, N.J., *Lawrence*, XXI (Feb. 27, 1901), 1.

Two News Reports

[March 2, 1901]

PRINCETONIAN BANQUET.

Third Annual Banquet Held
at the Inn Last Night.

The third annual banquet of the DAILY PRINCETONIAN board was held last evening at the Princeton Inn. The banquet began at about half-past eight and closing [closed] with the toast by Professor Woodrow Wilson.

The list of toasts was as follows:
The Outgoing Board—W. E. Hope 1901.
The Incoming Board—A. J. Barron 1902.
The *Yale Nsws* [*News*]—N. H. Mason.[1]
French Journalism—Professor A. G. Cameron.
College Men in Politics—Professor J. H. Finley.
The Faculty—Dr. Henry van Dyke.
Princeton University—Professor Woodrow Wilson.

J. W. Jameson, business manager of the 1901 board, acted as toast master. After a few remarks, he introduced W. E. Hope, editor-in-chief of the 1901 board, who spoke briefly of the responsibilities of the PRINCETONIAN toward the University and of the undergraduate body toward the PRINCETONIAN. A. J. Barron was then introduced and outlined the ambitions and purposes of the incoming board. Mr. N. H. Mason, of the *Yale News* followed. He conveyed the good wishes of the *Yale News* toward the DAILY PRINCETONIAN and related the scheme of work pursued on the Yale paper.

Professor A. G. Cameron was the next speaker, and dwelt upon the wit and high literary standards of the French papers and the excellent political journalism displayed in their columns.

Professor J. H. Finley spoke of the duties and responsibilities which college men will meet in the politics of the country after their graduation.

Professor Henry van Dyke followed and spoke on behalf of the faculty, emphasizing the importance of a spirit of the closest sympathy between the faculty and the undergraduate body and dwelling particularly upon the desire which the faculty has for extending such a relation.

The closing speech was made by Professor Woodrow Wilson. He spoke of Princeton as a place of preparation, not as a place of achievement, and of the necessity of getting in college ideas which will give the alumnus a mind trained to cope with the problems of life in all of its aspects.

Immediately after the remarks by Professor Wilson, the banquet was closed by the singing of "Old Nassau." . . .

Printed in the *Daily Princetonian*, March 2, 1901.
1 Norman Howell Mason, Yale, 1902.

[March 2, 1901]

DEBATING TEAM CHOSEN

Princeton has chosen the negative of the question to be argued with Yale on March 27—Resolved that a system of subsidies, other than the present mail subsidies, should be adopted by the United States to encourage our ship-building and ocean-carrying trades. At the final trials this week the following men were chosen to debate for Princeton: Walter Ewing Hope '01, of New York; Robert Service Steen '01, of Pennsylvania, and Axtell Julius Byles '03, of Pennsylvania.

Of the sixty men who entered the preliminary trials in the Halls, the following four from each Hall were retained: Whig— R. S. Steen '01, C. Campbell '02, J. G. Sims '02, W. P. Vail '02. Clio—F. W. Fort '01, W. E. Hope '01, R. F. Pitcairn '01, A. J. Byles '03. These eight, with A. S. Weston P.G.,[1] took part in the final trials, which were held in Murray Hall on Feb. 25. Professors Woodrow Wilson '79, J. H. Finley, H. B. Fine '80, W. M. Daniels '88 and H. F. Covington '92[2] were the judges, and chose the team of three men named above—Hope, Steen and Byles. For the second or scrub team the judges selected A. S. Weston P.G., F. W. Fort '01, R. F. Pitcairn '01, and J. G. Sims '02. Practice debates are now being held between the first and second teams, under the direction of Prof. Covington.[3]

The Spencer Trask ('66) prize of $50, which is awarded each year in these trials, to the man who delivers the best debate, exclusive of those who have won the prize in former years, was won by W. E. Hope '01. Previous winners of the Trask prize are A. S. Weston '99, Harvard trials, 1899; J. A. Jones '00, Harvard trials, 1900, and J. H. Hill '00, Yale trials, 1900. . . .

Printed in the *Princeton Alumni Weekly*, 1 (March 2, 1901), 546.
  [1] That is, postgraduate.
  [2] Harry Franklin Covington, Assistant Professor of Oratory.
  [3] For the outcome of the Princeton-Yale debate, see the news report printed at March 30, 1901.

To Laurence Hutton

My dear Mr. Hutton,   Princeton, 3 March, 1901

   I certainly "played in hard luck" in the matter of your lectures! Every one of them except the second, which I greatly enjoyed, fell upon a night on which I had some engagement, in Princeton or out of it, made before the lecture date was announced and not to be escaped from. I know how much the lectures have been appreciated, and, by the same token, how much I have lost.

   I hope the lectures did not too much fatigue you; and that another season you will feel like doing us the same kindness again.

   With warm regards,
                           Sincerely Yours,   Woodrow Wilson

ALS (WC, NjP).

From Laurence Hutton

My Dear Mr Wilson   Princeton March 4th 1901

   Let me thank you for your two notes, which touch and encourage me

   When the Harpers rejected the "Oxford," for book, as well as for periodical, form, on the ground that it appealed to an audience so "select" that it could not meet with financial success, I felt that there was no good left in me. But the select of Princeton have done not a little to cheer and comfort me.

   Believe me   Very sincerely yours   Laurence Hutton.

ALS (WP, DLC).

From Orin Grant Libby[1]

Dear Sir: Madison, Wis. Mar. 4, 1901.

Yours of the 18th ult. at hand. I shall be pleased to let you have any map you care to use in that monograph of mine.[2] I have been looking over the material and have found several mistakes in maps of the different states. Unless you are in a hurry I should like to make a number of corrections, especially in New England and North Carolina. Would it be worth your while to have these alterations provided for in the reprint? I regard your work as of the only really substantial and permanent sort that is being done in American History. Most of our writers lack either power of expression or the ability to investigate and discover, and I feel somewhat certain that their work will be soon entirely forgotten. I am very much pleased to have the opportunity to express my appreciation of what you are doing. I hope you will not be satisfied until you have given us a complete and authoritative history of the United States. Bancroft's, Von Holst's, and Schouler's are no longer to be taken as truly national histories, and McMaster's is only a brilliant experiment. This is my deliberate judgment after several years of seminary work in my advanced classes. We have traversed the ground carefully more than once and the fundamental errors stated or allowed to pass are numerous enough to attract the attention of every student. If we could have a history as carefully done as your "State" and showing in the treatment of the social, economic and political problems the insight which you show in "Division and Reunion," it would go a long way toward filling the gap so painfully apparent just now in our general histories.

                        Very Truly Yours   O. G. Libby

ALS (WP, DLC).

[1] A former doctoral student of Frederick Jackson Turner at the University of Wisconsin, Libby at this time was Instructor in History at the same institution.

[2] Orin Grant Libby, *The Geographical Distribution of the Vote of the Thirteen States on the Federal Constitution, 1787-8* (Madison, Wisc., 1894).

To Edward Ingle

My dear Ingle,   Princeton, New Jersey, 5 March, 1901.

I thank you most sincerely for your letter of February twenty-first. I had not forgotten that you had a paper on Richard Ingle but at the time I was writing the passage you refer to I could not put my hand on it. I had forgotten just where it was printed. I shall be sure to look it up before the articles get into book form, and to reconsider the passage carefully. I am sorry to have fallen into error, and grateful to you for having called my attention to it.

It was very pleasant to hear from you again. I have your "Southern Side Lights,"[1] and have followed you as well as I could through these years of separation. There is a great deal of pleasure in looking back to those old days at the Hopkins, which I dare say no one of us is likely to forget.

With much regard,

Sincerely Yours,   Woodrow Wilson

WWTLS (E. Ingle Papers, MdHi).
[1] Edward Ingle, *Southern Sidelights: A Picture of Social and Economic Life in the South a Generation Before the War* (New York and Boston, 1896). A copy of this book is in the Wilson Library, DLC.

From Howard Pyle

Dear Professor Wilson: Wilmington, Del., March 6th. 1901.

For this number (7) of the History I would like very much indeed to paint a maritime picture of the battle between the "Serapis and the Bonhomme Richard." I think there is nothing in the paper referring to the very insufficient navy of the Revolutionary period[.] Do you think it would be feasible for me to interpolate such a subject—or would it be possible for you to slide a sentence into the text that I could pin such a picture to? I know this sounds like a great piece of assurance on my part, but it seems to me that such a subject would much embellish the number.

I am not so wedded to it, however, but that I would relinquish it very readily if it is impracticable. I hope, however, you will let me know your verdict at as an early a moment as you conveniently can.

When do you come to Wilmington again? Do not forget that the next time you are to stay with me.

Sincerely yours,   Howard Pyle

TLS (WP, DLC).

To Howard Pyle

My dear Mr. Pyle,   Princeton, New Jersey, 7 March, 1901.

Unfortunately the proofs of No. VII. long since went through my hands for final revision, and it is now too late to add even a sentence about Paul Jones; but I intend to mention him in the book when it comes, and the picture you suggest is most attractive. It can easily enough be got in without a text, as the picture of Drummond and Berkeley was got in in [*sic*] the March number of the Magazine, by giving it a brief explanatory text of its own instead of a simple title. Will you not do that? The title can easily be changed when it comes to making up the book.

Thank you very much for saying what you do about my staying with you the next time I come to Wilmington. The idea is most attractive. May the thing some day happen!

In haste,

With much regard,

Sincerely Yours,   Woodrow Wilson

WWTLS (de Coppet Coll., NjP).

An Announcement

[March 7, 1901]

FACULTY NEWS.

Professor Woodrow Wilson, head of the Jurisprudence and Politics Department, who had intended to take advantage of his year's leave of absence next year and spend it abroad, has changed his plans and will defer his trip until some future date. This will alter the arrangements already made to have Professor Finley take charge of Professor Wilson's department and classes next year, as Professor Wilson will continue his regular course of lectures. . . .

Printed in the *Daily Princetonian*, March 7, 1901.

From James Wilson Woodrow[1]

Mapimí, Estado de Durango, México.

My dear Cousin Woodrow: March 10th 1901.

When you can do so conveniently, will you very kindly ascertain for me whether or not I am properly an *Alumnus* of Princeton.

In the Engineering Dep't. of the class of 1886, I was in good standing, and in the technical branches particularly I was in very excellent standing, until, in December 1895 [1885], my senior year, I was called home by father's illness. His death occurred on the 22nd of the following February, and I was detained at home so long that the second term of the year's course was practically completed when I returned to Princeton.

The last term of the Senior year was short and somewhat informal. It would have required some study during the summer, and a return to Princeton, to take the examinations which I had missed while at home. At that time it seemed to me not worth while to do this, and Prof. McMillan,[2] the chief of the Dep't. of Engineering[,] endorsed my decision in this respect. I received testimonials from the professors of the Eng. Dep't. with an endorsement by Dr. McCosh. Since graduation (i.e. of my class) I have occasionally corresponded with Prof. McMillan, who is to an extent acquainted with my subsequent career. I believe no one in my class has followed Engineering *quite* as uninterruptedly as I have done. I began Engineering work two months after leaving Princeton, and have since followed it without intermission. I have for a number of years, in South America, Colorado, and Mexico, been Engineer in Charge—either as Superintendent or Manager.

Of late years I have regretted deeply that I did not secure my degree, for reasons of sentiment. And I feel a sense of very slight injustice of Fate that after taking the Princeton C.E. course all but three months, and then having devoted myself earnestly and with fair success to the Engineering profession, that I nevertheless cannot claim to be C.E. of Princeton.

The immediate cause of this letter is the enclosed blank, which you perceive I cannot fill. Does the absence of a degree deter me from being an alumnus? If so is there any way in which I can still obtain the degree without returning to Princeton. I do not care for the degree particularly, but I would like much to be enrolled among the alumni.[3]

With kindest regards to yourself and family
Your affectionate cousin   J. Wilson Woodrow.

ALS (WP, DLC) with WWhw notation on env.: "Ans. 28 Mar. 1901." Enc. missing.

[1] Son of Thomas Woodrow, Jr., and Helen Sill Woodrow of Chillicothe, Ohio, and Wilson's first cousin. At this time James Wilson Woodrow was a mining engineer in Mexico.

[2] Charles McMillan, Professor of Civil Engineering and Applied Mathematics at Princeton since 1875.

[3] The degree of Civil Engineer was conferred on Woodrow in June 1901.

From Joseph R. Wilson, Jr.

My dearest Brother: Clarksville, Tennessee, 3/11 1901

It has been so long since I last wrote to you that it is distasteful to me to be forced to write only a business note at this time, but I am in a close place financially and my first impulse is to turn to those I love and who love me for help. Yet I hesitate to do so now, because I cannot tell how you may be situated and how convenient it may be for you to help me. My collections have been so very hard of late that I have found it necessary to obtain temporary relief by borrowing for say twelve months $100.00. It mortifies me, my dear brother, to ask this of you, and if it was not for my business I would not do so, but I find it will be absolutely necessary for me to get this amount by the end of this week, Saturday, and I hope that I am not asking more than you can grant. If I was not closely pressed I would not write so to you. I want this to be a business matter, and will send a note for the amount I ask. If you cannot grant the loan requested, could you let me have at least a part of it?

Do not condemn me for thus writing. It is not extravagance that makes it necessary, but my failure to realize on my outstanding accounts. If you can make the loan, I would ask you to telegraph the money and I will remit to cover the charges if you will advise me as to the amount of same.

We are all well and send a great deal of love to you and yours.

Your aff. bro.   Joseph.

ALS (WP, DLC).

From James Edward Webb[1]

My Dear Sir: Birmingham, Ala., March 11th 1901

You will remember that three years ago I had some correspondence with you in reference to the Presidency of the University of Ala.[2] You could not then see your way clear to accept the Presidency: and, the Board of Trustees, elected Dr James K. Powers. Dr Powers was active, and enthusiastically energetic. As a result the number of students increased from about 175 (not including in that number about 150 medical students in the Medical Department located at Mobile) to over 250. The Faculty also has been added to and greatly strengthened. The Academic and Law Students, now in attendance number 250. At the meeting of Board of Trustees in Jany last, Dr Powers resigned to take effect in June next: and the Board of Trustees is looking for a President. The annual income is from $38000.00 to $40000.00. There is a slight variation in the income, which grows out of the fact, that the royalty, which is paid it, by lessees of some of its coal lands, is not always the same. The Board has fixed the Presidents salary at $4,000.00 (payable $333.33 monthly) per annum, and Presidents mansion free of rent.

If you are in a position at this time to favorably consider a proposition to accept the Presidency, I will be much pleased to hear from you.

I will ask that what I have written shall be between you and me. We are not lacking in parties seeking the place: but we are not looking for men who are seeking place.[3]

With great respect, I am,

very truly, yours   James E Webb

ALS (WP, DLC).

[1] Lawyer of Birmingham, Ala., and trustee of the University of Alabama since 1886.

[2] Richard Channing Jones had resigned the presidency of the University of Alabama in March 1897 after an extended controversy over his administration and had been replaced in June 1897 by James Knox Powers. Hence Webb's correspondence must have occurred four years prior to the date of this letter. This correspondence is missing, and there is no reference in the Wilson Papers to an offer to Wilson of the presidency of the University of Alabama.

[3] Wilson's reply is missing, but he obviously declined to permit his name to be considered. The Alabama trustees ultimately elected William Stokes Wyman, Professor of Latin at the University of Alabama since 1855, who had often served as acting president.

From John Norris Miller

Dear Prof. Wilson: [New York, c. March 15, 1901]

I am in receipt of your letter of some days ago and am glad that you approve of our plan. I must however apologize for the delay in sending you the Formal Notification for your signature and approval. The drawing up of this document I left to Mr. Hedges. I have called upon him twice but each time he has said that his business prevented him from giving it his attention but has always promised to write me the next day. Tonight I have written him and if I do not receive the notification in a few days, I shall myself attempt to draw one up.

We are particularly fortunate in having secured a copy of the old Treaty, which will greatly assist us in the formation of the new one. Through the assistance of a member of the senior class, that valuable document has been found and a typewritten copy will be made immediately.

I am particularly sorry for this, which seems to me, unnecessary delay but I trust that matters will in a few days progress more smoothly. With very best regards, I am

Very cordially,   J. Norris Miller.

ALS (WP, DLC).

A News Item

[March 16, 1901]

The seniors graduated in Whig Hall last week,[1] and besides the serious business, there was a smoker and some fun. Prof. Woodrow Wilson '79 and Prof. John Grier Hibben '82 made speeches; Prof. George M. Harper '84 told a stirring story of personal adventure, and William H. McLauchlan,[2] of the department of chemistry, made several humorous remarks.

Printed in the *Princeton Alumni Weekly*, 1 (March 16, 1901), 580.
    [1] It was an old custom to have a "graduation" ceremony for the seniors of Whig Hall.
    [2] William Henry McLauchlan, Assistant in General Chemistry.

From Daniel Coit Gilman

My dear Wilson,   Baltimore   Mch. 16 [1901]

To fill the place of Dr. Adams at the head of our historical studies,[1] there is no one to whom our thoughts turn so naturally as to you, whom we know & honor as scholar, teacher, writer, thinker,—and as a man. "People" say 'you cannot get him!' but what do "people" know? You only can answer my question. I am quite ready to nominate you, & I believe that the nomination would be heartily & at once confirmed by the Trustees & the Faculty. Will you come & survey the situation & put your questions to me?

On Tuesday next, in the afternoon, Professor John Bassett Moore is to give us a lecture[2] & I am asking a few gentlemen to meet him at dinner at half past seven o'clock. Will you come & meet him? If so come at once to my house where a room awaits you. If you can come, send me a line by telegraph.[3]

Yours Sincerely   D. C. Gilman

ALS (WP, DLC).
    [1] Herbert Baxter Adams's health had been declining since 1899. His resignation as Professor of American and Institutional History and his promotion to the rank of Professor Emeritus were made public on February 22, 1901. He died at Amherst, Mass., on July 30, 1901.
    [2] At this time, Moore was Hamilton Fish Professor of International Law and Diplomacy at Columbia University. He gave two lectures at the Johns Hopkins during the academic year 1900-1901 on "International Questions of the Day." The first was entitled "Our Treaty with Spain"; the second, "Our Policy in the Far East."
    [3] As D. C. Gilman to WW, March 20, 1901, discloses, Wilson sent a telegram declining the invitation to dinner.

From Edward Graham Elliott

My dear Professor Wilson,   [Berlin] March 17th [1901]

The official close of my first semester was Friday—the actual close on the previous Saturday. I am, as you see, still in Berlin and will remain till about the first of April, when I hope to take a ten days vacation before going to H[eidelberg], part of the time most probably in Dresden with George. Since I last wrote you, I have gotten an 'Anzeige' of the lectures for the coming semester in Heidelberg and am much pleased with the prospect. Prof. Jellinek gives the following—

Einführung in die Rechtswissenschaft—4 hours

Geschichte der politischen und socialen Theorien—2 hours

Allgemeines und deutsches Reichs- und Landesstaatsrecht— 6 hours

Uebungen in öffentlichen Recht (Staats- Völker- und Vervaltungsrecht) mit schriftlichen Arbeiten—2 hours.

In all fourteen hours. To be sure it covers in large measure the same ground as did the courses I've had here in Berlin, but my German was so deficient during the first half of the semester, that I do not feel altogether as if I would be merely repeating for the sake of Prof. Jellinek's views. Perhaps I may make an exception of the allgemeines und deutsches Reichs- und Landesstaatsrecht. I got more out of my course under Prof. Gierke in that subject than out of any other course. In addition I am spending these three weeks in reading Laband, Meyer, & Schulze[1] and working over my notes in connection, so that I will have some idea of the deutsches and preussisches. The allgemeines you can imagine plays a relatively small part. There is still another reason, and really the most important one, why I may not take that course—viz. that it conflicts with the only course in the System des römischen Privatrechts. Having taken a course here this term in römische Rechtsgeschichte, I feel that I should continue in it. I should be very glad to hear if you have any advise [advice] to give on the subject.

The other courses I thought of taking were these—

Professor Strauch[2]—

Grundzüge der Rechtphilosophie 2 hrs.

Völkerrecht nach seinem Grundrisse 4 hrs.

Perhaps also these—

Dr. Hatschek[3]

Geschichte des constitutionellen Staatsrechts (I Teil: der amerikanisch-französische constitutionalismus. II Teil: die Reception des englischen Staatsrechts in Deutschland). 2 hrs.

Englische Verfassungsgeschichte der drei letzten Jahrhunderte. Prof. Strauch: Anleitung zur Benützung der wichtigsten Rechtsquellen, insbesondere des corp. jur. civ. und des corp. jur. cons: 1 hr.

Völkerrechtliche Uebungen—1 hr.

I do not want to take more courses than I can profitably attend and whether or not I take them all will depend largely on how much work the seminars require.

I am trying to follow out as best I can the general direction you gave me, and I send you my contemplated work in detail that you may know exactly what I am doing and can then add any other suggestions you may choose.

I expect to reach H. by the 15th of April at the latest. That will give me a few days in which to get located before the lectures begin. With very kindest regards to Mrs. Wilson,

Most sincerely yours   Edward G. Elliott

My address in H. will be Filiale der Rheinischen Credit Bank.

ALS (WP, DLC).
   1 Paul Laband (1838-1918), Georg Meyer (1841-1900), and Hermann Johann Friedrich Schulze (1824-88), political scientists often used and cited by Wilson.
   2 Hermann Strauch, long-time professor at Heidelberg, whose birth and death dates cannot be found.
   3 Julius Hatschek (1872-1926) of Heidelberg.

To Daniel Coit Gilman

My dear Mr. Gilman,   Princeton, New Jersey, 18 March, 1901.

I need not tell you how deeply your letter about the filling of Dr. Adams's place has gratified me, or how sorry I am to be obliged to say that I cannot consider the matter. The fact is, that I am under obligations here which I do not feel at liberty to turn away from or disregard. The Princeton people have so bound me to the place by every kindness and favour and honour, and have on several recent occasions made such a point of my staying here that I should really be ashamed to leave, as if I had not found my interests sufficiently advanced by them, or were weary of their service. There would be points of delicacy for me about accepting a chair elsewhere which I confess I should not know how to meet.

This letter of yours will always be a gratification for me to think of, as a very substantial proof of your confidence in me as a scholar and as a man; and I thank you for it most heartily. It is no easy matter to return this sort of answer to it.

I am sure you know how irreparable I think the loss of the

Un[i]versity in losing you. Your work and your individuality cannot be duplicated.

With warmest regard,

Loyally and sincerely Yours,   Woodrow Wilson

WWTLS (D. C. Gilman Papers, MdBJ).

A News Report of a Lecture

[March 19, 1901]

MONDAY NIGHT CLUB.[1]

Professor Woodrow Wilson addressed the Monday Night Club last evening in 3 S. W. Brown,[2] taking as his subject "Alexis De Tocqueville." Professor Wilson began his talk with a discussion of M. De Tocqueville's book, "Democracy in America," considering the contents of the book, the circumstances under which the material for it was collected, the Frenchman's prejudice against democracy which the author had to overcome, and De Tocqueville's purpose in writing the book, which was to show that democracy, though not an alleviator of all the difficulties of government, was yet in no way detrimental to government. He referred to De Tocqueville's intimacy with the English people and to his belief that their power of government was due to the strain of Norman rather than of Saxon blood.

As an instance of the courageous spirit of the author's family, he mentioned the fact that the De Tocqueville was one of the few royal families who remained in France during the Revolution. Professor Wilson characterized De Tocqueville as a man of high and clear ideas, but of comparatively small influence; as a profound thinker rather than a leader; as one who, though unfitted to take an active part in current politics, judged conditions fairly and prescribed remedies wisely.[3]

Printed in the *Daily Princetonian*, March 19, 1901.
[1] About this undergraduate organization, see n. 1 to the news report printed at April 20, 1900, Vol. 11.
[2] A dormitory on the Princeton campus.
[3] For this lecture, Wilson was using the notes for his University Extension lecture on de Tocqueville. About Wilson's University Extension series, see the Editorial Note, "Wilson's Lectures on Great Leaders of Political Thought," Vol. 9.

To William Rainey Harper

My dear Sir,   Princeton, New Jersey, 20 March, 1901.

I very much appreciate your kind invitation to lecture at Chicago next summer, particularly as you tell me I am the first

Princeton man to whom you have extended such an invitation. I am sure that it would be both pleasant and profitable to be associated with the work of the University, and that I should enjoy a great many features of the experience.

But not being in harness in the summer, I feel that I must not let my vacations be invaded by work like the winter's work. I have already declined several invitations of this kind which were in every other way most attractive; and the reason is as imperative and conclusive in this case as in the others.

Allow me to thank you very warmly.

With much regard,

Sincerely Yours,   Woodrow Wilson

WWTLS (ICU).

From Daniel Coit Gilman

My dear Wilson   Baltimore Mch. 20, 1901

I was very sorry to receive your telegram, more sorry to receive your letter, most sorry, superlatively, to believe, as you force me to believe, that there is no chance of our persuading you to come here as a Professor. You are happy in your temperament & in your environment & I do not wonder that you are reluctant to move. But there is a good deal that we could say, if you would only lend us an ear!

In less than ninety days I shall be a free man but I have bought this freedom at a great price, one item in the account being that I love my office, my colleagues, & my opportunities, all of which I now part from.

Ever yours with the highest regards   D. C. Gilman

ALS (WP, DLC).

From Henry Mills Alden

My dear Mr. Wilson: New York City March 22, 1901.

I am returning herewith Miss [Florence Stevens] Hoyt's poems which I thank you for letting me see.[1] They have unusual merit. Some passages are really remarkable disclosures of poetic power, and if, in any of the poems, the whole rose to the level of these parts, the result would be something meeting our needs and for which we should be grateful. This, unfortunately, is not the case.

We inquired into the matter of John Fiske's illustrated histories and found that the cost of them would be between fifty and sixty dollars. This being the case, it would seem better that you should have recourse to some library for the selection of illustrations. We shall be obliged to have such recourse ourselves in following out your suggestions for pictures.

With cordial regard, I remain

Yours sincerely,   H. M. Alden

TLS (WP, DLC).
[1] Wilson must have returned them to Miss Hoyt.

To Burton Egbert Stevenson[1]

My dear Mr. Stevenson,   Princeton, 25 Mar., 1901

Allow me to thank you for your thoughtful kindness in sending me a copy of your "Soldier of Virginia,"[2] and for the card which accompanied it. I have already begun to read it, and shall look forward to the rest with zest. I congratulate you on your success; and am very much pleased to know that my "Washington" helped you.

With much regard,

Sincerely Yours,   Woodrow Wilson

ALS (B. E. Stevenson Papers, DLC).
[1] Born and reared in Chillicothe, Ohio; student at Princeton, 1890-93; librarian of the Chillicothe Public Library, 1899-1957; prolific editor and author of fiction and non-fiction.
[2] Burton Egbert Stevenson, *A Soldier of Virginia: A Tale of Colonel Washington and Braddock's Defeat* (Boston and New York, 1901). A copy of this book is in the Wilson Library, DLC.

To Houghton, Mifflin and Company

My dear Sirs,   Princeton, New Jersey, 26 March, 1901.

I very heartily appreciate your kindness in offering to let me have the illustrated edition of Mr. John Fiske's works at the liberal discount of 33 1/3%, and gladly avail myself of the offer.

The six volumes so far published[1] foot up twenty-four dollars. Enclosed you will find my cheque for sixteen dollars. I would be obliged if you would ship them by Express at my expense.

Very sincerely Yours,   Woodrow Wilson

TCL (Houghton Mifflin Letter Files, MH).
[1] See H. M. Alden to WW, Jan. 28, 1901, n. 1.

From Job Elmer Hedges

Dear Sir: New York City. March 27th, 1901.

Enclosed please find copy of notice to be served on the Clio-sophic Society,[1] signed by Mr. Miller and myself, with copy for you to keep for reference, as the probabilities are that you will be called into discussion with some local member or graduate of Clio. If the notice as herewith sent meets your approval, it only remains for you to annex your signature thereto and serve it upon the proper person. As soon as you hear from the Clio, will you kindly notify Mr. Miller.

For your information I enclose copy of the treaty.[2]

Respectfully yours,   Job E Hedges

TLS (WP, DLC) with WWhw notation on env.: "Hall Treaty—Ans. 4/2/01."
  [1] It is missing.
  [2] It is also missing. As J. N. Miller to WW, June 2, 1901, indicates, the notice of the abrogation of the treaty by Whig was not delivered to Clio until June 1901. In accordance with a provision of the treaty, the abrogation did not take effect until February 1902. By the latter date a new treaty had been drawn up, and it was signed on February 25, 1902, by committees of undergraduates representing the two societies and by Wilson for Whig and Theodore Whitefield Hunt for Clio. The *Daily Princetonian*, March 1, 1902, summarized the differences between the old treaty and the new one, as follows:
"The original inter-hall treaty was adopted in 1892. It was rendered necessary by the extreme methods in use to secure members for the Halls. This treaty provided for absolutely no campaigning by representatives of either Hall, but was recently abrogated, as both Halls felt that while it would be unwise to permit indiscriminate campaigning, campaigning [might] be done in a modified manner. The salient point in which the new treaty differs from the old is that it provides for the soliciting [of] members by representatives from both Halls acting together. Under it, each Hall will appoint a committee on membership, containing thirty men, ten from each of the three upper classes. These committees will coöperate with each other, and the proper officials in each Hall will see that every entering undergraduate is conferred with by a member from the committee of each Hall, acting coöperatively, between the opening of college in September and the fall initiations in October. This campaigning may also take place before the second initiations at the wish of either Hall."

A Memorandum

Wednesday, March 27, 1901

At eight this evening Mr. Cleveland read the first of his lectures on the Venezuelan Boundary Controversy in Alexander Hall.[1]

I introduced him as follows: Ladies and Gentlemen, we are to have the pleasure this evening of hearing Mr. Cleveland speak on the Venezuelan boundary controversy,—a controversy wh. had a lively sequel in our own history. This is the third lecture delivered on the Stafford Little Foundation,[2] and reminds us both of Mr. Cleveland's great kindness in rendering the University this repeated service and of the thoughtful generosity of one of the best and most esteemed friends of Princeton. My function is, not

to introduce Mr. Cleveland,—that were superfluous anywhere,—
but, rather, to say, on behalf of the University, how important
an occasion it always seems to us when he is to speak. He has
chosen to make Princeton the home of his retirement from
office; but there are a few men of essential and intrusive force
who cannot retire from power. We rejoice that one of these has
made this his place of thought and of public utterance.

WWhw memorandum (WP, DLC).
  [1] About these lectures, see the second news report printed at March 30, 1901.
  [2] About which, see F. L. Patton to G. Cleveland, March 23, 1899, n. 2, Vol. 11.

From Howard Pyle

Dear Professor Wilson: [Wilmington, Del.] March 28th. 1901.

For illustrating Part VIII of "Colonies and Nations," I would
like very much to amend the list of subjects that you have given
so that I might do the following
  1. Washington refusing the offer to make him King.
  2. Some subject in Shay's Rebellion.
  3. Inauguration of Washington.
The first two subjects I should choose because they typify that
period of Anarchy following the Revolutionary War so critical,
apparently, to the life of the country. The last subject is obvious.
I have already made an illustration for it for McMaster's article,[1]
but I think I could represent the street in front of the old State
House, a crowd of people and Washington on the balcony.

Will you kindly let me know if you approve of these subjects?
                    Very truly yours,   [Howard Pyle]

CCL (de Coppet Coll., NjP).
  [1] John Bach McMaster, "Washington's Inauguration," *Harper's Magazine*,
LXXVIII (April 1889), 683.

A News Report of a Victory Celebration

[March 30, 1901]

The news of Princeton's victory over Yale in debate on the evening of March 27 reached here after eleven o'clock, but that was
not too late for the undergraduates to show how they felt about
it. They seemed to feel about it very much as they do over winning
athletic championships. First there was a burst of loud "yeas"
from the crowd waiting in front of the Daily Princetonian bulletin
board, followed by organized cheering, for Princeton, the members of the team and the coach, Prof. H. F. Covington '92, who,
it will be remembered, successfully coached last year's debaters.

Then, while the bell on Old North[1] rang energetically, and shot-
guns, cannon firecrackers and tin horns were rejoicing out of
the dormitory windows, a parade began to form, colored lights
were touched off, and a detachment of the fife and drum corps
turned up. A line of students five or six hundred strong then
paraded about the town for awhile in order to wake up whoever
might still be asleep and in order to give some of the faculty a
chance to say something about it. President Patton was out of
town, but Professors Woodrow Wilson '79, Henry van Dyke '73
and John H. Finley were called upon and responded in "a few
well-chosen words" and garments. It is worth while telling all
this by way of convincing Princeton pessimists, if there be any
left, that the modern undergraduate takes interest in other
things than athletics.

Printed in the *Princeton Alumni Weekly*, 1 (March 30, 1901), 605.
 [1] Nassau Hall.

A News Report

[March 30, 1901]

THE STAFFORD LITTLE LECTURES

The Honorable Grover Cleveland delivered the annual Stafford
Little Lectures on Public Affairs in Alexander Hall on the evenings of March 27 and 28. His subject was The Venezuelan
Boundary Dispute, and his lectures were a notable contribution
to unwritten history by the chief maker of that history. The hall
was crowded on both evenings. In addition to the members of the
college, many visitors came to hear the lectures. The Honorable
Henry Stafford Little '44, the founder of the lectureship, was
present with a number of his friends from Trenton.

Mr. Cleveland was felicitously introduced by Prof. Woodrow
Wilson '79, who said that all public men must sooner or later
retire from office, but that there were some who could never
retire from power, and such an one he had the pleasure of introducing. During the second lecture President Patton sat upon the
platform, and at its conclusion, he expressed the gratitude of
Princeton to Mr. Cleveland and Mr. Little, for an opportunity of
hearing at first hand the narration of the important history of
the Venezuelan controversy, in which, he said, Mr. Cleveland took
so conspicuous a part and with which his name would always be
inseparably connected. He expressed the hope that for many
years to come the Stafford Little Lectures would be delivered by
Mr. Cleveland. . . .

Printed in the *Princeton Alumni Weekly*, 1 (March 30, 1901), 611.

To Howard Pyle

My dear Mr. Pyle,   Princeton, New Jersey, 1 April, 1901.

I literally have not had ten minutes to consider your letter of March twenty-eighth until this morning. I hope that you will pardon the delay.

I like two of the subjects you suggest very much indeed, but not the first. I should think it a little dangerous, historically, to make a scene out of Washington's refusal to be made dictator. It was really an incident of correspondence. I should fear that, in making a picture of it, we should be in danger of putting in too large an imaginative element.

I had rather set my heart on having you do a group of emigrating loyalists in the northern forests, a subject that appeals greatly to the imagination; or one of your delightful character sketches of a rural group (this time on the western frontier) debating Jay's treaty.

The scene from Shays' rebellion and the inauguration of Washington I entirely like.

In haste,

With warm regard,

Sincerely Yours,   Woodrow Wilson

WWTLS (photostat in RSB Coll., DLC).

From Stockton Axson

The Colonnade Hotel, Philadelphia.

My dear Brother Woodrow: Tuesday afternoon [April 2, 1901]

We are most comfortably situated at the hospital in a cheerful front room on a quiet street.[1] Jessie is as bright as a cricket (she has been put to bed) and Sister seems perfectly cheerful, and has promised to go to the theatre with me tomorrow afternoon.

The operation will be at half-past ten (10.30) Thursday morning. I will meet the train at 8.57 (the 7.05 from Princeton) and go out with you if you come on that train. There is really no reason however why you should leave Princeton before 8.24—as this gets here at 9.35 nearly an hour before the operation. I may meet that train also. If I don't you will be able to find the place easily—it is about two blocks north of Race Street—and to get there you will take the 16th St. car. It is only about 10 or 12 short blocks from the Broad St. station.

Sister asked me, in case she should fail to get a letter off to you in the evening mail, to ask you to open the letter which will come from Mrs. Tedcastle,[2] and if Madge[3] is invited, to telegraph

Mrs. T. the time at which Madge will arrive at Boston. I think Mrs. T's address is 50 Commonwealth Ave., but I remember Sister said that she puts the address in every letter.

Everything is as cheerful and hopeful as possible. With best love   Yours affectionately always   Stockton Axson

P.S. I am at the Colonnade Hotel as you see by this paper.

ALS (WP, DLC).
   [1] As this and subsequent letters reveal, Mrs. Wilson and Stockton Axson had taken Jessie Wilson to the Philadelphia Orthopaedic Hospital, 1701 Summer St. A fragmentary letter, EAW to Anna Harris, Feb. 12, 1907, Vol. 17, discloses that the operation was for removal of tubercular glands in the neck.
   [2] Agnes Vaughn (Mrs. Arthur W.) Tedcastle of Boston.
   [3] Margaret Randolph Axson, then a student at the Woman's College of Baltimore, was going to Cambridge to attend Edward William Axson's marriage to Florence Choate Leach on April 9, 1901.

From Ellen Axson Wilson

My own darling,   [Philadelphia] Tuesday night [April 2, 1901]

As I have no ink and only the light of the high chandelier I will not try to write a long letter,—especially as Stockton has already written you to tell you the hour of the operation, &c. It is to be at 10.30 Thursday morning. They have put Jessie to bed already, but she does not seem to mind. We have a large cheerful room with two beds, and everything is going pleasantly and smoothly. We have had a very peaceful, restful day. Jessie is in excellent spirits, and Stockton is all attention. You must not worry about us at all. The place of course is very comfortable. If I could only have a lamp to read & write by there would be nothing to desire; but apparently they never heard of a lamp! so the evenings bid fair to hang heavy on my hands and Jessie's, for this light hurts my eyes badly.

Jessie sends her love to all. She is a perfect little angel! As for me I dare not try to say how much I love you all. My own *darling*! my Woodrow—my dear, *dear* love. Always & altogether,
                                          Your own   Eileen.

Open Agnes letter & telegraph her when to expect Madge.

ALS (WC, NjP).

To Ellen Axson Wilson

                          Princeton, Tuesday night. 2 April, 1901

Just a line, my sweet love, to say that all has gone well with us to-day. I lectured twice, wrote letters, did errands, and quite successfully made believe that my heart was not heavy. Nell goes to a party to-morrow afternoon at Dorothy's,[1] about which, she says, she quite forgot to tell you. To-day she lunched with the Fines. We love you and think of you both every minute. I do so hope that you are thoroughly comfortable.

With unspeakable devotion   Your Lover

ALS (WC, NjP).
[1] Dorothea van Dyke, daughter of Henry van Dyke.

To Edward Graham Elliott

My dear Mr. Elliott,   Princeton, New Jersey, 2 April, 1901.

Your letter of the seventeenth was most welcome and most satisfactory. I think of you a great deal; and if I do not write oftener it is because I have nothing to say.

The schedule of courses you map out for yourself at Heidelberg is excellent. My only criticism would be that perhaps you are attempting too many. And my only admonition would be: do not forget to go as early and as deeply as possible into International Law. I know that that is the chief thing that the President has set his heart on your teaching; and our use for International Law over here is certainly increasing very rapidly! You seem to me to be managing excellently, under stimulating men.

I suppose you see the Alumni Weekly. That contains all the news we produce. All is going a[s] usual. We are well; Professor Finley has made a great hit; and the "fellows" seem pretty well pleased with the Department which you are to join!

With warm regard and perfect confidence,
Faithfully Yours,   Woodrow Wilson

WWTLS (WC, NjP).

From Ellen Axson Wilson

[Philadelphia]
My own darling,   Friday afternoon [April 5, 1901]

Stockton will tell you in detail how we do, yet I will scribble a few lines to send by him. We have had a perfectly peaceful comfortable day. Jessie has complained of nothing except a little trouble in swallowing, which they tell me is inevitable. Her lips are so red and her cheeks so rosy that I would think her feverish if I did not know that her temperature has been normal from the first. She also had a remarkably good night "for an ether case." Has also slept most of the time since twelve today,—while I have read and worked button-holes. I slept ten hours last night and am as well as possible. Wrote to Ed[1] & Minnie[2] last night and then went to bed at half past eight; am staying in the room with Jessie again.

Please open my letters & answer if necessary. Love and kisses to the darlings. I love you, dearest, beyond all words! With all my heart　　　　　　　　　　　Your little wife,　Eileen.

ALS (WC, NjP).
　[1] Her brother, Edward William Axson.
　[2] Her first cousin, Mary Eloise Hoyt, who was keeping house for Wilson in Princeton.

To Ellen Axson Wilson

My precious darling,　　　　　　　　Princeton, 7 April, 1901

Thank you with all my heart for your telegram.[1] Dr. Freeman's[2] reassuring opinion clears things up, and I hope restores my darling to complete ease of mind again. It is a great comfort to me,—not because I *thought* the swelling serious, but because I did not *know* whether it was or not.

We reached home all right. I found Stock. and Mr. Graham[3] at the house, about to take dinner with Cousin Mary. We have been to church, and Margaret has gone to Stock's room, to try to get the pair to come around to dinner to-day again, so that *I* can see them. (They came) I went over to dine with the Fines, you know; and, although I was tired, I enjoyed myself very much indeed,—because it was a company of intimate friends: the McCormicks,[4] the Finleys, the Magies. We made a very cosey, easy-going company, and I was rather less tired when the evening was over than when it began,—as much rested as I could have been at home *without you*.

Dr. Duffield,[5] it seems, has fallen very suddenly and distressingly ill, since Friday, and they are keeping him alive to-day only by the use of oxygen. I have not been able to learn the exact nature of the attack. I do not know whether it is pneumonia or not. They evidently do not,—at any rate, *did* not this morning,—expect him to survive.[6]

Mrs. Brown,[7] after a rather bad week, is better again, but still weak and in bed. She and Mrs. Minor[8] make the most particular and affectionate inquiries after dear Jessie and you, and send you both a great deal of love. Indeed, it is very delightful, the number and the nature of the inquiries and the affectionate messages which always accompany them. A great deal of loving thought goes from Princeton to 1700 Summer St., to two dear little women, a sweet, brave little patient and her brave, sweet mother. This dear home seems very, very empty without them!

We are quite well and of quiet minds, my sweet pet. My thoughts fall short of *happiness*, of course; and yet there is a sort of poignant joy in thinking of you where you now are. A sense of your exquisite motherly sweetness and tenderness penetrates me now, perhaps, in an especial degree. You seem for a little to belong to *all* whom you love and to whom your love is a means of life, rather than specially and exclusively to me. My selfish desire to have you for myself is a little rebuked: my love and admiration for you are as it were broadened to the full measure of your perfect womanhood; and with a new ardour I am

Your own   Woodrow

Love unmeasured fr. all to Jess.
The only address of Lil's[9] I find in your desk is, Mrs. Wm. R. White, Berwyn, Penn. It is in her own handwriting.

ALS (WC, NjP).
  [1] It is missing.
  [2] Walter Jackson Freeman, M.D., 1718 Locust St., Philadelphia.
  [3] James Chandler Graham, a classmate of Stockton Axson's at Wesleyan, who was teaching at the Phillips Academy, Andover, Mass.
  [4] The Cyrus Hall McCormicks of Chicago.
  [5] The Rev. Dr. John Thomas Duffield, Professor Emeritus of Mathematics.
  [6] He died on April 10, 1901.
  [7] Susan Dod (Mrs. David) Brown, of 65 Stockton St.
  [8] Mary D. Minor, who kept house for Mrs. Brown.
  [9] Mrs. Wilson's first cousin, Lillian Hoyt White.

From Ellen Axson Wilson

[Philadelphia]

My own darling,   Sunday afternoon 3 P.M. [April 7, 1901]

All is going going [*sic*] well and quietly with us today. Jessie had a *very* good night. Her breathing was hard, as the night before, but she could not have been suffering for she slept almost without waking at all. Her voice is no better than on yesterday but it hurts her a good deal less to swallow. Dr. Freeman came just after breakfast—was out of town yesterday. He found a large swelling low down on one side but the other was quite free, so there is no danger from suffocation. He is treating it by inhalations and does'nt want her to speak at *all*,—a whispered word occasionally, but would prefer she should write her wants. That sounds a little serious, but if there is any cause for anxiety he did not admit it to me,—and I don't think he is famous for discretion either;—for instance he said before Jessie that it didnt matter for boys but he did so hate to see young girls scarred by this operation. And by the way Dr. Keen[1] speaks of it as "a very serious operation"! He dressed the wound today and it is doing beautifully. Jessie seems very much brighter and more like herself than she was yesterday. Her room is full of flowers. Dr Keen sent her a superb pot of Easter lilies, and two of the patients sent her beautiful bunches of flowers,—splendid La France roses, &c.

I am well except for a little cold in the head,—effect of the cold room(!) The weather is still dreary,—havn't been out yet but will walk out shortly and mail this.

Love to Minnie and Stockton; love & kisses for the darlings.

With unspeakable love for my dear love, my Woodrow, I am always and altogether,   Your own   Eileen.

ALS (WC, NjP).
  [1] William Williams Keen, noted Philadelphia surgeon and Professor of Surgery at the Jefferson Medical College. Perhaps he had been recommended to the Wilsons by Grover Cleveland; Keen had assisted at an operation on President Cleveland in 1893.

To Ellen Axson Wilson

My own darling,   Princeton, 8 April, 1901

I have mismanaged my time this morning, and left only a little bit in which to write to the dear ones who engross all my thoughts. I leave for N. Y. on the 1:20,[1] have lunch at 12:30, tried to answer a lot of business letters, shave, pack, and attend to several things about the house, and am belated.

Your sweet letter of yesterday tells me so much more than the telegraph and is, on the whole, so satisfactory that I go away in excellent spirits,—except for the weight that I cannot put off till my darlings are safe at home again,—the weight of *longing*. Anxiety is neither here nor there,—I practically feel no anxiety at all,—but the longing for my dear ones is unspeakably intense.

We are all perfectly well. I have written to Dr. Küsel.[2]

Dr. Duffield is a little better.

Stockton went to N. Y. this morning with Mr. Graham, and goes to Boston to-night.[3]

I am to stay with the [Moses Taylor] Pynes (42 W. 53rd.) I shall come home to-morrow just as soon as their breakfast arrangements will allow.

The envelope which brought the Easter card was marked R. A. DuB.,[4] Asheville. I love you more than I dare say. Unspeakable love to J.   Your own   Woodrow

ALS (WC, NjP).
  [1] For a speech to the St. Nicholas Society that evening, about which see the notes printed at April 8, 1901.

2 Dr. George C. Küsel, dentist of 733 N. 43rd St., Philadelphia.
3 To attend Edward Axson's wedding.
4 Rosalie Anderson (Mrs. McNeely) Dubose.

Two Letters from Ellen Axson Wilson

[Philadelphia]

My own darling,   Monday 12.45 A.M. [April 8, 1901]

Dr. Keen has just gone. He did little more than look at Jessie, being very busy, (has just performed an operation) but says she is doing well. I suppose he will come again this afternoon and look at the wound. Dr. Freeman is to come again if possible later in the day. Jessie's throat gives her practically no trouble in swallowing but her voice has still that strange broken-winded sound. She had a fine night,—slept about eleven hours. I have been reading to her most of the morning and she seems quite comfortable and happy.

I am very well,—have almost thrown off my cold. Your sweet letter and little Margaret's came this morning and were right welcome. Please tell her to let May[1] know that I *do* want the time she mentions. And will you please let Margaret take this note to Miss Winn at once,—I forget her initials and address. Perhaps Maggie[2] can tell you them and in that case you can mail it to her.

I am glad you enjoyed the dinner and are seeing plenty of company. The children are certainly in a whirl of gaiety.

I am very sorry about poor old Dr. Duffield. With all his drawbacks he will be a great loss to our church.[3] Give the family my love and sympathy. Tell Minnie her Bertha is all that she said; also that I am hoping to see her here en route to Bryn Mawr.[4] Tell her it is near the station. With heartfelt love to all you dear ones and Stockton, from us both, and with love *inexpressible* for my darling, I as am ever,   Your own   Eileen.

1 Mary Winn, dressmaker of 46 Charlton St., Princeton.
2 Maggie Foley, long-time servant who lived with the Wilsons.
3 The Second Presbyterian Church of Princeton.
4 That is, when she went to visit her sister, Florence, who was living in Bryn Mawr.

[Philadelphia]

My own darling,   Monday 3.20 P.M. [April 8, 1901]

Dr. Freeman has just been here & says Jessie is a good deal better and will soon be all right. The strange sound of her voice is due to a large swelling like a great water blister pressing on the vocal chords and preventing their vibration. He *could* prick it, and will if it does not soon disappear but "it is best not to be too energetic," he says. I had been making myself pretty miserable imagining permanent injury, from the operation, to the vocal chords, and Jessie doomed to go through life talking like old Mrs. Garland.[1] I thought he looked grave before and was rather evasive. But he was perfectly satisfactory today and entirely reassuring; says he doesn't think there is the *slightest* danger of any such thing, and explained as above the cause of the queer sounds. So now I am in fine spirits. I am afraid, though I did not intend it, that my letter this morning may have sounded a little depressed. So I hasten to supplement it with this.

Jessie is very bright and happy. Dr Keen has not been back. With devoted love,   Your little wife,   Eileen.

ALS (WC, NjP).
[1] Mary Stebbins (Mrs. M. J. G.) Garland, of 86 Stockton St.

Notes for an After-Dinner Speech[1]

8 April 1901

St. Nicholas Society
(A society of descendants of old New York families)

Generations through, you have sat here, at this great gate and receipt of custom, and seen all the world come and go. Your impression has not been of the America that abides so much as of the Am. which fr. age to age is transformed.

It is in these gatherings, "social" we properly call them, that we, consciously or unconsciously, renew our sense of comradeship and remind one another of our ideals,—ideals of our common life.

Thus we renew our *simplicity* of thought:
"Heaven lies about us in our infancy"; in old age we lie about ourselves.

Many elements amongst us: Substantial, tenacious, quiet-thinking Dutch,—no "indecent exposure of private opinions"; pragmatical English stuff; effervescent, incalculable, volatile Irish; hard-headed Scots; adaptable, persistent Scots-Irish; new stuffs mixed of every nation,—and yet a consistent tradition.

Quart cup. Small beginnings, no personal recollection of the first time, but an unbroken and abiding life.

Preeminently an active and talking race, rather than a literary,—of whom it is *not* true that we can "talk on our hands but not on our feet."

Familiar and yet ever strange aspects of our life: "Yes, my dear. Whom did you expect?"

Tennessee Scots elder's prayer.

"These lines were written," &c.

WWhw MS. (WP, DLC).
[1] The St. Nicholas Society celebrated its Easter festival dinner at Delmonico's in New York on April 8, 1901. The notable feature of the occasion was the

exhibition of a loving cup to be presented by the society to Queen Wilhelmina of the Netherlands as a wedding gift. There were at least five speakers, including Henry van Dyke. The fullest report of this affair, which appeared in the *New York Tribune*, April 9, 1901, said about Wilson's address only that he "spoke of the tenacity of character of the Dutch."

To Ellen Axson Wilson

My own precious darling,   Princeton, 9 April, 1901

Cousin Mary is to carry this letter to you. The only drawback to that arrangement is, that you will get no letter to-morrow.

I am just back from New York, tired, but all right. The Pyne's entertained me most pleasantly, and my speech at the St. Nicholas dinner was quite a success.

Your *two* letters of yesterday I found waiting for me. The second was a very comforting supplement to the first.

Cousin Mary will tell you all you want to know about us. We are all right; and this note is only my private whisper of love into my sweet one's ear,—the message which no lover can entrust to another. No messages will ever convey even a faint sense of my devotion, my infinite love for my darling; but it is always a relief to *try* to put into words what my heart seems unable to hold, pent up and unsatisfied. God bless you, my Eileen. Tell Jessie how much we all love and long for her, and remind yourself every minute what you are to   Your own   Woodrow

ALS (WC, NjP).

From Ellen Axson Wilson

[Philadelphia]

My own darling,   Tuesday, 5 P.M., [April 9, 1901]

I have been waiting all day for the doctor's visit so that I could send a satisfactory report of the wound, for he has not looked at it for two days, and today he was to take out the stitches. But he has not come yet. I will leave this open until he does. He had to rush away as soon as he finished a serious operation which kept him all the morning. By the way, it was the pale young woman, and the nurse tells me that all has gone well with her and that it did not turn out to be what they feared but something less serious. It was abdominal.

Jessie has been up for three hours partly in the easy chair, partly on the lounge, and has just gone back to bed. She was very glad to be up and is quite bright and happy[.] Her voice too is gradually improving. She is not as weak as I expected, for of course she has not been able to eat any solid food on account of her throat. She is so delighted at all the flowers that have been sent. Will you please ask Stockton to thank Mr. Graham for us both for the beautiful roses. I would write myself at once if I knew his address.

I suppose that Ed is actually married now! It makes my heart go pit-a-pat with something like dread to think of it! Marriage is a tremendous sort of chance to take, isn't it. I suppose he has written you that they will stop here for two hours on Thursday and *not* at Princeton. The other children will be sadly disappointed but they could not do both & of course this is best.

By the way, I dont believe there is any chance of our getting off before Saturday, (since Jessie is *just* sitting up a little now) so you may as well arrange with Dr. Küsel on that basis.

I am very well,—just a slight cold. I cannot get out regularly as you wished, dear, and you must not scold me for it is not my fault,—I am kept in all day waiting for the doctors to make their visits and besides Jessie is *so* lonely when I leave her.

7.30 The doctor arrived at this point, and a moment after Mary Hoyt who has just left. It was delightful to see her and hear from home.

The doctor found the wound in fine condition. He took out half the stitches—six—will leave the rest until Thursday. He says we can go home on Saturday.

Goodnight, darling. Thank you for the sweet note Mary brought. Am so glad the speech was a success.

With devoted love,   Your little wife,   Eileen.

Excuse scrawl,—have to write standing & holding paper in one hand!

ALS (WC, NjP).

To Ellen Axson Wilson

My precious sweetheart,   Princeton, 10 April, '01

I am so glad you had a chance to see Cousin Mary, and that you will have a glimpse of Ed. and Florence. Madge arrived this morning a little after ten, repacked, took lunch with us, and then left on the 2:10 train for Baltimore. She gave a glowing account of the wedding,—which seems to have been a brilliant success. Ed. was as cool as you please,—and exclaimed to Stock., just after the event, when they went up-stairs to dress, "Gad, I'm a married man!" in true boyish fashion[.] The presents, it seems, were numerous and beautiful. Madge looked *very* bright and well, and had evidently had an extremely enjoyable trip.

There was a *double* wedding in the family yesterday: Richard[1] was married in the evening. Do try, dear, to get down street before you come away and buy something suitable for a wedding present. I don't know whether they are going to keep house or not. Richard has been extremely shy and reticent about the whole affair!

We are all very well indeed, and as serene in mind and life as we can be so long as you and dear little Jess. are away. How far away Saturday seems! But your letters are a great comfort, my sweet one.

Cousin Mary probably told you of Mr. Conover's death yesterday morning.[2] This morning about eight Dr. Duffield died. How strange it will seem without him,—and how one's heart bleeds for poor Mrs. Duffield! He was, it seems, only seventy-eight,—just dear Father's age.

Father, by the way, writes that he cannot start north before the first of May,—when he will have some escort. He seems far from well,—and the Wilmington doctor wants him to see a liver specialist.

I am busy to-day with correspondence and with getting ready for the Trustee's committee meeting on Friday.[3] To-morrow I mean to try to begin on Part XII.

Good-bye, my sweet, lovely darling. I love you to distraction and am wholly and in everything

Your own   Woodrow

Margaret and Nellie were *so* pleased with dear Jessie's letter; and we all send her more love than she will know what to do with.

ALS (WC, NjP).
 [1] The Wilsons' yard man. His last name is unknown.
 [2] Francis Stevens Conover of 10 Bayard Lane. A former naval officer, he had sailed with Perry to Japan and served in the Civil War.
 [3] No extant records shed any light on this matter.

From Ellen Axson Wilson

[Philadelphia]

My own darling,   Wednesday 4.30 P.M. [April 10, 1901]

All is going as well as possible with us. Jessie's throat and voice are much better and she is beginning to have solid food,—soft toast and egg. Moreover she has just walked upstairs very steadily indeed and is sitting in the sun-parlour. And there is actually some sun too; it is the first fairly good day there has been since we came,—though not much to brag of yet, for it is cold and very windy. I took my exercise today, went down to Wanamaker's indeed and did my errands. I found a "sale" going on of something that has been on my list for a year, viz. yellow & green candle shades for dinner parties, very chead [cheap] indeed; which will explain the express package to follow.

We had a nice long visit from Mary and enjoyed it very much. Jessie was delighted to hear all about the fancy dress party. Now we are looking forward eagerly to Ed's arrival about one o'clock tomorrow,—to remain two hours. *Then* Saturday will be near at hand and the happy home-coming! Ah, *how* good that will be! ah! how we love you all! Jessie sends love & kisses without number. And I love *you*, my darling with love unspeakable.

Your little wife   Eileen.

I am very well—cold almost all gone, in the best of spirits.

ALS (WC, NjP).

To Ellen Axson Wilson

My own darling,   Princeton, 11 April, 1901

Stock. will come down for you on Saturday. I have been asked to be one of the ("honorary") pall bearers at Dr. Duffield's funeral at three o'clock that afternoon,[1] and it is an invitation which it would be peculiarly awkward and indelicate,—not to say impossible,—to decline. Much against my will, therefore, I resign the delight of bringing you and our precious Jessie home again. Margaret and Nellie, Dr. Küsel says, need neither of them come in till *next* week Saturday, the 20th.

Mr. Conover's funeral is taking place this afternoon,—is probably just over as I write.

I had a delightful surprise this morning. Dr. and Mrs. Hazen,[2] and Maynard, turned up,—from New York,—to spend an hour or two in Princeton! You may depend upon it that I spent that hour or two with them, showing them all through the University. They went off on the 1:20. It was most refreshing to see them again. Mrs. Hazen brought us a well-rooted little vine of ivy, brought from Clovelly, at the time I met them there.[3] It looks very hardy and promising, and I shall attach a very high *pretium affectionis* to it if it grows,—as I sincerely hope it will. I tried to get them to stay, if only to lunch,—but they would stick to their plan of "only between trains." They of course left most affectionate messages for you. Their faces fell sadly when they learned that you were away,—and *where* you were. Mrs. Hazen is looking *very* well and strong, and Maynard is much grown and filled out. Mr. Hazen looks as always, except that he has disfigured himself with an abominable, picayune *mustache*, crossing from side whisker to side whisker!

Your sweet, bright little note of yesterday did not come by the morning's mail, and has just been handed to me. How glad I am to get it, and how its sweet note of cheer goes to my heart and echoes there! Ah, I love you unspeakably, my Eileen,—and my darling Jessie. Saturday will be a day thrice blessed to us all,— but to me once more the end of a bitter space of life suspended.

We are all perfectly well, and when you get back shall be perfectly happy.

With love beyond all words,   Your own   Woodrow

More messages of love to Jess than she could count between this and Saturday

ALS (WC, NjP).
[1] There is a full account of Dr. Duffield's funeral in the *Princeton Alumni Weekly*, 1 (April 20, 1901), 655.
[2] The Rev. Dr. and Mrs. Azel Washburn Hazen and their son, Maynard.
[3] See WW to A. W. Hazen, July 18, 1900, n. 3, Vol. 11.

From Ellen Axson Wilson

[Philadelphia]

My own darling,   Thursday [April 11, 1901]

I write at the end of a very different day from any we have spent before, a day of constant occupation and change. Sal & Lil[1] came to see us first and just as they were leaving Ed & Florence arrived; so they were all here for a little, Sal and Lil delighted at the chance to see Florence;—who by the way looked *lovely*. She had a beautiful colour, was perfectly dressed[,] her figure was charming and she looked several years younger than when she was in Princeton. And she was *so* sweet! Lil and Sal were evidently charmed with her.

They had to leave just before three you know & I went to the station with them to get a pair of bon-bon dishes which they had left in their valise there and which they wished me to exchange for them, as they have about ten bon-bon dishes Uncle Tom & Aunt Saidie[2] sent them. I hurried back from the station to take Jessie out for a little walk before the sun lost its strength, the Dr. having ordered her out. Then I rushed down to Wanamakers to get some things for Miss Winn the dressmaker as I will have no other chance. Then supper and here I am trying to write standing up by the high light. Will write more satisfactorily in the morning,—am racing to get this mailed. Jessie looks and seems *well*—all the stitches out. With devoted love

                                                Your own   Eileen.

ALS (WC, NjP).
  [1] Her first cousins, Alice Hoyt Truehart and Lillian Hoyt White.
  [2] Rev. Dr. and Mrs. Thomas Alexander Hoyt.

From Annie Wilson Howe

My darling Brother: Dresden, April 11th 1901

. . . Your letter was a great comfort to me, dear brother. It relieved my anxiety about father to a great extent, and I am greatly relieved to know that it is really *better* for you to put off your trip until next year. I will depend on you to keep your promise to send for me to come home if it suits you to come over next summer. Thank you for the promise. It *is* a terrible disappointment that you are not to come while I am here—I did not realize how much I had depended on having you all *near* me if not with me.

George leaves in a few days now. Jean [Flinn] will sail for Baltimore on the first of August. I will go with her to Bremen, and after she sails probably to Eisenach where we will stay until October. Our landlord here says we should go to the seashore this summer instead of to the mountains—but Eisenach is so near Halle that I think we will go there. It is said to be a beautiful place in summer. We have a plan for next winter which I think will be an improvement on any we have yet considered both as to cheapness and comfort. I have a great curiosity to see how cheaply one *can* live in Germany and be comfortable. Having Jean with me and its being necessary for us to have rooms where she could practise has made it impossible to manage things just as I would like this past winter. We are more comfortably fixed now than we have been since we left Wernigerode and hope we can stay where we are so long as we are in Dresden. . . .

So Ed is married! I suppose you are just back from the wedding. It hurt George dreadfully that he could not be there and that he could not even send a wedding present. We found the duty so high on everything we wanted to send that we finally gave it up and decided to bring our presents with us. They will be late but I am sure Ed will understand. George feels it very much, but is not foolish about it. He wrote to Ed, and I added a few lines, hoping that the letter would reach him on his wedding day.

Please tell Fraülein Clara[1] that I received her letter and will answer it very soon. I wrote the letter she asked me to write and sent it by the first mail after hers was received. With a heart full of love for dear Ellie, the children and your precious self,

Your devoted sister,   Annie

George and Annie[2] send warm love to you all.

ALS (WP, DLC).
[1] Clara Böhm, former governess of the Wilson children.
[2] Her daughter, born in 1891.

From Ellen Axson Wilson

[Philadelphia]
My own darling,   Friday 12.15 P.M. [April 12, 1901]

Jessie is to be a very enterprising young person today! Lil is to take her driving in the Park and then to lunch with her and to lie down and rest there until four—all with the doctor's warm approval who says it "will do her good." Isnt *that* progress! She is already [all ready] to start now and my only fear is that she will get tired beforehand waiting for that unpu[n]ctual Lil who was to be here at 12. She does look so pretty,—yesterday in a new pink cambric wrapper I bought for her (the flannel being *so* hot) she was a picture. Lil and Sal were charmed with her. The bandages are all removed from her throat,—only adhesive plaster left.

While she is with Lil I go out to Bryn Mawr to see poor Florence.[1] Woodrow, the poor child is to lose her leg, it must be amputated above the knee, her very life depends on it. Isn't it dreadful! It will probably be done next Tuesday. Of course when one gets over the first intolerable shock of it there is much to comfort one. She will really be *well* when it is all over, no more of that awful pain, able to work and to make something of her life.

Jessie is off and I must hurry off too to make the 1.15 train, it is now quarter of one. I want to see Uncle Tom too while in Bryn Mawr. They are settled there now. Uncle T. much better, Margaret Hoyt[2] staying there. With dear love to all and above all to you   Your devoted little wife   Eileen

I am *so* sorry you can't come tomorrow, but glad you won't lose your morning.

ALS (WC, NjP).
[1] Florence Stevens Hoyt, who was suffering from tuberculosis of the bone.
[2] Probably Margaret Bliss Hoyt, daughter of Dr. William Dearing Hoyt of Rome, Ga.

An Announcement

[April 13, 1901]

UNIVERSITY BULLETIN
SUNDAY, APRIL 14.

... 6.50 p.m. 1904 class prayer meeting in the lower east room, Dodge Hall, addressed by Professor Woodrow Wilson.[1]

Printed in the *Daily Princetonian*, April 13, 1901.
[1] For this talk, Wilson used the notes referred to in n. 1 to the news report printed at April 2, 1897, Vol. 10.

From Azel Washburn Hazen

My dear Dr. Wilson,   Middletown. Conn. 15 April. 1901

Pray let me thank you once more for your generous kindness to us on Thursday. Mrs. Hazen said last evening—"The visit to Princeton is like a dream to me. I shall remember it as long as I live. The absolute sincerity and beauty of that man are very winning. How graciously he gave us two hours!"

These words so aptly expressed my own feeling that I took them down at once and can swear to their accuracy.

Do let me say for myself that I never meet you without genuine profit as well as abiding pleasure. You are very good to include one who has so little to impart among your friends.

We were distressed by the cause of Mrs. Wilson's absence, and are eager to hear from the dear girl who has suffered so much

Mrs. Hazen joins me in gratitude and love to you all. Our glimpse of your charming home will long remain with us as a benediction.

Believe me always Affectionately yours   A. W. Hazen

ALS (WP, DLC).

A News Item

[April 18, 1901]

FINAL DEBATE TRIALS

The final trials for the team to represent Princeton in the Harvard debate were held last night in Murray Hall. Professor J. G. Hibben presided, and Professors H. B. Fine, Woodrow Wilson, W. M. Daniels, J. H. Finley, and H. F. Covington acted as judges.

The team as final[ly] chosen will be made up as follows: W. A.

Babson 1901, W. E. Hope 1901, and R. S. Steen 1901. Alternates
—A. J. Byles 1903, F. W. Fort 1901, S. B. Scott 1900, and R. W.
Sutton. . . .[1]

Printed in the *Daily Princetonian*, April 18, 1901; one editorial heading omitted.
  [1] The seventh annual Princeton-Harvard debate took place in Alexander Hall
on May 10, 1901. The question was "Resolved, That Congress was justified in
imposing the terms embodied in the Platt amendment to the Army Appropriation
Bill, as conditions precedent to leaving the government and control of Cuba to
its people. (The condition with regard to the title to the Isle of Pines being ex-
cepted.)" Princeton argued the affirmative and lost.

To Cyrus Hall McCormick

My dear Cyrus,   Princeton, New Jersey, 20 April, 1901.

Will you not let me know before you come East again where I
may meet you and have a talk with you on important University
matters? I did not have half a chance at you while you were here;
and the matters about which I wish to confer with you had not
then developed as they have developed since.

I was so much engrossed by my little party at the hospital in
Philadelphia while you were here that I feel as if I had hardly
seen you at all. I had the great pleasure of spending an evening
with Mrs. McCormick after you left; but of her too I saw too little;
and Mrs. Wilson missed the pleasure of seeing either of you.

  With warmest regard to you both from us both,
    As ever,
      Faithfully and cordially Yours,   Woodrow Wilson

WWTLS (WP, DLC).

From Cyrus Hall McCormick

My Dear Woodrow: [Chicago] April 22, 1901.

Your letter of the 20th is received and I shall be very glad to
see you whenever I am in the east. At any time, it will always
give me the greatest pleasure to confer with you fully about any
matters which are of interest to you personally or to Princeton.
I realize that a party at dinner, such as we enjoyed so pleasantly
at Prof. Fines's, is not just the place for quiet consultation.

  I trust that your dear one at the hospital is improving!
  I am,   Very sincerely yours,   Cyrus H. McCormick.

CCL (C. H. McCormick Papers, WHi).

From Henry Mills Alden

Dear Sir: New York City April 24, 1901.

Will you kindly let us know, as near as may be, the number of words you intend to have in the book-form of "Colonies and Nation," so that we can make a close estimate of the whole number of pages before beginning the composition of the book.

Shall you make many changes in the work, or can we set from the *Magazine*? And how many illustrations and maps have you planned for the book in addition to those which appear in the *Magazine*? Kindly let us hear from you at your convenience.

Very truly yours,   Harper & Brothers per *a*

ALS (WP, DLC).

Notes for a Letter to Harper and Brothers

[April 26, 1901]

Harper Bros.

Text will be changed all thr. by infinite number of small touches, by little character sketches.

Number of words as nearly as I can guess, 261,000

Illustrations (See Art Dept.) Shall ask for a few more, but especially for a few different—full-page portraits in best possible style. Superb or nothing

Subscription?

Should personally prefer unillustrated, *popular* edition first—my original purpose, but defer to their *commercial* judgment.

WWhw and WWsh MS. (WP, DLC). Att.: WWhw two-page computation of word length.

From Edward Graham Elliott

My dear Professor Wilson,   Heidelberg April 26th [1901]

I found your letter of the 2nd inst. awaiting me upon my arrival here on the 14th, and was much gratified to know that my course so far met with your approbation. My proposed courses for this semester have been materially modified since my arrival here and particularly in regard to the International Law, the very subject you advise me to go into as deeply as possible.

The only course in International Law offered here this semester is that by Prof. Strauch, four hours, which I had intended to take. My first proceeding was to call on Prof. Jellinek, who, upon spring of 1610, as Governor and Captain-General for the company. But it needed a radically new policy to give it ~~it~~ real life; and that ~~new policy was adopted at last by~~ Sir Thomas Dale, ~~who~~ came the next year (1611), after Lord Delaware had gone home stricken with fever. The new policy it needed was one which should give it expansion and a natural vitality of its own. It was necessary that new towns should be built upon the river which should not be, like Jamestown, mere stations where men worked at tasks for the company, but ~~which should be~~ veritable communities in which men should be allowed to have land of their own, and should be given ~~time enough~~ to work for themselves as well as for the incorporators in London. For five years (1611-1616) Sir Thomas Dale and Sir Thomas Gates pushed this new policy forward; and it was their new and better way of doing things that really made Virginia. "Henrico," "Hampton," "New Bermuda," and other new settlements like them, were added to Jamestown, each with its fort and its stockade, its military commander and discipline, and each with its group or virtually independent land-owners, free to work for themselves.

to Such an enterprise

it did not get till

leave

and established
us/

Most of the colonists, it is true, were ~~still held~~ at Jamestown to serve the Company, and driven to their work, as little better than slaves, by their new task-masters.. Gates and Dale came with authority to rule by martial law, without let or mercy, and colonists of the poorer sort got nothing but blows and rations for their bitter toil. Those who mutinied or ran away were put to death or to the torture, if need were, to keep the discipline of toil and order which the Company's Treasurer ~~was~~ *and merchant adventurers were* now steadfastly minded should be wrung from it. But the new plantations showed the way to a new life. There were independent settlers here and there upon the river, as well as men who were mere servants of the Company. The better sort

Even of the men whom the Company had ~~set~~ sent out were given their patches of land and their time, — if it were only a month, — to do work for themselves, — in order that the new plans might thrive. A strong root as of a little commonwealth was planted at last.

A page of the manuscript of Chapter II of "A History of the American People," showing Wilson's emendations and additions to the "Harper's" article

learning that I was from Princeton and studying here under your direction—I took the liberty of thus far using your name—was more than ordinarily polite—in fact quite surprised me by his cordiality especially as I was prepared to face a lion in his den in view of what you had once written me regarding his personal characteristics. He entered into quite a conversation, in the course of which he paid you a very high compliment, incidentally remarked that he had an Honorary Degree from Princeton[1] and was glad to have American students. You can easily see that my first impressions were pleasant ones. He inquired what other courses—other than his—I intended taking. Upon my replying Prof. Strauch, Völkerrecht und Rechtsphilosophie, he asked me if I had ever studied any Völkerrecht at all and upon learning that I had Hübler in Berlin more recently, he advised me *not* to take Prof. Strauch, and further said that in the next semester he himself would read on those same subjects. I was a little surprised at his making such a statement, viz. that I wouldn't learn anything from Prof. Strauch, till I called upon that gentleman today in reference to the seminar—then I perceived that it was an act of kindness on Prof. Jellinek's part to an ignorant stranger. Strauch is old to begin with and in addition his mouth is apparently deformed so that it would have been almost an impossibility for me to have profited by his course. I regret very much there is no other course in Int. Law but I shall devote some time to it nevertheless.

I am so far delighted with Prof. Jellinek—he has given the introductory lectures to all three of his courses and he *far* surpasses any man I heard in Berlin unless it be Schmoller, and he was not in my line. Prof. Jellinek is of medium height, inclined to be stout, wears a full beard which is 'sandy' in color, is quite bald and wears the conventional German noseglass. His eyes are dark brown, his mouth full, often breaking into a pleasant smile as he lectures. His manner of lecturing, too, is splendid—full of vigor and life, yet mild and devoid of all that ranting which is more or less common to German professors. Gierke, for instance, could be heard a block away easily. Contrary to my expectations, I am highly pleased with Prof. Jellinek in every particular.

I have been to see him about the seminar work too. There, he said, was where I would learn most. I am awaiting a little impatiently the first meeting on next Tuesday to see if I shall be as much pleased in this particular as in others. He was very cordial in his offers to help me—said if there was anything I wanted to know, come to see him—a state of affairs difficult to attain in Berlin.

In accordance with your suggestion that I might be taking too much, I shall probably devote myself exclusively to Prof. Jellinek —Lectures 12 hours per week—Seminar 2.

There is another matter—my fellowship for next year—about which I write at this time in view of your contemplated absence from Princeton and this is what I would like to ask of you inasmuch as it has been with you alone that I have had any conversation regarding the financial part of the arrangements—that, if convenient, you would make before your departure some arrangement, with the Treasurer, Mr. [Edwin Curtis] Osborn, I presume, by which it would be sent me by some set time, say the first of August.

I don't write this because of any specially contemplated need at that particular time, but because with you out of Princeton I would be at a complete loss as to the proper person to whom to write—the President, I suppose. I hope this will not be asking anything that may consume your time, now so peculiarly valuable.

Heidelberg itself deserves all that may have been said in its praise.

"Alt. Heidelberg, du feine, du Stadt an Ehren reich,
Am Neckar und am Rheine, kein' andre kommt dir gleich."
For the next month I shall try the student plan of furnis[h]ed room and restaurant meals. I miss the opportunities for speaking German that I had in Berlin, but they may come later.

With my warmest regards to Mrs. Wilson and yourself,
    Most sincerely yours,   Edward G. Elliott.

ALS (WP, DLC) with WWhw notation on env.: "Ans."
1 Jellinek was confused. There is no record indicating that Princeton ever awarded him an honorary degree.

To Azel Washburn Hazen

My dear Friend,   Princeton, 29 April, 1901

Of course I have wanted ever since your delightful note of the 15th came to write and acknowledge it. That I have not done so sooner shows simply that I have been at a loss for the proper terms. It touched and delighted me more than I can say that Mrs. Hazen should have said such a thing about me and that you should have echoed it,—and yet to thank her, and you, for it seems like accepting it as true. I please myself with believing that it *is* true as coming from your *hearts*, and that it means that you both derive as much pleasure in being with me as I derive from being with you. That glimpse of you was an unmixed gratification—and the little space of time I devoted to sticking to you while you saw the University, instead of being a sacrifice of any kind, was a mere indulgence. I only regret, as she does most heartily, that Mrs. Wilson was not here to share it with me. We unite in all messages of affection to you both, and I am, as ever,

Faithfully Yours,   Woodrow Wilson

ALS (in possession of Frances Hazen Bulkeley).

To Houghton, Mifflin and Company

My dear Sirs,   Princeton, New Jersey, 29 April, 1901

Some time ago you were kind enough to ship me a set of the illustrated edition of Mr. John Fiske's histories. When I opened the package I found all except "The American Revolution" bound in red; that was bound in *Green*. I take the liberty of sending these two volumes back to-day by Express, with the request that you will kindly exchange them for copies in *red*. I have, of course, not cut the leaves or otherwise used the volumes.

Very truly Yours,   Woodrow Wilson

ALS (Houghton Mifflin Letter Files, MH).

An Announcement

[April 30, 1901]

BANQUET OF THE UNIVERSITY PRESS
CLUB TO-NIGHT.

The first annual banquet of the University Press Club will be held at the Princeton Inn this evening at eight o'clock, covers being laid for thirty. H. L. Bowlby,[1] president of the club, will preside as toast-master. The following is the list of toasts:—

"The Press Club," E. B. Wilson 1901; "Qualifications of a Correspondent," A. F. Eastman 1901; "Athletics," H. R. Reiter;[2] "Journalism as it Really is," Jesse Lynch Williams; "The Newspaper as an Educator," Professor A. G. Cameron; "The College Man in Journalism," Professor Woodrow Wilson; "My Inexperience as a Reporter," Dr. Henry van Dyke.

The menu cards are designed by Dreka, of Philadelphia. The outside cover presents a small seal of the University and an etching of Nassau Hall.

Printed in the *Daily Princetonian*, April 30, 1901.
[1] Harry Laity Bowlby '01.

2 Howard Roland Reiter '98, at this time a student at Princeton Theological Seminary, who had played on the football team as an undergraduate.

Notes for an After-Dinner Talk

Univ. Press Club.   30 April, 1901
The College Man in Journalism

He cannot, at any rate at once, shape the profession to his ideals; but he *can carry ideals into it*.
A certain distinction
   Of *accuracy*,—a careful eye.
   Of *good form*,—cultivated, but not pedantic, expression,—sense of flavour.
   Of *intelligent comprehension* of each thing as *a whole*.
   Of *outlook* upon other things which give or receive light.
   Of *sense of social responsibility*.
These will tell, not only for *self-respect* and *self-development*, but also for *success*.

WWhw MS. (WP, DLC).

To Robert Bridges

My dear Bobby,   Princeton, New Jersey, 2 May, 1901.

Mr. Kellogg,[1] the new head of the *Lit.* board, delights me with the news that you are coming up to speak at the *Lit.* Banquet next Monday evening. Hurrah for that! And hurrah for the chance to have you with us. Mrs. Wilson and I will be wofully disappointed if you do not stay with us, and come as early and stay as long as you can. I am to be toast-master at the feast, and so my [may] be considered in command. This is my command to you. See that thou obey.

Mrs. Wilson joins me in warmest regard, and I am, as ever,
   Faithfully and affectionately Yours,   Woodrow Wilson

WWTLS (WC, NjP).
[1] Edwin Henry Kellogg '02.

A Report of an Address on Gladstone

[May 3, 1901]
PROFESSOR WOODROW WILSON'S ADDRESS.

Professor Woodrow Wilson addressed the regular meeting of the Philadelphian Society in Murray Hall last night on "Gladstone." After a few prefatory remarks, Professor Wilson said in part:

Of Gladstone's individual greatness everyone speaks, even those who differed from him politically. All men were moved by him, and whether the sensation was that of attraction or repulsion, they recognized in him a master spirit. Yet this was not because of any pose of greatness in the man—on the contrary, his character was one of marked simplicity. At the age of thirty, when intrusted with the revision of the tariff laws, Gladstone took up the work and by personal investigation carried out the task assigned to him simply and without ostentation.

Never was there a man possessed of so great variety of power. This he obtained by growth and steady development of the mind. Not only did he possess variety, but the force of his intellect was apparent to everyone. He stood for the type of what a man may make of himself when fired by high ambition and resolve. To some Gladstone appeared to possess a certain degree of arrogance, and yet it was only the self-confidence arising from long study and training—a sort of arrogance which any man may well have. In the presence of questions concerning man's relation to God, this self-confidence was entirely lacking, as though he recognized that he was but a child in the presence of the Infinite. Many of his political mistakes were made through his strict adherence to religious affairs—through his desire to follow what he considered the right.

The strongest element in his whole character was his genuineness, the most forcible trait that can be possessed. He possessed absolute intellectual honesty and, though not a model, was a truly great man. It was his moral force that enabled him to fill the benches of the House of Commons for hours at a time, it was his moral force which gave him his marvellous power over his fellow men, and finally it was this same force which made him the equal, if not the superior of any constitutional statesman in his time.

Printed in the *Daily Princetonian*, May 3, 1901.

A News Report

[May 7, 1901]

ANNUAL LIT. BANQUET.

The annual banquet of the *Nassau Literary Magazine* was held at the Inn last night. The guests included several members of former boards and a representative from the *Yale Literary Maga-*

zine. Professor Woodrow Wilson acted as toastmaster and introduced the following speakers:

R. P. Swofford, managing editor of the 1901 board, spoke in
behalf of the retiring editors, and was followed by E. H. Kellogg,
managing editor of the present board, who outlined the policy
of the *Lit.* for the coming year. Mr. Bradley A. Welch, a representative of the *Yale Literary Magazine*, spoke of the work of the
Yale Lit. R. S. Steen 1901, spoke on the subject, "Princeton Debating." He laid especial emphasis on the relation of literary work
to debating. Professor G. M. Harper, managing editor of the '84
board, discussed the *Lit.* and the *Alumni* [*Weekly*] and mentioned
the interest taken in the magazine by the graduates. Robert
Bridges '79, then spoke on "Princeton and Literature." Professor
J. H. Finley followed, taking for his subject "Letters and Politics,"
laying especial stress on the necessity for college men interesting
themselves in affairs of the day. Professor A. Guyot Cameron
closed the list of toasts with an address on "Princeton University." . . .

Printed in the *Daily Princetonian*, May 7, 1901; one editorial heading omitted.

From Harriet Hammond McCormick

[Chicago] May 7th, 1901.
Many thanks. Am more than delighted. Can hardly keep secret
until sixteenth.[1]   Harriet McCormick.

TC tel. (C. H. McCormick Papers, WHi).
[1] See C. H. McCormick to WW, May 21, 1901, second letter of that date.

From William Nelson

My Dear Professor: Paterson, N.J.   May 7, 1901
I have been reading with much interest your extremely entertaining and admirable story of "Colonies and Nation," in Harper's,
and of course have been specially interested in what you say of
New Jersey. It occurs to me that perhaps an erroneous impression
might arise in the minds of some readers in perusing the brief
statement on page 907: "New Jersey became subject, as a whole,
to the rule of the king's governor in New York,—once more a single
territory." As I read this first the thought suggested was that New
York and New Jersey became "once more a single territory." Of
course, a careful reading shows plainly enough that the statement
is that East and West Jersey became once more a single territory.
But permit me to suggest that the statement that New Jersey

became subject to "the rule of the king's governor in New York" while correct in a sense is not strictly accurate in at least the legal or technical sense. The governor of New Jersey [New York] was not ex officio governor of New Jersey. It is true that for thirty-five years one person was at the same time governor of both Provinces, but a separate commission and separate instructions were issued to the governor of New York and to the governor of New Jersey, and each Province gave him peculiar troubles. Possibly—I venture this with hesitation—a preferable reading would be something like this: "New Jersey, once more a single territory, received a royal governor, in the person of Lord Cornbury, who at the same time was also commissioned governor of New York." I appreciate the difficulty you must have in condensing so extensive a narrative in such brief compass, with precision of statement, but the success with which you have thus far accomplished this feat leads me to take the liberty of this letter, which is rather in the nature of a suggestion than a criticism.

Very truly yours,   Wm. Nelson

TLS (WP, DLC) with WWhw notation on first page: "Correction embodied in book MS. W. W."

From Harper and Brothers

Dear Sir: New York City   May 8, 1901

We have your letter of the 26th ulto. and note that there will be about 260,000 words in the revised Ms. for book-form of "Colonies and Nation," and that the illustrations, with few exceptions, will be according to the lists now in our hands.

We are so impressed with the importance and charm of your work that, after careful consideration, we have concluded that it is best to issue it first in four volumes—uniform with our subscription edition of *Green's History of England*.

We look upon your History as a monumental, permanent work, and we shall spare no pains or expense in making the setting worthy of the matter. The illustrations would be a telling feature for the subscription agents, and from that point of view we would say that the drawings would suffer if much reduced; consequently it is important that they should have ample space, and the enlarged page will not only better accommodate the pictures, but will lend dignity to the work. We would propose to have the four volumes on the market early next spring.

Mr Alden suggests that we conclude the *Magazine* articles in the December or January number, and we think that the book-form will have a wider market than if the History were published complete in the *Magazine*; while the subscription method of publication would be materially benefitted by the wide advertising given by the serial publication if the work were brought out the first of next year.

Assuming that our proposed plan will appeal as strongly to you as it has to us, we remain

Sincerely yours,　Harper & Brothers.

ALS (WP, DLC).

To William Nelson

My dear Mr. Nelson,　　　Princeton, New Jersey, 13 May, 1901.

I am sincerely obliged to you for your kind letter of the seventh. The sentence to which you call my attention is certainly most misleading, and I am ashamed to have constructed it so carelessly. In the revision, for book form, I shall take pleasure in giving the passage an evident correspondence with the facts! The pitfalls of condensation are indeed many; and I am not a little pleased that you think that on on [*sic*] the whole my condensation has been successful.

I hope that you will do me the favour to call my attention to any other infelicity or error that may come under your eye. Covering so large a space, I feel peculiarly liable to minor mistakes, and feel that such letters as this of yours are real acts of friendship.

With much regard,

Sincerely yours,　Woodrow Wilson

WWTLS (NjHi).

To John Franklin Genung

My dear Professor Genung,　　　Princeton, 20 May, 1901

I am sincerely obliged to you for your thoughtful courtesy in sending me a copy of your very interesting and suggestive "Working Principles of Rhetoric." I have looked through it with a great deal of pleasure and instruction; and must say that I am as much pleased as surprised to find how much I illustrate! You have certainly done my modest little essay a great honour, and have gratified its author very much.[1]

Sincerely Yours,　Woodrow Wilson

ALS (de Coppet Coll., NjP).

[1] In the revised version of his book, *The Working Principles of Rhetoric Ex-*

amined in Their Literary Relations (Boston, 1901), Genung made extensive use of Wilson's essay, "The Truth of the Matter" (printed in this series under its original title, "On the Writing of History," at June 17, 1895, Vol. 9), to illustrate various principles of rhetoric. He illustrated the importance of a central idea or theme in literary composition by quoting (pp. 423-24) Wilson's formulation of the theme of his essay as stated in Wilson's letter to Genung of May 30, 1900, Vol. 11. Genung included a one-page outline of Wilson's essay composed by himself but revised and approved by Wilson (pp. 438-39; see also J. F. Genung to WW, June 11, 1900, Vol. 11). Genung also printed Wilson's opening paragraph (p. 453) as an example of a successful introduction and his closing one (p. 455) as that of a good summarizing conclusion. Additionally, he selected (pp. 457-58) several of Wilson's sentences to illustrate transitions. Finally, he used Wilson's paragraph condemning Macaulay for his Whig bias as an example of argumentation (p. 605). The copy of *The Working Principles of Rhetoric* which Genung sent to Wilson remains in the Wilson Library, DLC.

To Robert Randolph Henderson

My dear Bob: Princeton, 20 May, 1901

I need not tell you that your letter of the twelfth would have been answered long ago, had I been in a position to answer it. I was away in North Carolina when it came, with my father. His health, I am grieved to say, has not improved. On the contrary, I am afraid it is not in a way to improve; and I went down to bring him to Princeton, where I can myself have a direct hand in taking care of him. Now that we have him in hand, we shall hope to see him grow stronger; but we dare not plan to be away in June. Your invitation pleased and tempted us more than I can say. I know of nothing I should rather do than visit that delightful home and place again,—and Mrs. Wilson is as eager as I am. But we are held by a plain duty, and cannot think of our own pleasure. We can only express the deep gratification your invitation has given us. Thank you, my dear fellow, from the bottom of my heart. The older I get the more friendship seems to me the principal thing,—and you and Mrs. Henderson are friends of the sort that make life worth living.

                    Your affectionate friend,   Woodrow Wilson

ALS (WC, NjP).

Two Letters from Cyrus Hall McCormick

My Dear Woodrow: Chicago. May 21st, 1901.

Ambassador [Jules] Cambon from France is in Chicago making a visit of a few days. He has been most warmly received and has created a very strong impression here both as to his force of character and ability as a man and as to his interesting personality.

I have learned that Harvard has already conferred upon him the degree of L.L.D. and I wonder whether or not it would be well for Princeton at the coming Commencement to confer upon him also this degree of L.L.D. Before mentioning it to anyone I wish to consult you confidentially as to the merits of such a recommendation to the Board of Trustees.

Mr. Cambon, as you know, is a man who stands at the top of the diplomatic corps in France. His service in negotiating the Spanish-American Treaty would seem to me to warrant such an honor being conferred upon him by any American university. It is possible that the University of Chicago may confer the degree of L.L.D. upon him at the Commencement which occurs from June 15th to 17th. If our Commencement which comes on the 11th were to confer upon him the degree of L.L.D., he would no doubt go to Princeton for that occasion.

France is just now in a reasonable way making overtures to this country for close relationships on all subjects of mutual interest and it occurs to me that it would be fitting for this country to reciprocate whenever it can reasonably be done. I would not for a moment suggest the conferring of this degree by Princeton unless it seemed a wise and fitting thing to do purely for the interests of the University. Will you let me know frankly just how the matter appears to you? If you care to do so, you might consult Henry Van Dyke or Dr. Patton on the subject, but if you have a clear opinion yourself either way, please let me hear from you.

Very sincerely yours,   Cyrus H. McCormick.

My Dear Woodrow: Chicago. May 21st, 1901.

I cannot tell you what a pleasant surprise it was on my birthday to receive from Mrs. McCormick one of the choicest gifts imaginable, a set of your works with your autograph in each volume. I prize this not only from the sentiment of its coming to me on my birthday, but also because it is so closely connected with you personally.

With many thanks for your kindness in writing in these books and returning them so quickly to Mrs. McCormick, I am

Very sincerely your friend,   Cyrus H. McCormick

TLS (WP, DLC).

To Cyrus Hall McCormick

My dear Cyrus,   Princeton, 23 May, 1901.

I am distinctly of the opinion that it would be entirely appropriate and very graceful and timely for us to confer an LL.D. on M. Cambon. It strikes me as an excellent idea. I have not conferred with any one else [   ][1] practical judgment), but the matter seems clear to me.[2]

I am sincerely gratified that my small part in your birthday present from Mrs. McCormick should have pleased you so. You may be sure I did it with real satisfaction, out of a real affection, upon which you may count. I was very much complimented that Mrs. McCormick asked me to do it.

With warmest regards to you all,
          Cordially and faithfully Yours,   Woodrow Wilson

WWTLS (WP, DLC).
    [1] A portion of this sentence has been excised.
    [2] For reasons which are unknown, Princeton did not confer an honorary degree on Jules Cambon.

From Harper and Brothers

Dear Sir: New York City   May 24, 1901.

We have gone very carefully into the matter of the publication of "Colonies and Nation," in book-form, and in view of the fact that you cannot give us the complete copy this year, we find that we shall be obliged to defer the publication of the work until September, 1902, as we are satisfied that the four volumes must be published together.

It will take four or five months to manufacture the work, and meanwhile we should much like to get it under way, and beg leave to ask that, as soon as you have definitely determined upon the amount of material for the work, you would let us have the first volume to begin on. Kindly let us know when we may have volume I, and the probable dates when you will send us the complete copy for vols. II, III and IV.

          Very truly yours,   Harper & Brothers.

ALS (WP, DLC) with WWhw notation on env.: "Ans. 4 June 1901: Time of delivery of copy[:] vols. I., II., 1 Jany '02[;] vols. III., IV., 1 Apr. '02."

Ellen Axson Wilson to Thomas L. Snow

My dear Mr. Snow,   Princeton, May 27, 1901

Until the last few days we have been thinking that it would be quite impossible for us to get to Canada this summer on account of the poor health of Mr. Wilson's father. But he is not only much better, but he has now decided that he wants to spend the summer at the Danville "Sanatorium,"[1] which leaves us free to make plans for ourselves.

Mr. Wilson's desires prove to be all for Canada and he wishes me to write and make some enquiries as to rooms. If we are able to go so far from Father,—of course we cannot speak with entire certainty so long ahead,—we would like to be there for six weeks, viz., August and two weeks of Sept., and to have the three upper rooms that we had last year.

I know that our friend Miss Young has probably engaged *one* and possibly *two* of those upper rooms. If she has taken *two* we would like the other two and the one on the lower floor nearest the steps facing the lake. Possibly however you have built the "addition" to the house that you planned, and have now other "upper rooms" to offer us where we could in any case have three together. We would like to hear from you on the subject.[2]

Hoping that you have entirely recovered from your attack of blood-poisoning and that all the rest are well, I am, with kindest regards to all, in which Mr. Wilson joins me,

Yours most cordially,   Ellen A. Wilson.

TCL (RSB Coll., DLC).
  [1] It is impossible to determine in which of the numerous Danvilles this sanatorium was located.
  [2] As it turned out, Snow did not have rooms to offer the Wilsons, and they stayed instead at a resort called Heimera at Rosseau Falls, Ont., run by H. J. Gregory Allen.

From Annie Wilson Howe, with Enclosure

My darling Brother,   Dresden, June 2nd, 1901

Your letter brought comfort and great pleasure, as your letters always do, but the news about dear father distressed me, of course, sorely. It is a great comfort to know that he is with you and dear Ellie, and I feel very hopeful that Dr. Nesbit[1] will be able to find out what the trouble is, and do something to relieve it. At the same time I feel as if I would like to be with him, to nurse and care for him, if possible.

I have talked a good deal lately of our all going back to America in the fall and returning to Germany next summer. Some of George's classmates are going to Harvard next winter in order to get some instruction which they feel the need of and cannot get here. I talked with George about it, but he said no he would stay here and try to get what he needed alone—unless I really wished him to go—although he acknowledged that he believed it would be much easier for him to take his degree if he could have the year at Harvard. A catalogue from Harvard was received by one of the students and he was informed that if he applied in May he could get a scholarship certainly—possibly later. Now I know you and Ellie think I am very foolish—and that I think George *needs* me. I have no such feeling. I know I can make him more comfortable, and can help him to pass his holidays—but the secret of it is that *I need* him. He will be married as soon as possible you know after his return, and the next two years are all I will have. My idea is that if we can get a scholarship for George at Harvard we will all go home at the end of this semester and either all of us or George alone can come back next summer and spend another year. His work would be easier and I could be with dear father and you all. I have not been very strong this winter and I cannot bear the idea of going back and leaving George here. I suppose I am somewhat morbid about it and ought to overcome the feeling and will if necessary—but the above mentioned plan would make us so much happier that, if it is *possible* and *meets with your approval*, I would like to carry it out. We could come home in August on the Baltimore line for fifty dollars a ticket. None of us have the restless homesick feeling we had for the first few months, and George is completely absorbed in his work—exceedingly interested and anxious to learn in the best manner, not in order to get through quickly, but because he loves his work and wants to make a fine teacher of himself. I have asked him to write a note to be enclosed in this letter explaining what I mean about the work at Harvard. I am sorry to worry you with this while you are so busy, and fear you will think we are foolish. George fears you may think he is homesick again, but it is not so.

I am sorry to hear that you have had so much to do with doctors during the winter. I thought you were all unusually well. . . .

The weather is exceedingly hot now and we would leave the city if it were not for Jean's music lessons, which will continue until the end of July.

Beg Ellie to write to me, won't you? I have not had a letter from her for months. No one has told us anything about Ed's wedding. Of course he will not write for a long time and I doubt whether he could tell us much about it anyway.

You do not say anything about your health, dear. I am afraid the winters work and the anxiety you have had have been very hard on you.

If you approve of my plan would it be possible to apply at once for a scholarship at Harvard without waiting to answer my letter? Of course unless we could secure the scholarship I could not afford to send George to Harvard.

Please tell dear father that I think of him constantly, and long to be with him. I have felt anxious because he did not answer my last letter. He is generally so prompt in answering. I feel sure that the change and the pleasure of being with you all will do him more good than medicine. I know that happiness has more to do with my health than anything else.

I have written this in great haste, dear, because I must catch next mail. If you have not time to write and tell me what Dr. Nesbit says, beg Ellie or one of the girls to do so please, dear. Unbounded love from all three of us to you all, and to dear father. Jean sends warm regards. I have still to be careful with my eyes, or I would write more frequently. With a heart full of love

Your devoted sister,   Annie.

[1] J. Douglas Nisbet, M.D., 103 E. 43rd St., New York.

ENCLOSURE

From George Howe III

Dear Uncle Woodrow,   Halle a/S, June 2, 1901

Your good letter came a long time ago and I have never yet thanked you for it except by a postal card.[1] That does not mean want of gratitude but simply a sort of ignorance as to how I should answer. Of course you set me straight again—I confess I had got away from the track—and I see now that my whole point of view at that time was wrong. Since then it has changed to a much more wholesome one not only from having learned that haste was not the chief thing to be striven for, but also from the great interest in my study which has increased steadily ever since I made up my mind to master as much as I possibly could. Before I was thinking how I could get through most quickly; now, how I can accomplish most in the short time of preparation I have at my disposal.

All this introduction because of another question I want to ask you, and I don't want you to think I ask it now for any reason of homesickness or impatience or discouragement. Of course I have experienced all three in full measure, I suppose, but in thinking of any change I know I have not let them have any weight at all—the proof of which is that I am not only ready but eager to abide by whatever you advise. The two reasons I have for asking are on mother's account and because I am in doubt as to just what is wise in my own work.

As to the first, mother will explain that better than I can. In fact I am writing this for the sake of explaining the second, and at her request.

The other thing was brought before my notice by my inability to keep pace with the classes here & by Randolph[2] (an American in my branch of study, a little more advanced than I am, but with whom I do most of my work). This is his second semester here and is to be his last, for the present, because he has made up his mind to go back to Harvard for more elementary work. Whether that is a wise move for me or not is what I want you to tell me.

The truth of the matter is that we—the most of us Americans both in the branch of Philology and in others—have jumped into the midst of advanced work when we have not yet got hold of the fundamentals. For instance, the only thing we get here is higher criticism, text criticism, lectures on literature and history & once in a while on stray topics from the grammar or on meters. As for the *language* that is not at all taught—all students are supposed to have mastered the languages of Greek and Latin before they entered the university, and that is precisely what we have not done. In the meantime we must try to learn to read & write Latin & Greek while we keep up with the lectures and you know what slow work that is alone. Not only is it slow, but never sure because there is no one to tell us when we are right & when we are wrong, & if wrong how to get out of the difficulty. It must all be dug out alone which takes lots of time and must be done with books in a strange language. Further we want to get as many of the old Latin & Greek authors as possible and you can never guess how many are offered to us in a semester. Last semester we had lectures on *one* Latin author and *one* Greek—on Catullus and on Bacchilides. This semester we have Juvenal and a history of the criticism on Homer. Plato was also offered but I have followed in every case Prof. Wissowa's[3] advice & he told me not to take it— that it would be poor because offered by one of the lesser professors. In contrast to this the Harvard catalogue shows works in almost every single Greek & Latin author & while we could take only a few at one time still we could take more than one. In three years here six authors would not be enough—that would mean we would have to get the others on our own hook, while we did not have time enough even to keep up with the authors lectured on.

I don't know how to make this clear to you, but perhaps you can understand from an illustration or two. A while ago two whole lectures were spent on an accent over a single word in Homer. It seems to me that before I get to that stage I want to learn to read that line in which the mysterious accent occurs. Again, Wissowa began a course in the meters of Sophocles, said he would begin at the *very* beginning so that it would all be clear to us, went on to say "of course you understand all the rules for the ordinary forms of meter & for the Bacchic & the Aeolic & the Cretic and the Paramiscus—I need not repeat that." So his "from the very beginning" was two or three semesters ahead of me. All I could do was to try to find a place to dig out those unheard of simple things & long before I have caught up to his place of beginning he has left me way behind groping in the dark & not understanding his lectures at all. This is a fair sample, not a whit exaggerated, though, of course, it is not always so. Lectures on history & the history of literature I can always keep up with beautifully. But when, sometimes, a couple of lectures are spent on a discussion as to whether a word in the MS ends in o or e and I don't know even the meaning or declension of the word, I realize that I am not prepared for higher criticism. I don't mean to exaggerate my ignorance either. I have worked hard & read a great deal & it has become quite easy for me to read most Latin prose. Poetry remains as hard as ever & Greek seems impossible with every new author I pick up.

In other words I think the methods here and at home are wholly different. If I were in Harvard for a year, say, I should be drilled & drilled in the actual grammar & reading & writing of both languages until that became more or less an easy matter, & at the same time the text criticism would be combined with that drill. This is what we gather from the catalogue. Of course the text criticism would not be as fine at home, because here we are hearing the very men who have done most of that work—; but if we are not understanding it what good does their fame do. In fact Blass,[4] the most famous man in Germany for Greek, is so dull & uninteresting that his classes number scarcely a dozen men—one can't learn from him, he talks so far above our heads. If we could get the summary of his work by a man who knew our needs and also how to talk a good civilized language (for half of Blass's lectures will be a rattling off of Greek sentences which no one understands) we should learn more I think. Their seminar work here which should teach us most is conducted, of course, in Latin &, except the Professor & one or two old students, no one understands what is forward. At home we would get that drill work in English.

I don't want you to misunderstand, Uncle Woodrow. I have painted that black side, because that is what we have to struggle against without any light to help us. It is needless to say that I have learned a great deal here, that I have acquired a permanent interest in my work which I know will always spur me on, that there are many advantages here which we could not get at Harvard. Nor do I want you to think I am urging Harvard for any other reason than those I mentioned above. There is hardly any doubt in my mind that I can get the degree here in the time mapped out for it, but the question, (honestly, for I have thought it over carefully & honestly) is whether when I get that degree I will be as well prepared for my work in America as I might be. We do not teach much higher criticism at home—at Princeton, which is representative enough, I hardly knew what the word meant, & I had no idea what a MS was like and while it is necessary to know something of these things, is it not more necessary for my future work to know thoroughly the languages and the literatures first? We can get the literatures here but we can not get the languages unless we get them for ourselves without guidance. I have sought advice once or twice from the professors and each time they talked way above my head & I came away more confused than when I went. If I only had that preliminary work I would delight in what is given us here. Mr. Carter when he came was far better prepared than I am—Prentice[5] is said by the students here who knew him to have gone back home without knowing much more Latin & Greek than when he came. I am not alone in this way of looking at it. As I said, all Americans agree on this point. There are two professors here—Saunders from the Univ. of Miss[.] & Owen from the Univ. of Chicago[6]—and they say that for them the study here is fine because they have gone over the preliminary ground, but that otherwise it would be more or less waste of time. Randolph has made up his mind to return and learn first what he needs at present & then to return for the still more advanced work afterwards. Would it be wise for me to have a year at Harvard where I would be drilled & guided by the experience of others (for all the work there seems to [be] mapped out for the student, while here we are left absolutely at sea to do as we please) and then to return? I could get my degree in the same time, I am quite sure. Or would it be better to go back & take my degree at Harvard? Or would it be best to remain here & go through without interruption to the end. Of course you know better than I do & Mr. [Andrew Fleming] West must have known what he was advising me, and I am *perfectly* willing—don't doubt that for a moment—to do whatever is best. It is not a case of vacillation—it is merely that I am now interested in my work and want to do the very best I can in preparing myself for the work & methods at home. I am sure you will not attribute it to homesickness this time—the actual *blow* of that is over, tho' the time drags itself out sometimes almost unbearably.

That is the side of the question mother wanted me to explain. She will speak of the rest of it. I think mother would be better off in America where she could have friends, could be near Grandfather (& that with her is the chief thing now) & could put Annie to school & give her companions. But to be home without me—that goes against the grain. Therefore if such a change as I suggest should be as good or better for me, it could be made to fit in with mother's arrangements perfectly. As to my expenses at home, a Bostonian here assures me that he could fix me up almost as cheaply as I live here & a scholarship, if I could get it, would make it cheaper. I want to know only what is wisest. And I hope this will not take too much of your time. When you answer tell me frankly exactly what you think and whatever it is I shall appreciate & be grateful from the bottom of my heart. And if you can answer at once it will help us very much in making our plans.[7]

The news—there is very little. I have just returned from Dresden where I spent the ten days of Pfingsten holiday. (By-the-way, we have more holiday[s] here than workdays—& I would be kept at it more at home). The weather has turned excessively hot and I do not see how hard study is to be done in the coming months. I found the folks *pretty* well, not perfectly. Mother seems to continue to have her old dizziness, tho' she always looks well. Jean Flinn is to go home in the Fall, or, if we or mother & Annie should go sooner, sometime in the Summer. If I remain here after this semester Kimbrough[8] (the Mississippian who rooms next to me—a fine fellow) and I will be only two representatives of the American Club here. Davie Magie[9] will make a third.

I cannot say how sorry I am to hear of Grandfather's failing health. I can only hope that he will soon be made strong again by your good care & Dr. Nesbit's skill. We are all very much upset by your news. It is another thing that has made me want to get back home again—among the reasons apart from my work.

I suppose Ed must be too happy to write, because he has treated me worse than he has you by a long shot. He does not write to me even at intervals. I don't know that I blame him very much. I certainly did wish that I could be at his wedding—it wasn't quite right that he should get married when I was 4000 miles away. At least, I felt that way. I shall not be able to fully realize that he is a Benedick till I see him as such.

Please give a great great deal of love to all, individually & collectively. We love you all more than we can say, & you are always in our hearts although so much distance does lie between. Let me thank you again for all your goodness to me.

Lovingly   George Howe.

ALS (WP, DLC).

1 It is missing.
2 Charles Brewster Randolph, A.B., Wabash College, 1896; A.M., Harvard, 1902; Ph.D. in Philology, Harvard, 1905.
3 Georg Wissowa (1859-1931), Professor of the Philosophical Faculty at Halle.
4 Friedrich Wilhelm Blass (1843-1907), Professor of the Philosophical Faculty at Halle.
5 William Kelly Prentice, Assistant Professor of Greek at Princeton.
6 Paul Hill Saunders, Professor of Greek Language and Literature at the University of Mississippi, and William Bishop Owen, Assistant Professor of Greek at the University of Chicago.
7 George Howe decided to remain at Halle, where he received his Ph.D. in 1903.
8 The Editors have not been able to identify Kimbrough.
9 Princeton '97; Instructor in Latin, Princeton, 1899-1901. He received the Ph.D. from Halle in 1904.

From John Norris Miller, with Enclosure

"Ye Old Greenwich Inn," Sound Beach
My Dear Prof. Wilson: [Long Island, N. Y.], June 2, 1901

I inclose to you a letter from Mr. Trowbridge, which I received some days ago, but owing to the fact that I was in the midst of my examinations at Columbia, was unable to correspond with you upon the matter. With Mr. Trowbridge I have been in communication, the result of which is shown in the enclosed letter. It was rather unfortunate that the undergraduate body should have interfered and delayed us as they have but now that everything is settled and entrusted to us, I think that it would be best to deliver our notification of the abrogation of the Treaty to Clio immediately; of course that is provided that the notification meets with your approbation.

I am here resting up a little after passing very successfully a series of rather difficult examinations in law. In a few days I return to New York and trust to hear from you there in regard to the above. Very probably I shall return to Princeton for Commencement and hope to have the pleasure of seeing you. With my very best regards, I am

Faithfully yours,   J. Norris Miller.

ENCLOSURE

Stephen van Rensselaer Trowbridge[1]
to John Norris Miller

American Whig Society
Dear sir,   Princeton, N. J.   May 20th 1901.

The Whig Hall undergraduates have passed a resolution withdrawing their order to the Secretary of Foreign Affairs to notify Clio Hall of the Abrogation. This leaves the matter entirely in your hands. But one clause in the treaty states that six months notice must be served to the other Hall by the Hall breaking the treaty. Hence the abrogation cannot go in force until February 1902.

Yours truly,   Stephen van R. Trowbridge
for the Society.

ALS (WP, DLC).
[1] Princeton, 1902.

From Harper and Brothers

Dear Sir: New York City   June 5, 1901.

We beg leave to acknowledge the receipt of your letter of yesterday, and note that you say you can confidently promise the copy for Volumes I and II of "Colonies & Nation" by January 1st 1902. We shall esteem it a favor if you can see your way to letting us have the revised copy of Volume I at the earliest possible date, so that we can arrange the plan for the volumes with the utmost deliberation. We should also be pleased to receive, at your earliest convenience, the revised list of illustrations for Volumes I and II—as they will be the most difficult to find, and we may have to send to London for them—in order that we may have them processed, and ready, when the composition begins.

Very truly yours,   Harper & Brothers.

ALS (WP, DLC).

From the Minutes of the Princeton University Faculty

5 5′ P.M., Wednesday, June 5, 1901.

. . . Professors Brackett, Woodrow Wilson and Fine were elected by ballot a Committee to appear before and confer with the Trustees if required.

From the Minutes of the Board of Trustees of Princeton University

June 10, 1901.

FACULTY COMMITTEE APPEARS

The Faculty Committee consisting of Professors Woodrow Wilson and H. B. Fine appeared before the Trustees.

TIME OF APPEARANCE OF FACULTY COMMITTEE

After an informal talk it was

"Resolved that hereafter the Faculty Committee shall appear before the Trustees immediately after the President has made his report."

"Minutes of the Trustees of Princeton University, June 1901-Jan. 1908," bound minute book (UA, NjP).

From Richard Austin Rice[1]

Confidential   Williamstown, Mass.
My dear Mr. Wilson   10th of June 1901.

You know that the choice of a president is agitating this college. The question was proposed in a committee of which I am a member: "if the choice is to go outside of the graduates of this college, whose name would you suggest?" I said "Woodrow Wilson." This was greeted with such (unanimous) approval that I was asked to write to you—and ask you whether under any circumstances you would consider favorably the proposition.

You will readily understand that this question is entirely informal and unofficial, personal if you prefer,—as the committee of the Faculty has no *power* in the matter and can act only as advisory to the Board of Trustees.

It is composed however of these elements: three Yale men, one Harvard, one Amherst, and one Williams man, and none of us doubt, if it were left to the professors to decide, there being say ten others, mostly Williams men, that a unanimous vote would be given in your favor.

This is not saying that if there were a Williams graduate on whom all could agree it would not be better to elect him—but it may be easier to *agree* upon a man outside the circle of graduates.

If then you would be willing under any conditions to consider favorably an offer from the Trustees, and if you feel disposed to give an immediate answer, would you kindly telegraph "Yes" simply, so that I might get it in time for our next meeting on

Wednesday (June 12) at noon: please telegraph at my expense, "Yes" or "no,"—*then burn this letter.*

Yours very sincerely   Richard A. Rice

ALS (WP, DLC).
[1] J. Leland Miller Professor of American History, Literature and Eloquence at Williams College.

To Richard Austin Rice

My dear Professor Rice,   Princeton, New Jersey, 11 June, 1901.

I need hardly tell you how much I appreciate your kind letter of yesterday, which reached me this afternoon, or that it was with the greatest reluctance that I sent the telegram I sent in reply. I am very deeply gratified indeed that your Faculty should have so great a feeling of personal confidence in me as to wish to see me, rather than any other outsider, the President of Williams. These are the things that hearten a man, and make him try to deserve confidence.

I sent the answer I did send, not because I should not have liked to say Yes: but because this question has during the past three or four years come to me over and over again from other quarters, and I have been obliged to make up my mind very definitely, at any rate for the present, whether I wish to write or wish to devote myself to administrative duties. I should greatly relish doing both; but that is, of course, impossible; and I must finish what I have embarked upon.

With warm regards and deep appreciation,

Sincerely Yours,   Woodrow Wilson

TCL (RSB Coll., DLC).

From Edward Augustus Woods[1]

My Dear Sir: Pittsburg, Pa. June 11, 1901.

I have seldom read anything with so much delight, or with a feeling that there was so much real meat to it as to your article on "When a man comes to himself" in the current number of "The Century."[2] This ought to be published separately in small form and I should like to purchase one or two hundred copies to send where it will do good, I know. Will it be so published, or could any arrangement be made by which, if sufficient orders were given, it could be published in such form that it could be more easily circulated?[3] It is something that every man, and particularly every young man, should read.

Very truly yours,   Edw. A. Woods

TLS (WP, DLC).
1 Insurance executive of Pittsburgh. Wilson had stayed at Woods's home in Sewickley, Pa., when he lectured there in 1897.
2 It is printed in this series at Nov. 1, 1899, Vol. 11.
3 See WW to R. U. Johnson, June 15, 1901, n. 2.

A News Report

[June 15, 1901]

THE 154TH ANNUAL COMMENCEMENT

Two hundred and eighteen '01 men received the bachelor's degree at the 154th Annual Commencement, held on Wednesday, June 12. The gowned and hooded academic procession, marshalled by Prof. William Libbey '77 and headed by President Patton and the Honorable Foster M. Voorhees, Governor of New Jersey, made a stately picture marching under the old elms from Nassau Hall to Alexander. The usual Commencement visitors filled the building—with dignitaries on the platform, the graduating class in the horse shoe, their friends and families in the circle, the townspeople in the gallery and the undergraduates and alumni wedged in anywhere or peeking in the doors and windows.

. . . The honorary degree of Doctor of Laws was conferred upon the Honorable Foster M. Voorhees, Governor of New Jersey, and the Honorable John R. Emory [Emery] '61, Vice-Chancellor of New Jersey. The candidates were presented by Prof. Woodrow Wilson '79. . . .

Printed in the *Princeton Alumni Weekly*, 1 (June 15, 1901), 804.

To Robert Underwood Johnson

My dear Mr. Johnson,   Princeton, New Jersey, 15 June, 1901.

Thank you very much for the refunded dinner fee.[1] I had had [not] expected it at all, sending you notice so late as I did. It was kind of you to think of it.

With much regard,

Sincerely Yours,   Woodrow Wilson

You never reprint articles separately, do you? I [A] gentleman in Pittsburgh writes me to ask whether he could get (say) two hundred copies of "When A Man Comes to Himself" in some separate form, for distribution "where it will do most good"![2] W. W.

WWTLS (Berg. Coll., NN).
1 For the annual dinner of the Institute of Arts and Letters on March 12, 1901.
2 Johnson wrote the following instructions on Wilson's letter: "Tell him that we find this inexpedient as we rely on the influence of special articles to increase our circulation." However, Harper and Brothers published the essay in book form in 1915.

To Edward Graham Elliott

My dear Mr. Elliott,   Princeton, New Jersey, 17 June, 1901.

I fear that my long silence must have seemed to you quite inexplicable, particularly in view of the important item of business contained in your last letter to me. The fact is that I have been absorbed, as never before in my life, by illness in my family. All has come out well, I am thankful to say, but we have had an anxious time of it; and I am only just now ready to turn to ordinary things.

My father's failing health has led to a postponement of my trip to Europe for at least a year; so that I can attend to your money very well. Just as I was about to see to it, and write you what to expect, Mr. Osborn, our Treasurer died suddenly of a stroke of apoplexy[1] (one of the most serious blows the University has received within my recollection, for he was truly indispensable) and all business is temporarily in confusion. But I can safely promise to have it straigthened [straightened] out in time to let you have the $750.00 to your credit by the first of August.

I will write again, of course. This is only a preliminary note of explanation and apology.

With warm regard,

      Cordially Yours,   Woodrow Wilson

WWTLS (WC, NjP).
[1] Edwin Curtis Osborn, connected with Princeton since 1877 as Assistant Treasurer and Treasurer, died suddenly of heart failure on June 15. Only fifty-one, he was to have been married on June 17.

From Charles Williston McAlpin[1]

My dear Prof. Wilson: Princeton, N. J., June 21, 1901.

A letter addressed to Dr. Patton by Fred'k. T. Saussy[2] has been referred to me: in this Mr. Saussy states "I returned to Savannah this morning and found a letter from Mr. Woodrow Wilson informing me that the committee on degrees had recommended that I be awarded the A.M. degree." Can you throw any light on this matter? I have no record of such a degree having been conferred and I can find no trace of it in the Minutes of the Faculty. You may remember having spoken to me on March 28th about your cousin Mr. Wilson Woodrow who had been restored to his class, '86, by vote of the Scientific Faculty. The announcement was not made at Commencement and his name has not come to me, but in look[ing] through the Minutes of the University Faculty I find that the degree was voted to him.

I simply mention this in order to bring it to your attention.

Sincerely yours,   [C. W. McAlpin]

CCL (McAlpin File, UA, NjP).
  [1] Princeton, 1888, he had been elected as the first Secretary of the University by the Board of Trustees on December 13, 1900.
  [2] Frederick Tupper Saussy '96.

To Charles Williston McAlpin

My dear Mr. McAlpin,   Princeton, 22 June, 1901.

Mr. Saussy sent in a thesis for the Master's degree which I read and accepted. So soon as his application could be acted on, with the rest, I notified him that his thesis was accepted and that upon his filing a formal application with Professor Magie, the Secretary of the Committee on Higher Degrees, and the payment of the fee to the University Treasurer, he would be recommended for the degree. Before my letter reached Savannah, as I now learn from a letter from Mr. Saussy to me, he had left town for a trip of some duration. He did not return until after Commencement (having meanwhile been here without seeing me). When he returned he sent on the application and the fee. Before another Trustee meeting all things will be in course to complete the business by conferring the degree; but in the meanwhile, I am afraid, he must wait.[1]

I am much obliged to you for mentioning the matter of my cousin, Wilson Woodrow. I noticed at Commencement that his name was not mentioned. There has been some slip or omission, I fear, in the transmission of names from the University Faculty to the Board of Trustees. I will call the matter up again as soon as possible next Autumn.

With much regard,

Sincerely Yours,   Woodrow Wilson

WWTLS (McAlpin File, UA, NjP).
  [1] He was awarded the A.M. degree later in the year.

From Edward Graham Elliott

My dear Professor Wilson,   Heidelberg, June 25th '01.

I have just heard from George news of the illness of your father and your consequent detention in America—both were learned with much regret and I sincerely trust your father may be by this time much improved. Had I known you were still at home I

would have written before to tell you how very much pleased I am
with Prof. Jellinek. There is no comparison to be made between
him and the men in Berlin—he stands head and shoulders above
them all. His lectures are really inspiring and a pleasure to listen
to,—but it is in the Seminar naturally that one comes in closest
contact with him and sees what he represents,—his method and
his teaching. On June 4th I read a paper on the Monroe Doctrine,
largely a historical sketch as both time and material were lacking
to treat it from any other standpoint. He suggested however that
it had never received any other treatment and that it would be
an interesting and profitable work to discuss its relations to International Law—to treat it from the legal standpoint. Such a discussion would naturally include the effects of our own insular
possessions and position thereby assumed—in greater or less degree—of a "world-power" upon the Doctrine and our foreign
policy. I haven't done anything further in the matter both because
I have been busy with other matters and because I wished to hear
first if you thought such a work would be profitable. The semester
closes the first week in August. My plans for the vacation are
very indefinite. I shall probably loaf more or less consistently
during August but I expect to be at work again by the first of
September.

I am so pleased with my work here with Jellinek that with
your consent I shall spend the rest of my time here. I learned
from him the other day that Max Farrand was a pupil of his and
has recently translated "Erklärung der Menschen- und Bürger-
Rechte."[1] I am just now reading his last book "Das Recht des
modernen Staates."[2] I enclose a newspaper clipping which is self-
explanatory and I thought perhaps it might interest you.

With very kindest regards to Mrs. Wilson, I am,
Very sincerely yours   Edward G Elliott

ALS (WP, DLC) with WWhw notation on env.: "Ans." Enc.: clipping from the
Vienna *Neue Freie Presse*, June 15, 1901, of an article about Jellinek on the occasion of his fiftieth birthday.

[1] Georg Jellinek, *The Declaration of the Rights of Man and of Citizens: A Contribution to Modern Constitutional History*, trans. by Max Farrand (New York,
1901).

[2] *Das Recht des modernen Staates* (Berlin, 1900).

To Charles Williston McAlpin

My dear Mr. McAlpin,   Princeton, New Jersey, 29 June, 1901.

I hope that you will pardon my delay in returning these slips.
I sincerely hope that it has not interfered with your plans for the
issue of the catalogue. I have had so much work piled on me

during the last five weeks, and so much sickness in my little household, that I have allowed too many matters of business to wait.

With much regard,

Sincerely Yours,   Woodrow Wilson

WWTLS (McAlpin File, UA, NjP).

To Edward Graham Elliott

My dear Mr. Elliott,   Princeton, New Jersey, 8 July, 1901.

I take pleasure in enclosing a draft for seven hundred and fifty dollars, which Ed. Howe[1] has translated into three thousand one hundred and twenty-five marks. I hope that it will prove to be in a convenient form for use. It was the best I could do here.

Had you heard of the death of Mr. Osborn, the University Treasurer? He died very suddenly of apoplexy. It is really a tremendous blow to us. He came as near being indispensable as any man I ever knew. His place simply cannot be filled. The trustees will have, I fear, to farm out his functions among inferior men.

I am delighted to hear you speak with such enthusiasm of Professor Jellinek. What I had told you of him was simply what others who had been his pupils had reported to me. Your plan of staying with him for the remainder of your time abroad I am quite willing to agree to, since you are finding so exactly what you want.

As for the Monroe Doctrine, I fear that our national affairs are just now in so unformulated a condition with regard to international relations that it would be impossible to give any definite account of our own present notions about the significance of it. It would furnish, however, a very convenient topic indeed about which to group studies of international law in respect both of our past and of our prospective position among the nations. I think it would be very well for you to take it up, if you gave to your study of it scope enough.

With warm regard, and heartiest good wishes.

Faithfully Yours,   Woodrow Wilson

WWTLS (WC, NjP).
  [1] Edward Howe, president of the Princeton Bank (now the Princeton Bank and Trust Co.).

Wilson at the time of his election as President of Princeton

President Patton

James Waddel Alexander

Grover Cleveland

David Benton Jones

Cyrus Hall McCormick

Cornelius Cuyler Cuyler

Moses Taylor Pyne

Henry van Dyke

William Francis Magie

Stockton Axson

John Huston Finley

A recently discovered photograph of
Ellen Louise Axson as a young girl

Edith Gittings Reid

To Edward Ingle

My dear Ingle,   Princeton, New Jersey, 8 July, 1901.

I have turned about to the task of revising my history for book form, and, having reached Master Richard Ingle, find to my great surprise and disappointment that our library does not contain your monograph. Have you a copy which you could lend me, or is there one which I could borrow, or that you could borrow for me?

I am sorry to trouble you, but I am anxious to get as many flaws out of my story as possible; and would be very much indebted to you if you would get me a copy of the monograph which I could keep for a week or so.

With much regard, and renewed thanks for having called my attention to the matter,

Sincerely Yours,   Woodrow Wilson

WWTLS (E. Ingle Papers, MdHi).

From Jenny Davidson Hibben

My dear Mr. Wilson,   Redfield, N.Y.   July 14, 1901

I write hurriedly to-day, just before leaving to give you my friends address in Buffalo. Her card which I had kept for you I unfortunately have packed in my trunk. This is it, I *think*. Miss Lura B. Lord, 34 Highland Ave   *Buffalo*. If I find this is wrong, when I reach Elizabeth I will send you word again. I hope that you & Mrs. Wilson stay with her,[1] for she is a refined woman & to see you both would be lovely for her.

We are all very well. Our days here have been delightful. Jack has fished & we have all tramped the forests, & played tennis & lived out of doors.

Beth & I have ridden our bird hobby to our hearts' content, & have seen many rare birds. We go to Mantoloking [N.J.] on July 22nd. Our address there will be "The Breakers." Many thanks for your letter. We were so glad to hear from you. Isn't it delightful that the Ricketts'[2] are *all* going to Europe. Mr. West wrote us of the death of Mrs. Richardson's baby[3]—how pitiful that is! The news of it came just as we were rejoicing over the Ricketts. I hope that your dear Jessie is doing well & that your father is no worse. In your next letter, tell us that you are all on your way to your beloved lake, for the rest you & Mrs. Wilson need. With love for you all,

Believe me,   Ever yours,   Jenny Davidson Hibben

ALS (WP, DLC).
    1 While en route to Rosseau Falls, Ont., where they were to spend their vacation.
    2 Eliza Getty (Mrs. Palmer Chamberlaine) Ricketts and her daughter, Henrietta, lived at 80 Stockton St., Princeton. The other surviving members of the family were her sons, Palmer Chamberlaine Ricketts, Jr., President of Rensselaer Polytechnic Institute, and Louis Davidson Ricketts, Princeton, 1881, at this time a consulting engineer for Phelps, Dodge & Co. and other mining concerns in Arizona.
    3 Mary Ely Richardson, daughter of Ernest Cushing and Grace Ely Richardson, died at Lyme, Conn., on July 5, 1901, at the age of eight months.

From Edward Ingle

My Dear Wilson: Baltimore, July 15th, 1901.

    Here is the pamphlet on Richard Ingle. I shall send you the later study in a day or two. When you have used them please return them to me at 1606 Linden Ave, Baltimore, Md.

                    Sincerely yours,   Edward Ingle

TLS (WP, DLC).

From Theodore Roosevelt

My dear Prof. Wilson: Oyster Bay, N.Y, July 18th, 1901.

    Are you any where in this neighborhood now? Could you come out here and spend the night of Friday the 26th inst? There are some matters I want to talk over with you in connection with trying to arouse our young college students, and especially the seniors, to an active interest in politics. If you can come, take the 4.30 P.M. train from Long Island City for Oyster Bay. The last ferry leaves foot of E. 34th St., N.Y. at 4.20 P.M.

                    Sincerely yours,   Theodore Roosevelt

TLS (Letterpress Books, T. Roosevelt Papers, DLC).

An Introduction to *The Autobiography of Benjamin Franklin*

[*July 18, 1901*[1]]

    This famous book needs an introduction as little as any I know. Its frank pages reveal the man who wrote them more vividly, more completely, more naturally than any comment could reveal him. It is not even necessary to set a stage upon which to place him; you catch the air of the world in which he lived from his own sentences, and see the affairs he handled as he saw them. You meet him here as you might have met him in some Philadelphia coffee-house a hundred and twenty years ago, and your curiosity as to what he was and what he concerned himself with is satisfied out of his own talk. Here is his authentic flavor, to be had for the tasting.

And yet there is something more to be said. It is not easy to leave off when once you have begun to speak of Benjamin Franklin. When you have closed the book and he is gone, the genial figure lingers in your thought. Half peasant, only half man of the world, and yet a statesman, philanthropist, scientist, man of letters, his broad, plain, sunny nature fertile in every part of whatsoever is fit to nourish or be serviceable to the race, his thought running always upon conduct or upon affairs or upon the forces of the physical universe, the door is hardly shut upon him before we fall to comment and comparison, praise and thoughtful assessment.

Such a man, we say, could hardly have been born or brought to the full light of fame anywhere but in America. He is racy of the soil and of the institutions, not of Northamptonshire nor even of Massachusetts, but of the English colonies in America. In England, we feel (can we be mistaken?), he might have been such another as his uncle Thomas, the "ingenious" scrivener, who was "a chief mover of all public-spirited undertakings for the county or town of Northampton and his own village"; but hardly the chief figure of a whole nation for sagacity and for all the thoughts that make for enlightenment and quiet progress. Such a career bespeaks a country in which all things are making and to be made. No one who reads these pages can doubt that Franklin had the literary gift: you cannot mistake the career he describes or the country whose affairs set it about. For all it is so plain in diction and keeps in so businesslike a way to the quiet path of narrative, the book has flavor, smacks of men and things, and is touched throughout not only with the originality and the distinctive personal qualities of the man himself, but also with the qualities of a country and a time. All his writings attest Franklin a man gifted in no common measure with the power of expression. The firm, clear strokes define and clarify everything he touches. His sentences assemble with admirable precision, support one another without hesitation or confusion of movement; and when he is done the field clears at once, and you perfectly understand what you have seen. He can convince with excellent cogency; he can persuade with an art you shall not easily escape. And yet there is nowhere in what he writes any note of distinction. You tread always, while you walk with him, the levels of the ordinary world. The path does not rise; the air stirs with no breath from distant uplands or the vast extended sea. It is always the street or the counting-house, the country road or the council-chamber, the laboratory or the tradesman's counter, that lies before you, and the man who speaks is intent upon the business of the place,—not upon principles so much as upon transactions and upon all the means, great and small, by which men may be led to take part in them.

Is not this lack of the full flavor of letters, this air of being always engaged upon some new piece of business, one of the characteristics of the man which make us think of him as distinctively a product of America? American letters have so far lacked the full-throated power and the amplitude of tone which have made the literatures of many other countries rich and various and full of the qualities that move and refresh. The writings of Franklin do not, indeed, stand for all. There have been men amongst us who greatly excelled him in the range and efficacy of their power in letters. We have had among our writers men of unmistakable charm, men of power fit for the handling of great themes, men of vision, men who had caught not a little of the music of our mother-tongue. But in candid moods we are fain to admit that there has been, on the whole, a certain tameness in our better authors, something less than an easy mastery of theme and manner, a certain thinness where we could have wished for richness and depth of tone.

If we desired an explanation, we might turn to Franklin for it. Our genius has been of the practical type demanded of us by our tasks. We have had to subdue a virgin continent from sea to sea, construct institutions suitable for life upon it, whether as wilderness or settled country-side, get sustenance from its soil, and the resources of our wealth from its forests and mines and quarries. The task has not dulled our wits; it has quickened them, rather; but it has not been a business to stir our imaginations deeply. It has made us thoughtful of means, ingenious, inventive, men to look before and after and make good every stroke of constructive work; but we have accomplished the thing we set ourselves to do, not in armies under command, under no master's eye, with no breath of large plans, consciously thought out and perfected, in our nostrils, but singly, rather, each man for himself, hand and thought close to the immediate task,—by an instinct and mastery which operated from day to day, upon one thing at a time, no one keeping the whole pattern of the complex business in his eye the while, or directing with authority how it should be completed and brought to perfection. And our writing has matched our life and circumstances. Franklin's writing stands typical and significant of our whole intellectual history as a nation. It is letters in business garb, literature with its apron on, addressing itself to the task, which in this country is every man's, of setting free the processes of growth, giving them facility and speed and efficacy. It speaks in phrases of exposition and counsel, of debate, analysis, discussion. It looks upon the world as a laboratory and upon thought and the expression of it as a scientific, not a creative, process.

One is struck by nothing in this book so much as by the all-round efficiency of the man who wrote it. He was as practical, as thorough, as businesslike, as successful, in supplying General Braddock with wagons and teamsters for his ill-fated expedition against Duquesne as in organizing fire companies or a circulating library or a Philosophical Society; kept the same cool business head and the same shrewd eye upon individual men in diplomacy that had made him so sure of success in his printing-office and his book-shop; approached nature and got her secrets from her as calmly and easily as he dealt with governors or with subscribers, using as simple means,—a common kite to draw the electricity from the clouds,—and kept the exact and quiet mind in everything. His success lay, by an almost accidental choice, in the staid town of Philadelphia, and the things he did were the things natural sagacity and quick insight into human nature suggested in such a place, where the common interests of an ordered community waited to be served; but he would have succeeded anywhere in America, on the frontier as readily as in the settled town. Indeed, that is the characteristic and final test for a man of whom we say that he was a typical American. Would he have been fit for the frontier; would he have made as great a figure out in the forests or upon the untilled plains, where the rough first work of civilization was to be done? No one can doubt the answer in Franklin's case. The work would have been less rough and less slow for his presence. He would have studied and captained it like a scientist and a master.

And yet Franklin was no provincial, but belonged in many a characteristic to the whole large world of his time as well as to America. It was the man's range and variety that made him great. Nothing that he does or says, but only his plain dress, marks him a man out of place even in a Parisian drawing-room. Indeed, it is odd to see how close kin the man seems to the French savants and thinkers of his day, and yet how different he is. He unmistakably belongs in thought and life to the European eighteenth century no less than to the American. He has all the cool rationalism of the time, dissents without passion, surmises without enthusiasm, makes reason, not belief, the guide and critic of conduct, enacts a list of virtues and a set of maxims as his code of morality, is above all things speculative, and fills his days with little scrutinies and ingenious tests of thought and practice. There were not many heart-searching doubts in the philosophy of the eighteenth century. It abounds in pettifogging difficulties and cool dissents; its motive is curiosity, its method criticism and amateur experiment, its only enthusiasm for those who have none. The Reason which the French would have enthroned at their Revolution was not the reason of the fully sentient mind, but a thing as abstract, as separate from life and the real forces that must ever move the world, as the word-puzzles of the schoolmen in an age gone by and among the French despised. They played at laying all the elements of mind and nature bare in cold analysis, and missed the secrets of the very things they meditated upon. Franklin salted their philosophy with sound American sense and a practical sagacity not easily to be misled, used it for the most part only upon the objects it was really suited to elucidate, made it an instrument of practical prudence, and left its vagaries to the French who invented them.

Mr. Abel James and Mr. Benjamin Vaughan urged Franklin to publish his memoirs as a source of inspiration and guidance to the young men of America who should come after him and who should need what he had used with so consummate an art for their advancement in the world: the sobriety, the diligence, the prudence, the thorough habit of learning, that had put him in a way to succeed in a country where every man must be useful and make his own career. No doubt in its day the plain-spoken book served that purpose, and many a man steadied his life by means of its precepts and took heart from its example. But we feel, as we read it now, that its usefulness in that kind is no longer very great or very vital. Prudence is at best a dull motive. Only men of the eighteenth century or still under its spell and influence could dwell with unction upon those saving details of moral commonplace or take inspiration from the precepts of expediency. Of course prudence and expediency are not all that Franklin has to offer to support his principles of morality. A motive played through his life at once noble and deeply moving, the desire to serve his fellow-men, to turn them to a better way of living, to higher comforts and more elevated interests, to a life of thought and aspiration, of civic virtue and domestic honesty, as well as of toil and the heaping up of goods. But there is something singularly cool in his attitude toward it all. Mere increase of knowledge and of material comfort and con-

venience plays a noticeably large part in his conception of welfare,—seems oftentimes, indeed, to constitute the whole of it.
Men do not take fire from such thoughts, unless something
deeper, which is missing here, shine through them. We are
not content to order our lives by maxims or square our prudence by the saws of "Poor Richard's Almanac." There seems to
us now something very pale and thin about the morality which is
founded upon them. What may have seemed to the eighteenth
century a system of morals seems to us nothing more vital than a
collection of the precepts of good sense and sound conduct, the
old-time "wisdom of the world."

What redeems it from pettiness in this book is the scope of
power and of usefulness to be seen in Franklin himself, who set
these standards up in all seriousness and candor for his own life.
His little precepts take dignity from their author. Had he been a
man no greater than Lord Chesterfield was, his morality might
have seemed as shallow as Chesterfield's, the mere perfected good
judgment of a practised man of the world. But Franklin was a
really great man. You shall find yourself deeming him such, as
you read, even in the midst of trivial passages and unpleasing
disclosures. He was no mere philosopher walking among men to
dole out shrewd comment and kindly suggestion. He was a practical master in the mechanics of society, as well as in the mechanics
of the material universe and in the sophistries of the human
mind. He was in nothing greater than in the achievement which
comes by organization and from the concerted effort of many
men moving in voluntary accord. He not only conceived projects
that would better society, but also persuaded men of their utility,
drew them together to carry them out, and gave to their action
a vitality which did not flag when his hand was withdrawn. He
had that saving sense of what is practicable which makes reformers no reformers at all, but effectual leaders, rather, who
can quicken progress at will. Reformers will often convince you
that they are right; but leaders will take hold on you and persuade
you to action, will point out to you practicable modes of achievement, will begin with what a few can do, and wait for enterprises
to get their natural and wholesome growth. Probably no man
ever better understood how to handle a subscription paper or
how to give a society its first organization and sufficient impulse
than Franklin did. This is the power in him that takes your
imagination, this power to rule other men. This is his incom-
municable secret. This is the field of achievement which no
maxims good for business behind a counter can bound or contain.

The whole essence and object of this book is to explain, for the instruction of others, how Mr. Franklin, the son of a tallow-chandler of Boston, came to cut so notable a figure in the world. "My father," says he, "having, among his instructions to me when a boy, frequently repeated a proverb of Solomon, 'Seest thou a man diligent in his calling? he shall stand before kings; he shall not stand before mean men,' I from thence considered industry as a means of obtaining wealth and distinction, which encouraged me, tho' I did not think that I should ever literally *stand before kings*, which, however, has since happened; for I have stood before *five*, and even had the honor of sitting down with one, the King of Denmark, to dinner." How priggish and self-satisfied such a sentence sounds thus divorced from its context and set off by itself; how essentially self-laudatory the whole motive of such a narrative of one's own success! And yet the surprising and delightful thing about this book is that, take it all in all, it has not the low tone of conceit, but is a stanch man's sober and unaffected assessment of himself and the circumstances of his career. Here is the nicest possible test of how generous, large, and substantial the real bulk of the man's character and achievement was. He was cool, sober-minded, judicious enough to be trusted to look at himself objectively, without affectation of modesty, without excess of self-appreciation. There could be no finer or more conclusive proof of sanity and perfect balance. No just critic can call this book a piece of vanity; no man of right judgment can lay it down without esteeming Franklin, not less, but more.

Moreover, the undisguised personal equation is the chief charm in writing of this kind. The salt of Franklin's own good sense keeps the matter sound and untainted. Another man, as great, as large of mind, as sane, might have done such a piece of biography exceeding ill, to the deep offending of all good taste. A more intense man, a more ponderous mind, a less detached and nicely poised nature, unable really to hold aloof from itself and look at its own acts in the temper of the scientific observer, might have bungled sadly this delicate task of self-assessment. Franklin had just the right equipoise and temperament. The book, as a consequence, is flavored to the taste of the most critical and judicious. It is by common consent a classic in its kind, and must ever charm those who read it with its authentic image, intimate and from the life, of a figure which all men must account one of the most distinctive and notable in an age of creation and achievement.

WOODROW WILSON

Printed in [John Bigelow (ed.)] *The Autobiography of Benjamin Franklin* (New York, 1901), v-xix.
¹ The composition date at the end of Wilson's typescript of this introduction in WP, DLC. Wilson's shorthand draft, dated July 17, 1901, is also in WP, DLC.

To Edward Ingle

My dear Ingle,   Princeton, New Jersey, 22 July, 1901.

Under another cover, I return your pamphlets, with my warm thanks for the use of them.

When all is said and considered, Ingle does not seem a very estimable character, to say the least; perhaps it is impossible to form any but negative conclusions about him; but I have expunged opprobrious epithets from my narrative, have given a new tone to it, and have, I hope avoided injustice.

Again thanking you,

                    Very sincerely Yours,   Woodrow Wilson

WWTLS (E. Ingle Papers, MdHi).

From James Wilson Woodrow

                        Mapimí, Estado de Durango, México.
My dear Cousin Woodrow: July 24th, 1901

As my wife is now writing magazine articles under the name of "Mrs. Wilson Woodrow,"¹ I feel that I can no longer avoid the painful duty of advising you that about a year and a half ago Nancy deserted me under circumstances that rendered such an act peculiarly wicked. For my own part I suffered a blow that for [a] time threatened to seriously affect my health—but that is now past. I can take no action in court to effect a legal separation until I shall have returned to the United States and acquired legally a residence there, of not less than one year. All of the family emphatically uphold me in postponing this course until I shall have the opportunity of adopting it without serious injury to my professional work and prospects. Such a protracted interruption in my work would at the present time cause the practical severance of valuable business connections in Mexico.

I have never omitted the "J." in my name. Under the circumstances the fact that Nancy now uses the name "Mrs. Wilson Woodrow" (for purposes too obvious to mention) fills me, I assure you, with the deepest chagrin.

Although it is only right that you should know the facts in any case, I would probably have refrained from mentioning them until I had effected the legal separation, but I do advise you now, in order to assure you that the use of my incomplete name in the manner described is totally without my sanction, and is a surprise to me as well.

Affectionately   Your cousin   J. Wilson Woodrow.

ALS (WP, DLC).

[1] Nancy Mann Waddel Woodrow, who had married James Wilson Woodrow on August 4, 1897.

To Theodore Roosevelt

My dear Mr. Roosevelt,   Princeton, 28 July, 1901

Dr. Abbott, Trent,[1] and I journeyed to town together yesterday morning very contented men, agreeing that we had had a most delightful and refreshing time at Oyster Bay. I reached home much heartened in many ideals, and shall not, I am sure, need to be reminded, when the next term opens, to take in hand the scheme we discussed. I hope and believe that it will come to something, and I thank you for having made me a partner in the matter[2]

Thanking you also for the pleasure of Friday,

With warm regard,

Sincerely Yours,   Woodrow Wilson

ALS (Roosevelt Memorial Association Papers, MH).

[1] Lyman Abbott, Editor of the New York *Outlook*, and William Peterfield Trent, Professor of English Literature at Columbia University.

[2] As T. Roosevelt to WW, July 18, 1901, indicates, the purpose of the meeting at Oyster Bay on July 26-27, 1901, was to discuss ways and means of involving college men in reform politics in both major parties. It was Roosevelt's idea that committees of five or six men, including faculty members, recent graduates, and members of the senior classes, be appointed at Harvard, Yale, and Princeton to take charge of the movement at their respective institutions. He also believed that there should be about two large meetings a year on each campus at which active reform leaders would speak. See T. Roosevelt to Endicott Peabody, July 12, 1901; T. Roosevelt to Malcolm Donald, July 18, 1901; and T. Roosevelt to Lyman Abbott, Aug. 26, 1901, all in the Theodore Roosevelt Papers, DLC. Roosevelt's plan was never implemented at Princeton.

To James Wilson Woodrow

My dear Cousin,   Princeton, New Jersey, 30 July, 1901.

Your letter of the twenty-fourth reached me last evening, and brought me the keenest distress,—not, I assure you, my dear fellow, on my own account, but on yours. The fact that she is using a name so like my own in the magazines is, of course, a serious annoyance; but I never should have thought of blaming *you* in any case; and at worst it is only an annoyance.

What went to the quick with me was the news of your own

deep suffering and humiliation. I know that you do not wish to speak of it now; but I beg that you will let me say how profoundly I feel for you, and how deep into my heart it goes that you should have had such a dreadful thing come into your life. For really, my dear cousin, I have a deeper affection for you, and a closer sense of identification, than I have ever been able to express.

Of course you are right in not sacrificing your business opportunities for the sake of procuring a divorce. My judgment corresponds with that of all the rest in that matter.

May God grant you some day such happiness as will make all this easy to forget. All join me in affectionate messages, and I am ever,

Faithfully and affectionately

Your cousin,   Woodrow Wilson

Would you mind telling me what she writes, and for what magazines?

WWTLS (photostat in RSB Coll., DLC).

A News Item

[Aug. 10, 1901]

Governor Voorhees[1] has appointed Professor Woodrow Wilson, of Princeton University, to be a member of the State commission which has for its object action with other States to secure uniformity of laws. Professor Wilson will take the place on the commission of Supreme Court Justice J. Franklin Fort, who resigned. Professor Wilson has signified his willingness to accept a place on the commission.[2]

Printed in the *Princeton Press*, Aug. 10, 1901.

[1] Foster MacGowan Voorhees, Governor of New Jersey, 1899-1902.

[2] An "Act to Provide for the Appointment of Commissioners for the Promotion of Uniformity of Legislation in the United States" was approved by the New Jersey legislature on March 22, 1895. Three commissioners were appointed for five-year terms by the Governor with the approval of the Senate. The commissioners in 1901 were, in addition to Wilson, John R. Hardin and Frank Bergen, both of Newark. Wilson served one full term and a portion of a second, resigning in 1909. No reports by the commissioners have been found in the New Jersey State Library. Wilson's name was carried in the *Proceedings of the Annual Conference of Commissioners on Uniform State Laws* until 1909, but he was never listed as a participant in these meetings.

Two Letters from Charles White Merrill[1]

Dear Professor Wilson: Indianapolis, August 13–1901.

The Contemporary Club of Indianapolis[2] in arranging for its next season's program hopes that it may be possible to include your name. May I ask whether, if time and terms be satisfactorily settled, you would look favorably upon giving us the pleasure of hearing you?

Very truly yours,   C. W. Merrill   Secretary

[1] Treasurer of the Bobbs-Merrill Company, publishers of Indianapolis.
[2] About this organization, see WW to May Wright Sewall, Sept. 19, 1899, n. 1, Vol. 11.

My dear Mr. Wilson: Indianapolis, Aug. 22, 1901.

Your kind letter of Aug. 18th duly reaches me, and causes me, and I know will cause our board much pleasure. That board however, is now scattered for vacation and will not be gathered together for some weeks. On their return your letter will be spread before them.[1]

Thanking you for your courtesy, I beg to remain,
Very sincerely yours,   Charles W Merrill

TLS (WP, DLC).
[1] See C. W. Merrill to WW, Oct. 1, 1901.

To Daniel Coit Gilman

Heim[e]ra, Muskoka Dist.,
Mr. dear Mr. Gilman,   Ontario, Canada, 25 Aug., 1901

Your very kind letter of the nineteenth has reached me here,[1] and has gratified me very deeply. I have taken a day to think it over, and you may be sure I would not decline the commission it lays upon me were it so much as *possible* for me to accept. Dr. Adams was indeed a remarkable man, and did a lasting service of the most important kind to historical scholarship in this country. He deserves commemoration of a sort it is, unhappily, literally out of my power to give him.[2]

You ought, of course, to know the reason very explicitly,—for I realize that it is no light matter to decline such a request. I have filled next winter with work which I fear it will not be long enough to contain. The Harpers are to issue my history in four sumptuous volumes; I am to expand all the matter which has appeared in the *Magazine* and to add chapters bringing the narrative down to the end of the century; there are bibliographies and lists of carefully selected illustrations to be supplied, —and I have promised the whole thing by the earliest date justifiable by a most sanguine calculation as to my rate of production. I am not a little anxious as to the outcome,—and know that this task, added to my college work and the outside lectures (not new lectures, fortunately, but requiring frequent and more or less protracted absences from home) will tax my strength and *bottom* to the utmost. I *dare* not add more. It would be pale wording indeed to say that I am sorry. I am genuinely distressed; but I have no choice.

I thank you with all my heart for repeating again the suggestion that I allow the trustees to consider my name as Dr. Adams's successor, but in that matter I feel that the considerations I mentioned when first you asked me the question are imperative. Princeton has, morally, put me under bonds!

With deepest appreciation and affectionate regard,

Sincerely Yours, · Woodrow Wilson

ALS (D. C. Gilman Papers, MdBJ).
¹ It is missing.
² Gilman had asked Wilson to write a memorial to Herbert Baxter Adams in the book that was published as *Herbert B. Adams: Tributes of Friends . . .* (Baltimore, 1902).

A Political Essay[1]

[*c. Aug. 31, 1901*]

THE REAL IDEA OF DEMOCRACY:
A Talk

We think of democracy as at least as old as the republics of Greece and Rome, a thing based upon very ancient practices of the race and sanctioned from of old by the doctrines of political philosophers. And yet as a matter of fact democracy as we know it is no older than the end of the eighteenth century. The doctrines which sustain it can scarcely be said to derive any support at all from the practices of the classical states, or any countenance whatever from the principles of classical statesmen and philosophers. The citizens who constituted the "people" of the ancient republics were, when most numerous, a mere privileged class, a ruling minority of the population taken as a whole. Under their domination slaves abounded, and citizenship and even the privileges of the courts of justice were reserved for men of a particular blood and lineage. It never entered into the thought of any ancient republican to conceive of all men as equally entitled to take part in any government,

¹ No correspondence or documentary materials relating to the following essay are extant. The book in which it appeared was copyrighted Nov. 2, 1901. Other contributors were Grover Cleveland, Henry Demarest Lloyd, and Henry Jones Ford.

or even in the control of any government, by votes cast or lots drawn. Those who were in the ranks of privileged citizenship despised those who were not, guarded their ranks very jealously against intruders, and used their power as a right singular and exclusive, theirs, not as men, but as Athenians of authentic extraction, as Romans of old patrician blood.

Modern democracy wears a very different aspect, and rests upon principles separated by the whole heaven from those of the Roman or Grecian democrat. Its theory is of equal rights without respect of blood or breeding. It knows nothing of a citizenship won by privilege or inherited through lines of descent which cannot be changed or broadened. Its thought is of a society without castes or classes, of an equality of political birthright which is without bound or limitation. Its foundations are set in a philosophy that would extend to all mankind an equal emancipation, make citizens of all men, and cut away everywhere exceptional privilege. "All men are born free and equal" is the classical sentence of its creed, and its dream is always of a state in which no man shall have mastery over another without his willing acquiescence and consent. It speaks always of the sovereignty of the people, and of rulers as the people's servants.

The real problem of modern democracy, whether for those who work it out or for those who think it out, is how practicable means are to be found for putting such ideals into actual use in the conduct of governments. These are obviously ideals set very high. They have been very nobly expressed by some of the greatest thinkers of the race. The language in which they have been set for the thought of the world rings keen in the ear, as with a music of peace and good-will, and yet quick also with the energy of fine endeavor, lifting the thoughts to some of the highest conceptions of human progress. Their spell is upon us still, though they were first uttered long generations ago. And yet we halt, and know that we halt, at giving them effect in our lives, in the government of the communities we have set up since we gave ear to them.

The truth is that these ideals by which we seek and profess to live were formulated before the democracy of which they speak with so fine a fervor had anywhere come into existence. They were the song which beguiled the infancy of democracy, and, like other cradle songs, bear the marks of literary genius rather than of hard experience. We ought long ago to have remarked that they are touched with the visionary genius of the French rather than with the masculine and practical genius of the English mind—just as we ought long ago to have realized that when we speak of spring or summer or autumn we are speaking, not out of our own observation, but in the phrases of poets bred in the little English isle set in the northern seas, far away from the changeful ardors of the great continent whose sharp extremes of heat and cold give us seasons of our own. When we turn from the dreams of the French Revolution to the sober sentences which philosophers and statesmen of our own race and our own experience have spoken with regard to liberty and the institutions which make men free, the air clears at once and we can see our footing, alike for thought and for action. They spoke, before the French phrases crept in upon them, not of *the sovereignty of the people*, but of the *consent of the governed*; and the difference between the phrases is as wide as that between the political experiences of the two races.

In the conception of English writers, when English writers write like statesmen as well as like philosophers—as Locke did and our own Thomas Hooker—democracy is the antithesis of all government by privilege. It excludes all hereditary right to rule, whether in a single family or in a single class or in any combination of classes. It makes the general welfare of society the end and object of law, and declares that no class, no aristocratic minority, no single group of men, however numerous, however capable, however enlightened, can see broadly enough or sufficiently free itself from bias to perceive a nation's needs in their entirety or guide its destinies for the benefit of all. The consent of the governed must at every turn check and determine the action of those who make and execute the laws.

Every government is in fact conducted, when conducted with success, upon some calculation, more or less accurately made, of the assent of its subjects. The most unquestioned despot knows that revolution lies in wait for him upon more than one path which he might pursue, and to avoid it studies as he can the temper, the disposition, the interests, and even the passing inclinations of his people. Let him blunder too grossly in the calculation and his throne goes down. His task is infinitely hazardous, failure is more probable than success, and not many absolute monarchs have stayed the nineteenth century out. Governments have been liberalized. Representative assemblies have been chosen out of the body of the people, and by their suffrages, to advise with those who rule with regard to the needs and temper and interests of the nation, and to make sure beforehand of its cordial assent to every measure of government. The consent of the governed is no longer guessed at or risked upon some blind calculation. It is systematically ascertained. That is "constitutional government." When we speak of a constitutional government we mean a government so constituted that those who governed and those who are governed are brought by some systematic and efficient means into concord and counsel; and in which law, accordingly, is made and enforced in conformity with principles and by methods agreed upon between them.

Democracy, as statesmen of our race have understood and practised it, is simply the most advanced form of constitutional government: the form under which we no longer speak of "rulers" and "subjects," but only of citizens and the governors to whom they have given authority, of the people and their representatives, whether in council or in executive office. We speak of *the sovereignty of the people* quite in the manner of the French, but we do not interpret the phrase as Rousseau interpreted it. We understand it rather as Locke and Hooker would have used it. We have seen the world, and we know that sovereignty is not a thing merely of consent and approval, but a thing of initiative and of action. Those whom the people have chosen exercise sovereignty: select the policy of the nation, propose, formulate, and modify its law, determine its relations with other nations and its place of leadership or mastery in the world—subject always to the consent and approval of the people, by whose voice their acts are to be sanctioned or reversed, but not subject to their initiative and suggestion. It were impossible for the people to originate measures, except through their representative bodies; it were impossible for the people as a whole to consult. It is their part to choose between leaders, to accept or reject what their chosen governors or the organizers of their parties propose. Modern democracy is government subject to systematic popular control.

The real problem of democracy, therefore, is how to devise and maintain in full efficiency the best means of intimate counsel between those who are to make and administer the laws and those who are to obey them, and yet not destroy leadership or render government less real or less authoritative. It is as important for the progress of the race that governments should retain their power as it is that they should be free—no tyranny, but merely the chief guiding force of a free people. The problem of every government is leadership: the choice and control of statesmen and the scope that shall be given to their originative part in affairs; and for democracy it is a problem of peculiar difficulty. Many questions of government are in the highest degree technical and full of obscure perplexities; many require such study and experience for their proper handling as only trained public men of long and responsible service can give; all call for consultation, sifting, discussion, examination upon this side and upon that; none can be wisely decided by voters scattered at the polls and informed only by partisan newspapers. A democracy, by reason of the very multitude of its voters and their infinite variety in capacity, environment, information, and circumstance, is peculiarly dependent upon its leaders. The real test of its excellence as a form of government is the training, the opportunities, the authority, the rewards which its constitutional arrangements afford those who seek to lead it faithfully and well. It does not get the full profit of its own characteristic principles and ideals unless it use the best men in it, without regard to their blood or breeding. It cannot use them unless it call them into service by adequate rewards of greatness and of power. Its problem is to control its leaders and yet not hamper or humiliate them; to make them its servants and yet give them leave to be masters too, not in name merely but in fact, of the policy of a great nation—types of a power that comes by genius and not by favor.

Woodrow Wilson

Printed in Seymour Eaton and Frederic W. Speirs (eds.), *Problems in Modern Democracy* (Philadelphia, 1901), pp. 59-67.

A Preface to an Historical Encyclopedia[1]

Princeton, New Jersey, September 9, 1901.[2]

THE SIGNIFICANCE OF AMERICAN HISTORY

The study of American history has changed its whole tone and aspect within a generation. Once a plain and simple tale,—though heroic withal,—of a virgin continent discovered in the West, new homes for the English made upon it, a new polity set up, a new nation made of a sudden in the hot crucible of war, a life and a government apart,—a thing isolated, singular, original, as if it were the story of a separate precinct and parish of the great world,—the history of the United States has now been brought at last into perspective, to be seen as what it is, an integral portion of the general history of civilization; a free working-out upon a clear field, indeed, of selected forces generated long ago in England and the old European world, but no irregular invention, no

[1] Wilson's shorthand draft of this preface, dated Sept. 7, 1901, and his longhand draft, dated Sept. 9, 1901, are in WP, DLC.
[2] Actually, Wilson wrote this at Heimera, Rosseau Falls, Ont.

histrionic vindication of the Rights of Man. It has not lost its unique significance by the change, but gained, rather, a hundredfold both in interest and in value. It seemed once a school exercise in puritan theory and cavalier pride; it seems now a chapter written for grown men in the natural history of politics and society, a perfect exposition of what the European civilization of the seventeenth and eighteenth centuries was to produce in the nineteenth century. What formerly appeared to be only a by-product of the creative forces of society is now clearly enough seen to be the epitome of a whole age. We see it all, now that America, having come out of her days of adolescence and preparation, has taken her place among the powers of the world, fresh and still in her youth, but no stranger among the peoples,—a leader, rather, and pace-maker in the wide field of affairs.

The history of the United States is modern history in broad and open analysis, stripped of a thousand elements which, upon the European stage, confuse the eye and lead the judgment astray. It spans a whole age of the world's transformation, from the discoveries, the adventure, the romance of the sixteenth century, with its dreams of unbounded wealth in the far Indies and marvels at the ends of the earth, to the sober commerce and material might of the twentieth, with its altered dreams, of a world mastered, if not united, by the power of armed fleets patrolling it from end to end, in the interests of peace and European and American trade.

At its outset American history discloses a novel picture of men out of an old world set upon the coasts of a new to do the work of pioneers, without suitable training either of thought or hand,—men schooled in an old civilization, puzzled, even daunted, by the wilderness in which they found themselves as by a strange and alien thing, ignorant of its real character, lacking all the knowledge and craft of the primitive world, lacking everything but courage, sagacity, and a steadfast will to succeed. As they pushed their gigantic task they were themselves transformed. The unsuitable habits of an old world fell away from them. Their old blood bred a new stock, and the youth of the race to which they belonged was renewed. And yet they did not break with the past, were for long scarcely conscious of their own transformation, held their thoughts to old channels, were frontiersmen with traditions not of the frontier, traditions which they cherished and held very dear, of a world in which there were only ancient kingdoms and a civilization set up and perfected time out of mind. Their muscles hardened to the work of the wilderness, they learned woodcraft and ranged the forests like men with the breeding, the quick instincts, the ready resource in time of danger of the Indian himself, and yet thought upon deep problems of religion, pondered the philosophy of the universities, were partisans and followers of statesmen and parties over sea, looked to have their fashions of dress sent to them, with every other old-world trapping they could pay for, by the European ships which diligently plied to their ports. Nowhere else, perhaps, is there so open and legible a record of the stiffness of thought and the flexibility of action in men, the union of youth and age, the dominion of habit reconciled with an unspoiled freshness of bold initiative.

And with the transplantation of men out of the old world into a wilderness went also the transplantation of institutions,—with the same result. The new way of life and association thrust upon these men reduced the complex things of government to their simples. Within those untouched forests they resumed again, as if by an unconscious instinct, the simple organization of village communities familiar to their race long centuries before, or here and there put palisades about a group of huts meant to serve for refuge and fortress against savage enemies lurking near at hand in the coverts, and lived in their "hundreds" again under captains, to spread at last slowly into counties with familiar sheriffs and quarter-sessions. It was as if they had brought their old-time polity with them, not in the mature root nor even in the young cutting, but in the seed merely, to renew its youth and yield itself to the influences of a new soil and a new environment. It was drawn back to its essential qualities, stripped of its elaborate growth of habits, as they themselves were. All things were touched, as it were, by the light of an earlier age returned. The study of American history furnishes, as a consequence, materials such as can be found nowhere else for a discrimination between what is accidental and what is essential in English political practice. Principles developed by the long and intricate processes of the history of one country are here put to experimental test in another, where every element of life is simplified, every problem of government reduced to its fundamental formulæ. There is here the best possible point of departure, for the student who can keep his head and who knows his European history as intimately as he knows his American, for a comparative study of institutions which may some day yield us a sane philosophy of politics which shall forever put out of school the thin and sentimental theories of the disciples of Rousseau.

This is the new riches which the study of American history is to afford in the light that now shines upon it: not national pride merely, nor merely an heroic picture of men wise beyond previous example in building States, and uniting them under a government at once free and strong, but a real understanding of the nature of liberty, of the essential character and determining circumstances of self-government, the fundamental contrasts of race and social development, of temper and of opportunity, which of themselves make governments or mar them. It may well yield us, at any rate, a few of the first principles of the natural history of institutions.

The political history of America was the outcome of a constitutional struggle which concerned Englishmen in England no less deeply than it concerned Englishmen in the colonies, a struggle whose motives were compounded both of questions of conscience and of questions of civil liberty, of longings to be free to think and of longings to be free to act. And Englishmen on the two sides of the sea were not wholly divorced in the issue of that struggle. Not America alone, but the power to rule without principle and restraint at home as well, was once for all cut off from the crown of England. But there was sharp contrast, too, between the effects wrought in England and the effects wrought in America. On one side the sea an ancient people won their final battle for constitutional government; on the other side a new people was created,—a people set free to work out a new experience both in the liberty of its churches and in its political arrangements, to gain a new consciousness, take on a distinctive character, transform itself from a body of loosely associated English colonies into a great commonwealth, not English nor yet colonial merely, but transmuted, within little more than a generation, into a veritable nation, marked out for an independent and striking career.

At the Revolution the American States did hardly more than disengage themselves from the English dominion. Their thoughts, their imaginations, were still held subject to policy and opinion over sea. By the close of the War of 1812, these last, impalpable bonds were also thrown off. American statesmen had got their freedom of thought, and, within a generation, were the leaders of a nation and a people apart. One has only to contrast the persistent English quality and point of view of the English colonies of to-day, self-governing communities though most of them are, which have led their own lives for generations together under parliaments and ministers of their own free choosing, with the distinctive character of the United States to realize how much of the history of nations is spiritual, not material, a thing, not of institutions, but of the heart and the imagination. This is one of the secrets American history opens to the student, the deepest of all secrets, the genesis of nationality, the play of spirit in the processes of history.

Of course the present separateness and distinctive character of the United States among the nations is due in part to the mixture of races in the make-up of their people. Men out of every European race, men out of Asia, men out of Africa have crowded in, to the bewilderment alike of the statesmen and of the historian. An infinite crossing of strains has made a new race. And yet there is a mystery here withal. Where, when, in what way, have our institutions and our life as a people been turned to new forms and into new channels by this new union and chemistry of bloods? There has been no break in our constitutional development. Nothing has been done of which we can confidently say, This would not have been done had we kept the pure Saxon strain. All peoples have come to dwell among us, but they have merged their individuality in a national character already formed; have been dominated, changed, absorbed. We keep until now some of the characteristic differences of organization and action transplanted to this continent when races were separate upon it. We single out the Dutch element in the history of New York, the French element in the history of Louisiana, the Spanish influence in the far West. But these things remain from a time when Dutch and French and Spanish had their seats and their power apart and were independent rivals for the possession of the continent. Since they were fused they have given us nothing which we can distinguish as their own. The French who have come to us since that final settlement on the heights of Quebec have contributed nothing distinctive to our civilization or our order of government. The Dutch who have been immigrants amongst us since New Netherlands became New York have no doubt strengthened our stock, but they have adopted our character and point of view. No foreign stock long keeps its identity in our affairs.

The fact should a little daunt those who make much of physical heredity and speak of the persistence of race characteristics as a thing fixed and invariable, if they are to apply their theory to communities which are dominated by one and the same national idea, and fused to make a common stock. It is where races act separately that they act in character and with individual distinction. In this again the history of the United States demonstrates the spiritual aspects of political development. Nations grow by spirit, not by blood; and nowhere can the significant principle of their growth be seen more clearly, upon a more fair and open page, than in the history of the United States. It is this principle which throws a light as if of veritable revelation upon the real nature of liberty, as a thing bred, not of institutions nor of the benevolent inventions of statesmen, but of the spiritual forces of which institutions themselves are the offspring and creation. To talk of giving to one people the liberties of another is to talk of making a gift of character, a thing built up by the contrivance of no single generation, but by the slow providence which binds generations together by a common training.

From whatever point of view you approach it, American history gives some old lesson a new plainness, clarification, and breadth. It is an offshoot of European history and has all its antecedents on the other side of the sea, and yet it is so much more than a mere offshoot. Its processes are so freshened and clarified, its records are so abundant and so accessible, it is spread upon so wide, so open, so visible a field of observation, that it seems like a plain first chapter in the history of a new age. As a stage in the economic development of modern civilization, the history of America constitutes the natural, and invaluable, subject-matter and book of praxis of the political economist. Here is industrial development worked out with incomparable logical swiftness, simplicity, and precision,—a swiftness, simplicity, and precision impossible amidst the rigid social order of any ancient kingdom. It is a study, moreover, not merely of the make-up and setting forth of a new people, but also of its marvellous expansion, of processes of growth, both spiritual and material, hurried forward from stage to stage as if under the experimental touch of some social philosopher, some political scientist making of a nation's history his laboratory and place of demonstration.

The twentieth century will show another face. The stage of America grows crowded like the stage of Europe. The life of the new world grows as complex as the life of the old. A nation hitherto wholly devoted to domestic development now finds its first task roughly finished and turns about to look curiously into the tasks of the great world at large, seeking its special part and place of power. A new age has come which no man may forecast. But the past is the key to it; and the past of America lies at the centre of modern history.   Woodrow Wilson

Printed in *Harper's Encyclopædia of United States History* (10 vols., New York, 1902), I, xxvii-xxxii.

From the Minutes of the Princeton University Faculty

3 P.M., Wednesday, September 18, 1901.

. . . The President appointed . . .

Also the following Committee on the Graduate School; The Dean of the Graduate School ex officio as Chairman, The President of the University ex officio, and Professors Brackett, Magie, Fine, Woodrow Wilson, Scott, Harper & Thompson.

Remarks on the Assassination of President McKinley[1]

[[Sept. 19, 1901]]

How still this hour seems! Is it not singular that a nation should sit thus quiet in its churches in an hour like this; and yet may we not hope that it is characteristic that this nation should sit with still minds in its places of worship and ask counsel of God, what shall be done in such a crisis? The crisis is not one of affairs or of force or of immediate danger to the nation; it is a crisis of spirit— for it seems to me that we should make this an hour of reckoning with ourselves. This pestiferous thing that has grown in our soil must have had some air to feed upon, and we may well ask ourselves, have we supplied any of the air that has fed the fatal plant of anarchy in America? We had dared to hope that this was the place in all the world where men were free enough to think the thoughts of soberness in place of the thoughts of revolution, and where, because the law made the course of reform open, men would not with dastardly cunning seek the sudden way of force to gain their objects. If we have been deceived, if we may not believe this is a thing singular and isolated which cannot happen again, shall we not ask ourselves, what is our own duty in this time?

There could not be a time in which the question could be better asked; for there has been a hush of all party strife. The single comfort of this moment is the thrilling sense that we have forgotten for the time being to which party we have belonged, and know only that a blow has been struck at the institutions we ourselves have erected. In this moment of united spirits we may ask ourselves, if there be any common way of thought amongst us which we should correct? This is not the place, and I am not the man to read a lesson to this company or to any part of this nation; but I think that any man may exhort his fellow-citizens to cultivate that spirit of moderation which will make the air sweet and safe for controversy; that any man may beg of his fellow-citizens to check in any way that they can the factional spirit, in order that the air may be wholesome to breathe.

Even in days of political controversy I think we can succeed in checking to some extent the tendency to argue upon rumor. The air is full of rumors. This wretched man who did this tragic thing had fed his heart upon rumors of things that were not true; and I know there is many a man who says intemperate words, who has, without looking into them, repeated things that he has heard which were not true. There are men who have been moved, particularly at this critical stage of our country, to get at a conclusion and achieve a victory rather than use arguments meant to seek out the truth.

Shall a University not make the ascertainment of the real truth of every social situation the object of its inquiries, and of its controversies even, so that we may go slowly, sanely, temperately at work, seeking that every man should have the same spirit in getting his due, that every man should seek to advance toward the thing that is true rather than towards the thing which may set forward the special objects of his own ambition and of his own party? This awful tragedy will not be without a benefit to us if it so quiets our tempers, so sobers our judgments, so steadies our views that hereafter we shall be able to deal with this thing which eats at our vitals, not in a spirit of haste and passion but in a spirit, as it were, of kindly science, sending the knife where it will cut away that which is diseased, and not sending the knife where it will imperil the vital organs themselves.

I believe that it would be in the spirit of the assassin himself to pursue any set of men for their opinions, no matter what those opinions might be; but it will be in the true spirit of the institutions of this country to check that which is wrong and intemperate, and to stop that with the hand of force which is against the slow processes of reform and which makes for the quick process of revolution; and in quietness and fairness to make up our minds together what shall be done.

We say the President was killed, but the government lives. Aye, but institutions have no more vitality than the sentiments which sustain them, aud [and] the immortality of the Constitution of the United States is in our hearts and in our minds, and in no law written in any book. It is a law received out of the immaterial traditions of the race. It is the law which has made our minds free that has made our institutions free also. Let us not put our minds in thraldom to fear; let us not make haste; let us be slow and temperate and wise, and so give the world new credentials that this is a free nation where men may speak their minds and yet must keep the law.[2]

Printed in the *Princeton University Bulletin*, XIII (Oct. 1901), 5-6.

[1] Made at a special convocation in Alexander Hall in Princeton on September 19, 1901, at which Grover Cleveland and John Huston Finley also spoke. President McKinley had been shot in Buffalo, N.Y., by the anarchist Leon F. Czolgosz on September 6, 1901, and had died on September 14. For a report of this convocation, see the *Princeton University Bulletin*, XIII (Oct. 1901), 3-8.

[2] There is a WWhw outline of these remarks, dated Sept. 19, 1901, in WP, DLC.

A Report of an Interview

[Sept. 23, 1901]

JERSEY WOULD MOVE TO EXTERMINATE ANARCHY
PROF. WILSON'S ADVICE IS TO MAKE HASTE SLOWLY.

New Jersey will not be behind her sister states in the enactment of laws for the suppression of anarchy and the proper punishment of anarchists.

Since public sentiment throughout the land has been aroused by the assassination of the President, foremost citizens and eminent jurists of the state have been considering the problem presented by the existence of anarchy, and it is a safe prediction that prompt and decisive action will be the result.

As to the best means for accomplishing the desired result there is some difference of opinion, but all are united in the determination that something must be done.

Among the most eminent authorities in the state who has the matter under consideration is Professor Woodrow Wilson, Ph.D., LL.D., professor of jurisprudence in Princeton University.

Professor Wilson has a national reputation as a jurist and as a writer on economic and historical subjects. He is a member of the American Bar Association and is one of the committee of three appointed from New Jersey to act in conjunction with similar committees from other states to secure uniformity of state laws, the other New Jersey members being John R. Hardin and Frank Bergen.

This committee has been asked to confer with the committees from the other states with a view of preparing laws for the suppression of anarchy.

Professor Wilson was seen at his home in Princeton by a True American representative and talked freely upon the absorbing topic of anarchy, but at the same time said he was not prepared to express any opinion as to what should be done.

The subject, he said, was a broad one, and one requiring the most careful consideration before anything definite is done. That steps should be taken for the protection of society from anarchists, Professor Wilson is convinced; that the immediate present is not the time to do this he is equally certain. In explaining his position in this respect professor Wilson said:

"We are too angry today to give the subject the calm and deliberate consideration it demands. We are not in a frame of mind to form a just and sufficiently moderate law which will hold water.

"There is no question as to what we want, but there is of the method to be employed in accomplishing it. I would like to reach these scoundrels as much as any one, but whatever law is passed must stand not only the constitutional test but must not be liable to public condemnation, otherwise it will not accomplish its end.

"There are evidently obstacles in the way of such a measure and these must be carefully weighed in framing a law so that it will not prove faulty. For example, the right of free speech must be borne in mind, and care must be taken that this fundamental principle of our government is not violated."

Professor Wilson's conversation indicated that he would favor a stringent law, but at the same time he said there were so many things to guard against that it would probably take a long time to draft a measure which would stand the test and at the same time prove effective.

Professor Wilson was positive that the proper course of procedure was action by the individual states rather than by any attempt at federal legislation. Any law, he said, to meet the approval of any number of the states must be of such a character as to stand the requisite test.

While in the present state of the public mind an individual state might pass a faulty measure, Professor Wilson thought that the sanction of a number of the states would be a sufficient guarantee as to its soundness. He also thought that the matter was one which should be considered not by a few but by many of those competent to pass upon such matters.

In discussing the probable work of the committee of which he is a member, Professor Wilson said he had not been informed personally that the committee was to be called upon, although he considered the suggestion an excellent one. The committees from the several states, he said, had not considered thus far in their work any amendment to the criminal laws, so that any action in the present instance they may be called upon to make will be along new lines entirely.

Printed in the *Daily Trenton True American*, Sept. 23, 1901; several editorial headings omitted.

From Edward Augustus Woods

My dear Dr. Wilson: Pittsburg, Pa.   September 24, 1901.

I should be glad to know on what train you intend to reach Pittsburg for your talk before the Club on the evening of October third,[1] and also to know if there is anything I can do to serve your convenience in engaging return accommodations, etc. Perhaps the most convenient train for arriving in Pittsburg is No. 19, the Cleveland and Cincinnati Express, which I judge from the schedule you can conveniently make by leaving Princeton at 9:35 P.M., arriving in Philadelphia at 10:38, leaving there at 11:05 and reaching Pittsburg at 8:30 in the morning, breakfasting either on the train or after you get here, as you may prefer. If you will let me know when you must return and what train you prefer, or leave it to me to get accommodations in advance, I will arrange it so that you will have comfortable quarters in returning.

As you know, we expect you to stop at our house, and my wife[2] also hopes that Mrs. Wilson will come with you.

Anticipating your visit here with much pleasure, I am

Yours sincerely,   Edward A. Woods

TLS (WP, DLC).
    [1] The list of deliveries of the address, "Americanism," appended to the notes for it printed at Dec. 6, 1900, reveals that Wilson gave this speech at Sewickley, Pa., on Oct. 3, 1901. Woods's letter indicates that Wilson spoke to the Woman's Club of Sewickley. Files of the *Sewickley Valley*, the only local newspaper at this time, are not available for October 1901. No extant Pittsburgh newspaper carried an announcement or report of Wilson's address.
    [2] Gertrude Macrum Woods.

To an Unidentified Person

[Dear Sir,]   [Princeton, N.J., c. Oct. 1, 1901]

Knowing that I should not keep you waiting any longer than was absolutely necessary for my decision upon the matter you were kind [enough], with Judge Woodruff,[1] to lay before me this afternoon,[2] I have considered it very thoroughly, thus having arrived at the conclusion which I shall take the liberty of expressing as candidly as possible.

I find myself so far from sympathizing with the general attitude of the national Democratic party upon many of the chief articles of its creed, as the country understands it, that I feel that it would not be candid of me to identify myself with it in a local contest until it has regained its balance in those matters before the country. It will not be understood to have regained its balance by using the names of men like myself: it can regain it only by the speech and action of men whom the country has accepted as its spokesmen. I must in these matters regard not only my own personal position but also my responsibility as a university instructor.

I am deeply sensible of the compliment paid me in the invitation to allow myself to be put in nomination as state senator. I should sincerely like to serve the party in so good a cause as it now seems to be about to turn to; but I am convinced, because of the considerations I have already urged, that I ought to decline.[3]

With warm regards and thanks both for Judge Woodruff and yourself,

Sincerely yours,   [Woodrow Wilson]

Transcript of WWshL (WP, DLC).
[1] Robert Spencer Woodruff, lawyer and judge of the Court of Common Pleas of Mercer County, 1890-1900.
[2] That is, that Wilson accept the Democratic nomination for state senator from Mercer County. No Trenton or Princeton newspaper noted that this conference had occurred or, for that matter, that Wilson had ever been suggested as a possible candidate.
[3] Woodruff himself was nominated by the Democratic county convention at Hightstown on October 16. He was defeated by the Republican incumbent, Elijah C. Hutchinson, in the election on November 5, 1901.

From Charles White Merrill

Dear Mr. Wilson: Indianapolis October 1—1901.

Your kind letter of the 18th August is before me, and is entirely pleasing to our board.

April appeals [appears] to us a very desirable time, as this will fit in nicely with our other plans. The fourth Wednesday in each month is our regular meeting, but since you prefer Fridays in April, we have placed the date at the Friday following the fourth Wednesday, or April 25th. We trust this will be entirely agreeable to you.

We will write you later concerning our decision on the subject. All of those you mention are interesting to our Club.[1]

Thanking you for your courtesies, we beg to remain
Very truly yours,   THE CONTEMPORARY CLUB
Charles W Merrill Secretary

TLS (WP, DLC).
[1] See C. W. Merrill to WW, Nov. 20, 1901.

From Alois P. Swoboda[1]

My Dear Sir: Chicago, Oct. 2, 1901.

Your favor of recent date, enclosing $20.00 as full payment for course of instructions is at hand, for which please accept my thanks. I have noted your remarks and measurements and accordingly enclose exercises for your FIRST LESSON, which I trust you will follow conscientiously.

Begin exercise "P" by using the rim of the bath tub or some suitable piece of furniture of about that height for your hands, instead of the floor. The cut on this page illustrates the exercise as modified by the above suggestion.

Your trouble is due to lack of blood and nervous force, therefore in addition to the exercise make a practice of drinking at least four pints of water every day—a glassful the first thing on arising, one with each meal and one before retiring. Do not drink immediately after your meals, but drink freely after your food is well digested. This will add to the quantity of your blood and increase your weight materially. Drink hot water night and morning, instead of cold.

To derive the greatest amount of benefit from the instructions it is necessary to make a business of them as you would of anything else from which you expected the best results and I trust you will apply this principle to your work.

It is hardly necessary to state that as you proceed you will increase in the rigidity and consequently in your ability to improve your physical condition.[2]

Yours very truly,   Alois P Swoboda   ·

TLS (WP, DLC). Enc.: two-page mimeographed set of instructions entitled "The Swoboda System of Physiological Exercise."

[1] A physical therapist and quack of Chicago, active at least until the early 1920's in spite of frequent investigations by the American Medical Association.

[2] Swoboda's further letters of instruction—A. P. Swoboda to WW, Oct. 21, Nov. 15, and Dec. 20, 1901, and April 2, 1902, all typed letters in WP, DLC—will not be printed in this series.

From the Minutes of the Princeton University Faculty

5 5′ P.M., Wednesday, October 9th, 1901.

. . . Upon recommendation of the Committee on The Graduate School it was Resolved (1) That all existing Graduate Courses terminate at the close of this Academic year.

(2) That the Courses to be given in the Graduate School be constituted according to standards which may be adopted by the Trustees on recommendation of the University Faculty. . . .

The former Committee, Professors Brackett, Woodrow Wilson and Fine, to appear before and confer with the Trustees if required, was continued.

To Josephine Hunt Cutter[1]

My dear Mrs. Cutter,   Princeton, New Jersey, 11 October, 1901

I accept with the greatest pleasure the Woman's Club's invitation for the new date in January, and wish to assure you that I appreciate most deeply the very unusual compliment the Club has paid me by its action.

The new date you name, the twenty-eighth of January, is, I notice, a Tuesday,—while the other dates you named were both Wednesdays. Is it possible that it was a slip of the pen for Wednesday, the twenty-*ninth*? The latter date would suit me quite as well as the twenty-eighth,—indeed better,—so that you need have no hesitation in correcting the error, if it was one.

Have you any preference as to a choice of subject from those I suggested in my first letter ("Patriotism," "Americanism," "Political Liberty," "Alexis de Tocqueville")? I think my own choice would fall upon the first.

With renewed expressions of warm gratitude for the circumstances and the unusual cordiality of your invitation,

Most Sincerely Yours,   Woodrow Wilson

ALS (de Coppet Coll., NjP).
[1] Mrs. John C. Cutter of 520 Pleasant St., Worcester, Mass., chairman of the History Committee of the Worcester Woman's Club.

From the Minutes of the Board of Trustees of Princeton University

October 15, 1901.

FACULTY COMMITTEE APPEARS

The Committee from the Faculty, Professors Brackett, Fine, and Woodrow Wilson, appeared before the Trustees and spoke on matters of interest connected with the work of the University.

To Josephine Hunt Cutter

My dear Mrs. Cutter,   Princeton, New Jersey, 16 October, 1901

Thank you very much indeed for your kind letter of the thirteenth, with all its cordial hospitality.

The programme it suggests for my visit to Worcester on the twenty-ninth of January is most acceptable.[1] If you will be kind enough to take me to the "Bay State" for luncheon (from the 1:50 train) I will be at the hall at three; and it will give me great pleasure to dine with you at such hour as you may appoint.

Thanking you for your thoughtful kindness, and with confident expectations of enjoyment,

Sincerely Yours,   Woodrow Wilson

ALS (de Coppet Coll., NjP).

[1] Wilson gave his lecture, "Patriotism." See the news report printed at Jan. 30, 1902.

From Abram Woodruff Halsey[1]

My Dear Wilson,   Enid, Oklahoma T[erritory] Oct. 25. 1901.

In this far away corner of our great domain I read of the honor Yale conferred upon you at the Centennial celebration on Wednesday.[2] My hearty congratulations on so justly deserved recognition of good workmanship.

One of the bright members of my sometime parish said to me after reading your "Washington," "Professor Wilson should devote his entire time to literature." I confess to sympathizing a trifle with this view. I recognize however the wide scope given you in your present position and rejoice in the success attending your labors.

Somewhere you have written that men never tire of listening "to the incomparable music of perfected human speech." You are a master musician in this subtle art. May you have many added years in which to "exercise the gift that is within you"

It is with great personal pleasure and a pardonable '79 pride that I join with your many friends in felicitating you on this happy event.   Always Yours   A. W. Halsey

ALS (WP, DLC).

[1] Wilson's classmate at Princeton, at this time Secretary of the Board of Foreign Missions of the Presbyterian Church in the U.S.A.

[2] About this affair, see the following news report.

A News Report of the Yale Bicentennial

[Oct. 26, 1901]

Princeton's contingent in Yale's Bicentennial parade made a hit. A well known painter of New York who happened to be present remarked to the writer that the tiger costumes were the best thing in the whole show. However that may be, they were very striking, and the hospitable crowd cheered all along the line. Of the other universities, though hundreds of them from Tokyo to Padua sent delegates to the more dignified functions, the only ones represented in the parade were Harvard, Princeton, Wesleyan and Trinity. Each sent a squad of about twenty-five undergraduates, costumed more or less dignifiedly in the colors of the college represented. Altogether the parade was probably the greatest academic procession this country has ever seen. Though marching six abreast, it stretched out over two miles in length. There was a pleasing variety in the costumes, the several Yale classes, for instance, representing various periods in the 200 years of the college's and country's history. The celebration was a great success, from the religious exercises which began it on Sunday to the presentation of degrees and the farewell reception on Wednesday. The amount of Yale enthusiasm displayed can best be conveyed to the readers of this paper by saying that the scene reminded a Princeton man of the same dates in October five years ago.[1] . . .

At the concluding ceremonies Yale University conferred the degree of LL.D. upon President Patton, and the degree of Litt.D. upon Prof. Woodrow Wilson '79.[2] Also Basil Lanneau Gildersleeve '49, Professor of Greek at Johns Hopkins, and Ogden N. Rood '52, Professor of Physics at Columbia, received the LL.D. degree, and so did Prof. Caspar Rene Gregory of the University of Leipsic, a graduate of Princeton Theological Seminary.[3]

Printed in the *Princeton Alumni Weekly*, II (Oct. 26, 1901), 67-68.
[1] When Princeton celebrated her Sesquicentennial.
[2] Wilson's citation read: "On you who, like Blackstone, have made the studies of the jurist the pleasure of the gentleman, and have clothed political investigations in the form of true literature, we confer the degree of Doctor of Letters and admit you to all its rights and privileges." *Yale Alumni Weekly*, XI (Jan. 1902), 136.
[3] Among the other recipients of honorary degrees were President Theodore Roosevelt, Samuel Langhorne Clemens, William Dean Howells, Chief Justice Melville Weston Fuller, James Ford Rhodes, Richard Olney, Seth Low, and Richard Watson Gilder.

From Varnum Lansing Collins

My dear Professor Wilson   Princeton, N.J., Nov. 4. 01.

I propose to send the following books to Elliott subject to any amendments you may make to the list. We would not like to send our Benton's Abridgement of Debates for the period nor the U.S. Documents concerning Calhoun; but I shall mention them to Elliott and shall also remind him of Winsor's volume 7.

Very truly yours   V. Lansing Collins

Calhoun's Works
Calhoun's Letters (Am. Hist Assoc.)
Thomas[,] Carolina tribute to C.
Jenkins[,] Life of C.
Death & funeral ceremonies of C.

Van Holst[,] Life of C.
Southern Quart. Rev. 1850
Democratic Rev. vols 2, 12, 14, 16, 26
American Rev. vols 7, 12.
Littell's Living Age vol 70
N. Amer. Rev. vol 101.

ALS (Collins Scrapbooks, Vol. 1, UA, NjP).

To Edward Graham Elliott

My dear Mr. Elliott,   Princeton, New Jersey, 5 November, 1901.

Of course you may stay and take your degree. Of course there is work here waiting for [you], and I am anxious to see you back. I had hoped that, should I get away for my year abroad next college year, you would be here to keep the program of our department from falling blank of a sudden. But I do not think that we ought to hale you back if you can afford another year and can get your permanent label, the commercial value of which I deeply appreciate. Stay, therefore, by all means.

You do not say, in plain terms, that taking a degree would involve a whole additional year, but that of course, I suppose. It would be a good idea, if you did not embarrass the degree thereby, to put in a part of the year at Oxford, getting the atmosphere of their class rooms in international law particularly.[1]

Mr. Collins is getting the Calhoun books ready. There are painfully few of them, but the Life and the works and letters are, after all, what you chiefly need.

In haste,

With warm regards and Godspeed,

                     Faithfully Yours,   Woodrow Wilson

WWTLS (WC, NjP).
[1] Actually, Elliott received his Ph.D. at Heidelberg in 1902 and returned to Princeton to begin teaching in September of that year.

To Henry van Dyke

My dear van Dyke,   Princeton, 10 Nov., '01

After I left you this morning it came upon me that I had spoken rather brusquely about your reference to the honour system. I was thinking only of the *thing*, which lies very close to my heart, and did not consider *how* I spoke. Pray forgive the bluntness for the cause's sake.

                     Sincerely Yours,   Woodrow Wilson

ALS (facsimile printed in Ray Stannard Baker, *Woodrow Wilson: Life and Letters* [8 vols., Garden City, N.Y., 1927-39], II, 55).

To Edith Gittings Reid

My dear Friend,   Princeton, 13 Nov., 1901

Only half an hour ago did I hear of the death of Mrs. Gittings, whom Mrs. Wilson and I had learned to love very deeply, and with the sort of pleasure which only such women can give. We have felt the shock very keenly, and I write, not because I know how to speak words of comfort that will avail, but because I would, if I may and can, express my own sense of loss.

Mrs. Gittings was one of those rare women who belong, not to the generation with which they are contemporary, but to the generation with which they *live*, be it early in life or late. Her apprehension of all that went on about her was so keen, her sympathies were so quick and genuine, her mind had such a sweet friendliness for all who came near her, new friends or old, she was so essentially and permanently young in heart and nature, that I did not feel as if she belonged to a generation that was passing away. Her death affects me as the death of some one of my own generation whom I had loved, like something that has gone out of my life that *might* have continued to be part of it. Little as I knew her, reckoning by time and by actual intercourse, my sense of her sweetness and appreciative penetration and depth of nature was as keen as if I had known her with a real intimacy. Perhaps I knew her in part through you; perhaps I knew her in part by means of the unnumbered delightful things I had heard about her. I only know that the knowledge that she is gone comes to me like a personal grief, and that I would give anything I know of for some word sufficient to express my sympathy for you

With all affectionate messages from us both

Sincerely Yours,   Woodrow Wilson

ALS (WC, NjP).

To Varnum Lansing Collins

My dear Mr. Collins,   [Princeton, N.J., c. Nov. 15, 1901]

I have kept this letter all this while, it turns out, to suggest only one book "A Critical Study of Nullification in South Carolina" by David F. Houston, Longmans, 1896 (Harvard Historical

Studies, III). None of the other books I've thought of could well
be sent.   Yours faithfully   W. Wilson

ALS written on V. L. Collins to WW, Nov. 4, 1901 (Collins Scrapbooks, Vol. 1,
UA, NjP).

From Edith Gittings Reid

My dear dear friend   [Baltimore, c. Nov. 15, 1901]

I cared so much for your note, I know that you are sorry for
me.

I think, think, think day after day night after night—simply
this—what does it all mean?

I never know what a day of such travail of soul will bring
me—sometimes it is rest sometimes despair.

I go over laboriously all the dreadful details[.] I uncover the
ground. I know every inch, until I reach the beautiful dead face
with the faded pansies and the pitiful little tokens of affection
& then as I look at it all minutely sparing myself not an atom of
suffering there will come beating about my ears her living words &
thoughts[,] the charm of her manner—herself—and the grave
fills up[.] The beautiful dead figure is not my mother—and the
mind staggers in trying to comprehend this old old sorrow coming over & over again[,] cutting at the roots of things[,] the awful
mystery of life & death.

Some people write that she had reached the full measure of
womans life—just as if that didn't make the tragedy deeper. It
was not just a promise with her but the fulfillment of every
beauty of mind & soul & body. When she was cut down what a
fall of memories & beauties—what a poor place this house is
without her[,] what a low growth we all seem. The people who
met her for the first time this summer spoke of her great personal
beauty and how hard it was to realize that she was blind & I
said that we who lived with her did not think of it[,] she saw so
much more than we did. Her friends when they had new gowns
wanted to show them to her first because no one enjoyed them
so much—blind indeed! I can hear her now asking if the jet on
some gown was on the right side, & her "Oh! how lovely so much
prettier than if it were on the left side" & how we all laughed—
"and did it go to the very bottom[?]" ["]Well nothing was ever so
handsome"—and what fun we made of her. But oh! how pleasant
the atmosphere and how delightful the gown after such talking
over.

I have cared to write you all this. It has been a relief to me from the lonely mental problems. No one can save me from suffering but if I live through all this and am not a mental wreck perhaps I may be a more serviceable woman. I will certainly be kinder. My love to Mrs. Wilson. This is the only letter I have written since my mothers death. I hardly know why I have written so much except that you are among my dearest & I love to talk to you   Faithfully   Edith Gittings Reid

ALS (WP, DLC).

To Edith Gittings Reid

My dear, dear Friend,   Princeton, 17 Nov., 1901

How I wish I knew how to give you some proof of my appreciation of your letter about your dear mother! It has moved me more deeply than I know how to say. Certainly it was founded on a true instinct. My little note prompted it because, if ever a letter was, it was the expression of sympathy as direct and as profound as ever one friend felt for another whom he loved.

All that you say of your mother is so true,—it is the heart of your sorrow! It is as true as what you say of yourself is heartbreaking! And yet I hope,—I earnestly believe, that what is in store for you is, not despair or any breakdown, but the great strengthening, which you yourself even now dimly foresee. The very fact that that life from which you seem suddenly cut off *was* complete in all that can touch either character or person with beauty makes it more completely your ideal possession,—an image by the light and inspiration and confidence of which to live. What I love in you, what makes your friendship an inestimable pleasure, is your poise, your sanity, your look beneath the surface, no less than your delight in playing with moods and subjects in such a way as more perfectly to light them up. You make genuineness seem so natural, and so obviously the best thing in character and intercourse, and talk so perfect a means of the close friendship which is of the mind as well as of the heart;—your play is so upon the matter and not upon the person (for all it sometimes looks the other way), that no one can doubt where you got what you have only to perfect to carry on the true tradition of the beautiful life from which yours came.

I don't know how to say these things, but I would rather blunder than not try to say in *some* fashion, what is the only conceivable comfort in such a case, that death need not break this beautiful tradition, and that there is a way in which the old communion may be kept perpetually.

I know that this will not sound mystical to you. Certainly such things are to me as tangible as any reality. I know that I could not frame my own life if I lived by no model of actual human lives that have touched me and become part of mine; if there were upon me no compulsion of spiritual breeding, no near constraint of emulation.

Forgive me if I hurt you more than I help you by such half-expressed thoughts. I never before tried to put them into words. But I believe so thoroughly in you, and I accept so entirely all that your letter says of the mystery and the unspeakable tragedy of your loss that I could not rest until I had at least tried to think it out with you. I cannot say how I am touched that you should have found it some relief to talk to me of so sacred a thing.

Faithfully Yours,   Woodrow Wilson

ALS (WC, NjP).

From Edith Gittings Reid

My dear Mr. Wilson   [Baltimore, c. Nov. 19, 1901]

Your letter meant more to me than I can at all tell you.

I hate to have given you pain. Suffer I must but I should be silent, and indeed I have been to everyone but yourself. Patience, endurance, courage, self control—I must have—& will. One thing is perfectly clear to me. No one is justified in making the people around them suffer if it can be prevented.

And so let me tell you of the things that are giving me interest —Harry[1] & his glacial work which is growing into a dignified serious form and will mean when he puts it down a little permanent contribution to knowledge—the children & their possibilities—you & your work which means something that will endure and is altogether wonderful to me. But if any of you whom I have mentioned should have a finger ache I should I imagine think the work of little consequence. So first of all keep well. Please give my love to Mrs. Wilson and say to her that though I can speak to no one as I speak to you it is no slight tribute to her that such is the case. Do not be anxious about me. The long days & nights of pain will bring me into submission & already have brought to me a sympathy with the suffering world and the many phases that sorrow takes that was quite beyond me a few months ago. I thank God for my friends, and remember, though I am trying to talk bravely, I always need your help.

Faithfully yours   Edith G. Reid

ALS (WP, DLC).

[1] Her husband, Harry Fielding Reid, Professor of Geological Physics at the Johns Hopkins.

From Charles White Merrill

Dear Mr. Wilson: Indianapolis, Indiana   November 20—1901.

The Board of Directors of the Contemporary Club asks me to say to you that we shall hope to have you keep your engagement with us to address the Club April 25th as arranged. The subject "What it Means to be an American" appeals particularly to our members, and we shall look forward with pleasure to having you address us on that subject.[1]

Will you kindly advise us if this arrangement is entirely satisfactory to you? We remain

Very truly yours,   THE CONTEMPORARY CLUB
Chas W Merrill   Secretary

TLS (WP, DLC).
[1] A news report of this address is printed at April 26, 1902.

Notes for a Talk to the St. Louis Alumni

St. Louis, 21 Nov., '01

Stage of transition, of course, akin to that thr. wh. the country is passing.

Ideals difficult to maintain without constant recurrence to constituents
  Alumni trustees[1]

Growth and *Reorganization* require *Statesmanship* as well as ideals
  Bagehot's definition

The small college and the large
  Sometimes envy Prex. of small college
  Only substitute in larger inst. a dominating ideal,—*personified.*
  College men now public men

Present trend, Princeton.—Coördination.
  Choice of groups of studies, rather than of individual studies[2]

WWhw MS. (WP, DLC).
[1] The subject of direct alumni representation on the Board of Trustees of Princeton University had come up periodically since the presidency of James McCosh. However, the matter seemed to acquire a new urgency in the late 1890's. Most of the members of the co-optative Board of Trustees were alumni of the university, but large numbers of alumni began to feel and say that they should play a direct role in the selection of at least a portion of the board.
  On June 12, 1899, the Princeton Club of New York submitted to the trustees a proposal providing that, at every third vacancy on the board, the alumni should nominate three men from whom the trustees would then select one alumni trustee. There were obvious difficulties inherent in this plan, and the trustees took no action on it. In March of 1900, the Princeton Club of St. Louis, under the leadership of its president, John David Davis '72, called for a meeting of representatives of the Princeton alumni associations west of the Allegheny Mountains to form a Western Association of Princeton Clubs. In its first issue, of April 7, 1900, the *Princeton Alumni Weekly* endorsed this move and suggested that some form of alumni representation on the Board of Trustees should be part of the new association's first order of business. A plan was hammered out at the first meeting of the Western Association of Alumni Clubs on April 27, 1900. It provided for the enlargement of the board by adding five trustees to be elected by direct vote of the alumni. At the first election, five trustees would be chosen to serve one, two, three, four, and five years, respectively, as drawn by lot after

election. Each year thereafter, one alumni trustee would be elected to serve a five-year term. Alumni trustees were to be eligible for re-election. Only graduates of ten years' standing were to be eligible candidates, but all former students could serve as electors upon enrollment of their names and payment of an annual fee of one dollar to cover expenses. The plan also provided for the mode of nomination and election.

At their meeting on June 11, 1900, the trustees approved the "principle" of alumni representation and referred the St. Louis plan to a special committee composed of John Aikman Stewart, James W. Alexander '60, Simon J. McPherson '74, James Bayard Henry '76, and Moses Taylor Pyne '77, chairman. Reporting to the board on October 19, 1900, this committee presented a plan essentially the same as the St. Louis proposal except for stipulating that only graduates of the university should be entitled to vote. At their meeting on December 13, 1900, the trustees changed this provision to permit only graduates of three years' standing to participate in the elections. The trustees accepted the modified plan on October 19, and arrangements were made to submit a bill to the New Jersey legislature to amend the university's charter to implement the new arrangement. The legislature passed the enabling legislation in February 1901. A total of ten candidates were nominated by the first deadline of May 1, 1901, and the first alumni trustees elected were John Lambert Cadwalader '56 of New York, John D. Davis '72 of St. Louis, David Benton Jones '76 of Chicago, James Laughlin, Jr., '68 of Pittsburgh, and Alexander Van Rensselaer '71 of Philadelphia.

The above discussion is based on the "Minutes of the Trustees of Princeton University, Dec. 1898-Mar. 1901" (bound minute book, UA, NjP), June 12, 1899, Oct. 20, 1899, March 8, 1900, June 11, 1900, Oct. 19, 1900, and Dec. 13, 1900, and the *Princeton Alumni Weekly*, 1: April 7, 1900, pp. 7-8; May 5, 1900, p. 69; Sept. 29, 1900, pp. 176-77; Oct. 27, 1900, pp. 243-44, 246-48; Feb. 16, 1901, p. 487; Feb. 23, 1901, pp. 507-508, 512-16; May 4, 1901, p. 689; May 11, 1901, pp. 707-708; and June 15, 1901, pp. 795-96.

[2] Wilson here referred to a matter that had long been under discussion by the Princeton faculty.

At the meeting of the Academic Faculty of Princeton University on November 7, 1900, a resolution was presented, by whom the minutes do not say, for the appointment of a committee "to consider the condition of the scholarship of the Academic Department." It was made the first order of business for the next meeting. On November 21, 1900, the resolution was considered, amended, and adopted as follows: "Resolved, That a Committee be appointed to consider the question of the scholarship of the Academic Department, and to propose such measures as seem suited to promote a high standard thereof, including any changes which seem advisable in the regulations concerning conditions." The committee, appointed during the same meeting, consisted of President Patton, *ex officio*, William F. Magie, chairman, Dean Winans, Paul van Dyke, Henry B. Fine, Andrew F. West, Jesse Benedict Carter, Edmund Yard Robbins, and Alexander T. Ormond. At a meeting on January 16, 1901, John H. Westcott was added to the membership.

Although it appears that President Patton was never very enthusiastic about the committee or its work, it was he who gave the best indication that we have of what lay behind its appointment. Undergraduate work, he said in his report to the Board of Trustees on December 13, 1900, was going on in a fairly satisfactory manner. However, he continued, "There is a feeling in the Faculty that the Elective System which controls the third and fourth years of the University curriculum is working badly in regard to the students who constitute the lower half of the class in those years. Far too little work is done, and there is a very general disposition among the students to defer study in the departments where instruction is given by lecture, and cram for examinations toward the end of the term. It should be said, however, that while this state of things exists, it is also true that the better men in the Junior and Senior years are doing more and better work than the men in those years have ever done before. This is freely admitted by those in the Faculty who are most alive to the evil under notice." The evil, Patton said, was probably incurable and was the inevitable result of the elective system that was in vogue in all the leading universities of the country. However, the situation might be remedied by so restricting the choice of electives as to secure a unified course of study for men who were disposed to do serious intellectual work. "And it may be necessary," he went on, "to go so far as to confine the privilege of election to very narrow limits for those who reveal their unfitness for making good use of it, by their lack of interest in study." The whole question regarding the condition of scholarship in the undergraduate department, he concluded, was in the hands of a strong committee and was being investigated with great thoroughness.

As Patton's remarks make clear, his attitude toward the committee and the problem to which it was addressing itself was ambiguous at best. Henry W. Bragdon, in his *Woodrow Wilson: The Academic Years* (Cambridge, Mass., 1967), pp. 274-75, 459, writes that the formation of the faculty committee represented a "rebellion" by a "cabal" of faculty members led by Magie and West against Patton's slack administration, and that Patton succeeded in preventing any real reform through the spring of 1901. Bragdon's account, which is based largely on interviews and reminiscences of faculty members many years after the event, also mentions in passing that Wilson took no part in the faculty discussions.

The preliminary report presented by the committee to the Academic Faculty on June 5, 1901, lends some support to the view that Patton had succeeded in delaying action up to that point. Although the committee had met some twenty times, its preliminary report covered only the relatively innocuous topics of conditions, excuses from university exercises on Sundays, excessive use of medical excuses for absence from class, and absence from examinations.

The Academic Faculty's committee on scholarship continued to function during the autumn of 1901. On October 23, 1901, the Faculty of the School of Science resolved "that the President be requested to appoint a Committee of this Faculty to confer with the Committee on Scholarship of the Academic Faculty." Acting with characteristic deliberate speed, Patton did not appoint the School of Science committee until December 11, 1901, when he named Henry B. Cornwall, Charles G. Rockwood, Fred Neher, Herbert S. S. Smith, and Walter M. Rankin.

What turned out to be the final report of the combined "University Committee on Scholarship" was presented to the University Faculty at its meeting on March 26, 1902. For the debates which took place on that and subsequent dates, as well as the University Faculty's action on the report, see the extracts from the University Faculty Minutes printed at March 26 and April 9, 11, 14, and 16, 1902. The report of the committee is included as part of the extract printed at April 16.

The above discussion is based upon "Minutes of the Academic Faculty of Princeton University, 1898-1904" (bound minute book, UA, NjP), Nov. 7 and 21, 1900, and June 5, 1901; "Minutes of the School of Science Faculty, 1898-1904, Princeton University" (bound minute book, UA, NjP), Oct. 23 and Dec. 11, 1901; "Minutes of the Trustees of Princeton University, Dec. 1898-Mar. 1901" (bound minute book, UA, NjP), Dec. 13, 1900; and the Minutes of the University Faculty cited above.

A News Report of a Talk to the Princeton Alumni of St. Louis

[Nov. 22, 1901]

HISTORIAN WOODROW WILSON SPEAKS
AT SMOKER IN HIS HONOR.

Historian Woodrow Wilson, who is one of the leading professors of Princeton University, talked entertainingly Thursday night to about forty Princeton alumni at the smoker given in his honor at the University Club.

Prof. Wilson discussed the attitude of the university toward the activities of the present day, especially national activities. He thought that the university should look back to the past and while fitting young men for useful work should especially build up characters and instill into them the best ideas of the part [past] and the principles which have guided men to the highest achievements.

... Mr. Lionberger,[1] Mr. John D. Davis and others made brief addresses and with the songs of Princeton the evening passed pleasantly.

Printed in the *St. Louis Post-Dispatch*, Nov. 22, 1901; one editorial heading omitted.
  [1] Isaac Henry Lionberger '75, lawyer of St. Louis.

To Noah Cornwell Rogers[1]

My dear Mr. Rogers,   Princeton, New Jersey 24 Nov., 1901

Mrs. Wilson and I greatly appreciate your kind invitation to be guests of honour at the Annual Dinner of the Presbyterian Union on the evening of December second, and are really deeply disappointed that we are obliged to decline.

Literally all of my college work in the class-room comes on Mondays and Tuesdays, and I cannot meet an engagement at a distance on either of those evenings without a positive and serious neglect of duty.

Pray express to the Executive Committee of the Union our warm thanks and deep regrets. I am sure that they will deem me no worse Presbyterian for preferring my university duties to so tempting a pleasure.

With much regard,
                    Sincerely Yours,   Woodrow Wilson

ALS (in possession of Henry Bartholomew Cox).
  [1] New York lawyer, president of the Presbyterian Union of New York, an organization composed largely of laymen that met monthly for literary and religious discussions.

An Announcement of a Lecture in Greenville, South Carolina

[Nov. 29, 1901]

DR. WILSON TONIGHT.
A Princeton Professor Lectures
at the Grand Opera House.

The Lyceum has been fortunate in securing Dr. Woodrow Wilson who lectures in the Grand opera house this evening.

Dr. Wilson visits only two places in the State on this tour— Greenville and Spartanburg. He lectured before the Wofford College Lyceum last night[1] and arrives here this morning on the 11 o'clock train from Spartanburg.

This talented man ought to be given a hearty reception by the Greenville people. The opera house should be filled.

Tickets are on sale at Lewis & Hartzog's. General admission 50 cents, reserved seats 75 cents, students of the various schools and colleges will be given a special rate of 35 cents. Members of the Lyceum are again cautioned against leaving their membership cards at home.

Printed in the *Greenville*, S.C., *News*, Nov. 29, 1901.
  [1] No Spartanburg newspaper or Wofford College publication is extant for this period.

A Report of a Public Lecture

[Nov. 30, 1901]

LOGICAL AND INSTRUCTIVE.

It was a large audience that heard the lecture last night at the Grand opera house by Dr. Woodrow Wilson.

The subject was "Patriotism" and the speaker handled it remarkably well, presenting a strong, clear, logical and instructive address. Dr. Wilson is an eloquent speaker and held the closest attention of his hearers during the entire time of his address which was without doubt one of the best delivered in this city in some time.

Dr. Wilson's address was given under the auspices of the Greenville Lyceum Association, each member of which was thoroughly pleased with the evening's entertainment. The association is to be congratulated on having such a high class attraction as the lecture of Dr. Wilson last night.

Printed in the *Greenville*, S.C., *News*, Nov. 30, 1901.

To Rebecca Caroline Webb Hoyt[1]

My dear Mrs. Hoyt,   Princeton, New Jersey, 3 December, 1901

I was a very tired man when I reached home early Sunday morning, but a very deeply contented one. Added to the pleasure of getting home again was the delightful, abiding sense of all the kindness I had met with on my visit to you,—your and Colonel Hoyt's[2] natural, unstinted, and altogether delightful hospitality; the new friendships made; the cordial open-heartedness of all whom I had had the good fortune to meet and exchange words with. I have to thank you for one of the most enjoyable trips that I remember.

Mrs. Wilson joins me in all cordial messages to her cousins,[1] her little glimpse of whom she remembers with lively pleasure.[3]

With warm regard,

Sincerely Yours,   Woodrow Wilson

ALS (WP, DLC).

[1] Wife of James Alfred Hoyt, identified in the next note.

[2] James Alfred Hoyt, born Oct. 11, 1837, son of Jane Johnson Hoyt and Jonathan Perkins Hoyt, a younger brother of Mrs. Wilson's grandfather, the Rev. Nathan Hoyt. A printer and newspaper editor in South Carolina before the Civil War, James Alfred Hoyt rose from the rank of private to colonel in the Confederate Army. Returning to newspaper work after the war, he settled in Greenville, S.C., in 1879 as editor of the *Baptist Courier* and later of the Greenville *Mountaineer*. Active in politics, he was chairman of the Democratic state committee in 1890 and ran unsuccessfully for governor on the Prohibition ticket in 1900. He was also president of the South Carolina Baptist Convention, 1885-94, and a vice president of the Southern Baptist Convention. He died in Greenville on May 27, 1904. Mrs. Wilson's first cousin once removed, Hoyt is incorrectly identified in Volume 7 as the son of Henry Francis Hoyt and Mrs. Wilson's first cousin.

[3] When she visited them in Greenville on April 22, 1892. See EAW to WW, April 20, 21, and 22, 1892, Vol. 7.

From the Minutes of the Princeton University Faculty

5 5 P.M., Wednesday, December 4th, 1901.

. . . The former Committee, Professors Brackett, Woodrow Wilson and Fine, to appear before and confer with the Trustees if required, was continued.[1]

[1] They did not confer with the trustees at their meeting in December 1901.

To Charles Andrew Talcott

My dear Charlie,   Princeton, 4 Dec., 1901

Hurrah for the reunion at Isham's on the 13th![1] You *must* be there, we have all set our hearts on having you. We are getting to be mature men, my dear fellow, more and more deeply absorbed in affairs, and if we do not do these things how shall we keep close together? And the boys especially want *you*. There is universal rejoicing among them that you have been so signally honoured in Republican Utica,[2] and they all want a grip of your hand,—especially the inner group—all of whom, I think, are to be there—who most love you, of whom, and chief among whom, is

Yours most affectionately,   Woodrow Wilson

ALS (WC, NjP).

[1] That is, the annual Isham dinner in New York.

[2] Talcott, a Democrat, had just been elected Mayor of Utica, N.Y.

To Robert Bridges

My dear Bobby,   Princeton, 4 Dec., 1901

I've written to Talcott in my most persuasive vein, and will stay with you on the night of the 13th with the greatest pleasure. It promises to be an affair to warm the cockles of the heart!

Affectionately Yours,   Woodrow Wilson

ALS (Meyer Coll., DLC).

From Harper and Brothers

Dear Professor: New York City Dec. 5, 1901.

As the time is drawing near when we shall begin the setting of your work for book-form, the idea has occurred to me that, as it is to be put on the market through subscription channels, "Colonies and Nation," as a title, seems to be hardly complete and comprehensive enough to aid our people on their canvass. Do you think you could work in the word "history" in some way? Say, "The History of Colonies and Nation," or possibly, "The History of the United States Colonies and Nation," which would tell the story of the work perfectly, and would roll off the tongues of our travelling men most easily and glibly.

We would ask, without being importunate, if you can now let us know how soon we may expect the complete MS and list of illustrations for Volume I.? We are very desirous of getting at the work at the earliest possible moment. Can you give us a date when you will be able to send it?

Sincerely yours,   Harper & Brothers.

ALS (WP, DLC).

To Mrs. Alexander F. Jameson[1]

My dear Mrs. Jameson,   Princeton, 17 Dec., 1901

I very much appreciate the wish of the ladies of the Woman's Branch of the New Jersey Historical Society to have me address them, and the kind note in which you convey their invitation; but I am sorry to say that I have made as many engagements for this academic year as I dare make,—many more than I should have made, and I simply have no choice but to decline.

Pray convey to the Committee of the Branch my very warm

thanks for the compliment they have paid me, and my very sincere regret that I cannot accept.

With much regard, both to Mr. Jameson and yourself, from us both,   Sincerely Yours,   Woodrow Wilson

ALS (NjHi).
[1] It has been impossible to identify Mrs. Jameson other than that she lived in Lawrenceville, N.J., and became a life member of the New Jersey Historical Society in May 1901.

From the Minutes of the Princeton University Faculty

4 10′ P.M., Wednesday, Dec. 18, 1901

The Faculty met in compliance with the following call of the President:

"Princeton, December 14, 1901.

A special meeting of the University Faculty to receive and consider The Report of the Committee on the Graduate S[c]hool in regard to Standards of Graduate Work will be held at four o'clock Wednesday afternoon, December eighteenth,

Francis L. Patton, President."

The Dean presided in the absence of the President through illness.

The Committee presented its Report, dated December 9. 1901, and it was explained by the Dean of the Graduate School. It was then discussed, certain amendments were made and the first Six Sections were adopted.

The Faculty then adjourned to meet at 4 P.M., Wednesday, January 8th, 1902, for the further consideration of the Report[1] and other business.

[1] There was subsequent discussion of this report, which appears in its approved form in the University Faculty Minutes printed at Jan. 15, 1902.

From Harper and Brothers

Dear Professor: New York City Dec. 24. 1901.

We have carefully considered your letter of the 7th inst. and in the matter of the title we have thought that "A History of the American People," might appeal to you favorably as a general title to the work. How does it strike you?

We note with pleasure that we are to have the complete MSS. of Volumes I and II, next week, and on its receipt we shall at once put it in hand and submit the specimen pages to you before proceeding with the work.

Sincerely yours,   Harper & Brothers.

ALS (WP, DLC).

To Varnum Lansing Collins

[Princeton, N.J., c. Dec. 25, 1901]

With the compliments of Woodrow Wilson, who is to contribute a so-called "oration" to the said literary exercises, but who is thought by the Committee in charge to have only *male* friends and has been sent only stage tickets.

AL (V. L. Collins Scrapbooks, Vol. I, UA, NjP). Enc.: one stage ticket to the "Literary Exercises" of the 125th Anniversary of the Battle of Trenton, Taylor Opera House, Trenton, N.J., Dec. 26, 1901, 3 P.M.

A Commemorative Address[1]

[[Dec. 26, 1901]]

THE IDEALS OF AMERICA.

We do not think or speak of the War for Independence as if we were aged men who, amidst alien scenes of change, comfort themselves with talk of great things done in days long gone by, the like of which they may never hope to see again. The spirit of the old days is not dead. If it were, who amongst us would care for its memory and distant, ghostly voice? It is the distinguishing mark, nay the very principle of life in a nation alive and quick in every fibre, as ours is, that all its days are great days,—are to its thought single and of a piece. Its past it feels to have been but the prelude and earnest of its present. It is from its memories of days old and new that it gets its sense of identity, takes its spirit of action, assures itself of its power and its capacity, and knows its place in the world. Old colony days, and those sudden days of revolution when debate turned to action and heady winds as if of destiny blew with mighty breath the long continent through, were our own days, the days of our childhood and our headstrong youth. We have not forgotten. Our memories make no effort to recall the time. The battle of Trenton is as real to us as the battle of San Juan hill.

---

[1] Delivered at the Literary Exercises commemorating the 125th anniversary of the Battle of Trenton at the Taylor Opera House in Trenton, N.J., at 3 P.M. on December 26, 1901. There is a WWsh draft of "Ideals of America," with the composition date "21 Dec. 1901," in WP, DLC. [This and following notes by the Eds.]

We remember the chill, and the ardor too, of that gray morning when we came upon the startled outposts of the town, the driving sleet beating at our backs; the cries and hurrying of men in the street, the confused muster at our front, the sweeping fire of our guns and the rush of our men, Sullivan coming up by the road from the river, Washington at the north, where the road to Princeton is; the showy Hessian colonel shot from his horse amidst his bewildered men; the surrender; the unceasing storm. And then the anxious days that followed: the recrossing of the icy river before even we had rested; the troop of surly prisoners to be cared for and sent forward to Philadelphia; the enemy all the while to be thought of, and the way to use our advantage.

How much it meant a third time to cross the river, and wait here in the town for the regiments Sir William Howe should send against us! How sharp and clear the night was when we gave Cornwallis the slip and took the silent, frosty road to Allentown and Princeton! Those eighteen miles between bedtime and morning are not easily forgot, nor that sharp brush with the redcoats at Princeton: the moving fight upon the sloping hillside, the cannon planted in the streets, the gray old building where the last rally was made,—and then the road to Brunswick, Cornwallis at our heels!

How the face of things was changed in those brief days! There had been despair till then. It was but a few short weeks since the men of the Jersey towns and farms had seen us driven south across the river like fugitives; now we came back an army again, the Hessians who had but the other day harried and despoiled that countryside beaten and scattered before us, and they knew not whether to believe their eyes or not. As we pushed forward to the heights at Morristown we drew in the British lines behind us, and New Jersey was free of the redcoats again. The Revolution had had its turning point. It was easy then to believe that General Washington could hold his own against any adversary in that terrible game of war. A new heart was in everything!

And yet what differences of opinion there were, and how hot and emphatic every turn of the war made them among men who really spoke their minds and dissembled nothing! It was but six months since the Congress had ventured its Declaration of Independence, and the brave words of that defiance halted on many lips that read them. There were men enough and to spare who would not speak them at all; who deemed the whole thing madness and deep folly, and even black treason. Men whose names all the colonies knew held off and would take no part in armed resistance to the ancient crown whose immemorial sovereignty kept a great empire together. Men of substance at the ports of trade were almost all against the Revolution; and where men of means and principle led, base men who played for their own interest were sure to follow. Every movement of the patriotic leaders was spied upon and betrayed; everywhere the army moved there were men of the very countryside it occupied to be kept close watch against.

Those were indeed "times that tried men's souls"! It was no light matter to put the feeling as of a nation into those scattered settlements: to bring the high-spirited planters of the Carolinas, who thought for themselves, or their humble neighbors on the upland farms, who ordered their lives as they pleased, to the same principles and point of view that the leaders of Virginia and Massachusetts professed and occupied,—the point of view from which everything wore so obvious an aspect of hopeful revolt, where men planned the war at the north. There were great families at Philadelphia and in Boston itself who were as hard to win, and plain men without number in New York and the Jerseys who would not come for the beckoning. Opinion was always making and to be made, and the campaign of mind was as hard as that of arms.

To think of those days of doubt and stress, of the swaying of opinion this way and that, of counsels distracted and plans to be made anew at every turn of the arduous business, takes one's thoughts forward to those other days, as full of doubt, when the war had at last been fought out and a government was to be made. No doubt that crisis was the greatest of all. Opinion will form for a war, in the face of manifest provocation and of precious rights called in question. But the making of a government is another matter. And the government to be made then was to take the place of the government cast off: there was the rub. It was difficult to want any common government at all after fighting to be quit of restraint and overlordship altogether; and it went infinitely hard to be obliged to make it strong, with a right to command and a power to rule. Then it was that we knew that even the long war, with its bitter training of the thoughts and its hard discipline of union, had not made a nation, but only freed a group of colonies. The debt is the more incalculable which we owe to the little band of sagacious men who labored the summer through, in that far year 1787, to give us a constitution that those heady little commonwealths could be persuaded to accept, and which should yet be a framework within which the real powers of a nation might grow in the fullness of time, and gather head with the growth of a mighty people.

They gave us but the outline, the formula, the broad and general programme of our life, and left us to fill it in with such rich store of achievement and sober experience as we should be able to gather in the days to come. Not battles or any stirring scene of days of action, but the slow processes by which we grew and made our thought and formed our purpose in quiet days of peace, are what we find it hard to make real to our minds again, now that we are mature and have fared far upon the road. Our life is so broad and various now, and was so simple then; the thoughts of those first days seem crude to us now and unreal. We smile upon the simple dreams of our youth a bit incredulously, and seem cut off from them by a great space. And yet it was by those dreams we were formed. The lineage of our thoughts is unbroken. The nation that was making then was the nation which yesterday intervened in the affairs of Cuba, and to-day troubles the trade and the diplomacy of the world.

It was clear to us even then, in those first days when we were at the outset of our life, with what spirit and mission we had come into the world. Clear-sighted men over sea saw it too, whose eyes were not holden by passion or dimmed by looking steadfastly only upon things near at hand. We shall not forget those deathless passages of great speech, compact of music and high sense, in which Edmund Burke justified us and gave us out of his riches our philosophy of right action in affairs of state. Chatham rejoiced that we had resisted. Fox clapped his hands when he heard that Cornwallis had been trapped and taken at Yorktown. Dull men without vision, small men who stood upon no place of elevation in their thoughts, once cried treason against these men,—though no man dared speak such a taunt to the passionate Chatham's face; but now all men speak as Fox spoke, and our Washington is become one of the heroes of the English race. What did it mean that the greatest Englishmen should thus cheer us to revolt at the very moment of our rebellion? What is it that has brought us at last the verdict of the world?

It means that in our stroke for independence we struck a blow for all the world. Some men saw it then; all men see it now. The very generation of Englishmen who stood against us in that day of our struggling birth lived to see the liberating light of that day shine about their own path before they made an end and were gone. They had deep reason before their own day was out to know what it was that Burke had meant when he said, "We cannot falsify the pedigree of this fierce people, and persuade them that they are not sprung from a nation in whose veins the blood of freedom circulates. The language in which they would hear you tell them this tale would detect the imposition, your speech would betray you. An Englishman is the unfittest person on earth to argue another Englishman into slavery." . . . "For, in order to prove that the Americans have no right to their liberties, we are every day endeavoring to subvert the maxims which preserve the whole spirit of our own. To prove that the Americans ought not to be free, we are obliged to depreciate the value of freedom itself; and we never seem to gain a paltry advantage over them in debate, without attacking some of those principles, or deriding some of those feelings, for which our ancestors have shed their blood."[2]

It turned out that the long struggle in America had been the first act in the drama whose end and culmination should be the final establishment of constitutional government for England and for English communities everywhere. It is easy now, at this quiet distance, for the closeted student to be puzzled how to set up the legal case of the colonists against the authority of Parliament. It is possible now to respect the scruples of the better loyalists, and even to give all honor to the sober ardor of self-sacrifice with which they stood four-square against the Revolution. We no longer challenge their right. Neither do we search out the motives of the mass of common men who acted upon the one side or the other. Like men in all ages and at every crisis of affairs, they acted each according to his sentiment, his fear, his interest, or his lust. We ask, rather, why did the noble gentlemen to whom it fell to lead America seek great action and embark all their honor in such a cause? What was it they fought for?

A lawyer is puzzled to frame the answer; but no statesman need be. "If I were sure," said Burke, "that the colonists had, at their leaving this country, sealed a regular compact of servitude, that they had solemnly abjured all the rights of citizens, that they had made a vow to renounce all ideas of liberty for them and their posterity to all generations, yet I should hold myself obliged to conform to the temper I found universally prevalent in my own day, and to govern two millions of men, impatient of servitude, on the principles of freedom. I am not determining a point of law; . . . the general character and situation of a people must determine what sort of government is fit for them."[3] It was no abstract point of governmental theory the leaders of the colonies took the field to expound. Washington, Henry, Adams, Hancock, Franklin, Morris, Boudinot, Livingston, Rutledge, Pinckney,—

2 Edmund Burke, "Speech on Moving His Resolutions for Conciliation with the Colonies, March 22, 1775," in *The Works of the Right Honorable Edmund Burke*, 5th edn. (12 vols., Boston, 1877), II, 130, 133.
3 *ibid.*, p. 141.

these were men of affairs, who thought less of books than of principles of action. They fought for the plain right of self-government, which any man could understand. The government over sea had broken faith with them,—not the faith of law, but the faith that is in precedents and ancient understandings, though they be tacit and nowhere spoken in any charter. Hitherto the colonies had been let live their own lives according to their own genius, and vote their own supplies to the crown as if their assemblies were so many parliaments. Now, of a sudden, the Parliament in England was to thrust their assemblies aside and itself lay their taxes. Here was too new a thing. Government without precedent was government without license or limit. It was government by innovation, not government by agreement. Old ways were the only ways acceptable to English feet. The revolutionists stood for no revolution at all, but for the maintenance of accepted practices, for the inviolable understandings of precedent,—in brief, for *constitutional government.*

That sinister change which filled the air of America with storm darkened the skies of England too. Not in America only did George, the king, and his counselors make light of and willfully set aside the ancient understandings which were the very stuff of liberty in English eyes. That unrepresentative Parliament, full of place-men, which had taxed America, contained majorities which the king could bestow at his will upon this minister or that; and the men who set America by the ears came or went from their places at his bidding. It was he, not the Parliament, that made and unmade ministries. Behind the nominal ministers of the crown stood men whom Parliament did not deal with, and the nation did not see who were the king's favorites, and therefore the actual rulers of England. There was here the real revolution. America, with her sensitive make-up, her assemblies that were the real representatives of her people, had but felt sooner than the mass of Englishmen at home the unhappy change of air which seemed about to corrupt the constitution itself. Burke felt it in England, and Fox, and every man whose thoughts looked soberly forth upon the signs of the times. And presently, when the American war was over, the nation itself began to see what light the notable thing done in America shed upon its own affairs. The king was to be grappled with at home, the Parliament was to be freed from his power, and the ministers who ruled England were to be made the real servants of the people. Constitutional government was to be made a reality again. We had begun the work of freeing England when we completed the work of freeing ourselves.

The great contest which followed over sea, and which was nothing less than the capital and last process of making and confirming the constitution of England, kept covert beneath the surface of affairs while the wars of the French Revolution swept the world. Not until 1832 was representation in Parliament at last reformed, and the Commons made a veritable instrument of the nation's will. Days of revolution, when ancient kingdoms seemed tottering to their fall, were no days in which to be tinkering the constitution of old England. Her statesmen grew slow and circumspect and moved in all things with infinite prudence, and even with a novel timidity. But when the times fell quiet again, opinion, gathering head for a generation, moved forward at last to its object; and government was once more by consent in England. The Parliament spoke the real mind of the nation, and the leaders whom the Commons approved were of necessity also the ministers of the crown. Men could then look back and see that America had given England the shock, and the crown the opportune defeat, which had awakened her to save her constitution from corruption.

Meanwhile, what of America herself? How had she used the independence she had demanded and won? For a little while she had found it a grievous thing to be free, with no common power set over her to hold her to a settled course of life which should give her energy and bring her peace and honor and increase of wealth. Even when the convention at Philadelphia had given her the admirable framework of a definite constitution, she found it infinitely hard to hit upon a common way of progress under a mere printed law which had no sanction of custom or affection, which no ease of old habit sustained, and no familiar light of old tradition made plain to follow. This new law had yet to be filled with its meanings, had yet to be given its texture of life. Our whole history, from that day of our youth to this day of our glad maturity, has been filled with the process.

It took the war of 1812 to give us spirit and full consciousness and pride of station as a nation. That was the real war of independence for our political parties. It was then we cut our parties and our passions loose from politics over sea, and set ourselves to make a career which should be indeed our own. That accomplished, and our weak youth turned to callow manhood, we stretched our hand forth again to the west, set forth with a new zest and energy upon the western rivers and the rough trails that led across the mountains and down to the waters of the Mississippi. There lay a continent to be possessed. In the very day of first union Virginia and her sister states had ceded to the common government all the great stretches of western land that lay between the mountains and that mighty river into which all the western waters gathered head. While we were yet weak and struggling for our place among the nations, Mr. Jefferson had added the vast bulk of Louisiana, beyond the river, whose boundaries no man certainly knew. All the great spaces of the continent from Canada round about by the great Rockies to the warm waters of the southern Gulf lay open to the feet of our young men. The forests rang with their noisy march. What seemed a new race deployed into those broad valleys and out upon those long, unending plains which were the common domain, where no man knew any government but the government of the whole people. That was to be the real making of the nation.

There sprang up the lusty states which now, in these days of our full stature, outnumber almost threefold the thirteen commonwealths which formed the Union. Their growth set the pace of our life; forced the slavery question to a final issue; gave us the civil war with its stupendous upheaval and its resettlement of the very foundations of the government; spread our strength from sea to sea; created us a free and mighty people, whose destinies daunt the imagination of the Old World looking on. That increase, that endless accretion, that rolling, resistless tide, incalculable in its strength, infinite in its variety, has made us what we are; has put the resources of a huge continent at our disposal; has provoked us to invention and given us mighty captains of industry. This great pressure of a people moving always to new frontiers, in search of new lands, new power, the full freedom of a virgin world, has ruled our course and formed our policies like a Fate. It gave us, not Louisiana alone, but Florida also. It forced war with Mexico upon us, and gave us the coasts of the Pacific. It swept Texas into the Union. It made far Alaska a territory of the United States. Who shall say where it will end?

The census takers of 1890 informed us, when their task was done, that they could no longer find any frontier upon this continent; that they must draw their maps as if the mighty process of settlement that had gone on, ceaseless, dramatic, the century through, were now ended and complete, the nation made from sea to sea. We had not pondered their report a single decade before we made new frontiers for ourselves beyond the seas, accounting the seven thousand miles of ocean that lie between us and the Philippine Islands no more than the three thousand which once lay between us and the coasts of the Pacific. No doubt there is here a great revolution in our lives. No war ever transformed us quite as the war with Spain transformed us. No previous years ever ran with so swift a change as the years since 1898. We have witnessed a new revolution. We have seen the transformation of America completed. That little group of states, which one hundred and twenty-five years ago cast the sovereignty of Britain off, is now grown into a mighty power. That little confederation has now massed and organized its energies. A confederacy is transformed into a nation. The battle of Trenton was not more significant than the battle of Manila. The nation that was one hundred and twenty-five years in the making has now stepped forth into the open arena of the world.

I ask you to stand with me at this new turning-point of our life, that we may look before and after, and judge ourselves alike in the light of that old battle fought here in these streets, and in the light of all the mighty processes of our history that have followed. We cannot too often give ourselves such challenge of self-examination. It will hearten, it will steady, it will moralize us to reassess our hopes, restate our ideals, and make manifest to ourselves again the principles and the purposes upon which we act. We are else without chart upon a novel voyage.

What are our thoughts now, as we look back from this altered age to the Revolution which to-day we celebrate? How do we think of its principles and of its example? Do they seem remote and of a time not our own, or do they still seem stuff of our thinking, principles near and intimate, and woven into the very texture of our institutions? What say we now of liberty and of self-government, its embodiment? What lessons have we read of it on our journey hither to this high point of outlook at the beginning of a new century? Do those old conceptions seem to us now an ideal modified, of altered face, and of a mien not shown in the simple days when the government was formed?

Of course forms have changed. The form of the Union itself is altered, to the model that was in Hamilton's thought rather than to that which Jefferson once held before us, adorned, transfigured, in words that led the mind captive. Our ways of life are profoundly changed since that dawn. The balance of the states against the Federal government, however it may strike us now as of capital convenience in the distribution of powers and the quick and various exercise of the energies of the people, no longer seems central to our conceptions of governmental structure, no longer seems of the essence of the people's liberty. We are no longer strenuous about the niceties of constitutional law; no longer dream that a written law shall save us, or that by ceremonial cleanliness we may lift our lives above corruption. But has the substance of things changed with us, also? Wherein now do we deem the life and very vital principle of self-government to lie? Where is that point of principle at which we should wish to make our stand and take again the final risk of revolution? What other crisis do we dream of that might bring in its train another battle of Trenton?

These are intensely practical questions. We fought but the other day to give Cuba self-government. It is a point of conscience with us that the Philippines shall have it, too, when our work there is done and they are ready. But when will our work there be done, and how shall we know when they are ready? How, when our hand is withdrawn from her capitals and she plays her game of destiny apart and for herself, shall we be sure that Cuba has this blessing of liberty and self-government, for which battles are justly fought and revolutions righteously set afoot? If we be apostles of liberty and of self-government, surely we know what they are, in their essence and without disguise of form, and shall not be deceived in the principles of their application by mere differences between this race and that. We have given pledges to the world and must redeem them as we can.

Some nice tests of theory are before us,—are even now at hand. There are those amongst us who have spoken of the Filipinos as standing where we stood when we were in the throes of that great war which was turned from fear to hope again in that battle here in the streets of Trenton which we are met to speak of, and who have called Aguinaldo, the winning, subtile youth now a prisoner in our hands at Manila, a second Washington. Have they, then, forgot that tragic contrast upon which the world gazed in the days when our Washington was President: on the one side of the sea, in America, peace, an ordered government, a people busy with the tasks of mart and home, a group of commonwealths bound together by strong cords of their own weaving, institutions sealed and confirmed by debate and the suffrages of free men, but not by the pouring out of blood in civil strife,—on the other, in France, a nation frenzied, distempered, seeking it knew not what,—a nation which poured its best blood out in a vain sacrifice, which cried of liberty and self-government until the heavens rang and yet ran straight and swift to anarchy, to give itself at last, with an almost glad relief, to the masterful tyranny of a soldier? "I should suspend my congratulations on the new liberty of France," said Burke, the master who had known our liberty for what it was, and knew this set up in France to be spurious,—"I should suspend my congratulations on the new liberty of France until I was informed how it had been combined with government; with public force; with the discipline and obedience of armies; with the collection of an effective and well-distributed revenue; with morality and religion; with the solidity of property; with peace and order; with social and civil manners."[4] Has it not taken France a century to effect the combination; and are all men sure that she has found it even now? And yet were not these things combined with liberty amongst us from the very first?

How interesting a light shines upon the matter of our thought out of that sentence of Burke's! How liberty had been combined with government! Is there here a difficulty, then? Are the two things not kindly disposed toward one another? Does it require any nice art and adjustment to unite and reconcile them? Is there here some cardinal test which those amiable persons have overlooked, who have dared to cheer the Filipino rebels on in their stubborn resistance to the very government they themselves live under and owe fealty to? Think of Washington's passion for order, for authority, for some righteous public force which should teach individuals their place under government, for the solidity of property, for morality and sober counsel. It was plain that he cared not a whit for liberty without these things to sustain and give it dignity. "You talk, my good sir," he exclaimed, writing to Henry Lee in Congress, "you talk of employing influence to appease the present tumults in Massachusetts. I know not where that influence is to be found, or, if attainable, that it would be a proper remedy for the disorders. *Influence* is no *government*. Let us have one by which our lives, liberties, and properties will be secured, or let us know the worst at once."[5] In brief, the fact is this, that liberty is the privilege of maturity, of self-control, of self-mastery and a thoughtful care for righteous dealings,—that some peoples may have it, therefore, and others may not.

We look back to the great men who made our government as to a generation, not of revolutionists, but of statesmen. They fought, not to pull down, but to preserve,—not for some fair and far-off thing they wished for, but for a familiar thing they had and meant to keep. Ask any candid student of the history of English liberty, and he will tell you that these men were of the lineage of Pym and Hampden, of Pitt and Fox; that they were men who consecrated their lives to the preservation intact of what had been wrought out in blood and sweat by the countless generations of sturdy freemen who had gone before them.

Look for a moment at what self-government really meant in

4 *Reflections on the Revolution in France*, as reprinted in *ibid.*, III, 241-42.
5 George Washington to Henry Lee, Oct. 31, 1786, in Worthington Chauncey Ford (ed.), *The Writings of George Washington* (14 vols., New York, 1889-93), XI, 77.

their time. Take English history for your test. I know not where else you may find an answer to the question. We speak, all the world speaks, of England as the mother of liberty and self-government; and the beginning of her liberty we place in the great year that saw Magna Charta signed, that immortal document whose phrases ring again in all our own Bills of Rights. Her liberty is in fact older than that signal year; but 1215 we set up as a shining mark to hold the eye. And yet we know, for all we boast the date so early, for how many a long generation after that the monarch ruled and the Commons cringed; haughty Plantagenets had their way, and indomitable Tudors played the master to all men's fear, till the fated Stuarts went their stupid way to exile and the scaffold. Kings were none the less kings because their subjects were free men.

Local self-government in England consisted until 1888 of government by almost omnipotent Justices of the Peace appointed by the Lord Chancellor. They were laymen, however. They were country gentlemen and served without pay. They were of the neighborhood and used their power for its benefit as their lights served them; but no man had a vote or choice as to which of the country gentlemen of his county should be set over him; and the power of the Justices sitting in Quarter Sessions covered almost every point of justice and administration not directly undertaken by the officers of the crown itself. "Long ago," laughs an English writer, "lawyers abandoned the hope of describing the duties of a Justice in any methodic fashion, and the alphabet has become the only possible connecting thread. A Justice must have something to do with 'Railroads, Rape, Rates, Recognizances, Records, and Recreation Grounds'; with 'Perjury, Petroleum, Piracy, and Playhouses'; with 'Disorderly Houses, Dissenters, Dogs, and Drainage.'" And yet Englishmen themselves called their life under these lay masters self-government.

The English House of Commons was for many a generation, many a century even, no House of the Commons at all, but a house full of country gentlemen and rich burghers, the aristocracy of the English counties and the English towns; and yet it was from this House, and not from that reformed since 1832, that the world drew, through Montesquieu, its models of representative self-government in the days when our own Union was set up.

In America, and in America alone, did self-government mean an organization self-originated, and of the stuff of the people themselves. America had gone a step beyond her mother country. Her people were for the most part picked men: such men as have the energy and the initiative to leave old homes and old friends, and go to far frontiers to make a new life for themselves. They were men of a certain initiative, to take the world into their own hands. The king had given them their charters, but within the broad definitions of those charters they had built as they pleased, and common men were partners in the government of their little commonwealths. At home, in the old country, there was need, no doubt, that the hand of the king's government should keep men within its reach. The countrysides were full of yokels who would have been brutes to deal with else. The counties were in fact represented very well by the country gentlemen who ruled them: for they were full of broad estates where men were tenants, not freehold farmers, and the interests of masters were generally enough the interests of their men. The towns had charters of their own. There was here no democratic community, and no one said or thought that the only self-government was democratic self-government. In America the whole constitution of society was democratic, inevitably and of course. Men lay close to their simple governments, and the new life brought to a new expression the immemorial English principle, that the intimate affairs of local administration and the common interests that were to be served in the making of laws should be committed to laymen, who would look at the government critically and from without, and not to the king's agents, who would look at it professionally and from within. England had had self-government time out of mind; but in America English self-government had become *popular* self-government.

"Almost all the civilized states derive their national unity," says a great English writer of our generation, "from common subjection, past or present, to royal power; the Americans of the United States, for example, are a nation because they once obeyed a king." That example in such a passage comes upon us with a shock: it is very unexpected,—"the Americans of the United States, for example, are a nation because they once obeyed a king"! And yet, upon reflection, can we deny the example? It is plain enough that the reason why the English in America got self-government and knew how to use it, and the French in America did not, was, that the English had had a training under the kings of England and the French under the kings of France. In the one country men did all things at the bidding of officers of the crown; in the other, officers of the crown listened, were constrained to listen, to the counsels of laymen drawn out of the general body of the nation. And yet the kings of England were no less kings than the kings of France. Obedience is everywhere the basis of government, and the English were not ready either in their life or in their thought for a free régime under which they should choose their kings by ballot. For that régime they could be made ready only by the long drill which should make them respect above all things the law and the authority of governors. Discipline—discipline generations deep—had first to give them an ineradicable love of order, the poise of men self-commanded, the spirit of men who obey and yet speak their minds and are free, before they could be Americans.

No doubt a king did hold us together until we learned how to hold together of ourselves. No doubt our unity as a nation does come from the fact that we once obeyed a king. No one can look at the processes of English history and doubt that the throne has been its centre of poise, though not in our days its centre of force. Steadied by the throne, the effective part of the nation has, at every stage of its development, dealt with and controlled the government in the name of the whole. The king and his subjects have been partners in the great undertaking. At last, in our country, in this best trained portion of the nation, set off by itself, the whole became fit to act for itself, by veritable popular representation, without the makeweight of a throne. That is the history of our liberty. You have the spirit of English history, and of English royalty, from King Harry's mouth upon the field of Agincourt:—

> "We few, we happy few, we band of brothers;
> For he to-day that sheds his blood with me
> Shall be my brother; be he ne'er so vile,
> This day shall gentle his condition:
> And gentlemen in England now a-bed
> Shall think themselves accursed they were not here,
> And hold their manhoods cheap whiles any speaks
> That fought with us upon Saint Crispin's day."

It is thus the spirit of English life has made comrades of us all to be a nation.

This is what Burke meant by combining government with liberty,—the spirit of obedience with the spirit of free action. Liberty is not itself government. In the wrong hands,—in hands unpracticed, undisciplined,—it is incompatible with government. Discipline must precede it,—if necessary, the discipline of being under masters. Then will self-control make it a thing of life and not a thing of tumult, a tonic, not an insurgent madness in the blood. Shall we doubt, then, what the conditions precedent to liberty and self-government are, and what their invariable support and accompaniment must be, in the countries whose administration we have taken over in trust, and particularly in those far Philippine Islands whose government is our chief anxiety? We cannot give them any quittance of the debt ourselves have paid. They can have liberty no cheaper than we got it. They must first take the discipline of law, must first love order and instinctively yield to it. It is the heathen, not the free citizen of a self-governed country, who "in his blindness bows down to wood and stone, and don't obey no orders unless they is his own." We are old in this learning and must be their tutors.

But we may set them upon the way with an advantage we did not have until our hard journey was more than half made. We can see to it that the law which teaches them obedience is just law and even-handed. We can see to it that justice be free and unpurchasable among them. We can make order lovely by making it the friend of every man and not merely the shield of some. We can teach them by our fairness in administration that there may be a power in government which, though imperative and irresistible by those who would cross or thwart it, does not act for its own aggrandizement, but is the guarantee that all shall fare alike. That will infinitely shorten their painful tutelage. Our pride, our conscience will not suffer us to give them less.

And, if we are indeed bent upon service and not mastery, we shall give them more. We shall take them into our confidence and suffer them to teach us, as our critics. No man can deem himself free from whom the government hides its action, or who is forbidden to speak his mind about affairs, as if government were a private thing which concerned the governors alone. Whatever the power of government, if it is just, there may be publicity of governmental action and freedom of opinion; and public opinion gathers head effectively only by concerted public agitation. These are the things—knowledge of what the government is doing and liberty to speak of it—that have made Englishmen feel like free men, whether they liked their governors or not: the right to know and the right to speak out,—to speak out in plain words and in open counsel. Privacy, official reticence, governors hedged about and inaccessible,—these are the marks of arbitrary government, under which spirited men grow restive and resentful. The mere right to criticise and to have matters explained to them cools men's tempers and gives them understanding in affairs. This is what we seek among our new subjects: that they shall understand us, and after free conference shall trust us: that they shall perceive that we are not afraid of criticism, and that we are ready to explain and to take suggestions from all who are ready, when the conference is over, to obey.

There will be a wrong done, not if we govern and govern as we will, govern with a strong hand that will brook no resistance, and according to principles of right gathered from our own experience, not from theirs, which has never yet touched the vital matter we are concerned with; but only if we govern in the spirit of autocrats and of those who serve themselves, not their subjects. The whole solution lies less in our methods than in our temper. We must govern as those who learn; and they must obey as those who are in tutelage. They are children and we are men in these deep matters of government and justice. If we have not learned the substance of these things no nation is ever likely to learn it, for it is taken from life, and not from books. But though children must be foolish, impulsive, headstrong, unreasonable, men may be arbitrary, self-opinionated, impervious, impossible, as the English were in their Oriental colonies until they learned. We should be inexcusable to repeat their blunders and wait as long as they waited to learn how to serve the peoples whom we govern. It is plain we shall have a great deal to learn; it is to be hoped we shall learn it fast.

There are, unhappily, some indications that we have ourselves yet to learn the things we would teach. You have but to think of the large number of persons of your own kith and acquaintance who have for the past two years been demanding, in print and out of it, with moderation and the air of reason and without it, that we give the Philippines independence and self-government now, at once, out of hand. It were easy enough to give them independence, if by independence you mean only disconnection with any government outside the islands, the independence of a rudderless boat adrift. But self-government? How is that "given"? *Can* it be given? Is it not gained, earned, graduated into from the hard school of life? We have reason to think so. I have just now been trying to give the reasons we have for thinking so.

There are many things, things slow and difficult to come at, which we have found to be conditions precedent to liberty,—to the liberty which can be combined with government; and we cannot, in our present situation, too often remind ourselves of these things, in order that we may look steadily and wisely upon liberty, not in the uncertain light of theory, but in the broad, sunlike, disillusioning light of experience. We know, for one thing, that it rests at bottom upon a clear experimental knowledge of what are in fact the just rights of individuals, of what is the equal and profitable balance to be maintained between the right of the individual to serve himself and the duty of government to serve society. I say, not merely a *clear* knowledge of these, but a clear *experimental* knowledge of them as well. We hold it, for example, an indisputable principle of law in a free state that there should be freedom of speech, and yet we have a law of libel. No man, we say, may speak that which wounds his neighbor's reputation unless there be public need to speak it. Moreover, we will judge of that need in a rough and ready fashion. Let twelve ordinary men, empaneled as a jury, say whether the wound was justly given and of necessity. "The truth of the matter is very simple when stripped of all ornaments of speech," says an eminent English judge. "It is neither more nor less than this: that a man may publish anything which twelve of his fellow countrymen think is not blamable." It is plain, therefore, that in this case at least we do not inquire curiously concerning the Rights of Man, which do not seem susceptible of being stated in terms of social obligation, but content ourselves with asking, "What are the rights of men living together, amongst whom there must be order and fair give and take?" And our law of libel is only one instance out of many. We treat all rights in like practical fashion. But a people must obviously have had experience to treat them so. You have here one image in the mirror of self-government.

Do not leave the mirror before you see another. You cannot call a miscellaneous people, unknit, scattered, diverse of race and speech and habit, a nation, a community. That, at least, we got by serving under kings: we got the feeling and the organic structure of a community. No people can form a community or be wisely subjected to common forms of government who are as diverse and as heterogeneous as the people of the Philippine Islands. They are in no wise knit together. They are of many races, of many stages of development, economically, socially, politically disintegrate, without community of feeling because without community of life, contrasted alike in experience and in habit, having nothing in common except that they have lived for hundreds of years together under a government which held them always where they were when it first arrested their development. You may imagine the problem of self-government and of growth for such a people,—if so be you have an imagination and are no doctrinaire. If there is difficulty in our own government here at home because the several sections of our own country are disparate and at different stages of development, what shall we expect, and what patience shall we not demand of ourselves, with regard to our belated wards beyond the Pacific? We have here among ourselves hardly sufficient equality of social and economic conditions to breed full community of feeling. We have learned of our own experience what the problem of self-government is in such a case.

That liberty and self-government are things of infinite difficulty and nice accommodation we above all other peoples ought to know who have had every adventure in their practice. Our very discontent with the means we have taken to keep our people clear-eyed and steady in the use of their institutions is evidence of our appreciation of what is required to sustain them. We have set up an elaborate system of popular education, and have made the maintenance of that system a function of government, upon the theory that only systematic training can give the quick intelligence, the "variety of information and excellence of discretion" needed by a self-governed people. We expect as much from schoolteachers as from governors in the Philippines and in Porto Rico: we expect from them the *morale* that is to sustain our work there. And yet, when teachers have done their utmost and the school bills are paid, we doubt, and know that we have reason to doubt, the efficacy of what we have done. Books can but set the mind free, can but give it the freedom of the world of thought. The world of affairs has yet to be attempted, and the schooling of action must supplement the schooling of the written page. Men who have an actual hand in government, men who vote and sustain by their thoughts the whole movement of affairs, men who have the making or the confirming of policies, must have reasonable hopes, must act within the reasonable bounds set by hard experience.

By education, no doubt, you acquaint men, while they are yet young and quick to take impressions, with the character and spirit of the polity they live under; give them some sentiment of respect for it, put them in the air that has always lain about it, and prepare them to take the experience that awaits them. But it is from the polity itself and their own contact with it that they must get their actual usefulness in affairs, and only that contact, intelligently made use of, makes good citizens. We would not have them remain children always and act always on the preconceptions taken out of the books they have studied. Life is their real master and tutor in affairs.

And so the character of the polity men live under has always had a deep significance in our thoughts. Our greater statesmen have been men steeped in a thoughtful philosophy of politics, men who pondered the effect of this institution and that upon morals and the life of society, and thought of character when they spoke of affairs. They have taught us that the best polity is that which most certainly produces the habit and the spirit of civic duty, and which calls with the most stirring and persuasive voice to the leading characters of the nation to come forth and give it direction. It must be a polity which shall stimulate, which shall breed emulation, which shall make men seek honor by seeking service. These are the ideals which have formed our institutions, and which shall mend them when they need reform. We need good leaders more than an excellent mechanism of action in charters and constitutions. We need men of devotion as much as we need good laws. The two cannot be divorced and self-government survive.

It is this thought that distresses us when we look upon our cities and our states and see them ruled by bosses. Our methods of party organization have produced bosses, and they are as natural and inevitable a product of our politics, no doubt, at any rate for the time being and until we can see our way to better things, as the walking delegate and the union president are of the contest between capital and federated labor. Both the masters of strikes and the masters of caucuses are able men, too, with whom we must needs deal with our best wits about us. But they are not, if they will pardon me for saying so, the leading characters I had in mind when I said that the excellence of a polity might be judged by the success with which it calls the leading characters of a nation forth to its posts of command. The polity which breeds bosses breeds managing talents rather than leading characters,—very excellent things in themselves, but not the highest flower of politics. The power to govern and direct primaries, combine primaries for the control of conventions, and use conventions for the nomination of candidates and the formulation of platforms agreed upon beforehand is an eminently useful thing in itself, and cannot be dispensed with, it may be, in democratic countries, where men must act, not helter skelter, but in parties, and with a certain party discipline, not easily thrown off; but it is not the first product of our politics we should wish to export to Porto Rico and the Philippines.

No doubt our study of these things which lie at the front of our own lives, and which must be handled in our own progress, will teach us how to be better masters and tutors to those whom we govern. We have come to full maturity with this new century of our national existence and to full self-consciousness as a nation. And the day of our isolation is past. We shall learn much ourselves now that we stand closer to other nations and compare ourselves first with one and again with another. Moreover, the centre of gravity has shifted in the action of our Federal government. It has shifted back to where it was at the opening of the last century, in that early day when we were passing from the gristle to the bone of our growth. For the first twenty-six years that we lived under our Federal constitution foreign affairs, the sentiment and policy of nations over sea, dominated our politics, and our Presidents were our leaders. And now the same thing has come about again. Once more it is our place among the nations that we think of; once more our Presidents are our leaders.

The centre of our party management shifts accordingly. We no longer stop upon questions of what this state wants or that, what this section will demand or the other, what this boss or that may do to attach his machine to the government. The scale of our thought is national again. We are sensitive to airs that come to us from off the seas. The President and his advisers stand upon our chief coign of observation, and we mark their words as we did not till this change came. And this centring of our thoughts, this looking for guidance in things which mere managing talents cannot handle, this union of our hopes, will not leave us what we were when first it came. Here is a new world for us. Here is a new life to which to adjust our ideals.

It is by the widening of vision that nations, as men, grow and are made great. We need not fear the expanding scene. It was plain destiny that we should come to this, and if we have kept our ideals clear, unmarred, commanding through the great century and the moving scenes that made us a nation, we may keep them also through the century that shall see us a great power in the world. Let us put our leading characters at the front; let us pray that vision may come with power; let us ponder our duties like men of conscience and temper our ambitions like men who seek to serve, not to subdue, the world; let us lift our thoughts to the level of the great tasks that await us, and bring a great age in with the coming of our day of strength.

Woodrow Wilson.

Printed in the *Atlantic Monthly*, xc (Dec. 1902), 721-34.

From John Alexander Campbell[1]

My Dear Wilson: Trenton, N.J. Dec. 28, 1901

I want to thank you personally, and officially, for the magnificent address which you gave us on the 26th.

The amount of hard work done by you in the preparation of this oration cannot be estimated by any of us, because we know nothing of the amount of mental strain necessary to reach such a high point as this.

I can only say that I have heard most flattering opinions expressed with reference to the address.

My own dominie said to his boy on coming out of the Opera House (and the boy is now at Lawrenceville, in line for Princeton)

"John, you want to remember this occasion, because it will be many a long year before you are called upon to listen to a more finished, and thoughtful oration than that you have listened to to-day."

I think that you can certainly feel that your work has been fully appreciated here, by those whose opinion you would naturally value, and it is not confined, by any means, to professional men, because I have heard the opinion of a great many others to whom a finished address would not always naturally appeal.

No doubt you will hear from the Committee themselves in a very short time, as soon as they are able to meet for the final reports.

I enjoyed your visit very much, and wish you would so state to the members of your immediate family, to your sister and Miss [Henrietta] Ricketts.

My wife also greatly enjoyed having your family on that day, and we trust that none of you received any bad effects from your visit with the accompanying rain.

With very best wishes,

Yours sincerely,   John A. Campbell

TLS (WP, DLC).
1 Princeton '77, General Manager of the Trenton Potteries Co. He was a member of the committee of fifty men appointed by Mayor Frank O. Briggs of Trenton to organize the celebration of the anniversary.

From Cyrus Hall McCormick

Dear Woodrow: [Chicago] January 2nd, 1902.

I send you a short history of the United States which perhaps you may not have seen in your researches on this subject.[1] As it is profusely illustrated, it will, no doubt, be used as an interesting souvenir for Christmas or New Years, and I send it to you with the compliments of the season.

With kind regards to Mrs. Wilson, I am,

Very sincerely yours,   [Cyrus H. McCormick]

CCL (C. H. McCormick Papers, WHi).
1 As Wilson's reply of January 13, 1902, discloses, this was a work by the

humorist, George Ade, probably his highly successful *Fables in Slang* (Chicago and New York, 1900). A copy of this book is in the Wilson Library, DLC.

From Albert Bushnell Hart

My dear Professor Wilson:

Cambridge, Massachusetts
January 3, 1902.

For some years it has been in the air that the time had come to organize the historical forces of the country into the preparation of a scientific history of the United States on a cooperative basis. It is twenty-one years since Mr. Winsor began his *Narrative and Critical History*, and that series covers only a part of the field, and is not of much service to the general reader. The American Historical Association has for two years had the matter under discussion as an Association job, but finally concluded not to undertake it. I have therefore ventured to make an arrangement with Harpers to publish such a series in twenty-five small volumes, of about 75,000 words each.[1] Is there not somewhere within this extensive range a volume which you would be willing to write? Many years ago you prepared a volume at my solicitation, for which you were not extravagantly paid;[2] indeed, neither of the three writers[3] nor the publishers ever supposed that a hundred thousand volumes would eventually be sold out of the series. I think from a money point of view the present series would be better worth taking part in. I know how busy you are and how much your time is worth to you and to your readers; but it would give me great personal pleasure and would be an element of strength in the series if you could come in. I may say that I have reason to suppose that the writers of this series will include some of the most distinguished authors on American history, and will make up a company in which even Woodrow Wilson will find himself at home.

Sincerely your friend,   Albert Bushnell Hart

TLS (WP, DLC).
[1] Harper's "American Nation" series, edited by Hart, was to run to a total of twenty-eight volumes. Twenty-seven were published from 1904 to 1908, and one additional volume, covering the period 1907-17, came out in 1918. The authors included many of the most prominent professional historians in the United States.
[2] *Division and Reunion*, published by Longmans, Green in the "Epochs of American History" series, edited by Hart, for which Wilson had been paid a flat fee of $500. See the Editorial Note, "Wilson's *Division and Reunion*," Vol. 8.
[3] Reuben Gold Thwaites, Hart, and Wilson.

From Joseph Henry Harper

My dear Mr. Wilson,   New York Jan. 7, 1902.

Mr. Sears[1] has just told me that you are considering—& he hopes favorably—co-operating with Prof. Hart in his series of small volumes on American History.

I sincerely hope that we may be able to include your name among the contributors, there would be a feeling of "Hamlet left out" should you decline.

Very sincerely yours,   J. Henry Harper.

ALS (WP, DLC).
[1] Joseph Hamblen Sears, an editor at Harper and Brothers.

From George Brinton McClellan Harvey

Dear Professor Wilson: New York City January 7, 1902

I am very much gratified to learn that you are favorably considering the possibility of writing one of the volumes in our proposed monographic history of the United States. I know how busy you are and how you naturally dislike taking up additionally [additional] work; and yet we feel that a great history of this country by leading historians must include your name. For this reason & because we want to enlarge our present pleasant relations with you, I frankly urge you to undertake at least one volume.

Sincerely yours   George Harvey
President of Harper & Brothers

ALS (WP, DLC) with WWhw notation on env.: "Ans. 1/12/02."

From the Minutes of the Princeton University Faculty

4 10′ P.M., Wednesday, January 8, 1902.

... The Report on Graduate Work was again considered, certain amendments were made and Sections 7th-11th were adopted. Section 12th was considered and action upon it was postponed.

The Faculty adjourned to meet at 4 P.M., Wednesday, January 15th for further consideration of the Report.

To Thomas Nelson Page

My dear Mr. Page,   Princeton, New Jersey, 10 January, 1902

Alas, my most important mid-year examination has been set for nine o'clock on the morning of the twenty-fifth instant, and that puts an "evening off" for me on the twenty-fourth out of the question.

I am *very* sorry. To be your guest and to meet the men of the good old University[1] which I love so much would be pleasures it goes very hard to miss. But, in the language of the great Washington, "I am tied by the leg," and to kick would only be to chafe the member.

Accept my warm thanks for your kind invitation, give the men who gather on the twenty-fourth my heartiest greetings, and believe me

With much regard,

Cordially Yours,   Woodrow Wilson

ALS (T. N. Page Papers, NcD).
   [1] The University of Virginia.

A News Account of an Alumni Banquet

[Jan. 11, 1902]

The sixteenth annual banquet of the Princeton Alumni Association of Northeastern Pennsylvania was held at the Hotel Sterling, Wilkes-Barre, on the evening of December 23;[1] it was the largest and most successful meeting this association has had, about fifty members being present. Benjamin F. Dorrance '68, the retiring President, was toastmaster, and the toasts responded to were: Princeton—Herself, Professor Woodrow Wilson '79; Princeton—Her Guests, Hon. George S. Ferris '74; Princeton—Her Rivals, Hon. Frank W. Wheaton; Princeton—Her Sisters, Rev. Horace H. Hayden; Princeton—Her Alumni, H. A. Fuller '74; Princeton—Her Influence, Henry W. Dunning '82. Preceding the dinner the business meeting was held and the following officers were elected for the ensuing year: President, S. B. Price '70; Treasurer, John H. Brooks '95; Secretary, Edwin Shortz, Jr., '97; Chairman of Executive Committee, H. H. Welles, Jr., '82.

Printed in the *Princeton Alumni Weekly*, II (Jan. 11, 1902), 226-27.
   [1] There is a printed program of this affair with WWhw cues for jokes in WP, DLC.

To Albert Bushnell Hart

Princeton, New Jersey,

My dear Professor Hart,   12 January, 1902.

Your kind letter of the third was followed by a visit from Mr. Sears and letters from Mr. J. Henry Harper and Colonel Harvey.

You may be sure I very heartily appreciate the interesting invitation which is thus so cordially pressed upon me. It would be a real pleasure to work under your editorship again, and I should feel it an honour to colaborate with such a group of men as those whom Mr. Sears named to me.

But the mere fact of the matter is, that I have just now reached a point at which I know that the next ten or twelve years of my life (these and no others) must be devoted to an entirely different task, for which I have all along been in training, and for which now, if ever, I am ready.[1] I should not be content to write only a single volume of the series you are planning: the measure of space would be too cramping: a fellow could not show the real pattern of his thought in it; and yet even a single volume would rob me of at least a year, as I work, and that I simply cannot spare.

I am very sorry. I feel a distinct sense of loss in declining: loss of stimulating companionship in the work, loss of the satisfaction of doing a thorough piece of work in the best company and under the best conditions. But job work, of however high an order, is for the present out of the question for me. I must go my own way for a while, and see what I am made of.

With warmest regards and appreciation,

Sincerely Yours,   Woodrow Wilson[2]

WWTLS (photostat in WP, DLC).
[1] That is, the writing of his projected magnum opus, "The Philosophy of Politics."
[2] There is a WWsh draft of this letter dated Jan. 12, 1902, in WP, DLC.

To George Brinton McClellan Harvey

My dear Mr. Harvey,   [Princeton, N.J.] 12 Jan'y, 1902

I have taken the liberty of delaying my reply to your kind letter of the 7th for several days because the importance of the matter it dealt with made it necessary that I should give it very careful consideration.

I have found it very difficult indeed to decide what I should say. I was not only very much attracted by the scheme Professor Hart and Mr. Sears outlined to me, but I was also sincerely desirous of meeting your wishes and the wishes of the house with which I have been so pleasantly associated. You may be sure I would have said Yes had it been possible.

But the facts are simply these. It would not be satisfactory to write a single volume of the series: the connections of things are too long and too complex to make it possible to weave so small a piece of the whole with good text; and yet I know just how long it takes me, working at my best, to discharge a piece of work and I know that even a single volume would throw me out of all calculations for my future work. I have a piece of work plotted which will take at least ten years in the doing; what I have done so far was only to get my hand in for that. I must take a year off to get my head clear for it and then I must do it at once, while my powers are at their best. To promise this new piece of work in Prof. Hart's series would be to postpone beginning what I can do best until the close neighborhood of my 50th birthday and that I cannot in prudence and good sense do.

I know that you will consider these reasons sound and conclusive. I shall best serve my own interests as a writer, and perhaps in the long run the interests of the house as well, by going my own way for the next ten or twelve years.

With much regard and appreciation,

Sincerely yours,   Woodrow Wilson

Transcript of WWshLS   (WP, DLC).

To Joseph Henry Harper

My dear Mr. Harper,   [Princeton, N.J.]   12 Jan'y, 1902

I am sure you will attribute my delay in replying to your kind letter of the 7th to the real cause, my sense of its importance. It is no little matter to decline a task so congenial and so well worth doing.

But, as I have just written to Colonel Harvey, to do it would appear certain to mar plans I have had ever since I set out as a writer. I am now about to begin the piece of writing for which I am best suited. It will take, I should say, at the least ten years; a man whose forty-fifth birthday has just been passed knows that, intellectually speaking, the next ten or twelve years of his life are the best.

It is not as if I could do what you ask easily. I know just what time and pains it would cost. I should not be content to write only one of the volumes planned either: that would be too small a piece to spread any plan of thought or exposition upon; and yet even a single volume would consume a long time and I have not even a short time to spare.

I would do this book for you, if it were possible, if only because you wish it; but, reckoning possibility by any standard of wisdom or prudence, it is out of the question. I feel sure that you will see the force and the exclusiveness of the reason.

With warmest regards and warm thanks for the very cordial
way in which you have pressed this undertaking upon me,
                          Faithfully yours,   Woodrow Wilson

Transcript of WWshLS (WP, DLC).

To Cyrus Hall McCormick

My dear Cyrus,   Princeton, 13 Jan'y, 1902

Truly I am abashed that there should have existed so striking
an authority on the history of the United States of which I knew
nothing! It was an act of genuine kindness and thoughtful courtesy on your part to call my attention to it now, in this private
way, instead of waiting till my book appeared and then calling
attention to the fact that I evidently know nothing of at least one
distinguished authority, Mr. Geo. Ade!

Good luck to you, and the heartiest good wishes for the New
Year to Mrs. McCormick, the children, and yourself from us both.
                          Faithfully Yours,   Woodrow Wilson

ALS (WP, DLC).

From Harper and Brothers

Dear Sir: New York City   Jan. 13. 1902.

Will you kindly let us know to what year you bring your "History of the American People"? We think it very important to carry
it, if possible, to the death of President McKinley. There is no
complete American history, of any prominence, now published
—as far as we know. Please let us hear what your judgment is on
this point.

We send you enclosed herewith, proofs of two pages, the size of
Fiske's volumes. In this form your work will make six volumes.
Kindly let us know if this meets with your approval.
                          Sincerely yours,   Harper & Brothers

ALS (WP, DLC). Att.: three-page WWhw memorandum concerning the length of
A History of the American People, calculating 301,249 words divided into five
volumes.

From George Brinton McClellan Harvey

My dear Professor Wilson: New York City   January 14, 1902.

I am very sorry to hear of your decision not to undertake a
volume or two in the Monographic American History, but I can

understand your kind note and we must respect your point of view, much as we regret not including you among the authors.

The long work you have in mind interests me, and I trust that the last sentence of your note of Sunday means that, when the time comes and you are ready to talk over the plan, you will still look to us as your publishers.

Sincerely yours,   George Harvey

TLS (WP, DLC).

From the Minutes of the Princeton University Faculty

4 5′ P.M., Wednesday, January 15, 1902.

. . . Section 12th of the Report on Graduate Work was again considered, amended and a[d]opted.

The entire report as amended was then adopted and is as follows; (a Correct Copy with all the amendments to be given to the Clerk by the Dean of the Graduate School)

Standards of Graduate Work
in
The Graduate School
of
Princeton University

I.

It is assumed that the object aimed at in the graduate work is primarily the development of a body of scholars possessing liberal culture and mastery of the special subjects of their studies.

II.

The general liberal culture is the guarantee of an open-minded appreciation of the place of the student's special subject of study in the general body of knowledge.

III.

The mastery of special subjects starts with the acquisition of extensive and exact knowledge, develops by the use of correct methods, and results in the ability to exercise independent scholarly judgment and prosecute original research.

IV.

The surest evidence of the possession of independent scholarly judgment is the ability to distinguish, appropriate and use the most valuable material in any subject, in contrast to what is of less relevancy and value. Not the mere accumulation of information, nor the possession of mere formal skill, nor merely a large quantity of work done faithfully and patiently but with little intellectual effort should be considered as satisfying our standards of graduate study.

V.

Graduate instruction should, in the main, be given by means of courses in important subjects, rather than by courses in minor parts or sketchs of subjects. So far as our resources permit, the graduate instruction should be planned so that the leading courses given have the character of subjects. Ample schedule time should be allotted for their free development by the Professor. While courses having less schedule time may be allowed, they should be regarded as supplementary and not central to the proper graduate work of any department.

VI.

In order to maintain graduate as distinguished from undergraduate standards, a body of purely graduate courses is necessary. If graduates desire nothing but undergraduate courses, they should, as a rule, be enrolled as undergraduates. A graduate should devote at least his main effort to work in graduate courses, seminaries or laboratories. In case, however, graduates are admitted to undergraduate courses, their studies in those courses should be especially directed and enlarged by means agreed upon by conference between the Dean of the Graduate School and the Professor conducting the course.

VII.

Each graduate course should be in charge of one person. Otherwise responsibility cannot be satisfactorily located. It is, of course understood that one professor should be free to assist in another's course, if occasion arises.

VIII.

The graduate work should be classified under three heads.

　　　　1. Courses.
　　　　2. Seminaries.
　　　　3. Laboratories.

An exact line cannot be drawn between courses and seminaries, but in general it may be said that the courses are in the nature of exposition and instruction, involving collateral work on the part of the student, while the seminaries train students individually in the methods of research and are accompanied by a large amount of outside, independent study. In either case the student ought to do a great deal on his own initiative, helped by the Professor's advice. The nature of laboratory work needs no special description. It is analogous to that of Seminary work.

IX.

The graduate course (outside of the distinctively seminary and laboratory work) consists of lectures and conferences; some courses being composed entirely of lectures, others of lectures accompanied by colloquies with the students, and others consisting mainly or wholly of conferences.

X.

The aim of the distinctively seminary work should be to enable the studentual [individual] student, at first under the guidance of his professor and then on his own initiative,

1. To find and use the literature of his subject, including important older monographs and editions, as well as the current journals;

2. To enlarge his acquaintance with his field of study by continuous reading, observation and reflection;

3. To trace and estimate the evidence regarding particular problems;

4. To acquire the methods of exact research, to develop them by his own inventive effort, and to apply them in investigation;

5. To subject all his conclusions to the test of rigorous criticism;

6. To perceive the relation which each investigation pursued bears to the whole of which that investigation forms a part;

7. To distinguish the real issues in a question, and to perceive where the discovery of truth hitherto unknown is possible

It is not expected that any seminary will be able to realize all or most of these aims at once or that all subjects will be capable of similar treatment. But a graduate student devoting himself to seminary work for two or three years ought to be able at the end of that time to appropriate all these aims of the seminary training.

XI.

The character of graduate work involves more independent intellectual effort and more time on the part of the student and the instructor than is involved in the work of undergraduate courses of equal length. If the character of the graduate courses is sound, the greater quantity of work is inevitable, and although the large quantity of work may not be evidence of itself that a course is controlled by graduate standards, a small quantity of work may be taken as evidence that the course is unsatisfactory.

XII.

A graduate course shall, as a rule, occupy three hours a week for a term. Every department offering graduate courses is expected to offer at least on[e] such course each term on some centrally important subject in the department. By permission of the University Faculty, on recommendation of the Committee on the Graduate School, additional briefer courses of lectures, not necessarily accompanied by outside investigation on the part of the student, may be given on special themes.[1]

[1] The trustees approved this report at their meeting on March 13, 1902.

A Report of an Address in Reading, Pennsylvania

[Jan. 17, 1902]

WOODROW WILSON'S LECTURE.

What it Means to be an American.

Prof. Woodrow Wilson, of Princeton, gave an interesting lecture on "What it means to be an American" before an audience of several hundred at Rajah Temple.

Prof. Wilson said former ages produced men who were splendid workers, thinkers and idealists, but they were not confined to one generation or century. America has, on the other hand, produced men of the same kind who had mastered the arts, sciences and metaphysics, and could produce in a generation what their fellow men of former ages required years, if not centuries, to accomplish.

The reason Americans receive contracts in the old country is because they can furnish the material and deliver it at a given place in a shorter period of time than any other nation on earth.

He referred to the making of the federal government as one of the finest pieces of work ever accomplished by man and one that can stand because it possesses the tensile strength and the elasticity to conform to all the requirements of new ideas and thoughts. America has always had and to-day possesses the most intelligent and best reasoning men in the world. It is a nation of builders, first and last.

In referring to the reason for American success, he said it was because our national officials were men capable of coping with any subject successfully.

In the army and navy the same rule prevails, because the officers would make good privates and the latter were fully competent to become officers and acquit themselves creditably. This was only true of the United States.

He referred to the manner of speaking and said Americans speak more on the dead level than any other nation, the English, for instance, varying the tone of voice almost an octave in one sentence.

Above all, Americans possess sound hearts. He said that the American government was not founded on laws, but was entwined in the lives and characters of the men who propounded and enacted them. The President, Cabinet and Congress were the government; there was the government written, not in books, but in the hearts and minds of these representatives of the people.

Printed in the *Reading*, Pa., *Eagle*, Jan. 17, 1902.

To Robert Bridges

My dear Bobby,   Princeton, New Jersey, 20 January, 1902.

It was kind of you, and characteristic, to think of this pleasure for me. It would be just the kind of recreation I covet to spend such an evening with you at the Aldine,[1] with nothing to do myself but have a good time; and I have kept your note trying to figure it out that it would be possible to manage it. But, alas! the book drags too much, my engagements away from home are already too many, and I must deny myself all recreation, apparently, between this and Commencement.

I am deeply disappointed, and very grateful to you. What in the name of thunder is the use of another "History of the American People" anyway?

As ever,

Affectionately and faithfully Yrs.,   Woodrow Wilson

WWTLS (WC, NjP).
[1] The Aldine Association, a men's literary club in New York.

To Frederick Jackson Turner

My dear Turner,   Princeton, New Jersey, 21 January, 1902.

I have just declined an invitation from President Harper to lecture during their next summer term, and writing the letter has made me feel that there somehow ought to go with it a letter to you.

The only thing about the invitation that tempted me was the idea that perhaps to accept it would be to go somewhere in the neighbourhood of where you would be. Declining it made me think, too, of another piece of work I had said I could not do, but which I had considered long and with not a little disinclination to say No because it would bring me into association with you, if only indirectly and at a distance. I mean Hart's coöperative history of the United States. It gave me real pleasure to learn that you had accepted a part in its preparation; and the presence of your name on the list went far toward forcing my hand.[1] There was no one else on it with whom I felt I could have anything like the same sense of comradeship.

I had to say No, if I am to do the work I really seem to have been cut out for. I was forty-five three weeks ago, and between forty-five and fifty-five, I take it, is when a man ought to do the work into which he expects to put most of himself. I love history and think that there are few things so directly rewarding and worth while for their own sakes as to scan the history of one's own country with a careful eye, and write of it with the all absorbing desire to get its cream and spirit out. But, after all, I was born a politician, and must be at the task for which, by means of my historical writing, I have all these years been in training. If I finish at fifty-five, shall I not have fifteen richly contemplative years left, if the Lord be good to me! But, then, the Lord may prefer to be good to the world!

I am enlarging, and I hope enriching, the papers I have recently been contributing to Harper's for their appearance in book form; and shall bring the narrative down through the Spanish war. It was of course my earnest wish, as all who know me must know that it would be, to have the first form of the book a single volume without illustrations, and wait for an illustrated edition until the book had won some standing,—if it is to win it. But, alas! what is man as against his publishers! Once sign a contract and you have signed away the right to have any choice as to the visible form of your book. This poor modest child of mine is to appear first, if you please, tricked out in five sumptuous subscription volumes (may the Lord have mercy on it), and its author is to seem, I fear, the most pretentious of mortals. Let us hope that his friends at least will detect the imposition, and will not misjudge him; but it is a sore cross to him, none the less. He has almost lost pleasure in the book.

It is not the book you and I talked over in the delightful days when talk between us was possible. My plans have undergone transformations many, under the mysterious dispensations of Providence, and the present plan is not as good as the original one. But no doubt the thing is as good as I know how to make it in that kind, for all its painful defects.

If you have discovered any blunders in "Division and Reunion" since I saw you, pray communicate them to me in kindness, lest I fall into the like in this new narrative.

But I do not write this to get "tips." I write merely out of the fullness of my desire to hear from and about you again, and keep warm one of the friendship[s] I value most as the years go by, and would be most rewarded to turn into an intimacy.

Mrs. Wilson joins me in all cordial messages to you both, and I am, in all affection,

Faithfully Yours,   Woodrow Wilson

WWTLS (F. J. Turner Papers, MH).
¹ For the "American Nation" series, Turner wrote *Rise of the New West, 1819-1829* (New York and London, 1906).

Léon Duguit's¹ Preface to the French Edition of *The State*

PRÉFACE   [Jan. 24, 1902]

MM. Boucard et Jèze me demandent de présenter au public français la traduction du livre de M. Woodrow Wilson. Je le fais bien volontiers. Ce m'est en effet une occasion de remercier les traducteurs du signalé service rendu par leur bibliothèque internationale de droit public; un moyen aussi de dire tout le bien que je pense du bel ouvrage de M. Wilson. Enfin (on me pardonnera cette considération personnelle), j'ai ainsi la bonne fortune de pouvoir mettre sous l'autorité du savant auteur américain quelques idées qui me sont chères.

Le livre de M. Wilson occupe une place à part dans la littérature anglo-américaine du droit public. Dédaigneux des théories et des généralisations, les juristes anglais et américains se bornent en général à l'exposé analytique des législations positives qu'ils étudient; aussi bien, ils ne manquent point de marquer le rôle social des institutions politiques et les déformations qu'elles reçoivent sous l'influence des faits. Mais de constructions juridiques à la manière allemande, de conceptions politico-métaphysiques à la manière française, de synthèses sociologiques, on n'en

¹ Professor of Constitutional Law at the University of Bordeaux, prolific author in the fields of public law, international law, the history of law, and comparative constitutional law.

trouvera point dans l'œuvre de ces publicistes. Pour eux le droit politique, comme la politique elle-même, doit être essentiellement réaliste. Qu'importe ces longues théories sur la personnalité et la souveraineté de l'Etat, sur le but et les fonctions de l'Etat, sur la nature intrinsèque de la loi, sur le fondement juridique des contrats d'Etat? Ce sont là jeux d'esprit sans portée, qui n'ont point de place dans les écrits de Story, de MM. Todd, Cooley, Anson, Dicey ou Bryce. Leur but est seulement d'exposer clairement les règles du droit public anglais et américain, leur relation avec l'Etat social du pays, les avantages ou les inconvénients pratiques de telle ou telle institution. La question elle-même, qui nous paraît capitale, du caractère obligatoire de la loi positive pour les volontés individuelles, leur échappe entièrement, et un jurisconsulte éminent, comme M. Dicey, ne trouvera d'autre critérium à la loi positive que l'obligation où est toute cour de justice d'en faire l'application. M. Wilson lui-même dans son livre célèbre, *le Gouvernement congressionnel*, ne s'était point départi de cette tradition; il y démonte pièce à pièce les rouages du parlementarisme américain, en montre les avantages et les inconvénients, les défauts et les qualités, la manière dont en usent les hommes politiques. Rien de plus. Tout cela n'est point d'ailleurs pour diminuer dans ma pensée la valeur de ces divers écrits. Des livres comme ceux de Story, de MM. Bryce, Dicey, Wilson sont des ouvrages de premier ordre; et après tout, les juristes anglo-américains ont peut-être raison de répugner aux théories abstraites, aux conceptions métaphysiques, aux généralisations sociologiques et de se complaire à l'observation purement réaliste des institutions politiques.

Dans son ouvrage sur l'Etat, M. Wilson a rompu avec ces procédés et ne voit dans l'étude des institutions politiques positives qu'un moyen d'arriver à une compréhension scientifique du droit politique en général. La première moitié de l'unique volume de l'édition américaine et tout le premier volume de l'édition française (qui en comprendra deux) sont remplis par l'analyse des institutions politiques de la Grèce et de Rome, de la France, de l'Allemagne, de l'Autriche-Hongrie, de la Suède et Norvège et de la Suisse. Mais ce n'est là qu'un préambule, et comme le recueil des documents, qui permettront à l'auteur de formuler des conclusions générales sur la nature de l'Etat et du gouvernement, sur les lois qui ont présidé à leur développement historique, sur la puissance de la loi positive, sur l'objet du gouvernement et sur les limites apportées à cet objet. Pour tout dire d'un mot, M. Wilson a voulu écrire un traité de *sociologie politique*. Je ne saurais trop vivement l'en féliciter. Cependant, en qualifiant ainsi ce bel ouvrage, j'en marque les qualités éminentes, mais aussi les imperfections et les lacunes. Je les signalerai avec une entière franchise, que M. Wilson voudra bien excuser.

I

Dire que l'ouvrage de M. Wilson est un véritable traité de sociologie politique, c'est indiquer d'abord tout le mérite du livre. Suivant une rigoureuse méthode scientifique, l'auteur écarte toutes les hypothèses métaphysiques ou religieuses sur l'origine de l'Etat. "La question de l'origine probable de l'idée de gouvernement, déclare-t-il dès la première page du volume, est une question de fait à déterminer historiquement et non par des hypothèses." Non seulement on doit écarter le dogme du droit divin, mais encore les hypothèses métaphysiques qui se résument dans le contrat social, réalisant la conscience collective de la société et formant l'Etat souverain. Dogmes et conceptions *a priori* sont sans valeur scientifique, et le sociologue doit les ignorer. Il recherche seulement, par les procédés de la préhistoire et de la critique historique, comment s'est établie, dans les sociétés anciennes la différenciation entre gouvernants et gouvernés, laquelle résume toutes les formations politiques. De cette étude, M. Wilson donne un substantiel aperçu, mais trop succinct à mon gré; il le restreint d'ailleurs aux sociétés dites aryennes, parce que, dit-il, elles sont les mieux connues et paraissent s'être élevées au plus haut stade de la civilisation. Peut-être cependant serait-il bien téméraire de généraliser et de dire que l'évolution politique de la plupart des sociétés ait eu les mêmes origines, ait suivi les mêmes étapes que celle des peuples indo-européens. Mais le point n'est pas là. L'essentiel est d'affirmer que toutes les doctrines *a priori* sur l'origine de l'Etat et des gouvernements doivent être rejetées parce qu'elles sont anti-scientifiques, et faire place à l'étude objective des faits historiques et pré-historiques. M. Wilson n'y a point manqué.

Quoiqu'on pense des doctrines sociologiques modernes, on ne saurait contester qu'elles ont montré d'une manière définitive que les groupements humains sont des faits généraux, naturels et spontanés et non des créations accidentelles, artificielles et volontaires. Cette idée féconde domine tout l'ouvrage de notre auteur. Que l'homme ne s'est pas rapproché des autres hommes par un acte de volonté claire et réfléchie, qu'il n'a point crée la société comme le sculpteur modèle une figure, qu'il n'a point établi par une combinaison consciente les divérses institutions sociales, qu'il ne peut point créer et accorder les rouages de la machine politique, comme le mécanicien fait d'une machine électrique, voilà des idées qu'on n'affirmera jamais assez haut, surtout en France, où les doctrines de Rousseau ont si profondément pénetré les esprits, et où les mécaniciens politiques, depuis Siéyès, n'ont jamais manqué. Aussi M. Wilson a-t-il cent fois raison d'écrire: "La société n'est en aucun sens artificielle; elle est aussi vraiment naturelle et organique que l'homme individuel lui-même" (n° 1392).[2] Et encore: "Le choix humain à tous les âges du grand développement de la politique dans le monde a eu sa part dans la formation des institutions; mais il n'a jamais été en son pouvoir de procéder par sauts et par bonds; il s'est borné à une adataption [adaptation] entièrement exclusive d'une invention propre. Les institutions, comme les morales, comme toutes les autres formes de vie et de conduite, ont eu à subir la lente, la presque imperceptible formation de la coutume. Les monarques les plus absolus ont eu à apprendre les moeurs, à observer les traditions, à respecter les préjugés de leurs sujets; les plus ardents réformateurs ont eu à apprendre que trop dépasser les masses les plus indolentes, c'était se rendre eux-mêmes impuissants. Une révolution a toujours été suivie par une réaction. . . . La croissance politique se refuse à être forcée; et les institutions ont grandi avec le lent accroissement des relations sociales; elles se sont transformées non d'après de nouvelles théories, mais d'après de nouvelles circonstances" (n° 1352). Par cette citation on aperçoit l'esprit qui remplit tout le livre de M. Wilson: développement spontané des institutions politiques et juridiques, précarité des institutions créées [crées] par l'arbitraire du législateur et qui ne correspondent pas aux traditions, aux moeurs, aux tendances, aux besoins du pays auquel elles s'adressent. Ces vues éminemment justes, publicistes et hommes politiques de tous pays les oublient trop souvent. Puisse ce beau livre les leur rappeler et leur montrer tout le danger de ne s'y point conformer!

Il convient encore de féliciter hautement l'auteur de n'avoir point fait de place aux constructions juridiques de l'école allemande, sans doute ingénieuses et subtiles toujours, mais artificielles et vaines souvent. Désireux de faire rentrer les relations politiques dans les vieux cadres du droit subjectif et de la personnalité juridique qui lui sert de sujet, les juristes allemands ont édifié la théorie de l'Etat-personne, sujet du droit subjectif de puissance publique et tenté de ramener tout le droit public à la combinaison des droits subjectifs de l'Etat avec ceux des autres personnes publiques ou privées. Quelques auteurs français sont

[2] Here and in following such cases, Duguit refers to section numbers of *The State*.

entrés dans cette voie. Tout ce que peuvent inventer l'ingéniosité du raisonnement, le raffinement de l'esprit scolastique, occupe une bonne partie des écrits publiés récemment sur le droit public en France et en Allemagne. La personnalité juridique de l'Etat est-elle une abstraction ou une fiction? Les gouvernants et les agents de l'Etat sont des représentants. Mais sont-ils des organes juridiques ou des mandataires? La souveraineté est-elle le caractère de la volonté qui ne se détermine que par elle-même? Toutes ces questions, qui se prêtent aisément à de subtiles dissertations (gymnastique intellectuelle qui n'est pas d'ailleurs sans agrément pour l'esprit), M. Wilson les ignore entièrement. Ce n'est point qu'il conteste la réalité du fait social, bien au contraire; l'existence naturelle et réelle du lien qui unit entre eux les membres d'un même groupe social, l'auteur la met souvent en relief. Mais il ne daigne même pas discuter cette conception des juristes allemands, qui, derrière les manifestations de la puissance publique, placent je ne sais quelle substance métaphysique, qui serait l'Etat, personne juridique, titulaire des droits subjectifs de puissance. Résurrection d'un substantialisme scolastique, que le réalisme moderne paraissait cependant avoir définitivement condamné. Le lecteur verra comment M. Wilson montre clairement que l'Etat n'est autre chose qu'un groupe social, où certains individus, détenteurs de la force, l'ont monopolisée et l'ont organisée, "que la caractéristique de tout gouvernement, quelle que soit sa forme, est l'autorité, qu'il doit y avoir en définitive d'une part des gouvernants et d'autre part ceux qui sont gouvernés, que l'autorité des gouvernants, directement ou indirectement, repose dans tous les cas finalement sur la *force*; qu'en dernière analyse, le gouvernement c'est la force organisée" (n° 1387).

II

Jusqu'ici j'ai résumé les idées essentielles de M. Wilson, en les approuvant sans réserve. On voudra bien m'excuser si je ne borne pas là mon rôle de préfacier. La haute valeur du livre mérite en effet que celui qui le présente au public dise sans détour les réserves et les critiques qu'une lecture attentive lui a suggérées. D'ailleurs réserves et critiques s'adressent bien moins à l'ouvrage lui-même en particulier, qu'aux doctrines sociologiques en général. Voulant constituer de toutes pièces une science des sociétés, les sociologues modernes ont naturellement tenté de faire entrer dans des formules synthétiques les éléments si complexes, si variables du développement social, étudiés par plus de dix sciences spéciales. De là des généralisations artificielles et hâtives, qui contiennent sans doute une grande part de vérité, mais souvent aussi une part non moins grande d'erreur. La chose était inévitable. Les œuvres de puissants esprits, comme Auguste Comte et Herbert Spencer en sont la preuve. Les généralisations hâtives abondent dans l'ouvrage de M. Wilson. Ainsi, au dire de l'auteur, la famille aurait été la forme première de l'Etat dans toutes les sociétés indo-européennes; et le fondement premier de l'organization et de l'autorité sociale aurait été la parenté. Il n'est point impossible qu'il en ait été ainsi; mais la preuve n'est pas faite et vraisemblablement ne le sera jamais. En tout cas, si la parenté a été un facteur du groupement social et de la distinction des gouvernants et des gouvernés, il est incontestable que d'autres éléments ont aussi puissamment agi. Bien plus, la parenté n'a dû être primitivement qu'une cause temporaire d'association, unissant à leurs auteurs les descendants pendant la période seulement où ceux-ci avaient besoin d'aide et de protection. La permanence des groupements sociaux, leur structure politique sont dues certainement à d'autres causes que la parenté seule. L'autorité du parent n'a pu s'imposer qu'à une époque où la consanguinité était socialement et régulièrement constatée et où les sentiments de déférence vis-à-vis des ancêtres ou des aînés avaient pénétré l'esprit des hommes. Or tout cela implique un long stade d'évolution, pendant lequel une authorité politique existait assurément. On ne résout point le problème de la différenciation politique dans les sociétés indo-européennes en disant que la forme première de la société politique y a été partout la famille. C'est là une formule générale, qui méconnaît la complexité du problème et qui, je le crains bien, n'a rien de scientifique. Et cependant M. Wilson va plus loin encore: il estime que la famille patriarcale et monogamique a été de très bonne heure, dans le lointain passé de la préhistoire, la forme unique de la société politique; il en voit la preuve "dans l'instinct monogamique très fort que l'homme possède et avec lui les bêtes les plus haut placées dans l'ordre animal, et qui a tendu à exclure des relations sexuelles communes ou multiples et à constituer des familles distinctes basées sur des mariages monogamiques" (n° 7). A la vérité, il n'y a point là de preuve bien convaincante. Ne peut-on pas dire avec autant de vraisemblance que l'instinct monogamique est au contraire le produit d'une civilisation relativement avancée?

Dans l'état actuel des études préhistoriques, on ne peut rien affirmer. Il paraît vrai cependant qu'à une certaine époque historique, très variable, dans les sociétés du type aryen, la famille était en général patriarcale et monogamique, et formait une société politique complète, fortement intégrée par les liens de soli-

darité étroite, qui en unissait les membres, fortement différenciée
par l'autorité reconnue au chef de famille; que le groupement de
ces familles, en Grèce et à Rome, a donné naissance à la cité, type
par excellence de l'Etat ancien. Aller plus loin, c'est formuler de
pures hypothèses; c'est méconnaître ce fait incontestable que la
forme patriarcale suppose une conscience juridique parvenue
déjà à une haut degré de développement, après de longs siècles
d'efforts, accomplis sous l'influence des causes les plus diverses.

N'est-ce pas encore une généralisation un peu téméraire que
d'opposer, comme le fait M. Wilson, au socialisme des cités antiques l'individualisme des races germaniques et du christianisme?
Anciennement, dit-il, "la société était l'unité; l'individu la fraction.
L'homme existait pour la société. . . . L'Etat était le seul individu.
Pendant des siècles, il n'y a pas eu de changement essentiel dans
cette idée. . . . Il n'y avait pas de droits privés existant contre
l'Etat. Postérieurement diverses influences se sont combinées
pour briser cette vieille conception. Ces influences ont été au
premier chef le christianisme et les institutions des conquérants
germains du ve siècle" (n°s 1408 et 1409). Pareille proposition
a été bien souvent formulée. Il est aisé de montrer cependant
combien peu elle répond à la réalité des choses. Pour qu'elle fût
vraie, il faudrait établir que les hommes des cités antiques n'ont
point eu conscience de leur valeur propre comme individus,
qu'aucune doctrine ancienne n'est venue affirmer la puissance
du moi individuel. D'autre part il faudrait démontrer que la conception de solidarité sociale était inconnue des populations germaniques et des fondateurs du christianisme. Or rien de tout
cela n'est vrai. Il est exact que ni les Romains ni les Grecs n'ont
eu la notion, même approchée, de droits individuels au sens
moderne et qu'ils ont reconnu à la cité le droit de demander à
chacun le sacrifice de sa personne et de ses biens dans l'intérêt
de tous. Mais est-ce à dire que les institutions antiques aient
entièrement méconnu les droits de l'individu? Hermann a montré,
il y a déjà longtemps, que le respect de l'individualité a toujours
existé en Grèce et à Rome et se traduisait dans cette idée que la
cité pouvait tout demander aux individus à la condition qu'elle
demandât à tous le même sacrifice.[3] En un mot la liberté con-
sistait dans l'égalité. Mais il n'y a d'égalité qu'entre des valeurs;
l'individualité était donc une valeur dont la cité reconnaissait tout
le prix. Peut-on dire qu'un peuple qui a enfanté le stoïcisme, n'ait
pas compris l'éminente dignité de la personne humaine, n'ait
pas reconnu l'autonomie de la volonté individuelle? Et le droit

---

[3] Hermann, *Lehrbuch der griechischen Rechtsalterthümer*, 1884, p. 28. [This
and the following notes by Duguit. They have been renumbered.]

romain classique, dérivé de la philosophie stoïcienne, n'est-il pas tout entier fondé sur le respect de la personne libre et de ses droits? Il n'est pas vrai non plus que les institutions germaniques et les idées chrétiennes aient été avant tout individualistes. Il suffit, pour prouver le contraire, de rappeler la persistance de la propriété collective dans les populations d'origine germanique, et la solidarité étroite, qui réunissait les membres d'une même famille et peut-être d'un même *pagus*, au cas d'offense faite à l'un d'eux. Enfin s'il est une doctrine qui ait contribué à faire pénétrer dans l'esprit des hommes l'idée de solidarité sociale, c'est assurément le christianisme. La transmission héréditaire de la faute originelle, la rédemption du péché par la sacrifice du Christ, le juste par excellence, la communion des saints et le rachat des pécheurs par la souffrance et la prière des justes, voilà toute la théologie chrétienne. Il n'est pas de doctrine qui affirme plus hautement la solidarité de tous, le principe social par excellence. Il serait hors de propos d'insister davantage sur tout cela. Mais on conviendra qu'une proposition qui oppose tout simplement l'individualisme germanique et chrétien au socialisme des cités antiques, mérite quelques réserves.

Je dois aussi signaler certains rapprochements artificiels, certaines comparaisons suspectes, certaines explications simplistes, notamment le long parallèle que fait M. Wilson entre Rome et l'Angleterre. Il n'est personne assurément qui n'ait été frappé par une certaine similitude entre les procédés diplomatiques, militaires et coloniaux des Grecs et des Romains, et aussi par l'esprit conservateur, qui se retrouve à un haut degré chez les deux peuples. Il y a là un rapprochement qui peut illustrer avantageusement un livre de vulgarisation, éveiller l'attention des auditeurs dans une conférence publique, mais qui ne mérite point d'occuper dans un ouvrage scientifique la place importante que lui a faite notre auteur. Profond admirateur de la politique réaliste toujours pratiquée par les Romains et les Anglais, M. Wilson pense que c'est à elle que les deux nations doivent d'avoir pu fonder et conserver un immense empire. Ce sont, dit-il, les deux nations impériales (nº 1358); elles marchent à la tête de la civilisation, parce qu'elles ont conquis le monde et su le gouverner. Que Rome et l'Angleterre aient fondé de puissants empires, qu'elles aient puisé leur force dans une fusion de l'esprit conservateur et d'une hardiesse réaliste, que le droit privé de Rome et les institutions politiques de l'Angleterre aient servi de modèle à bien des pays, je n'y contredis point. Mais sont-elles pour cela les deux premières nations du monde? Je suis de ceux qui pensent qu'un peuple est vraiment grand, moins par la conquête, le gouvernement, l'ingéniosité de ses institutions, l'habileté de ses procédés politiques, que par les idées dont il a doté le patrimoine moral et intellectuel de l'humanité. Le peuple juif, disséminé aux quatre coins du monde, reste une nation impériale, pour employer l'expression de M. Wilson, parce qu'il a enfanté le prophétisme et le christianisme. Et si la France devait un jour perdre son rang de grande puissance, il lui resterait toujours la gloire impériale d'avoir imposé à l'attention du monde la déclaration des droits de l'homme.

Artificielle, l'assimilation que fait l'auteur entre Rome et l'Angleterre; non moins artificielle, l'opposition qu'il signale entre les deux peuples. Quelques habiles, dit-il, qu'aient été les Romains dans le choix des procédés politiques, ils n'ont jamais pratiqué ni connu le système représentatif "qui permet d'étendre l'organisation de la nation sans perte de vitalité" (n° 1361). Les Anglais ont au contraire connu et pratiqué de très bonne heure ce merveilleux système. Ils l'ont trouvé, au dire du savant auteur, dans les institutions germaniques, qui se sont développées librement en Angleterre, parce que, à la différence du continent, elle avait échappé à l'influence romaine. Ces institutions représentatives, empruntées aux Germains, développées et précisées par le génie anglais, sont ensuite passées sur le continent pour constituer le fonds commun des régimes politiques dans les Etats civilisés.— Montesquieu avait dit en effet en parlant du régime représentatif: "Ce beau régime a été trouvé dans les bois."[4] Mais depuis Montesquieu, la critique historique a fait des progrès. Elle a montré d'une manière irréfutable que les assemblées des anciens Germains n'avaient rien de commun avec nos assemblées représentatives modernes. Je suis loin de méconnaître que l'Angleterre ait joué un rôle actif dans la formation du système représentatif. Mais la part de la France a-t-elle été moindre? Chez nous, il est vrai, le développement des institutions représentatives a été entravé par l'absolutisme royal, dû à des causes particulières à notre pays. L'idée de représentation est née en Angleterre et en France à des époques concomitantes; et ni l'une ni l'autre ne l'ont empruntée aux Germains: elle dérivait de causes sensiblement analogues dans les deux pays. En tout cas, le régime représentatif moderne est un fait historique trop complexe, pour qu'on puisse résoudre le problème de son origine en affirmant dans quelques lignes qu'il est une importation germanique, se développant librement sur sol anglais, à l'abri des influences romaines.

Je demande aussi la permission à M. Wilson de mettre le lecteur français en garde contre quelques inexactitudes de détail.

[4] *Esprit des Lois*, Liv. XI, chap. vi.

Ainsi, voulant marquer l'opposition du système social des Germains et des Romains, l'auteur écrit: "Le système teuton était essentiellement personnel; le système romain essentiellement impersonnel. Ni le soldat romain, ni le citoyen romain n'ont jamais rien connu de la fidélité personnelle, qui est la base de l'Etat politique primitif en Germanie" (nᵒˢ 292 et 1409). M. Wilson oublie l'institution romaine de la clientèle, qui créait certainement un devoir de fidélité personnelle, due par le client à son patron; l'opposition n'est donc pas si complète entre les conceptions germaniques et les idées romaines. Ce rapprochement de la fidélité que doit le client au patron et du service personnel que doit l'homme d'armes à son chef a été d'ailleurs aperçu depuis longtemps, puisque Tacite même n'a point manqué de le signaler.[5]

M. Wilson consacre d'assez nombreuses pages à la féodalité et parle à diverses reprises du morcellement social qui aurait été la caractéristique de ce régime (nᵒ 311). Le savant auteur, nous semble-t-il, n'a pas aperçu que la féodalité a été au contraire un puissant mouvement d'intégration sociale. Le lieu était bien ici de tenter une généralisation et de rechercher si la forme féodale n'est pas une étape par laquelle doit passer toute société avant d'arriver à l'unité nationale. Mais l'écrivain n'a vu ni la prédominance, à l'époque féodale, de l'idée de contrat, ni l'intégration sociale puissante, ni la solidarité profonde entre les hommes, que réalise la pure conception féodale, ni, spécialement en France, la permanence d'un pouvoir royal chargé de maintenir pour tous et contre tous, grands vassaux et hommes du commun, le principe supérieur de justice. D'ailleurs, dans sa bibliographie, M. Wilson ne cite, comne [comme] ouvrages français sur la féodalité, que les livres de Guizot, bien vieillis aujourd'hui et le petit manuel scolaire d'histoire du moyen âge, publié par M. Duruy. Les savants travaux de MM. Fustel de Coulanges et Luchaire, pour ne citer que ces noms, paraissent lui être inconnus. Je signale encore quelques erreurs de détail dans le chapitre relatif au gouvernement actuel de la France, erreurs bien excusables au reste, chez un écrivain étranger.

III

Je ne puis clore cette préface, déjà trop longue cependant, sans faire une dernière réserve sur un point qui me semble capital. Après un quart de siècle consacré à l'étude du droit et de la politique, je suis arrivé à cette conviction profonde que toute recherche sociale n'a de raison d'être et de valeur que si elle peut

---

[5] *Annales*, I, 37.

formuler une règle de conduite qui s'impose au respect des gouvernants. M. Wilson parait être resté tout à fait étranger à cette préoccupation. Dès lors son livre, rempli d'aperçus ingénieux et de fortes pensées, présente le défaut commun à toutes les doctrines de sociologie pure: l'impuissance à fonder une morale politique et sociale aussi bien qu'une morale individuelle. Sans doute le savant auteur écrit: "Le gouvernement doit servir la société; par aucun moyen, il ne doit la régir et ni la dominer. Le gouvernement n'est pas une fin en soi; il est seulement un moyen, —un moyen d'assurer les meilleurs intérêts de l'organisme social. L'Etat existe pour le but de la société et non la société pour le but de l'Etat" (n° 1528). Mais si je comprends bien la pensée de M. Wilson, il y a là une simple limite de fait à l'action du gouvernement, et non point une règle de conduite supérieure, s'imposant, par sa vertu propre, aux détenteurs de la force; à chaque page en effet, l'auteur affirme que tout gouvernement est impuissant, s'il méconnait la structure, les mœurs, les conditions d'existence, les aspirations et les besoins de la société; que s'il les respecte au contraire, il trouve alors sa force dans l'acquiescement du plus grand nombre, dans l'opinion publique plus ou moins consciente d'elle-même; que le gouvernement est seulement l'organe exécutif de la société, l'organe par lequel sa coutume agit, sa volonté opère, "par lequel la société s'adapte à son milieu et réalise une vie plus effective"; que cette volonté de la collectivité n'est pas autre chose que la volonté de la majorité, volonté d'abord inconsciente et prenant conscience d'elle-même dans les pays civilisés, que cette volonté de la majorité, inconsciente ou consciente, donne toute sa force au droit, aux créations du gouvernement, aux ordres de la loi; qu'il n'y a pas de despote, quelque puissant qu'il soit, qui puisse se maintenir, s'il ne s'appuie pas sur cette volonté de la majorité (v. surtout n° 1389).

Mais tout cela ressemble bien à la vieille doctrine du contrat social et du *moi commun* de Jean-Jacques Rousseau. Au reste, dans un article récent, M. Espinas, l'éminent sociologue français, aboutit à une conclusion sensiblement analogue.[6] Cinquante ans après la mort d'Auguste Comte, on pouvait espérer que la sociologie trouverait un autre fondement à la politique scientifique que l'hypothèse surannée du contrat social. En résumé, disciples de Rousseau et sociologues expliquent la puissance politique par l'assentiment tacite de la collectivité, par l'acquiescement de la conscience sociale, qui se traduit à l'extérieur dans les manifestations de la majorité. Toutes ces doctrines ont un vice irrémédia-

6 Espinas, *Être ou ne pas être, Revue philosophique*, mai 1901, p. 478.

ble: elles négligent l'acte de volonté individuelle. Il y a là cependant un fait; une sociologie objective ne peut le méconnaître. On aura beau affirmer la seule valeur de la volonté et de la conscience sociales; en fait, il y a et il y a toujours eu des volontés et des consciences individuelles qui s'insurgent contre le moi social. Si l'on ne tient pas compte de cette opposition, on n'a qu'une compréhension tout-à-fait incomplète des faits sociaux. Si, au contraire, on la reconnaît, il faut l'expliquer et déterminer comment elle se comporte au regard de la conscience et de la volonté sociales.

On ne saurait nier d'abord que le gouvernant, détenteur de la force, peut toujours ordonner et en fait a souvent ordonné des choses contraires à la volonté consciente ou inconsciente de la société. Quelle sera la valeur, quel sera l'effet d'un pareil ordre? M. Wilson répond: cet ordre pourra s'imposer pour un temps par la force; mais l'effet n'en est point durable, et le despote qui voudrait l'imposer définitivement, disparaîtrait sans y réussir. Fort bien. Mais cet acte individuel de la volonté gouvernante n'en est pas moins un fait qui agit sur les autres hommes, et par suite un fait social, que le sociologue ne peut négliger. Ce commandement arbitraire n'aura, je le veux bien, qu'une action réduite et temporaire; mais il aura cependant un effet, ne serait-ce que la révolution qu'il provoque. La révolution apaisée, l'état social qui la suit sera certainement différent de ce qu'il était auparavant. L'acte individuel et arbitraire d'un gouvernant n'est donc jamais une quantité négligeable. L'acte individuel et arbitraire d'un Napoléon ou d'un Bismarck est une réalité, et même une réalité sociale; le sociologue ne saurait en faire abstraction. Que cet acte individuel soit déterminé par le milieu, par l'hérédité du personnage, par son éducation, par son tempérament physique, c'est très probable, mais cela n'est point démontré. A coup sûr, il nous apparaît, non point comme une manifestation de la conscience sociale, mais comme une insurrection contre elle, et malgré cela il produit un effet incontestable sur l'état social, sur la formation du droit, sur la direction politique. Le droit se développe spontanément, sans contredit; mais l'action individuelle des gouvernants n'est point étrangère à ce développement, ne serait-elle qu'une cause perturbatrice. Ihering a d'ailleurs clairement démontré qu'il y avait plus que cela; il a établi contre l'école historique orthodoxe l'action certaine de la volonté raisonnée des gouvernants, au moins sur la partie constructive, l'anatomie du droit. M. Wilson paraît nier tout cela; je tiens à l'affirmer au contraire. "La vraie science sociale, comme le dit M. Tarde, doit montrer l'inanité des prétendues formules, des prétendues lois historiques, qui opposeraient des obstacles infranchissables aux volontés des individus."[7]

Comme celle des gouvernants, la volonté individuelle des gouvernés et même d'un seul gouverné, exerce une action sociale. S'inspirant des doctrines sociologiques courantes, M. Wilson explique la force obligatoire de la loi positive en disant qu'elle est l'expression de la conscience collective; Rousseau avait dit, ce qui est la même chose, l'expression de la volonté générale. Par là tout commandement conforme à cette conscience collective, à cette volonté générale, tout commandement adéquat au moi commun s'impose à tous les gouvernés. "C'est pourquoi, dit notre auteur, l'intervention disciplinaire du gouvernement, pour faire respecter les décisions qu'il prend comme organe de la volonté générale est, en fin de compte, exceptionnelle" (nº 1393). Mais M. Wilson, comme Rousseau, comme tous les sociologues, est bien obligé de reconnaître que cette prétendue volonté générale ne peut être que la volonté de la majorité, qu'il peut toujours y avoir des volontés individuelles réfractaires aux décisions de cette volonté générale. Cette insurrection possible d'une ou plusieurs volontés individuelles est un fait social, puisqu'elle réagit sur d'autres volontés, ne serait-ce qu'en provoquant l'emploi de la force pour imposer directement ou indirectement l'obéissance.

Ainsi se pose le problème sur lequel doivent à mon sens converger tous les efforts de la science politique et qu'elle doit forcément résoudre. Pourquoi et quand la volonté générale, dont, par hypothèse, le gouvernement est l'organe, peut-elle imposer, même par la force, aux volontés individuelles réfractaires, les décisions qu'elle a prises? Tout le problème de la science politique est là. Il n'a point échappé à la sagace pénétration de M. Wilson. "C'est, dit-il, seulement l'individu exceptionnel qui ne s'en tient pas forcément à l'habitude commune de la courtoisie et des devoirs sociaux" (nº 1393; rap. nº 1440). Rousseau avait déjà dit: "Hors le contrat primitif, la voix du plus grand nombre oblige toujours tous les autres. . . . Quand donc l'avis contraire au mien l'emporte, cela ne prouve autre chose sinon que je m'étais trompé et que ce que j'estimais être la volonté générale ne l'était point."[8] La volonté individuelle réfractaire aux décisions de la majorité est une volonté malade, une volonté qui se trompe. L'explication est en vérité trop facile. Encore ici les sociologues n'ont rien inventé depuis Rousseau.

Le problème ne sera résolu que lorsqu'on aura déterminé les conditions sous lesquelles la décision des gouvernants, même

[7] Tarde, *La réalité sociale, Revue philosophique*, novembre 1901, p. 464.
[8] *Contrat social*, Liv. IV, Chap. ii.

approuvée par la quasi-unanimité des gouvernés, est légitime en soi; ces conditions ne peuvent se trouver que dans la reconnais· sance d'une règle de conduite, supérieure aux gouvernants, et qui commande, dirige et limite leur action. Sans doute M. Wilson et les sociologues déclarent que les gouvernants doivent se conformer aux besoins de la société à la tête de laquelle ils sont placés. "Si les gouvernants sont des envahisseurs ou des usurpateurs, ils éviteront prudemment de briser les préjugés et les longues habitudes de la nation. . . . Ils font arbitrairement des décrets sur les individus; mais ils sont dépourvus du pouvoir d'atteindre la vie la masse: ceci, ils ne peuvent le faire que par de lentes et d'habiles mesures, qui presque insensiblement modifient la coutume du peuple. . . . La coutume de la nation est la matière sur laquelle travaille le législateur, et son caractère constitue la limite de son pouvoir" (n° 1442). Assurément. Mais j'ai déjà montré que ce n'était là qu'une limite de fait, et une limite illusoire, puisque, je l'ai dit plus haut, l'acte individuel du gouvernant qui viole la coutume traditionelle de la nation, a cependant des conséquences sociales et atteint par là, suivant l'expression de l'auteur, la vie de la masse. D'autre part cette formule est purement négative; elle borne l'intervention du gouvernement, elle ne lui impose pas une action. Or il ne suffit pas de marquer ce que l'homme d'Etat ne peut pas faire, il faut préciser ce qu'il est obligé de faire. Et puis, il resterait à prouver que toute décision du gouvernant est légitime quand elle est conforme à la coutume nationale, à la volonté de la majorité. Cette preuve n'est point faite. On n'établit pas davantage qu'une décision est toujours illégitime quand elle est contraire à la coutume, à la volonté générale; ce serait cependant l'essentiel. Il est possible que cette décision n'ait qu'une durée éphémère; mais ne serait-elle appliquée qu'une seule fois, il faudrait démontrer que contraire à la coutume, elle est toujours illégitime; on ne prouve point que la volonté générale ait toujours raison, et le gouvernement toujours tort quand il ne se conforme pas à cette volonté générale.

En fait n'y a t-il pas des exemples nombreux où cet acte individuel du gouvernant, à son origine manifestement contraire à la coutume, devient le point de départ d'une coutume nouvelle? Comme le dit très judicieusement M. Tarde,[9] "toute coutume est une série d'actes répétes; et toute série suppose un premier terme et ce premier terme est forcément un acte individuel." Dire que

[9] *La réalité sociale, loc. cit.,* p. 465.

toute décision conforme à la coutume s'impose à tous, c'est reconnaître légitime toute coutume établie: et cependant cette légitimité ne peut s'apprécier que par la valeur de l'acte individuel, quel qu'il soit, qui lui a servi de point de départ. Il faut, coûte que coûte, trouver un critérium que permette d'apprécier la valeur d'un acte gouvernemental. Ce critérium, la coutume sociale est impuissante à le fournir, parce qu'on ne peut établir la légitimité de la coutume qu'en démontrant la valeur de l'acte individuel initial, "de l'acte de spontanéité relative, auquel l'habitude est suspendue comme au premier anneau de sa chaîne."[10]

M. Wilson est le premier à reconnaître que l'Etat moderne est caractérisé par l'intervention volontaire, consciente et continuelle des gouvernants, qui ont une mission civilisatrice et sont, dit-il, "un instrument pour employer tous les moyens par lesquels une société peut être perfectionée, par lesquels tous les droits individuels peuvent être adaptés et harmonisés avec les devoirs publics, par lesquels le self-développement individuel peut servir et compléter le développement social, un instrument pour façonner d'anciens usages en de nouveaux, modifier de vieux moyens en vue de fins nouvelles" (n°s 1519 et 1536).—La mise en œuvre de ces moyens implique donc une intervention volontaire et individelle des gouvernants. Il faut par suite de toute nécessité formuler une règle qui soit la norme de cette action gouvernementale, qui la commande, la limite et la dirige et qui soit le critérium de sa légitimité. Pour tout dire d'un mot, il n'y aura de science politique que lorsqu'on aura trouvé le principe d'une morale politique. Nos anciens l'avaient bien compris en donnant aux sciences sociales ce beau nom de sciences morales et politiques; ce principe ne peut se trouver dans les contingences d'un prétendu développement social, indépendant des activités individuelles, puisque ce sont celles-ci, et au premier chef celles des gouvernants, qui provoquent et dirigent ce développement.

Tout cela n'a certainement pas échappé à l'esprit si pénétrant de M. Wilson. C'est assurément en pleine connaissance de cause qu'il a laissé dans l'ombre l'élément moral, qui doit, à mon sens, occuper la première place dans la science et l'art politiques. Le savant auteur a voulu faire une œuvre scientifique; il a pensé qu'il n'y avait de science sociale que celle qui niait la réalité de l'acte proprement individuel et reconnaisait seulement les manifestations de la conscience collective, en marquait l'ordre de succession et de coexistence, et d'art politique que celui qui adaptait exactement ses procédés aux faits sociaux ainsi compris. Je suis

[10] Tarde, *loc. cit.*, p. 466.

de ceux qui pensent au contraire que le fait primordial, auquel se rattachent toutes les manifestations sociales, est un acte de conscience individuelle, qu'en tout cas l'écrivain politique ne remplit toute sa tâche que s'il tente de déterminer, à la lumière de la raison et de l'experience, le principe stable et permanent d'une règle de conduite, s'imposant aux gouvernants, fixant leurs devoirs et limitant leur action.

M. Wilson voudra bien voir dans ces critiques et ces réserves une preuve de la haute estime que j'ai pour sa personne, sa science profonde et son grand talent. Le lecteur mesurera à la longueur de cette préface l'importance et l'intérêt captivant du livre. Je souhaite vivement que ce bel ouvrage trouve dans le public de langue française l'accueil empressé que lui ont fait l'Amérique et l'Angleterre. Il le mérite à tous égards.

Léon Duguit
Professor de droit constitutionnel
à l'Université de Bordeaux.

Bordeaux, 24 janvier 1902.

Printed in Woodrow Wilson, *L'État: Éléments d'Histoire & de Pratique Politique*, translated by J. Wilhelm, in "Bibliothèque Internationale de Droit Public," published under the direction of Max Boucard of the Conseil d'État and Gaston Jèze of the University of Lille (2 vols., Paris, 1902), pp. vii-xxv.

From the Minutes of the Princeton University Faculty

5 5′ P.M., Wednesday, January 29th, 1902.
. . . An Invitation was received [from The Johns Hopkins University] requesting the President and the Faculty to attend the Celebration of the Twenty Fifth Anniversary of the Founding of the University and to be present at the Inauguration of Professor Remsen, LL.D. as President of the University. To represent the Faculty Principals & Alternates Professors Brackett, Woodrow Wilson; McCay and Fine were appointed the Committee to represent this University. . . .[1]

The President then stated the precise object of the special meeting and read the Suggestions which he had presented to The Honorable The Board of Trustees in his report at their last meeting and which had been discussed by the Committee on the Curriculum and certain members of the Faculty.

SUGGESTIONS TO THE TRUSTEES BY THE PRESIDENT.

"In view of certain tendencies in the leading universities in this country that look toward a shortening of the curriculum and the widening of the range of elective studies, I think it is important for the Trustees to consider whether action should not be taken by this University in the direction of these tendencies. I do not think that we should act hastily, and I should hope that whatever it may be best to do will be with the full concurrence and support of the Faculty; but I feel confident that some decided modification of our existing curriculum must be made in the near future, unless we are ready to face the probability of a decided falling off in the number of our students.

The changes which I should favor are these:

1. That provision should be made for such increase in our Faculty as shall enable us to offer a thorough course in Human Anatomy and Physiology and also a course in the Common Law, so that those who so desire may have in the studies of Senior Year the full equivalent of one year of professional study in Medicine or Law.

2. That it may be possible for those who are willing to take an additional amount of work, making it twenty hours instead of fifteen hours per week, to take their Bachelor's degree in three years.

3. That some modification of the curriculum of the Sophomore year in the Academic department be effected, whereby a wider range of choice may be open to the student after he has completed the Freshman year."

After a discussion of the Suggestions as presented the following Members of the Faculty were elected a Committee to confer with the Trustee Committee in reference to the matter:

Dean Winans, Dean West, Professors Magie, Westcott, W. Wilson, Thompson, Fine and Humphreys of the Academical Department, and Professors Cornwall and [Elmer Howard] Loomis of the Scientific Department.[2]

[1] For accounts of this affair that focus on the part that Wilson played, see the news reports printed at Feb. 22 and 23, 1902.

[2] President Patton had included his suggestions for modification of the curriculum in his report to the Board of Trustees on March 14, 1901. It seems quite likely that he intended them to be a kind of counter-project to the investigation of the condition of undergraduate scholarship then being carried on by a special committee of the Academic Faculty (about which, see n. 2 to the notes for a talk printed at Nov. 21, 1901). Patton's suggestions were referred to the trustees' Committee on the Curriculum, enlarged into a special committee to include James Bayard Henry, James W. Alexander, and Moses Taylor Pyne. This special committee reported "progress" in its consideration of Patton's recommendations at the trustees' meeting on June 10, 1901. At this meeting, Cyrus H. McCormick proposed that the special committee "be requested to hear fully the opinions of the Faculty on the subject through a Committee appointed by the Faculty for this purpose." The resolution passed, but Patton apparently chose to delay bringing the matter before the University Faculty until the special meeting on January 29, 1902.

The appointment of the faculty committee was announced to the trustees at their meeting on March 13, 1902. At the next meeting of the trustees, on June 9, 1902, the special committee reported that it had had a "prolonged conference" with the faculty committee and was now considering a printed report of the said committee. Wilson's commentary on Patton's proposals is printed at June 1, 1902.

The special committee expected to make its final report to the Board in October 1902. However, the committee reported at this meeting, on October 21, that illness had prevented final action. As WW to E. R. Craven, Dec. 3, 1902, Vol. 14, indicates, Wilson, as the newly elected President of Princeton University, then took a decisive hand in the matter by suggesting that the special committee either suspend its activities indefinitely or else ask to be discharged. The committee chose the latter course and was discharged at the trustees' meeting on December 11, 1902.

The above note is based on "Minutes of the Trustees of Princeton University, Dec. 1898-Mar. 1901" and "Minutes of the Trustees of Princeton University, June 1901-Jan. 1908" (bound minute books in UA, NjP), at the dates mentioned.

A Newspaper Report of a Speech on Patriotism in Worcester, Massachusetts

[Jan. 30, 1902]

FLAG WORSHIP IS CRIED DOWN.

Prof. Woodrow Wilson Goes Deep Into His Subject.

Prof. Woodrow Wilson of the chair of jurisprudence at Princeton university, delivered an address yesterday afternoon in Association hall, before the members of the Worcester womans club, and a number of invited guests. His subject was "Patriotism," and while it might be more appropriate to an audience of men rather than of women, more especially as it touched on politics and the ways of politicians and the framing of laws, in which men are more especially interested, members of the club were much interested in and edified by what he said. . . .

Prof. Wilson, in the course of his address, said:—

"It is one of the pleasures of living in a country of free thought that we can meet and consult on those matters of common interest. We are for the most part of the same motive and we can consult on the subject and ideals of patriotism. There are words which seem to us like living things, the very mention of which sends a thrill along the blood. Patriotism is one of these words and liberty is another. Men speak them as if they were the summing up in them the great history of achievement and speak with memories of things heroically done in the past and also with memories of things basely done because of blood having spilled which should not have been.

"Our first feeling about patriotism is that it is practically impossible to expound or impart it, because we talk it, because it is a sentiment, and there are some sentiments you can't breathe in men's minds by deliberate processes. You can make men fear you if you have power enough, but you can't make men love you, at any rate, some of us tried to make men love us, but we found it was not a thing that could be done by compulsion, and many a man has played a subtle part by being a better looking fellow than he really is.

"We take it for granted we all love the country in which we live. Patriotism expresses itself in sentiment, but it is itself a principle of action. When I say I am a man's friend, I say something more than that, I intend affection for him. If I be his friend, I have a principle of action toward him. There are some wild fellows whose conduct I cannot approve and which is leading them to the bad, but I love these wild fellows. My taste is for the wild fellow, with the quick impulses, and with the lusty sort of quality. But when I say I am their friend, I am not to indulge my taste by letting me run riot with them. My duty is to take out of them some of the quality which in my heart I admire. The principle of friendship is different from the taste of friendship. I must serve them according to their quality, not according to their preferences, and I am not a true friend when I yield to their impulses of indulgence. We speak of some men as noble.

"It is necessary a man should serve his own interests, for the business of the world must be conducted. Men cannot live on altruistic principle in all they do. They must preserve their own families, and it is honorable for men to serve their own interests, and if they do that honestly they will be advancing the interests of the community in which they live. So soon as men spread a fine character over a large area of surface, we ascribe to them nobility, and not before, and one of the things which heartens a men [man] is that he can bestow nobility upon himself by right and by the plaudits of his fellow-men. It is your choice to be noble, and it is that nobility which puts the fine energy in this nation.

"Patriotism comes when a man is of big enough range of affection to take the country in. It is friendship writ large. It is fellowship with many sides, which expends itself in service to all mankind joined in the same citizenship, and who are bound up in the same principles of civilization. Men have dreamed of international patriotism, and they have spoken of the provincialism of the patriotism we have professed, and of the narrowness of keeping our patriotism to ourselves. And there's a boundary to it. It is easier for us to feel a quick impulse of sympathy with the nation across the ocean because its people speaks the same language that we do, and because so many threads of history are run into our past, which is also their past, and there is the idea of kinship and solidarity of interests and purpose and ideals which lie at the bottom of it all.

["]It has been said that patriotism is a more serious matter to the American than to any other person in the world, because of the government under which we live. The polity under which we live is a polity of discussion, and where everything must be done as near as possible on the merits of the case. Remember, I don't say that everything is done on the merits of the case. That is another story: and that is because it is so difficult to do all these things because of the different minds and different environments. But even that does not withhold us from seeing the ideal. You will see that we have been doing some very ridiculous things in this country. It is becoming a habit in a great many of our public schools to go through the elaborate performance of worshipping the flag of the United States. I don't know what it is if it is not worship. I have seen the same thing happen in the capital of the emperor of Germany before the colors and standards of the empire,[1] and we smile at the thing which the young emperor requires his troops to do.

"I don't think we can afford to smile so long as we make our school children do what they are doing every day of the week before the flag of the United States. I have not the slightest objection to that worship, provided you teach the children what the flag stands for. There are old charters in the flag, and permanent conceptions of human rights in that flag, and everything that stands for the dignity and independence of men, in political thinking, and if the flag does not stand for that, it is not worthy of being worshipped.

"I fou [If you] want to carry out anything in a democratic country, you must have a majority, and you must fish for that majority, or you will go home with an empty basket. And the duty of every man is to make his opinions known. Things are not settled in this country because men throw their hats in the air and huzzah. What the nation is after is character, and some of us weaken our intellectual characters by saying that there is another world to brace up in, and that we have the rest of eternity to straighten out in. This is all the stage the world will ever have. I don't believe in a great deal of the object of the individual being character. A man who is bent all the time on his being a personal character is a precious prig. This world was not created for such as him. This world was created for another thing. And the way individual character is formed is by the self-forgetful perform-

___

[1] That is, Wilson had seen flag worship in Berlin in his mind's eye. He had never been there.

ance of duty, for if you do what is right, your character will take care of itself.

"Your character is no more to live for than is your dress. Your dress is your standard for self-respect, and your character should be the product of living according to the principles of rectitude. Men are instruments in this world and not objects. Men avoid employments they are best fitted for because they are afraid their healths will suffer. They are going to die sometime, and it is better to die doing the best service for the world than in some employment which is not fitted to them. We are all tools in the hands of the master, and we should yield ourselves.

"Systematic writers are very dangerous fellows, and give the impression of knowing more than they do know, but system seems the negative of inspiration. I have learned a good deal more out of poetry than out of all the systematic prose writers have put together. And I make no apology for drawing my points of inspiration from Tennyson, in the lines beginning 'A nation, yet the rulers and the ruled.'[2] I do not know of any better lines on which they could hang their morals on.

"Sectionalism is the negation of nationality. It comes from different degrees and kinds of development. We are disrespectful to our grandfathers, and don't recognize the very steps on which the people to whom we are nearest and dearest once passed.

"I was born and bred in the South, and even now there are certain things which I can perfectly understand in my heart and not justify in my mind. I know of able men who believe in the free coinage of silver, but I cannot conceive of the intellectual basis for that belief. But I know these men, and I should feel myself ashamed if I dared to condemn them. They must have got their ideas from the stage of economic developments of the people among whom they live, and I have a great respect for their minds when I place mine alongside theirs.

"We talk as if this government was conducted by the people. I have a great and profound affection for nonsense. I would not stop talking nonsense for anything, but I would prefer to know when I am talking it, and I would prefer, when I hear people talking government by the people to realize that they are talking nonsense.

"No government ever was conducted by the people. We select persons to do the governing for us, and during the time they are in office, if we be sovereign[,] we are like the god Baal, we are asleep, because we are on the journey. We are called an astro-

2 From "The Princess: Conclusion."

nomical government, because after so many revolutions of the seasons, we are consulted, and we are made subjects of the government just as much as any who are living under a despotic government.

"We have rulers and rules, and it pays to have a certain respect for our rulers. I have no objection to calling an interesting gentleman "Teddy" when he is not president of the United States. But when he is, I think it is a distinct discredit to call him by any nickname whatever. (Applause.)

"He is president of the United States, and so far forth our master. He is in the place of a king, by our choice, and the place which kings might envy, because it is a place to rule, and one in which he really determines an important part of the destinies of the world.

"Our present president is a sort of composite photograph of an American. When we look at some phases of the picture, we like it, and at some others we don't like it. And here is another picture of him, which appeared in a paper:

"Snatch of Lord Cromer, Jeff Davis a touch of him.
A little of Lincoln, but not very much of him;
Kitchener, Bismarck, Germany's Will,
Jupiter, Chamberlain, Buffalo Bill."[3]

(Laughter). "There's enough truth in this likeness to make it very interesting, of the larger, composite character of a very interesting arnd [and] a very strong man.

"Then we have some reverence for the laws of the country, and one of the inconveniences of a country like ours is extravagant reverence for laws. I believe we should not reverence laws so far as that they could not be changed. If you are convinced the law is wrong, and even if it be in the constitution of the United States, it should be changed, and you should say so. That may be something unusual to advocate, but I have suffered the penalty of making such a suggestion as that, and I have been called things for saying so. But you don't like to be regarded as a freak because you see a kind of disproportion between you and the constitution of the United States. It looks much like a pigmy challenging a giant, and still there have been times when pigmies and giants came together, and the giants got the worst of it.

"There have been no finer exhibitions of moral courage than in times of excitement, when one man has stood up against a mob, and rebuked them with cool words of wisdom. Such as the case of the town clerk who came out among the multitude who

---

[3] The author of this doggerel verse, widely circulated at the time, is unknown.

were yelling: 'Great is Diana of the Ephesians.' The town clerk said there was no one questioning the greatness of Diana, but for making such a tumult they would be held responsible by the government. Those idiots had been crying out for two hours: 'Great is Diana of the Ephesians,' and I think that town clerk was a consummate politician in that time.

"Patriotism is an active wisdom. We should be studious of the life of the nation. One of the things that keeps this country back is that men who have opinions don't put them into practical politics. We have not practical consciences. Most people will not yield an inch of principle. The man in this country who strikes for ideals by short cuts and suggestions, shows himself incapable of citizenship. You must go forward, shoulder to shoulder, in organized force. Every progress in history has been by inches, and the conditions of men who have advocated revolutionary methods as a general thing have sunk back further than they were before they started the movement. Practical politics is getting what you can by co-operation, and co-operation is yielding to too many dull fellows. People suggest that going into politics is going into office, and if you tell a young fellow he must go into practical politics he gets the idea that he must look for office.

"One of the things which made Theodore Roosevelt president of the United States is that it did not make any difference if you put him out of office, he stayed in politics, and there is nothing so inconvenient for the politician as for honest men to stay in politics. John Quincy Adams went to congress after he had been president of the United States.

"We should not allow ourselves to be clouded in our minds by what we read or be duped by men. It may seem unusual counsel from a college professor to warn you against books, but people have been misled by books. Don't be confused by thinking that life looks like the books written about it. Book writers are plausible men, and they are also some of them good fellows, but don't be deceived by smooth or rough-speaking. Know your fellowmen and know the world. The reason that books are necessary is that we know the men and women of our new generation, and in order to know the things of the past generations, they have [been] written down, because we were not there to see for ourselves. Know the men by rubbing shoulders with them, and not by getting ideas out of newspapers and books.

"The only way to get a good government is to elect good men to conduct it, and then get good men to interpret it. We have bred in this country a race of subtle lawyers, and they read the statutes very subtlely, and you cannot frame a law in American grammar and punctuation, but he can get out of it and drive a coach and six horses through it, and then he will make you believe that was the law which was meant." . . .

Mrs. Cutter entertained Prof. Wilson to dinner at 6 o'clock at her home, at 520 Pleasant street, and later Prof. L. P. Kinnicutt[4] entertained him at the Worcester club.

Printed in *Worcester*, Mass., *Daily Telegram*, Jan. 30, 1902; two editorial headings omitted.
[4] Leonard Parker Kinnicutt, Professor of Chemistry at Worcester Polytechnic Institute.

To Joseph Benson Gilder[1]

Princeton, New Jersey,
My dear Mr. Gilder,   30 January, 1902.

Since your letter leaves me in the dark as to what you want with him, it is a little difficult for me to answer the question, Who is the coming man in American history? But on the general question no man who knows the field need hesitate a moment for the answer. He is Professor Frederick J. Turner, of the University of Wisconsin. Both in knowledge and in the gift of expression he is already in the first class. He has not yet published a book. When he does various other writers to [in] the country will be willingly accorded a back seat.

Very truly Yours,   Woodrow Wilson

WWTLS (WHi).
[1] Co-editor of the New York *Critic*, literary adviser to the Century Company, and brother of Richard Watson Gilder.

To Richard Theodore Ely

My dear Dr. Ely,   Princeton, New Jersey, 30 January, 1902.

I wish very much that I had time to give careful formulation to my estimate of Dr. Adams's gifts and services. As it is, I can give only a few hasty sentences to what I should like to dwell upon at length; but I do so with with [sic] a cordiality of feeling which may, I hope, make up in part for the inadequate form.

If I were to sum up my impression of Dr. Adams, I should call him a great Captain of Industry,—a captain in the field of systematic and organized scholarship. I think all his pupils would accord him mastery in the formulation of historical inquiry, in the suggestive stimulation of research, in the communication of methods and ideals. His head was a veritable clearing house of ideas in the field of historical study, and no one ever seriously studied under him who did not get, in its most serviceable form, the modern ideals of work upon the sources; and not the ideals merely, but also a very definite principle of concrete application in daily study. The thesis work done under him may fairly be said to have set the pace for university work in history throughout the United States. That is the whole thing in a nutshell; and it makes a reputation which can never be justly obscured.[1]

Hoping that this is what you wanted, as nearly as I have time to furnish it,

> Faithfully and cordially Yours,   Woodrow Wilson

WWTLS (R. T. Ely Papers, WHi).

[1] Ely reproduced Wilson's letter, beginning with the first paragraph, up to this point in "A Sketch of the Life and Services of Herbert Baxter Adams," *Herbert B. Adams: Trubutes of Friends* . . . (Baltimore, 1902), p. 46.

A News Item

> [Feb. 1, 1902]

Prof. Woodrow Wilson lectured on What it Means to be an American, before the Peninsula Twentieth Century Club at Fort Monroe, Va., on Jan. 24. Thomas Tabb '56, Rev. L. C. Cooley '97, E. S. Alexander '97 and Louis Heffelfinger '00 are members of that club. On Jan. 25, Prof. Wilson visited Hampton Institute, and made a brief address to the students.[1]

Printed in the *Princeton Alumni Weekly*, II (Feb. 1, 1902), 283.

[1] No announcement or report of these addresses appeared in any extant Norfolk, Newport News, or Hampton newspaper, and the monthly publication of Hampton Institute did not note Wilson's visit to the campus of that institution. E. G. Murphy to WW, Feb. 5, 1904, Vol. 15, recalls Wilson's address at Fort Monroe.

From Houghton, Mifflin and Company

Dear Sir: Boston, February 1, 1902

It is a pleasure to see by this statement of the sales of your two books[1] in the past half year that they rather more than keep their place. And we are glad to take the opportunity that the transmission of this statement gives us of re-enforcing the suggestion Mr. Scudder made you last summer of our interest in the larger projects you may take in hand.[2]

> Yours sincerely,   Houghton Mifflin & Co.   W.B.P.

TLS (WP, DLC).

[1] *Congressional Government* and *Mere Literature and Other Essays.*

[2] This correspondence between Wilson and Horace Elisha Scudder is missing.

To Thomas Randolph Ball[1]

My dear Sir,   Princeton, New Jersey, 4 February, 1902.

Allow me, through you, to express my thanks to the authirities [authorities] of the University for their invitation to be present at the celebration of the twenty-fifth anniversary of the founding of the University and the inauguration of President Remsen; and to say that I shall be present at the public exercises both of the twenty-first and of the twenty-second. I should be obliged if you would kindly send me cards of admission.

Very truly Yours,   Woodrow Wilson

WWTLS (MdBJ).
  [1] Registrar of The Johns Hopkins University.

From Walter Ewing Hope[1]

Dear Professor Wilson,   New York. February 6, 1902.

I have no desire to add to your voluminous mail, especially at this time when you probably have quite sufficient reading, but I have an item of news which I thought might interest you, and which perhaps will furnish an excuse for this letter.

You may remember that Bob Steen[2] went out to Beirut, Syria, to teach in the college there. Well I have been in continuous correspondence with him throughout the fall and winter, and only the other day I had a very interesting letter from him. After discussing at some length his experience in teaching the "heathen" of all nationalities, he concluded with the following: "Do you know, I find that the few things that have stuck in my mind as a result of Woodrow Wilson's courses are just about the most useful things I learned during my four year's college course. The more I see of things out here, the more I agree with the general principles that he used to lay down for good government and progress. It is all so new to some of these boys that one feels as though he had a clean slate upon which to write whatever he wishes."

I have taken the liberty of sending you this because it has always seemed to me that the unconscious compliment, as it were, which was written without the slightest idea that it would reach other ears is worth a dozen of the ordinary forms of flattery. And Bob Steen is no poor judge.

I trust that you are having an enjoyable year and that you are surviving the semi-annual deluge of examination papers.

Yours very sincerely   Walter Ewing Hope

ALS (WP, DLC).
  [1] Princeton, 1901, at this time a student at the New York Law School.
  [2] Robert Service Steen, Princeton, 1901, instructor at the Syrian Protestant College, Beirut.

From Harper and Brothers

Dear Sir: New York City   Feb. 7, 1902.

We have your favor of yesterday with regard to spelling, and shall follow gladly your wishes in the matter of hyphens and most of the other suggestions; but as to the spelling of such words as labour, colour, ardour, etc. we beg leave to say that such spelling runs directly counter to every current and tendency of the age, and to the best modern usage. We respectfully suggest that this is not advisable. We are quite aware that the Century and the Standard dictionaries make such spelling permissible, but the best usage here and in England, is toward the elimination of all unnecessary letters. It is, however, against the long established and carefully considered rule of the house to use the English spelling in any case, and we feel convinced, in view of the strides that have been made towards the simplification of the language, that in a few years from now such spelling will be obsolete on both sides of the Atlantic.

In a work like yours which will, without doubt, take its place as an authoritative and standard work, we think it would be a mistake to hamper it with what, from our standpoint, would be a blemish. We beg that you will kindly give consideration to this point of view, and trust that you may come to agree with it.[1]

Very truly yours,   Harper & Brothers.

ALS (WP, DLC).
  [1] Wilson gave in to this point of view in the forms of spelling used in his *A History of the American People.*

A Fragmentary Report of a Lincoln Birthday Dinner

[Feb. 13, 1902]

37TH BANQUET IN HONOR OF LINCOLN

Jersey City Club Filled with Members of the Country's Pioneer Lincoln Ass'n.

Two Virginians paid tribute to the memory of Abraham Lincoln last night at the thirty-seventh annual banquet of the Lincoln Association of Jersey City, the pioneer organization of its kind in the country. The banquet was held at the Jersey City Club.

They were of different types and they looked at Lincoln from different viewpoints. Hugh Gordon Miller,[1] who declared that he represented "Young America and the new South," claimed for his native State all the credit for what was good and noble and patriotic in Lincoln. He endeavored to show not only that Lincoln came of Virginia parentage, but that he took for his inspiration, his ideal, his model in life, the greatest of all Virginians, George Washington.

The other Virginian, Prof. Woodrow Wilson, who is now an adopted Jerseyman, being one of the faculty of Princeton University, did not claim as much for Virginia—in fact, he declared that not Virginia, but the time in which Lincoln lived and his own indomitable pluck and perseverance, despite the drawbacks from which he suffered, because of lack of early advantages of education, made him the man he was—the typical American.

Hugh Gordon Miller's speech was a plea for the new South. "Had Lincoln lived," he said, "the reconstruction of my country would have been easy and not so burdensome as it is now. Had he lived he would have been loved and respected by the old South as well as the new."

Mr. Miller spoke of the condition of Virginia, of her struggle to regain the prestige and prosperity she lost through civil strife. "I take your invitation to be here to-night," he said, "as a tribute to the ability of my generation to repair the old flagship of all the fleet of her sister States until she shall regain her place in the nation. I talk not for the old Virginia, but of the Virginia of to-day, which is rising from the ruin and ashes of the old Virginia— the ruin of war."

Mr. Miller reviewed the achievements of Virginians in the early days of the nation and of the close bond of sympathy which existed between New Jersey and his native State, the two most patriotic of the thirteen colonies. He declared that while New Jersey produced her Frelinghuysen, Forman and other great men, Virginia contributed Washington, Jefferson, Madison and Lighthorse Harry Lee.

"I bring you," said the speaker, "the assurance of the good will and loyalty of the people of the South to the government and the flag that protects us all."

Mr. Miller claimed that Gen. Washington, a Virginian, was the first American to propagate the doctrine of anti-slavery. He told how in his will he provided for the emancipation of all his slaves and how he declared to Jefferson that he would like to see slavery abolished.

[1] Of the law firm of Miller and Coleman of Norfolk, Va.

The subject assigned Mr. Miller was "Lincoln and Lee."

Of Robert E. Lee he said that he was one of the greatest generals the world has ever produced. He rapidly sketched his career from West Point to Mexico, through the hard campaigns there, in one of which he was seriously wounded, through the Civil War to Appomattox, and then to Washington [Lexington, Va.], where he spent the remainder of the days of his life, instructing the youth of both North and South. He spoke feelingly of the great magnanimity of Gen. Grant at the surrender of the army of Lee, when he permitted the Southern officers to retain their side arms.

"That," said Mr. Miller, "was the grandest, the most magnanimous thing a warrior ever did. It placed your great Northern general higher in the halls of fame than Caesar, Alexander, Charlemagne or Napoleon. Grant rose to fame because he was opposed in Virginia by Robert E. Lee, one of the greatest commanders the world has ever seen. As Wellington became great because he was opposed and defeated Napoleon, so Grant became great because of his hard-earned victory over Lee." The speaker commented on the fact that in the Spanish-American war a grandson of Lincoln and a nephew of Lee rode side by side to battle.

In conclusion he said that the reuniting of the North with the South was a guarantee that "the last vestige of European tyranny and imperialism would disappear forever in the new countries of the world."

Prof. Woodrow Wilson, who is an authority on the history of the United States, took exception to some of the historical and biographical statements made by Mr. Miller. While a Virginian and proud of his native State, he did not claim so much for it.

He created a hearty laugh at the expense of Mr. Miller by alluding to a few of his digressions from the strict truth in his endeavor to prove Virginia the greatest State in the Union. He declared that Mr. Miller's speech reminded him of the epitaph of one, William Stacy, who died in a Western State. It read, he said: "This here to the memory of William Stacy, who came to his death by a Colt's revolver, old style, brass mounted. Of such is the Kingdom of Heaven."

"Mr. Miller's oratory," said Prof. Wilson, "is old style, brass mounted—an excellent specimen of brass work."

He declared, for instance, that the "Life of Washington," from which Mr. Miller had declared Lincoln must have received his inspiration, it, with Aesop's fables, the Bible and Pilgrim's Progress, having been the only books he had to read until after he had reached the formative period of life, was written by Parson Weems and was purely a work of the imagination and of little historical value. In commenting upon the true blue Unionism of Gen. Wheeler at San Juan, to which Mr. Miller had alluded in glowing terms, Prof. Wilson remarked that Mr. Miller had forgotten that in the excitement of the charge Gen. Wheeler was heard to yell "Give it to the damn Yankees, boys; give it to them!"

"That remark," said the speaker, "did not show any disrespect to the Yankees, but was merely illustrative of how impersonal every born soldier becomes when involved in a fight, and it is that we admire in him."

Prof. Wilson declared that at that late hour [–] he rose to speak after 11 o'clock, [–] he did not feel that he should say more. He, however, added that he hadn't the objections of the old Methodist Negro he once heard about. The Negro's master was an Episcopalian and he induced the Negro to attend the Episcopalian Church. The Negro was regular in attendance at the services for some time, but he finally returned to the Methodist Church. His master asked him why he did not attend his church any more, and the old fellow replied, "Well, master, it takes too much time to read the minutes ob de prebious meetin'."

After declaring that his hearers had heard about all the anecdotes of Lincoln he thought they could stand in one evening, Prof. Wilson took his seat. Then something happened which was unprecedented in the history of the Lincoln Association gatherings. With one accord the audience cheered and cheered again until their voices gave out. They clapped their hands and cried "Wilson, Wilson; more, more!"

After fully five minutes of this Prof. Wilson yielded to the popular demand and announced that he would give [p]art of the address which he had prepared for the occasion, but had decided not to deliver because of the sufficiency of oratory that had preceded his introduction.

The tosat [toast] assigned him was "Lincoln, the Scholar."

"I come," he said, "from an institution of learning, of which I am a member of the Faculty, and if I am not a scholar I ought to be, and as a scholar I ought to be able to know a scholar when I find one. It is the common belief that Abraham Lincoln was no scholar, so an attempt to treat on the subject assigned me might be considered somewhat like examining the interior machinery of a minus quantity or the intestines of a nonentity. Although my profession is that of teaching young men to study books, after all Lincoln was perhaps the best kind of scholar.

"The best way to learn things is by direct contact. If I could have lived with the men who were men in the past generations, I would not read books about them. It is because I was[2]

Undated fragmentary clipping (WP, DLC); some editorial headings omitted.
[2] The Editors have been unable to find the balance of this report in any Jersey City, New York, or Trenton newspaper. It seems most likely that the report appeared in the Jersey City *Jersey Journal*, Feb. 13, 1902, but no files of the newspaper for this period are extant.

From John Albert Blair[1]

My dear Prof,   Jersey City, N.J. Feby 13, 1902

Though I did not fail to show my enjoyment of your speech last night, I cannot refrain from repeating to you in this short note how much I was delighted. It was so clean cut, direct, and to the point, in such marked contrast with its somewhat diffuse predecessor—and withal so good-humoured, that it afforded us all very distinct pleasure. I am sure I express herein the feelings of the whole Association.

I hope you healed Mr. Miller's wounds, if he realized that he was hurt.[2]   Very respectfully   John A. Blair

ALS (WP, DLC).
[1] Princeton, 1866, Presiding Judge of the Hudson County, N.J., Court of Common Pleas.
[2] He did indeed. See H. G. Miller to WW, March 24, 1902.

From Basil Lanneau Gildersleeve

Dear Professor Wilson: Baltimore Feb. 14, 1902

May I not hope to have the pleasure of your company at dinner on Friday, February 20th at half past seven o'clock? I have seen so little of you in all these years & yet there is no one among your many friends who takes more pride and pleasure in your work than I do.   Yours sincerely   B. L. Gildersleeve

ALS (WP, DLC).

To Basil Lanneau Gildersleeve

Princeton, New Jersey,
My dear Professor Gildersleeve,   16 February, 1902

Thank you most sincerely for your kind note of Friday. It gives me real pleasure to accept the invitation it brings. It will be no small part of the enjoyment of the approaching celebration that

I am to have the opportunity thus to see you, for something more than a glimpse.

    With warm regard and appreciation
                Cordially Yours,   Woodrow Wilson

ALS (B. L. Gildersleeve Papers, MdBJ).

To Edith Gittings Reid

My dear Friend,   Princeton, 16 February, 1902

    I reproached myself after leaving you two weeks ago for not having written out the enclosed lines for you.[1] Perhaps they will seem all the fresher to you now that you have had time to forget them. I don't remember which of the English papers I saw them quoted from.

    I am looking forward with the keenest pleasure to seeing you at the end of this week. I wish there were going to be less celebration and more time for the *real* pleasure on Cathedral St. I have just been obliged, for lack of wit enough to think of any way of escape, to accept an invitation from Professor Gildersleeve to dine with him on Friday evening. He put the invitation to me with such cordial compliment that I could not but suppose that he really wanted me; and I should have felt cheap to invent an excuse for declining. And yet how difficult it is to read the utterance of a radically vain man and be *sure* you know what he means!

    Sometimes I am a bit ashamed of myself when I think how few friends I have amidst a host of acquaintances. Plenty of people offer me their friendship; but, partly because I am reserved and shy, and partly because I am fastidious and have a narrow, uncatholic taste in friends, I reject the offer in almost every case; and then am dismayed to look about and see how few persons in the world stand near me and know me as I am,—in such wise that they can give me sympathy and close support of heart. Perhaps it is because when I give at all I want to give my whole heart, and I feel that so few want it all, or would return measure for measure. Am I wrong, do you think, in that feeling? And can one as deeply covetous of friendship and close affection as I am afford to act upon such a feeling? In any case, you may know why such a friendship as yours is a priceless treasure to me,— and the distance between Princeton and Baltimore a misfortune.

    I mean to traverse that distance on Friday forenoon between the hours of eight and one, reaching Baltimore at 12:30,—until which time good-bye.

Mrs. Wilson is well again, and joins me in all cordial messages to you both.   Faithfully and sincerely your friend,
Woodrow Wilson

ALS (WC, NjP).
¹ This enclosure is missing.

Notes for a Religious Talk

Philadelphian Soc'y., 20 Feb'y, 1902.

"*No man can serve two masters.*" Matt., VI., 24.
   Subject—the Christian in public life, a propos Washington's Birth-day.

Two ideals of Christian life
   (1) That which *shuts out the world* entirely
   (2) That which seeks to *realize Christ in the world*,—in the thick of its work.

The most difficult field in which to realize the second is *the field of public life.*
   The Standards: (1) *The spirit of Christ*, i.e. of self-abnegation, of service, of fidelity to God.
   (2) *A reasonable, instructed conscience*,—instructed, i.e., in the conditions of moral progress,—in *the moralities of* (not compromise) the combination of wills and of good motives which are feasible in *concert of action.*

Washington: the *singular* impression of *balance* about the man, of moral rather than intellectual greatness. He was, in fact, *the principled man of the world.*

WWhw MS. (WP, DLC).

A News Report of a Religious Talk

[Feb. 21, 1902]
PHILADELPHIAN SOCIETY ADDRESSED
BY PROFESSOR WOODROW WILSON.

Professor Woodrow Wilson addressed the regular meeting of the Philadelphian Society in Murray Hall last evening. Taking as his subject, "No man can serve two masters," Professor Wilson applied it practically to a Christian in public life. He spoke of the opinion generally prevailing that there is no field worse for a Christian than public life, and said if that were so, then public life is condemned beforehand, and there is something radically wrong in the foundation of our state. The harm resulting from public service, he said, was due to the fact that a man had one motive in his public life and another motive in his Christian life; a man should have the same motive pervading both his Christian and his public life.

He spoke next of the two ideas which the world had concerning a Christian life; the first, the older one, was that a man should shut out the world and live apart from it, while the later idea held that a man must live his life in the world and help his fellow men. He said the first idea had long since been set aside, and in speaking of the second idea, he drew the vivid picture of a pure character, uncontaminated by the filth around it. Professor Wilson showed how a Christian life was inconsistent with a public life, only when personal ambition was the incentive, instead of unselfish service for the people. After speaking of vanity and its evils, and of the grandness of a life free from self-consciousness, he spoke of the practical Christian public life. He showed how necessary it was, for practical good, that a reformer should be content with one step forward at a time, be it ever so small. He said that the man who lives his public life for personal glory or gain is the one who makes the public and the Christian life inconsistent.

Professor Wilson stated that the subject of his address was chosen on account of the nearness of Washington's Birthday, also stating that the thing one enjoys in looking back at Washington's character is that he was entirely consistent, though not a brilliant man. A peculiar feature about Washington's character was its absolute symmetry. The genius of symmetry is better than the genius of brilliancy, and the line of force is the line of unity of purpose.

Printed in the *Daily Princetonian*, Feb. 21, 1902.

A Presentation Address[1]

[[Feb. 21, 1902]]

Doctor Gilman, the part I have to play is very small, but very gratifying. I hold in my hand a beautiful volume in which is engrossed an address from the Alumni, Graduates and Faculty of the Johns Hopkins University. It is an address of affection and congratulation, and I esteem it, Sir, one of the most pleasureable privileges and honors of my life that I should have been asked to represent such a body of men, for, in representing them,—as you yourself have said,—I feel that I am representing men who have taken from this University an ideal which has lifted their lives to

[1] A news account of this affair is printed below.

a plane they might not otherwise have attained; an ideal, Sir, of the service of truth not only, but of the service through truth, of the country of which they are citizens.

It is a significant thing, Sir, that the service of this University, inconspicuous in its methods, should nevertheless have drawn the attention of the nation upon it, and have led the government of this country to call upon men of the Johns Hopkins to assist in pushing forward the affairs of the nation. For, Sir, in encouraging the kind of study for which the Johns Hopkins has stood, the study which has its face forward toward the future and whose object is the extension of the realm of knowledge, it has been made evident that knowledge lives; that it is but a part of the power of achievement, fit to serve the nation in the present and in the future. America is not a child of books, she is a child of action,—and the sort of learning which you have fostered, is learning in action, not in reminiscence. If men have tired of classical study, it is because they have forgotten,—and sometimes even those who profess those ancient studies have themselves forgotten,—that though the language is dead, the stuff of thought which the language carries is still an integral part of the stuff of the world's thinking. They have here seen the classical learning live again, and it is for this reason that you and others who have stood with you have been honored by being called into the counsels of the nation; for at last learning is abroad, it has not kept within its cloister. And this, Sir, it seems to me, is the significance of this address,—coming from these men, some of them themselves distinguished, who thus come back to the source of their inspiration to show with friendly affection and acknowledge the signal obligations under which you have placed them.

Congratulatory Address.

"To Daniel Coit Gilman, Bachelor of Arts, Master of Arts, Doctor of Laws, formerly Professor in Yale University and President of the University of California, organizer and first President of the Johns Hopkins University in Baltimore, on the occasion of his retirement from the presidency. Presented on commemoration day, the twenty-second of February, in the year of our Lord, 1902.

"We, members of the Johns Hopkins University, upon this, the occasion of your laying down the burdens of your high office, greatly desiring to make formal acknowledgment of our personal obligation to you, unite in a common testimonial of our respect, our gratitude and our affection.

"We believe that the services which you have rendered to education have not been surpassed by those of any other American.

If it be true that Thomas Jefferson first laid the broad foundation for American universities in his plans for the University of Virginia, it is no less true that you were the first to create and organize in America a university in which the discovery and dissemination of new truths were conceded a rank superior to mere instruction, and in which the efficiency and value of research as an educational instrument were exemplified in the training of many investigators. In this, your greatest achievement, you established in America a new and higher university ideal, whose essential feature was not stately edifices, nor yet the mere association of pupils with learned and eminent teachers, but rather the education of trained and vigorous young minds through the search for truth under the guidance and with the co-operation of master investigators—*societas magistrorum et discipulorum.* That your conception was intrinsically sound is attested not only by the fruitfulness of the institution in which it was embodied at Baltimore, but also by its influence upon the development of the university ideal throughout our country, and notably at our oldest and most distinguished seats of learning.

"Your catholicity of spirit was such that you looked at each part of the university in its relation to the whole, at the whole university in its relation to the whole system of American education, and at that system of education as a vital force in the life of the State. Moreover, it has brought to you opportunities of varied and public service, of which you have honorably acquitted yourself—now from a learned society, again from an organization of some of the most patriotic of your fellow citizens; now from the City of Baltimore, again from the State of Maryland, yet again from the Chief Magistrate of the United States.

"We affirm that through the influence of the Johns Hopkins University the whole country has been led to place a higher and juster estimate upon the 'improvement of natural knowledge, the cultivation of liberal learning and the development of power in culture.[']

"We affirm that your wisdom and ability in the choice of those who should aid you in the making of the new university were extraordinary. You also first recognized the importance of publication as a function and a duty of a modern university, and by your demonstration of its feasibility and value you set a quickening example which has been widely followed.

"We affirm that you displayed remarkable insight in appreciating the necessity and practicability of providing for the highest medical education and more abundant medical investigation in America, and we rejoice that you had the foresight and the patience to wait until the Johns Hopkins Hospital and the Johns Hopkins Medical School could be so established, organized and equipped that they should forthwith exert a commanding influence upon the methods and aims of medical education in the United States.

"You have encouraged the study of languages, literature and poetry; you have guarded the interest of religion: you have stimulated the development of the exact sciences; you have promoted the wider exploration of the heavens and of the earth, and you have been influential in diffusing a better knowledge of the world.

"These and many other things you have done. And now that you have chosen to lay down the honorable but heavy burdens of leadership in our beloved University and to seek in well-earned retirement the quiet and repose which befit the afternoon of life, we, who have served under you—we, who have been disciples of so admirable a master—do give you hail, and tender to you our loyal, filial devotion. Your ideals have become our inspiration.

"Your sympathy in its fullness and kindliness has been an unspeakable help and blessing to more of your colleagues and students than you can ever know. Undaunted in adversity you have given us the example of resourcefulness and cheerful confidence. In your position as a leader of men, who were themselves to become leaders, your course has been informed by a masterful courage, a lofty faith and a noble idealism which will continue to illumine our land when you and we are no longer here.

"And in token of our confidence in the validity and permanence of the ideals which you have set before us, and in grateful acknowledgment of all that you have done for us and for the world, we have hereunto subscribed our names."

Then follow, Sir, the signatures of one thousand and twelve men. Some of them are here in body; all are here in spirit.

This address, Sir, has spoken of your having retired to enjoy the afternoon of life. I venture to say, Sir, in view of your new and responsible undertaking,[2] that that afternoon promises to be like our generous autumn in this country, which seems to contain all the tonic of the year for a long season through, in which men rejoice to be strong.

We not only give you hail, but we give you God-speed.

Printed in Johns Hopkins University, *Celebration of the Twenty-Fifth Anniversary of the Founding of the University and Inauguration of Ira Remsen, LL.D. as President of the University* (Baltimore, 1902), pp. 37-43.

[2] Gilman in 1901 had become the first President of the newly established Carnegie Institution of Washington.

A News Account of a Tribute to Daniel Coit Gilman

[Feb. 22, 1902]

ALL HAIL HOPKINS
Eminent Scholars Join in Celebrating
Jubilee of University.
PRAISE FOR DR. GILMAN

Scholars of wirld- [world-] wide reputation, representatives of the foremost educational institutions in North America, city and State officials, representative clergymen and men of prominence in the literary, artistic and social life of the city joined with the faculty, the trustees, the alumni and the students of the Johns Hopkins University in paying tribute to that center of learning, either by their presence or by spoken words, yesterday afternoon at the Music Hall at the opening exercises of the jubilee celebration in honor of the university's twenty-fifth birthday.

Though yesterday's exercises had been announced as the commemorative and retrospective ones of the celebration, there was no note of sadness in the addresses. Instead an undercurrent of jubilation ran through all and more than once the note of prophecy was struck and the promise of a new era in which adversity would have no part was made. Discouragements of the past were touched upon lightly, or were ignored altogether; the marvelous achievements of the university in the past quarter of a century and the bright prospects for the future formed the keynote for the addresses.

And even Dr. Gilman's address—though it was the last that he will make before the title of president emeritus becomes his in actual fact—showed none of the sadness of farewell. President emeritus the program had it—"the man of many titles, but best of them all is 'our president,' " Dr. Remsen said, in introducing the man to whom every subsequent speaker paid homage, as the one to whom the credit belongs for the establishment and the development, not only of the Johns Hopkins University, but for the erection of the new ideal in university methods.

Dr. Gilman said that while the temptation to recount the memories of the infancy of the university was strong, such reminiscences would have but slight interest for the majority in the audience, and the consideration of the grave problems of education which have engaged the attention of the leading educators in the past quarter of a century was a more appropriate subject for consideration.

He sketched briefly the conditions which prevailed when the

university was founded and touched in passing upon the educational problems, directly connected with the development of the university, which have solved themselves in the past 25 years.

Again and again the applause broke forth, as he paid tribute to the high scholarship and unselfish loyalty of the men—members of the faculty and alumni—who have won for the Johns Hopkins University the reputation it has in the world of science and of letters.

Applause was not sufficient to satisfy the junior element in the audience, and under the leadership of one of their marshals, both before the address and at its close, the boys gave good rousing yells, ending in "Gilman! Gilman! Gilman!"

It was President Gilman's day from beginning to end. Dr. Remsen presided and introduced the speakers, but effaced himself otherwise as far as possible and in every way contributed toward securing for Dr. Gilman recognition as the central figure of the exercises of the afternoon. After the address some music by the orchestra—the minuet from the Mozart symphony, in E flat—gave the boys a chance to cool down, and then Dr. Woodrow Wilson, a Johns Hopkins Ph.D. of 1886 and now professor at Princeton, presented the testimonial gift from the alumni. In accepting the volume, with its testimonial address and the signatures of over a thousand students, Dr. Gilman said, pointing to the faculty: "It was their work, not mine. I wish I had a thousand hands so that I could shake hands with everyone of you. Go on and on my fellows; carry the banner of the university wherever you go, and may God's blessing be with you wherever you are." . . .

MEMORIAL TO DR. GILMAN
Alumni Acknowledge His Services
To The University.

Dr. Woodrow Wilson, Ph.D., Johns Hopkins, 1886, now professor at Princeton, presented the testimonial from the alumni, a volume beautifully bound in white and gold, and engrossed on its covers with the seal of the university. The gift contains the commemorative address prepared by the alumni, together with the signatures of over a thousand graduates of the Johns Hopkins, many of whom are now occupying positions of responsibility in distant fields of work.

After speaking of the significance of the gift, and of the love and affection which it represented, Dr. Wilson said that while the 1,012 donors were not all present in the body, all were there in spirit. "The address refers," he added, "to your having retired to enjoy the quiet of the afternoon of life. We feel that with you, and especially in your entrance on your new duties, the afternoon of life will be like the beautiful autumn which the country gives us, the season which contains the tonic and glow of the whole year."

The complete address was read by Dr. Wilson. . . .

Printed in the Baltimore *Sun*, Feb. 22, 1902; some editorial headings omitted.

A News Report of the Ceremonies at
The Johns Hopkins University

[Feb. 23, 1902]
PRESIDENT REMSEN IS INAUGURATED.

. . . Dr. Ira Remsen yesterday took upon his shoulders the honors, cares and responsibility of the presidency of the Johns Hopkins University.

The exercises took place at Music Hall, beginning at 11 A.M. The occasion was no less impressive than the exercises on Friday afternoon, and it was rendered even more momentous by the formal induction into office of President Remsen and the conferring of the degree of doctor of laws upon 23 of the most eminent educators of America, and of master of arts upon 10 former students who pursued advanced studies at the university, the majority of them being prominent Baltimoreans. . . .

CONFERRING OF DEGREES
President-Emeritus Gilman Presents The Names.

Next came the "Finale" from Haydn's symphony in D major by the orchestra and this was followed by the conferring of degrees. President-Emeritus Gilman presented the names, with a few complimentary words to each, and as the recipients stood before him President Remsen said:

"By the authority of the State of Maryland granted to this university and committed to me I admit you to the degree of doctor of laws."

The words "master of arts" were, of course, used in regard to those on whom that degree was conferred.

In presenting the names Dr. Gilman said:

"From time immemorial it has been the custom of universities at festive celebrations to bestow upon men of learning personal tokens of admiration and gratitude. In conformity with this usage our university desires to place upon its honor list the names of scholars who have been engaged with us in the promotion of literature, science and education. In accordance with the request of the Academic Council and in their name I have the honor and the privilege of presenting to the president of the Johns Hopkins University those whose names I shall now produce, asking their enrollment as members of this 'Societas Magistrorum et Discipulorum.' . . .

"Mr. President, I have now the honor of presenting to you, one by one, a number of eminent men, recommended by a committee of the professors, and of asking you to admit them to the degree of Doctor of Laws, *honoris causa*, in the Johns Hopkins University.

"Three of these scholars were friends and counsellors of the trustees before any member of this faculty was chosen. They pointed out the dangers to be avoided, the charts to be followed, and during seven and twenty years they have been honored friends, by whose experience we have been guided, by whose example we have been inspired.

"CHARLES WILLIAM ELIOT, president of Harvard University, oldest and most comprehensive of American institutions—the chief, whose wisdom, vigor and devotion to education have brought him honors which we gladly acknowledge, which we cannot augment.

"JAMES BURRILL ANGELL, teacher, writer, diplomatist, scholar, excellent in every calling, whose crowning distinction is his service in developing the University of Michigan.

"ANDREW DICKSON WHITE, honored Ambassador of the United States in Germany, the organizer of Cornell University.

"With these early friends I now present to you several men who have been associated with us in carrying on the work of this university:

"JOHN SHAW BILLINGS, able adviser of the trustees of the Johns Hopkins Hospital respecting its construction, an authority on the history of medicine, a promoter of public hygiene, a famous bibliographer and the wise administrator of public libraries in the city of New York.

"GRANVILLE STANLEY HALL, who planned and directed the first laboratory of experimental psychology in the United States, and who left a professorship among us to become first president of Clark University, in Worcester.

"JAMES SCHOULER, successful lecturer and writer on law and history, a lover of truth, a diligent explorer of the historical archives of this country, author of a history of the United States, comprehensive and trustworthy.

"JOHN WILLIAM MALLET, of the University of Virginia, one of

that brilliant band of lecturers to whom we listened in the winter of 1876-77, an ornament of the university founded by Jefferson.

"CHARLES DOOLITTLE WALCOTT, superintendent of the United States Geological Survey, a Government bureau of the highest standing, that extends its investigations to every part of the land, securing for other States, as it does for Maryland, an accurate knowledge of the structure and resources of the earth.

"SIMON NEWCOMB, professor of mathematics in the United States Navy, once professor here, who has carried forward the researches initiated by Copernicus. His astronomical memoirs, above the ken of ordinary minds, have caused his name to be enrolled in the learned academies of Europe among the great investigators of celestial laws.

"I have now the honor to present to you two scholars from a neighboring commonwealth, the Dominion of Canada, the representative of the University of Toronto and the representative of the McGill University, in Montreal, who came to rejoice with us in this our festival—JAMES LOUDON and WILLIAM PETERSON. We welcome them in the brotherhood of scholarship, which knows of no political bounds.

"It is not easy to discriminate among our own alumni, so many of whom we honor and admire, but on this occasion I have been asked to present four candidates, all of whom are widely known as scholars.

"JOSIAH ROYCE, a graduate of the University of California, one of the first to be called to a fellowship among us, and one of the first four doctors of philosophy of this university, doctor subtilis, now professor in Harvard University, Gifford lecturer in two of the Scotch universities, historian, man of letters and philosopher.

"JOHN FRANKLIN JAMESON, of the University of Chicago, one of the most accurate and serviceable students of the constitutional history of this country.

"EDMUND B. WILSON, of Columbia University, a profound investigator and an acknowledged authority in biological science.

"WOODROW WILSON, of Princeton University, writer and speaker of grace and force, whose vision is so broad that it includes both North and South, a master of the principles which underlie a free government, whom we would gladly enroll among us as a professor of historical and political science.[1]

"FRANCIS LANDEY PATTON, under whose presidency 'Old Nassau Hall,' the College of New Jersey, has become the University of Princeton, revered as a preacher of righteousness, admired as an Abelard in dialectics, beloved as an inspiring teacher of theology and philosophy.

"WILLIAM RAINEY HARPER, interpreter of the Sacred Scriptures, a fearless leader, a skillful organizer, who has brought into the front rank the University of Chicago.

"CHARLES WILLIAM DABNEY, of the University of Tennessee, a man of science, and EDWARD [EDWIN] A. ALDERMAN, of Tulane University in New Orleans, a man of letters.

"NICHOLAS MURRAY BUTLER, whose enthusiasm, energy and knowledge of principles and methods of education have given him distinction throughout the land and have led to his promotion to the presidency of Columbia University in the city of New York.

"HENRY SMITH PRITCHETT, astronomer and geodesist, who has been the distinguished head of the United States Coast Survey and is now the head of a vigorous foundation in Boston, the Massachusetts Institute of Technology.

"I present to you the two representatives of learning and scholarship in 'the new world beyond the new world,' a Grecian and a student of natural history, BENJAMIN IDE WHEELER, president of the University of California—an idealist worthy to represent the aspirations of Berkeley, and DAVID STARR JORDAN, the naturalist, who has led in the organization of the Stanford University, chiefs of two harmonious institutions, one of which was founded by private bounty, the other by the munificence of a prosperous State.

"As this roll began with Harvard it ends with Yale. I present to you finally one of the strongest and most brilliant of this strong and brilliant company—ARTHUR TWINING HADLEY—a writer and thinker of acknowledged authority on the principles of finance and administration, the honorable successor of Timothy Dwight as president of Yale University."

Printed in the Baltimore *Sun*, Feb. 23, 1902; one editorial heading omitted.

1 "The name most cheered was that of Professor Woodrow Wilson of Princeton University. When Dr. Gilman mentioned him, the applause continued unbroken for nearly five minutes and as it died away and before Dr. Gilman could resume, a group of alumni composed of members of one of Professor Wilson's old Hopkins classes, struck up the old class yell. . . . Professor Wilson arose from his seat as if the sound had touched something dear in his past, and bowed to them, and then the audience cheered again." *Baltimore News*, Feb. 22, 1902.

To Edith Gittings Reid

My dear Friend,   Princeton, New Jersey, 25 February, 1902

I reached home without adventure, notwithstanding the wreckage the storm had wrought all along the route. My train was only some fifteen minutes behind hand at the end of the journey, though the telegraph wires were down and it was running without the usual signals.

When I reached home I found that my apprehensions had been well founded. My dear father was in the midst of one of his attacks. It is over with now, and he is as well as usual; but I feel much safer at his side.

The scene of desolation that met me here when I got back was quite indescribable. Princeton is almost stripped of its glory. Its real glory was its trees; and the weight of ice piled upon them by the fine rain and chill airs of the storm stripped and tore them as if some malicious giant had studiously broken every branch away upon which their dignity and grace and symmetry depended,—and done it with a vicious wrench at that, so that the wound might be as deep and ragged and lasting as possible. Our own little place has suffered so much that it is fairly heart-breaking,—I have had the blues deep in me ever since I saw it first in the dim, beclouded, dismal moonlight of Saturday night! One or two of our finest, stateliest trees are now mere scarecrows, and much of what we most loved about the place is gone,—and Ellen and I are worshippers of trees,—chose this spot for the splendid fellows who are gone!

But why should I burden you with all this? We are happy, none the less, in this dear home; and I have still strong upon me the delight of having been with you and Mr. Reid. It was tantalising to be there and see so *little* of you, but that little was infinitely refreshing. The delightful reception given my little address and the announcement of my degree, deeply as it gratified me, did not go as deep as the delight of being with those I love. Mrs. Wilson smiled with deep complacence over your sweet note,[1] and sends you warm love[.] Our warmest greetings to Mr. Reid and the children.

With all my heart your friend,   Woodrow Wilson

ALS (WC, NjP).
[1] It is missing.

From John Bach McMaster

My dear Professor,   Philadelphia   March 1 1902

The next meeting of the American Historical Association will be held in this good town on the 29th-30th and 31st of December 1902.

We are most desirous to have them made red letter days and appeal to you to help us in this laudable purpose.

Will you not give us a fifteen or twenty minute talk on any subject you think proper? Why not the influence of Lock[e], and Montesquieu in forming the political ideas of our revolutionary leaders? Don't say no! Say yes!![1]

Faithfully   John Bach McMaster
3805 Locust St

ALS (WP, DLC) with WWhw notation on env.: "Ans."
[1] Wilson did not participate in the annual meeting of the American Historical Association in December 1902.

From Harper and Brothers

Dear Sir: New York City   March 4, 1902.

We beg leave to acknowledge the receipt of the MS. of part of Vol. III, of your "History of the American People."

Very truly yours,   Harper & Brothers.

TLS (WP, DLC).

Notes for an After-Dinner Talk

Princetonian dinner, 4 March, 1902

Pray for ideas.
Two frogs in watered milk
Princeton's gifts to public life:
  Thoughtfulness
  Sympathy with democracy.
Nothing needed more in this country than public life without office
  Spoken patriotic truth.
Local bully and circus tiger.
Heaven lies about us in our infancy
"Past redemption."

WWhw MS. (WP, DLC).

A News Report

[March 5, 1902]

PRINCETONIAN BANQUET.

The fourth annual banquet of *The Daily Princetonian* Board was held last evening at the Princeton Inn. The dinner began about half after eight, and closed with the toast by President Patton.

The list of toasts was as follows:

"The Retiring Board"–A. J. Barron 1902.
"The Incoming Board"–J. G. Armstrong 1903.
"The *Yale News*"–Louis G. Coleman.
"The *Harvard Crimson*"–R. J. Bulkley.
"Princeton in Literature"–Professor Stockton Axson.
"Princeton of the Past"–Professor A. G. Cameron.
"Princeton of the Future"–Professor A. F. West.
"Princeton Men in Public Life"–Professor Woodrow Wilson.
"Princeton University"–President Patton. . . .

Printed in the *Daily Princetonian*, March 5, 1902; one editorial heading omitted.

From the Minutes of the Princeton University Faculty

5 5' P.M., Wednesday, March 5, 1902

. . . Professors Brackett, Woodrow Wilson and Fine were elected by ballot a Committee to appear before and confer with the Trustees if required.[1]

[1] See the Minutes of the Trustees printed at March 13, 1902.

An Announcement

[March 8, 1902]

UNIVERSITY BULLETIN.
SUNDAY, MARCH 2 [9], 1902.

. . . 5 p.m. Vesper Service in Marquand Chapel, conducted by Professor Woodrow Wilson.

Printed in the *Daily Princetonian*, March 8, 1902.

Notes for a Chapel Talk

Afternoon Chapel, 9 March, 1902. Prov. IV., 18.

"The path of the just is as the shining light, that shineth more and more unto the perfect day."

Every normal man cares for conduct, whatever else he may be indifferent about, whether intellectual or spiritual.

If we do not understand the law of character *we are without excuse*. It is written plain in this and in a score of other passages of the Bible.

"Just" here means more than *righteous*. It means *righteous with a certain fine perfection*, balance, completeness,–a certain *poise of motive*.

Hence Light. Light, *not heat*, the law of Christian character. Not lack of warmth, but lack of warping heat.

And so the real Christian leaves this shining path, this *wake of light,*– making men see when he has passed their way how simple, after all, the problems of conduct are.

A perfect image: the light of day, of the full, the perfect day, not narrow but diffused, not concentrated but general.

A perfect example: Christ–in the broadening light of his path all nations walk.

"Then shall the righteous shine forth as the sun in the Kingdom of their Father." Matt. XIII., 43.

WWhw MS. (WP, DLC).

A Testimonial

Princeton, N.J., 10 March, 1902

It is with very keen and special pleasure that I make my own acknowledgement of the debt of praise and honour due Professor Smith.[1] I did not enjoy the privilege of being his pupil, but I did enjoy the privilege of feeling his influence. No man could be at the University and not feel the fine compulsion of his courtesy, his high example both in conduct and in learning; and I am personally grateful to him for what he has contributed to the life and the fame of the University of Virginia.

Woodrow Wilson

HwS testimonial in bound volume entitled "Prof. Francis H. Smith from His Friends and Pupils, 1852-1902" (Tucker-Harrison-Smith Coll., ViU).

[1] Wilson's old friend, Professor Francis Henry Smith, Professor of Natural Philosophy at the University of Virginia from 1853 to 1907.

From the Minutes of the Board of Trustees of Princeton University

March 13, 1902.

COMMITTEE FROM THE FACULTY

The Clerk of the Faculty reported that Professors Brackett, Woodrow Wilson, and Fine had been elected by ballot to appear before and confer with the Trustees if desired. Also that the following resolution had been adopted by the Faculty:

Resolved, That the Faculty instruct their committee to report that there are no matters which they desire their committee to present to the consideration of the Board at this meeting.

This resolution was received and the committee did not appear.

From David Benton Jones[1]

Hotel Manhattan
My dear Mr. Wilson,   [New York, March 13, 1902]

I should have asked you, as I promised to do, whether you could come to Chicago to speak at a dinner of the Princeton Club on April 7th. The President of the Club[2] authorized me to make the inquiry.[3]

I am ashamed to confess as I do in the above statement that it is time for me to "retire," and that like some other people I still hold on. My only excuse for the oversight is that Princeton and not Chicago was in my mind and I know you will forgive much on that account. If you will please drop me a line on receiving this addressed to 1104 Marquette Building Chicago it will reach me Monday morning in time to save my reputation in Chicago. That is something.

I was very sorry not to be able to tell you of todays events.[4] On the surface "nothing but peace and gentle visitation" but I hope for much if matters are followed up. If they develop as I hope Princeton will owe more than it can ever repay to you, Mr. Fine and Dr. Brackett for your cool, clear-visioned advice.[5] It is really unfortunate we could not remain to explain fully so the matter could be fully in your minds. It will require careful consideration and other things besides *Care*. If Mr. McCormick and I or either of us can be of service we should be "commandeered." I could respond after May 1st.

Please excuse this hurried statement.

Very Sincerely   David B. Jones

I shall write from Chicago in a few days if matters work out into some definite shape in my mind.

ALS (WP, DLC).
    [1] Jones was born in Pembrokeshire, Wales, on September 1, 1848, and emigrated to Wisconsin with his parents soon afterward. A.B., College of New Jersey, 1876; A.M., 1879. Studied at the University of Leipzig, 1876-77. Jones then studied law privately and went into practice in Chicago. He was president of the Mineral Point Zinc Company of Wisconsin from 1883 until its consolidation with the New Jersey Zinc Company in 1897 and director of the latter corporation from 1897 to 1908. Elected as one of the first alumni trustees of Princeton University in 1901, he drew a two-year term by lot and was then re-elected for a full five-year term. He and his brother, Thomas Davies Jones, also of the Class of 1876, were frequent benefactors of Princeton. David B. Jones died on August 22, 1923.
    [2] John Cass Mathis '86.
    [3] Wilson in fact spoke to the Princeton Club of Chicago on April 24, 1902. A report of this affair is printed at April 25, 1902.
    [4] D. B. Jones to WW, March 17, 1902, describes them fully.
    [5] As subsequent documents will soon make clear, the following events had taken place: Jones and Cyrus H. McCormick had conferred with Wilson, Fine, and Brackett on March 12, probably during the evening, before the meeting of the Board of Trustees on the following day. The three professors had described what

they said was the acute crisis in the university resulting from Patton's inaction, low standards, and utter failure to provide any leadership. Indeed, they had told Jones and McCormick that only drastic action could save Princeton from serious decline or, as Wilson later put it, "fatal deterioration." McCormick then suggested the establishment of an executive committee, composed of three faculty members, to take control of Princeton out of Patton's hands and thereby rescue the university. The nature and powers of this proposed executive committee, the membership of which was later expanded at Grover Cleveland's suggestion to include two trustees, will soon be fully revealed in the documents. The Editorial Note which follows describes the development of the crisis in presidential leadership at Princeton to mid-March of 1902.

EDITORIAL NOTE

THE CRISIS IN PRESIDENTIAL LEADERSHIP AT PRINCETON

David B. Jones's letter, just printed, gives the first intimation that the long-standing discontent with President Patton's leadership had reached the point at which a crisis in the affairs of Princeton University was inevitable. The documents which follow in this volume constitute a nearly complete record of the development of that crisis to its unexpected solution, one that would be immensely significant for the university and Woodrow Wilson. These documents also make it abundantly clear why a group of faculty members and trustees had lost confidence in Patton.

Actually, the crisis had been brewing for several years, at least since the Sesquicentennial Celebration in 1896. In announcing then that the "College of New Jersey shall in all future time be known as Princeton University," Patton raised hopes among all friends of the university that a new era had begun in which Princeton would soon take its place among the nation's great institutions of higher learning. What is more, the trustees, on December 10, 1896, had responded promptly to a memorial from the faculty urging the establishment of a Graduate School by appointing a committee to work with the faculty toward that end.[1] And at the same meeting, the trustees—sensitive to the implications of the university's new title—had appointed a special committee to "inquire into the affairs of this University, to consider what changes if any are desirable in the policy, methods of administration, curriculum, or corps of instructors."[2]

As these hopes were gradually dispelled, they gave way to bitter discontent. The record of this disillusionment is scanty, but we can glimpse the growing unrest in letters already printed in this series and —by reading between the lines—in cryptic faculty and trustee minutes and reports which have also appeared in these volumes.

President Patton naturally drew much of the criticism, but some was directed against the Board of Trustees, the real center of power in the university. That Patton was in many ways derelict in meeting his responsibilities cannot be doubted, although it is difficult at this distance to pinpoint specific administrative failures. Wilson had had an early taste of Patton's methods during his futile discussions with the President concerning the establishment of a School of Law.[3] In a

[1] See n. 1 to the memorial to the Board of Trustees printed at Dec. 2, 1896, Vol. 10.

[2] See the Trustees Minutes printed at Dec. 10, 1896, *ibid.*

[3] See the Editorial Note, "Wilson's Plans for a School of Law at Princeton," Vol. 7.

letter to the historian, Frederick Jackson Turner, on November 15, 1896, Wilson aptly characterized Patton's administration: "We are under the reign of 'King Log' rather than 'King Stork' here, so far as our president is concerned." When Patton and the trustees backed away from appointing Turner to a history professorship because he was a Unitarian, Wilson, in another letter to Turner on December 15, 1896, accused the trustees of "sudden timidity" and said of Patton, "Our President does not bother us by having a mistaken policy, he daunts us by having no will or policy at all."[4]

Wilson's first direct manifestation of displeasure was his resignation from the Discipline Committee in June 1899, in which he was soon joined by John Grier Hibben and Charles Augustus Young. This action was provoked by Patton's recent appointment of Samuel Ross Winans to succeed the late James Ormsbee Murray as Dean of the Faculty. To the resignees, Winans clearly represented Patton and more of his do-nothing policies.

How discouraged Wilson, Hibben, and others were can be discerned from the remarks that they exchanged during the summer of 1899. "In my present state of mind about the sinister influences at present dominant in the administration of the College," Wilson wrote to Jenny Davidson Hibben on June 26, "it would be easy for me to leave Princeton if it were not for 'the Hibbens.' " Mrs. Hibben replied on July 11: "Mr. West we see constantly. . . . He *nightly* mutters, on our side porch as he smokes over Dr. Patton & 'Dean Winans.' " "We have had several informal gatherings of the Faculty malcontents on Wests porch," Hibben reported to Wilson on July 20. "The excitement of the early days of the summer has subsided, and a sullen resentment seems to have taken its place in reference to the powers that be."

Later in the same month, Wilson, who was then in the British Isles, sounded out several English scholars about possible candidates for a new professorship of politics at Princeton, but he did so with little enthusiasm. "How I *hate* business," he complained to his wife on July 31, 1899, "particularly the business of appointments, now that I *know* that Dr. P[atton]. cannot be depended on for anything at all."[5]

These contemporary criticisms are confirmed by a strong oral tradition at Princeton to the effect that Patton was dilatory, lacked initiative in important matters of policy, generally resisted meaningful efforts to improve the curriculum, had low scholarly standards, and failed to appoint the best men available to faculty vacancies.[6] Thus discontent with Patton stemmed not from one or two specific failures but from conditions which seemed endemic to his entire administration. By every test, he had proved unable to provide the kind of dynamic leadership required for the transformation of a college into a modern university. What was worse, from the point of view

[4] The two letters to Turner quoted in this paragraph are printed in Vol. 10.

[5] All the letters quoted in this and the preceding paragraph are printed in Vol. 11.

[6] This tradition was best recorded by Henry W. Bragdon in memoranda, now in WC, NjP, of interviews with a number of faculty members active during Patton's presidency. Among others, Bragdon interviewed Winthrop M. Daniels, Henry G. Duffield, George M. Harper, William F. Magie, Bliss Perry, Williamson U. Vreeland, Andrew F. West, and John H. Westcott.

of the faculty rebels, was the fact that Patton, an exceedingly clever politician, usually managed to head off or defeat efforts at reform.

Owing largely to Patton, the work of the Committee on the Affairs of the University came virtually to naught. By the time that it made its first report on June 14, 1897,[7] that committee had heard testimony highly critical of the administration from Wilson and many other members of the faculty. The committee admitted that there had been "decided adverse criticism" and recommended that "discipline be administered with firmer hand; that studies be better co-ordinated; and methods of administration be somewhat changed in order to greater efficiency." However, the committee defended Patton, claiming that it was very clear to the members that "he had a full and comprehensive grasp of the situation . . . and broad, intelligent, and forceful views of the lines on which the logical development of Princeton University should proceed." Furthermore, the committee suggested that Patton be added to its membership, and this was done.

The committee broadened its review during the following year and, on June 13, 1898, submitted a lengthy report[8] in which Patton's influence was plainly evident. The committee recognized the pressing need for a Secretary of the University, improvement of the physical plant, and additions to the Departments of History and Economics, but in every case put these needs aside on the grounds of insufficient funds. It flatly rejected the suggestion by many faculty members that a system of deans be instituted. The committee did recommend establishment of two sub-faculties, the Academic and School of Science Faculties, in the hope that this would promote more efficient administration. Also recommended, among other things, were expansion of the honors program and establishment of professorships in architecture and politics. But the report, for all its length, was far from being bold and imaginative and could hardly be said to reflect "forceful views" about the future development of the university. Nor could it be said to have fulfilled the promise of 1896 and the reasons then given for launching such an investigation—"consideration of the fact that this institution has recently assumed the title of Princeton University and entered upon a new era in its history."

Two issues on which faculty discontent tended to focus between 1898 and 1902 were the establishment of a Graduate School and alleged low standards of the undergraduate work at the university. On these two issues, the rebels coalesced around Andrew Fleming West and William Francis Magie, respectively.

The first trustee committee on the Graduate School was unable to raise an adequate endowment,[9] and Patton was able to block establishment of this institution for a time. However, the faculty persevered and gained reconsideration by the Board of Trustees in June 1900. The result was the appointment of another special trustee committee and a faculty counterpart whose joint work led in December 1900 to the establishment of the Princeton Graduate School and West's election as its first Dean.[10]

[7] See the Trustees Minutes printed at June 14, 1897, Vol. 10.
[8] See the Trustees Minutes printed at June 13, 1898, *ibid.*
[9] See n. 1 to the memorial to the Board of Trustees printed at Dec. 2, 1896, *ibid.*
[10] See J. G. Hibben to WW, Nov. 25, 1900, n. 1.

Establishment of the Graduate School was a significant milestone in the transformation of Princeton from a college into a university. However, the administrative structure devised for the Graduate School revealed the conviction that it was necessary to circumvent Patton because of his penchant for delay and his antipathy to reform. The plan of organization stipulated that the Dean was to be elected by the Board of Trustees and to hold office at its pleasure. He was also given nearly autonomous powers in operating the School.

Discontent with low academic standards led the Academic Faculty in November 1900 to appoint a committee to consider the "condition of the scholarship" in the Academic Department. A similar committee was constituted by the Science Faculty in the autumn of 1901. The two committees then combined to form the University Committee on Scholarship under Magie's chairmanship. It submitted a long report on March 26, 1902, calling for drastic reforms in the curriculum. The report was discussed and amended during five University Faculty meetings in March and April, but, as it turned out, Patton's will prevailed again, and the entire report was recommitted to the committee.[11]

These efforts at reform by the faculty, however frustrating, were not entirely fruitless. Not the least important of their results was the fact that members of the Board of Trustees began to give increasingly sympathetic attention to evidences of faculty unrest. In fact, significant changes in the composition of the Board during the late 1890's and early 1900's had created a substantially new governing body by the time that the crisis in presidential leadership erupted at Princeton in the spring of 1902.

Sixteen new trustees were elected between 1896 and 1901. Of these, one was West's intimate friend, Grover Cleveland, and no less than eight had been graduated during the 1870's, when James Mc-Cosh was in his prime, busily seeking to instill discipline and a spirit of learning into his charges, all the while holding out the promise of future greatness as a university. If one adds to these nine trustees Moses Taylor Pyne '77 and Cyrus Hall McCormick '79, who were elected to the Board of Trustees in 1885 and 1889, respectively, and were leaders of the younger trustees, it becomes evident that a nucleus for change was developing even as Patton rounded out his first decade as President. This is not to say that all the newer trustees were hostile to Patton, or that all the older members supported him. It simply means that by 1902 the composition of the Board of Trustees was such that Patton's methods, insofar as they continued to be exposed by the faculty, would probably not have been tolerated for long in any case. Most of the newer and younger members were successful lawyers and businessmen who valued success and thought in large terms. Many of them were in direct and frequent communication with Patton's critics on the faculty. Clearly the day was ending when trustees would be more concerned with the religious welfare of students than with their secular education, and with the denominational affiliations of prospective faculty members than with their scholarly distinction. It is interesting to observe that McCosh at the end of his tenure had struggled with a conservative Board of Trustees

11 See n. 2 to the notes for a talk printed at Nov. 21, 1901, and the University Faculty Minutes printed at March 26 and April 9, 11, 14, and 16, 1902.

with which Patton might have worked in harmony, while Patton was faced with an increasingly forward-looking and progressive board which, it may be imagined, would have delighted McCosh.

From Robert Erskine Ely[1]

My dear Mr. Wilson: New York   March 14th, 1902.

The program of the League for Political Education is now being arranged for next year. Could you lecture before the League some Saturday morning at 11 o'clock, in November or December next? The dates are, November 8th, 15th, 22nd and 29th, and December 6th and 13th. It is possible that either the 8th or 15th will be taken by Dr. Carroll D. Wright, of the Department of Labor.

The League for Political Education has a Saturday morning course through the season from November to April. Our audience numbers from 300 to 500, and is composed of people of influence. The educational value of these lectures is considerable.

The lectures are free to members of the League, with an admission fee to non-members. We cannot offer anything like adequate remuneration, but would ask you to accept thirty dollars for expenses.[2]

As to the subject, that can be decided later. Mrs. Robert Abbe,[3] President of the City History Club, unites with the League for Political Education in desiring to have you lecture. We should like to have the subject one which would appeal to the City History Club as well as to the League for Political Education. Believe me,   Very truly yours,   Robert Erskine Ely

P.S. I take pleasure in sending you herewith a copy of the Political Primer of New York City and State, just issued by our League.[4] I should be very much obliged for your opinion of this little book, with permission to quote what you say if it seems desirable to do so.

TLS (WP, DLC).
 [1] Director of the League for Political Education of New York City, 1901-37. The League was founded in 1894 by several prominent New York women for the purpose of educating women in public affairs in the hope that they might thus qualify for the suffrage. However, the organization soon took in male members and broadened its objective to include the political education of all who wished to participate.
 [2] Wilson's reply is missing; however, he did not deliver the lecture.
 [3] Catherine Amory Palmer Abbe, wife of a distinguished New York surgeon.
 [4] Adele Marion Fielde, *Political Primer of New York City and State; The City Under the Revised Charter of 1902* (New York, 1902).

From James Monroe Taylor[1]

Dear Sir,   Poughkeepsie, N. Y. March 16, 1902.

With the concurrence of the Committee on our Founder's Day, I write to invite you to deliver the annual address on that occasion. The date is the second of May. The address will be in the afternoon, followed in the evening by a social function. I hope that we may be more successful in inducing you to come to us than we have been on several occasions when I have had the pleasure of asking you, but I want to assure you that we shall give you a most hearty welcome if you can come to us, and an interested audience.

We should entertain you at the College during your stay, and the College provides an honorarium of one hundred dollars for this service.[2]

Hoping for a favorable and early reply, I am
                              Cordially yours,   J. M. Taylor

TLS (WP, DLC).
  1 President of Vassar College.
  2 Wilson gave this Founder's Day Address, a news report of which is printed at May 3, 1902.

To Robert Bridges

My dear Bobby,   Princeton, 17 March, 1902

Thank you with all my heart for the book.[1] It does my heart good. The blessed thing about poetry is, that a lot of a man's *self* has *got* to go into it or it isn't poetry at all; and so, I dare say, those of us who are your real, inside friends get more of the authentic flavour of the man we love in these little pages of verse than we could get from *any* prose, however fine and straightaway. We need not tell you what we think of the man who here stands revealed!

In all affection
          As ever   Your old, old friend,   Woodrow Wilson

ALS (Meyer Coll., DLC).
  1 Robert Bridges, *Bramble Brae* (New York, 1902).

From David Benton Jones

My Dear Professor: Chicago March 17th, 1902.

I am very sorry you cannot come to us on the 7th of April. I shall attempt to-day to see those in charge of Princeton matters here, hoping they can name a day that will meet your convenience.

If only as a matter of interest, I was very sorry not to be able to stay over and tell you of what took place Thursday afternoon [March 13], both at the Inn and, later, at the President's house. It was all interesting, some of it exciting, even if nothing should come of it. That nothing should come of it is quite impossible. The subject has been placed upon the operating table; the operation or operations will follow. My anxiety was largely limited to that preliminary step.

I met Mr. McCormick Saturday forenoon[1] (he did not arrive until very late Friday night) and briefly stated to him the condition of things at Princeton. I told him that if the Trustess [Trustees] were fully informed as to the general situation their self-respect would do the rest, resulting either in wholesale resignations or in some step of efficient reformation. I further told him that no matter at what point one started in ones examination of affairs it always led to the same place. In our further talk of what should be done the suggestion of an Executive Committee was considered. At that point you and Mr. Fine were, as you know, briefly consulted.[2]

Immediately upon the adjournment of the Board in the afternoon[3] a limited conference was held at the Inn, where Mr. Cleveland,[4] Mr. Pyne, Mr. Davis,[5] Dr. McPherson,[6] Mr. McCormick and myself were present. The matter was stated to Mr. Cleveland, and while he was less impetuous than the rest of us, he was heartily in accord with the suggestion if it could be carried out without humiliation. Mr. Cleveland felt that the Executive Committee should consist of three members of the faculty, two from the Academic and one from the Scientific faculty, with two members of the Board added. These members, of course, would be largely acting in an advisory capacity. Mr. Cleveland and Dr. McPherson were mentioned as the only members available, as both were near at hand and could be consulted at any time when the faculty members of the committee desired a conference.

This suggestion of Mr. Cleveland's has some strong things to recommend it. It will be much easier to carry it into effect or, if it must be, to "jam it through" the Board. It would give the faculty members of the committee an appearance of authority which possibly the University faculty would not as readily recognize if only men from their own numbers were selected.

At the close of the conference we all felt that since sentiment was so unanimous in support of the suggestion no time should be lost in bringing the matter to the President's attention. Whether because we were on the point of leaving town or for some other reason, they all felt that Mr. McCormick and myself were the only ones who could see him. We naturally felt that any other two would be the proper persons. We immediately started for Prospect and were at once given an opportunity to present the matter, although he was at the time engaged.

The Doctor heard us in silence for some time. In the opening statement the need of additional executive machinery was based in part upon the growth of the University in numbers, the great extension of the curriculum and the enlargement of the faculty, making it difficult for one man to properly administer its affairs. The first question he asked was, "Will the President be a member of this Executive Committee?" I said "No," and gave him my reasons for it. He went directly to the point in stating that it might result in taking away from the executive head of the University all his functions except that of a figurehead. At this point Mr. McCormick intervened. As my letter is already too long I will tell you of that when I see you.

He expressed a willingness to consider the matter carefully and went so far as to say that his first impression regarding it was favorable; that he would talk to the members of the Board whom we named as having been consulted. He will, of course, talk to other members, and will doubtless attempt to work up a sentiment against it.

The scheme will save his face and should do much for the situation if it is vigorously pushed, as it must be.

My time is solidly mortgaged until about the first of May. But the chief thing is to get such a platform drawn up as will make the committee thoroughly efficient to do the work which must be done. In many ways it is better that the work should be done by a committee than by a new head to the institution. The agency is more impersonal, and when the Doctor's successor is to be named it will not throw upon him so much disagreeable work, and he will find the University better equipped and organized than if he should take hold of it at the present time.

As to the makeup of the committee, the present faculty committee[7] would seem to be the natural members of the new Executive Committee. The two members named from the Board, Mr. Cleveland and Dr. McPherson, would make a harmonious body.

Anything I can do at this distance I shall be glad to do between this and the first of May. After that time I can even arrange to spend a week there at Princeton if I can in any way help matters along. We must, however, have the scheme matured and prepared for presentation at the June meeting of the Board. It should be matured as long before the meeting as possible, as missionary work with individuals may be required to insure a majority vote. I do not think there is any difficulty on this point. A statement which the Doctor made can be used as the basis of more radical action if he balks as to this scheme, and that without external disturbance. He indicated his readiness to step aside, which I could not very well encourage after stating that I thought the Executive Committee would meet the requirements of the situation. But if the Executive Committee scheme should fail I shall certainly recall to him the statement he made and tell him that my own firm conviction is that one solution or the other must be adopted.   Very sincerely yours,   David B. Jones

If above is of interest to Mr. Fine you may find it convenient to show it to him & so avoid duplication.

TLS (WP, DLC).
¹ In Chicago on March 15.
² Apparently by telephone.
³ Thursday afternoon, March 13.
⁴ Grover Cleveland had been elected to the Princeton Board of Trustees in 1901.
⁵ John David Davis of St. Louis, an alumni trustee.
⁶ Simon John McPherson, D.D., Headmaster of the Lawrenceville School and a member of the Board of Trustees.
⁷ The three men customarily chosen by the faculty to confer with the Board of Trustees—Wilson, Fine, and Brackett.

Cyrus Hall McCormick to David Benton Jones

My dear Friend: [Chicago] March 17, 1902.
    I send you herewith proposed letter to Prof. Woodrow Wilson. Will you look it over, and make such changes or additions in it as you think best? I do not wish to send it until it has met with your approval.
            Yours very sincerely,   Cyrus H. McCormick.

CCL (C. H. McCormick Papers, WHi).

From Cyrus Hall McCormick

My dear Woodrow: Chicago March 19, 1902:
    I should like to have seen you to inform you of the very satisfactory and interesting conference that David Jones and I had with Dr. Patton with regard to the improvement of the executive machinery at Princeton. It has been proposed by a small committee—(Cleveland, Davis, Jones, Pine [Pyne], Cuyler, [Bayard] Henry, McPherson, McCormick)—that an executive committee of five should be appointed, three from the faculty and two from the trustees; that this committee should be charged with the execu-

tive work so far as the internal affairs are concerned which now devolve upon the president, and that the plan of appointment of this committee and the outline of what duties are to be devolved upon them shall be proposed by Dr. Patton to the trustees at the June meeting.

David Jones and I have volunteered our services to help bring about such a much needed addition to the present machinery of the University, and we desire to make such original suggestions along this line as we feel will be of practical help in organizing the faculty and attending to its proper carrying out. In order to prepare a working plan I write to request that you and Prof. Fine will give us confidentially your views as to just what duties could properly be assigned to an executive committee. Our idea is that Mr. Cleveland and Dr. McPherson would be the two best members of the trustees to act upon such a committee. If you can give us your views upon the subject, we will put them in shape so that we can present them to the other members of our volunteer committee as our own ideas, thus relieving you of any responsibility in suggesting them.

Hoping to hear from you at your convenience on this subject, I am   Very sincerely yours,   Cyrus H McCormick

TLS (WP, DLC).

To David Benton Jones, with Enclosure

My dear Mr. Jones: Princeton, N.J. March 19, 1902.

I received your kind and very interesting letter of the 17th this morning, and thank you for it most sincerely. It is very kind of you to wish to change the date of the alumni dinner in order that I may be present. That is hardly worth while so far as the Chicago alumni in general are concerned; but I must say I should very much like an opportunity to have a little further talk with you and Cyrus McCormick about the difficult and delicate business we now have in hand.

Fine and I acted very promptly on the suggestions conveyed to us by our brief conversation with you and McCormick on the day of the Trustees' meeting[1] and by your recent letters to him and to me. We took Professor Brackett into our confidence, of course, and the enclosed memorandum is the result of our conferences, which have been long, earnest, and, I believe, thorough.

The memorandum no doubt explains itself. You will see from it that we have merely put into definite statement the powers which we understood you and McCormick plainly to suggest.

They are sweeping enough in all conscience! but we have been punctiliously careful to include nothing which we did not feel certain was part of your plan; because we think it imperative for the subsequent peace of mind of the *Faculty* that this plan shall be clearly understood on all hands to have originated wholly with the Trustees, and not with any member or members of the Faculty ambitious of power. I say nothing about *our* peace of mind; it is out of the question that the men who put this plan into execution shall have any until the work is done; and even then, no doubt, the most that they can hope for is peace of *conscience*!

For the same reason we have phrased each power except the last, with which the Faculty has in practice had nothing to do, in terms which must satisfy all reasonable expectations of co-operation on the Faculty's part. If the Executive Committee is to play the part of President in all matters lying within its functions, it ought, of course, to play the part of a wise President; and a wise President carries his Faculty with him in every educational reform, unless he seems to have a body of servants and not a body of willing colleagues about him.

The "vagueness" which you very wisely suggested should characterize the formation of these ticklish plans, ought, it seems to us, to be characteristic of them only in respect of the relations of the Executive Committee to the President. Those are clearly not susceptible of definition. They must work themselves out through the good sense and moderation of all concerned. As a member of the Board, he can suggest what he pleases; the Committee must suggest whatever it lies within its province to suggest; and the Trustees must take the suggestion which seems to them best. It will, in any event, trust and follow the Committee only if the Committee proves trustworthy and worth following. The *voluntary* relations of the President and the Committee will, if the committee men are wise men, be of the frankest, friendliest, most cordial character. The Committee ought constantly to seek an expression of his views on every matter of importance which it is called upon to handle; and it ought to fall in with his views whenever it can do so without detriment to what it conceives to be the integrity of the necessary reforms. But it ought never to be required or expected to take his advice unless that advice commends itself to it on its merits. Is not all of that a matter which tact and discretion and manly good feeling, with polite firmness, will settle without rules?

We are greatly heartened by a prospect of the settlement of some of the questions which lie nearest the heart of the situation.

We pity the men who are to constitute the Executive Committee, but their duty is plain; and we trust the members of the Board will handle this delicate business as true friends of the University and true friends of the men whom they mean to ask to cooperate with them.

With the most cordial regard and appreciation,

Faithfully yours,   Woodrow Wilson.[2]

TCL (C. H. McCormick Papers, WHi).
[1] On March 13, when Jones and McCormick had informed Wilson about the decision to enlarge the proposed executive committee and asked Wilson, Fine, and Brackett to put the proposal for such a committee into written form.
[2] There is a WWsh draft of this letter in WP, DLC.

ENCLOSURE

[March 19, 1902]

MEMORANDUM

A COMMITTEE consisting of three members of the Faculty and two members of the Board of Trustees, appointed by the Board, to hold at its pleasure, and empowered

(1) To formulate and recommend to the Faculty and Board of Trustees such changes in the curriculum and in the co-ordination of studies as may seem best for the University;

(2) To formulate and recommend to the Faculty and Board of Trustees such measures as may seem best adapted to increase the efficiency of instruction in the studies of the curriculum, whether singly or as parts of a system; and to superintend the administration of such measures when adopted;

(3) To formulate and recommend to the Faculty and Board of Trustees such regulations as may seem wise for maintaining a reasonably high standard of study among the students of the University and a reasonably strict system of discipline for failure in study; and to see to the enforcement of such regulations;

(4) To propose to the Board of Trustees all changes in or additions to the *personnel* of the Faculty of the University; and to take such action in the matter as the Board may direct.

Mem.—Nothing to be said about the relationship of the Committee to the President of the University.

Mem.—The privilege of attendance and right to debate in the Board of Trustees to be accorded the Faculty members of the Committee by the by-laws of the Board whenever matters lying within the field of the Committee's functions are under consideration.[1]

TC memorandum (C. H. McCormick Papers, WHi).
[1] There is a WWT draft of this memorandum in WP, DLC.

From Franklin William Hooper[1]

My dear Professor Wilson: Brooklyn, March 20th, 1902.

I beg leave to inquire whether it will not be possible for you to undertake to give a course of lectures during the coming year, 1902-03, before the Institute?

We are now beginning to make up a tentative schedule of lecture courses, and in case you would be willing to consider a proposition to give a course, we should be glad to reserve some dates for you. This inquiry is an informal one and is not intended to commit the Institute to any specific proposition.

We have on Tuesday evenings beginning in October and ending in May, courses of lectures in progress, and Tuesday evenings, November 18th, 25th, December 2nd, 9th, 16th and 23rd we should be glad to reserve for you.

Very faithfully yours, Franklin W. Hooper.

TLS (WP, DLC) with WWhw notation on env.: "Ans. No."
[1] Director of the Brooklyn Institute of Arts and Sciences.

Notes for a Talk to the Alumni of Union County, New Jersey[1]

Plainfield, 20 March, 1902
The University and the Country,—the Age.

Thought: Stage of transition, of course, like that wh. the country and the whole age are passing thr.,—but the function of a University is, to supply atmosphere, balance, recollection, the temper of thoughtfulness in the midst of change

Growth and Reorganization require
Statesmanship as well as ideals.
Bagehot's definition of a constitutional statesman.

The small college and the large,—
Only substitute for personal contact, a manifest, dominating ideal, personified.

Choice and coördination of groups, instead of individual studies.

Stories:
Old woman who saw a man read thr. a two-inch board.
Manners *very* familiar.

Two frogs in watered milk.
Princeton don't need to pray for power. "Pray for ideas."

"Heaven lies about us in our infancy;
In old age we lie about ourselves."

WWhw MS. (WP, DLC).
  ¹ About this affair, see the news report printed at March 29, 1902.

To Cyrus Hall McCormick

My dear Cyrus,   Princeton, New Jersey, 21 March, 1902.

Your kind letter of the nineteenth reached me this morning, and I thank you most sincerely for it. We are, of course, anxious to learn as much as possible of the progress of the critical business now afoot.

Mr. Jones had already written both to Fine and to me. We understood, not only from his letters, but also from the brief interviews we had with you and him on the day the Trustees met, the confidential part you expected us to play. We therefore called Professor Brackett into conference and got immediately to work to prepare a memorandum as to the necessary powers of the proposed committee. I sent it to Mr. Jones yesterday.

Put in explicit terms, as they are in that memorandum, the powers seem very great; but we see no safe way to make them smaller. Any one of them without the rest would be inefficacious and cause more mischief than relief. Probably Mr. Jones has already shown you the memorandum. It seems to us that the adjustment of power between the proposed committee and the other powers that be should be a matter of evolution, the result of manliness and forbearance on all hands; but that it would be fatal to start without a very plain statement of what the powers of the committee are to be.

We anxiously and ardently hope that the business will issue in some substantial and lasting good to the University which we all love and would save from fatal deterioration! We thank you with all our hearts for the part you have played in the matter.

With warmest regards and appreciation,
    As ever,
        Cordially and faithfully Yours,   Woodrow Wilson¹

WWTLS (C. H. McCormick Papers, WHi).
  ¹ There is a WWsh draft of this letter in WP, DLC.

From David Benton Jones to Cyrus Hall McCormick

My Dear Mr. McCormick: Chicago March 21st, 1902.

I enclose copy of letter and memorandum just received from Woodrow Wilson.

As I told you, I had written him exactly in the same meaning as your letter which followed. This, I take it, is in reply virtually to both your letter and mine. The first paragraph refers to my negotiations with him, carried on at Mr. Mathis' suggestion, in regard to his coming out to the next Princeton dinner. I volunteered to see what could be done in the way of changing the date to suit his convenience. I make this statement that you may understand the opening paragraph.

They have very wisely omitted attempting to formulate an exact relationship between the contemplated Committee and the executive. They have simply stated affirmatively the functions to be exercised by this Committee. I have as yet had no time to consider them very carefully, but I question whether knowledge exists outside of the Faculty which would enable anyone to pass judgment upon them, except to determine wherein, if at all, the suggestions were objectionable.

The principle underlying the scheme is certainly sound, regardless of the condition which led to the suggestion. There is nothing in any one of the four heads which anyone should shy at or object to, as far as I understand them, and if some such a plan can be adopted I am convinced that your suggestion of an Executive Committee to meet the situation will result in more good to Princeton's internal work and organization than all that has been done for the past ten years. And it has this very great advantage, that it is constructive, and not surgical, in character.

Very truly yours,   David B. Jones.

TLS (C. H. McCormick Papers, WHi).

A News Report

[March 22, 1902]

The Halls, by the way, are doing a pretty good business, in spite of the patriarchs who are always telling them that there are no days like the old days. For instance, one of them had its senior graduation the other night, which was the occasion of a smoker and incidentally a general jollification. Besides singing by a quartet of the glee club, there were speeches by Professors Woodrow Wilson '79, A. T. Ormond '77, G. M. Harper '84 and

Stockton Axson; and Andrew C. Imbrie '95 came down from New York (between business hours) to tell the undergraduates how much better the Halls were not conducted in his day.

Printed in the *Princeton Alumni Weekly*, ɪɪ (March 22, 1902), 396.

From David Benton Jones

My Dear Professor: Chicago March 22nd, 1902.

Your letter of the 19th inst. is received, enclosing memorandum. I at once sent copies of both to Mr. McCormick, thinking possibly you had not had time to do so.

I am delighted with the brevity and summary character of the statement defining the functions and provinces of the Committee. Your omission of any reference to the relationship of the Committee to the President is so much better than my suggested "vagueness" that it gave me a distinct sense of relief when I saw it. I feared that difficulty more than anything else, but now fully agree with you that it is much better to trust to the discretion and good feeling of all concerned.

I have not as yet been able to see Mr. McCormick to talk the matter over with him. We have not, of course, such knowledge of the situation as will enable us to judge as to whether the points indicated are sufficiently comprehensive or not. They would seem to me to be so; and what is more important, they seem to make interference impossible, as the relationship between the Committee and the Board is and must remain direct.

I am sending you this as an acknowledgment of the receipt of your letter and memorandum more than in the way of consideration of the subject. My conviction has been steadily growing, and is now quite established after reading your memorandum, that the scheme can be made operative at the next meeting of the Board. As soon as I have been able to see Mr. McCormick I will write you again.

For myself and for all lovers of Princeton, if they knew what you were doing, I want to thank you and those who have labored with you in this matter for what you have done.

Very sincerely yours,   David B. Jones

TLS (WP, DLC).

Cyrus Hall McCormick to David Benton Jones

My dear Mr. Jones: [Chicago] March 24, 1902.

I thank you for your note enclosing the suggestions from Fine and Woodrow Wilson. I think the plan they have projected is admirable, and I cannot add anything to it. I send you a letter on the same subject from Woodrow Wilson to me, and I will be glad to confer with you as to what is the next step to be taken.

Very sincerely yours,   Cyrus H. McCormick F.A.S.[1]

TLS (McCormick Letterpress Books, WHi).
[1] Frederick A. Steuert, McCormick's private secretary.

From Cyrus Hall McCormick

My dear Woodrow: Chicago March 24, 1902.

I thank you for your letter of March 21st and for your communication on the same subject to Mr. Jones, which he showed me. I think the suggestions made are admirable, and I will confer with Mr. Jones about the matter before long. I am strong in the belief that something good will come out of this movement.

I am   Cordially yours,   Cyrus H. McCormick

TLS (WP, DLC).

From William G. Starr[1]

My dear Sir;   Ashland, Va., March 24, 1902

You have been selected by the Faculty and students of our College to deliver our Annual Address—at 12 oclock—June 19, 1902.

Will you kindly consent to come. You will receive a most enthusiastic welcome—and render a great service to the cause of education in the South.

Your expenses to and from your home will be promptly met. Hoping soon to receive your reply,[2] I am

Fraternally yours   W. G. Starr.

ALS (WP, DLC) with WWhw notation on env.: "Ans."
[1] The Rev. Dr. William G. Starr, President of Randolph-Macon College, 1899-1902.
[2] Wilson's reply is missing; however, he had to decline.

From George Hutcheson Denny[1]

My dear Sir: Lexington, Virginia   March 24, 1902.

I am writing to ask you, in the name of the Corporation, to be present at my installation, Tuesday, June 17th, at 11 A.M., and deliver one of the three addresses of greeting.

It is not expected that you will speak more than five or ten minutes, and there will be no tax upon your time in making preparation. Your presence here under these circumstances will be gratifying and helpful to us, and I believe may be made fruitful to your University.

Dr. Cameron was with us at Mr. Wilson's installation.[2] I shall be glad to hear from you soon.[3]

Yours very truly,   George H. Denny.   President.

TLS (WP, DLC) with WWhw notation on env.: "Ans."
   [1] Professor of Latin and newly elected President of Washington and Lee University.
   [2] That is, Professor Henry Clay Cameron of Princeton had been present at the inauguration of William Lyne Wilson as President of Washington and Lee on September 15, 1897.
   [3] Wilson's reply is missing. However, as G. H. Denny to WW, Aug. 14, 1902, Vol. 14, reveals, Wilson persuaded Andrew Fleming West to go in his place.

From Hugh Gordon Miller

My Dear Mr. Wilson: Norfolk, Virginia. March 24, 1902.

I suppose you have already read the enclosed clipping.[1] I personally enjoyed your very able and witty speech on the occasion very much, as did every one else, but some of my political enemies down here have circulated the report that you meant to charge me with plagiarism, ignorance, and about everything else that was mean. Of course, I care nothing personally about such remarks coming from such sources, but this morning the Hon. Geo. E. Bowden, Clerk of the United States Court here, and Republican National Committeemen from this State, called the matter up in a very offensive and insulting manner.[2]

Now you would do me a great favor if you would write him telling him how the matter was intended and the way the whole thing was taken by every body. These people would have it appear that I had made an ass of myself through an exposure of ignorance, and that you, besides, charged me with plagiarism. Being the innocent cause of this embarassment, I hope you will do me this kindness. Write to the gentlemen in question *and send me a copy of the letter* if you will.

Thanking you in advance, I am

Yours very sincerely,   Hugh Gordon Miller

This unfortunate incident has caused me no little embarrassment and I hope you will administer to the party in question a stinging rebuke. I know you can do it if you will. As young Virginians the charge is unjust to both of us. Of course you are a man of settled reputation and nothing of the kind could do you any harm but it is really injurious to me.

Just begin by saying that you "have been informed of the insinuation."[3]   H.G.M.

TLS (WP, DLC).
    [1] The fragmentary news report printed at Feb. 13, 1902.
    [2] The extant Norfolk newspapers do not mention this matter.
    [3] Wilson's letter to Bowden and his reply to Miller, if he ever wrote them, have not been found.

From Harper and Brothers

Dear Sir: New York City Mar. 25. 1902

We have your letter of yesterday, and beg leave to say that we have given explicit instructions to the composing room to follow your capitalization and punctuation in the setting of your history.

We return by to day's express, prepaid, the volume of the Joy geneology[1] from which we have copied the "First Boston Town Hall."   Sincerely yours,   Harper & Brothers.

ALS (WP, DLC).
    [1] James Richard Joy, *Thomas Joy and His Descendants* . . . (New York, 1900).

From the Minutes of the Princeton University Faculty

3 05′ P.M., Wednesday, March 26, 1902

The Faculty met at the call of the President to receive and consider

The Report of the University Committee on
Scholarship.[1]

Present thirty-six Professors and ten Instructors. The Report of the Committee was presented by the Chairman, Professor Magie.

The President called the Dean to the Chair and, upon the motion to adopt the Report, proceeded to discuss it.

After further discussion by Professors Magie, A. Guyot Cameron, West and Ormond, the Faculty adjourned to meet at 3 P.M., Wednesday, April 9th, 1902 in the Lecture Room of the Chemical Laboratory.

    [1] For the background and membership of this committee, see n. 2 to the notes for a talk printed at Nov. 21, 1901. For additional debates on the committee's report, see the extracts from the University Faculty Minutes printed at April 9, 11,

14, and 16, 1902. For the report itself, see the extract from the University Faculty Minutes printed at April 16, 1902.

From William Goodell Frost[1]

My dear Friend: Berea, Ky., Mar. 26, 1903 [1902].

For two years I have given my main attention to developing the internal work of our school, and have not troubled my friends with calls, except by letter. The growth of the work compels me to start out once more for resources for current expenses, and I write to ask your aid, which has been so generously extended in the past. I have in my desk a letter of yours bearing date in '99, which has assisted me greatly in securing attention and help.[2] It would still be of service were it not for the last century date!

You may have seen a copy of the enclosed engraving.[3] When boys come on foot 150 miles, they cannot be turned back. This winter we have been lodging many of our students four in a room.

You have a right to real satisfaction in feeling that you are in such a position that a few strokes of your pen can benefit a wide region.[4]

Most gratefully and faithfully yours,

Wm. Goodell Frost.

TLS (WP, DLC) with WWhw notation on env.: "Ans. 28 Mar., '02."
   [1] President of Berea College.
   [2] WW to W. G. Frost, Dec. 27, 1899, printed as an addendum in Vol. 11.
   [3] It is missing.
   [4] Wilson's reply of March 28, 1902, is missing in the Frost Papers in the Berea College Library.

Cyrus Hall McCormick to Francis Landey Patton, with Enclosure

Dear Dr. Patton: [Chicago] March 27th, 1902.

Referring to the subject about which Mr. David Jones and I conferred with you after the last meeting of the Board of Trustees he and I have spent a good deal of time on it since our return. Believing that you would be glad to have such practical suggestions as we might submit for your consideration and that of the Board of Trustees, I hand you herewith a schedule embodying as briefly as possible our ideas of what such an Executive Committee could advantageously do if it were given the proper authority.

We have not gone much into detail as to the work of such an Executive Committee, but we have assigned to the Committee definite powers, because if they are men of ability and well chosen, they should be able to do strong and useful work along executive lines, and this they could not do unless they were properly so empowered.

It would seem to us proper that the privilege of attendance and the right to debate in the Board of Trustees should be accorded the faculty members of this Committee whenever matters coming within the jurisdiction of this Committee are under consideration, and, if necessary to this end, the by-laws of the Board of Trustees should be amended. Such a privilege might not require an amendment to the by-laws.

In thinking of the names of those who might serve on this Committee, we realize that (so far as the Trustees are concerned) locality is an important feature, and we would suggest Mr. Cleveland and Dr. McPherson. A natural selection for the faculty members would be the Committee appointed by the faculty itself to confer with the Board of Trustees, viz: Professors Brackett, Wilson and Fine. The faculty having already appointed them for conference with the Trustees, no new questions or issues would be raised by their appointment on this Executive Committee, the work of which is one which the Trustees must be continually in touch with.

Mr. Jones and I feel that we ought to submit this outline to you personally so that you may consider it most fully at your earliest convenience, and we have no objection to your consulting on the subject any one whom you may desire. It might be appropriate, if it is your pleasure, to consult with any of those with whom we talked on the matter while at Princeton. These gentlemen were Messrs. Cleveland, Pyne, McPherson, Cuyler, Bayard, Henry [Bayard Henry] and Davis. We shall be glad to have you make use of this letter in any way that you think may promote the best interests of this movement which we have deeply at heart, believing it to be one of distinct assistance to you and of vital importance to the Trustees and the University in general.

In order that this matter may have ample consideration and personal consultation before the June meeting of the Board of Trustees, Mr. Jones and I will endeavor to spend a few days in Princeton, reaching there on Monday, May the fifth. I will endeavor to so arrange my business that I can be there then, and Mr. Jones informs me that in any event he will arrange his matters so that he can be there. We shall hope to find you at home at that time, and will understand that you expect to be in Princeton then, unless we hear from you soon to the contrary.

Trusting that you will accept these suggestions in the spirit of cordial and sympathetic assistance in which they are given and

that you may write us on the subject at your earliest convenience,
I am   Very sincerely yours,   Cyrus H. McCormick.

CCL (C. H. McCormick Papers, WHi).

E N C L O S U R E

MEMORANDUM

A COMMITTEE consisting of two members of the Board of Trustees and three members of the Faculty, appointed by the Board, to continue in office at its pleasure, and empowered
(1) To formulate and recommend to the Faculty and Board of Trustees such changes in the curriculum and in the coordination of studies as may seem best for the University;
(2) To formulate and recommend to the Faculty and Board of Trustees such measures as may seem best adapted to increase the efficiency of instruction in the studies of the curriculum, whether singly or as parts of a system; and to superintend the administration of such measures when adopted;
(3) To formulate and recommend to the Faculty and Board of Trustees such regulations as may seem wise for maintaining a reasonably high standard of study among the students of the University and a reasonably strict system of discipline for failure in study; and to see to the enforcement of such regulations;
(4) To propose to the Board of Trustees all changes in or additions to the *personnel* of the Faculty of the University; and to take such action in the matter as the Board may direct.

TC memorandum (C. H. McCormick Papers, WHi).

From David Benton Jones

My Dear Professor: Chicago March 28th, 1902.
     You will probably receive by the same mail a copy of Mr. McCormick's letter to Dr. Patton enclosing draft of plan. His letter covers the subject admirably and very directly.
     It seemed to me vital that he, and not I, should write the letter and forward the scheme. His real objection was that the letter and scheme would bear conclusive evidence that they did not originate from the same source. But I was able to show him that a scheme of that kind always had to be worked over and whipped into its simplest terms and by different people; that the plan as drawn up was really only an embodment of his suggestion, and that he was the proper man to transmit it. This I not only thoroughly believe, but consider of great importance.

You will see that the letter also provides for a conference at Princeton in early May. Mr. McCormick's calendar is very full about that time and I very much fear that he may not be able to go. I shall return to Chicago from the West on April 26th, and unless unforeseen obstacles arise I shall make the trip, if I can only remain a day or two. This leaves ample time for consideration before the conference and after the conference before the June meeting.

After Dr. Patton gives his adherence much work will then remain to be done with the individual members of the Board. A majority must be definitely committed to the scheme before the meeting of the Board, and as large a majority as possible.

If subterranean currents are not stronger than I think likely I see no danger of defeat ahead. I have not had time to examine the rules and by-laws as to the competency of acting upon a proposition of that kind at the meeting at which it is proposed. This, of course, must be looked into.

This letter needs no reply, but after you have received a copy of Mr. McCormick's letter to Dr. Patton I should be very glad to have you write Mr. McCormick in approval. The thing was not only well done, but was a very important step in our progress, and I know he values your approval very highly.

Very sincerely yours,   David B. Jones.

TLS (WP, DLC).

A News Report of a Victory Celebration

[March 29, 1902]

"Princeton wins by unanimous decision in ten minutes."—The jubilant yell that welcomed the arrival of that message at the telegraph office in Princeton a few minutes before midnight last Wednesday, was enough to put all the pessimists out of business for the rest of their natural lives.

For after seven years of unbroken defeats, Princeton conquered Harvard in their eighth annual debate at Cambridge on the evening of March 26.[1]

Good news, this was, to the two or three hundred undergraduates who had not left for the Easter recess. And they immediately celebrated in the usual fashion—with a pee-rade. It was sufficiently noiseful if not as numerous as it would have been if most of the undergraduates had not been out of town. Headed by a suddenly improvised bugle and drum corps, they marched to Prospect and got a congratulatory speech from the President;

then out to Bayard Lane to the house of Professor Henry van Dyke '73, who was still up waiting for news of the debate; Professors A. G. Cameron '86 and Woodrow Wilson '79 were also called upon and made brief balcony speeches, properly punctuated with Y-E-A—s from the crowd below. This nocturnal celebration lasted till two a.m.

Printed in the *Princeton Alumni Weekly*, II (March 29, 1902), 411.
  [1] The question was "Resolved, That Mayor Low should strictly enforce the Excise Law in New York City." The members of the victorious Princeton team, who supported the affirmative side of the question, were Robert Andrew Blair, M.A., 1903, Alexander Johnston Barron '02, and Robert Warren Anthony '02.

A News Report of an Alumni Dinner

[March 29, 1902]

Union County, New Jersey, has a Princeton alumni club all to itself. Thirty-eight alumni were present at the annual dinner of this flourishing club, held at the Park Avenue Hotel, Plainfield, N.J., on March 20. George C. Thomas '79 presided, and the speeches were by Professor Woodrow Wilson '79, Professor Alfred G. Reeves '84, of the New York Law School, Professor Wilson Farrand '86, of the Newark Academy, and Judge William N. Runyon, of Plainfield, representing Yale. Also, a quintette of the University Glee Club was present and helped on the entertainment. . . .

Printed in the *Princeton Alumni Weekly*, II (March 29, 1902), 417.

From David Benton Jones

My dear Mr. Wilson,   Chicago   March 29 1902
    The President of The Princeton Club of Chicago has just called to say that they were writing you officially asking you to come to a Princeton meeting to be held in Chicago the latter half of April and they wanted me to write also urging your acceptance.
    You need no urging when there is work to be done for Princeton. It would also give you an opportunity to talk to Mr. McCormick. It is impossible for me to be here between April 7 and 26[.] I need no convincing as to Princetons needs, nor does Mr McCormick, but to have you tell him how great the needs are would be of very great value. He is not being driven or carried along in this matter. But he has not had time to look into the situation as fully as he might and you know how effective a force he is when fully informed and enlisted. He will eat a hearty

dinner after doing things that would put me to bed. I would not say this to any one likely to misunderstand. I know your friendship for him and I have worked with him here in many things and my respect for his efficiency has steadily grown as I see more of him. A frank talk with him would be of the greatest possible help in any event and especially if he can go east with me in May. Dr. Patton is to be at Lake Forest in early, very early June, or late in May—at Harlan's inauguration.[1] The whole situation is full of humor which I can tell you of someday. So you see Mr. McC. will see Dr. Patton before June meeting even if he cannot join me. The surrender may be so complete that I need not make the May trip at all. I hope the surrender will be sent in writing to Mr McC.   Very Sincerely   David B. Jones.

ALS (WP, DLC).
  [1] That is, the inauguration of the Rev. Richard Davenport Harlan '81 as President of Lake Forest College on June 4, 1902.

From Harper and Brothers

Dear Sir: New York City   March 31, 1902.
    . . . We duly received the closing chapters of Volume IV.
    We note what you say about the portraits which we propose to print in brown on a tint, and are pleased to learn that your judgment coincides with ours. We thank you for your cordial expressions and would assure you that we shall do our utmost to obtain the best results.   Very truly yours,   Harper & Brothers.

TLS (WP, DLC).

From George Walter Prothero[1]

Dear Sir,   London, W.C.   2 April '02
    You are perhaps aware that Ld. Acton has been obliged by ill-health to resign his editorship of the Camb. Mod. History,[2] which has been entrusted by the Syndics of the Press to the three editors[3] whose names appear above. I have undertaken the special charge of Vol. VII, to which you were good enough to contribute a chapter on "State Rights."[4] That is now in type, & I presume you have seen & corrected it; but of this I am not sure, and it is unfortunately impossible to communicate with Ld. Acton. Will you therefore be good enough to let me know whether you wish to see the proof or not? I see it is not accompanied by a bibliography, such as is intended to accompany each chapter of the book. Can

you tell me when I may expect this addition to your chapter?[5]

We hope to publish the volume about April 1903.

Yours faithfully   G. W. Prothero

ALS (WP, DLC).
[1] Historian, at this time editor of the London *Quarterly Review*.
[2] Acton had suffered a paralytic stroke and died on June 19, 1902.
[3] They were, in addition to Prothero, Adolphus William Ward, Master of Peterhouse, Cambridge, and Stanley Mordaunt Leathes, Lecturer in History, Trinity College, Cambridge.
[4] It is printed at Dec. 20, 1899, Vol. 11.
[5] See G. W. Prothero to WW, June 19, 1902.

To Cyrus Hall McCormick

My dear Cyrus,   Princeton, 3 April, 1902

Several days ago I received a letter from Mr. Jones saying that you had written to Dr. Patton, sending him a copy of the plan, and that I would probably receive from you a copy of the letter. Was he mistaken as to your intention? I have received nothing from you, and am a little nervous lest the letter should have been sent and have gone astray.

Of course it would be of great service to Fine and me to see what you had said to the President, in order that we might be guided by it in anything we may ultimately have to do or say.

We value your initiative and action in this vital matter more than I can say.

With warmest regard,

Faithfully Yours,   Woodrow Wilson

ALS (C. H. McCormick Papers, WHi).

From Caleb Thomas Winchester

My dear Professor Wilson,   Middletown, Conn., Apr. 3d 1902

Let me assure you that your favorable decision on the Wesley [Bicentennial] Commemoration address has given very great pleasure to all your friends here.[1] You must let us think it in part a personal favor to us, and another proof of the place we still have in your kind remembrance. And then we know that at least *one* thing in the Commemoration will be done as it should be. I only wish we may be able [to] find other speakers as worthy [of] the theme and the occasion.

As fast as the arrangements for the Commemoration are made, I will send you announcements of them.

Mrs. Winchester joins me in kindest remembrances to Mrs.

Wilson and yourself; and we should like to be remembered also to Mr. Axson.   Very cordially yours,   C. T. Winchester.

ALS (WP, DLC).
  1 Wilson's address at Wesleyan University, "John Wesley's Place in History," is printed at June 30, 1903, Vol. 14.

From Cyrus Hall McCormick

My dear Woodrow: Chicago April 3rd, 1902.

I enclose you herewith copy of a letter I sent to Dr. Patton and a summary which embodies David Jones' and my ideas as to the construction and operation of such an Executive Committee as was talked of personally with you for a few moments at Princeton. I am sending copies of this letter and the memorandum to Messrs. Cleveland, Pyne, McPherson, Cuyler, Bayard Henry and Davis, and trust that this matter may receive careful attention, in order that something may be done along this line at the June meeting of the Board.

Kindly consider this confidential except so far as you may desire to consult Professors Brackett and Fine, the other members of your Committee appointed to confer with the Trustees. You will notice that we have suggested that your Committee act in this matter with two representatives from the Board of Trustees.

I am   Very sincerely yours,   Cyrus H McCormick

TLS (WP, DLC). Encs.: C. H. McCormick to F. L. Patton, March 27, 1902, TCL (WP, DLC); C. H. McCormick to G. Cleveland, April 3, 1902, TCL (WP, DLC); and memorandum in re executive committee, TC (WP, DLC).

Cyrus Hall McCormick to Grover Cleveland

Dear Mr. Cleveland: [Chicago] April 3rd, 1902.

Following up the thought expressed in the little private conference held in Princeton Inn after the last Trustees' meeting, David Jones and I have given some careful attention to this matter, and I enclose herewith copy of a letter I have written to Dr. Patton on the subject, together with an outline which I sent to Dr. Patton, embodying the views David Jones and I held on the practical organization and work of such an Executive Committee as was proposed.

If you happen to be at home about May 5th, when we come to Princeton, we shall give ourselves the pleasure of conferring with you on this subject. And in the meantime I trust that you can consider this letter to Dr. Patton and the outline of the duties of the Executive Committee in order that you may suggest such amendments or additions as may seem to you wise before the matter is brought before the Trustees at the next meeting, as I certainly hope it can be.

I am   Very sincerely yours,   Cyrus H. McCormick.

TLS (McCormick Letterpress Books, WHi).

Cyrus Hall McCormick to Cornelius Cuyler Cuyler

My dear Mr. Cuyler: [Chicago] April 3rd, 1902.

I enclose you herewith copies of letters to Mr. Cleveland and Dr. Patton, and a schedule showing David Jones' and my ideas of the organization and work of this Executive Committee. Please consider the matter carefully and we will confer with you early in May. Even if I cannot come to Princeton, David Jones will make the trip. This, I consider, is one of the most important matters we have on hand.

I am   Very sincerely yours,   Cyrus H. McCormick.

This form of letter sent to each of those who were consulted. I hope this will stir up the matter. Jones and I have put a good deal of time on it.

TLS (McCormick Letterpress Books, WHi).

Cornelius Cuyler Cuyler to Cyrus Hall McCormick

My dear Cyrus: New York. Apl 3/02

Much to my surprise Dr. Patton called on me the other afternoon and spent an hour with me going over the matter which you and Jones discussed with him and he also showed me your letter and memorandum. He is in a very disturbed state of mind and I should advise you as well as Jones not to press the matter any further, particularly by correspondence, but when you are on in May talk the matter over quietly with him. The point that seems to be worrying him most is the fact that under your plan he is being almost entirely disregarded. He feels that he should at least be a member of the Executive Committee. Confidentially matters look to me very serious and as if they were coming rapidly to a point—by that I mean a disturbance—and the tendency in that direction is more marked than at any time since I came on the Board. I realize the gravity of the situation and the absolute need of something being done—at the same time we shall have to be exceedingly careful in every way to handle this matter so that there will be the least possible friction.

I have no objections to your showing this letter to Jones, and meantime with kind regards, I am

Yours faithfully,   C C Cuyler

ALS (C. H. McCormick Papers, WHi).

From David Benton Jones

My Dear Mr. Wilson: Chicago   April 5th, 1902.

I enclose copy of a letter which explains itself. It is only an example of the same things which have paralyzed Princeton for some time and must not be allowed to stand in the way of progress. Please limit its use to Dr. Brackett, Mr. Fine and yourself, and this in strict confidence, as I have not been able to see Mr. McCormick since he sent me the copy.

I very deeply regret the fact that I leave on Monday next to be gone for three weeks, as otherwise I should be inclined to go east.

If he is not chairman of the contemplated Executive Committee would it in any way diminish the effectiveness of the Committee for good if he is a member of it? He must not be chairman. There could be no Committee, certainly composed of the men we have in mind, if he were to be Chairman. In a former letter you stated that the Committee would, of course, freely confer with Dr. Patton as President of the University. The members might not feel that his presence on the Committee would in any way hamper its activity or efficiency, so that he is not Chairman. We could support that position by any number of citations from the business world where the President of a corporation is not Chairman of the Board or of the Executive Committee, though a member of both.

I certainly hope Cuyler is right in what he says, that the tendency toward a disturbance is more marked than at any time since he came on the Board. It would be discreditable as well as hopeless if that were not true. Dr. Patton is the cause of the very difficulty we are seeking to remedy, and because he is disturbed is no reason why we should do nothing. He must be disturbed before anything can be done, and if he is not satisfied with a mere disturbance, then he should step aside and allow some other form of remedy to be applied.

I hope the real friends of the institution will show enough courage and good judgment to take advantage of the present situation and resolutely insist upon an effective remedy, either of reform or of an entire removal of the obstruction.

Very sincerely yours,   David B. Jones.

P.S. Since dictating the foregoing Mr. McCormick called me up on the telephone, and I stated to him that the only concession which should be even considered was that the President of the University should be ex officio a member of the Executive Committee, but that even this should be conditional upon the willingness of the three men I have mentioned to act on the Committee to carry on its work with the President as a member, but under a Chairman of its own choosing.

Mr. McCormick is anxious to confer Monday before I leave (at 10 in the evening), and we would like very much to know whether you, Dr. Brackett and Mr. Fine would be willing to serve as members of the Executive Committee with the President of the University as a member of it, but not its Chairman. I should take your willingness to serve as tantamount to an opinion that his presence would not seriously, if at all, impair its efficiency. Can you confer Monday as promptly as may be with Dr. Brackett and Mr. Fine and telegraph me your opinion as to whether it is wise and safe to concede membership on the Committee to the President of the University? In case of an affirmative opinion you can simply say, "I shall be glad to meet the new condition." If in the negative your telegram can read, "Regret I cannot comply with your request."

I give these forms merely for the purpose of avoiding any wording there which might possibly cause trouble. In case you desire to add anything further you can safely word it, but I will understand your approval or disapproval of the suggestion if only these words are used, as I shall have a copy of this letter before me.   D. B. J.

TLS (WP, DLC). Enc.: C. C. Cuyler to C. H. McCormick, April 3, 1902, TCL (WP, DLC).

Cornelius Cuyler Cuyler to Cyrus Hall McCormick

My Dear Cyrus: New York. April 5/02

I have yours of April 3d with correspondence with Dr. Patton and also memorandum of suggestions for consideration. You may be sure I shall give them very careful thought.

Sincerely yours,   C C Cuyler

ALS (C. H. McCormick Papers, WHi).

Francis Landey Patton to James Waddel Alexander

My dear Mr. Alexander: [Princeton, N.J.] April 5th, 1902.

. . . . In regard to the other point raised in your letter, I have no objection at all to your writing to Mr. McCormick in respect to the Executive Committee, and let me say to you that while the plan as outlined to [by] him is open to criticism, his letter may furnish occasion for important modifications in respect to the administration of the University. My only desire would be that such modification should go on in accordance with strictly academic ideals and precedents and in a way that would conserve the traditional spirit of Princeton University. I am sure that the whole matter can be wisely adjusted and that the attainment of good results can be looked for as a result of a conference between a few men of the Board of Trustees and perhaps also of the Faculty.

Very sincerely yours,   Francis L. Patton

TLS (Patton Letterpress Books, UA, NjP).

Cyrus Hall McCormick to Cornelius Cuyler Cuyler

[Chicago] April 7, 1902.

Letter third received. Important I see you, Pyne and if possible Wilson New York next Saturday. I go Willard's Hotel Washington tomorrow for Thursday Friday. Writing.

Cyrus H. McCormick.

CC telegram (C. H. McCormick Papers, WHi).

Cyrus Hall McCormick to Cornelius Cuyler Cuyler

My dear C.C.—   [Chicago] April 7, 1902.

I have your letters of April 3rd and 5th. I quite agree with you that correspondence is not a favorable manner of prosecuting a delicate but important question of this kind, but I am convinced that it is absolutely essential for the welfare of the faculty work and the success of our curriculum, and the standing of the intellectual work to be done by the various departments, that some radical improvement must be made over the present condition of things, and this improvement cannot be made unless the trustees take hold of the matter energetically. There has been, at least for two or three years, great apathy on this matter, and both David Jones and I feel firmly the necessity of persistent effort to work out some improvement, which will be practical and which, at the same time, must be effectual.

Dr. Patton need not feel that he is to be, "almost entirely disregarded." Our plan simply relieves him of an immense amount of detail, which I should think he would be glad to be relieved of, and which at the present time he is quite unable to attend to.

So important do I regard this whole matter that I am willing to go to New York for the purpose of seeing you and M. T. P. [Moses Taylor Pyne] on this subject, and I would like, if possible, to have Woodrow Wilson join us, so that we four may have a heart to heart discussion of the situation. I have had very little talk with Woodrow Wilson, and would be very glad to hear what he has to say about the facts of the present situation and how best to make an improvement. A personal conference of this kind would be more efficacious than much writing, and I will ask you to find out whether M. P. T. can meet with you and me in New York on next Saturday, the 12th. I will be at your disposal morning or afternoon as you may prefer. I think that New York would be a better place to meet than Princeton, because if Dr. Patton should hear that I was in Princeton he might feel that I overlooked him in not conferring with him, and it does not strike me that we are ready just yet for me to see him further about the matter. Our plans must be well made before too many people are taken into consultation. Furthermore, Jones and I expect to be in Princeton the week beginning May 5th, and we will have ample time then to go into the matter fully with Dr. Patton.

You will get this letter on Wednesday, and I shall reach Willard's Hotel, Washington, on Wednesday evening at 6:30. If you have not already telegraphed me before I leave here, will you wire me at that address so we can arrange about a meeting Saturday, also, write me on Wednesday, so I shall hear from you at Willard's hotel on Thursday morning. My plan is to remain in Washington on Thursday and Friday, and be in New York on Saturday morning, returning home Saturday night. As this is a matter of the deepest importance, and as I am going out of my way a good deal, when other matters are pressing me, to go to New York to see you I hope that you and M. T. P. will be able to arrange a conference with me, even though at some little inconvenience to yourselves. For instance, I could meet you as early in the morning as you like—we could even breakfast together down town, or if you wish to meet me in the afternoon I can suit myself to your engagement.

I am sending a copy of this letter to Mo,[1] so that he will be ready for a telephone message from you.

I am,   Very sincerely yours,   Cyrus H. McCormick.

TLS (McCormick Letterpress Books, WHi).
[1] That is, Moses Taylor Pyne.

James Waddel Alexander to Cyrus Hall McCormick

My Dear Mr. McCormick: New York, April 7, 1902.

President Patton told me the other day that he had received a letter, I think from you and Jones, outlining a plan for an Executive Committee of Princeton University, consisting partly of Trustees and partly members of the Faculty (but exclusive of the President), who should have authority to manage practically all the affairs of the institution.

While I am alive to the fact that improvements can be made, I want to say to you that as I feel at present, I could not support such a revolutionary measure. No matter who the President of the University is, I think he should not be stripped of his dignity, and, indeed, there are other objections in my mind to the plan proposed. President Patton tells me that he thinks that the proposition from you may furnish occasion for important modifications in respect to the administration of the University, but that his desire is that such modification should go on in accordance with strictly academic ideals and precedents, and in a way that would conserve the traditional spirit of Princeton University. He thinks the whole matter can be wisely adjusted, and that the attainment of good results can be looked for as the result of a conference between a few men of the Board of Trustees and perhaps also of the Faculty, so that good may come of your movement; but, in its present bald state, I want to be frank to say that I could not support it, and I think many others of the Trustees would feel the same.

Sincerely yours,   James W Alexander

TLS (C. H. McCormick Papers, WHi).

From David Benton Jones

My Dear Mr. Wilson: Chicago April 7th, 1902.

Mr. McCormick will be in New York next Friday and expects to communicate with you in regard to meeting him in New York.

I am sending you this merely to urge you to meet him if possible. He requires only to be fully informed. He is not lacking in courage or determination. I hope you will talk to him with perfect freedom and endeavor to show him how important it is to find a remedy for the present situation.

Very truly yours,   David B Jones   T.[1]

TLS (WP, DLC).
[1] Thomas Davies Jones, who signed this letter for his brother.

From Thomas Davies Jones

My dear Professor   [Chicago, April 8, 1902]

The foregoing note was dictated by my brother last night just before he left for the Southwest. This morning there came to his office a copy of a letter written by Mr McCormick to Mr C. C. C. in reply to Mr C's letter to Mr McC. copy of which last mentioned letter was sent to you. I know that my my [sic] brother desires to keep you and Professors Brackett and Fine posted as to the situation: and I think I am warranted in sending on to you a copy of Mr McC's reply. I hardly need to ask you to consider it as confidential (except as to Profs B. & F.)[.] It is obviously of the utmost importance to support Mr. McCormick in his present attitude; and I trust you will have an opportunity to do so in New York   Faithfully yours   Thomas D. Jones.

ALS, written on D. B. Jones to WW, April 7, 1902. Enc.: C. H. McCormick to C. C. Cuyler, April 7, 1902, TCL (WP, DLC).

To Cyrus Hall McCormick

My dear Cyrus,   Princeton, New Jersey, 8 April, 1902.

Fine and Brackett and I read your letter to Dr. Patton with real gratification. It puts the matter kindly, but in the most effective way, and ought to bring the business to a head without serious friction.

Mr. Jones's later letter, which reached me yesterday, inclosing a copy of Cuyler's letter to you, he will have told you about. Just so soon as I had read it, I found Dr. Brackett and Fine, and we went into conference. The result was the telegram Mr. Jones will have shown and explained to you.[1] We were absolutely unanimous in our judgment about the question it was meant to answer. It seems useless to try any experiments which will have in them the same elements, or, at best, the same possibilities, of ineffi-

ciency, that make the present administration of affairs unsatisfactory. We have had abundant experience of that sort of
cooperation. The constant overriding of the chief officer of the
University, in Committee, the constant necessity for debate and
persuasion, the constant possibility of misunderstanding and of
the introduction of outside influences of all sorts would make the
burden of such a method quite intolerable. Worse than that, they
would really rob the method of efficiency and singleness of purpose. We would have been false counsellors to have answered
otherwise than we did. We are clear in our judgment that the
new method ought to be tried as you first conceived it in order
to get anything like the best results.

I wish you knew how much we value all that you and Mr.
Jones and the rest of you are doing, and with how entirely kindly
a feeling toward Dr. P. we are willing to coöperate in making the
plan effective.

   With warmest regard,
         Cordially and faithfully Yours,   Woodrow Wilson

We must have a talk when I come to Chicago on the 24th for the
alumni dinner

WWTLS (C. H. McCormick Papers, WHi).
  [1] No copy of this telegram has been found.

Cornelius Cuyler Cuyler to Cyrus Hall McCormick

My Dear Cyrus: New York. Apr 8/02
   I received your telegram yesterday afternoon and at once
called up Pyne's office but he was not down. I shall try to see him
today. I am also writing to Wilson and will try to have him meet
us Saturday. I will arrange the meeting for my office unless you
hear to the contrary for 12 o'clock Saturday. Awaiting your letter,
I am, with kind regards   Your faithfully,   C C Cuyler

ALS (C. H. McCormick Papers, WHi).

From Cornelius Cuyler Cuyler

My Dear Woodrow: New York. Apl 8/02
   I received a wire from McCormick yesterday afternoon stating
that it was important for him to see you, Pyne and myself on
Saturday, so I have named my office as the place and 12 o'clock

as the hour for the meeting. Evidently he has something very important to discuss with us. Hoping you can be here, I am,

Yours sincerely   C C Cuyler

ALS (WP, DLC).

Simon John McPherson to Cyrus Hall McCormick

Lawrenceville, New Jersey,

My dear Mr. McCormick: Tuesday, April 8th, 1902.

Let me thank you sincerely for your note of April 3d, enclosing the copies of the letter to Mr. Cleveland, the letter to Dr. Patton, and the memorandum prepared by yourself and Mr. Jones. I have read all these papers with the deepest interest. I think your letters are very cordially and wisely worded. If the matter in view is to be arranged for by a committee, I think that the committee from the Faculty, already appointed, would be as good as we could possibly get. But I should most seriously object to taking a place on such a committee myself for two reasons: in the first place, because my time and attention are so fully engrossed here; and, secondly, because I fear that a man in my position, as the head of a secondary school, might be *persona non grata* to many in the Faculty of a University, whether it be that of Princeton or another.

I have been questioning in my mind since the day of the little meeting at the Inn, whether a committee after all is the best thing. Rome found that even two consuls made a difficult team to drive. The committee might work the more harmoniously from the fact that three come from the Faculty and would virtually decide all important questions that might come before it; but one man, if the right one could be found, could, I think, do the work required better than five men. What would you think of one or other of these alternatives [alternative] plans. First, to appoint, or not, as seemed wise, a dean of the School of Science. If that were done we should then have three deans of the usual sort: One in charge of the academic department, another in the scientific department, and a third in charge of the graduate department. Then appoint a dean of the university, to whom should be given the powers and responsibilities outlined in your memorandum. Or, secondly, leaving everything else as it is now, appoint a Vice-President with prescribed and limited functions, roughly outlined in the memorandum.

There can be no difference of opinion amongst us, I take it, as to the desirability of accomplishing the common end that we all have in view. The way by which that can be accomplished is a question which disturbs me.

I am especially glad that you have submitted this whole matter to the president. He has a right to know of every step that is taken and I should want to act only, as you say, in the spirit of cordial and sympathetic assistance to him in anything that is done.   Very sincerely yours,   S. J. McPherson.

TCL (C. H. McCormick Papers, WHi).

Notes for an After-Dinner Talk

8 April, 1902

Trenton Alumni dinner,

The *private* vs. the *state* institution.

The former can choose what contribution it will make to the power of the country, and *keep its individuality*. The nation best served by *variety* in institutions as in individuals.

Stole their bait.

Princeton's contribution: the spirit of institutions along with the spirit of the age.

Lawd told Moses to come fo'th

Bagehot's definition of a "constitutional statesman." *Not novelties, but atmosphere, esprit*, balance, the temper of thoughtfulness in the midst of change.

Pray for power as well as for ideas

The sort of public life to be supplied by the university man, public life without desire for office, light without heat.

Frogs in the watered milk

The small college and *the large*:

Only possible substitute for the personal contact of the small college, a manifest, all-pervasive, spirit, ideal, dominant throughout.

Little, but O, Lawd!

Choice and coördination of groups, instead of scattered choice of studies.

WWhw MS. (WP, DLC).

A Report of a Meeting of the Trenton Alumni

[April 9, 1902]

BANQUET OF PRINCETON CLUB

The Princeton Club of Trenton held its annual banquet last evening at the Trenton House.

Mayor Frank S. Katzenbach[1] was the first speaker of the evening. President Patton spoke on the necessity of financial support of old Nassau. Dr. Smith[2] made a cheerful address of which "Princeton Spirit" was the theme.

Dr. Wilson confined his remarks to "The Ideal Princeton Student."

Dr. [Henry] Van Dyke made the closing speech and his talk was on "Good Fellowship."

Governor [Franklin] Murphy was present as an invited guest.

Printed in the *Trenton Times*, April 9, 1902; one editorial heading omitted.
[1] Frank Snowden Katzenbach, Jr., '89, Mayor of Trenton.
[2] The Rev. Dr. Wilton Merle Smith '77, pastor of the Central Presbyterian Church of New York.

From the Minutes of the Princeton University Faculty

3 05′ P.M., Wednesday, April 9th, 1902.

The Faculty met according to adjournment.

Present forty four Professors and twenty four Instructors.

The discussion of the Report [of the University Committee on Scholarship] was continued by Professors Baldwin, Paul Van Dyke, Ormond, Shields, A. Guyot Cameron, West, Young, Brackett, McCloskie, Winans, Baldwin, Magie and Ormond.

The Faculty adjourned to meet at the same place at 8 P.M., Friday, April 11th, 1902.

To Thomas Davies Jones

My dear Mr. Jones,   Princeton, New Jersey, 10 April, 1902.

Thank you most sincerely for your thoughtful kindness in sending me the copy of Mr. McCormick's letter which you enclose in your brother's letter received this morning. It will help us materially to have seen it.

Cuyler wrote me of McCormick's wish to consult me, and I have arranged to be at Cuyler's office at noon on Saturday, to meet the three men mentioned

With warm regard and appreciation,
Cordially Yours,   Woodrow Wilson

WWTLS (Mineral Point, Wisc., Public Library).

From the Minutes of the Princeton University Faculty

8 05′ P.M., Friday, April 11th, 1902.

The Faculty met according to adjournment in the Chemical Room.

Present forty seven Professors and nineteen Instructors.

The Chairman of the Committee [Professor Magie] gave notice of intention to present certain proposals in addition to those contained in the Report [of the University Committee on Scholarship].

The discussion of the Report was then continued by Professors Dahlgren, Humphries, West, Magie, Marquand, Cornwall, Hibben, A. Guyot Cameron, Fine, Wyckoff, Shields, Young, Hoskins,[1] Magie, Paul Van Dyke, Ormond, Harper, Shields, Winans, Loomis, Young, Baldwin[,] Smith,[2] Neher[3] and Cornwall.

After full discussion two amendments were adopted and No. 6. was changed to read as follows, viz:

6 Courses in Junior and Senior Years should ordinarily occupy three hours weekly instead of two hours weekly as at present. The extra hour thus provided is available for a quiz.

The weekly Schedule of Studies shall not be less than fifteen hours.

The Faculty adjourned to meet in the same room at 8 P.M., Monday, April 14th, 1902.

[1] John Preston Hoskins, Assistant Professor of German.
[2] Herbert Stearns Squier Smith, Professor of Applied Mechanics.
[3] Fred Neher, Assistant Professor of Analytical and Organic Chemistry.

Francis Landey Patton to Cyrus Hall McCormick

My dear Mr. McCormick: Princeton, N.J.   April 12th, 1902.

I am in your debt for two letters. In the first place let me say in respect to your letter enclosing a memorandum of suggestions made by Mr. Jones and yourself, that the points covered by the memorandum involve changes so different from anything which I had contemplated in my conversation with you the day that the Trustees met that I feel that no progress could be made in the discussion of them except by means of conversation. When you and Mr. Jones come on in May, I shall be very happy to go over the whole ground with you, and we will see then what can be done. In respect to the date mentioned, I may say that I am under engagements which will take me away from home on Monday, Tuesday and Wednesday, the 5th, 6th and 7th of May, but I shall be at home on Thursday, Friday and Saturday of that week and shall be very happy to see you and Mr. Jones on any of these days. . . .   Very faithfully yours,   Francis L Patton

TLS (C. H. McCormick Papers, WHi).

A News Item

[April 12, 1902]

PRESBYTERIAL APPOINTMENTS.

The Princeton ministers and elders not noted elsewhere as having been appointed on the standing committees of the Presbytery of New Brunswick are as follows: . . . the [Rev.] Henry C. Cameron, D.D., chairman, and Elder Woodrow Wilson, on the Committee on the Historical Society. . . .

Printed in the *Princeton Press*, April 12, 1902.

Notes for a Talk

12 April, 1902

University of Va. Alumni, New York City.[1]

My *somewhat* varied college experience—*Jane Collier*
Don't regret it,—don't feel the sentiment of the Confederate soldier—
"Never love another country."
In what capacity do I appear? "Sugar coat your head"?
If I could only have brought away fr. each a touch of its distinction.
   Individuality the capital of the university as of the person
   University had a great deal. One might fancy it the individuality of
      Mr. Jefferson
      Change has come, of course,—*whistle to your lobster*,—but not
         change of principle.
      No imitation,—*stole their bait.*
      Election, but of substantial *subjects*, not innumerable *courses*,—
         and the whole cycle required for a degree[2]
      Subjected to the wisdom of the world
         Not a horse; a hobby (Keats)
            "Then felt I like some watcher of the skies
            When a new planet swims into his ken;
            Or like stout Cortez when with eagle eyes
            He stared at the Pacific—and all his men
            looked at each other with a wild surmise—
            Silent upon a peak in Darien."[3]

WWhw MS. (WP, DLC).
   [1] The *New York Times*, April 13, 1902, in a brief report of this meeting, said about Wilson only that he responded to the toast, "The University of Virginia."
   [2] Here Wilson seems to have been setting forth his own ideas about the elective system and the ideal university curriculum. The University of Virginia's undergraduate curriculum and degree requirements had always conformed generally to these ideas, and the standard history of the university does not indicate that there had been any major changes there in recent years. See Philip Alexander Bruce, *History of the University of Virginia, 1819-1919* (5 vols., New York, 1920-1922), IV, 282-87.
   [3] From John Keats, "On First Looking into Chapman's Homer."

From the Minutes of the Princeton University Faculty

8 05′ P.M., Monday, April 14th, 1902

The Faculty met according to adjournment & continued the consideration of the Report [of the University Committee on Scholarship].

The attendance was about the same as at the last meeting[,] about two thirds being Professors & one third Instructors

The motion to adopt Section 9. "All Junior-Senior Courses should be abolished. But on i[n]dividual &" was discussed by Professors West, W. B. Scott, Hunt, West, Baldwin, Humphreys, Magie, West, Ormond, Shields, Marquand, W. B. Scott, Harper, Cornwall, Hibben, Baldwin, Dahlgren, Winans, Hibben and Mac-Closkie. Certain motions were presented and discussed and by general consent were allowed to be withdrawn.

The President called Prof. H. C. Cameron to the Chair and proceeded to discuss the Section 9 and the following proposed amendment, "To strike out the word 'All' in the first line and to add to the paragraph—'Junior-Senior Courses involving small classes conducted mainly by recitation methods or their equivalents may be allowed on recommendation of the Committee on Electives.' "

After further discussion by Professors West, Loomis, Ormond and Baldwin the amendment was carried by a vote of twenty four (24) to sixteen (16). Section 9 as amended was then adopted by a vote of twenty to fifteen

The Faculty adjourned to meet in the same place at 3 P.M. Wednesday, April 16th, 1902.

Cornelius Cuyler Cuyler to Cyrus Hall McCormick

My dear Cyrus: New York. Apr 14/02

Referring to our conversation of Saturday last in rê formation of Executive Committee for Princeton University, I feel that as you and Jones had the first talk with Dr. Patton it would be better, if you are not able to be personally present on May 5th, to defer the visit to Dr. Patton until such time as you and Jones can be present together. I think I can do more good for the cause by not being brought directly into the interview with Dr. Patton. I want to oblige you in every way possible but believe that in talking it over with Jones you will conclude that it is best not to bring any outsider into the interview with Dr. Patton but to confine it to the two who originally had the conversation with him. I think we are now on the right track but the matter requires the utmost tact and careful handling at every step. Awaiting your further advices, I am,   Yours faithfully,   C C Cuyler

ALS (C. H. McCormick Papers, WHi).

To Cyrus Hall McCormick

My dear Cyrus,   Princeton, New Jersey, 14 April, 1902.

We have had our conference, and Brackett and Fine see the business necessity, so to say, of allowing membership on the Committee to the President as you made me see it on Saturday. They authorize me to say, therefore, that we will fall in with your wishes in the matter, critical as we fear the change of plan will make the method of our action after the Committee is officially constituted. Do not understand me to mean that our acquiescence is not cordial. It is. We are ready to do anything that circumstances show to be necessary to secure an effective means of saving the University; we are ready to sacrifice even some measure of efficiency in the means, if the concession really does not prevent substantial results. We shall have to ask your very jealous and watchful assistance,—that's all.

No small part of our willingness to do this springs out of your suggestion that Mr. Cleveland be made chairman of the Committee. We would like to urge that he be made chairman by action of the Board itself; and that Dr. McPherson be made vice chairman in the same way, in view of Mr. Cleveland's frequent absences from home and our earnest desire to avoid the necessity of deliberately excluding the President from the chairmanship or vice chairmanship by the votes of members of the faculty. We feel that you should manage this for us, in order to save unnecessary embarrassments.

I shall hope to see you next week in Chicago.

With warmest regard,
                    Faithfully Yours,   Woodrow Wilson[1]

WWTLS (C. H. McCormick Papers, WHi).
[1] There is a WWT draft of this letter in WP, DLC.

A News Report of a Lecture on Sir Henry Maine

[April 15, 1902]

ADDRESS BEFORE MONDAY NIGHT CLUB.

At a meeting of the Monday Night Club, held in 11 North Dod last night, Professor Woodrow Wilson read a paper on "Sir Henry

Maine." Sir Henry Maine, he said, was a lawyer, yet he wrote literature, a thing which many people find hard to believe. His personality had its effect on his work in which appear his broad view, his genius—not only touched with art, but art itself. As a speaker he was brilliant and forceful, but as a writer calm and deliberate. Professor Wilson gave a brief sketch of Sir Henry's life and described his university career, and his work as tutor and professor. After he gave up university life, he turned to the law and later took up writing. "Ancient Law" was his first and best book. It shows much of the style and character of his later works. Professor Wilson told what these works had done for the law. His greatness, he said, lay in the art and mystery of derivation. He was a master of interpretation. He often got his material second-hand, but he always added something of his own. The lawyer's great work for India was next discussed, his many honors in public life, and his political views. Professor Wilson then gave a brief review of Sir Henry's later writings, and concluded with a summary of his character and his life work.[1]

Printed in the *Daily Princetonian*, April 15, 1902.
[1] Wilson obviously read the lecture printed at Feb. 25, 1898, Vol. 10, which was published as "A Lawyer with a Style," *Atlantic Monthly*, LXXXII (Sept. 1898), 363-74.

From the Minutes of the Princeton University Faculty

3 05 P.M., Wednesday, April 16, 1902

The Faculty met according to adjournment.

The Minutes of the last four meetings were read and approved.

There were present fifty eight (58) members of the Faculty of whom forty five (45) were Professors and thirteen (13) were Instructors.

Pending a motion to adopt Section 3 of the Report [of the University Committee on Scholarship] discussed by Professors Magie and Baldwin a Resolution to recommit the Report to the Committee was presented and after discussion by Professors Baldwin, MacCloskie, West, Ormond, Wilson, the President, Professors Cornwall, West, Magie, Neher, Winans and Ormond, It was Resolved That the Report be recommitted to the Committee.

Report of
The University Committee on Scholarship.

Your Committee is convinced that the condition of scholarship among our students at the present time is one of demorilization, especially in the two upper years. In our judgment the present plan of studies is not and cannot be applied effectively and beneficially. The most obvious fault of the system now in operation is the abundant opportunity it offers for taking courses in which study is not exacted, and cannot be exacted so long as these courses have to be conducted almost entirely by lectures. The majority of Juniors and Seniors make up their elective lists mainly from these courses, some of which are common to both classes, thus increasing the difficulty. We also think that the number of studies which must now be taken simultaneously by a student is too large, and that the time allotted to each study separately is too small. This scatters the student's interest and dissipates his energies instead of combining them upon a few studies each of which has enough time assigned to it to make it really su[b]stantial & valuable. Moreover, as the choice of electives is often determined by the convenience of the hours at which the exercises are held, as well as by a preference for the easier courses, the result is frequently an entire abandonment of a serious or even coherent plan of study

We therefore propose a revision of the un[d]ergraduate Academic course and of the course in General Science on the following basis:

1. The required and elective courses should be co-ordinated in such a way as to provide a curriculum of liberal education of the purely collegiate type throughout the first three years.

2. Instruction in Freshman and Sophomore years should be given by recitation courses in which the classes recite orally in small divisions. The only exception to this should be courses in science requiring experimental illustration or laboratory work. But even such courses should consist in part of oral recitations.

3. The studies of the Academic Freshman Year should remain as at present.

4. Some elective extension may be allowed in the Academic Sophomore Year, provided the courses are conducted by oral recitations in small divisions. But the amount of required Classics and Mathematics should be maintained undim[in]ished and the time allotted to required English increased and devoted to training in rhetoric and writing.

5. In all courses of Junior and Senior Years a considerable portion of the time should be devoted to oral and written recitations. If the classes are large they should be divided into small sections for this purpose. The Committee strongly recommends the oral recitation in preference to the written recitation

6. All courses in Junior and Senior Years should occupy three

hours weekly instead of two hours weekly as at present. The extra hour thus provided is available for a quiz. The number of courses taken simultaneously on a three hour basis will be five, instead of seven as at present.

7. All courses open to Juniors should be of a general, and not of a specialized character. The number of these general courses should be limited so as to include only leading subjects of importance in a liberal education.

8. Every Junior should be required to take throughout the year one course in Philosophy and one course in Science. This leave[s] three elective courses.

9. All Junior-Senior courses should be abolished. But on individual petition a Senior may be allowed to take a Junior course. In every case, however, it should be shown that the request is based on some reasonable plan of study.

10. To secure uniformity in the ranking system and make more feasible a plan for Special Honors in leading subjects of study, all four classes should be ranked on a basis of five groups.

11. General Honors for general excellence should be maintained, but more efficient provision should be made for Special Honors as an inducement both to coherency and to serious purpose in the choice of electives.

12. As soon as our resources permit, a four course (twelve hour) schedule is desirable for our best men in Junior and Senior Years, but is not recommended at present because of the impossibility with our limited Faculty of providing the necessary extra courses.

13. A Committee of the University Faculty should be appointed to exercise supervision of the choice of electives and awarding of Honors.

14. It is desirable that the revised course of study here proposed go into effect the coming Academic Year, if possible.

Sections 6 & 9 as amended.

6. Courses in Junior and Senior Years should ordinarily occupy three hours weekly instead of two hours weekly as at present. The extra hour thus provided is available for a quiz.

9. Junior-Seniour courses should be abolished. But on individual petition a Senior may be allowed to take a Junior course. In every case, however, it should be shown that the request is based on some reasonable plan of study.—Junior-Senior Courses involving small classes conducted mainly by recitation methods or their equivalents may be allowed on recommendation of the Committee on Electives.

The Arrangement of Courses in Detail.

The Committee makes the following recommendations regarding the nature and arrangement of courses, in the belief that they embody the above principles more satisfactorily than any other plan at present feasible:

Academic Department.

Freshman Year. To remain as at present.

Sophomore Year. The required subjects to be

1st Term.		2nd Term.	
Latin,	2	Latin,	2
Greek,	2	Greek,	2
Mathematics,	3	Mechanics,	3
English,	2	Logic,	2
	9		9

Each student shall be required to choose three of the following elective subjects:

Latin,	2	Latin,	2
Greek,	2	Greek,	2
Mathematics,	2	Mathematics,	2
French,	2 (3)*	French,	2 (3)*
German,	2 (3)*	German,	2 (3)*
Chemistry,	2	Chemistry,	2
	15		15

All Sophomore courses are to be recitation courses, except Chemistry which should consist of lectures and recitations.

* Beginner's courses in French and German will be offered in addition to the regular electives in those languages. They are to be taken for the year. Three recitations a week in these courses are to count as two on the schedule.

Junior Year.

The studies of the Junior Year to be organized under the following Groups. Each student to take five elective courses of three hours each, of which one at least must be chosen from the Group in Philosophy and one at least from the Group in Science.

I. Philosophy.	II. Politics & History.	
Ethics, 3 Psychology, 3	History,	3 3
History of Philosophy, 3 3	Politics,	3 3
	Economics,	3 3

III. Science.			IV. Languages & Literature.		
Mathematics,	3	3	Greek,	3	3
Physics,	3	3	Latin,	3	3
Laboratory Chemistry	3	3	Italian,	3	3
Biology,		3 3	Spanish,	3	3
Astronomy 3 Geology, 3			French,	3	3
			German,	3	3
3 3 = both Terms.			English Liter.	3	3

Senior Year.

Students to take five elective courses of three hours each.

Further details of Senior Year are to be left to the Committees on Schedule of Studies, on Weekly Schedules and on the Graduate School.

Course in General Science.

Freshman Year. As adopted in 1901.

Sophomore Year.*

1st Term.

Mathematics,	3	Required of all students.
English,	3	Required of all students.
Latin,	3	
French,	3	One to be taken and carried through both terms.
German,	3	
Mineralogy,	3	
Biology,	3	One to be taken.
Physics,	3	

One additional subject to be chosen from among the following:

Latin,	3.	Mineralogy,	3.
French,	3.	Biology,	3.
German,	3.	Graphics,	3.

* For further details see Report of Special Committee of the School of Science Faculty.

2nd Term.

Logic, 2. Required of all students.

Students to take four other courses of three (or four) hours each to be chosen under the restrictions indicated from the following:

Latin,	3.		Chemistry,	4.	
French,	3.	One to be taken.	Biology,	3.	One to be taken.
German,	3.		Physics,	3.	

Two additional subjects to be chosen from among the following:

Latin,	3.	Mathematics,	3.
French,	3.	Physics,	3.
German,	3.	Chemistry,	4.
English,	3.	Biology,	3.

Junior Year.

The studies of Junior Year to be organized under the same Groups as on the Academic Side. Each student to take five courses of three hours each, of which one at least must be chosen from the Group in Philosophy and one at least from the Group in Science, the second course in Physics remaining a required subject for all students who have not taken it in Sophomore Year.

I. Philosophy.

As above under Junior Year, Academic Department.

II. Politics & History.

As above under Junior Year, Academic Department.

III. Science.

Mathematics,	3 3.	Chemistry,	3 3.
Physics,	3 3.	Astronomy, 3. Geology,	3.
(To be four hours until the		Biology,	3 3.
preliminary course has		Graphics,	3 3.
been introduced).			

IV. Languages & Literature.

Latin,	3 3	Italian,	3 3.
(Distinct from Academic		Spanish,	3 3.
Latin courses)		English Lit'rat're	3. 3.
French,	3 3.	3 3 = both terms. (Distinct
German,	3 3.	from Academic Junior
		English Lit.)

Senior Year.

The studies of Senior Year to be organized under the same Groups as those of the Academic Senior Year, omitting Classics. Students take five elective courses of three hours each.

Further details to be left to the Committees on Schedule of Studies, on Weekly Schedules, and on the Graduate School.

Classification of Courses.

All courses in the Graduate and Undergraduate Department shall be classified and published in the Catalogue as stated below:

I.—Faculty of Philosophy

  1. Division of Philosophy
  2. Division of History & Politics.
History, Jurisprudence and Politics, Economics.
  3. Division of Art & Archaeology.

II.—Faculty of Literature

  4. Division of Semitics.
  5. Division of Ancient Languages.
      Classics, Indo-Iranian.
  6. Division of Modern Languages.
      Romance, Germanic, English.

III.—Faculty of Science.

  7. Division of Mathematics.
  8. Division of Physical Science.
      Astronomy, Physics, Chemistry.
  9. Division of Natural Science.
Biology, Geology, Physical Geography.

HONORS.

I. General Honors.

General Honors shall be given for general excellence

The Group System of marking shall be employed, and students ranked in each subject throughout the four undergraduate years on the basis of five groups. The percentage of the entire class that may be placed in each group in any subject is

First Group,   10 per cent.   Second Group,   20 per c't
Third Group,   35 per cent.   Fourth Group,   25 per c't
           Fifth Group, 25 per cent.

Academic and School of Science Students are to be grouped separately.

The limits of the General Groups shall be determined on the same principles as at present.

The names of students standing in the First General Group at graduation shall be printed on the Commencement Programs, in the Catalogue, &., as receiving High Honors; those of men in the Second General Group as receiving Honors. The distinctions

summa cum laude, magna cum laude, and cum laude shall hereafter be reserved for graduate students taking the Doctor's degree.

II. Special Honors.

Special Honors shall be awarded as follows:

A. Second Year Honors in Latin, Greek and Mathematics in
the Academic Department, and in Languages, Mathematics, and
Science in the School of Science.

B. Final Honors in

1. Philosophy.
2. History & Politics.
3. Art & Archaeology.
4. Classics.
5. Romance Languages.
6. Germanic Languages.
7. English.
8. Mathematics.
9. Physical Sciences.
10. Natural Sciences.

For Final Special Honors the requirements are as follows:

To receive High Honors:

(1) The student's general rank must be above the Fourth General Group.

(2) He must have pursued two Junior and two Senior Courses
each term in the subject.

(3) The sum of his group numbers in these courses must not
exceed ten (10).

To receive Honors:

The student must have the same general rank and pursue
the same number of courses as for High Honors, and the sum
of his group numbers in these courses must not exceed seventeen (17).

In subjects in which the Junior Schedule does not provide the
full number of courses required by the above regulations, the
candidate for Honors must choose the additional courses from
the same group.

Candidates for Honors in Art and Archaeology must pursue in
the Junior year courses in Classics or in Classics combined with
Modern Languages.

Additional Recommendation.

It is recommended that the sentence in the University Catalogue Page 74, under the head of "Standing," which reads "The
maximum mark in each study is one hundred; the minimum or
passing mark is fifty" be stricken out.

As stated above. . . It was resolved, That the Report be recommitted to the Committee.[1] On motion the Faculty adjourned.

¹ After reporting briefly on November 12, 1902, that it had circularized the faculty on curricular reform in the spring of 1902 and felt unable to take effective action because of its limited mandate, the University Committee on Scholarship asked to be discharged. The request was granted. "Minutes of the University Faculty of Princeton University, Beginning September, 1902[,] Ending June, 1914" (bound minute book, UA, NjP), Nov. 12, 1904.

From Cyrus Hall McCormick

My dear Woodrow: Chicago   April 16, 1902.

I have your letter of the 14th, and am glad to know that Professors Brackett and Fine have agreed with us that it is expedient for the President to be on the Executive Committee, making a committee of six. While I appreciate that this may make somewhat more difficult, for the time being, the work in the Committee, I am convinced that it will greatly expedite the operation of the Executive Committee's plans as soon as they are brought to the Board. Furthermore, it will greatly minimize the obstacles to be encountered in securing the adoption by the Board of the general plan of the Executive Committee. In fact, without putting the president on the Committee, we should have a difficult path before us. This is a matter where we are all willing to sacrifice, for the time being, some personal interests, and we are doing it for the sake of the ultimate good of the University. Both David Jones and I appreciate as fully as possible how much Professors Brackett and Fine and you are doing to help in this noble enterprise. We feel sure that this concession will not really prevent substantial results. Not only Mr. Jones and I, but others who are deeply concerned for the success of this movement, will give watchful attention and assistance to the progress of matters, and we will endeavor to keep in close touch with all that goes on under the new regime.

We will do all that we can to make Mr. Cleveland chairman of the Committee. Whether so small a Committee needs a vice chairman or not will remain to be seen. I should think a vice chairman would not be necessary. It might be more difficult to persuade Dr. McPherson to be vice chairman than it would to make Mr. Cleveland chairman. All this we will go into most carefully when we are at Princeton in May, and we will save you all the unnecessary embarrassment that is possible.

Mr. Jones is in the West, so I cannot write my letter to Dr. Patton, proposing that he be on the Executive Committee, until I hear from Mr. Jones, but I will do this without delay.

I am   Very sincerely yours,   Cyrus H McCormick

TLS (WP, DLC).

Cyrus Hall McCormick to David Benton Jones

[Chicago] April 16th, 1902.
New York interview decided request Wilson persuade Brackett, Fine to admit President on Executive. Letter from Wilson says others agree. Do you acquiesce? If so I will write President tomorrow stating on reflection you and I suggest him making Executive Committee of six. Telegraph reply. Important letter mailed you tonight Palace Hotel Denver.

Cyrus H. McCormick.

TC telegram (C. H. McCormick Papers, WHi).

Cyrus Hall McCormick to David Benton Jones

My dear Friend: [Chicago] April 16, 1902.
    Matters are becoming warm with regard to the questions which we have started at Princeton. I send you copies of some documents which will be of deep interest, and which will show you that the situation requires tact as well as firmness and persistence. In the first place to report about my interview at New York. I met Wilson, Pyne and Cuyler, and Cuyler gave us a recital of his interview with Dr. Patton, going more fully into the details than his letter could. He said he was satisfied that Dr. Patton was ready to resign at any time; that he felt the humiliation of the proposal made in my letter and did not wish to be pushed out of any place where he was not wanted.* He said that Dr. Patton felt that the reflection upon him in not naming him as an ex officio member of the Committee was very great. He said that in Dr. Patton's frame of mind he (Cuyler) felt very sympathetic with him and felt that we must temporize or else he would array against us those who were personal friends of Dr. Patton. Pyne, Cuyler and I agreed that the thing to do, under the circumstances, was to make Dr. Patton a member of the Executive Committee. I gave no indication that any expression had been made beforehand on this subject, but went at the matter openly with Wilson to show him the advantages to be gained by such a method. I told him that we had two horns to the dilemma and must choose which to take. *One horn* would be to put Dr. Patton on the Executive Committee and thus satisfy him and make a proposal which could, with Dr. Patton's support, be adopted by the Board without much friction. The drawback to this would be, as we all knew, that Dr. Patton might be like a wet blanket in the Executive Committee and so might retard the work, but

being only one to five (particularly if a strong man like Mr. Cleveland should be chairman of the Committee) Dr. Patton's vote could not carry with the Executive Committee, and they could continually over-rule him. I predicted, however, that there would not be need to do much over-ruling because in view of the trend that affairs are now taking he would not make objection to the proposals of the faculty members of the Executive Committee, but would fall in and agree with them more times than he would disagree.

The other horn of the dilemma would be to leave Dr. Patton off, and try to push through the present proposal which you and I have made. This would make it easier working in the Committee, but would multiply indefinitely the difficulties of having the program adopted by the Board of Trustees and the difficulty of handling matters that might come to the Board from the Executive Committee. In my judgment, the first plan is far the wisest, and we all suggested that he go back and see Brackett and Fine, and persuade them to agree to have Dr. Patton on the Committee. This he said he would do, and I came away well satisfied with my visit and the meeting, which was a most interesting and important one.

Now I enclose to you copy of Wilson's reply to me after seeing Brackett and Fine. It was understood that if they gave their consent, I was to consult you and if you agree, I am then to write Dr. Patton proposing that he should be on the Executive Committee. This will greatly help to make easier the other steps in the program. I enclose to you also copy of my reply to Wilson. I do not think it wise to send a copy to Wilson of Alexander's letter or copy of McPherson's letter, for I do not wish to discourage or dishearten them. Let us make each move one step at a time. If we should insist upon a vice chairman for the Committee some one would be sure to propose Dr. Patton for that position, whereas no one could object to Mr. Cleveland being chairman. Furthermore, it is doubtful whether he will even serve on the Executive Committee, in view of what he [Patton] says in his letter, but we must try and persuade him to change his mind.

I enclose to you copy of letter of April 15th [14th] from Cuyler, received this morning, in which he wishes to postpone action unless I can be personally present on May 5th. This is because when I was there that I had an understanding with him that if I could not be present he would go with you to see Dr. Patton. In my judgment, it would be a very great mistake to postpone this matter simply because I cannot go to New York on May 5th, and at present it does not seem possible that I can do this. On May the eighth Dr. Patton is to dine at New York at a dinner given John A. Stewart,[1] and he is to make an address; and I had thought that he would be particularly happy if we could have reached a conclusion in this matter before he went to that dinner, for no doubt he would speak with more enthusiasm after this burden is off his mind, but I regret to learn from his letter of April 12th, copy of which I enclose, that he will not be in Princeton the 5th, 6th, or 7th, but will be there Thursday, Friday and Saturday of that week. Now I should like to know from you whether you do not think it better to push forward this matter while it is possible for you to be in Princeton rather than to hold it up indefinitely until I could be there. It is possible I could not be there till the end of May if then.

I enclose copy of letter just received from Jas. Alexander which you will see emphasizes the necessity of having the President on the Executive Committee. Dr. Patton has evidently been to see Alexander and has worked upon his sympathies without Alexander having heard the other side of the case. I will reply to Alexander as soon as I learn from you whether you approve putting Dr. Patton on the Executive Committee.

I enclose herewith also copy of letter from Dr. McPherson, to which I will reply as soon as I have heard from you. My judgment is that unpleasant as it may be to Dr. McPherson, we should endeavor to hold him to the necessity of serving upon the Executive Committee, for I cannot think of any one else near at hand who would do as well under all the circumstances as he. Please let me hear from you by telegram and letter as soon as you have considered these enclosures. I am quite willing with you to take the brunt of this whole matter, believing that it is one of the greatest importance to Princeton, and my reason for preferring that action should be taken in the matter as early as possible, even though I cannot be at Princeton with you, is because the longer this is in an unsettled state the worse it is for Dr. Patton, the more likely it is to creep out in the form of gossip and the more difficult it would be for us to stem the tide of sympathy which will be aroused for Dr. Patton's position by those who do not know all sides of the question.

I omitted to say that Cuyler reported that Dr. Patton believes that most of the criticisms against him comes from Professor

---

[1] John Aikman Stewart, a member of the Princeton Board of Trustees since 1868.

West. He expressed himself as thoroughly satisfied with the high position taken on all these questions by Woodrow Wilson.

    I am   Yours very sincerely,   Cyrus H. McCormick.

* He says in any event he thinks Dr. P. will resign within two years.

TLS (McCormick Letterpress Books, WHi).

Two Telegrams from David Benton Jones
to Cyrus Hall McCormick

Canon City Colo Apl 16 02

Efficiency of Committee cant be impaired and it will greatly help us if executive is included if they will serve I strongly favor it.

David B Jones

Denver Colo Apl 18 [1902]

You have made great progress outlook very promising am working to shorten my stay hope to reach home Wednesday could go earlier if you can and president is at home. Unwise to delay

David B Jones

Hw telegram (C. H. McCormick Papers, WHi).

Cyrus Hall McCormick to Francis Landey Patton

Dear Dr. Patton: [Chicago] April 18th, 1902.

    I have your letter of April 12th and thank you for the kind and full consideration which you have given and are giving to the letter which I sent you after consultation with Mr. David Jones.

    It was not our intention to expand the suggestions offered by the memorandum beyond the thoughts outlined in our conversation with you at Princeton, but naturally in reducing suggestions of this kind to writing they must appear more in detail.

    I agree with you that correspondence is not a good method of considering matters of this kind, and we shall take pleasure in going over the whole ground with you more in detail when we see you. In the meantime, allow me to supplement the suggestions given in the memorandum in such a way that your name will be added to the Committee. It seems to both Mr. Jones and to me that it would be quite important that you should be not only ex-officio a member, but actually a participant in the work of the Committee and we would, therefore, amend our former suggestion by making the Committee six, placing your name with the other five we have mentioned.

We will telegraph and write you later as to the exact date when we can be in Princeton after I hear from Mr. Jones, who at present is absent from the city.

With kind regards, I am,

Very sincerely yours,   Cyrus H. McCormick.

TLS (McCormick Letterpress Books, WHi).

From Frederick A. Steuert

Dear Sir: [Chicago] April 18th, 1902.

Mr. Cyrus H. McCormick wishes me to hand you herewith a copy of a letter which he has received from Dr. Patton, together with his reply thereto mailed to-day.

I am,

Very respectfully yours,   F. A. Steuert   Secretary.

TLS (McCormick Letterpress Books, WHi).

Frederick A. Steuert to Bayard Henry

Dear Sir: [Chicago] April 18th, 1902.

Mr. Cyrus H. McCormick wishes me to hand you herewith a copy of a letter which he has received from Dr. Patton, together with his reply thereto which he is sending to-day. You will remember that on April 3rd Mr. McCormick sent you a copy of his letter of March 27th to Dr. Patton referring to the matter mentioned in the correspondence.

I am,

Very respectfully yours,   F. A. Steuert   Secretary.

TLS (McCormick Letterpress Books, WHi).

Cyrus Hall McCormick to James Waddel Alexander

My dear Mr. Alexander: [Chicago] April 18th, 1902.

In reply to your favor of April 7th, I believe your impression as received from Dr. Patton regarding the suggestions made by David Jones and by me are rather broader than were the terms of the suggestions we made. The Executive Committee, we suggested, would not have "authority to manage practically all the affairs of the institution." You will see by the copy of the letters I enclose herewith that this Executive Committee was expected to deal primarily with the Faculty and the matters of the curriculum. I enclose also a copy of my letter of March 27th to Dr. Patton and Dr. Patton's reply to me, and the letter I am sending him to-day, which, I think you will agree with me, alters the complexion of the matter considerably. It was not our intention to strip Dr. Patton of his dignity, but to supplement his efforts in a way that would add to his force as President of the University, and assure to the Board of Trustees the progress of certain work which at present is not being attended to. I shall hope to have the opportunity of talking with you fully over this matter, as you may be sure that nothing of such importance as this will progress very far without your careful attention being given to it and your judgment and assistance being enlisted.*

It is our idea to so shape matters that *the President himself* will be willing to make any proposals that are made at the June meeting of the Board.

I am,　　Very sincerely yours,　Cyrus H. McCormick.

* Had you been present at the March meeting I should have consulted you, as I did several others. I am sorry you were not there.

TLS (McCormick Letterpress Books, WHi).

From Cyrus Hall McCormick

[Chicago] April 19th, 1902.
Hope you will be our guest our house during your stay in Chicago.
Cyrus H. McCormick

TC telegram (C. H. McCormick Papers, WHi).

From Frederick A. Steuert

Dear Sir:　　　　　　　　　[Chicago] April 19th, 1902.

Mr. and Mrs. Cyrus H. McCormick hope you will be their guest while you are in Chicago on April 24th. If you are able to accept their invitation, may I ask you to advise me on what train you expect to arrive.

I am,
Very respectfully yours,　F. A. Steuert　Secretary.

CCL (C. H. McCormick Papers, WHi).

To Frederick A. Steuert

My dear Sir,   Princeton, New Jersey, 21 April, 1902

I accepted Mr. McCormick's kind invitation by telegram.[1] I shall expect to reach Chicago by the Pennsylvania Limited Express at 8.55 on Thursday morning.

Very truly Yours,   Woodrow Wilson

ALS (C. H. McCormick Papers, WHi).
[1] It is missing.

Cyrus Hall McCormick to Simon John McPherson

My dear Dr. McPherson: [Chicago] April 22, 1902.

Answering that portion of your letter of April 8th, relative to the matter of Princeton, I do not see exactly how the object we wish to attain could be secured by a vice president, neither do I feel that the appointment of a dean of the School of Science would answer the purpose. I think you will find when you come to examine the details of the question a little more closely that the Executive Committee we have suggested is the most feasible and practical plan, and Mr. Jones and I have added another thought which should make the appointment of this Executive Committee less difficult. We have suggested that Dr. Patton be a member of the Committee, making six, and it is our idea that Mr. Cleveland should be chairman of that Committee.

I enclose you copy of my letter to Dr. Patton on this subject, and, also, send you copy of letter received from James Alexander who, as you remember, was not present at the Trustees' meeting, and has not heard our side of the question. The letter of Mr. Alexander will show how important it is that we move carefully and altogether. I enclose you also copy of my reply to Mr. Alexander.

I trust that you will not make a point of your unwillingness to serve on this Committee for even if you do not do much work, I think it is most important that you should be on the Committee,— at least that is the idea that Mr. Jones and I have. If you will look over the list of trustees, you will find no other name which could serve the purpose of this position as well as yourself. To take a man from some other neighborhood, where he could not be easily reached for a meeting, would not attain the necessary end.

Mr. Jones and I hope to be in Princeton early in May, and will consult you about the matter further.

I am   Very sincerely yours,   Cyrus H. McCormick.

TLS (McCormick Letterpress Books, WHi).

To Edward Herrick Griffin[1]

My dear Dr. Griffin,   Princeton, New Jersey, 22 April, 1902.

Thank you for letting me see this report.[2] It meant little enough as it stood, and made me very much ashamed; but I think I have managed to make it read as if it were sense. It's poor at best; but I have not felt at liberty to doctor it.[3]

I am very much interested to learn of the volume you intend to issue.[4] It ought to interest a wide circle.

With warm regard,

Sincerely Yours,   Woodrow Wilson

WWTLS (MdBJ).
[1] Professor of the History of Philosophy and Dean of the College Faculty, The Johns Hopkins University.
[2] Of Wilson's speech of February 21, 1902, presenting the testimonial volume to Dr. Gilman.
[3] Wilson's revised speech is printed at Feb. 21, 1902.
[4] Johns Hopkins University, *Celebration of the Twenty-Fifth Anniversary of the Founding of the University and Inauguration of Ira Remsen, LL.D. as President of the University* (Baltimore, 1902).

Simon John McPherson to Cyrus Hall McCormick

                                    Lawrenceville, New Jersey
My dear Mr. McCormick: Thursday, April 24, 1902

Let me thank you for your kind letter of April 22d, with its three enclosures.

I shall be very glad indeed to talk the matter over with you when you and Mr. Jones come.

My idea with regard to the Vice-presidency is that the duties of the President should be to some extent divided. If those that he relinquishes were put in the single power of another man's hands I think the work would be far more efficiently handled than by so large a committee as you suggest. The question of a Dean for the School of Science was only indirectly ad rem.

I sincerely sympathize with your point, and that of Mr. Alexander, that the President should be in no sense stripped of his dignity, but the office has come to have so much more work committed to it than formerly that I think there should be some division of the work that would be helpful to the President and promote the efficiency of the administration.

Very sincerely yours,   S. J. McPherson.

TLS (C. H. McCormick Papers, WHi).

Notes for a Lecture[1]

24 Apr. 1902

Mem. for Lake Forest.

The *Man* and the Man of *Letters*
(or the *Scholar*)

Attitude of the "practical" man (and of the world in general) toward university education. The "self-made man"

The "academic point of view": the world a body of phenomena, the student a detached observer. Right for the time being, but not to be persisted in.

The democratic law of mind, thr. which the university is to serve the Community,—like the Church of the Middle Ages

WWhw MS. (WP, DLC).

[1] There is no mention of Wilson's address in any Chicago newspaper or Lake Forest College publication.

A Report of a Meeting of the Chicago Alumni

[April 25, 1902]

ALUMNI OF PRINCETON HOLD ANNUAL DINNER.
Chicago Graduates of Old Nassau Meet
and Make Merry After Listening to
Address by Prof. Woodrow Wilson.

Alumni of Princeton now living in Chicago ate, drank, and made merry at the University club last evening on the occasion of the annual dinner of the Princeton club. Professor Woodrow Wilson of the Princeton faculty was there to talk to his former pupils, and he had many things to say about the past glories of the college and the greater ones to come.

Professor Wilson made it clear that the idea that an election of studies which would allow a man to slip through college on the lines of least resistance was not the idea ruling the New Jersey institution. He also reminded his hearers that it rested with the alumni whether Princeton kept its place in the ranks of colleges, and his audience was standing most of the time in appreciation of his clever admixture of wit and wisdom.[1]

Henry E. Mason replied on behalf of Yale, David B. Jones told of the difficulties of the resident trustee, while Richard D. Harlan, who is 6 feet 4, said he was sorry he could not speak for his "big little brother." Then there was a smoker, and Cyrus H. McCormick, Lawrence A. Young, John Maynard Harlan, John C. Mathis, Thomas D. Jones, W. H. Forsyth, William Alton, and others of the elders gathered around the cleared tables and encouraged the youngsters at the piano to sing "Nellie Gray."

Printed in the *Chicago Daily Tribune*, April 25, 1902.
1 There are brief WWhw notes for this address, entitled "*Chicago*, 1902," in WP, DLC.

Cyrus Hall McCormick to Francis Landey Patton

Dear Dr. Patton: Cleveland, Ohio, April 25, 1902.

Inasmuch as you are not to be in Princeton until March [May] 8th, we will fix that date or the 9th for the visit which Mr. Jones and I are planning.   Cyrus H. McCormick.

TLS (McCormick Letterpress Books, WHi).

Cyrus Hall McCormick to Moses Taylor Pyne

My dear Mo: Cleveland, Ohio, April 25, 1902.

I am making every effort to arrange to go with David Jones to Princeton to be there May 8th, the date fixed by Dr. Patton. Should I find it impossible, however, Jones and I feel it is far better not to delay the matter longer. We both feel that you would be the best man to go with Jones since C. C. Cuyler wishes to be excused. He will do most of the talking, but your presence will be a great help. I think I understand from your letter that you have already spoken to Dr. Patton of the need of more executive work connected with faculty matters.

Yours respectfully,   Cyrus H. McCormick.

TLS (McCormick Letterpress Books, WHi).

An Item from an Indianapolis Newspaper

[April 25, 1902]

Prof. Woodrow Wilson arrived to-day at noon, and is the guest of Booth Tarkington. He will speak at the Contemporary Club this evening.

Printed in the *Indianapolis News*, April 25, 1902.

News Reports of Two Public Addresses in Indianapolis

[April 26, 1902]

WOODROW WILSON'S TALK

Prof. Woodrow Wilson, of Princeton University, spoke this morning, in the assembly room of the Benjamin Harrison school, to an audience composed of teachers. His subject was "The Teaching of Patriotism in the Schools."

True patriotism, he held, consists in forgetfulness of self. Patriotism is a sort of enlarged friendship. Sometimes in true friendship it is necessary to do painful things, to rebuke your friend, to show him paths in which he ought to have walked, but in which he has not walked.

He said that patriotism could best be taught to children through biography. It was hardly the thing to make genuf[l]ections to the flag without knowing what the flag stands for, what is and was behind it. "The flag," he said, "originated in a huge kick against government. It was made the national flag of this country because the people of this country were not satisfied with the government they were living under. It stands for the right of any man to rise in any company and challenge the opinion of the company or the country, it may be. If we teach them that it stands for no questions to be asked, we teach them a mistake.

"The liberty of this country stands in the first place for self-government. The government of a democracy must be conducted by a very small minority. The whole impulse of government must come from small groups of men. They come from those groups which are unlike the average of the nation. The average man is not prepared to conduct government; he does not know enough to do so.

"One of the misfortunes of this country is that we have to pay our public servants. The purest motive of public service is the desire for service and the desire for honor—not the desire for homage, not the desire to have men cheer you, but to know in your heart that you are to serve the people and that the people know this. Men are dignified by desiring to be honored by their fellow-citizens.

"It is absolutely false teaching to teach the children of this country that Abraham Lincoln was a man of the people. We never would have heard of Lincoln if he had not been different from other men. He ceased to belong to the rank and file and lifted himself out of the mass of common [men]. He reached a place that none can reach unless he strive as Lincoln did. Don't teach anybody to become common. Every man has a chance to lift himself out of the ranks and lead in the service of his country. And self-government will not be satisfied except by this process of self-selection.

"Your freedom is made in adjustment with the laws of nature. You know the terms of your physical liberty. If you take too many liberties she will put you in thraldom. Emerson says you must hitch your wagon to a star. It pays to go in the direction in which the solar system is going. The freest people is the people that has the best adjustment to the forces of law. It is the people that is not subject to the whimsical, arbitrary, unreasonable purposes of a governing minority.

"There are other things precedent to liberty. Order is one of these, obedience and discipline are others. Without religion, with[out] the solidity of property relations, there can be no adjustment of liberty. The first thing is the orderly movement of society; a democracy without order leads only to anarchy.

"Equality does not mean that if a number of boys start in a foot race they must all get to the goal in the same order in which they started. All that is meant is a free field and no favors; that the boys shall be started equal and you cheer the one at the goal. If you said to the swift, you shall not outrun the slow, he would not run at all. What we want out of men is the best that is in them, and we must provoke that best by competition.

"The only equality is that we should see that there is no fouling on the course, no man put at an artificial disadvantage; that the man humbly born is as free to make his way to the front as the man born in the privileged class.

"Patriotism is not the plant, it is the flower of the plant. No amount of cheering will sustain a government like this. It rests upon ancient understanding; upon what has gone before. When we cease to be a thinking race we shall cease to be a free and achieving race."

✧

MR. WILSON'S ADDRESS

The address delivered last night in the Contemporary Club by Woodrow Wilson, of Princeton University, is regarded by the club as being exceptionally brilliant and forceful. Mr. Wilson took for his address a large subject, "What It Means to Be an American," and met its demands with strength, wit, dignity and marked personal charm.

On being introduced by Mrs. William L. Elder,[1] in the terms

[1] Laura Bowman Elder, wife of an Indianapolis businessman active in real estate.

of a phrase of his own, as a "critical optimist," Mr. Wilson at once gained his audience by telling a frog story. A milkman, who, as milkmen sometimes do, once watered his milk, inadvertently put in also two frogs. One frog, who must have been of foreign birth, immediately exclaimed "Got to die," and died. The other frog began stretching himself, and said, "Got to do something," and the next morning this frog happily reposed on a cake of butter. This was an American frog.

Mr. Wilson said that it was unnecessary to prove that Americans are the greatest nation on earth, since they themselves frankly admit it. We have always felt this, he said, but we feel it now with a difference. Once we pretended not to mind criticism at all; we were like the young fellow just beginning to go out in society who wants to appear impeccably dressed and perfectly at ease, though he is very far from it.

We had then the self-consciousness of youth. Now we are characterized by the self-consciousness of maturity. We are aware that there has been a fresh shift of things. A new play is on, we are at the center of the stage, and we are not afraid that we can not fill our part.

"We know," continued Mr. Wilson, "that we are inquisitive, inventive, that we hate monotony and we love change. The reason that we love change is that we have always had it. An American never considers himself rooted to any spot, he is ever ready to get up and move on. We are accommodating, adaptable.

"Foreigners say we have no reverence, that we do not realize the dignity that age imparts. Admitting the truth of this stricture, it is still better that we should be as we are than that we should sit at home and nurse a narrow spirit. It has been our destiny always to be pioneers, and it might be said that only the man that would make a good pioneer is a good American. Our history has been a history of beginnings, which, roughly speaking, may be marked off in centuries—first, a century of colonization, then a century of subduing the continent by wars, then a century of independence from Great Britain and of nation building. Now we face the fourth century, before which stands a big interrogation mark.

"One thing that this century ought to see remedied is our city governments. We don't say much about them out where it will be heard, but in our hearts we know that they are bad, that they are colossal failures. They are one of the things we did not take time to do well when we made them. They are like our streets. Whenever we have been forced to pave streets, we have paved them, but only there, and often not well even there, because we have said to ourselves that we have not time now to finish this particular city, we have got to get on to that other city out beyond on the plains.

"America has produced individual writers of merit, but no strong body of writers, because of this defect in the national make-up, this aversion to finishing things. We are ashamed, apparently, to burn the midnight oil in polishing our phrases, but it is only the finished and perfect phrase that is immortal—all others perish."

Mr. Wilson said that one could read into the constitution of the United States almost anything that he liked, simply because it is living, not dead. A man that insists nowadays on holding to the strict interpretations of it made by the first Americans is a fossil; he has not grown with his times.

This is perhaps a dangerous statement for a lawyer to make, he said, but as long as the fibers of the constitution are not mutilated, it is all right to stretch it to accommodate our new conditions.

We need to beware of sentimentality, a very different thing from sentiment. Sentimentality is sentiment gone to seed. Every good man has sentiment in him, though he is shy to confess it. Ask a man why he goes to a certain church and he will say, "Oh, my people have always gone there, just habit," when really he has a particular fondness for this church and is only afraid of uncovering a deep well of sentiment, a well from which all the water comes that gushes through him and sweetens and purifies him. A man of sentiment will, if it is necessary, do a repulsive work, whereas the sentimental man will hang back and say, "No, that will soil my hands." Many sensible people to the contrary, it is sentimental to withhold the infliction of the death penalty. Society is of more importance than the individual, and the man that has injured society by a foul murder should hang for it.

A real American is a man that can with equal ease boss a job or do it himself. Many Americans have actually done both. And this is what makes foreigners fear us. No one fears the man that tells him to do a certain thing which he can not do himself. But other nations know that we can ourselves do all that we insist on. Alexander Hamilton was not a typical American. He thought and worked in the atmosphere of an older society, his sympathies were aristocratic. He thought the constitution a dangerously liberal document. Benjamin Franklin, though equally used to sophisticated society, and having a remarkably sophisticated mind, was truly American. He could put his mind to any problem that came before him, from sweeping the streets of Philadelphia, which have never been so well swept since, to bringing down lightning from heaven with a kite. He ran the entire gamut in respect of nature.

Mr. Wilson hoped that Americans would grow less intolerant. They are inclined to view as dangerous people that hold views different from theirs. Yet the American believes that nothing is impossible; he is ready for everything. The "isms" of Boston are not representatively American. Americans like something big enough to spread out all over the continent and plain enough to be talked about in everyday language.

Culture does not consist, as someone has harmoniously said, in being able to quote freely from Walter Pater and in knowing the other ten persons in the "Blessed Damezel," but in power to think, to think on the run even, as most Americans do think. Democracy is an awkward form of government, but it more than compensates for its awkwardness in giving every man a splendid chance to make the most of himself.

At the closing of his address, Mr. Wilson was generally felicitated on it. He spoke this morning to the city teachers at the Benjamin Harrison school.

Printed in the *Indianapolis News*, April 26, 1902; several editorial headings omitted.

James Waddel Alexander to Cyrus Hall McCormick

My dear Mr. McCormick: New York, Apl. 28, 1902.

I thank you for yours of April 18th, which I have read with care.

I am glad to see by your letter of the 18th to Dr. Patton that you propose to make him a member of your Committee.

Any measure that is considered important by you and Mr. Jones must, of course, receive very careful consideration from me, and I shall hold my opinion in the balance. While I know that there are many things that need improvement, I am conservative enough to hesitate about starting a new plan which may not be workable, and which may not "improve." I have very grave doubts as to whether it is wise to have a Committee composed of Trustees and Faculty both. The old motto of Princeton is, "The Trustees rule the Faculty, and the Faculty rule the College." So far as I am concerned, I shall have no other motive than the good of the institution.

Sincerely yours,   James W. Alexander

TLS (C. H. McCormick Papers, WHi).

Moses Taylor Pyne to Cyrus Hall McCormick

My Dear Cyrus: Princeton, N.J. April 28, 1902.

Of course I shall be glad to do all I can on the 8th, but I would suggest that Cuyler be there also as I think his facility in conversation and the delicate way in which he can handle these things would be valuable to men like Jones and myself.

Very sincerely yours,   M Taylor Pyne

TLS (C. H. McCormick Papers, WHi).

Frederick A. Steuert to Cornelius Cuyler Cuyler

Dear Sir: [Chicago] April 29, 1902

Mr. McCormick wishes me to hand you herewith a copy of his letter of April 18th to Mr. Jas. W. Alexander.

I am,   Yours respectfully,   F. A. Steuert   Secretary.

TLS (McCormick Letterpress Books, WHi).

To Laura Bowman Elder

My dear Mrs. Elder,   Princeton, 29 April, 02

I want to thank you (there seemed to be no suitable opportunity—or was I too shy!—on Friday evening or Saturday morning) for the words, with which you introduced me to the Contemporary Club.

You said of me just what I should like to believe to be true. I am not so inexperienced or so unkind as to hold introducers responsible for what they say in compliment to a guest, but when exactly the most pleasing thing possible is said, I deem it only decent—as well as a great pleasure—to give my hearty thanks for what is, at least, a most delightful invention.

With warm regard

Sincerely Yours,   Woodrow Wilson

TCL (RSB Coll., DLC).

Two Letters from Frederick A. Steuert to David Benton Jones

Dear Sir,   [Chicago] April 30, 1902.

Mr. Cyrus H. McCormick wishes me to hand you the attached copy of the letter of April 24th, which he has received from Dr. McPherson. Mr. McCormick wishes me to say that Dr. McPherson evidently has in his mind included him in the statement of Mr. Alexander, that the President should not be stripped of his dignity. This idea he did not get from Mr. McCormick's letter, but from Mr. Alexander's letter.

Yours truly,　F. A. Steuert　Secretary.

Dear Sir:　　　　　　　　　　　　[Chicago] April 30th, 1902.

Mr. Cyrus H. McCormick wishes me to hand you herewith copy of a letter of April 28th from Mr. M. Taylor Pyne, also a copy of a letter written to him on the same date by Mr. James W. Alexander, with reference to the proposed Special Executive Committee for Princeton University.

I am,　Very respectfully　F. A. Steuert　Secretary.

TLS (McCormick Letterpress Books, WHi).

Francis Landey Patton to Cyrus Hall McCormick

My dear Mr. McCormick　　　Pittsburgh, Pa. 30 April 1902

Yours of 25 was sent to me here. I think it better to say May 9 for our conference. I have to be in New York on Thursday night to attend the dinner in honour of Mr John A. Stewart. I shall be at home by 1 P.M. & at any time after that shall be glad to see you & Mr. Jones.

Very sincerely yours　Francis L. Patton

ALS (C. H. McCormick Papers, WHi).

An Old-Fashioned Democrat to the Editor of the *Indianapolis News*

To the Editor of The News
Sir:　　　　　　　　　　Indianapolis, May 1 [1902]

Many men would be glad to vote the Democratic ticket in 1904, if they could be sure that the man for whom they voted would be worthy of their confidence. Hundreds of thousands of Democrats are longing for a chance to fight a good, old-fashioned Democratic campaign. It has been ten years since those men have had an opportunity to voice their exact sentiments with any hope of winning. And these are all eager for a chance to make another fight in behalf of the old principles to the defense and propagation of which they have devoted their lives. And I believe that there are many Republicans, wearied of the excessive commercialism of these days and somewhat alarmed by imperialistic tendencies, who could be induced to vote for such a man as Grover Cleveland. The trouble is to find the man. Of course, Mr. Bryan is out of the question. Mr. Hill,[1] though a man of ability, and though he is esteemed much more highly than he was ten years ago, is, nevertheless, somewhat distrusted. Senator Gorman,[2] to whom many people are looking with a sort of timid and shamefaced hopefulness, is merely a machine politician, without any of the qualifications, moral or intellectual, which a great popular leader ought to possess. There is talk of Judge Parker,[3] of New York, of Mr. Olney[4] and of Mr. Shepard,[5] the Tammany candidate for mayor of New York city last fall. These are all good men, but somehow the mention of their names does not arouse enthusiasm. If Mr. Olney were younger—he will be seventy years old, lacking six months, by the time of the inauguration of the next President—he would be an exceedingly formidable candidate. But a man of seventy is felt to be too old to assume the arduous duties of the presidency.

It seems to me that this would be a good time for the Democrats to break entirely away from the older men, and to take one wholly unidentified with past quarrels. And if in doing so they could find a man of ability and character, one who has a profound conviction of the truth of Democratic principles, and who has the advantage of knowing what these principles are, they should esteem themselves fortunate. The type of man that I have in mind is represented by Prof. Woodrow Wilson, of Princeton University, who lectured in this city a few days ago. I do not even know whether Mr. Wilson is a Democrat. But as he was born in Virginia, studied law at the University of Virginia, has lived in Georgia and has degrees from two Southern colleges[6] in addition to the one awarded him by Thomas Jefferson's famous university, it is perhaps safe to assume that he is not unfriendly to the Democratic philosophy. Would not some such man as this arouse enthusiasm among the people of the country? Mr. Wilson is a good deal more than a mere college professor. He is a man of affairs, a scholar, a patriot, and a man whose very presence inspires enthusiastic devotion. It is worth a good deal to have a party leader in these days who knows something of the history and the ideals of the country. We are all of us more or less tired of politicians and so-called statesmen. More and more, we like to believe, the people are coming to appreciate the value of learning and knowledge. We need more than a business man to administer the affairs of this Government. Executive ability is, of course, of prime importance, but there are other things to be taken into account. It is important that a man should know when a policy is proposed whether it has ever been tried before, and how it has worked. A deep acquaintance with the principles by which our Government has been guided is most desirable in the man who is called on to administer its affairs. The business of government is not simply a business—it is a science as well, and it should be so considered. There is a place for the college professor in our politics—provided he be the right kind of college professor.

Of course, I understand that a suggestion like this will be deemed strange and fanciful by many people who have come to take a distressingly practical view of our politics. But if there ever was a time when an infusion of imagination and idealism was needed in our politics it is in these days of railroad mergers, shipping trusts, beef trusts and steel combinations. We need to get back to the old ideals, and in order to get back to them we must enlist under a man before whose eyes they gleam with undimmed brightness. We should try to think of our Government, not merely as a great business enterprise, but as the champion of sacred and abiding principles, which it is its first business to defend. Prosperity is good and essential, but it is not the only thing to be sought. Righteousness still "exalteth a nation," and now as always "sin is a reproach to any people." We ought to get firmly in our minds some such vision of our country as that which flashed before the inspired eyes of Lowell when he wrote:

> O Beautiful my Country! ours once more!
> Smoothing thy gold of war-disheveled hair
> O'er such sweet brows as never other wore,
>   And letting thy sweet lips,
>   Freed from wrath's pale eclipse,
> The rosy edges of their smile lay bare.
> What words divine of lover or of poet
> Could tell our love and make thee know it
> Among the nations bright beyond compare?
>   What were our lives without thee?
>   What all our lives to save thee?
>   We reck not what we gave thee;
>   We will not dare to doubt thee,
> But ask whatever else and we will dare![7]

OLD-FASHIONED DEMOCRAT.[8]

Printed in the *Indianapolis News*, May 5, 1902.

[1] David Bennett Hill, Governor of New York, 1885-91, United States Senator from New York, 1892-97.

[2] Arthur Pue Gorman, United States Senator from Maryland.

[3] Alton Brooks Parker, Democratic presidential nominee in 1904.

⁴ Richard Olney of Massachusetts, former Attorney General and Secretary of State.

⁵ Edward Morse Shepard.

⁶ That is, honorary degrees from Wake Forest College and Tulane University.

⁷ From James Russell Lowell, "Ode Recited at the Harvard Commemoration, July 21, 1865."

⁸ Ray Stannard Baker has suggested that this letter was written by Louis Howland, then on the staff of the *Indianapolis News* and later its editor, and revised by Charles Richard Williams, Princeton 1875, at this time editor of the *News*. See R. S. Baker, *Woodrow Wilson: Life and Letters* (8 vols., Garden City, N. Y., 1927-39), III, 8, n.1.

Frederick A. Steuert to David Benton Jones

Dear Sir: [Chicago] May 2nd, 1902.

Mr. Cyrus H. McCormick wishes me to hand you herewith copy of a letter he has received from Dr. Patton written April 30th. with reference to the date he would be in Princeton, and could take up personally the matter under discussion.

I am,

Very respectfully yours,   F. A. Steuert   Secretary

CCL (C. H. McCormick Papers, WHi).

A News Report of a Founder's Day Address at Vassar College

[May 3, 1902]

ADDRESS BY WOODROW WILSON

The 31st anniversary of Founder's Day at Vassar College was celebrated Friday [May 2] and was made notable by the announcement that the college is to have a new library.[1] The day marks not the celebration of the founding of the college, but, as nearly as calendar conveniency permits, the birthday of the founder.[2] The day is set apart as a holiday and this in itself is commemoration but like observances are far from ending here. In the afternoon at four o'clock came the address by Prof. Woodrow Wilson, of Princeton, introduced by Miss Caroline Sperry, president of the Students' Association, the Choral Club rendering several numbers, the first of which was specially composed for the occasion by Prof. Gow.[3] . . .

¹ This was presumably the first public announcement of a gift from Mary Clark (Mrs. Frederick Ferris) Thompson in memory of her husband. The Frederick Ferris Thompson Memorial Library, with a seating capacity of 360 readers and a book capacity of 150,000 volumes, was dedicated on June 12, 1905.

² Matthew Vassar, born April 29, 1792.

³ George Coleman Gow, Professor of Music at Vassar College.

The address by Professor Woodrow Wilson, of Princeton University, dealt another blow to the old theory that writers and teachers of history are usually of the "dry-as-dust variety." The subject was Americanism, and Prof. Wilson was very happy in describing our national characteristics, in setting forth the good things about our country, and pointing out the bad things without becoming pessimistic about them. He rev[e]aled himself as a believer in the new American policy of taking our place among the nations, and spoke of the government's Philippine policy as inevitable. The keynote of his description of our country was that it is "unfinished," and that it is a characteristic trait of the American people to leave things unfinished. We have not left any considerable body of literature that has impressed the world, because we haven't had time to give the last touches that cause many writings to be prized for their style, even when the subject matter is not of great importance. The address itself was a fair example of the characteristic mentioned. Charmingly delivered, straight to the point, abounding in happy, practical illustration, taking high ground with a genuine true ring that left an impression, it was, nevertheless, not one of the carefully constructed and elaborately polished addresses that one frequently hears on such an occasion, and certainly most of the auditors were glad it wasn't. It was spoken without notes in a free, flowing, almost colloqui[a]l style, with plenty of digressions and many humorous stories for purposes of illustration.

After a few introductory words and a reference to the present scare in Europe over the absorbing greatness of America in commercial matters, Prof. Wilson plunged at once into his subject. He pointed to our city governments as a shining illustration of something unfinished. He hoped at least that they are unfinished, for if they are finished, then we have failed in one important matter of government. We pride ourselves on our ability to make governments and have abundant confidence in ourselves. People say the trouble with our city governments is the bad blood in them, by which they mean blood not our own. They say the trouble is due to the presence of so many foreigners. I don't think that's what is the matter, but believe we have made some damaging mistakes in their construction.

Prof. Wilson summed up our history as having consisted roughly in a century of colonization, a century of wars by which we cleared away those who didn't know the job of governing (the French, the Dutch, the Spanish, etc.), and a century of nation building after we had asserted our independence. Now having builded a nation roughly, we have broken away from our old habits and traditions to make use of the nation among other nations, and for this century a big interrogation point is stalking in front of us.

One of our peculiar points as a nation is the elasticity of American institutions. This Prof. Wilson illustrated by reference to the characteristically American steel structures, the tall buildings in which every part is put together so that it will give a little after the manner of the Kipling story of "The Ship That Found Herself." We have a written constitution, but let no man suppose that it is the same as when it first came out of the shop in 1787. It wasn't the same before the Civil War, and the war may be said to have been caused by the fact that the South thought it was while the North knew it wasn't. Our constitutional [lawyers] knew it wasn't. Our constitutional lawyers have been said to be like good corporation lawyers. Given [Give them] a charter containing a few general provisions and they will read almost anything in it. A constitution cannot be a mere document. It must be a thing of life.

A large part of our effort as a nation has been expended in spreading over our own territory, and a test of the Americanism of any man of the past may be made by asking, "How would he have fared on a frontier?" Let a frontiersman see a man dressed in a certain way and he is perfectly certain no human being can make use of that man. Certain otherwise useful men are dependent upon civilization for their usefulness. They have no hands adapted to grappling with frontier difficulties. Apply this test to Benjamin Franklin and you know instantly that he was a frontiersman, though equally at home in the philosophical societies. He was practically serviceable in meeting all problems and felt the zest of solving them. James Madison, I take it, would not have been serviceable on a frontier. His was the European type of student mind, thoughtful, but not practical, not characteristically American. His career as president illustrates this. Though he rendered great service to the country in the writing of the constitution, as president he was generally dominated by other men. The same may be said of Alexander Hamilton. Washington was bred on the frontier and always kept in touch with it.

The characteristic American again is the man who can either be a boss or a workingman—a man who can take off his coat and show his men how to do the job and rather likes the idea of doing it. Hence it comes about that the members of each of our different economic classes are able to see things from the point of view of others, and this interlacing makes us homogeneous, for we are sufficiently homogeneous to accomplish what we set out to.

The American has ideals without sentimentality. The last is the beginning of the end. It is what inspires women to send roses to condemned criminals. Sentimentality is a feeling that hasn't got any work in it. But there is in every American a deep well of sentiment. There is where the living water comes from, but we are not accustomed to parading our sentiment. Ask an average man why he attends a certain church and he will at once assume an air of indifference and say it is habit, or because his parents attended it. He will not reveal to you that he is held to that church by ties the strongest and deepest. Men are driven not so much for money as by sentiment, by hopes, many of which will never be realized. Ideals are paraded only on the Fourth of July, when certain well-recognized stock phrases are used.

I wish I could say we have principles without bigot[r]y, but I believe we are a most bigoted people. We get this from the race from which most of us are descended. An Englishman has very definite opinions, and this is what makes him draw a sharp distinction between a college professor and a man of sense. From the English, however, we get the feeling that it isn't necessary to be consistent with our principles, and so our bigotry doesn't hurt us much. Truth is no invalid and isn't hurt by rough handling. Some gentlemen who are violent anti-imperialists, whatever that means, tell us we are damaging our own natures by our treatment of the Philippines. They don't talk to us about Porto Rico, where everybody appears to be happy, but the Philippines. They say we are inconsistent with our principles. I am not here to defend our Philippine policy, though I think it inevitable, but if we do right anywhere we shant damage our principles. They must hold water, real wet water, or they must be mended so they will.

Though we must not give up any of our faith in liberty, we ought not to be so cock-sure that we know the only kind of liberty. We are learning from present experience that for different stages of development in civilization there are different stages of liberty. Our own history teaches us this. A Congress is not necessary to liberty. We have the same sort of human nature that Adam had. We have arranged so that the person who misbehaves catches it worse than of old, but we haven't succeeded in exterminating the tendency to misbehave. In developing liberty we have to learn how to hold certain persons in check without choking them to death.

Printed in the *Poughkeepsie*, N.Y., *Daily Eagle*, May 3, 1902; several editorial headings omitted.

David Benton Jones to Cyrus Hall McCormick, with Enclosure

My Dear Mr. McCormick,   Chicago May 3rd, 1902.

I have just received a copy of Dr. Patton's note of April 30th, indicating May 9th as the time of conference and that he will be at home by 1 P.M. of that day. I enclose letter just received from Mr. Fine. It indicates that they are somewhat disturbed by the situation.

I have been housed all the week by a very nasty attack of bronchitis and am still in a very unfit condition. Notwithstanding this loss of a week's time by illness, I shall make the trip to Princeton if I am able to be about.

As I see it, the conference will practically determine the success or failure of the movement, and I am very sorry you do not find it possible to go east. It will require not only determination on the part of those interested, but it will also be necessary to convince the Doctor that the matter has proceeded too far to be reconsidered; that, in fact, it has been determined upon, and that the conference is simply for the purpose of settling the manner of its presentation. Nothing short of essential position will convince him or carry the measure. I doubt whether Cuyler or Pyne or both together will back that position. If those two show weakness or a tendency to compromise or postpone, the conference will simply serve to place the Doctor firmly in the saddle and enable him to ride a winning race once more, with Princeton a greater sufferer than ever because of the inevitable discouragement it will bring to the representative men in the faculty.

In case of final need I shall, of course, tell the Doctor that if his ultimate determination is not to present the scheme to the Board I shall do so and accompany it with a statement of the necessity for some such a plan, and that I shall ask the Board to summon the Faculty Committee to be present to hear the statement, in order that they may confirm or deny the truth of the situation presented. This I desire to avoid if possible. If you could be present I think both of us could brace up Cuyler and Pyne as to carry the day without the danger of an open contest and without even telling Dr. Patton that the matter will be presented whether he chooses to do so or not.

I am sending you this extended statement hoping your affairs may so shape themselves as to enable you to go east say Wednesday night; or even Tuesday noon might meet the case.

Very truly yours,   David B. Jones   by RMH

TLS (C. H. McCormick Papers, WHi).

E N C L O S U R E

Henry Burchard Fine to David Benton Jones

My dear Mr. Jones: Princeton, May 1, 1902.

Dr. Patton's letter to Mr. McCormick (Apr. 12) and Mr. McC's reply (Apr. 18) have been shown me by Mr. Wilson. They have caused us some uneasiness. It is of fundamental importance from our point of view that it be made clear to Dr. Patton that in the proposed Executive Com. he is to be merely one of six members, and *not* its Chairman or leader. It will require a *flat* statement to make the points clear to him.

He writes (Apr. 12) that he got no such conception of your meaning from his interview with you as that embodied in Mr. McC's memorandum. Unless at the coming interview he gets the point I now write about, he will plead a similar misunderstanding at the meeting of the Board and stampede the Board by one of those clever speeches of his into making him Chairman of the proposed Committee—an arrangement which would be absolutely *intolerable to us.*

The long and short of the matter is this:

Quite against our best judgment, Brackett, Wilson and I have acquiesced in Dr. Patton's presence on the Committee. Having made that one concession, we have fears that you may count on our making another—if you find yourselves put to it to carry your scheme through in its present form. Please dont make that mistake—if you have us in mind (or others like us) for the Com.

To be members of that Committee under the chairmanship of Dr. Patton or his leadership in any form, is more than we are willing to subject ourselves to. It would be to make a great personal sacrifice without real benefit to the University.

If carrying your scheme through is going to involve the addition of that feature, it is our opinion better to abandon it altogether and get the President's resignation when you think the proper time has come.

With much pleasure in the prospect of seeing you,

Sincerely yours,   H. B. Fine

TCL (C. H. McCormick Papers, WHi).

A Memorandum on Leadership

5 May 1902

LEADERSHIP eludes analysis. It is only by the action of leading minds that the organic will of a community is stirred to the exercise of either originative purpose or guiding control in affairs.

Definition: Leadership is the practicable formulation of action, and the successful arousal and guidance of motive in social development.

Its forms and *its objects* will be as various as the forms of political organization under which it is exercised.

Family government,

Military government,

Royal government, by a single hereditary or elective ruler,

Government by a class,

Government by discussion and free concert of action must each produle [produce] its characteristic type of individual initiative and influence.

There must also be one form and method of leadership or another according as the field in question is

Counsel or

　　　Action

These require *different gifts and qualities,* and the one or the other will be at the front of the political stage according to circumstances and the development of the particular body politic in question. But there are common elements in all leadership:

Common Elements: Ordinary ideas, extraordinary abilities (W. Bagehot). The habitual ideas of the governing group or class or of the existing task as performed in the past, and a power of effective presentation, progressive modification, a power to conceive and execute the next forward step and to organize the force of the State for the movement.

This, upon analysis, *presupposes*

The *sensitive,*

　the *conceiving,* the interpreting,

　　the *initiative* mind

with the addition of will power or of such subtle persistency as will put strong wills at the disposal of the managing intellect.

WWT MS. (WP, DLC).

A. S. Hammond[1] to David Benton Jones

Dear Sir: [Chicago] May 5, 1902.

At the request of Mr. Cyrus H. McCormick, I am sending you by to-night's mail several carbon copies of letters dictated by Mr. McCormick, and which he wishes you to freely criticise and comment upon as you see fit, and he will then have the letters re-written, if necessary, and he will sign them in their amended form. Mr. McCormick desires you to change them as you think best, as he wishes them to be strong and also to be in accordance with your desires.

Mr. McCormick says that if you want him to put in any sentence stating that Mr. Pyne will accompany you, he will do so, but it is Mr. McCormick's opinion that you had better take Mr. Pyne along on your own motion.

Will you kindly correct these, and then either send same back to Mr. McCormick, or telephone to this office, and we will have a boy call for them at any time you may specify?

Very truly yours,   A. S. Hammond

CCL (C. H. McCormick Papers, WHi).
 [1] Another of McCormick's secretaries.

David Benton Jones to Cyrus Hall McCormick

My dear Mr. McCormick: Chicago May 6th, 1902.

The letters that you have written Dr. Patton, McPherson, Pyne and Fine, leave the situation in as complete a condition as possibly can be made by correspondence.

You will be glad to know that I have received a telegram from Dr. Patton, stating that he can see us Tuesday, May 13th, instead of Friday of this week. I have therefore made arrangements to arrive in Princeton on Monday night and shall communicate with McPherson, Pyne and Fine, so as to have a preliminary conference before I see Dr. Patton on Tuesday. I feel more hopeful of convincing the Doctor in a quiet friendly way than I did, probably because I am feeling better myself.

I think it may seem more considerate if we suggest calling on Mr. Cleveland after I arrive at Princeton, instead of attempting to make an appointment with him merely by correspondence.

Very sincerely yours,   David B. Jones

TLS (C. H. McCormick Papers, WHi).

Cyrus Hall McCormick to Francis Landey Patton

Dear Dr. Patton: [Chicago] May 7, 1902.

I have been endeavoring to so arrange my matters here that I could go with Mr. Jones to see you upon the very interesting subject which has been under consideration between us. I regret to find at the last moment that I cannot go East now and also be at Princeton at the Trustees' Meeting early in June. I am, therefore, informing Mr. Jones that it will be necessary for him to go alone, and I trust that the conference which he will have with you will reach the same results which might have been attained had I been able to have had the pleasure of accompanying him.

I am Very faithfully yours, Cyrus H. McCormick.

TLS (McCormick Letterpress Books, WHi).

Cyrus Hall McCormick to Moses Taylor Pyne

My dear Friend: [Chicago] May 7, 1902.

I regret to find at the last moment that it is impossible for me to go to Princeton now and also to be there at commencement. Under these circumstances, I have suggested to Mr. Jones that he consult with Mr. Cleveland, Dr. McPherson and you as to how best to present the case most forcibly, and yet kindly, to Dr. Patton. In my judgment, this is not a case where there can be any retrograde movement. It is absolutely necessary that something be done or the condition of things will be deplorable during the next year. I beg you to do all you can in a firm, but kind way, to form this Executive Committee with Dr. Patton's acquiescence, and it would be best, if possible, that Dr. Patton should propose the plan. This he ought to be willing to do, especially since he is to be on the Committee himself, but it is of the utmost importance that he be not chairman, and, therefore, we suggest Mr. Cleveland for that position.

I commend this matter to you, believing that no more important question has been for years submitted to the Board of Trustees, and when I am at the meeting during commencement I will do all I can to promote the success of this measure.

I am Very sincerely yours, Cyrus H. McCormick

TLS (McCormick Letterpress Books, WHi).

Cyrus Hall McCormick to Simon John McPherson

Dear Dr. McPherson: [Chicago] May 7, 1902.

I regret to find at the last moment that it is impossible for me to go to Princeton now and also to be there at the Trustees' Meeting which occurs early in June. Therefore, under these circumstances, I trust you will do everything in your power to help the cause in which Mr. Jones and I are enlisted. I have suggested that he confer with you and Mr. Cleveland and Mr. Pyne before seeing Dr. Patton.

I am   Very sincerely yours,   Cyrus H. McCormick.

TLS (McCormick Letterpress Books, WHi).

Simon John McPherson to Cyrus Hall McCormick

Lawrenceville, New Jersey
Dear Mr. McCormick: Friday, May 9, 1902

It is a great loss to us all that you cannot be in Princeton at the close of this week or at the meeting in June. I shall do what I can about the matter in hand.

Very sincerely yours,   S. J. McPherson

TLS (C. H. McCormick Papers, WHi).

A Newspaper Report

[May 13, 1902]
LIT. BANQUET.

The annual banquet of *The Nassau Literary Magazine* was held at the Princeton Inn last evening. The dinner began about half after eight and ended shortly before midnight with the toast by Professor Ormond. President Patton acted as toastmaster and introduced the speakers.

E. H. Kellogg, managing editor of the 1902 board, spoke in behalf of the retiring editors, and was followed by Pax. P. Hibben, managing editor of the 1903 board, who outlined the policy to be followed by the *Lit.* during the coming year. Mr. Antonio Waring, a representative of *The Yale Literary Magazine*, spoke of the ideals which the *Lit.* stands for at Yale. Professor T. M. Parrott[1] spoke on the subject, *"The Nassau Literary Magazine of the Past,"* laying especial emphasis on the records which so many editors of the magazine have achieved in American literature. Professor George McL. Harper, managing editor of the '84 board, discussed "Journalism and Literature," with especial reference to the wide field of activity which lies open to the college graduate in these professions. Professor Woodrow Wilson then spoke on "The Value of *The Nassau Literary Magazine.*" Professor A. T. Ormond closed the list of toasts with an address on *"The Nassau Literary Magazine* of the Future." . . .

Printed in the *Daily Princetonian*, May 13, 1902; one editorial heading omitted.
[1] Thomas Marc Parrott '88, Assistant Professor of English.

From Edward Graham Elliott

My dear Professor Wilson,   Heidelberg, May 15th, '02.

I have today officially turned my Arbeit over to the Faculty and in the course of a couple of weeks or such a matter will learn definitely whether or not I will be admitted to the examination. The Dekan[1] said he thought there would be no trouble about it—the only thing lacking in the way of testimonials being one to the effect that I was instructor for two years at Princeton. I shall write by this same mail to Dean Winans in regard to such a certificate as I imagine it can properly be given by him and will perhaps receive more prompt attention than if sent to the President. At the same time I will take advantage of the occasion to make inquiry as to the possibility of my getting one of the dormitory rooms regularly assigned to instructors for next year.

It is quite probable that the date of my examination will fall in the week beginning July 13th—and in the event I am admitted and come through successfully, I hope to sail for America on Aug. 3rd and after a day in Princeton, run down to Tennessee to spend a few weeks with my mother.

Should either my application be refused or my effort to pass unsuccessful I should want to stay another semester. I am *hoping* all will go well. Is it possible that you will be in Princeton as late as the middle of August?

Not having heard what I may be expected to teach next year, I am trying to prepare myself for whatever may turn up—in other words I'm taking Roman Law—then too I'm continuing my course in International Law, this time Prof. Anschütz,[2] 3 hrs. per week. I am taking but four hours with Jellinek this semester. The Seminar gives promise of being unusually interesting. There are a number of older men taking part.

With very kindest regards, I am,
              Most sincerely yours   Edward G. Elliott

ALS (WP, DLC) with WWhw notation on env.: "Ans."
[1] That is, the Dean. There were several professors at Heidelberg with this title.
[2] Gerhard Anschütz (1867-1948), Professor at Heidelberg.

To Thomas L. Snow

My dear Mr. Snow,   Princeton, 17 May, 1902

I received the other day, from Messrs Royce and Henderson, the deed to the new piece of land, executed in due form, and I now take pleasure in sending you a draft on New York for the remaining three hundred dollars ($300.00) of the purchase money.

Will you not be kind enough to notify Messrs. Royce and Henderson of its receipt, so as to conclude their responsibility in the matter?

Allow me to express again my warm appreciation of your courtesy and willingness to serve me in this purchase, and my pleasure in being able, on never so small a scale, to assist in setting forward your plans of improvement at The Bluff.

Mrs. Wilson and my daughters join me in warmest regards to you all.   Cordially Yours,   Woodrow Wilson

ALS (photostat in RSB Coll., DLC).

From Charles Williston McAlpin

My dear Professor Wilson: [Princeton, N.J.] May 19, 1902.

Dr. Patton has asked me to request you to present the candidates for the honorary degree of LL.D. at the Annual Commencement June 11th. Please advise me if you will accept the appointment and I will furnish you with the names of those upon whom it has been voted to confer the degree.[1]

I remain,
          Sincerely yours,   [C. W. McAlpin]   Secretary.

CCL (McAlpin File, UA, NjP).
[1] See C. W. McAlpin to WW, May 22, 1902.

Cornelius Cuyler Cuyler to Cyrus Hall McCormick

New York   May 20-02

Please wire John A. Stewart asking him to confer with president Patton am writing   C. C. Cuyler

T telegram (C. H. McCormick Papers, WHi).

Cyrus Hall McCormick to Cornelius Cuyler Cuyler

[Chicago] May 20th, 1902.

Cannot understand telegram. Prefer to await receipt your letter. Will act immediately on receipt.   C. H. McCormick.

TC telegram (McCormick Letterpress Books, WHi).

Cornelius Cuyler Cuyler to Cyrus Hall McCormick

My dear Cyrus: New York. May 20/02

Confirming my wire of this date in which I asked you to wire Mr Stewart requesting him to see Dr. Patton, I would state that Pyne has today seen Mr Stewart who showed a willingness to confer with Dr. Patton on the matter which we have had under consideration. I am following this up by a letter to Mr. Stewart and a wire from you along the same lines will undoubtedly bring about an interview as desired.

Yours sincerely   C C Cuyler

Since writing this letter circumstances have arisen which render it unnecessary for me to write to Mr. Stewart.

ALS (C. H. McCormick Papers, WHi).

Frederick A. Steuert to Cyrus Hall McCormick

Mr. McCormick: [Chicago] May 20th [1902].

I have spoken to Mr. David B. Jones about writing the substance of his mission to Princeton[1] to Mr. Cuyler and he wishes me to say that his judgment is against doing this. He called to see Mr. Cuyler when passing through New York but did not find him at his office and it is his opinion that the less that is written about this matter before Dr. Patton comes to Chicago for the conference which Mr. Jones has mentioned to you,[2] the better it will be. Mr. Jones adds that the New York gentlemen are great talkers and it is his judgment that Dr. Patton has seen Mr. Cuyler.

F. A. Steuert

TL (C. H. McCormick Papers, WHi).

[1] Unaccompanied by McCormick, Jones had seen President Patton in Princeton on May 13. During this conference, Patton had not only intimated that he was contemplating resigning the presidency of Princeton University but had also outlined conditions and terms which would make an early retirement attractive to him. For the details of their meeting and the terms suggested by Patton, see D. B. Jones to F. L. Patton, May 23, 1902, and F. L. Patton to D. B. Jones, May 31, 1902; also B. Henry to C. H. McCormick, May 26, 1902.

Patton's suggestion of his possible early resignation ended all discussion of the proposal for an Executive Committee.

2 As has been noted earlier, Patton was to attend Richard Davenport Harlan's inauguration as President of Lake Forest College on June 4, and Jones had arranged for a conference among Patton, McCormick, and himself in Chicago on June 3 to discuss Patton's possible retirement.

Cyrus Hall McCormick to Simon John McPherson

Dear Dr. McPherson: [Chicago] May 21st, 1902.

I regret that I did not word my letter clearly. I was unable to go to Princeton last week with David Jones, because I especially wanted to be there at the June meeting and I could not do both. I will make every effort to be at the June meeting and hope nothing will occur to prevent my doing so, as I feel that the matters to come before the Board at this meeting are of the utmost importance.

I am
    Verey [Very] sincerely yours,   Cyrus H. McCormick.

TLS (McCormick Letterpress Books, WHi).

Cornelius Cuyler Cuyler to Cyrus Hall McCormick

New York, My 21, 1902.

Do not act on my letter and wire of yesterday but await my letter of today.   C. C. Cuyler

T telegram (C. H. McCormick Papers, WHi).

Cornelius Cuyler Cuyler to Cyrus Hall McCormick

My dear Cyrus: New York. May 21/02

I have your wire reading: "Cannot understand telegram—prefer to await receipt of your letter," which I note. The whole matter has taken on a new aspect and President Patton denies absolutely that he ever made such a proposition as Jones thought and stated that he did. The consequence is that we have agreed here in New York to let the thing drop until such time as you and Jones can be here for a day or two before Commencement when we can canvass the entire subject and try to put it in good shape. I am sorry to say that at present there seems to be a great deal of misunderstanding in the premises and I fear some needless friction may arise which a little diplomatic handling will obviate.

In view of this situation I strongly urge that Jones and you take no further step of any kind until after you have had a full conference with some of the prominent Trustees here as to the means best adapted to bring about the desired result.

  With kind regards, I am,

                              Yours faithfully   C C Cuyler

I have today wired you not to act on my wire and letter of yester-day but to await my letter of this date.

ALS (C. H. McCormick Papers, WHi).

David Benton Jones to Cyrus Hall McCormick, with Enclosure

My Dear Mr. McCormick: Chicago May 21st, 1902.

  I enclose copy of letter which I spoke of. It is a little unfor-tunate that those having the same point of view should be some-what widely scattered, while those on the other side are reason-ably compact, geographically speaking.

                    Very sincerely yours,   David B. Jones.

TLS (C. H. McCormick Papers, WHi).

                    E N C L O S U R E

Henry Burchard Fine to David Benton Jones

[Dear Mr. Jones,]   [Princeton, N.J., c. May 19, 1902]

  At the risk of being thought a borrower of needless trouble I am going to drop you a line regarding the situation.

  In one way and another we see indications that Patton is think-ing of [Henry] van Dyke as his successor and that a like thought is not absent from van Dyke's mind. To anyone who knows van Dyke the very possibility of his election seems absurd; but most people *don't* know him, and to them he is the embodiment of the most brilliant intellectual powers and the most charming per-sonal virtues. The Board of Trustees, moreover, has been known, as in the Winans case,[1] to act with unexpected haste and without regard to the wishes of the faculty. And plainly Patton, one of the cleverest of men, must see that if he wants van Dyke elected his best chance is to rush the matter through with the greatest possible celerity at the meeting when he presents his own resigna-tion, if that can be done.

  John A. Stewart is a warm admirer of van Dyke; so are Morris K. Jesup and Carnegie,[2] from whom some of our trustees are

hoping for money for Princeton. Cuyler also thinks most highly
of him. Patton and van Dyke continue to avoid all differences in
faculty, and recently Patton has taken every opportunity to flatter
van Dyke in public and to show him marks of special esteem.
I am reciting some of the indications which have set us thinking.
None of us believe that van Dyke can be elected if time is taken
to weigh men; but time has not always been taken. I should think
at all events that it was only a safe precaution for the liberals
on the Board to have a common understanding as to what might
and must be done to prevent catastrophies in the case of this or
a similar emergency. It would not be amiss if the Liberals could
agree on their man right away. Brackett and I are ready to be
asked for suggestions under that head if you want them; but I
will venture to say without being asked that neither we nor anyone else in the Princeton faculty want Henry van Dyke, barring
Henry himself and Paul [van Dyke] and the Pattons.[3]

                     [Sincerely yours, H. B. Fine]

(If the last sentence is correct statement then he is clearly impossible. You can see what he means by saying "Brackett and I."
The omission of the third member of the trio is an implied suggestion)[4]

TCL (C. H. McCormick Papers, WHi).
    [1] That is, when Patton had secured the election of Winans as Dean of the
Faculty in 1899.
    [2] Morris Ketchum Jesup, the New York philanthropist, and Andrew Carnegie,
who was just beginning his career in philanthropy after retiring from the steel
business.
    [3] President Patton and his son, George Stevenson Patton, Assistant Professor
of Moral Philosophy and Secretary to the President.
    [4] Jones's handwritten comment. The implied suggestion was the election of
Wilson.

Cyrus Hall McCormick to Moses Taylor Pyne

My dear Mo: [Chicago] May 22, 1902.
    David Jones, Bayard Henry and I have had a long conversation
to-day over the situation which is so important to Princeton. It
was understood between Mr. Jones and Dr. Patton that when the
latter came to Lake Forest on June 3rd this matter[1] would be
taken up and settled—that is, so far as Dr. Patton is concerned.
Now inasmuch as the details must be reduced to writing and,
at least, tentatively got in shape, subject to the approval of the
Board, both Jones and I feel the great importance of your presence with us in concluding this arrangement with Dr. Patton.
He is to arrive on Tuesday morning, June 3rd. Can you not arrive

either Monday afternoon on the Lake Shore Limited, at 4:30,—leaving New York at 5:30 Sunday afternoon; or can you not arrive Tuesday morning and spend the day here helping us to consummate this agreement, returning Tuesday afternoon? This is a matter of such magnitude and vital importance that it does not seem wise to leave it entirely to Jones and me, and the time is getting so short that we cannot postpone this agreement beyond the 3rd of June, as there will only then be a few days before the meeting of the Board and in that time it will be necessary for you men, who are in the East, to consult confidentially as many members of the Board as possible, so that the whole matter will not come up at the meeting of the Board without the members having been apprised of the situation beforehand.

Please write to me or write Jones in any event what you think of the terms proposed by Dr. Patton. It seems to us if the full resignation can be accomplished at the present meeting, that is better than arranging it a year from now. I hope you will think that this matter is of sufficient importance to warrant your taking the trip, for no one on the Board could be of as much help to us in concluding the arrangement as you could.

With a firm stand, if those of us who have been consulted agree, we can bring this about with harmony and success, and it will all be proposed by the President himself. The matter is of too much importance to be allowed to fail at this stage, and thus far I can see no reason why it should. We must remember to protect the feelings, dignity and position of the President at every point, and this will amply be done by the terms of the proposal which he has made.

While I should not feel disposed to urge it, I would regard it as a happy addition to the plan if the President could give some additional time to the Seminary, and receive a portion of his income from that source.

I am   Very sincerely yours,   Cyrus H. McCormick.

If you can stay longer than one day will you not bring Mrs. Pyne with you and stay with us?

TLS (McCormick Letterpress Books, WHi).
1 That is, the arrangements for Dr. Patton's resignation.

From Charles Williston McAlpin

My dear Professor Wilson: [Princeton, N.J.] May 22, 1902.

The names of those upon whom it has been voted to confer the honorary degree of LL.D. at the coming Commencement are the

Hon. Richard H. Alvey, Chief Justice of the Supreme Court of the District of Columbia; the Hon. William S. Gummere, Chief Justice of the Supreme Court of New Jersey; James H. Reed, Esq., of Pittsburgh, Pa.[1]; Morris K. Jesup, Esq. of New York City, President of the Chamber of Commerce, President of the American Museum of Natural History, etc.; Professor Henry Fairfield Osborn of New York City and Dr. Nicholas Murray Butler, President of Columbia University in the city of New York.

If I can be of further service to you please call on me.

I remain,

Sincerely yours,   [C. W. McAlpin]   Secretary.

CCL (McAlpin File, UA, NjP).
[1] James Hay Reed, former judge, distinguished corporation lawyer, and director of the United States Steel Corporation.

From Francis Landey Patton

Dear Sir: [Princeton, N.J.] May 23rd, 1902.

There will be a special meeting of the Faculty's Committee on schedule of studies in the Faculty Room, on Monday the 26th, at 12 o'clock. A full meeting of this Committee is desired for the preparation of a report to the University Faculty on Wednesday the 28th on new electives for the ensuing academic year.

Very sincerely yours,   Francis L. Patton

TLS (Patton Letterpress Books, UA, NjP).

David Benton Jones to Cyrus Hall McCormick, with Enclosure

My dear Mr. McCormick—   Chicago May 23, 1902

A Conference of Trustees suggested by Cuyler would be a good thing if they were prepared to act. The matter has gotten so far along that it lies with Dr. Patton and with him alone as to whether he will allow the matter to proceed quietly or not. If not then he knows or will know that the whole subject will be presented to the Board accompanied by a written statement of the present condition of things.

I shall be greatly surprised if the Doctor commits the fatal folly of resistance. The case is too strong against him, and even if it were less strong it would be fatal for him to attempt to hold on.

Very sincerely   David B. Jones.

ALS (C. H. McCormick Papers, WHi).

David Benton Jones to Francis Landey Patton

My dear Doctor: [Chicago, May 23, 1902]

I have conferred with Mr. McCormick and have heard from Mr. Pyne in regard to your suggestion made at our last interview.

We are all heartily in accord in our view of the financial conditions you named. The amount per annum in excess of the permanent salary of $4000. has already been assured. This, if satisfactory to you, will take the form of a written guarantee of $6000. a year in addition to the permanent salary and running for five years from June, 1903. The only modification suggested by Mr. McCormick and Mr. Pyne is that your resignation should become effective on the election of your successor, but not later than June, 1903. If it should become effective before June, 1903, then the conditions as to salary should begin at the time it became effective and run for the full term, that is, to June, 1908.

As the June meeting follows so closely upon your visit to Chicago we have asked Mr. Pyne to be here June 3rd, so that we may go over the matter with you in a more definite way.

Very sincerely,   D. B. J.

(The above was sent in script not typewritten)[1]

TCLI (C. H. McCormick Papers, WHi).
[1] Jones's handwritten comment.

Cyrus Hall McCormick to Cornelius Cuyler Cuyler

My dear C.C.:   [Chicago] May 24, 1902.

Your favors of the 20th and 21st are received, and also your telegram, which reached me on the 21st.

Inasmuch as Dr. Patton is to be in Chicago on June 3rd, Jones and I will confer with him about this important matter which is before us. You may rest assured that we will be discreet and tactful in any conference we have with Dr. Patton.

I have written to Pyne urging him to come to Chicago for the 3rd, believing that his presence at the conference would be most important. If he can join us I feel confident we can arrive at a solution of the present difficulties which will be satisfactory to the large majority of the Board of Trustees, and also greatly to the interest of Dr. Patton himself. I will advise you further as I learn more of this matter.

The Lake Forest commencement, for which Dr. Patton is to

be here, occurs on Wednesday 4th and Thursday the 5th of June, and the annual meeting of the Northwestern Directors[1] also occurs on the 5th, so that the very earliest moment at which I could leave the city would be by the Limited on Thursday afternoon, reaching Princeton or New York Friday evening. We will telegraph you fully after we see Dr. Patton on the 3rd, so that we may decide whether to have the meeting with the eastern members of the Board of Trustees on Friday evening or on Saturday evening. If the latter date will be satisfactory I could leave here on Friday afternoon, the 6th. We will do all we can at this end of the line to prevent and allay either misunderstanding or friction, but we must act together in this important matter with kindness, firmness and fidelity to the vital interests for which we are Trustees.

I am,

Very sincerely yours,   Cyrus H. McCormick, F.A.S.

P.S. Mr. McCormick was obliged to leave the office before signing this letter.

TLS (McCormick Letterpress Books, WHi).
    [1] The Board of Directors of the Chicago and North Western Railroad.

From Charles Williston McAlpin

My dear Professor Wilson: [Princeton, N.J.] May 26, 1902.

President Patton wishes you to present the two candidates for the honorary degree of A.M. at the coming Commencement in addition to the candidates for the degree of LL.D. They are:

Mr. John W[hite]. Alexander, of New York, the artist, and the Hon. James H. Eckels of Chicago.[1]

I remain,

Sincerely yours,   [C. W. McAlpin]   Secretary.

CCL (McAlpin File, UA, NjP).
    [1] James Herron Eckels, Comptroller of the Currency, 1893-97, at this time President of the Commercial National Bank of Chicago.

Cornelius Cuyler Cuyler to Cyrus Hall McCormick

My dear Cyrus,   New York. May 26/02

I have your favor of May 24th and note with interest all you say in rê Dr. Patton's visit to Chicago on June 3d. It seems unfortunate that he should have to be away at that particular time as there will be many people in Princeton from Friday on. I suppose of course he will leave Chicago on Thursday. I quite understand how tied down you are by meetings but hope you will not make the meeting with the Trustees, or with such of them as you want to meet, before Saturday night as I have an important meeting Friday night, already arranged for and evidently it would suit you better to leave on Friday than Thursday.

With kind regards, I am,

Yours faithfully   C C Cuyler

ALS (C. H. McCormick Papers, WHi).

Bayard Henry to Cyrus Hall McCormick

Confidential

My dear Cyrus: Philadelphia, Pa., May 26th, 1902.

The situation at Princeton is unsatisfactory. On Saturday one of the New York Trustees told me that Dr. Patton had stated to Mr. John A. Stewart that he had made no offer to Mr. Jones of any kind whatever to withdraw from the Presidency, but on the contrary said Mr. Jones had made certain suggestions to him as to salary and a professorship of ethics; that the only thing he had stated to Mr. Jones was that he did not intend to remain in the Presidency until he became an old man, but had said nothing about resigning or withdrawing at the present time or next year; that suggestion having come from Mr. Jones. It is of the utmost importance, therefore, when Dr. Patton is in Chicago he be seen by you and Mr. Jones *together*, and that any understanding or agreement arrived at be immediately put in writing, each party retaining signed copy. In the mean time as you can well see, nothing can be done, and it is unfortunate that no one was present at the interview between Mr. Jones and Dr. Patton. I am of opinion from what was said to me at Princeton by a Trustee (who did not wish his name mentioned) there will be no trouble in securing the guarantee suggested, provided it is acceptable and an agreement is reached. It would not be a bad idea for you to have a talk over the long distance 'phone with C. C. Cuyler, and discover the exact situation from a New Yorker's point of view. I have not seen him since I saw you, but believe he is fully conversant with the situation from Dr. Patton's standpoint. Momo Pyne said it would be impossible for him to go to Chicago next week, but he thought if any agreement was reached between you and Mr. Jones and Dr. Patton, you should immediately inform him, and you and Mr. Jones should be in Princeton *not later than Thursday, June 5th,* when we can have a conference or conferences to determine upon course of action to be pursued.

The whole future of the University is involved, and nothing could be more important than a satisfactory solution.

With kindest regards to Mr. Jones, I am

Yours sincerely,   Bayard Henry

TLS (C. H. McCormick Papers, WHi).

David Benton Jones to Cyrus Hall McCormick

My Dear Mr. McCormick: Chicago   May 26th, 1902.

I have just received a note from Mr. Fine referring to his former letter regarding Van Dyke, which is as follows:

"I had a talk with Pyne which quite allayed my fears. He assures me that the danger of which I wrote you was not real, but fancied; that he knew that John A. Stewart, Cuyler, Bayard Henry, all of them, favored Woodrow Wilson, and that he knows of no one who favored Van Dyke. But he is going to write you himself, so he told me, and you need not accept this reassurance at second hand.

"From what Pyne told me, it is clear that the President got no comfort out of his visit to New York; that neither John A. Stewart, Pyne nor Cuyler gave him any clew to a way of escape from the dilemma in which your interview placed him. And surely he only needs to be convinced that these men and others naturally associated with them and influenced by them agree with you and McCormick to accept the extraordinarily generous terms which are now open to him with as good a grace as possible."

As this note was written immediately after his conversation with Pyne it seems less unsatisfactory than Cuyler's letter would indicate. Cuyler is almost as much of a difficulty as Patton himself.   Very sincerely yours,   [David B. Jones]

TL (C. H. McCormick Papers, WHi).

To Charles Williston McAlpin

My dear Mr. McAlpin: Princeton, N. J., May 27th, 1902.

It will give me pleasure to present the candidates for the honorary A.M. at Commencement as the President requests.

Very sincerely yours,   Woodrow Wilson

TLS (McAlpin File, UA, NjP).

Moses Taylor Pyne to Cyrus Hall McCormick

My dear Cyrus: Princeton, N.J. May 27, 1902.

I have your letter of the 22nd, but cannot get out to Chicago. This matter of yours must be handled very delicately, and any suggestion must come from the President of his own accord and free will, as the Board of Trustees is a very difficult body to handle and unless things come in the regular way some one might raise an objection which would upset everything.

I am glad you are coming East before the meeting, and do not see how we can accomplish anything unless we have a conference with the Eastern men.

I have written Jones.

Very sincerely yours,   M. Taylor Pyne

TLS (C. H. McCormick Papers, WHi).

To Edward Graham Elliott

My dear Mr. Elliott,   Princeton, New Jersey, 29 May, 1902.

I fear that you have reason to feel hurt that I have not written you more definitely about next year; but the fact is, that I have not only been busier than I ever was before in my life,—more literally driven,—but that the courses are in process of wholesale revision,[1] and it has really been impossible to say definitely what you will be assigned. I think that I can say now, however, that it will pretty certainly be International Law.[2] Probably you will have very little lecture work to do the first year. At any rate you will not be forced to begin with too quick a pace or a full quota of lecture hours. We must induct you gradually.

Things go on here much as usual. A great many persons here inquire after you frequently with a great deal of interest. You certainly have plenty of friends, and ought to have a decidedly homelike feeling when you get here.

Of course you know me better than to conclude that because I have answered so few of your letters I was indifferent or did not follow what you were doing with the greatest attention. If there had been anything that did not meet with my approval, you may be sure I should have hastened to say so. I have felt all along that you could direct yourself much better there, on the spot, than I could direct you from this side the sea, and what you have done has seemed to me as well planned as the courses offered made possible.

You have made a record for speed and prompt success which

gives us great satisfaction. I hope that you have kept your health too and will not show yourself the worse for wear.

With much regard,

Cordially and faithfully Yours,   Woodrow Wilson

Pray present my compliments to Prof. Jellinek.

WWTLS (WC, NjP).
    [1] See n. 2 to the notes for a talk printed at Nov. 21, 1901, and the University Faculty Minutes printed at March 26 and April 9, 11, 14, and 16, 1902.
    [2] Elliott did offer the course in international law as a senior elective during the first term, 1902-1903.

From Bayard Henry

Personal

My dear Prof. Wilson: Philadelphia, Pa., May 29th, 1902.

One of your warm friends requested that I ask you to make a few remarks at our little luncheon on Saturday, and although there will be no speech-making, we would be gratified if you would give a warm welcome to the members of the Bar and business men to Princeton.[1] My thought is if Dr. Patton is present he should say a word or two of welcome, and that you should then give a few remarks, detailing some of the historical events associated with Princeton, referring to the battle, the meeting of Congress, Washington's visit, his portrait, Morven, Washington's Headquarters, the cemetery, the old offices of the Delaware & Rariton [Raritan] Canal, which was the precursor of the Camden & Amboy R.R. and the close relations always existing between Philadelphia, Pennsylvania and Princeton, closing with a statement that it has also now been selected as the future home of all ex-Presidents, giving short tribute to Mr. Cleveland; when if he is present (as I hope he will be) he will have an opportunity of bowing and saying a word or two, for I have told him there would be no speech-making.

I hope I am not asking too much of you to do this, and I will appreciate it more than I can tell you if you will say a few words. We are doing all in our power to develope Princeton's interests here, and now it looks as if we were well established and secure.

With best wishes, I am

Yours sincerely,   Bayard Henry

TLS (WP, DLC).
    [1] No Princeton newspaper reported on this affair, but intimations of its character can be gleaned from WW to EAW, June 1, 1902, and B. Henry to WW, June 2, 1902.

Cyrus Hall McCormick to Bayard Henry

My dear Bayard: [Chicago] May 29th, 1902.

Your favor of the 26th is received. I think you will find that matters are in better shape than you assume from what you have heard regarding the New York situation. Mr. Jones and I will see Dr. Patton in Chicago and will advise you promptly as to the result of our interview. It is our intention to leave here on Thursday afternoon, reaching Princeton or New York Friday evening. We will telegraph you after we have seen Dr. Patton and after we have arranged our plans for Princeton and New York.

I am,   Very sincerely yours,   Cyrus H. McCormick

TLS (McCormick Letterpress Books, WHi).

Cyrus Hall McCormick to Cornelius Cuyler Cuyler

My dear C.C.:   [Chicago] May 29th, 1902.

I have your favor of the 26th and note what you say with regard to Dr. Patton's visit to Chicago. I know nothing of the circumstances of his invitation to Lake Forest, or the details of how it was arranged. My supposition is that he will leave Chicago Wednesday afternoon and be in Princeton on Thursday evening.

It is my intention at present to leave here on Thursday June 5th, reaching Princeton or New York on Friday evening. Would it not be feasible to have a meeting with such parties as you suggest, in New York on Saturday morning? I fear that if it is left until Saturday evening it will make it rather late for the necessary conference in Princeton. Will you telegraph me the names of such parties as you feel Mr. Jones and I should consult at the New York interview? I assume they would include Pyne, Stewart, Alexander, Cadwalader and McCook.

I am,   Very truly yours,   Cyrus H. McCormick.

TLS (McCormick Letterpress Books, WHi).

Frederick A. Steuert to Cornelius Cuyler Cuyler

Dear Sir: [Chicago] May 29th, 1902.

In connection with Mr. McCormick's letter of even date he wishes me to ask if you will arrange to have the parties get together to meet Mr. Jones and himself at the time agreed upon by telegram?

I am,
          Very respectfully yours,   F. A. Steuert   Secretary.

CCL (C. H. McCormick Papers, WHi).

A News Report of a Meeting of the Village Improvement Society of Princeton[1]

[May 31, 1902]

The annual meeting of the Village Improvement Society of Princeton was held at the Princeton Inn, May 20th, 1902, at 8 o'clock P.M. There were about fifty persons present.

The retiring president, Mrs. Hutton, being unable to be present, Dr. [James H.] Wikoff called the meeting to order.

Mr. Leroy H. Anderson was elected chairman and Mrs. A. R. Burke secretary.

The minutes of the last annual meeting of May 7th, 1901, were read and approved.

The following resolution was presented by Mrs. [Allan] Marquand:

Resolved, That a vote of thanks be presented to Mrs. Hutton for her enterprise and public spirit in organizing the Village Improvement Society, her unselfish devotion to its aims and her untiring interest in its behalf during the three years she has served as its president.

A motion of Mrs. Leroy Anderson, to adopt the resolution, was seconded by Professor Woodrow Wilson, who said: Mr. Chairman, I take pleasure in seconding the motion. I wish to do something more than merely record my affirmative vote; we all feel the debt of gratitude we owe Mrs. Hutton; she had sagacity to observe what too many of us had overlooked, the needs of the community, and she had the initiative and energy to take the proper steps to meet them. It gives me peculiar satisfaction to have the opportunity to speak for myself and others these words of warm appreciation.

The resolution was unanimously adopted.

Printed in the *Princeton Press*, May 31, 1902; editorial headings omitted.

[1] Organized in 1899 by Eleanor Varnum Mitchell (Mrs. Laurence) Hutton, as its constitution put it, "to promote the cleanliness, beauty, and sanitary conditions of Princeton; to co-operate with the public authorities in the enforcement of existing ordinances; to suggest additional legislation when necessary; and to aid all efforts to improve the town in all its moral, educational, sanitary and artistic aspects."

David Benton Jones to Cyrus Hall McCormick, with Enclosures

My Dear Mr. McCormick: Chicago May 31st, 1902.

I enclose copy of some correspondence with Pyne, which shows that he has already "ratted."

It was a great tactical blunder on my part to have referred to him in my letter to Patton [of May 23, 1902]. As you will see by my letter to the Doctor in correction, I have made such amends as I can. The letter itself may have been a blunder, even, but was written after I heard that he denied my version of our interview.

I was warned at Princeton that you and I should be prepared to see the Pyne-Cuyler coterie "rat" at the last moment. I have not a word to say in justification of the use of his name, nor, for that matter, for the use of yours, except that we have been working together on it from the start. But the thing that fills me with disgust is Pyne's poltroonery. What does he object to, Patton's resignation? Or is it the financial conditions? As to all outside of the permanent salary—and in decency the Board cannot pay Patton less than half his regular salary, even as an emeritus retired president, and this was the basis of the salary he fixed for the professorship—Mr. Pyne need not contribute at all. Mr. Palmer[1] told me in New York that he would be glad to come in and see that the thing was financed. I would rather pay it all myself than to Jew Patton down. If he has to go out, he should go out feeling that the Board has met his conditions without curtailment. I shall not be a party to any movement looking toward a reduction of his terms except as to the retention of his son permanently as a professor. That would be clearly incompetent for the Board to do.[2]

The next to the closing paragraph of Pyne's letter is so amazingly simple minded that I was so saturated with contempt and disgust as to find it difficult to answer him at all.

He will probably as little enjoy reading my reply as I did his note. I have no justification whatever to make of the use of his name. It was extremely unwise. But the underlying spirit and point of view of his note is an amazing revelation to me and now fully explains the reasons why Princeton has been allowed to sink deeper and deeper into a disorganized and disheartened condition. Representative men on the Faculty are heart-broken. They have told me so in specific terms, and it is largely due to the contemptible poltroonery, as I have said, of those eastern men. They act as if they were trustees of Patton's feelings and position, and not trustees of Princeton University.

I hope I can recover from my disgust before going east.

Very sincerely yours,　David B. Jones.

Your plan of showing copies of letters in advance seems wiser to me now than it has in the past. My blunder would have been avoided had I taken time to send you a copy before mailing　DBJ.

TLS (C. H. McCormick Papers, WHi).

¹ Stephen Squires Palmer, railroad, utility, and mining magnate, trustee of Princeton University from 1908 to 1913, whose son, Edgar Palmer, was a junior at Princeton at this time.

² None the less, the Board of Trustees on June 9, 1902, promoted George Stevenson Patton from Assistant Professor of Moral Philosophy to Professor of Moral Philosophy.

E N C L O S U R E   I

Moses Taylor Pyne to David Benton Jones

Dear Jones: [Princeton, N.J.] May 27, 1902.

I have your letter asking me to come out to Chicago next week, but cannot do so, and even if I were able I do not see what power I have to close any such matter as you suggest.

I am amazed that you have used my name as you did in your letter to the President. I have authorized no such statement as you have attributed to me, nor do I believe this to be the proper method to arrive at the result you desire. The matter is in danger of falling into a very dangerous condition, causing a division in the Board, creating open scandal and defeating the very object we seek to attain. It seemed to me so important that I have called Mr. John A. Stewart and Mr. Cuyler together and we have discussed the matter fully.

After an extended discussion our conclusion is that should the President open the matter himself by presenting his resignation to the Full Board, when it could be referred to a strong Committee to consider and confer with him and report back to the Board, at the earliest possible moment, the whole thing could be arranged in a proper way, and we believe the best interests of the University would be subserved.

You must remember that you and Cyrus are acting as individuals, and that anything you may do will have to be referred to and receive the approval of the whole Board.

Very sincerely yours,   M. Taylor Pyne.

E N C L O S U R E   I I

David Benton Jones to Moses Taylor Pyne

My dear Mr. Pyne: [Chicago] May 29, 1902.

Your note of the 27th, just received, comes to me as a painful surprise.

I had supposed that you were in substantial accord with Mr. McCormick and myself, both as to the need of some radical change in the administration of affairs at Princeton and, in a general way, as to the best means of bringing about such a change without "creating open scandal."

You will hardly need my assurance that I have not deliberately misrepresented you. It is evident, however, that I have unwittingly done so, and the least that I can do in justice to you and to Dr. Patton is to write Dr. Patton at once, stating that in so far as my letter purported to express your views, as well as Mr. McCormick's and my own, it was unauthorized. I am writing Dr. Patton to that effect to-day and enclose a copy of my note herewith. Let me add my very deep regret that I should have made this mistake.

Now, as to the subject matter of the controversy: I have read your note with anxious care, and the more I consider it the more clear it seems to me that you intend to give me to understand that you range yourself squarely and unequivocally with Dr. Patton in maintaining the status quo at Princeton. That is, in my judgment, a calamity to Princeton of the first order. I cannot help feeling extremely depressed over it. But my conclusions have not been reached hastily. I believe that I know the real condition of things at Princeton pretty thoroughly. I have no animus against anyone connected with Princeton and my judgment is not biased by any personal considerations. It is my clear conviction, and I must in candor state frankly the conviction to you, that the course which you and your friends are pursuing makes "a division in the Board and the creation of an open scandal" practically certain. The condition of things at Princeton at present simply cannot be smothered up. I believe it to be my clear duty to do my utmost to bring the exact condition of things to the knowledge of every member of the Board if it should be necessary to resort to that extreme, and I say to you now that I am unalterably determined that unless an amicable adjustment of the affair can be reached along substantially the lines which I have hitherto indicated, a full statement shall be made to the Board of the deplorable condition of things as they now exist at Princeton. If with full knowledge of the facts the Board should let matters run along in the same old way I cannot help it.

I could scarcely have believed it possible, except for the direct statement of your note, that you conceive it as at all probable that President Patton will, of his own initiative, "open the matter himself by presenting his resignation to the full Board." I am entirely convinced that but for your attitude the President could have been persuaded that his interests, as well as the interests of the University, require such a course on his part at the present time, and that is precisely what Mr. McCormick and I have been trying to bring about. Time will show that Mr. McCormick and I and those who believe and act with us are, in the long run, Dr. Patton's best friends. Under the procedure outlined in your letter a resignation will doubtless come in time, but perhaps only after protracted and bitter controversy, which will be injurious both to Dr. Patton and to the University.

I quite acquit you of any intention to be offensive in reminding Mr. McCormick and myself that we are acting as individuals and that we do not constitute the whole Board. It does, however, imply a limited estimate of our intelligence, which is pitiful if not offensive.   [Sincerely yours,   David B. Jones]

ENCLOSURE III

David Benton Jones to Francis Landey Patton

My dear Doctor: [Chicago] May 29th, 1902.

I have just received a note from Mr. Pyne, stating that he will not be able to be here next week.

It appears from his note also that I was mistaken in believing that I was authorized in speaking for Mr. Pyne as well as for Mr. McCormick and myself in my letter to you of recent date, and I therefore desire, in justice to Mr. Pyne, to at once correct what I said by limiting it to Mr. McCormick and myself.

This in no way changes our purpose, nor does it alter what can be done as indicated in my note to you.

Very truly yours,   [David B. Jones]

TCL (C. H. McCormick Papers, WHi).

Two Letters from Francis Landey Patton
to David Benton Jones

My dear Mr. Jones   [Princeton, N.J.] 31 May 1902

I am writing you a long letter in reply to yours of May 23. You may show it to Mr. McCormick but I need not say how important it is that the matter be kept in strict confidence.

Yours   Francis L. Patton

My dear Mr. Jones: [Princeton, N.J.] May 31, 1902

I have received your letter of May 23rd . . . .[1]

. . . suggested by Mr. McCormick and yourself and in the course of which I intimated that I did not look with approval upon the idea of an executive committee, I went on to say to you that I had definitely fixed in my own mind the period of twenty years as the limit of what I regard as the length of my term of office as President of the University; that consequently I should not think of remaining in office more than six years from the present Commencement. I also said that I thought that I ought during that period to receive $10,000 per annum,[2] and that after that it would be my desire to enter upon the duties of a professorship at a salary of $4,000 per annum with the understanding here that my work should be done in one term. I said that in this plan I was considering the good of the University as well as my own comfort & that I was in it contemplating a kind of work which I wanted to do but was unable to do because of the administrative duties which now engross my time and thought.

It was when I made this statement to you that you replied by suggesting to me the plan outlined in your letter.[3] To that plan as suggested I replied by saying that I could not but be hospitable to it: but that of course I was not in a position to say whether I would or would not accept it. You then asked me to think the matter over and to let you know how I felt about it when I came to Chicago. I told you that I would do so.

It is, as I am sure you will see, of the utmost importance for all concerned that my position in this matter should be clearly understood: and particularly that the proposition which is the subject of your letter is one that you made to me and not one that I made to you.

This matter being made clear I am ready now to say a word more in regard to the proposition itself. In the first place let me say that while I had definitely determined not to remain [in] the presidency of the University after the expiration of twenty years of service, I am by no means unwilling to entertain the idea of leaving the Presidency within a much shorter period and I can well believe that it may be better for [the] University that I should do so.

I wish to say moreover that I appreciate very fully the kind way in which you spoke of the work which you think I could do and the service I could render if I were free from the burdens of administration; and I concur with you in feeling that such a plan as the one you propose would give me greater advantages for the prosecution of my literary & philosophical work that [than] my own plan as suggested by me to you.

I wish to say moreover that while I fully understand that your proposed plan for my support is prompted by what you regard as urgent needs in the matter of university reform, I at the same [time] appreciate very sincerely the fair, just and generous way in which you propose that I shall be treated.

I think I may go further and say that further reflection so far from creating in me any revulsion of feeling only confirms me in the belief that such an arrangement as the one you suggest may be not only of advantage to the University and [but] also a benefit to me.

At the same time I feel that this is too serious a matter to be concluded without more thought and particularly without the knowledge of the Board of Trustees.

I was elected by the unanimous vote of the Trustees to the Presidency of the University; and I do not feel that I would be treating the Trustees properly if I allowed myself to be committed to a proposition that would involve my resignation of the Presidency without first placing the matter before the Board.

I am sure that you will fully understand my position in this respect and that you will concur with me in feeling that if in my judgment the best interests of the University will be served by my resignation at an early date, the proper thing for me to do is to place the matter before the Board of Trustees in order that they may if they deem best appoint a committee to consider the whole subject and confer with me.

I am my dear Mr. Jones

Very faithfully yrs.   Francis L. Patton

ALS (Patton Letterpress Books UA, NjP).
  1 The balance of the first page of this letterpress copy is completely obliterated.
  2 Patton's salary at this time was $8,000 a year.
  3 That is, D. B. Jones to F. L. Patton, May 23, 1902.

To Ellen Axson Wilson[1]

My own darling,   Princeton, 1 June, 1902

Harry [Fine] had nothing new to tell me,—I don't know what Pyne can have been alluding to,—but after the luncheon at the Inn to-day (Bayard Henry had a numerous club of Philadelphia lawyers up here, and I lunched with them) C.C., who was also there, gave me this intimation: "It looks now, Tommy, as if you were going to have a great deal of responsibility." That was all,— in the midst of a crowd no explanation could be entered into,—but it was said in a very significant way and carries an obvious implication.[2]

When I came home after the lunch I found the new number of the *Alumni Weekly* on my desk. You may imagine how startled I was to find on the cover, in bold type, "Woodrow Wilson, '79, for President."³ My first thought was that some fool was taking a hand in college politics from the outside! But it turned out entirely harmless. Somebody has written to the Indianapolis *News* to suggest that the Democrats nominate me for the presidency of the United States,—that's all!⁴

The chapter was finished last night at ten o'clock, copying and all, according to schedule,—and I went to bed as happy a man as the circumstances in which I went to bed would permit. Now for the home-stretch!

I let Nellie go to Lawrenceville (!) yesterday, to lunch with Elizabeth Robinson, and was a very nervous parent until she got back, you may be sure.

Ah, my darling, with what pangs I love you,—with how full a heart I am   Your own   Woodrow

We are all perfectly well. Much love to the Reids.

ALS (WC, NjP).
  ¹ Mrs. Wilson had gone with her daughter, Margaret, to Baltimore to attend the graduation of her sister, Margaret Randolph Axson ("Madge"), from the Woman's College of Baltimore. Mrs. Wilson and Margaret were staying with the Harry Fielding Reids.
  ² This letter strongly indicates that Wilson had been kept abreast of recent developments in the presidential situation by Fine, who was of course in direct communication with David B. Jones.
  ³ *Princeton Alumni Weekly*, II (May 31, 1902).
  ⁴ An Old-Fashioned Democrat to the Editor of the *Indianapolis News*, May 1, 1902.

A Memorandum¹

[c. June 1, 1902]

Notes on the proposed changes in the Curriculum.

A THREE YEAR'S COURSE can be frankly and wisely provided for only by permitting graduation at the end of the present Junior year. But, if that is permitted, there ought to be such a reconsideration of the whole course of study as will make it more rounded, definite, and systematic throughout the three years, without making it less elastic.

A PROFESSIONAL YEAR could then be added, in connection with a systematic development of graduate study. But a graduate year in law or medicine would involve

(A) Amount of work, and kind.

(B) Technical studies which ought not to be allowed to count for any such academic degree as M.A. or Ph.D. These, like the baccalaureate degree, should be reserved for work strictly scholarly and liberal in character.

THE RECONSTRUCTION OF SOPHOMORE YEAR would necessarily accompany any change which resulted in permitting
graduation at the end of Junior year. Unless such a change is
made, however, Sophomore year can hardly be changed in any
material respect consistently with the preservation of the
standards and ideals which give Princeton its character and
prestige.

IN ANY CASE, a thorough reconsideration of the course of study
ought to take place such as is now being attempted by a select
committee of the Faculty,[2] in order that each student's studies
may be better coordinated and also rendered more thorough.

WWT memorandum (WP, DLC).
[1] Probably prepared for the meeting of the special trustee and faculty committee on a three-year curriculum, referred to in n. 2 to the extract from the
University Faculty Minutes printed at Jan. 29, 1902.
[2] About this committee, see n. 2 to the notes for a talk printed at Nov. 21,
1901.

From Ellen Axson Wilson

My own darling,   Baltimore, Md. June 2 [1902]

I have been getting quite miserable for want of an opportunity
to write to you. This is *literally* the first I have had! We had breakfast at nine yesterday. Had just finished and talked with Mrs.
Reid for a quarter of an hour when they came for me to go to
church, and I did not get back to the house until 10 at night!
I would have written then, tired as I was, if I had had a light that
I could see by. Then Madge insisted that we must be at the college
by 9.30 this morning to secure a seat, so I hurried through breakfast and was off at nine,—returned just in time for a half past one
dinner from which we have just arisen.

In spite of my early start yesterday we reached the church too
late to secure a seat out of the gallery, so that the services were
to me all dumb show. Afterwards I dined with Madge and her
friends in hall, then they[,] all fourteen of them, went to her
room to meet me. We really had a very pleasant time together,—
they are *very* attractive girls. At 3.30 I started to the hospital,
having been lucky enough to find a guide, a sweet young girl in
training there, the sister of one of the doctors. She belonged to
Madge's "fraternity" at the University of Wis. & was over at the
college to see her "sisters[.]" I spent a *delightful* hour and a half
with your Aunt.[1] She is *lovely*. And it was most fortunate I went
then, for she leaves for Chillicothe today. The doctor says there is
nothing the matter with her heart,—it is all "nerves." Then having

telephoned for a cab, I drove to Mary Hoyts to tea, and she brought me home at 9.45.

The exercises this morning were much more entertaining than the Princeton Class Days,—but that will keep. Margaret[2] came back to dinner with me. I am going to see Mrs. Bird presently and in the meantime am hoping against hope that Ed[3] will turn up. I am to have the carriage at 5.30 and it will be nice if I can find them to drive with me. In the morning at ten I take Margaret to the occulists. So you see in a way all goes well, though in another sense not at all, for Mrs. Reid is ill in bed & I havn't seen her since yesterday morning. She was almost speechless then with a heavy cold. And they are to sail for *Europe* on *Saturday*! It gives me the most unhappy sense of making a convenience of our friends to be here under such circumstances; though it is unnecessary to add that they seem to like being made a convenience of. They are *lovely*! But oh how glad I will be to get back to my darling! I havn't heard from you yet,—am hoping for a few lines by bedtime. I am a bit homesick to tell the truth,—I want my love more than tongue can tell.

But I must close and try to see the Birds. Margaret is very happy and sends love to all. She is here with me now. Dear love & kisses to the children, and for your dear self love beyond expression from   Your own   Eileen.

ALS (WP, DLC).
[1] Helen Sill (Mrs. Thomas) Woodrow, who was in The Johns Hopkins University Hospital for examination and diagnosis of what she thought was heart trouble.
[2] That is, her daughter, Margaret.
[3] Her brother, Edward William Axson.

From Bayard Henry

Personal

My dear Wilson: Phila. June 2nd, 1902.

Let me thank you again sincerely for the charming remarks you made at our lunch on Saturday. They were fine, and I cannot tell you how greatly they were appreciated by every one present. What you said gave a high tone to the whole affair, which even the delightful and piercing sarcasm of our friend [Isaac Wayne] McVeagh, only accentuated. Every member of the party enjoyed himself immensely, and I thank you for the large part you had in booming Princeton, which is connected so closely with many Colonial and Revolutionary events, it was not necessary for

Cornwallis to have surrendered to Washington on the site of Witherspoon Hall, to have made it famous.

Hoping to see you during Commencement, I am

Yours sincerely,   Bayard Henry

Postscript. By to-day's mail have sent you copy of Presbyterian Historical Journal containing Dr. Craven's article on the Log College.[1] Won't you kindly read it, and some time wish you would put some of your students at work reading up about the matter and get some facts as to relation between the Log College and the College of New Jersey. There must be some papers of the Tenants[2] as well as Whitfields[3] & others, either in manuscript or type, showing the close connection which existed between the two institutions.   B. H.

TLS (WP, DLC).
  [1] Elijah Richardson Craven, "The Log College of Neshaminy and Princeton University," *Journal of the Presbyterian Historical Society*, 1 (June 1902), 308-14.
  [2] The Rev. William Tennent, Sr., and his son, the Rev. Gilbert Tennent, founders of the famous Log College at Neshaminy, Pa.
  [3] George Whitefield, the eighteenth-century English evangelist.

From Jenny Davidson Hibben

My dear Mr. Wilson   Princeton, Monday [June 2, 1902].

Many thanks for your note.[1] I have the important personages well in mind, and shall listen to you with great interest on Commencement day.

I am afraid as Beth says "I was ruffled" yesterday. I won't put myself down in black and white as to whether I think you over critical, but will leave it until we meet, and you shall judge yourself.

With warmest regards, and appreciation of your note,
Believe me,

Ever your friend   Jenny Davidson Hibben.

ALS (WP, DLC).
  [1] It is missing.

Cornelius Cuyler Cuyler to Cyrus Hall McCormick

My Dear Cyrus: New York. June 2/02

In rê the Dr. Patton matter things look so much more favorable since I last wrote you that I think a short talk will be all that is required. I must be in Princeton Friday night and shall certainly want to be there Saturday. Saturday night I consider the best time for a few of us to get together, or even Monday morning. As matters now stand very little discussion should be necessary.

Yours faithfully   C C Cuyler

ALS (C. H. McCormick Papers, WHi).

Cyrus Hall McCormick to Francis Landey Patton

Dear Dr. Patton: [Chicago] June 3, 1902.

If agreeable to you, Mr. Jones and I would be glad to have a brief conference with you at any hour most convenient to you. We can call upon you at Dr. Notman's[1] or, if you prefer, my carriage can bring you over here to our office or we can go together to the Chicago Club. We do not wish to trespass upon your time which will be occupied with the preparation for the evening, but it seems as if it would be mutually desirable that we have a few moments together before your return to-morrow. If you prefer to see us this evening after the dinner I have no doubt that Mr. Jones would remain in from Lake Forest for that purpose. Kindly let me know your pleasure. The bearer will wait for an answer.

Sincerely yours,   Cyrus H. McCormick.

CCL (C. H. McCormick Papers, WHi).
[1] The Rev. Dr. William Robson Notman, pastor of the Fourth Presbyterian Church of Chicago.

Francis Landey Patton to Cyrus Hall McCormick

My dear Mr. McCormick   Chicago [June 3, 1902].

I shall be happy to see you & Mr. Jones this forenoon & on the whole I think it would be better for me to go to your office. I will be ready to leave here by eleven o'clock this forenoon & will wait the coming of your carriage.

Yrs sincerely   Francis L. Patton

ALS (C. H. McCormick Papers, WHi).

Cyrus Hall McCormick to Moses Taylor Pyne

My dear Mo.:   [Chicago] June 3, 1902.

Mr. Jones and I have had a very pleasant interview with Dr. Patton this morning, about which I feel it is proper I should write you in the fullest confidence, believing that you and C.C. should know just what passed.

We informed Dr. Patton that we desired to know the state of his mind on the present interesting subject now before us and we assured him that we stood in the relation purely of individuals who were loyally and deeply interested both in the welfare of the University and in him personally. After this he went on very freely and frankly to explain to us the present status as he understands the matter, and he did this in a tone and in a bearing that was most satisfactory in every way, and we believe that out of this will come the highest good to the interests of Princeton.

The only thing which we feel should be emphasized is the fact that all financial proposals must come from the Board and must not be supposed to originate with Dr. Patton. It is in his mind at present to make a statement to the Board, either in June or October, that he intends in due time to resign. This statement he thinks should not be in the form of a definite resignation handed in on the spot, but should be in the form of a general statement of his intention, which was formed sometime ago. He would then ask the Board to name a committee to take under consideration the whole matter and immediately then someone should be ready to propose a committee to take the whole matter under advisement, and Dr. Patton will then be ready to treat with this committee touching all the details of the subject.

Mr. Jones and I have been careful to reach no understanding with Dr. Patton on any of these points, except that we have taken it upon ourselves to assure him that if such a plan as is here outlined transpires we will guarantee him personally that the funds necessary will be forthcoming on the basis of the suggestion of which you are aware.

I hasten to give you the result of this deeply interesting interview so that you and C.C. may feel that nothing has been done here that is not in entire harmony with the general plan, to secure which we must all act together.

Dr. Patton tells us that he proposes to see Mr. John A. Stewart and Colonel McCook on Friday about this matter.

In view of this situation it seems to both Mr. Jones and to me that the proposed conference in New York, as was suggested for Cuyler to arrange, is entirely unnecessary, and with this view of matters I will probably not arrive until Saturday,—not unless you telegraph me that you think it still important for me to be there Friday night. I hope that you will telegraph me not later than Thursday morning what you think about this, as a day is very important to me here.

I am,   Very sincerely yours,   Cyrus H. McCormick.

TLS (McCormick Letterpress Books, WHi).

Moses Taylor Pyne to Cyrus Hall McCormick

Trenton, N.J. June 4-02

New york conference unnecessary come to Princeton soon as you conveniently can   M. Taylor Pyne

T telegram (C. H. McCormick Papers, WHi).

To Edith Gittings Reid

My dearest Friend,   Princeton, 5 June, '02

This is a line to thank you and Mr. Reid with all my heart for your kindness to a dear little lady who is very precious to me; to say how distressed I was to hear of your illness; and to wish you the best imaginable health and enjoyment on your trip. Our hearts shall follow you all summer.

It will be delightful to think of the pleasure you are having in those far northern countries which will be so novel, so interesting, so invigorating. May God keep you all!

With deep affection,

Faithfully Yours,   Woodrow Wilson

ALS (WC, NjP).

Cyrus Hall McCormick to Cornelius Cuyler Cuyler

My dear C.C.   [Chicago] June 5th, 1902.

Your letter of the 2nd is received. Since our first interview with Dr. Patton we have had another one yesterday with him which was even more satisfactory than the first. Everything, in my judgment, will turn out all right, for Dr. Patton's ideas are pretty well crystalized as to what he wishes to do.[1]

I will be in Princeton Saturday evening or early Sunday morning. In the meantime David Jones will be there Friday afternoon and will confer with you and Pyne as to what transpired here.

I am,   Very sincerely yours,   Cyrus H. McCormick.

TLS (McCormick Letterpress Books, WHi).
[1] That is, it seems safe to assume, Dr. Patton had told McCormick and Jones that he had decided to tender his resignation to the Board of Trustees when it met on June 9, 1902.

From the Minutes of the Board of Trustees
of Princeton University

June 9, 1902.

RESIGNATION OF PRESIDENT PATTON

The President of the University presented his resignation of that office and suggested that a committee be appointed to consider the matter and report to the Board.

COMMITTEE TO CONSIDER RESIGNATION OF PRESIDENT PATTON

On motion of Mr. John A. Stewart duly seconded it was

Resolved, That so much of the President's Report as has reference to his resignation be referred to a committee of the Trustees with instructions to consider and report what action should be taken upon such resignation and to make such recommendations to the Board as the circumstances of the case may suggest and as to said committee may seem wise and proper.

MR. JOHN A. STEWART CHAIRMAN OF COMMITTEE

On motion of Mr. McCormick seconded by Dr. [David Ruddach] Frazer it was

Resolved, That Mr. John A. Stewart be the chairman of said committee and be empowered to name the other members of the committee. . . .

COMMITTEE FROM THE FACULTY

The Secretary reported the following communication from the Committee of the Faculty [Professors Brackett, Woodrow Wilson, and Fine] appointed to appear before the Trustees:

The Committee appointed to represent the Faculty at this meeting of the Board has not received instructions to bring any particular items of Faculty business to the attention of the Board.

The Committee did not appear. . . .

COMMITTEE TO CONSIDER RESIGNATION OF PRESIDENT PATTON

Mr. John A. Stewart announced the appointment of Trustees Pyne, Frazer, McCormick, and Cadwalader as members of the Special Committee to consider the resignation of the President of the University. . . .

REPORT OF SPECIAL COMMITTEE ON CURRICULUM

The Special Committee consisting of the Committee on the Curriculum and Trustees Bayard Henry and Pyne reported progress as follows:

3. Your Special Committee [reports that] they have given care-

ful attention to the matter of changes in the Curriculum referred to them in June 1901. They have had a prolonged conference with the Committee on the Faculty, and have now under consideration a printed report of said Committee. It is their expectation to make a final report on the subject at the meeting of the Board in October. . . .[1]

COMMITTEE ON RESIGNATION OF PRESIDENT RETIRES

Permission was given to the Special Committee on the Resignation of the President of the University to retire. . . .

REPORT OF COMMITTEE ON RESIGNATION OF PRESIDENT

Mr. John A. Stewart stated that the Special Committee, of which he was chairman, had met with the President of the University and was prepared to report. The Report of the Committee was read by Mr. John L. Cadwalader and is as follows:

The Committee appointed by the resolution of the Board adopted this day in reference to the resignation of the President beg leave respectfully to report, that they have fully conferred with the President with reference to his proposed resignation and he has expressed an emphatic desire to be relieved of the administration of the affairs of the University as President. In view of this statement and the wishes of the President we are of the opinion and report that the resignation of President Patton should be accepted with a full recognition of his distinguished services in behalf of the University and the kindest wishes for his future welfare.

In making this recommendation, however, we are happy to be able to state that the President while desiring to be relieved of the administrative duties of his present office, is ready and proposes to continue in the service of the University as Professor of Ethics, under the arrangements now existing, it being understood that his services as such professor shall be rendered during the first term of the academic year.

We venture to express our opinion, in case the Board should deem it wise to accept the resignation of the President, that there should be no long interval before proceeding to the choice of a successor, and that it would be unwise to entirely defer the consideration of that subject until the opening of the next academic year.

We further suggest that the term of the succeeding President should commence at the end of the present fiscal year, August 1, 1902.

[1] About this matter, see n. 2 to the University Faculty Minutes printed at Jan. 29, 1902.

In conclusion we report that the President has fully and freely conferred with the Committee, that he has placed himself and his future services at the disposal of the University, and has assured us that his interest in and devotion to the University shall in no way be lessened by the termination of his services as President.

While fully conscious of the great and distinguished services rendered to the University by Dr. Patton during his long and brilliant career and the great credit to which he is entitled we assume that the Board will prefer to express itself fully on this subject in its own appropriate way.

For the Committee,

(Signed) John A. Stewart, Chairman

FORMAL RESIGNATION OF PRESIDENT PATTON

Dr. Craven, the Senior Trustee, having been called to the chair Dr. Patton formally tendered to the Trustees his resignation as President of Princeton University to take effect at the end of the Academic year, July 31, 1902.

REPORT OF COMMITTEE ON RESIGNATION OF PRESIDENT ADOPTED

On motion of Mr. John A. Stewart, seconded by Dr. Jacobus,[2] it was unanimously

Resolved, That the Report of the Special Committee appointed to report to the Board in reference to the resignation of the President of the University be adopted.

COMMITTEE TO DRAFT RESOLUTION ON RESIGNATION APPOINTED

After remarks in reference to the resignation of Dr. Patton by members of the Board on motion of Mr. Pyne, seconded by Mr. John A. Stewart, it was

Resolved, That a committee of five be appointed to draft suitable resolutions upon the resignation by Dr. Patton of the presidency of Princeton University. Mr. Pyne was appointed chairman of the committee with power to select the other members.

COMMITTEE TO CONFER WITH PRESIDENT PATTON
ABOUT HIS SUCCESSOR

On motion of Dr. McPherson, seconded by Mr. Davis, it was

Resolved, That the committee appointed to confer with the

2 Melancthon Williams Jacobus, born in Allegheny City, Pa., Dec. 15, 1855. A.B., College of New Jersey, 1877; Grad., Princeton Theological Seminary, 1881; studied at the Universities of Göttingen and Berlin, 1881-84. Ordained to the Presbyterian ministry, 1884; pastor, Oxford, Pa., 1884-91. Professor of New Testament Exegesis and Criticism, Hartford Theological Seminary, 1891-1928; Acting President, 1902-1903; Dean of the Faculty, 1903-27. Trustee of Lincoln University (Pa.), 1887-1904, and of the College of New Jersey and Princeton University, 1890-1937. Died on Oct. 31, 1937.

President be requested to hold further conference with him in order to obtain from him any suggestions that he may be willing to make as to a suitable successor. . . .

REPORT OF COMMITTEE ON CONFERENCE WITH PRESIDENT PATTON

Mr. John A. Stewart reported that in accordance with the resolution of the Board the Special Committee had conferred with the President as to his successor- and they were glad to find that the views of the President on that subject concurred with the opinion of the Committee viz. as to the propriety of the election of Woodrow Wilson, Ph. D., Litt.D. LL.D., McCormick Professor of Jurisprudence and Politics in Princeton University.

NOMINATION OF PROFESSOR WOODROW WILSON FOR PRESIDENT

Mr. John A. Stewart nominated Professor Woodrow Wilson for President of Princeton University and the nomination was seconded by Dr. McPherson. . . .

PROFESSOR WOODROW WILSON ELECTED PRESIDENT

The Board proceeded to ballot for a President of Princeton University. Messrs. Cuyler and Green were appointed Tellers and after scrutiny of the ballots reported that twenty-five Trustees were present, twenty-five ballots had been cast all of which were in favor of Professor Woodrow Wilson and he was thereupon declared elected unanimously.

COMMITTEE TO NOTIFY PROFESSOR WILSON OF HIS ELECTION

On motion of Mr. Cuyler, seconded by Mr. Henry, it was
Resolved, That a Committee consisting of President Patton and of those members who were students in the College of New Jersey at the same time that Professor Wilson was a student should be appointed to notify Professor Wilson of his election as President of the University.

COMMITTEE ON NOTIFICATION WITHDRAWS

The Committee consisting of President Patton and Trustees Pyne, McCormick, Jacobus, Bayard Henry, Cuyler and Jones withdrew.

COMMITTEE ON NOTIFICATION TO ACT AS COMMITTEE ON INAUGURATION

On motion of Mr. John A. Stewart duly seconded it was
Resolved, That the committee appointed to notify Professor Wilson of his election be further empowered to arrange for his inauguration. . . .

PROFESSOR WILSON ACCEPTS HIS ELECTION AS PRESIDENT

Professor Woodrow Wilson was presented to the Trustees by the committee appointed to notify him of his election and announced that he would accept the election as President of Princeton University.

The Board adjourned to meet at 10 A.M. Wednesday, June 11th.

An Inscription by Andrew Fleming West

Princeton June 9, 1902

To Woodrow Wilson—
Lover of Letters, Music and PRINCETON
from
Andrew F. West
Servus Inutilis

Hw inscription on cover of *The Triple Cheer, A Parting Song, Dedicated to the STUDENTS of PRINCETON* (n.p., n.d.) (WP, DLC).

From Edgar Odell Lovett

My dear Professor Wilson—   Princeton, 9 June 1902.

You will be overrun by hundreds who have more claims on you at this time than I, but would there by any impropriety should one alumnus of the University of Virginia say to another alumnus of the University of Virginia what the governor of one Carolina is said to have proposed to the governor of the other Carolina?

In all seriousness and great hopefulness for Princeton I beg to assure you of my loyalty.

Mrs. Lovett joins me in very cordial greetings to Mrs. Wilson and all of your house.

Yours most truly   Edgar Odell Lovett

ALS (WP, DLC).

From Richard Theodore Ely

My dear Professor Wilson: Madison, Wis. June 10, 1902.

I saw this morning the report in the paper of your election as President of Princeton University. I have already sent you a telegram of congratulations.[1] It affords me very great pleasure to see you elevated to this high office, which will give you increased opportunities for usefulness and will, I know, add to your fame.

I have not a shadow of a doubt about the large success which you will achieve in this new position. It is now about twenty years since I first met you, and during that time you have advanced steadily, step by step, in a manner which must be gratifying to you, as well as to all your friends. I cannot say that I have been surprised by your career as from the start I expected a great deal from you and for you. On this occasion I beg leave also to extend my congratulations to Mrs. Wilson, and remain,

Ever Sincerely yours,   [Richard T. Ely]

CCL (R. T. Ely Papers, WHi).
    [1] It is missing.

From Alfred Lewis Dennis, Jr.[1]

Dear Tommie   Newark, N. J. June 10th, 1902

This happy day I have long hoped for and I hasten to offer my heartiest congratulations.

You are so admirably endowed and equipped for the position of president of a great university that I feel that a new era is opening for Princeton and that she will become the greatest university in the land.

This is a great day of rejoicing for all your personal friends, for the Class of '79 and for all the true friends of Princeton.

Three cheers for the new President!

Sincerely yours   Alfred Lewis Dennis

ALS (WP, DLC).
    [1] Princeton, 1879, at this time a stockbroker in Newark.

From William Archibald Dunning[1]

My dear Professor Wilson,   Columbia University June 10, 1902

Let me add my congratulations also. Princeton is right in line with the rest of them. But when all the rest of the professors become presidents, who will do the professing? That's going to be a big problem for the presidents to solve. For of course there will never be a generation of scholars like those who became Ph.D's in the middle '80's. This, however, is no time for conundrums. Nunc est bibendum to your assured glory and success.

Sincerely yours,   Wm. A. Dunning

ALS (WP, DLC).
    [1] Professor of History at Columbia University and Managing Editor of the *Political Science Quarterly*.

From Abel McIver Fraser[1]

My dear Dr. Wilson: Staunton, Va. June 10th, 1902.

From the house in which you were born, I send you the congratulations of a former college mate on the new honor that came to you yesterday.

Many persons here remember your boyhood with pleasure and rejoice in your distinction and work.

Do not consume your valuable time by any reply to this greeting.   Most cordially yours   A. M. Fraser.

ALS (WP, DLC).
[1] A.B., Davidson College, 1876; pastor of the First Presbyterian Church of Staunton, Va., 1893-1931; and President of Mary Baldwin College, 1923-29.

From Harold Godwin

My dear Tommy: New York. June 10, 1902

It was so unexpected that I could hardly believe it true that you had achieved so much since '79. It reconciles me to Princeton to know there is such a strong heart and such an able head in command. I have felt a little indifferent these past years, for the old illiberality has kept me in a spirit of lukewarmness. That is over now and I feel an added pride in my Alma Mater. I can only send you a hasty line to tell you how overjoyed I am. With Hadley at Yale and Wilson at Princeton there has been a thoroughly modern change in both which assures the two colleges, or Universities a brilliant future. You can always count upon my sympathy and any help I can give you. I wish you a long and a happy administration.   Sincerely   Harold Godwin

ALS (WP, DLC).

From Albert Bushnell Hart

My dear Wilson,   Cambridge, Massachusetts June 10, 1902

The morning papers contain news for which I have been hopefully waiting for years—the appointment of Woodrow Wilson to be President of Princeton. It is a lofty task, and all your thousands of friends have confidence that it will be well performed.

The great Universities of America more and more tend to understand their common purpose and joint responsibility. We of Harvard feel that the advancement and growth of our neighbors is also advancement for Harvard: a strong administration in Princeton or Yale or Columbia is a buttress to the whole system of University education.

Indeed I think you have the most magnificent opportunity that can come to a man—the chance to set your stamp on a whole generation of Princeton men, and equally upon the American community. It rejoices my heart to see the right man in so splendid and so long a boulevard, the end of which no man can see.

Though I have seen Mrs. Wilson but few times, I hope she will allow me through you to express a warm personal congratulation on this official recognition of her husband's power and promise.

Sincerely your friend,   Albert Bushnell Hart

Don't answer this note—you will have a mountain of correspondence.

ALS (WP, DLC).

From Alexander Scott Bullitt[1]

My dear Prof. Wilson,   [Louisville, Ky.] June 10, 1902

Not having had the opportunity to see you before leaving Princeton, I take this means of adding my congratulations to the great number already received.

While in college I had the pleasure of taking every course offered by you and my only regret was that there were not more of them.

Simply as one of the countless alumni enthusiastic in your support, I desire to extend my heartiest congratulations and best wishes.

Since graduating I have not missed a single commencement and never expect to miss one. I know that you have no more loyal "rooters" than the young alumni. In political parlance they are "original Wilson men," every one of them.

With kindest regards

I am,   Yours Sincerely   Scott Bullitt.

ALS (WP, DLC).
  [1] Princeton, 1898; LL.B., University of Louisville, 1899; at this time practicing law in Louisville.

Annie Bliss Perry to Ellen Axson Wilson

Dear Mrs. Wilson—   Cambridge [Mass.], 10 June, 1902.

When Bliss rushed up from the breakfast-table this morning, paper in hand, exclaiming "What *do* you think is here!" I almost forgot I was indulging in "Shingles" of which acute neuralgia is the most important symptom. But it makes me homesick and blue to think that the event we had so often talked about and wished for has come to pass and we are outsiders, not there to enjoy it. *Do* tell me all about it—but I know you have so many relatives and southern friends to write to that you will not have time to write here for a long time. But it is so exciting and delightful and we are so overjoyed, if only you are sure Mr. Wilson is strong enough for it. In your last letter you say he is remarkably well, and that is a great pleasure to us. Oh, dear! oh, dear! I feel so far away. How long have you had it to think about? And how will you feel about giving up the dear house? And I suppose it must postpone your trip to Europe! I have not once mentioned in the most remote way what "it" is, and a third person would feel this a bit incoherent, but you understand. What wouldn't I give for two hours visit with you! I was just about to write you again when your delightful long letter came—if you write seldom, you certainly make up for it when you find time! And I have wished to write ever since; but I was not very well just then, and was bracing up to go to the hospital which I did as soon as Dr. thought I was up to the operation, and now I am on the high-road to being a new and better woman I think.

And you have had such a dreadful year, so much illness and your own suffering. But what a pleasure it is to be able to write that the children have been so well, which is just what I can chronicle. . . . Bliss is tremendously busy and very happy, tho' I can see clearly that having taught *first* and so many years teaching will always be his "first love," tho' it takes his nervous strength more than his present work. He is away a good deal lecturing, and as you say of Mr. Wilson, these trips in moderation are an excellent thing for him. But they are dreary for me, as I have been ill so much. He is on his way to Aurora, N.Y. now, and my wood fire is my only company.

I have been hoping to take two little outings soon, have really felt strong enough to anticipate them—the last of this week to my class reunion at Smith, and a week later to Pres. [Henry] Hopkins's inauguration at Williams. Well, there is one thing I *shall* plan for—front seats for us both (Mr. Perry and me) at Mr. Wilson's inauguration. I suppose it will come next fall. I wrote Mrs. Westcott not long ago that I expected to spend "weeks" with her next year. Now I shall have a definite time to plan for. I hope it will suit her! Good night and so much love, and congratulations & best wishes.

Always your affectionate friend,   Annie B. Perry

ALS (WP, DLC).

From Laurence Hutton

My Dear Wilson   Princeton, New Jersey. June 10th 1902

I can not resist the temptation of dropping the Mister, and calling you Wilson; because, in future, I can call you nothing but Mister President

This morning, when I met you, on the Campus, I could not call you anything. I could not say anything. I do not know whom to congratulate most, the Wilsons, the University or the Universe

Believe me,

Dear Mr. President,

Yours Faithfully to Command   Laurence Hutton

ALS (WP, DLC).

Jenny Davidson Hibben to Ellen Axson Wilson

My dear Mrs. Wilson,   [Princeton, N.J., c. June 10, 1902]

I want to tell you now what I could not this morning, that if *you* have a feeling of distrust about yourself, *we* have not, and we know that you will fill the place of the President's wife with the sweetness[,] distinction and grace which you already have— and we shall love you and be proud of you!

I am so very happy about it all and I feel it difficult to put in words all that I feel. You know how dear you & Mr. Wilson & your children are to us, and it will be more lovely than I can say to have you near us.[1]

With love, dear Mrs. Wilson,

Ever your friend,   Jenny Davidson Hibben.

ALS (WP, DLC).

[1] The Hibbens lived at 62 Washington Road, about a block away from Prospect, then the home of the President of Princeton University.

From William Burhans Isham, Jr.

My Dear Tommy,   New York, June 10 1902

I only wish to write my congratulations and press your hand and say "God bless you." Some "Westerner" thought the White House would do for you, but we know "Prospect" is much better. Dont forget our little University which meets here.[1] Death is required not elective and the last student taken was Jimmy Lord.[2] Dont fail to call on the Boys when you need us. And never forget first last & alway I am yours sincerely & 79ly

Wm. B. Isham Jr.

ALS (WP, DLC).
    [1] That is, the Isham Dinners.
    [2] James Brown Lord '79, New York architect, who died on June 1, 1902.

From Henry van Dyke

My dear Wilson,   Princeton, New Jersey. June 10, 1902

Hearty congratulations, to Princeton and to you, on your election as President. The news was brought to me in my sick-room last night by Cyrus McCormick. I wish you a long life and a large success in your new work. Don't take the trouble to answer this.   Faithfully Yours   Henry van Dyke

ALS (WP, DLC).

From Frank Mason North[1]

My dear President-Elect: New York, June 10, 1902

You will have bushels of letters and telegrams—but please do not let mine get lost until you get it in somewhere on your mind that Mrs. North and I are *delighted* and send you our greetings and congratulations.

It is altogether fine—the thing that was done and the way of it! And to the dear lady who has had a lot to do with making you equal to so noble a task we send greetings also—for we know that her heart is right too. We learned to like you both in those uncrowded days in Middletown and we have never recovered from the attack.[2]

God bless you and make you a great President!

With Enthusiasm
                    Yours always,   Frank Mason North

ALS (WP, DLC).
    [1] At this time Corresponding Secretary of the New York City Church Extension and Missionary Society of the Methodist Episcopal Church and editor of the *Christian City*.
    [2] See F. M. North to WW, Sept. 15, 1890, Vol. 7.

From Charles Andrew Talcott

My dear Tommy: Utica, N.Y. June 10, 1902

My best wish for Princeton is realized in your election to the presidency of the university. It will bring to Princeton, I believe, a great deal that Princeton has never had. Whatever of success and accomplishment the future can yield I hope will be yours. I feel all the joy and pride a friend can feel in the recognition of the worth of one whom he knows and loves.

As ever,   Affectionately Yours,   C. A. Talcott

ALS (WP, DLC).

From Edith Duer[1]

My dear Mr. Wilson   [Baltimore, c. June 10, 1902]

I cannot forbear sending you a line of most sincere & heartfelt congratulation, & I feel that Princeton is to be congratulated equally. You are just in your right place, & it is delightful to think that for once in this topsy-turvy world the square man is in the square hole. The office of a college President is such a magnificent opportunity & an opportunity to do work that is worth-while & none the less blessed because you will,—in the majority of cases, —never know what you have accomplished until the last great day when every man reaps his own harvest. Do not bother to answer this but believe I was so truly glad that I had to extend my hand.   Sincerely yours,   Edith Duer

Do you know I have a sneaking wonder whether you will not re-call who I am without an effort!

ALS (WP, DLC).
[1] Whom Wilson had met in Baltimore on February 12, 1894, and had de-scribed in WW to EAW, Feb. 19, 1894, Vol. 8.

From Adrian Hoffman Joline

Dear Dr Wilson: New York   June 10 1902

The venerable class of 1870 congratulates the University and its superannuated President pledges to you its devoted allegiance.

Great rejoicing among the alumni in this neighborhood.
                    Yrs. ever truly   Adrian H. Joline

This calls for *no* reply. You'll have to hire an office force if you answer all congratulatory messages.

ALS (WP, DLC).

From Frank Hathaway Kemper[1]

My Dear Sir: Cincinnati, O. June 10, 1902.

I congratulate the University upon your election as President. I have but this moment seen the news in this morning's paper, and it gives me the liveliest kind of satisfaction. I look for great things as the result of it all.

It has been many a long day, since back in 1878, we used to help produce the "Princetonian" of that era;[2] but from that time on, I have not been blind to what you have been doing. I rejoice in this honor which has come to you. I can think of no greater one.

With my heartiest wishes for your most abundant successes, I am, as ever,   Very truly yours,   Frank H. Kemper

TLS (WP, DLC).
    [1] Princeton, 1878; LL.B., Cincinnati Law School, 1880; lawyer in Cincinnati.
    [2] Kemper was on the Editorial Board of the *Princetonian* with Wilson.

From Alfred James Pollock McClure[1]

My dear Tommy: Philadelphia June 10, 1902.

I have just heard the news and write you in the quickest possible manner *my heartiest congratulations*. May you live long and have a prosperous reign. I am almost as proud as if I had gone and done it myself.

It means a new era for Princeton I am quite sure. May you have faith and courage and wisdom and tact, indeed all the virtues and vices of the characteristic men of the great and glorious class of '79.

I am coming up to Princeton perhaps the latter part of this week or next with my two boys to talk with you. With my salary I had made up my mind that it was impossible to get enough ahead for *two boys* at Princeton and so had them pass the examinations for Haverford, right in our own community. But Tommy, old man, this is too much for me. To have a member of my class President of the College breaks my back and I must see what can be done.

Why didn't you announce this thing before they took their examinations. I wrote to the Secretary and found the usual arrangement in regard to parsons sons i.e. $100 each or a remission of the Tuition, but they would have to have about $500 apiece, and a thousand over and above my needs were I considered quite impossible. However, I am afraid they will have to walk from Jenkintown to Princeton every morning now, for something has got to be done.

However, don't take this thing to heart as a personal matter at all. It is only the uppermost thing in my mind in the exuberance of my joy at your election.[2]

    Cordially and sincerely yours,   Alfred J. P. McClure

TLS (WP, DLC).

1 Member of the Class of 1879, at this time assistant treasurer and financial agent of the General Clergy Relief of the Protestant Episcopal Church.
2 His two sons, Jay Cooke McClure and Alfred James McClure, Jr., did come to Princeton and were both members of the Class of 1906.

From James Cowden Meyers[1]

My dear Professor: [New York] June 10th, 1902

When something happens to which one has been looking forward for a long time it is often a greater surprise than would otherwise be the case, and so it is with your election as President Patton's successor. This is the consummation of my hopes for the past eleven years, and during that time I know that I have made myself something of a bore to my fellow alumni by my advocacy and prophecy. I believe that this ushers in the Golden Age for Princeton, and I trust that your rule may cover many fruitful years. When you think that I can be of service to the Alma Mater pray command me.

Believe me   Yours sincerely,   James Cowden Meyers

TLS (WP, DLC).
1 Princeton, 1891; LL.B., New York Law School, 1893; lawyer in New York City.

From Francis Southmayd Phraner[1]

My dear "Tommy"   New York, June 10th, 1902

Just a line to congratulate you on your well deserved advancement. I had thought of it as a possibility but the suddenness of the change almost took my breath away, when I glanced at the paper this morning.

The unanimity of action on the part of the Board of Trustees must be very pleasing to you showing you that you have their entire confidence, and I am sure that the Alumni will back up the Trustees in what they have done. As an old alumnus (back of '79) expressed himself to me to-day "I felt like giving three cheers."

One more honor for the class of '79.

With hearty congratulations for yourself & also for Mrs. Wilson I remain

Your classmate (with all that it implies)

Francis S. Phraner

ALS (WP, DLC).
1 Princeton, 1879, in the warehouse business in New York.

From Legh Wilbur Reid[1]

Dear Professor Wilson: Haverford [Pa.], June 10th, 1902.

I heard the splendid news by telegraph last night and hope that you received promptly my message sent by telephone. There is absolutely nothing that could give me greater pleasure than to know that Princeton is to have you for its president.

Mrs. Reid joins me in sincerest congratulations to both yourself and Mrs. Wilson. She sends her love to Mrs. Wilson and asks me to say how much she enjoyed her visit.

It was a most delightful surprise and brightened Mrs. Reid up wonderfully.

With kindest regards for yourself, Mrs. Wilson and the children, believe me   Faithfully yours   Legh W. Reid.

ALS (WP, DLC).
[1] At this time Associate Professor of Mathematics at Haverford College.

From Bernard Christian Steiner

Dear Prof. Wilson: Baltimore, Maryland. June 10, 1902

Please give Princeton my hearty congratulations for her success in choosing the right man to succeed President Patton. We were greatly pleased to read the news this morning. May your shadow never grow less (the institution is the lengthened shadow of the man &c)

Had the pleasure of meeting Mrs. Wilson at the Woman's College Reception last week
                    Yours sincerely   Bernard C. Steiner.

ALS (WP, DLC).

William Royal Wilder[1] to Robert Randolph Henderson

My dear Henderson,   New York. June 10th. 1902.

Sound the loud tocsin,—operate violently the hew gag! A good sized mob of the boys is going down tomorrow to Princeton to violently and vociferously congratulate 'Tommy' Wilson. Don't fail to join the procession. He will not be inaugurated until next October, but this need not prevent our making a demonstration tomorrow. Take the earliest possible train and go down in large force.   Verily yours,   Wm. R. Wilder

TLS (WC, NjP).
[1] Secretary of the Class of 1879.

From the Minutes of the Board of Trustees
of Princeton University

June 11, 1902.

. . . The President of the University spoke and then introduced
Professor Woodrow Wilson, President-elect, who also spoke. Old
Nassau was sung and after the benediction the Board adjourned
to meet on Tuesday, October 21, 1902, at eleven A.M.

From Charles Wolf McFee[1]

Dear Mr. President,   Georgetown, Delaware, June 11, 1902.

Great Scott.—Just to think I can call the President of "me College" by his first name.

Dear old "Tommy," how proud we all are of you. I wish I could
see thee face to face, but as that is impossible, I hasten to send
you my warmest and most sincere congratulations.

Old '79 will stand by you and I know all the Alumni feel that
the University is safe in your hands.

God bless you always and believe me,

Faithfully yours,   Chas. W. McFee

TLS (WP, DLC).
   [1] Princeton, 1879, vice president of the Peninsular Incorporators Trust Co.
of Delaware.

From Azel Washburn Hazen

My dear Dr. Wilson—   Middletown, Conn.   11 June 1902

In the midst of all the congratulations which are showered
upon you this week, will you accept a rose from me—a humble,
yet genuine friend? Our boy Maynard, ever since your charming
courtesy to us in Princeton, has shared our admiration for you.
Hence when he went to the door for the morning paper yesterday,
he came back with much enthusiasm, exclaiming—"Papa, Woodrow Wilson is President of Princeton!" Mrs. Hazen and myself
at once shared his delight, saying, "The *expected* has happened
this time."

I have felt for some time that you would be the next head of the
University, though I did not anticipate the honor for you quite
so soon.

May I say that I rejoice with you in this deserved recognition
of your character and attainments? May I add that I congratulate

the University upon its good fortune? I love to think of your widened field of influence over so many young men of our time— a power for *good*, and that only.

Mrs. Hazen joins me in love and felicitations to Mrs. Wilson and yourself.

Believe me   Ever affectionately yours   A. W. Hazen

ALS (WP, DLC).

From A. Elizabeth Wilson Begges[1]

My dear Woodrow   Cleveland   June 11th [1902]

Having just seen the announcement of the highly honorable position which has been extended to you of the presidency of the grand old Princeton College I take pleasure in offering my most hearty congratulations. You will accept them won't you? It is a high honor, and for so young a man, wonderful. Is not your father greatly gratified—I would like much to hear of the state of his health. Do not judge this shameful handwriting please until I explain the reason—my hand can scarcely grasp a pen since last fall when I sustained a stroke of paralysis, from which I have only partially recovered, & has made me a very old woman. . . .

                Your true & faithful Aunt   Elizabeth Begges

ALS (WP, DLC).
   [1] Sister of Joseph Ruggles Wilson.

From Elmer Truesdell Merrill

My dear Wilson: Middletown, Conn. June 11, 1902.

I have just returned to Middletown after a brief absence out of the range of newspapers, to learn that you have been elected President of Princeton University. I hadn't even suspected that 'The King is dead,' & I've hardly caught sufficient breath yet to join in the shout of "Long live the King,"—but I do so nevertheless —you hear me?!

I hope you won't consider my gratification intrusive on account of my not being numbered in the Princeton family. I must shout with them nevertheless. Princeton must grant that the society of letters, & not merely the society of Princeton, is represented by the man she is raising to her Presidency,—and so I, wandering around the outskirts of that noble greater society, & standing a-tiptoe to catch some glimpse of the divine mysteries over the shoulders of my greaters must be allowed to join my 'Vivat! Floreat!' with the rest. *Homo sum, et nil humani–*, & I don't know when any academic distinction & recognition has appealed to my heart & my judgment more warmly. By Hercules, naught but the stately periods of the classic tongue will express my emotions! I will sit down incontinent & indite a Latin ode. Tremble not! The burdens of the presidential mortar-board shall not be augmented by the need of reading aught from my stylus but this letter. The ode shall disburden me of my swelling passion, & shall then be dropped, gently & unaffectedly, into that which my foot now toucheth.

But I wish I could shake hands & tell you how glad I am,–for Princeton's sake, & for your sake too, inasmuch as the election is a great mark of universal trust & confidence. The work of a University President is doubtless one of those honors & tasks that, as I think Cicero somewhere said, are neither to be greatly desired nor to be avoided by a good citizen. But no one could be better fitted to undertake it than you, nor could any one undertake it under better omens. And so again,

'Vivas! Floreas!'

Faithfully yours,   Elmer Truesdell Merrill.

ALS (WP, DLC).

From John H. Pearson[1]

Dear Sir,   Easton, Pa. June 11th, 1902.

In the basement of Mr Chas H. Barnwell's house in Columbia, S.C. which was used as a school room by Mr Barnwell, I had the honor of going to school with you, and while I have no idea you have the faintest recollection of me, as I was only one of a large class—some of its members having been Jim McMaster, John McMaster, Parker Waites, Sandy Childs & others, while you were taught alone—at any rate whether you remember me or not, you will not, I know, object to my taking the liberty of extending my congratulations on your recent elevation to the Presidency of Princeton as Dr. Patton's successor.

I am   Yours Sincerely   John H. Pearson.

ALS (WP, DLC).
[1] Nothing is known about Pearson at this time except that he was associated with the Lehigh Coal and Navigation Co. of Easton, Pa.

From Bowdre Phinizy[1]

My dear Mr. President: Augusta, Ga.   June 11/02

I can't tell you how glad I was yesterday to read the news of your election. Had I known anything like that was on the tapis, I had surely made the pilgrimage to Princeton.

As things now stand, we Augustans are having a little celebration & jollification all our own & we are industriously circulating all the details of your early career which was spent in our midst. I cant express how deep & sincere are my feelings of pleasure & congratulation. To my mind it means more to Princeton than it does to you, tho' I daresay Mrs Wilson will not join me in those sentiments. After the rush is over, as "the boys" say won't you tell me how it happened.

Give my love to your dear wife & with best wishes for yourself.
          Most sincerely   Bowdre Phinizy

ALS (WP, DLC).
[1] Princeton, 1892, at this time owner and publisher of the *Augusta*, Ga., *Herald*.

From Louis Clark Vanuxem

Philadelphia   11th June 1902.

Here's my hand, Tommy, and I am proud of you, our College and our Class; and myself, that I am your friend. It is needless to say that you can always count on my support. I don't believe you ever will need support; you are sufficiently strong and enthusiastic to carry all of the burden of your office on your own broad shoulders; but if you ever need encouragement, be sure that along with the rest of the '79 boys, it will give me the greatest pleasure to shout for our distinguished class-mate.
          Yours with affection,   L. C. Vanuxem

TLS (WP, DLC).

From Albert Shaw

My dear Wilson: New York   June 12, 1902

Robert Bridges is going to write an article about you for the next number of the Review of Reviews.[1] That means not very much time to turn around in. We shall, of course, be able to get the stock pictures of you up at Pach Brothers' shop; but we would like to make a new picture on our own account if you are coming to New York. Bridges says you are coming over to do several errands, such as to buy college president clothes, and the like. We want very much to run you in to a photographer's named Pirie MacDonald, who is down town at 141 Broadway, not far from the Cortlandt Street ferry. He takes remarkably good pictures, and I think we could promise Mrs. Wilson the finest photograph of you by far that ever was taken.[2]

Mr. James McCusker, of our office, would look after the whole affair, meet you at the ferry with a coach and four, and put the thing through expeditiously. Please send us just a line telling us whether or not you can coöperate in this way.

I shall add no congratulations, because you know well enough how all your friends feel, and because, after all, the position into which you have been thrust is, I know, from your own point of view one for hard work rather than for congratulations. I take it that Dr. Patton is really the man to be congratulated.

As ever,   Faithfully yours,   Albert Shaw   w. m.

TLS (WP, DLC).
[1] It is printed at July 1, 1902.
[2] The Pirie MacDonald portrait is reproduced in the photographic section of this volume.

From James Woodrow

My dear Woodrow: Columbia, S. C., June 12, 1902.

We have just heard the delightful news.

I congratulate you with all my heart. In view of the way in which honors have been showered on you, I cannot say that I am surprised; but certainly nothing could have been added to make the way of bestowing this last honor more gratifying.

I am not going to say anything about the "tremendous responsibility," etc., or to write a letter at all; I just want to tell you how glad we all are, and to wish you the very highest success.

With love to you all,
                    Your affectionate uncle,   James Woodrow.

ALS (WP, DLC).

From Harriet Woodrow Welles

My dear Woodrow: [Denver] June the twelfth [1902].

I cannot tell you how happy it made us to hear of the distinguished honor that has been conferred upon you. Ned[1] was reading the morning paper aloud, and when he came to the headlines announcing Dr. Patton's resignation I interrupted him by saying:

"Cousin Woodrow will fill that place some day, but he's too young for it yet." So you may imagine our delight when we found that, young or no, you had actually been *made* President!

I have thought so often of Uncle Joseph, and of how happy you must be that he has lived to see your ability recognized and rewarded. Give him my warmest love.

Is it true that you are contemplating a western trip this summer? I hope it is, and that you will be sure to bring Cousin Ellen with you. Of course we expect you to make our home your headquarters. You know we have been living in Denver for the past five years, and find it a delightful place of residence. We are looking forward with keenest pleasure to a visit from Mother[2] and Helen,[3] this Fall, on their way to Mexico.[4] Did mother write you that Dr. Thayer and Dr. Osler both say that there is nothing the matter with her heart?[5] Her trouble is simply one of nerves, and she can come to Colorado, and climb Pike's Peak to her heart's content. You can realize my joy on hearing this, when for this past two years we had supposed she could never risk this altitude again.

Give my love to Cousin Ellen and the dear girls, and let me know if we are to have the pleasure of a visit from you this summer.   Your affectionate cousin   Hattie

ALS (WP, DLC).
   [1] Her husband, Edward Freeman Welles.
   [2] Helen Sill (Mrs. Thomas) Woodrow of Chillicothe, Ohio.
   [3] Her sister, Helen Woodrow.
   [4] To visit her brother, James Wilson Woodrow.
   [5] William Sydney Thayer, M.D., Associate Professor of Medicine, and Sir William Osler, M.D., Professor of the Principles and Practice of Medicine at the Johns Hopkins.

From Helen Sill Woodrow

Dear Woodrow: Chillicothe O.   June 12th, 1902.

Let me too offer my congratulations on the high honor that has been, not sought, but thrust upon you. Surely your highest ambition has now been satisfied, since you can go no higher. And I do heartily rejoice with you and Ella.

It was so kind of the latter to visit me at the Hospital. She is more lovely even than you pictured her to me. Hoping that I may see you both some future day, in the old home in Chillicothe, I am,
                    Yours affectionately,   Aunt Helen

ALS (WP, DLC); P.S. omitted.

From Daniel Collamore Heath

My dear *President* Wilson: Boston   June 12, 1902.

The news has arrived. We are all saying "Princeton couldn't have done better," and I personally am saying, "I think the Amherst trustees will now believe that my recommendation to them of a few years ago was in no way overdone."[1] Of course they will say, "Well, Professor Wilson is a Princeton graduate and is a good person for Princeton, and then Harris[2] is a good president for Amherst because he is an Amherst graduate but wouldn't have answered so well for Princeton" etc. I predict and wish for you a long and happy career. I am sure your régime will be a successful one.

Don't trouble to answer this. You have too many others to answer, and I have written it because I couldn't very well help it.

Cordially yours,   D. C. Heath

TLS (WP, DLC).
[1] See EAW to WW, Oct. 29, 1898, n. 2, Vol. 11.
[2] George Harris, President of Amherst College, 1899-1912.

From James Sprunt

Dear Professor: Wilmington, N.C.   June 12th. 1902

We are all gratified by the news that you have been elected President of Princeton, because we know that it means much for that honoured institution, which will now forge ahead among the giants of education and its distinguished leader will be covered with fresh laurels from a grateful and admiring people.

We love you and your dear father so much that our hearts respond quickly to anything which affects the welfare of yourself and your family. I trust that this arrangement will not conflict with your purposed holidays abroad and that we may see you and the good Doctor when he finds it convenient to return to us here.

We have, as you know, been under a heavy weight of sorrow since last August[1] and I am preparing to leave on Monday next with my wife and son,[2] and my nephew—young Dr. Wood[3] who has just graduated at the Pennsylvania University, for a trip abroad. They will take some tours at their leisure but I must work during the whole time for the furtherance of our business connections in Europe.

Please remember me with love to your good father and kindest wishes for yourself and your family.

Yours very truly,   James Sprunt

TLS (WP, DLC).

1 The Sprunts' only daughter, Marian Murchison Sprunt, thirteen years old, died on August 30, 1901, in Asheville, N.C., of scarlet fever after a two-day illness.

2 James Laurence Sprunt.

3 Edward Jenner Wood, M.D., University of Pennsylvania, 1902, son of the late Dr. Thomas F. Wood of Wilmington, N.C.

From Lawrence Crane Woods[1]

My dear Doctor Wilson: Pittsburg, Pa. June 13, 1902.

I have been away for the past week and this is the first opportunity I have had to extend to you most hearty congratulations and cordial best wishes over your election to the Presidency of Princeton. Nothing has ever happened in connection with the University which has given me more genuine pleasure and absolute confidence that Old Nassau is now entering upon a period of prosperity such as she has never seen before, even in the days of good old Doctor McCosh. From the expressions I have heard from the alumni on all sides, you can feel confident of the most loyal support from this direction.

With renewed congratulations and assurances that I will work for Princeton with even more confidence and enthusiasm than ever under your administration, believe me

     Sincerely yours, Lawrence C. Woods '91

Harvard couldn't score a run after that announcement.[2]

TLS (WP, DLC).

1 Princeton, 1891, at this time Assistant Manager of the Equitable Life Assurance Society Agency in Pittsburgh.

2 Princeton defeated Harvard in baseball on June 11 by a score of 7 to 0.

A News Report of an Alumni Luncheon

[June 14, 1902]

At the annual alumni luncheon on Tuesday [June 10], Professor Wilson said:

"Fellow alumni, you know, you must know the feeling with which I rise upon an occasion like this. This thing has come to me as a thunderbolt out of a clear sky. How can a man who loves this place as I love it realize of a sudden that he has now the liberty to devote every power that is in him to its service. You must sympathize with me, I feel sure, in the feeling with which I realize that I am to be the successor of the brilliant man who has just addressed you. I know how great a part he has played in the councils of the church, in public opinion and in putting the truth in phrases that ring and last and cannot be forgotten. I can only speak for myself and my colleagues in the faculty when I say that I rejoice that he is not to leave Princeton. If he is not to be our leader, he is to continue to be our ornament, and therefore we shall not lose all of the brilliant service which he has rendered to this university during the fourteen years of his administration. I know that if there is any one power behind me it is the power of sympathy, the power of friendship, the power of comradeship in the great body of alumni among whom I count so many dear and personal friends. The objects that we seek in a university are not selfish objects. There is here no interest served which is a personal interest. We are here to serve our country and mankind, and we know that we can put selfishness behind us. The cordial handshakes, the unmistakably genuine look of good will and the good wishes that have come to me since this election was announced, are to me the most blessed augury for the future."[1]

The several hundred alumni at this luncheon received Dr. Patton and Professor Wilson with the most enthusiastic applause and cheering. In his speech, which preceded Professor Wilson's, Dr. Patton said, among other things:

"I realize that this university stands face to face with new problems of development. In respect to the new administration, the policy which is to be inaugurated is a policy that ought to be inaugurated by him who has every reason to look forward to twenty or twenty-five years of administrative service. It would ill become my good sense or any reputation I may have for wisdom if I should wish to inaugurate a movement that might trammel the freedom of him who must be my successor. I hope to enter upon those quiet pursuits of which I am fond, and to serve the university in the quiet capacity of teacher. And it is fitting that the administrative leadership should pass into other hands. I feel very happy in the action I have taken and very satisfied with reference to Princeton's future in view of the action which followed so spontaneously after the acceptance of my resignation. With my whole heart and with every element of my being I am in sympathy with the action of the trustees, in which I had the honor to participate, which has placed Woodrow Wilson in the leadership of Princeton University. God bless the university and God bless him in the great work that has been given him to do."

James W. Alexander '60 presided at the lu[n]cheon, and the speeches were unusually good, from the few simple but impressive words of the Rev. Dr. James Curtis Hepburn '32, the oldest living graduate, who still enjoys good health though in his 87th year, to the vigorous response of the Hon. John Glover Wilson, who spoke for the young class of '92. The Hon. Henry Stafford Little '44 was at the speakers' table, and told the alumni that he had got a lot of fun out of his gifts to the university and hoped they would take his word for it and try it. The other speakers were Judge James H. Reed of Pittsburgh, the Hon. H. B. Munn '47 of Washington; the Hon. W. C. Spruance '52 of the Supreme Court of Delaware; the Rev. Dr. W. W. Knox '62 of New Brunswick, N. J.; John D. Davis '72, M. Taylor Pyne '77 and J. W. Queen, Jr., '87. It was the largest alumni luncheon ever held.

Printed in the *Princeton Alumni Weekly*, II (June 14, 1902), 633-34.
  1 There is a brief WWhw outline of these remarks dated "Tuesday" [June 10, 1902] in WP, DLC.

A News Report of Commencement Exercises

[June 14, 1902]

THE 155TH ANNUAL COMMENCEMENT

At the one hundred and fifty-fifth annual Commencement in Alexander Hall on Wednesday, June 11, the bachelor's degree was conferred upon two hundred and forty-nine members of the graduating class—which breaks the record. This is thirty-one more than last year and twenty-four more than the largest former class, '96.

Alexander Hall was packed to the roof. In addition to the usual interest, it was known that this was the last time Dr. Patton would preside at Commencement as President of the university. At the President's right on the platform was ex-President Cleveland and at his left, President-elect Woodrow Wilson '79. The exercises opened with prayer by the Rev. Dr. J. Addison Henry '57, of the board of trustees. . . .

The Valedictory was delivered by Edwin Henry Kellogg of Pennsylvania, and after the graduating class had sung Old Nassau, there were notable addresses by President Patton and President-elect Wilson, both of whom were repeatedly applauded. Among other things Dr. Patton said:

"Personal infirmities have made it impossible for me to know men individually, but I think we understand each other and I am grateful beyond any words of mine to express it, for the confidence and the respectful treatment which I have uniformly received at the hands of the students of Princeton University. I have tried, with what measure of success others may say, but I have tried to see the students' side of the case. I suppose that in this respect I have not always held the scales of justice with an even hand. And I think that if I were to obey the categorical imperative of the present, it is my duty here and now to hear my heart make ample apology to my head. But in this respect I stand before you a stolid and hopeless impenitent."

The President referred to the several gifts to the university during the first years of his administration and paid a high tribute to the givers. He then announced his intention to remain a member of the faculty of the university, which was the occasion of the most enthusiastic applause, both from the audience and the trustees and members of the faculty on the platform. Referring to the latter he said: "They will give me the credit of being willing to say what I think and of being ready to defend what I think to be right on all occasions and of being content to stand, as I have often stood, in a very lonely sort of minority. We could give and take and after the freest speech and the largest license of debate we could go out of the faculty room and be as warm friends as we ever were before." He added: "The opportunity I have prayed [for] so long of having a leisure afternoon in life, so far as it is in the power of the board of trustees to give it to me, has been granted."

Dr. Patton said that "no large vision of achievement" filled his gaze, but that he hoped "to do such service to the university as limited resources and restricted energies may allow. When a man has passed as far beyond the meridian of life as I have passed," he said, "the experiences of a life-time are of little worth if they have not taught him that his heart is the biggest and best part of his body, and all I ever hope for and the utmost that I pray is that I may have a little share in the love of Princeton men.

"I regard it as a piece of Princeton's singular good fortune that the day which dates my resignation of office dates also the unanimous and enthusiastic election of my successor. Himself a son of Old Nassau, he will rally the spontaneous, unrestricted and unlimited enthusiasm of Princeton men all round the world. Ordained by the laying on of hands to the office of a ruling elder of the Presbyterian Church, that great church will not feel in his accession to the presidency that there has been such a breach in the tradition of Princeton as the public prints would have you to suppose. Born in the South and trained in the North, he is a fitting representative of the fusion of those social and political forces in new America which knows no South and no North. A student of political philosophy and a representative of the highest thought of the time in philosophical jurisprudence, he will serve and carry to still greater achievement the traditions of Princeton which were established by those great men who rocked the cradle of the Republic and who had so much to do in framing the constitutional basis of our national life. A master of speech with few equals in this land, he will represent Princeton wherever he goes with unfailing distinction. It is a matter on which I felicitate myself and on which I congratulate the university, that in passing out of office I hand over the insignia of that office to my friend and colleague Dr. Woodrow Wilson."

President-elect Wilson's response was brief, but he said enough to indicate his endorsement of the plans already adopted for the development of the university. "There are things which we hope to add to this university," he said, "and there are things which we hope will never be subtracted from it. We hope that men will open their hearts to us and will enable us to crown this university with a great graduate college."[1]

Printed in the *Princeton Alumni Weekly*, II (June 14, 1902), 631-33.
[1] There is a brief WWhw outline of these remarks, entitled "Commencement, 1902," in WP, DLC.

From Robert Ewing[1]

My Dear Sir,   Mannie, Tenn., June 14, 1902

Wont you accept from our entire household, who hold you in such affection, our sincerest congratulations? I need not tell you that from my first reading of Congressional Government, unto yesterday, I have noted your advancement with the keenest, friendliest interest and therefore this last great honor did not surprise me as you say it did you. How anxious I was, years ago, to have you come and accept the Presidency of the Peabody Normal! I wanted you for "our people."[2] You declined on the ground that acceptance might interfere with outside literary work, in which you were then engaged. I was disappointed then— but a careful reading of the books written since, has shown me very conclusively that your decision was a wise one. You must, even then, have "come to yourself" and known what you had to give us. I keep your teachings in the hands of my boys. You have now a great charge. May your health continue—and enable you to satisfy yourself! That you will all others, I do not doubt.

Very Cordially Yours,   R. Ewing

ALS (WP, DLC).
[1] Husband of Mrs. Wilson's first cousin, Harriet Hoyt Ewing, Robert Ewing was at this time general manager of the Buffalo Iron Co. of Mannie, Tenn.
[2] See R. Ewing to WW, May 28 and June 14, 1887, Vol. 5.

From James Alfred Hoyt

My Dear Sir: Greenville, S.C., June 14th, 1902

I wish to congratulate you and Princeton upon the action of the powers that be in making you president of the Uy. The news was received in our household with much gratification, and many friends in Greenville have expressed their pleasure to me. Mr. Hamlin Beattie[1] was especially delighted with the information.

Present our loving regards to Cousin Ellen Lou, and with a due share for yourself, I am,

Very Truly Yours,   James A. Hoyt

ALS (WP, DLC).
[1] Princeton, 1856, banker of Greenville, S. C.

From John Bell Henneman[1]

Dear Mr. Wilson,   Sewanee, Tennessee, June 14, 1902.

My friend, Mr. James Maynard jr., Princeton '02, sent me at once the good news of your election to the Presidency of Princeton University. Indeed, knowing my interest, he was kind enough to telegraph it with a Hurrah for Princeton and the Class of '02, the finest, etc. Old Nassau had ever sent forth. I think this is finely illustrative of the good will and enthusiasm with which the news has everywhere been received, and you will be pleased, I am sure, to know of this general spontaneous expression.

Kindly permit me, too, to join my hearty good wishes and congratulations. I feel convinced it means a great deal for Princeton, and despite the heavy responsibilities that to-day confront the Executive officer of a progressive institution, it will have its rewards for you.

Particularly I beg leave to offer my congratulations to Mrs. Wilson, and to express the pleasure it gave me to meet her during my exceedingly pleasant glimpse of Princeton and to be at her board with you and yours while you were still "Herr Professor."

Sincerely yours,   John Bell Henneman.

ALS (WP, DLC).
[1] Professor of English at the University of the South and Editor of the *Sewanee Review*, Henneman had written the first extensive biographical sketch of Wilson. It is printed at Feb. 1, 1895, Vol. 9.

From Edward Otis Stanley[1]

My dear Sir: New York, June 14th, 1902.

I beg that you will accept from an entire stranger, hearty congratulations upon your elevation to the Presidency of Princeton University.

In choosing a college to which to send my son,[2] I considered particularly those institutions where I believed the chairs of history, of economics and of biology to be filled with special ability, and a chief one of the deciding reasons in my selecting Princeton was the fact that you were at the head of a department whose courses I thought the most valuable of any in the curriculum. May I now express the hope that the duties of administration will not take you wholly from lectures, and in any event I feel sure that you will always have an especial care over those studies which have been so brilliantly illuminated by your own work.

While I am not in sympathy with offering a degree in arts for such miscellaneous courses as some of the colleges are now doing, I had wondered whether Princeton would see fit to offer a little broader course in the sophomore year, possibly not making the classics compulsory in that year.

Though of sound mind in a sound body, my son will not take athletic preeminence to his college, but where firm christian character, high ideals and good scholarship count, I believe he will be a welcome student. Of a graduating class of fifty-seven in the East Orange High School, scattering to many colleges, the two head boys of the class, of whom my son is one, will go to Princeton, that is, presuming them to have been successful in their examinations of yesterday and the day before, and by their reports I judged that these had no terrors for the well prepared student any more than did the preliminaries of last year, which these two so easily passed.

With a profound regard for the retiring President of your University, I am nevertheless very glad that the whole of my son's college course is to be under your administration.

Very respectfully yours,   E. O. Stanley.

TLS (WP, DLC).

[1] Treasurer of the Title Guarantee & Trust Co. of New York and a resident of East Orange, N. J.

[2] Edward Otis Stanley, Jr., Princeton, 1906.

To Richard Watson Gilder

My dear Mr. Gilder,   Princeton, 16 June, 1902

It was a most generous impulse that led you to write your kind note of the tenth![1] I believe I am more glad that you think something will be lost by my not writing than that you think that something will be gained by my being President of Princeton. I dare say my pen is only for "occasional addresses" for some years to come,—but some day, back to the thing I love. Meantime I am deeply the better for your note.

Faithfully and cordially Yours,   Woodrow Wilson

ALS (R. W. Gilder Papers, NN).
    [1] It is missing.

To Edward Perkins Clark[1]

My dear Mr. Clark: Princeton, N. J., June 16th, 1902.

Thank you most sincerely for your kind letter of congratulation.[2] Thank you also (or is it not you that I must thank) for all the many generous things which the "Evening Post" has said of me during the past few days.[3] If anything could make a man fairly believe in himself, it would be the support of such men as yourself and of such real friends of education as the "New York Evening Post." You have given me a great deal of pleasure and a great deal of courage.

Very sincerely yours,   Woodrow Wilson

TLS (Presidential Coll., CtY).
    [1] Editorial writer for the New York *Evening Post*.
    [2] It is missing.
    [3] See the New York *Evening Post*, June 10, 1902, particularly the editorial, "President Woodrow Wilson."

To John Franklin Jameson

My dear Jameson: Princeton, N. J. June 16th, 1902.

Your letter of congratulation[1] is delightful. Nothing has given me so much pleasure in respect to my election as President of Princeton as the delight and generous praise of my friends. They all seem just so much the nearer to me because of their praise and hearty friendship. One of the pleasant things to look forward to is that in the course of the many journeys to which a college President is doomed, I shall at least enjoy the great compensation of running upon dear friends like yourself. Mrs. Wilson joins me in the warmest regards.

Very sincerely yours,   Woodrow Wilson

TLS (J. F. Jameson Papers, DLC).
  1 It is missing.

To Barrett Wendell[1]

My dear Mr. Wendell,   Princeton, 16 June, '02

Your letter[2] has heartened and gratified me not a little: it was thoughtful and kind in you to write it. When a man is called to a post of great responsibility what he wants is not praise and applause but a quiet word of cheer and confidence from a few men who know and care and speak a sober meaning. I thank you most heartily,—and am deeply pleased to think that I can count you among my friends.

Cordially Yours,   Woodrow Wilson

ALS (in possession of Henry Bartholomew Cox).
  1 Professor of English at Harvard University.
  2 It is missing.

To Thomas Nelson Page

My dear Mr. Page,   Princeton, 16 June, '02

It was generous of you to write your kind letter of the thirteenth.[1] I value it more than I can say as an evidence of your confidence and friendship,—I believe I value most of all your high estimate of the value of my literary work. No doubt my pen must be laid by for some years to come,—except for "occasional addresses"!—but my "History of the American People," as the Harpers have made me call it, will, I hope, be finished within a couple of weeks, and published in the Autumn,—and I shall wait to see what the judicious think of that before I make up my own mind whether there is net loss in my silence.

Thank you for what you say about the headship of the University of Virginia. I *was* approached on the subject, and I shall ever account that one of the chief honours of my life.

I wish we might oftener see you here and make a real comrade of you.

With warmest appreciation and regard,

Faithfully Yours,   Woodrow Wilson

ALS (T. N. Page Papers, NcD).
  1 It is missing.

The very legations at Peking were invested in deadly ~~~~ *siege* by the insur-
gents; and America with the other nations whose representatives were threatened sent troops to their relief. America played her new part with conspicuous success. Her voice told for peace, conciliation, justice, and yet
for a firm vindication of sovereign rights, at every turn of the difficult
business; her troops were among the first to withdraw, to the Philippines,
when their presence became unnecessary; the world noted a calm poise of
judgment, a steady confidence as if of conscious power in the utterances of
the American Secretary of State; the new functions of America in the East
were plain enough for all to see. The old landmarks of politics within the
United States themselves seemed, meanwhile, submerged. The southern States
were readjusting their elective suffrage so as to exclude the illiterate
negroes and so in ~~large~~ part undo the mischief of reconstruction; and yet
the rest of the country withheld its hand from interference. Sections began to draw together with a new understanding of one another. Parties were
turning to the new days to come and to the common efforts of peace. States-
men knew that *it was to be their task to* ~~their task was to be the~~ release ~~of~~ the energies of the country for the great day of trade and of manufacture which was to change the
face of the world: to ease the processes of labour, govern capital in the
interest of those who were its servants in pushing the great industries of
the country to their final value and perfection, and make law the instrument, not of justice merely, but also of social progress.

*The final page of Wilson's own typescript
of "A History of the American People"*

From Elgin Ralston Lovell Gould[1]

My dear Wilson: [New York] June 16/02.

I cannot tell you how delighted I feel over your promotion. And it has been so worthily won! May you have complete success! You deserve it.

I had a talk with Mr. Alexander the other evening and I was delighted to learn that your election was entirely unanimous.

God bless you and give you wisdom and strength for your new and important duties.   Your old friend   E. R. L. Gould

ALS (WP, DLC).
[1] An old friend from Johns Hopkins days, at this time president of the City and Suburban Homes Co. of New York and City Chamberlain of New York.

From Daniel Moreau Barringer

My dear Wilson: Philadelphia, Pa. June 16, 1902.

About ten days ago I went with Ned Trotter[1] to look at some alleged mining properties in Virginia, and did not see a newspaper or hear anything that was going on in the outside world until my arrival at the University of Virginia, where I went to see my cousin and very intimate friend, Dr. Paul B. Barringer.[2] I learned there to my great joy that the great honor of President of Princeton University had been conferred upon you, and immediately went to the telegraph office and tried to give voice in a short telegram[3] to my feelings. I merely wish to confirm now what I said then,—that I congratulate you with all my heart that this great office has become yours. It is not only a great office but a great trust, the full importance of which no one can realize better than you. In wishing you "God speed" I do so with a great feeling of satisfaction, for I know that the interests of Princeton University will be always the nearest to your heart after those of your family. You have worked hard, and I am delighted to know that the world has recognized the value of your work in this manner.

I find a letter from Billy Wilder asking me to join in the procession that went to Princeton to congratulate you, and I only wish that it had been my good fortune to be one of them. Nevertheless I am with them in spirit.

I am sure that Mrs. Barringer,—whom I have not seen since my return,—will be almost as glad as I am that this great honor has been conferred upon you.

As always with kindest regards, and every good wish for you and yours, I am,

Your friend and classmate,   Daniel Moreau Barringer

TLS (WP, DLC).
[1] Edward Hough Trotter '79, dealer in and manufacturer of metals in Philadelphia.
[2] Paul Brandon Barringer, M.D., Professor of Physiology and Materia Medica at the University of Virginia since 1888 and Chairman of the Faculty of the same institution since 1896.
[3] It is missing.

From Robert Randolph Henderson

My dear Woodrow   Cumberland [Md.] June 16/02

My meager telegram[1] did not half express my great delight at your election. It was the sudden and unexpected realization of an ambition that your friends have cherished for you ever since you have been at Princeton, and coming as it did, it is an honor we are all proud of for you. I firmly believe that at last exactly the right man has been found for our dear old University, and I shall have all the greater love for her and pride in her to think that she is under your guidance. The news came when we were all very much troubled at my mothers serious illness, and it brightened and gladdened us not a little. I am thankful to say she now seems out of danger. I know how pleased Mrs. Wilson must be at this latest appreciation of your worth, and we have thought a great deal of her, too.

Please give her and accept for yourself our sincerest congratulations, and feel sure, my dear old boy, that every true Princetonian is enthusiastically behind you in your new responsibilities, and believe me, as ever your affectionate friend

Robert R. Henderson

Don't bother about answering this, but sometime when you have leisure, later on, send me a line to let us know how you all are.

R.R.H.

ALS (WP, DLC).
[1] It is missing.

From Edward Graham Elliott

My dear Professor Wilson,   Heidelberg, June 16th [1902]

I have just heard this morning from George [Howe] the good news that you have been elected President of the University, and

I hasten to send you my heartiest congratulations upon the acquirement of this new honor, and my best wishes for unbounded success in your new duties. But it is not only you who are to be congratulated. Princeton is at the same time most fortunate, and graduates, old and young, will rejoice when they hear of your election and will look forward to a new era of prosperity. Furthermore I believe they will be stirred to more exalted enthusiasm and more substantial assistance through the confidence they have in you.

I rejoice most heartily in this great honor that has been paid you and again congratulating you, and with all good wishes for your success in this new field, believe me
Most sincerely   Edward G. Elliott.

ALS (WP, DLC).

From Charles Richard Nisbet[1]

My dear Sir: Atlanta, Ga.   June 16th., 1902.

Allow me to add my congratulations to those which I know have poured in from your friends and admirers North & South.

Since it has seemed best to call one who is not a minister of the gospel to preside over this great institution, I rejoice that Princeton has had the good sense to select so worthy a man as yourself. Being a native of the South, your administration will doubtless attract Southern sympathy and support, and, as Princeton Seminary has for years been silently breaking down sectionalism in the Church,[2] so Princeton Univernity [University] may become a strong factor in breaking down this same spirit in the State. I should rejoice to see the conditions at Princeton as they were before the war.

I send under separate cover a marked copy of the Atlanta Constitution. Mr. Lucien L. Knight,[3] one of my Elders, and an editorial writer on the Constitution, gives you quite a complimentary notice in the same, which I thought you might be pleased to see, though his facts are a little twisted.[4] Mr. Knight will leave the journalistic field for the ministry, and expects to enter Princeton Seminary in September.[5]

Again extending congratulations upon your deserved elevation, and desiring to be remembered to Mrs. Wilson, I am,
Very sincerely,   Chas. R. Nisbet.

TLS (WP, DLC).
[1] Pastor of the Westminster Presbyterian Church of Atlanta.
[2] Nisbet had attended Princeton Theological Seminary in 1895-96 and 1897-98.
[3] Lucian Lamar Knight, at this time Literary Editor of the Atlanta *Constitu-*

tion. He afterward wrote the brief biographical sketch, *Woodrow Wilson, the Dreamer and the Dream* (Atlanta, 1924).

4 "Princeton's New President," editorial in the Atlanta *Constitution,* June 11, 1902. One of Knight's errors was to say that Mrs. Wilson was the daughter of the Rev. Dr. Isaac Stockton Keith Axson of Savannah.

5 Knight entered Princeton Theological Seminary in 1902 and was graduated in 1905. After a brief career as a Presbyterian minister, he retired until 1908, when he became editor of the *Atlanta Georgian.*

From Beverley Randolph Wellford, Jr.[1]

My Dear Sir   Richmond, Va., June 16. 1904 [1902]

Permit me as one of the oldest of the Southern Alumni of Princeton to express to you my great gratification at yr election as President of the University—& my earnest & prayerful hopes for a success in yr high office to be protracted for very many years.

Please present my kindest remembrances to your honored Father & believe me

Most Truly Yrs   B. R. Wellford Jr.

ALS (WP, DLC).
1 Princeton, 1847, Judge of the Circuit Court of the City of Richmond.

To Alexander James Kerr[1]

My dear Kerr: Princeton, N. J. June 17th, 1902.

Thank you most sincerely for your telegram of congratulation.[2] I appreciate most deeply the friendship and the thoughtful kindness which prompted it. It is such things that make a man take heart and go forward.

Very cordially yours,   Woodrow Wilson

TLS (in possession of Henry W. Bragdon).
1 Princeton, 1879, pastor of the Broome Street Tabernacle, New York, 1895-1902, and of the Memorial Church, Wilkes-Barre, Pa., 1902-17.
2 It is missing.

To Robert Randolph Henderson

My dear Bob: Princeton, N. J. June 17th, 1902

Thank you with all my heart for your telegram of June 11th.[1] It delights me more than I can say to have such support and endorsement from you and the other '79 men, who stand so close to me.

Faithfully and cordially yours,   Woodrow Wilson

TLS (WC, NjP).
1 It is missing.

To Cleveland Hoadley Dodge

My dear Cleve: Princeton, N. J. June 17th, 1902.

Thank you with all my heart for your telegram of June 11th.[1] It delights me more than I can say to have such support and endorsement from you and the other '79 men who stand so close to me.

     Faithfully and cordially yours,   Woodrow Wilson

TLS (WC, NjP).
[1] It is missing.

To Edward Washburn Hopkins[1]

My dear Hopkins: Princeton, N. J. June 17th, 1902.

Your cordial letter of the 10th[2] went to the right spot. It does me more good than I can say to know that the men who have been closest to me are the men that believe in me, and in my capacity to undertake the great task to which I have been appointed; and I value your letter no less as an evidence of friendship than as an evidence of confidence. Mrs. Wilson joins me in the warmest regard.

     Faithfully yours,   Woodrow Wilson

TCL (RSB Coll., DLC).
[1] Professor of Sanskrit and Comparative Philology at Yale University, who had taught with Wilson at Bryn Mawr College.
[2] It is missing.

To Richard Theodore Ely

My dear Dr. Ely: Princeton, N. J. June 17th, 1902.

It was very kind of you to write me in such cordial terms about my election to the presidency of my University, and I appreciate it both as a mark of friendship and a mark of confidence. I shall take the more heart in what I have to do because men like yourself are so generous in believing in me.

     Very cordially yours,   Woodrow Wilson

TLS (R. T. Ely Papers, WHi).

To Daniel Moreau Barringer

My dear Moreau: Princeton, N. J. June 17th, 1902.

Your telegram of the 15th gave me the greatest possible pleasure. I do not know of anything that pleases me more or gives me more hope in the unexpected situation in which I find myself, than the cordial and generous support which the men whom I trust and love have given me. Thank you with all my heart.

Where do you spend the winters? Now that I am to go about and not stick at my desk, cannot we not see something of each other?

Faithfully and cordially yours,   Woodrow Wilson

TLS (D. M. Barringer Papers, NjP).

To Walter Hines Page

My dear Page: Princeton, N. J. June 17th, 1902.

I am sincerely obliged to you for your letter of the 10th.[1] It was certainly a thoughtful kindness on your part to write it. I do not know of any man whose backing and confidence I would rather have than yours in the difficult thing I have now undertaken.

Faithfully and cordially yours,   Woodrow Wilson

TLS (W. H. Page Papers, MH).
  [1] It is missing.

From George Black Stewart

My Dear Prof. Wilson: Auburn, N. Y. June 17, 1902.

I have just returned from a trip to South Dakota where I was engaged during Princeton's Commencement week in meeting some important appointments. I take this first opportunity of extending to you my congratulations upon your election to the Presidency of Princeton University. I sincerely regret that I was not able to be present at the late meeting of the Board for it proved to be one of the most important meetings of that body. I, however, desire to assure you of my cordial and loyal support in your administration of the high office to which you have been elected and for which you have so many admirable qualifications. I trust and expect that your administration will be a brilliant and successful one and I hope it may be for a long period. You may always count upon my honest endeavor to cooperate with you to the extent of my ability to bring about the results which you in the administration of your office desire.

With kindest regards and best wishes, I remain,

Yours sincerely,   Geo. B. Stewart.

TLS (WP, DLC).

To Robert Bridges

My dear Bob: Princeton, N. J. June 18th, 1902.

I would a great deal rather write you a letter with my own
hand than dictate it, but I must take the shortest method for
the present.

I saw you on Saturday and you know what I think about your
pleasure and support in such a matter as my election to the
presidency; but I want to put down in a form more distinct and
permanent my feeling of deep gratitude and delight that I have
such close friends as yourself to stand by me and give me strength.
I shall both need and enjoy you more now than ever before. In
haste, but deep affection,

                    Faithfully yours,   Woodrow Wilson

TLS (WC, NjP).

To Frederick Jackson Turner

My dear Turner: Princeton, N. J. June 18th, 1902.

Thank you with all my heart for your telegram of congratulation.[1] I do not know any one from whom I would rather have
had so cordial a message. I hope that as a college President it
will be one of the rewards of having to go about a great deal to
the ends of the country, that I shall be able once in a while to
get hold of you and renew face to face the delightful friendship
which I so value. With warmest messages of friendship from
Mrs Wilson and myself for both Mrs. Turner and you, as ever,

                Cordially and faithfully yours,   Woodrow Wilson

TLS (Archives, WU).
[1] It is missing.

To Nicholas Murray Butler

My dear Dr. Butler: Princeton, N. J. June 18th, 1902.

I particularly appreciated the telegram which you sent me
immediately after reaching New York on the 9th.[1] It was, I
believe, the first that reached me, and came as a happy omen of
the comradship in college work which I hope will draw us closer
and closer together. Please thank Mrs. Butler for her share in
the congratulation, and believe me, with warmest regard,

                    Very cordially yours,   Woodrow Wilson

TLS (N. M. Butler Papers, NNC).
[1] It is missing.

To Sarah Baxter Bird

My dear Mrs. Bird: Princeton, N. J.   June 18th, 1902.

I know that you will pardon a very much rushed man for dictating a letter, and a short letter, when he would very much rather write a long one with his own hand. I am obliged to postpone that indulgence, but I cannot postpone expressing to you and to Mrs. Smith[1] my delight at the telegrams which you have sent me.[2] It a great deal heightens my pleasure in the great confidence the Trustees have shown in me, that my dear friends whose affection and confidence I particularly covet, should be so pleased at my promotion. I hope it will not be so very long before we may talk the matter over together, and I may see on your faces the delight in which I so greatly rejoice. With all affection,   Sincerely yours,   Woodrow Wilson

TLS (Berg Coll., NN).
  [1] Mrs. Bird's daughter, Saida Bird (Mrs. Victor) Smith.
  [2] Both telegrams are missing.

From Charles Howard Shinn[1]

My dear friend—   Niles, Calif.   June 18, 1902

I understood fully abt your position in reference to the Forestry matter but did not reply to your letter[2] earlier because there was no real news. I am only writing now to "hurra" over your new honors. No one in America is more justly where he belongs, by virtue of tact, love, & knowledge. It is a good thing for Princeton— I wish there were more of you—and another you for this side of the continent. When you have a photo "in gown" send it out, please. And some day come West & see us. . . .
          Yours as ever,   C. H. Shinn

ALS (WP, DLC).
  [1] An old friend from Johns Hopkins days, Shinn was at this time an agent of the United States Bureau of Forestry and was soon to be appointed head forest ranger, Department of the Interior, assigned to the Sierra Reserve in California.
  [2] It is missing.

From John James McCook

My dear Dr. Wilson: New York, June 18th. 1902.

I was present during the proceedings of the Board on Monday up to and including your election as President of the University, and I regret that my representative duties at West Point[1] deprived me of the pleasure of seeing you personally during some part of the Commencement proceedings to express my hearty congratulations.

I do not believe that a man was ever before brought to the head of a great American University with such absolutely cordial unanimity. You are entirely sure of the loyalty of the Board of Trustees and humanly speaking you can depend upon the hearty and sympathetic cooperation of the members of the Governing Body of the University.

With renewed congratulations, and hoping that when you next come to New York you will let me know a day in advance so that we may have the pleasure of lunching together at the Lawyers' Club, in this building[2] when we can talk over some matters of common interest.   Faithfully yours,   John J. McCook

TLS (WP, DLC).
   [1] McCook represented Princeton at the Centennial of the United States Military Academy at West Point, June 9 to June 12, 1902.
   [2] At 120 Broadway.

From Thomas Armstrong Jacobs[1]

Dear Sir.   Youngstown, Ohio, June 18' 02

Your letter of the 16' is at hand. I want to congratulate you upon your election to the presidency of Princeton. It is an honor to any man, and goes to show the good judgement of our committee in selecting you to lecture on our course. We are even more anxious to have you now.

Acting upon your suggestion to make some date the latter part of September, I give you from Sept. 15-19 and and [sic] Sept. 22 and 24. I trust you will find it possible to come to Youngstown and that one of these dates will be satisfactory to you.[2]

Very Truly Yours   Thomas A. Jacobs Secy

TLS (WP, DLC).
   [1] Secretary of the People's Institute of Youngstown, Ohio, and Assistant Cashier of the Mahoning National Bank of the same city.
   [2] Wilson's reply is missing; however, he did not lecture in Youngstown in 1902.

From David Fentress[1]

My dear Professor Wilson   Chicago, June 18th 1902.

The papers advise me of your recent election to the Presidency of Princeton. As a friend & admirer of yours, I write to extend my hearty congratulations & assurance of my belief in the progress & prosperity of the University under your guidance. Though

I cannot speak officially for "The Glorious Class of '96," yet I can, by right of intuition, pledge its loyalty to Princeton's new leader.

With kind regards for Mrs. Wilson—

I am—Sincerely & loyaly yours   David Fentress

ALS (WP, DLC).
[1] Princeton, 1896, at this time in the legal department of the Illinois Central Railroad in Chicago.

From Andrew Varick Stout Anthony[1]

My dear Professor: New York City   June 18, 1902.

I am in receipt of your letter of the 16th inst.[2] and the parcel.

It is certainly no burden for me to place the illustrations. My only fear was that, as many of the pictures are not directly referred to in the text, I might not place them according to your wishes. Such judgment as I have shall be most carefully exercised, and I can only hope that the result may please you.

I have seen Mr. Pallsitts,[3] at the Lenox Library, to secure his services in authenticating the various old plates and documents, and in the two hours I was with him I was led to marvel at his exhaustive knowledge in the matter of Americana. He is not certain that his engagements will permit him to do the work required, but when I undertake a commission of this sort I am fairly insistent, and I believe I interested him. I shall have his decision tomorrow.

While looking over the sheets of the volume, page by page, he made some notes that are very valuable, and even though he does not do what we wish he has certainly made the matter much easier for whoever does the work.

Kindly feel assured that I shall do my best in the interest of the new President and his History.

Sincerely Yours,   A. V. S. Anthony

ALS (WP, DLC).
[1] Artist, engraver, and magazine writer connected with the Literary Department of Harper and Brothers.
[2] It is missing.
[3] Victor Hugo Paltsits, Assistant Librarian of the Lenox Library in New York, author, editor, and historical writer.

To Andrew Varick Stout Anthony

My dear Mr. Anthony: Princeton, N. J.   June 19th, 1902.

Let me thank you for your unusually kind letter of yesterday. I have not the least uneasiness about your taste and judgment in the arrangement of the illustrations; and the generous kindness with which you undertake the whole burden of the matter, adds not a little to the great pleasure I have already had in being associated with you in the preparation of the book.

It is very encouraging to hear that you have some prospect of getting Mr. Pallsitz's services in the matter of discovering and authenticating illustrative matter. I hope that if he does undertake the task with you that you will express to him my own pleasure that we shall have the benefit of his invaluable services.

The writing of the last chapter of Volume V is coming slowly on amidst a great many interruptions; but I still hope to have almost all, if not all of it, finished by the 1st. of July. I shall then have left only the very entertaining task of preparing an index. With renewed expressions of regard and appreciation,
                        Very sincerely yours,   Woodrow Wilson

TLS (MH).

To Edward Ingle

My dear Ingle: Princeton, N. J.   June 19th, 1902.

Thank you very much indeed for your note of congratulation, and for the interesting and amusing clippings which you sent me.[1] It is very flattering to think that there should be a competition between different places to claim my boyhood.[2]
                        Very sincerely yours,   Woodrow Wilson

Mrs. Wilson especially enjoyed the clippings and would be most grateful for any others you may happen to see![3]

TLS (E. Ingle Papers, MdHi).
    [1] Ingle's letter and enclosures are missing. However, the clippings were probably editorials on Wilson's election to the presidency of Princeton from the Baltimore *Sun*, June 10, 1902; the *Baltimore News*, June 10, 1902; the *Baltimore American*, June 11, 1902; the *Nashville*, Tenn., *American*, June 11, 1902; and the *Richmond Times*, reprinted in the *Baltimore News*, June 14, 1902.
    [2] The *Nashville American* said that Wilson spent most of his boyhood and young manhood in Clarksville, Tenn.; the *Richmond Times*, that he was born and reared in Virginia, and was "a Virginian through and through."
    [3] EAWhw.

To Edward Otis Stanley

My dear Sir: Princeton, N. J.   June 19th, 1902.

I have been very much interested in your kind letter of the 14th, and shall look forward with interest to meeting your son. I am particularly interested by what you tell me of your reasons for choosing this University as the place of your son's education.

We are of the conservative school in education here, and I do not think we shall ever get too far away from the classical model; but I do think it probable that we shall make changes in our Sohpomore [Sophomore] year, which will render the course in many ways more elastic and attractive.

With sincere regard and appreciation,

Very truly yours,   Woodrow Wilson

TLS (WC, NjP).

From Moses Taylor Pyne

My dear Tommy   Princeton, N. J.   June 19/02

President Roosevelt writes—"Woodrow Wilson is a perfect trump. I am overjoyed at his election and unless my arrangements render it absolutely impossible to get back in time I will attend his inauguration with the utmost pleasure."[1] He has since, as you know, written Mr. Cleveland that he would certainly be present.[2]   Very truly yours   M. Taylor Pyne

ALS (WP, DLC) with WWhw figures on env.
  [1] T. Roosevelt to C. H. Dodge, June 16, 1902, Elting E. Morison *et al.* (eds.), *The Letters of Theodore Roosevelt* (8 vols., Cambridge, Mass., 1951-54), III, 275.
  [2] "Your letter pleased me. I had already written that if I could fix two or three appointments previously made I would come; but I now write without any reservation to say I certainly shall come. It is a real pleasure to do so, for I have long regarded Mr. Wilson as one of the men who had constructive scholarship and administrative ability; and I am very glad from every standpoint that he is to be the new President of Princeton." T. Roosevelt to G. Cleveland, June 17, 1902, *ibid.*, p. 277.

From William Royal Wilder

My dear 'Tommy' Wilson,   New York, June 19th. 1902.

Your note to hand.[1] Of course, you are aware that the Class Committee and which for the time being should be characterized as the 'Coronation Committee' is actively engaged in getting ready for the solemnities of October 25th.[2] Cuyler was to confer with you and find out whether a dinner on that evening, which I think is Saturday, to be given by the Class to you, will be regarded with favor. Let me hear from you as soon as possible. I think it would be easier to get the men there Saturday night than to have them Friday night.[3] I am sending out a general alarum.

I didn't think of speaking to you Wednesday about the site for our Building.[4] I agree with you that we should stand out for the Nassau Street site in front of Dickinson Hall if there is any possibility of getting it. I do hope that Cuyler will be able to settle with the Committee on Grounds and Buildings, the site between now and the opening of the College.

When next in the City I wish you would make it convenient, if possible, to drop in upon me.

Faithfully yours,   Wm. R. Wilder

TLS (WP, DLC).

[1] It is missing.

[2] That is, Wilson's inauguration as thirteenth President of Princeton University.

[3] The dinner was held on Saturday night, October 25.

[4] The Class of 1879 had decided to present a dormitory to the university as its twenty-fifth anniversary gift. This building, Seventy-Nine Hall, dedicated on June 11, 1904, stands on Washington Road below McCosh Hall.

From William Battle Phillips[1]

My dear Wilson: Austin, Texas, June 19 1902

I am just in from a long trip along the frontier between Mexico and Texas and have seen the notice of your election to the Presidency of Princeton. It has been some time since we sat in the class at Davidson College . . . and our work has led us in different directions. But whether in Canada, Nova Scotia, Cuba, New Mexico, Arizona, Old Mexico or Texas I have recalled you with a great deal of pleasure. In fact I am now posing as one of the sub-minor prophets, for I told some friends several years ago, when we were talking about you that we should see you President of Princeton. It has come to pass and I offer my congratulations both to yourself and to Princeton. . . .

With kindest regards,

I am very truly yours   Wm. B. Phillips.

TLS (WP, DLC).

[1] An old friend from Davidson College days, at this time Director of the University of Texas Mineral Survey.

From Frederick Morgan Davenport[1]

Dear Professor Wilson: Yonkers, N.Y., June 19, 1902.

It is a delight to me to know of your elevation to the Presidency of Princeton. I am sure that all Wesleyan men who knew you, as I did, for that all too brief time in the lecture-room and on the campus at Middletown, will rejoice with me. The boys want you to come up to New York, probably on the evening of the 8th of December next, as a guest of honor at the annual banquet of the Wesleyan Alumni Association, to be held at the Waldorf-Astoria.

We are planning for a big time this year, and we want you there. I will write you again in the fall, but we are letting you know about it early enough so that your other engagements can just be arranged accordingly.[2]

I am still at Columbia, in postgraduate work in sociology and economics, and hope to finish the work for my doctor's degree next year.[3]

> Very sincerely yours,   Frederick M. Davenport

ALS (WP, DLC).

[1] Wesleyan University, 1889, later Professor of Law and Politics at Hamilton College, member of the New York Senate, and Progressive candidate for Governor of New York in 1914.

[2] It is not known whether Wilson spoke to the Wesleyan Alumni Association in New York on December 8, 1902, or, indeed, whether the organization met at or near this time. Wilson left no notes for such a speech, and the New York newspapers and Wesleyan University publications do not mention a meeting of the Wesleyan Alumni Association in New York in December 1902.

[3] He actually received the Ph.D. from Columbia in 1905.

From George Walter Prothero

My dear Sir,   London, 19 June 1902

I am sending you herewith two copies of the text & bibliography of your chapter on "State Rights," & shall be much obliged if you would return them corrected as soon as you can conveniently do so. I also send a specimen bibliography—one that will appear in Vol. I, as a guide; & instructions showing how we want the bibliography arranged. I am afraid it will be rather troublesome to you to re-arrange your bibliography, so as to bring it into more or less of harmony with the rest; but it wd. be a very great convenience to us if you cd. do this, as it will be very difficult if not impossible for any one but the author to do this without making serious mistakes.

May I be allowed to express my admiration for the manner in which you have treated the subject in your chapter, & for the style in which it is written? In the latter respect, especially, it is certainly the most successful bit of work we have yet received for volume VII.   Yours very truly   G. W. Prothero

ALS (WP, DLC).

From Abram Winegardner Harris[1]

My dear President Wilson: Port Deposit Md.   19 June 1902

I write to extend you a cordial invitation to deliver the address upon Founder's Day at the Jacob Tome Institute. This will be

October 1. The exercises are usually held in the afternoon, and this year they will be in the memorial building just completed. This section and the Institute have a strong interest in Princeton and in yourself, and I very much hope you will find it possible to accept the invitation. The fee to cover expenses has usually been $50, but the Institute will be glad to place this at a figure that will be satisfactory to you.[2]

I mail under another cover a circular of the boarding school for boys.

I cannot neglect this opportunity to express my delight in your appointment to the great position as President of Princeton.

Yours very truly,   A. W. Harris

TLS (WP, DLC).
[1] Director of the Jacob Tome Institute, a boys' school in Port Deposit, Md., founded by Jacob Tome in 1889. Harris became President of Northwestern University in 1906.
[2] Wilson's reply is missing, but he declined the invitation.

To Robert Underwood Johnson

My dear Mr. Johnson: Princeton, N. J. June 20th, 1902.

I am sincerely obliged to you for your kind letter of congratulation.[1] You must know how much such spontaneous expressions of friendship and confidence put a man in heart. I dare say that my election to the presidency of Princeton will cut me off from some of the things that I love most; but probably if I should again have time to write I shall have more to write about than I should have had, had I sat still for many years more at my quiet desk. With warmest regard and appreciation,

Sincerely yours,   Woodrow Wilson

TLS (WC, NjP).
[1] It is missing.

Thomas Alexander Hoyt to Ellen Axson Wilson

My Darling Ellie,   Bryn Mawr [Pa.], June 20. 1902.

A day or two after you were here, I had a relapse, from which I am just recovering.

Our joy in the accession of dear Woodrow to the Presidency is very great. I congratulate him & you most warmly. It is what I expected, but its suddenness was a surprise. He has at length reached the position which I believed he would attain, & for which he is eminently fitted, & in which I predict for him great success.

Tell me how it happened at this time. Your promise to come next week holds out the hope of hearing all about it from your lips. Do not disappoint me. I wish Woodrow could come to see us, but this may be too much to expect

My attack was caused, the Dr. thinks, by distress at Dr. Palmer's death.[1] . . .

I am not strong enough to write more, but I wish you to know how deeply I sympathize with you in the great event which has lifted Woodrow to an office of such commanding influence.

With love to him & the children

Ever fondly & devotedly,   Uncle T

ALS (WP, DLC).
[1] The Rev. Dr. Benjamin Morgan Palmer, who had died in New Orleans on May 25, 1902.

From David Murray

Dear Sir   [New Brunswick, N. J.] June 20/02

At a meeting of the Trustees of Rutgers College held June 18, 1902, the honorary degree of doctor of laws was unanimously conferred upon you in recognition of your eminent services in the fields of education and literature.

Trusting that this action may be acceptable to you, believe me

Very sincerely yours   David Murray

Secretary of the Trustees

ALS (WP, DLC).

From Percy Rivington Pyne[1]

My dear Wilson   [New York] June 20 1902

I cannot tell you how much pleased I am to have you President of Princeton. I congratulate you on having one of the most delightful positions I can conceive of and congratulate all who are interested in Princeton in having you at the head of the University. Wishing you every success and with kind regards I am

Very sincerely yours   Percy R. Pyne.

Cleve Dodge, Harry Thompson[2] and I have just spent two days on Cleve's yacht and we drank your health with great delight.

ALS (WP, DLC).
[1] Princeton, 1878, Wall Street banker, and brother of Moses Taylor Pyne.
[2] Henry Burling Thompson, born, Darby, Pa., Aug. 6, 1857; B.S., College of New Jersey, 1877. Active in the cotton textile business, he was president of the United States Finishing Co., 1913-33. Chairman of the Delaware Republican State Committee, 1898-1902, and member of the Republican National Committee from Delaware in 1898. Trustee of Princeton University, 1906-35. Died Nov. 20, 1935.

From Orin Grant Libby

Dear Sir: Madison [Wisc.] June 20, 1902

I sent the maps today as I was delayed beyond my expectations.[1] I am not sure I should have had the courage to promise so thorough a revision of the old map had I known how much work was involved. The expert engineering labor alone cost me $12, and I had hardly counted on that at all. I have tried to revise in line with recent criticism. You will notice an effort to allow for scantiness of population and to show elevation and topography. I have asked to have the first copies of the map sent me, two of each, in order to complete my copyright. I presume there is no objection to having these original maps returned. Shall you have the work ready by next fall?

Yours truly   O. G. Libby

ALS (WP, DLC).
[1] Prints of Libby's revised maps of votes in the thirteen states on ratification of the Constitution are tipped in the third volume of *A History of the American People*, facing pp. 78 and 80.

From William Henry Roberts[1]

My dear Sir: Philadelphia, Pa., June 20 1902

Permit me at the beginning of this letter to tender to you my sincere congratulations upon your succession to the Presidency of Princeton University. This is a great responsibility, but I believe that you will be equal thereto. May the God of your fathers strengthen you for all duty, and enable you to render great service both to the cause of education and to the Presbyterian Church.

The Moderator of the General Assembly, Rev. Dr. Henry van Dyke, it gives me pleasure to state, has appointed you a member of the Assembly's Special Committee on Sustentation.[2] A list of the Committee is enclosed, and also a copy of the action of the Assembly appointing it.[3] I sincerely hope that you will be able to accept this appointment. As an Elder of our Church you must appreciate the need there is to give attention to the subject entrusted to the Committee, and we confidently look forward to your active participation in the work.[4]

I am, with sincere esteem and best wishes,

Yours very truly,   Wm. H. Roberts

TLS (WP, DLC).
[1] Stated Clerk of the General Assembly of the Presbyterian Church in the U.S.A.
[2] That is, for the care and relief of retired Presbyterian ministers.
[3] These enclosures are missing.

From Daniel Coit Gilman

My dear Wilson,   Berlin, June 21, 1902

My wife has just brought in an American paper of June 10, saying "did you know that President Patton has resigned & Woodrow Wilson is chosen in his place?" This is our first intimation of the great change & I have hastened to the room of our Ambassador, Mr. [Andrew Dickson] White, to give him this important & interesting piece of news.

Now, my dear friend, let me say to you that I greatly rejoice in your preferment. In every respect the choice seems to me most fitting and likely to add to the distinction of Princeton in the domain of scholarship & culture,—likely to increase your usefulness & happiness. I congratulate Princeton & I congratulate you,—& let me add the hope that five & twenty years hence, when you resign, there will be an orator with a silver tongue, ready to do you honor for a long & successful administration.[1]

Dr. Patton's resignation is a great surprise but I had suspected that some of the incidental duties of his chair had become irksome, & I can readily believe that he will be happier in a professorship & in the pulpit than he could be in the cares & perplexities which you, as a younger man will enter with a brave & exultant spirit.

Mrs. Gilman charges me to add her very warm regards & congratulations to you & Mrs. Wilson & I am

More than ever yours faithfully   D. C. Gilman

ALS (WP, DLC).
[1] He was of course referring to Wilson's tribute to him, printed at Feb. 21, 1902.

From Ira Remsen

My dear Dr. Wilson: Baltimore. June 21, 1902.

The news of your election to the Presidency of Princeton reached me at a time when my mind was very much occupied with home affairs, or I should have sent you a word of congratulation at once.

It is not surprising to me that your faculty and trustees should have selected you without hesitation. We who know you agree,

I am sure, that the right man has been chosen. Although a President of very short standing, I welcome you to the band, and hope we may have many opportunities to be of mutual help to each other.   Yours sincerely,   Ira Remsen

TLS (WP, DLC).

From Jabez Lamar Monroe Curry[1]

Dear Dr Wilson,   Evian-les-Bains, 21 June 1902

I have just read in an American paper of your election to the Presidency of the University of New Jersey. As a friend, as an American, as officially and intimately connected with education in the South I wish to express my sincere congratulations, and more my gratification that old Princeton has so honored herself and taken a still higher position in the great work.

For years I have wished and labored for your election as President of the University of Virginia. That being impossible I am glad that the old historic University has put you at its head.

My diplomatic and political career having closed forever I hope, with your good wishes and occasional help to do more and better work for free schools for all the people and higher education in the South.

I hope to reach home about the first of Sept
                    Yours faithfully   J. L. M. Curry.

ALS (WP, DLC).
   [1] Politician, educator, and diplomat, Curry in 1902 was Supervising Director of the Southern Education Board. When he wrote this letter, he was vacationing in Europe after having been a special envoy of the United States to Madrid on the occasion of the coming of age of Alfonso XIII.

From William Francis Magie

My dear "Tommy,"   Florence, Italy   June 21, 1902

Long before you get this you will have received my telegram,[1] & I hope have gathered from its somewhat meagre contents that I not only rejoice over the resignation, but most heartily and sincerely over your election & acceptance. I have heard nothing yet except from my Father,[2] to whom I had disclosed the situation as it stood on the day he came to take leave of me on the steamer. His account was complete so far as the formal actions of the Board went but of course there is still much that I want to know. I am hoping for a letter from Fine.

There is any amount of advice that I could give you that you don't need—but that can wait until it is wanted. You know that you can count on my loyal and earnest support in all the tasks which lie before you. We will do our best to make the Physics Department a credit to the University—and in all general Faculty business I will help all I can.

Mrs. Magie sends her congratulations too. After the steamer sailed I told her the situation & we have been anxiously waiting for news. We are very sorry for one thing—that you will have to give up your beautiful house, and that we shall lose you as neighbors. Will you give our kindest regards to Mrs. Wilson. . . .

I can't help saying that both Fine & I agreed, in the last talk we had together, that you were the one of all possible candidates whom we wished to be elected—only for West's sake I wouldn't say this to anyone else but you. You will not be able to set everything right in a day or a year, but we will stand by you until things *are* right—& I hope we shall have some years yet left to enjoy the fruits of our labors.

Your affectionate friend W. F. Magie

ALS (WP, DLC).
  [1] It is missing.
  [2] William Jay Magie, Princeton trustee and Chancellor of the State of New Jersey.

From St. Clair McKelway[1]

Reform Club 233 Fifth Avenue [New York]

Dear Dr. Wilson June 21 1902

While dining here and encountering the formidable picture of you in Harper's Weekly[2] I find myself impressed for at least the sixth time with a consciousness of having neglected a courtesy and postponed inclination in not sending to you my personal congratulations on your election to the Presidency of Princeton University. In my absence one of my staff did the Eagle's duty to its public on the event, in a sensible but lustreless way;[3] but that only made me realize that I should let you have a personal word.

I do most heartily congratulate you and wish you well. So does a lady who is a great admirer of your words and works—and a loving, loyal but not always encomiastic monitor of mine.

We have been a little puzzled about the forth puttings of the Sun[4] but have thought them to be unimportant, whether true, half-true or false, and rather think that dear Dr Van Dyke erred in jumping up, when jumping up was exactly the effect intended—which he should have serenely omitted[.] I like him very much but he is too visibly sensitive by half. My own conviction is that the attachment of mystery to your election is more ingenious than accurate[.] Good wine needs no bush. A right result requires no occult reason

You have cause to be satisfied with the salutations of the general press. I trust you have properly discounted the positive statements that you are to carry Princeton over from what it is to what it is to be. Princeton and you will carry one another to results that are doubtless predestined, but which I doubt can be infallibly predetermined. It doth not yet appear what we shall be here—as well as hereafter.

I have, frankly, but one misgiving. It involves the ability of Dr. Patton to let go, after you take hold—the liability of an unconsciousness of a duumvirate—where there should only be an autocratic presidency. This doubt is based on no disparagement of Dr. Patton[.] His is the most stimulating intellect I know of. He may be really unable to dam himself within the limitations of a chair where he has more than filled a throne. But that is for you to meet and manage. Let me know if I can be of any help to you, in your administration. As a regent my State makes its colleges in part my wards but my father's and brother's relations to Princeton[5] have always created for it a warm place in my heart. The plan was for me to enter it—when family finances broke down and the benefit of college study in residence was denied to me. But Old Nassau and her sons and her welfare have always been very precious to me.

Sincerely your Friend   St. Clair McKelway

ALS (WP, DLC).

1 Editor of the *Brooklyn Daily Eagle*.

2 On the cover of *Harper's Weekly*, XLVI (June 21, 1902).

3 In an editorial, "New President at Princeton," *Brooklyn Daily Eagle*, June 10, 1902.

4 The New York *Sun*, on June 10, 1902, received an anonymous letter, "typewritten and evidently composed by an educated man," which asserted that Patton had been " 'forced' out of the presidency as a bar to the progress of the university and as personally undesirable." Unfortunately, nothing more is known of the letter or its writer beyond what the *Sun* revealed in a description and summary of the letter in an editorial on June 13, 1902. The writer obviously either knew or had guessed at least a portion of the true story of the change of administration.

Following receipt of this letter, the *Sun* sent one or more reporters to Princeton and, between June 12 and June 14, 1902, published several sensational stories about the transfer of the university's chief executive office.

The *Sun* asserted in a front-page news story on June 12 that Patton, far from being forced out, had in fact deliberately planned to resign suddenly and to secure the speedy election of Wilson in order to foil a "clique" of trustees and faculty members who hoped to bring another man into the presidency. The *Sun* intimated that Henry van Dyke, Simon John McPherson, and Andrew Fleming West had had aspirations to the office and strongly hinted that van Dyke had been the leading contender of the trio. Patton, the *Sun* went on, was a "very progressive President in the last few months" who was advocating to a reluctant and divided faculty the broadening of the university's curriculum "especially as regards the choice of electives." The "clique" had been attempting to take advantage of the dissension in the faculty. "In selecting Dr. Wilson," the *Sun* continued, "President Patton found a man of such conservative tendencies that the opposition clique was robbed of the avenue of attack labelled 'too much progressiveness.' On the other hand, Dr. Wilson is sure to have a definite policy that will be independent of the caballing that is apt to grow up in a college community. Dr. Wilson has been distinguished in the present differences of opinion in the faculty by his consistent silence. The hotter the debates the tighter have his lips been held together."

However, the main argument of the *Sun*'s article of June 12 was that Patton, by his sudden resignation and nomination of Wilson, had foiled the "clique" and prevented an open scandal: "But had the election of the next President been deferred for twelve hours, so all students of the faculty politics of Princeton are now agreed, there would have been precipitated the most undignified scramble for President Patton's shoes that ever an American university saw."

Publication of this article caused van Dyke to issue a vigorous denial that he had ever been a candidate for the Princeton presidency. "The report," he said, "which connects my name with the Presidency of Princeton is absolutely and maliciously without truth. I have never considered the idea as a possible, much less a desirable, thing. If my name was discussed by any persons in authority, it was done entirely without my knowledge or consent. President Patton and Dr. Wilson both know this, and in the circumstances they owe it to themselves to say so." New York *Sun*, June 13, 1902.

Influenced perhaps by this strong statement, the *Sun*, in its second article published on June 13, shifted its ground and made West both the leading aspirant to the presidency and, with the aid of his friend, Grover Cleveland, the chief plotter of the "clique." Indeed, the writer of this article went so far as to suggest that West, in his capacity as a trustee of the Lawrenceville School, had "side-tracked" McPherson as a candidate for the Princeton presidency by having him brought from a highly successful pastorate in Chicago to be headmaster of the Lawrenceville School in 1899.

Finally, in a third article published on June 14, the *Sun* went even further to charge that West had forced out James Cameron Mackenzie, the first headmaster of the modern Lawrenceville School, in order to make a place for McPherson. Moreover, it specifically named McPherson and Cleveland as the trustees who were West's chief supporters in the "clique."

The *Sun* also printed an editorial on June 13 eulogizing Patton for his enlightened administration of Princeton and for his quick action to forestall the "clique." He had thus steered the institution "away from the hidden rocks of intrigue on which its honor and dignity might have been wrecked."

The *Sun*'s alleged revelations caused considerable stir. The New York *Evening Post* of June 14, 1902, printed an editorial ridiculing the *Sun*'s articles. The editors of the *Princeton Alumni Weekly*, understandably somewhat more disturbed, devoted two pages of the issue of June 14, 1902, to a refutation of the *Sun*'s charges.

5 His father, Dr. Alexander J. McKelway, had attended Princeton in 1830-31; his brother, John Ryan McKelway, was a member of the Class of 1857.

From Daniel Moreau Barringer

My dear Woodrow:　　　　　　　Philadelphia, Pa. June 21, 1902.

Many thanks, my dear friend, for your letter of yesterday.[1]

In answer to your question where I spend my winters, I can answer briefly. I have made my nest at Strafford, 16 miles from Philadelphia, where I have besides a mighty good wife three little birds of whom I am very proud,[2] all of whom I am anxious for you to know. I spend the greater part of my winters and summers at this place, and I hope it will not be long before you can pay us a visit. Mrs. Barringer most cordially unites with me in this invitation, and you may be sure that you will find a very hearty welcome whenever you care to pay us a visit. Any time will suit us. Telegraph me when you are coming and we shall be ready for you. Cannot you bring Mrs. Wilson with you?

Again congratulating you with all my heart, and Old Nassau as well, I am,

Faithfully your friend,   D. M. Barringer

P.S. Did you see the reference to yourself in the last Harper's?[3] Though brief it was admirable, and all of your friends say "Amen."   D. M. B.

TLS (WP, DLC).

[1] He meant "received yesterday." Wilson's letter was dated June 17, 1902.

[2] Brandon Barringer, born June 11, 1899; Daniel Moreau Barringer, Jr., born June 30, 1900; and Sarah Drew Barringer, born September 13, 1901.

[3] *Harper's Weekly*, XLVI (June 21, 1902), 777.

From Charles Howard McIlwain[1]

Dear Sir: Cambridge, Mass., June 21/1902.

I received your very kind letter in answer to mine inquiring about the degree of Ph.D. in history.

I cannot feel toward any other institution as I do toward Princeton, but I have decided to do as you suggested—stay here until I pass my general examination for the degree, which I hope to be able to do next year, and then try to get a position and come back here when I am ready for my special examination.[2]

I hope you will allow me to say how glad I was to hear of your election as President. The news gave me the greatest pleasure, as I knew it must have done to every Princeton man, especially those who have been in Princeton since 1891.

Very truly yours   C. H. McIlwain '94.

ALS (WP, DLC).

[1] Wilson's friend and former student, member of the Class of 1894.

[2] McIlwain received the A.M. degree in history from Harvard in 1903 and the Ph.D. in 1911 from the same institution.

From Franklin Woolman D'Olier[1]

My Dear Prof. Wilson   Burlington, N.J. 6/21/02

Being away from home on a short business trip, it was only yesterday that I heard of the change which had taken place at my Alma Mater.

Since I had the good luck to take your Law courses during

Junior & Senior year, I felt as though I knew you well enough, to write you a few lines & say to you in all sincerity that I know of no one, whom I would rather see at the head of Princeton, than yourself. Please excuse this short note, but I wished to congratulate you & also say how proud I feel, as a graduate, that you have accepted.

Very Sincerely Yours   Franklin W. D'Olier
Class of '98

ALS (WP, DLC).
₁ Princeton, 1898, at this time in business with his father in Burlington, N.J.

To Isaac Wayne MacVeagh

My dear Mr. McVeagh,   Princeton, 22 June, '02

I don't know any word of congratulation that has come to me that has done more than yours[1] to put me in heart,—and I thank you for it most warmly. After all it is the applause, not of the crowd, but of "the judicious" that we desire and strive to deserve, and your confidence outweighs a ton of ordinary congratulations. You may be sure that you have done a vast deal to put me in spirits to succeed.

With warmest regard and appreciation,

Sincerely Yours,   Woodrow Wilson

ALS (I. W. MacVeagh Papers, PHi).
₁ It is missing.

From Edith Gittings Reid

Cambridge June 22nd [1902]

The news has only been with me ten minutes of the great honor you are going to confer on Princeton. It is with very mixed feelings that I write my dear, dear friend. Of course I like the world to recognize what you are—but your strength & your history! I am glad that it is Princeton, if it must be, & not the Johns Hopkins[.] Your travail over the latter would certainly have been more disheartening—whereas there seems to be much buoyant youthful blood in Princeton's veins & it is inspiring to control eager willing steeds. I feel a little too anxious & serious to write. Harry wants me to tell you of his interest & pride in the matter. My dear love to Mrs. Wilson.

The marvelous beauty of Cambridge does me a world of good. "Ancient of days" are the words always in my mind

In looking at these great trees I thought of yours with fresh compassion. May all go well with you—and oh! take care of yourself   Ever your friend   Edith G. Reid

My address will be Brown Shiply London

ALS (WP, DLC).

From John Franklin Fort[1]

My Dear Dr Wilson   East Orange N.J.   June 22 1902

It is late, but with very great sincerity, that I extend my congratulations. Your election to the Presidency, I believe, means much for Princeton. The cordial way it has been received by the alumni and the public indicates universal approval. It must be quite gratifying to you.

The head of a great university in these days means much labor and great responsibility. The first of them is your delight, the latter I am sure you will meet and bear successfully.

I hope for your administration all that your ambition would have it, and for you personally good health and many years to accomplish it   Sincerely   J. Franklin Fort

ALS (WP, DLC).
[1] Justice of the Supreme Court of New Jersey and Wilson's predecessor as Governor of New Jersey.

From Theodore Roosevelt

My dear Mr. Wilson: White House. June 23, 1902.

As an American interested in that kind of productive scholarship which tends to statesmanship, I hail your election as President of Princeton, and I count myself fortunate in having the chance to be present to witness your inauguration.

With hearty regards and many thanks for your kind letter,[1] I am,   Faithfully yours,   Theodore Roosevelt

TLS (WP, DLC).
[1] It is missing.

From Franklin Murphy

                    State of New Jersey   Executive Department
My dear Mr. President,   [Trenton]   June twenty-third [1902].

If I am a little late in sending you a word of congratulation on your promotion, it is not because there has been any doubt in my mind as to your fitness for the distinguished place that has come to you, nor of the wisdom of the board in offering it to you, but because I have been away from home salmon fishing—that most alluring and attractive of all pursuits.

I met Mr. Cadwalader at Matepedia and he told me how hearty and unanimous the vote in the Board of Trustees was for your election. The promptness with which you were chosen and the oneness of sentiment as to your being the particular man for the place was most unusual and cannot be felt by you but as the highest possible compliment. I congratulate you most sincerely, and, with your many friends, hope for you a brilliant and successful administration.

I am informed that one of my privileges as Governor is to meet with the Board of Trustees,[1] and that I hope to be able to do in the future, and if in that or in any other way I can be of support or service to you, I hope you will feel free to command me at any time.   Sincerely yours,   Franklin Murphy

TLS (WP, DLC).
[1] The Governor of New Jersey was ex officio a member and President of the Board of Trustees of Princeton University. Murphy qualified as a trustee on October 25, 1902.

From Samuel Alexander[1]

My dear Woodrow: New York.   June 23rd, 1902.

I have just received your letter of June 20th in answer to mine of June 10th.[2] I want to assure you that so far as I know, your election to the presidency of the University has given great pleasure to all of Dr. Patton's many friends. The action of the Trustees in choosing a president was most wise. I am sure that your administration will begin with the united support of all the friends of Princeton.

Dr. Patton spent Sunday with me a week ago and is very enthusiastic in regard to your appointment. I take great pleasure in the knowledge that the great traditions of Princeton University as to sound learning and true religion are entrusted to you, and I have no doubt that so long as these traditions are in your hands they will stand, as they have done in the past, for what Princeton University really is.

I appreciate very much your very kind letter. I appreciate also the great responsibilities which your new office will bring, and I beg to assure you that you can always count upon the sympathy and support of those who bear the name of Alexander however unworthily.

I am,　　　　　　Very sincerely yours,　Sam. Alexander.

TLS (WP, DLC).
　[1] Princeton, 1879, at this time Professor of Diseases of the Genito-Urinary System at Cornell University Medical College in New York.
　[2] Both letters are missing.

From Jesse Lynch Williams

　　　　　　　　　　　　　　　　　　Princeton, New Jersey
Dear Prof. Wilson,　　　　　*Monday morning* [June 23, 1902]

If you care to read one more article about it, here is something from the Boston Transcript, June 14.[1] The mistakes are due to the fact that the copy had to be rushed off before things had cooled—but a request to write about Princeton for New Englanders is like a command, and something was better than nothing, I thought.

I was mighty glad to hear through Hibben that you approve of what The Weekly felt called upon to say.[2]

Again congratulating you (I enclose a sample of the letters I'm getting nowadays) I am

　　　　　　　　Yours Faithfully,　Jesse Lynch Williams

ALS (WP, DLC). Enc.: Lawrence C. Woods to J. L. Williams, June 21, 1902, TLS (WP, DLC).
　[1] This enclosure is missing, but it was a clipping of Jesse Lynch Williams, "Rulers of Princeton," *Boston Evening Transcript*, June 14, 1902.
　[2] In an extended commentary in the *Princeton Alumni Weekly*, II (June 14, 1902), 626-28, Williams vehemently denied the New York *Sun's* allegations that Patton had resigned so that Wilson could be elected, thereby foiling "a clique that was endeavoring to run in Dr. Henry van Dyke."

To Daniel Moreau Barringer

My dear Moreau:　　　　　Princeton, N. J.　June 24th, 1902.

Thank you for your prompt answer to my letter of the 20th. I do not at all know what my movements are to be during the next two or three months. But certainly I shall look out for an opportunity to visit friends, whom I so much wish to see.

　　With cordial regards and thanks,

　　　　　　　　Very sincerely yours,　Woodrow Wilson

TLS (D. M. Barringer Papers, NjP).

To Beverley Randolph Wellford, Jr.

My dear Judge Wellford: Princeton, N. J.   June 24th, 1902.

Allow me to express to you my very sincere appreciation of your kind letter of the 16th. You have done me a real kindness to extend to me so cordial a greeting to my new place in the University. I shall hope some time to see you in Princeton and have the pleasure of expressing my thanks in person.

My father joins me in warmest regards, and I am,
          Most sincerely yours,   Woodrow Wilson

TLS (NcD).

To David Fentress

My dear Mr. Fentress: Princeton, N. J.   June 24th, 1902.

I particularly appreciate your kind congratulations on my election to the Presidency. I know how close you stand to Dr. Patton,[1] and one of the most gratifying circumstances of the present change is that I come in as his accepted successor, and upon his initiative. Your words of satisfaction seem like an additional greeting from his own family.

With warmest regards from both Mrs. Wilson and myself to Mrs. Fentress and yourself,
          Cordially yours,   Woodrow Wilson

TLS (WC, NjP).
[1] Fentress's wife, Mabel Kingsbury Fentress, was a niece of Mrs. Patton.

From Samuel Bayard Dod[1]

My Dear Dr. Wilson   Hoboken, N. J.   June 25 1902

Beside the ballot that I had the pleasure of casting for you, I want to add my word of welcome to the universal acclaim that greets you, from all who have the prosperity of Princeton at heart.

While, with many others, I regret the foolish inventions with which some of the New York reporters sought to make a sensation, yet I am sure that they could not have marred your satisfaction in the manner of your choice.

I never saw so many men of many minds unite so promptly, without debate, without hesitation at the mere mention of a name. When the ballot was taken I thought that there might be one or two blanks; but every man had promptly cast his ballot without consultation, & when the vote was announced we agreed that it was the act of Providence.

Some time, next Fall, or in the early Winter, I would like to give you a reception at Orange.

Our Orange contingent at Princeton is too small. The residents are of a class whose sons go to college; but Yale & Harvard have the lead[.] I think a visit from you would do us good, and I know that it would afford all the Princeton men there very much pleasure   Yours very truly   S. Bayard Dod

ALS (WP, DLC).
    [1] Princeton, 1857, President of the First National Bank of Hoboken, N. J., a trustee of Princeton University, and president of the Board of Trustees of the Stevens Institute of Technology of Hoboken.

From Nancy Saunders Toy[1]

Dear Mr. Wilson   Leipzig, June 25th, 1902

In Berlin last week when Mr. Gilman told me the great news of Princeton's good fortune, I rushed at once to my room and directed this envelope preparatory to sending her my congratulations through you. And here it is Leipzig with Weimar in between before I have been able to express my enthusiasm. Just before I left home, a Princeton graduate—but you know Mr. Andrew,[2] don't you?—prophesied that his Alma Mater would eventually lead all American colleges in giving men an education—that Harvard & Yale were failing in that more & more in their efforts to teach a man to do his "job." I didn't believe him then. I do believe him now. And while you are telling Princeton for me how lucky she is, will you tell Mrs. Wilson for me how much I envy her? I'd rather be Mrs President of one of these three colleges than anything else in the world. Just now I'm rather homesick at the prospect of being over here for a year—did you ever hear of anything so foolish? With greetings to you & Mrs. Wilson,
    Believe me   Yours sincerely   Nancy Toy

ALS (WP, DLC).
    [1] Wife of Crawford Howell Toy, Hancock Professor of Hebrew and Other Oriental Languages and Dexter Lecturer in Biblical Literature at Harvard since 1880. Wilson had first met the Toys at Plymouth, Mass., in the summer of 1894. See WW to EAW, July 16, 1894, n. 1, Vol. 8.
    [2] Abram Piatt Andrew, Jr., Princeton, 1893; Ph.D., Harvard, 1900; at this time an Instructor in Economics at Harvard.

From James Gayley[1]

My dear Sir: New York, 25th June, 1902.

The United States Steel Corporation is well provided with reserves of raw material; has splendidly equipped works and an efficient organization, but in the matter of organization, we cannot, in the natural order of things, see as far into the future as we are able to with respect to raw material or equipment, and as the equipment of brains and energy are just as important to this corporation, we are desirous of working out some plan by which one or more of the most promising graduates each year, from the departments of Chemistry, Metallurgy, Engineering, &c., in certain Technical Schools, can be provided with employment in the constituent companies of this corporation, wherein they would have every opportunity to learn the practical and business side, and we would be securing the services of the best trained brains for the development of our manufacturing interests. As such men must compete for advancement with the young men, who are a product of the works and largely self educated, (and who, I might say, are to be found no mean competitors), we want such as are practical in their judgment and have a plentiful supply of common sense. We want men of brains and ambition, who are disposed to devote their energy in industrial lines; men with potential energy and originality. We do not want men whose primary claim to recognition lies in the attainment of high grades for recitation, as some men are quicker than others at absorbing information and reciting it, but not at digesting it. As many institutions have several technical departments, it is not our desire to take each year the best student in each course; but considering the courses in the aggregate, it is our desire to secure from such aggregation one or more of the men having qualifications as outlined above, to place them in departments for which they have been specially trained, and to give them special opportunities for one year at a stipulated salary. The future will take care of itself. We want ability; will recognize it, and pay for it.

We would be pleased to have your views as to such a plan, and any suggestions relating thereto.

Yours very truly,   James Gayley   First Vice President.

TLS (WP, DLC).
1 First Vice President of the United States Steel Corporation.

From Clarence Valentine Boyer[1]

My dear Mr. Wilson: Titusville Pa. June 25, 1902

You assured me when I left college that if I wrote you would advise me in regard to the purchase of some books, and I am taking advantage of your kindness. I have all the books we read during our courses with you, and wish to get quite a number of other books along the line of Political Science. If it will not be too much trouble I wish you would send me a list of ten or twelve books on that subject.[2] I would also like to have my thesis[3] if it will not bother you too much to send it.

Hoping that you are in the best of health, and with best wishes for a pleasant summer I remain

Very sincerely Yours   Clarence V. Boyer

ALS (WP, DLC) with WWhw list of authors and titles on verso of second page.
[1] Princeton, 1902, who was about to begin the study of law at the Pittsburgh Law School.
[2] See WW to C. V. Boyer, July 15, 1902, Vol. 14.
[3] He was probably referring to his essay on English colonial administration which won the Lyman H. Atwater Prize in Political Science in 1902.

To Laurence Hutton

My dear Hutton,   Princeton, 26 June, '02

Your note of congratulation,[1] take it outside and in, was delightfully compounded of jest and earnest. The jest gave authenticity to the earnestness,—for a man jests and plays only when he is sure of his meaning and his audience, and is not afraid that he will be deemed less sincere because he is not solemn.

It is a great thing to go to great tasks as I go, surrounded by friends, cordial, genuine friends,—and it makes my heart stout against dismay to think of them in connection with the future. I owe you deep thanks for having added so authentic a voice to the heartening chorus.

Always
Faithfully and Cordially Yours,   Woodrow Wilson

ALS (WC, NjP).
[1] L. Hutton to WW, June 10, 1902.

To Eleanor Varnum Mitchell Hutton

My dear Mrs. Hutton,   Princeton, 26 June, '02

I know that you will pardon me for not have [having] answered your delightful note sooner.[1] I have been dictating letters without number, but a few, like this of yours, I laid aside to answer with my own hand, with something of a more personal tone of gratitude and appreciation.

I have been specially pleased & strengthened by the cordial notes that have come to me from friends who know me near at hand and speak from the heart. It gives me courage, spirits, to be so welcomed to my new duties. The tonic of these good

words of confidence and cheer will not soon go out of my blood.
　With warmest regard and appreciation,
　　　　　　　　Cordially Yours,　Woodrow Wilson

ALS (WC, NjP).
　[1] Eleanor V. Hutton to WW, June 11, 1902, ALS (WP, DLC).

From Francis Landey Patton

My dear Professor Wilson:　　　[Princeton, N.J.] June 26th, 1902.
　I would like to make a few suggestions to you with reference
to certain odds and ends of administrative work.

　1st. On recommendation of the English Department, I have
written to Mr. A[ugustus] W[hite] Long, of the Lawrenceville
School, appointing him instructor in English for the next academic year in place of Mr. [Hardin] Craig, who is absent on leave,
and at Mr. Craig's salary. I had expected to ask the Trustees to
confirm this appointment at their October meeting. But I am
sure that you will have no hesitation in assuming this responsibility.[1]

　2nd. Mr. [Percy Robert] Colwell, one of the instructors in English, is receiving $800., and feels that his salary ought to be
increased to $1000. I agree with him in this respect and hope that
the way may be clear for him to have this increase; at all events,
that $100. may be added to his salary.[2] I think that I have given
no promises to any of the other instructors, and have no suggestions to make in regard to any other salaries.

　3rd. When I was in Pittsburgh in the Spring, I said to Dr.
[William Leonard] McEwan of the 3d Pres. Ch. that I would like
to have him preach in the Marquand Chapel during the first term
of the next academic year. Dr. McEwan holds such a relation,
not only to his own church, but to the men of influence in Pittsburgh, that I think it would be a very wise thing to ask him to
preach. And if you have no objection, I should like to keep my
promise with him, and arrange for him to supply the pulpit of
the Marquand Chapel some time during the months of October
and November.[3] I will be responsible for the payment of the
honorarium, $50.

　If for any reason these suggestions do not commend themselves to you, do not hesitate to let me know. I refer more particularly to the 2nd and 3rd. The first I look upon in the light of a
contract made under my own administration. I am
　　　　　　Very sincerely yours,　Francis L. Patton

TLS (Patton Letterpress Books, UA, NjP).

[1] On Wilson's recommendation, the trustees confirmed Long's appointment on October 21, 1902.
[2] Colwell did not get an increase in salary for 1902-1903.
[3] Dr. McEwan did not preach at the university during the autumn term of 1902-1903.

To Harriet Woodrow Welles

My dear Hattie,   Princeton, 27 June, 1902

It was truly delightful to get your letter[1] full of generous pleasure at my election to the presidency of the University. I am settling now very quietly to the thought of the new duties, but at first it was too big a surprise to adjust ourselves to very easily. I believe we are at present perversely and ungratefully bored at having to leave the delightful privacy of the beautiful home we have made for ourselves and move into the stately presidential mansion, "Prospect," where we shall be public personages. The pleasure and the real dignity will come with the *work*.

No, alas, there is no western trip in store for us for the present. Dr. Wheeler[2] invited me to go out to the University of California this summer, but I had to decline,—even before I knew that I was to be President. Now I have so much to learn, and to learn at once, that the nearer I stay to home the better.

I was *so* rejoiced to hear from dear Aunt Helen's doctors in Baltimore (Dr. Thatcher [Thayer] wrote to me directly) that there was no *trace* of organic trouble; and it is an additional pleasure to hear that she is going to visit you. Ellen enjoyed visiting her at the hospital most thoroughly.

Dear father is quite feeble, but in good spirits and it is a great blessing to have him with us.

Ellen joins me in warmest love to all.

Your affectionate cousin,   Woodrow

ALS (WC, NjP).
[1] Harriet W. Welles to WW, June 12, 1902.
[2] Benjamin Ide Wheeler, President of the University of California.

To Robert Bridges

My dear Bobby,   Princeton, New Jersey, 27 June, 1902.

I simply cannot figure it out this week: I am desperately finishing my history, to get my decks cleared. But I can manage it about the middle of next week, and will do so with great pleasure.

If I do not hear from you to the contrary, I will assume that that suits you, and will come in just as soon next week as possible, letting you know beforehand, and looking forward to the day with the finest hopes for a good, old-fashioned chat.

As ever,   Faithfully and affectionately Yours,
Woodrow Wilson

WWTLS (WC, NjP).

A News Item

[June 28, 1902]

PRESENTATION OF SILVER PITCHER.

Messrs. John A. Campbell and Elmer Ewing Green, representing the Trenton battle celebration committee, came to Princeton last Saturday[1] on a pleasant errand. This was to present to Dr. Woodrow Wilson, President-elect of the University, a testimonial for his part in the exercises of the battle of Trenton last December, when he delivered the address of the occasion in the Opera House.[2] The gift selected was a handsome silver pitcher, appropriately engraved. The presentation was entirely informal, by Mr. Green stating the appreciation of all concerned of the response of Dr. Wilson to the invitation of the committee and his patriotic and instructive address. Dr. Wilson responded briefly.

Printed in the *Princeton Press*, June 28, 1902.
[1] June 21, 1902.
[2] The address was "The Ideals of America," printed at Dec. 26, 1901. About the exercises, see n. 1 to this address.

Ellen Axson Wilson to Florence Stevens Hoyt

My dearest Florence,   Princeton, June 28, 1902

I don't think we will set a date for Margaret quite yet.[1] I am still at it "regulating" her teeth, also studying the effect of the glasses to report to Dr. Brown.[2] She did not begin to wear them until after the examinations, but we think they are having a fine effect already. The weather keeps so delightful that there is no hurry on that account; she is playing tennis a great deal and being quite "hygienic"!

Of course I have been wanting to write you ever since the election but perhaps you can imagine how things have been,—the interruptions of all sorts, the callers, the dinners &c., to "celebrate," besides the hundreds upon hundreds of congratulatory letters to Woodrow and many to me. The ones I have postponed longest are just those to my nearest and dearest because I did not want to write a brief note to them. The letters and the news-papers are both wonderful; the Alumni seem half mad with joy, and outsiders almost as enthusiastic. As for the Professors, stu-dents and Princeton people generally,—well, the scenes here were indescribable! It is enough to frighten a man to death to have people love & believe in him so and *expect* so much. Yet on the other hand it is like going in with the tide; he is only the leader of the Princeton forces and all this enthusiasm will surely be a strong power impelling the University forward. Of course you know he was unanimously elected on the first ballot,—something unique in college history. One of the Trustees told me that "those 26 men had never agreed on *any*thing in their lives before, yet in this they were *perfectly* unanimous from the *first*, no other name was ever proposed." Another Trustee writes, "I never saw so many men of many minds unite so promptly, without debate, without hesitation at the mere mention of a name. When the ballot was taken I thought that there might be one or two blanks; but every man had promptly cast his ballot without consultation, and when the vote was announced we agreed that it was the act of Providence."[3] Wasn't it wonderful,—especially when one thinks that Woodrow made no more effort to get it than *you* did!

Of course it envolves heavy sacrifices to people of our tempera-ment. His literary work must suffer greatly,—just how much remains to [be] seen, and we must leave our dear home and the sweet, almost ideal life when he was [a] simple "man of letters" and go and live in that great, stately troublesome "Prospect," and be forever giving huge receptions, state dinners, &c. &c. We are both rather heart-broken about this side of it, but I am trying now not to let my mind dwell on it. All these new duties and responsibilities it is "up to me" as the boys say to fulfill to the best of my ability, & I must "brook no continuance of weak-minded-ness." I will, as you desire, look up some paper giving an account of the first day, & enclose.

I go to Agnes[4] the 10th of July for two weeks, after that Wood-row goes away for five, & I take care of Father & get ready to move the 1st of Sept. With dear love to all, hurriedly,

Ellen.

There is a *fine* full page portrait of W. with a beautiful little notice in "Harper's Weekly" for *June 21st*.

ALS (WP, DLC).
    [1] That is, for Margaret's visit to Miss Hoyt, who was vacationing at Lavallette, a small resort community on the New Jersey shore.
    [2] A Baltimore oculist.
    [3] S. B. Dod to WW, June 25, 1902.

From James Ford Rhodes

Dear Mr. Wilson   Dresden   June 28 [1902]

I congratulate you on your election to the presidency of the University of Princeton. Literary men, to say nothing of a Scotch Irishman, are getting to the fore. I wish you what I know you will have [—] a great success. I hope that we shall still see you at the dinners of the Institute of Arts and Letters.

With kind regards and the expression of my high respect
I remain   Very truly yours   James Ford Rhodes

ALS (WP, DLC).

From Mary Gresham Machen

My dear Mr. Wilson,   Baltimore, June 28. 1902

Not many of your friends could have felt greater pride than I at your promotion to the exalted position of President of a great University. To me it seems one of the most honorable stations the whole world can offer, and with my whole heart I congratulate you and your sweet wife. Personally, I feel the greatest pride in you, as the representative of our South Land, as a son of our beloved Church, as a friend whom I may claim by the right of heredity and, I trust, by a more especial bond.

I waited until the great murmur of applause should have subsided that you might hear my piping voice.

My thoughts have turned especially to your father whose cup is full of blessed fruition of hope. How often do the noblest honors of this world fall at the feet of those who have not sought them!

Such a reward as many worldlings seek in vain for their children has come to the son of your father, whose aim was simply to do God's work and to have you do likewise. And how is the same truth illustrated in the case of Dr. [Benjamin Morgan] Palmer! A man who never thought of himself is called by the people of New Orleans their "*most* distinguished citizen."

I may have seemed ungrateful not to have expressed my thanks for your very kind letter in response to my inquiries for my son, Gresham.[1] Yet I did appreciate the pains which you took about such an apparently trivial matter. You might have thought—
"Why consult Peter in a simple case

Peter's wife's mother in her fever-fit
Might solve as readily."

But if you thought so, your detailed answer did not evidence it. And it was a comfort in that time of indecision to have a word from you. The Phi Kappa Psi[2] boys, among others, are much elated over your honors.

We love Dr. Patton and hope that this does not mean in any sense a breakdown for him. There always seemed to me to be an immense reserve of strength in his nature. Yet he did look tired sometimes after giving forth his best.

I wish you every blessing in your new duties. My only regret is that Hopkins has lost you. Give my love to your wife and believe —for both—in the sincere friendship of

Yours cordially,   Minnie Gresham Machen.

ALS (WP, DLC).

[1] After being graduated from the Johns Hopkins in 1901, John Gresham Machen had done graduate work in Greek for a year at the same institution. He came to Princeton Theological Seminary in 1902 and was graduated in 1905. After advanced study in Germany, he returned to teach at Princeton Theological Seminary in 1906 and in the 1920's became the storm center of a fundamentalist-liberal controversy that rocked the Presbyterian Church. A leader of the extremely conservative wing, Machen withdrew from Princeton Theological Seminary and helped to found Westminster Theological Seminary in Philadelphia in 1929. Mrs. Machen's letter about her son and Wilson's reply are both missing.

[2] Wilson's fraternity at the University of Virginia.

From Jesse Benedict Carter

My dear Mr. Wilson,   Göttingen. June 28, 1902.

I have just received the news of your election to the Presidency of Princeton—and I want to express to you my very hearty congratulations.

My personal relations with Dr. Patton have always been of such an intimate nature—(in many ways I have almost a filial feeling toward him)—that I have for some years fought my growing conviction that a change of administration would be for the best interests of Princeton. My absence for the last half year[1] has deprived me of the opportunity to watch the trend of events— and the announcement that the change had come, was a great surprise to me and would have been also a very considerable shock, had the *person* of the successor been as surprising to me as the *fact* of the succession.

The formal duty of assuring you of my cooperation is under the circumstances a sincere pleasure, feeling, as I do, that Policy as *well* as Personality, will enlist my heartiest sympathy—and that my feelings will not be divided against themselves.

With cordial regards to Mrs. Wilson in which Mrs. Carter joins, I am   Yours faithfully   Jesse Benedict Carter.

ALS (WP, DLC).
[1] Carter had been on leave, studying in Germany.

To Charles Franklin Thwing[1]

My dear President Thwing: Princeton, N. J. June 30th, 1902.

Allow me to thank you most sincerely for your kind letter of congratulation.[2] This common interest which binds us together, and which seems to be drawing all men interested in our education together, I look upon as one of the chief sources of strength to a man assuming such a position as that which I am about to occupy. I appreciate your greetings, therefore, as those of a comrade and fellow-counsellor in the duties which it shall be my study to perform.

Very sincerely yours,   Woodrow Wilson

TLS (FTU).
[1] President of Western Reserve University and Adelbert College since 1890.
[2] It is missing.

To James Gayley

My dear Sir: Princeton, N. J., June 30, 1902.

Your plan for the employment of young college men in the business of the Steel Corporation of course interests me very deeply. Our term is over, and the men who could give me the best advice in matters of this sort are not at home, being away for their summer outing. But I shall consult with them as soon as possible after their return in the autumn, and shall take pleasure in seeing what it is possible for us to suggest by way of co-operating with you, in plans which seem so sensible and so serviceable.[1]   Very sincerely yours,   Woodrow Wilson.

PCL (Archives, PPiUS).
[1] There is no further correspondence between Wilson and Gayley in either the Wilson Papers or the Archives of the United States Steel Corporation.

To Robert Bridges

My dear Bobby,   Princeton, 30 June, '02

Unless I have hard luck, I shall turn up at your office to-morrow, Tuesday, at about one o'clock, to lunch with you.

Thank you from the bottom of my heart for your all too generous but, as from you, delightful praise of me in the Review of Reviews!

In haste,   Affectionately Yours,   Woodrow Wilson

ALS (Meyer Coll., DLC).

An Article About Wilson

[July 1902]

PRESIDENT WOODROW WILSON.
By Robert Bridges.

By the election of Woodrow Wilson to be its president, Princeton has, for the first time in thirty-four years, one of its own graduates at the head of its affairs. Dr. Wilson is, moreover, representative of what is best in Princeton,—the Princeton re-created by McCosh, and admirably developed by Patton, out of the old Princeton which the Civil War had so terribly crippled. He also represents one of the most important elements in the life of that old ante-bellum Princeton,—the Southern man who once dominated the student life. Woodrow Wilson is a Virginian, with that inborn love of the study of statecraft which has been the heritage of so many Virginians from Madison and Henry to the present day.

But he is a great deal more than the product of a State or a section. His education represents many phases. He studied, first, at a North Carolina college [Davidson College]; he took his academic degree at Princeton, his law degree at the University of Virginia, and his doctorate of philosophy at Johns Hopkins. He practiced law in Atlanta, Ga.; he taught history at Bryn Mawr, in Pennsylvania; and then at Wesleyan, in New England. While there he began to be known as a public lecturer all over New England, in its most intellectual centers. With that openness of mind which is one of his chief characteristics, he absorbed from North and South what was best. With this cosmopolitan education and training, he is to-day the product of no section,—he is a representative American.

Though his education has been so varied, there has been no haphazard in his career. Every step that he has taken has been one of conscious choice, leading to a definite, logical end. No one who knew him intimately in his undergraduate days had any doubt about his aim in life, or, what is more remarkable, had they any doubt of his ultimate achievement. That a boy under twenty should so impress other boys under twenty is not unusual; but that his whole career should be an abundant fulfillment of the boy's ideal is the remarkable thing.

This choice of *the best thing for his own purpose* was the marked quality of Wilson in his student days. He knew exactly what he wanted to do, and he had very definite ideas as to what part of the curriculum would help him to do it. He worked hard at the thing he wanted and let the rest go. What relative rank in class this system of selection might bring him did not interest him in the least. He practiced the elective system in his own career ten years before Princeton had much of it in the curriculum.

Those who knew him well soon learned what he was driving at. He proposed to "study government and write about it." He knew that a necessary part of the preparation for it would be the study of law; but whether he should find the best opportunity to make himself a writer on Institutions through the practice of law, or through public life, or through teaching, he did not know. Of one thing he was sure,—if the practice of law did not give him the opportunity to write about government, by the application of law he would abandon it.

He also knew that not only must he be a good writer, but a good speaker and debater, if he was to make public affairs his career. Government is a device of men, and human nature is back of it and always present in its application. He showed an early intolerance for mere book knowledge; he wanted to understand the workings of men in the mass and individually. This science of government interested him because it was intensely human, and because he was himself intensely human. There never was a bit of the prig or "dig" about him. He was a marked man intellectually, but made no bones about it. He knew every kind of man in the class, and every kind of man knew him, and most of them liked him,—unless they were stupid or insincere. He was so intolerant of duplicity and impatient with stupidity that those people stayed out of his way.

He gathered around him a coterie of men who were interested in similar questions, and they debated them vigorously. In the literary Hall [the American Whig Society] he was always ready for a debate, and in the actual machinery of the government of that often unruly body of two hundred men he took the liveliest interest. A society founded by James Madison in his undergraduate days would naturally furnish a favorite forum for his mind. One thing we soon found out,—and that was that, although Wilson was always ready for debate, he would never argue on a side which he did not believe. And so when the preliminary contest for the greatest debating honor of the course came—the Lynde debate —and Wilson drew the side of a question in which he did not believe, he instantly withdrew from the competition.[1] He was easily the best debater we had, and it was giving up a certainty, but he never hesitated. He did not believe—and that was enough.

There was one question that he never tired of arguing; when all other topics failed, and a lively tilt was wanted, some one would broach the question of Cabinet government as opposed to Committee government. I don't think we cared much about the question, one way or the other, but it was fun to hear Wilson argue it. We could always draw fire also with Burke, Brougham, Bagehot, or Chatham. He used to read their speeches out loud in Potter's woods, in order to get the swing of their style. And to-day, if you will read Wilson's books, or hear him make a speech, you will see the part that those great Englishmen played in the making of his own style.

It is often easy to write this sort of thing about a man *after* the fact, and make it fit his achievements. But in this case it is a matter of record in black and white. His essay on Cabinet Government was written and accepted by the *International Review* while he was an undergraduate.[2] The old *Nassau Lit.* contained his famous essay on Earl Chatham,[3] which is good reading to-day, and several hundred men will vividly recall his brilliant oration on Richard Cobden.[4]

There was a definiteness of purpose, a maturity of achievement, about Wilson's undergraduate days which make them worth recalling. Moreover, he was always a good fellow, interested in every phase of college life,—president of the athletic association, editor of *The Princetonian*, a leader in social affairs, and the most loyal classmate and friend.

It was natural that, after graduating in 1879, Wilson should return to his native State, to the University of Virginia, to study law. There he left the same record of vigorous clearness in the pursuit of his aim as at Princeton. He practiced law in Atlanta, Ga., in 1882-83, in the same office with a man of congenial lit-

[1] See the Editorial Note, "Wilson's Refusal to Enter the Lynde Competition," Vol. 1.

[2] It is printed at Aug. 1, 1879, *ibid.*

[3] Printed at Oct. 1, 1878, *ibid.*

[4] Wilson delivered this oration, "Richard Cobden—An Historical Lesson," at Chapel Stage (about which, see n. 1 to Wilson's diary entry for Nov. 4, 1876, Vol. 1) on November 2, 1878. *Chapel Stage, Second Division. Saturday, November 2nd, 1878, 11 A.M.* (printed program in the Philippus William Miller Scrapbook, UA, NjP). This is the sole contemporary documentary record of Wilson's address, but see Henry W. Bragdon, *Woodrow Wilson: The Academic Years* (Cambridge, Mass., 1967), p. 42.

erary tastes.[5] The net result of that experiment was the conviction that for him at least the way to a knowledge of the science of government, and the opportunity to write about it, did not lie through the routine of law. But the experience has left with him a flexibility of mind, an easy adjustment to all kinds of audiences, and a fund of anecdote which unite to make him one of the most effective and graceful of after-dinner speakers, and a ready man in the emergencies of public life.

When he abandoned law practice, in 1883, he went to Johns Hopkins University, and found a stimulating atmosphere of vigorous mental life, the inspiration of which was "original research." Here he had the opportunity, as Fellow in History, to perfect his knowledge and polish his style in preparation for the final draft of his first book, at which he had been working since his undergraduate days. When completed it immediately found a publisher, and served also as the thesis on which Johns Hopkins granted him his Ph.D.

This book on "Congressional Government" (1885)[6] was the first attempt that any one had made to describe the actual workings of our system in practice as developed from the theory of the Constitution. There was a literary charm about its style and a fine moral enthusiasm in its argument that immediately made him a far larger audience than a book on politics is apt to gain. The book remains, after seventeen years, the standard authority on the subject, and was the acknowledged basis of Mr. Bryce's chapters on committee government. Wilson was not yet thirty years of age, but gained at a bound a recognized place, not only among students of politics, but as a man of letters.

His next book, "The State" (1889), was a feat of scholarship, and by the breadth of its subject and the necessity for condensation, allowed little opportunity for the graces of style,—except for that supreme grace of clearness. It was the first book in English to present the workings of all constitutional governments as they are carried on at the present day, and it has held its place ever since as a college text-book.

In the writing of history he first showed his skill in "Division and Reunion," a sketch of the period from 1829 to 1889, and a few years later he produced a brilliant popular biography of "George Washington" (1897). These books have led up to his "Colonies and Nations," a "History of the People of the United States," an elaborate work, in four volumes, which he has just completed, and which will be published this fall. The chapters

5 Edward Ireland Renick.
6 Printed at Jan. 24, 1885, Vol. 4.

from it which have appeared in *Harper's* show that he has written a history that is fascinating in style and scholarly in matter. It is the first important history of the United States written by a Southerner,—but it is not a Southern history. It represents *all* the elements that have gone to the making of this great country. The New England point of view has heretofore dominated our historical writers. Professor Wilson's point of view is broadly American.

Two volumes, collected from various periodicals,—"An Old Master" (1893) and "Mere Literature" (1896),—show Wilson's versatility, lightness of touch, and quality as an essayist.

Admirable as his achievement has been as scholar, historian, and essayist, it would not of itself designate him as the ideal man to be president of a university. Along with it goes a wonderful success as a teacher for a period of seventeen years. As lecturer on Administration at Johns Hopkins, for ten years, he was brought in contact with a picked body of students from all over the country, many of whom are now professors in the leading universities. At the same time he was lecturing on Constitutional Law at the New York Law School, before men of an entirely different cast of mind; and his elective classes at Princeton, since 1890, have been the largest in that institution. He has been in constant demand as a public lecturer for many years.

In purely executive work he has shown force, diplomacy, and acuteness as a member of the most important committees in the Princeton faculty. All his life he has studied executive problems, and his fitness for executive work has been so marked for years that he has received invitations from many important institutions to be their president. It was told on the Princeton campus the other day that one of the political parties had asked him, months ago, to run for State Senator,[7] and recently a Western newspaper pointed him out as the right kind of man to be a candidate for President of the United States.[8]

That is the man whom President Patton, with the intellectual acuteness which he always exhibits, designated as his successor and the trustees unanimously elected. Princeton has never grown more rapidly than under Dr. Patton's presidency. It has been reaching out in many directions toward what is best in the modern system of education. Schemes have been started that as yet are formless, and Dr. Patton, with wonderful clearness, recognized in Woodrow Wilson the man to guide them to efficient com-

[7] See WW to an Unidentified Person, Oct. 1, 1901.
[8] See an Old-Fashioned Democrat to the Editor of the *Indianapolis News*, May 1, 1902.

pleteness. At forty-five, Dr. Wilson takes up the great task with vigor, and a reasonable hope of years of successful labor. He knows the leading men and the best methods in universities here and abroad; the loyal body of Princeton alumni (and none are more loyal) throughout the country know him personally and trust him; and the undergraduates welcome him with cheers.

He has a great task, but he also has a great courage. And back of it lies the superb equipment founded on years of single-minded, persistent training in the science of government, leading up to this opportunity for applying it to the needs of Princeton University.

Printed in the New York *Review of Reviews*, XXVI (July 1902), 36-38.

From Frederick Jackson Turner

My dear Wilson: Madison July 1, 1902.

I am very glad of your letter, and am delighted that your new honors will give us reason to hope for more frequent occasions for meeting. If there is any possibility of your being in the West during the coming year, I should like to know of it, and, if possible, to arrange that our students may hear you. I am hoping before long to see the publication of your history. In spite of what you wrote of its illustrations, I am sure that no amount of picturesque effort on the part of the artist can interfere with its being the important work which the chapters which I have read in the magazines indicate.

As for me, I should be delighted if I could get out any book with or without artistic embellishment; but I seem to be rather under water with university engagements most of the time.

Mrs. Turner joins me in renewed congratulations and good wishes to Mrs. Wilson and yourself.

Very cordially yours, Frederick J. Turner

TLS (WP, DLC).

Cornelius Cuyler Cuyler to Cyrus Hall McCormick

THE F. L. PATTON FUND

My dear Cyrus: New York, July 2nd, 1902.

Referring to the action recently taken whereby it was determined to pay over to the Rev. F. L. Patton, D.D., a sum of money in cash, which, together with the salary of his Professorship, would equal for six years the amount annually received by him as President of Princeton University, I beg to advise that the amount now necessary to be secured is $31,500., of which you have generously agreed to contribute the sum of $5,000.[1] I shall be obliged by your kindly forwarding your cheque for this amount to me at this address before July 25th to order of Cuyler, Morgan & Co., who will keep the account and pay over the amount at the proper time to Mr. M. Taylor Pyne, who will attend to the details with Dr. Patton.   Yours faithfully,   C C Cuyler

TLS (C. H. McCormick Papers, WHi).
    [1] The contributors and the amounts of their contributions to the Patton Fund were De Witt C. Blair, $2,500; John L. Cadwalader, $1,000; John A. Stewart, $500; C. C. Cuyler, $1,000; Bayard Henry, $400; Rev. Charles Wood, $100; John D. Davis, $1,000; M. Taylor Pyne, $5,000; Albertina Pyne Russell, $1,000; Alexander Van Rensselaer, $2,500; Henry W. Green, $1,000; John J. McCook, $1,000; Stephen S. Palmer, $2,500; James W. Alexander, $1,000; David B. Jones and Thomas D. Jones, $5,000; Cyrus H. McCormick, $4,000; and Stanley McCormick, $1,000. "CONTRIBUTORS OF THE F. L. PATTON FUND," typed memorandum in the C. H. McCormick Papers (WHi), and F. A. Steuert to C. C. Cuyler, March 27, 1903, CCL (C. H. McCormick Papers, WHi).

A Religious Talk[1]

[[July 4, 1902]]

RELIGION AND PATRIOTISM

The many voices that we have heard here this evening all unite in a common theme, a theme which seems to me to make it almost an impertinence to speak of patriotism, as if men who felt the impulse of service and of love, love of God and service of men, needed to be preached to upon the lessons of patriotism. For I believe we mistake in conceiving of patriotism as a sentiment. No doubt patriotism breeds a noble sentiment, but patriotism itself is a sense of duty. It is a principle of devotion, a principle of devotion to some definite thing which we know and love, to that spirit which lifts a nation to the level of its duty, which lifts a nation along the way to its destiny. For it seems to me that you can conceive patriotism truly only when you have conceived it as a sort of larger, a sort of universal friendship. I have not served my friend unless I have told him the truth. I have not served my friend until I have learned to know my friend, know the needs of his nature, know how to tell him when he is wrong as well as how to cheer him when he is right. I serve my friend, if I deserve the name of friend myself, according to his character, according to his nature; and so it seems to me that patriotism would find hard shift to live in a country that was not self-governed, because only in a country which is self-governed is it a man's duty and privilege to know the nature of the polity under which he lives and serve his country according to the conceptions which were born and bred in him and in it; for there is many a time when a man must have some sense of duty, something of a faith, some reverence for the laws his own people have made, and upon occasion some civic manhood firm against the crowd.

The thing that keeps patriotism alive in this country is the right of every man to speak his real conviction and to conform to the opinion of nobody, and when I have heard men cried out against as un-American because they did not agree with the opinion of the majority in this country, I have wondered where our study of history had gone to. That flag which we honor in this country seems to me sometimes to be composed of stripes of parchment upon which are written the principles of the ancient liberty of the English speaking peoples, and stripes of blood, the blood which has flowed for the vindication of those principles. That flag started in a kick, in a rebellion, in a dissent; and if a man living under that flag has not the right to dissent, there is no flag that floats in the world under which men can utter their difference from the majority of their fellowmen. That flag is the flag of freedom of opinion, as the other flag yonder wound with it is also. That flag has been singularly dignified. Men have not felt it beneath them to honor a particular family with their reverence, and yet they have deemed it beneath their honor as men not to say to that family, You shall not do what we do not assent to your doing.

Liberty and reverence, obedience and free power are the things that these two nations have stood together to represent, and so it seems to me that we must conceive of patriotism as an energy of character which operates outside the narrow circle of self-interest. We do not blame men, we ought not to blame men that they work with all the energy that is in them for the advancement of their own legitimate interests, but we never keep the special words of praise for those men. If we describe a man as a noble man, do we mean that he is conspicuously successful in his private business? It would be inconceivable that we meant that. When we say that he is noble, we say that there is a fine surplus fund of character in that man which he can spend upon other men as well as upon himself, and that the men whose energy of character is greater than their own interests are the noble men of the world.

And so it seems to me that religion connects itself with patriotism, because religion is the energy of character which, instead of concentrating upon the man himself, concentrates upon a service which is greater than the man himself. And how a religious man can fail to have the fine impulse of patriotism I cannot conceive; for when you reflect upon it, the atmosphere we create is the atmosphere in which other men live, and national character is nothing but the atmosphere of motive and of action which we create for each other. We are making the men who are about us by creating that atmosphere. In proportion as we create the right corporate feeling in any body of men, we have lifted the individual man to the level of endeavor to which we desire to lift all men. And so it seems to me that religion unites itself with the patriotic purpose, because there is no motive which elevates like the religious motive; there is no other motive in the world which connects a man with the things so great that he cannot measure them by himself. The standard is the standard of universal providence; the goal is the goal of human progress itself, and men cannot once get that motive in their blood and then forget that they have fellowmen whom they are to serve. The spirit of service has made every leader that this race has ever known, and the spirit of religious service is the chief and crowning spirit of service for all men.

Did you ever reflect that a nation has only this life in which to live? You and I have deceived ourselves many a time by saying we shall have a last chance of repentance; there is an infinite mercy which will open the gates to us, and we have depended on that mercy. There is no mercy for a nation. A nation must save itself on this side of the grave; there is no other side for it. Its character must be made now and finished now; there is no other time of complete fruition. And so there is a responsibility laid upon us here which is greater than the responsibility of individual salvation. I believe it is every man's duty to be saved. I mean it is every man's duty to bring himself into such relations with the only Saviour of mankind that his own future is linked with all the plans of Providence. But there is a duty which crowns that, and that is the duty to lift other men along with him in that great process of elevation; and that is the patriotic duty just as much as it is the religious duty. You may cultivate patriotism. You cannot cultivate any sentiment that I know of in any other way than by cultivating your regard for the object of that sentiment.

Now you know there is a sentiment which everyone of us has tried—most of you are trying it now, I suppose—and that is to make another person love you. You have probably found out that there is no way of compelling another person to love you. Compulsion is no part of the rule of the game, and you know that the

only way in which you can make another person love you is by
seeming to be a fine fellow. That has saved the moral life of
many a chap. He found out that when he began the play business he had to keep it up, that it would be fatal after succeeding
to be found out, and that, therefore, he had to live up to the
fine play that he had set upon the board. And so a man knows
that he is the object of observation, and that the only way anybody is going to love him is by observing him and observing
him to be lovable. Well, now, that is a large contract. To go
about to be lovable is a large contract, because a man cannot
do it unless he gets some standard that is bigger than himself.
The standard that he generally gets—and the great good fortune
is that there is such a standard—is the character of the person
whose love he desires.

I admit that he sometimes makes a mistake about that. I do
not mean that he is ever mistaken in supposing that the object
is lovely, but he does not get the catalogue of the details of that
loveliness exactly right, and he sometimes finds out too late that
he has got hold of the wrong items in his bill; but in the meantime he has conformed his own character to the catalogue which
he supposed to be the catalogue of perfection, and so he has
lifted himself up so far forth into the sphere of the person whose
regard he would have.

You observe that our country is not an object which we can
look at in the flesh. The beauty of the country is neither here nor
there. I know that we have been a great deal laughed at by foreign nations, and I dare say with a great deal of weight and
justification, because we were bragging about the size of this
country, and we were reminded that we did not make it. We
were reminded of the weakness of another nation which, in
spite of all temptations to belong to other nations, remained
Englishmen. In other words, we have been reminded that nature
put us here and nature gave us what we possess. But the point
of the moral of that is that we do possess the great thing which
nature created. We were a big enough people to get a big thing.
The two nations which have become the imperial nations of the
world are as big as their own empires. It is that moral of Burke,
that a small mind and a great empire go ill together, and the
empire cannot be conducted by those who have small minds;
and so we have been expanded to the compass of a thing which
we never saw, of a nation whose faces we never looked upon,
of peoples whom we never visited, and we get that large aspect
of mind which goes with large undertakings, and are carried
into the sphere of ideals, of conceptions. No man ever saw a

nation. No man ever conceived of government as a physical thing. The whole matter is abstract and of the mind, and it is clothed with the ideals of the mind, and when those ideals are crowned with the ideals of religion you have the greatest compass, as it seems to me, of impulse that the human heart can desire. And so I have not come here to say to men like these, You ought to be servants of your country, but merely to remind men like these what it means to be servants of God and servants of their native land.

Printed in the *Northfield*, Mass., *Echoes*, IX (July 1902), 217-21.

¹ Delivered at the Northfield, Mass., Student Conference on July 4, 1902. About this conference, see C. H. Dodge to WW, Jan. 3, 1901, n. 1, and the news report printed at Aug. 23, 1902, Vol. 14.

To Robert Bridges

My dear Bobby,   Princeton, New Jersey, 8 July, 1902.

Mrs. Wilson and I will be in town, weather permitting, tomorrow, buying (official) furniture for Prospect. There is a little matter of business, connected with my book, about which I want your advice. In order to combine business with pleasure, I mean to be at your office sometime between one and half past to take you out to lunch with us.

As ever,

Faithfully and affectionately,   Woodrow Wilson

WWTLS (WC, NjP).

Cyrus Hall McCormick to Cornelius Cuyler Cuyler

My dear C.C.:   [Chicago] July 8th, 1902.

Your note of July 2nd is received, and I presume this is the form which you are sending to all the subscribers to the fund. If it does not trouble you too much, I would like to have some further particulars. Have you found that $31,500.00 is the sum necessary to fulfil our obligations toward Dr. Patton? In what form do you propose to have this fund put into the trusteeship? It is not convenient for me to send this money at the present time, but if you can advise me when it is to draw interest and in whose hands it is to be placed, as trustee, I will either forward a note for a short time, drawing the same rate of interest which you have agreed the general fund shall draw, or I will make some other provision for the payment. I judge from the fact that you are still counting my sum of $5,000.00, that you have

not been able to secure sufficient surplus to reduce my subscription. I am quite willing that it shall stand at this amount,
although I had hoped perhaps more would join in this fund so
that it would not be so necessary to have me put in so large an
amount. I am quite satisfied, however, with any arrangement
on this subject that you have made.

I am,

Very sincerely yours,   Cyrus H. McCormick   H.

CCL (C. H. McCormick Papers, WHi).

Moses Taylor Pyne to Cyrus Hall McCormick

My dear Cyrus: Princeton, N. J. July 11, 1902.

Your favor of the 8th inst. to Cuyler has been handed over to
me from his office as he is at present on his way to Europe.

We find that the sum necessary to fulfill our obligations
towards the President will be $31,500. This Fund is not to be
put in the hands of a Trust but to be paid over directly to him
on the date, if possible, of his resignation, to wit, the 31st of
this July.[1] We are figuring on the rate of interest at 5%. The
draft or note should be sent to Cuyler's office as the whole matter
is being attended to by them there. . . .

With kind regards, believe me,

Very sincerely yours,   M. Taylor Pyne

TLS (C. H. McCormick Papers, WHi).
[1] See F. L. Patton to Cuyler, Morgan and Co., Aug. 2, 1902, Vol. 14.

ADDENDUM

A Class Report

[c. Nov. 19, 1884]¹

Some Words upon An Essay
on the Early History of the Family, by A. Lang.

(Contemporary Review, Sept., 1883)²

Mr. Lang's article is so scant in its proportions, and his treatment of his subject is so light in its touch, that it cannot be said
that his article has contributed much to the discussion of the
origin of the family. It has, nevertheless, a very distinct value as
a landmark by which we may discover the stage at which the
controversy has arrived. In reviewing the debate from the standpoint of an out-sider, one receives the impression that this is a
tilt between hobby-riders and the greater champions of high-
booted scholarship. Sir Henry Maine and Mr. [Herbert] Spencer,
together with all their noble following, seem to be dispassionate
students of the course of social phenomena, whilst Mr. [John
Ferguson] McLennan and his fellows run eagerly about to estab-
lish a pet theory.

The range of the question, as indicated by Mr. Lang, is now
comparatively narrow. There are three leading interrogatories in
which the whole matter is summed up: (1) DID man originally
live in a patriarchal family, or in a more or less modified promiscuity, with uncertainty of blood ties and especially of male
parentage? Upon this point Mr. Lang, though inclined to the side
of McLennan, somewhat unexpectedly yields to the opinion of
Sir Henry Maine, granting that if man was created a perfect animal he probably at first paired off with a wife whom he claimed
and kept for himself.

So we are free to pass to the second question: (2) DID circumstances or customs compel or induce man (whatever his original
condition) to resort to practices which made paternity uncertain,
and so caused kinship to be reckoned through women? On this
point also there seems to be no direct issue joined: Sir Henry
Maine and all of his ilk admitting that some peoples did and do
husband their women with many men and leave their children
with doubtful paternity. So that the discussion now rests its whole
weight upon this third interrogatory, whether (3) granting that
some races have been thus reduced to matriarchal forms of the
family, there is any reason to suppose that the stronger peoples,
like the Aryans and the Semites, have passed through a stage of

culture in which female, not male, kinship was chiefly recognized, probably as a result of polyandry? Rallying here for the defence of this stronghold of the McLennan theories, Mr. Lang brings to bear not less than six batteries of proof, made up of many pieces of various caliber. Three of his guns do not carry very far. He is forced to admit that the inference drawn from the form of capture in bridal ceremonies (which form has been noted as running from India through Sparta to Wales) is a very questionable inference which looks in several directions; and he offers the evidence drawn from myth and legend with an apology for its dimness, and that drawn from direct historical statements as to the onetime prevalence of the matriarchal family with an apology for its scantness.

His first point of strength is the custom of exogamy, for Sir Henry Maine himself declares that "the barbarous Aryan is generally exogamous." Mr. Lang allows himself to fancy that the origin of exogamy is to be found in "some early superstition of which we have lost the touch," but he is not deterred by this fancy from founding upon exogamy an emphatic argument for the matriarchal family. Since the man of an exogamous tribe must seek his wife beyond the bounds of a very distant kinship and is hedged by tables of prohibition which extend their restrictions far beyond the possible course of blood relationship, through indefinite degrees of affinity, Mr. Lang concludes that this custom must have originated when men's ideas of kinship were confused by the practices of polyandry: for had they known kinship through a father they could have made the range of prohibition both narrower and more definite.

That this broad indefinite relationship could have originated in other ways he does not seem to have seen, nor can anyone see it clearly who has not entered that splendid storehouse of social facts which Sir Alfred Lyall has recently opened to the world, and which he has himself explored with his masterly capacity for discriminating observation. Sir Alfred Lyall has seen the Aryan race in its social infancy. He is the chief representative of the British government in Rajpútána, that vast region of North-western India which lies towards Afganistan between the Indus and the Ganges, and where the pure-blooded Aryan Rajpút seems to have preserved the tribal and family organizations possessed by our ancestors before they emerged into the view of history. Here amongst the lawless men of the border the processes of tribal organization are to be seen in actual operation, and one can *watch* the widening of the circles of affinity, but we see nothing of polyandry and hear nothing of the matriarchal family. Carlyle is quoted as having said that "the perplexing jungle of primitive society springs out of many roots, but the hero is the tap-root from which in a great degree all the rest were nourished and grown," and here is the illustration of it. Daring men draw around them desperate followers; success and its consequent prestige increase the subject company; the restless, the adventurous, the outcast, the excommunicate from every wind of heaven join the prosperous standard; and then a tribe is about to be born: each unit of the miscellaneous horde preserves in its name the tradition of its extraction, but the instinct of the race finally draws these units together into the characteristic tribal organization, which adopts the fiction of a common descent from its valourous founder and *thus* extends those circles of indefinite kinship which puzzle the later observer, and cause the crystalization of those marriage restrictions which so harass the later tribesman. But not in the oldest of the immemorial traditions of this race whose life-breath is tradition is there any rumour of maternal descent. The whole structure is agnatic

It is not in the tribe alone, however, that such combinations take place: similar groupings, similar inner and outer circles of reputed affinity, are to be observed in the religious brotherhoods, in cast[e]s which also adopt the fiction of a common descent and also respect vexatious and all-embracing tables of prohibition. With them also kinship is fictitious, at first consciously, though afterwards converted by tradition into a semblance of physical fact.

But how did the names of women creep into family genealogies? There is no proof that amongst the Rajpúts kinship ever was reckoned in the maternal line; but amongst other branches of Aryan and Semitic peoples there is occasionally to be found evidence of such a reckoning. This, by the aid of Sir Henry Maine, we may possibly understand, without suspecting our race of polyandry. The breaking away of that crust of Mohammedanism which has in South-western [southeastern] Europe for so long obscured the persistent life of the subsoils of Slavonian society, has revealed to us the Slavs of the Southern provinces still ruling themselves according to family forms which the heel of the Turk has not been able to crush out, and whose survival reminds us of those hardy habits of local self-government which our Anglo-Saxon forefathers kept alive through all the long, blighting winter of Norman feudalism. Southern Slavonian families of near kin are still to be seen dwelling together under a common roof, in House-communities which are ruled over by the eldest or wisest male of the direct descent. Under this house-lord there is a housemistress (generally the wife of the chief) who governs the women of the family community. There is in this family government an element of election, however. Rulership descends from father to son only when the son is capable and worthy; and it not infrequently happens that some woman of masterful genius is suffered to succeed her husband and herself take the seat of supreme authority. Such women are the mothers who are canonized amongst the worshipful ancestors of the primitive peoples, and whose names get into the family lineage; but no Slav ever dreams of counting kinship otherwise than through at least an original paternal line.

We are prepared, therefore, to regard as inconclusive Mr. Lang's other proofs of confused or mythical genealogy and of artificial kinship, and can enter with clearer lights upon the consideration of his next point of insistence, which is, evidences of totemism, especially as seen in the names and organization of the Roman gens and the Grecian γένος. True, Mr. Lang enters upon this subject with a big "if": "if the supposed survivals of totemism among Aryans be accepted as genuine"; but he thinks the facts significant. "Were the gentes really of different stocks, as their names would imply and as people believed?" asks Mr. McLennan. "If so, how came clans of different stocks to be united in the same tribe? how came a variety of such groups, of different stocks, to coalesce in a local tribe?" Our attention is also called to the fact that family ancestry was sometimes traced to Zeus in animal form, or to some other god in like disguise; that one Athenian γένος reverenced an ancestral plant, the asparagus; and that these indications tally with corresponding peculiarities of tribal organization amongst the Irish and the British. Well, Sir Alfred Lyall has answered Mr. McLennan's question. He has seen Aryan gentes of different stocks combining as tribes, and even coalescing as local tribes, without any confusion about paternity. And he has seen, besides, illustrations of that universal social, or rather political, fact which seems to make plain the way towards an explanation of those fantastic family trees which were originally family vegetables. That fact is man's strong imitative faculty. There is nothing at all improbable in the tradition which Grey [John Henry Gray] has noted: "One origin of family names ascribed by the natives," he says, "is that they were derived from some vegetable or animal being common in the district which the family inhabit." Certain tribes there were of real blood kin; other tribes there were which were formed in imitation of these, which were made up at first of unrelated groups who assumed the name of their leader or arbitrarily chose a fanciful, emblematic

ancestry from God or animal or useful plant. This imitative fac-
ulty is vital even unto this day with nations as well as with tribes.
It has made the British Constitution the model of the world, and
English legislative methods the prevailing fashion of the times.

Nor is this all. Amongst Romans, Greeks, and Indians alike,
along with these perplexing suggestions of a onetime promiscuity
of sexual relations, there existed from the very earliest times,
by force of the very oldest traditions and habits of the races, that
worship of ancestors which [Fustel de] Coulanges has made so
picturesque, and in which, until the later inventions of memorial
times, male ancestors alone were the objects of worship. The
priesthood descended from father to son in direct and unbroken
line, and there was no recollection of a time when women entered
the reverenced lineage, though in sterile families the lines were
sometimes extended by adoption and other kindred devices which
confuse the vision of modern students of these ancient social
systems.

These are meagre, unsatisfactory, inadequate hints as to the
range and interest of this great discussion. It is a field of wonderful and increasing interest, full of flowers of delight for the student of history, a field in which one would fain linger. I hope that
I have said enough to make at least these two things plain: (1)
That the chief strength of the school of polyandry, in their effort
to saddle our kin with this ugly institution of promiscuity, lies in
the wide-spread traces of confused ideas of relationship; and (2)
that if we follow the great scholarly students of primitive social
life, we can be made sure that this confusion is explicable in
many ways which enable us to preserve our respect and admiration for our forefathers, as at least fine savages.

N.B. "There seems, in truth, to be a form of family dependency
still more archaic than any of those we know from the primitive
records of organized society. The agnatic union of kindred in
ancient Roman Law, and a multitude of similar indications point
to a period at which all the ramifying branches of the family tree
held together in one organic whole; and it is no presumptuous
conjecture that, when the corporation thus formed by the kindred
was in itself an independent society, it was *governed by the oldest
male of the oldest line.* It is true we have no actual knowledge of
any such society."

"This extract was taken from the third edition of the Ancient
Law, published in 1866, and it is curious to remember that about
that very time the author must have been occasionally in the
company, at Simla or elsewhere in India, of chiefs who held pre-

cisely the position here described conjecturally at the head of societies of the very kind for which Mr. Maine was then searching. The passage is a fine example of successful deduction; since the conclusion that such an organization must have existed appears to have been reasoned out from the indication and structural characteristics of later forms, without any knowledge that the earlier species could actually be observed in existence. In Rajpútána the Chief is supposed to be the nearest legitimate descendant in direct line from the founder of the state according to the genealogy of the tribe; and the heads of the branches from this main stock form the leading Rajpút nobles, the pillars of the state."–Sir A. Lyall.

N.B. "Totems are, as a rule, objects which may be easily drawn or tat[t]ooed, and still more easily indicated in gesture language." A. Lang.

WWT MS. (WP, DLC).
    [1] It is impossible to be precise about the date of this document. It seems most likely that it was prepared for Herbert Baxter Adams's course at the Johns Hopkins, "History of Politics," which Wilson took in the autumn semester of 1884-85. His notes taken in this course are described at October 8, 1884, Vol. 3. Adams, on November 19, 1884, discussed Aristotle on the origins of the family, the relation of the family to political economy, and village communities. He might well have asked Wilson to report on the literature on the origins of the family and Lang's article on that subject at the class meeting on the same day, November 19. Hence the date ascribed to the document.
    [2] Wilson lists this article by Lang and the works of authors subsequently mentioned in this report in the bibliography printed at March 27, 1890, Vol. 6.

INDEX

NOTE ON THE INDEX

THE alphabetically arranged analytical table of contents at the front of the volume eliminates duplication, in both contents and index, of references to certain documents, such as letters. Letters are listed in the contents alphabetically by name, and chronologically within each name by page. The subject matter of all letters is, of course, indexed. The Editorial Notes and Wilson's writings are listed in the contents chronologically by page. In addition, the subject matter of both categories is indexed. The index covers all references to books and articles mentioned in text or notes. Footnotes are indexed. Page references to footnotes which place a comma between the page number and "n" cite both text and footnote, thus: "624,n3." On the other hand, absence of the comma indicates reference to the footnote only, thus: "55n2"—the page number denoting where the footnote appears. The letter "n" without a following digit signifies an unnumbered descriptive-location note.

An asterisk before an index reference designates identification or other particular information. Re-identification and repetitive annotation have been minimized to encourage use of these starred references. Where the identification appears in an earlier volume, it is indicated thus: "*1:212,n3." Therefore a page reference standing without a preceding volume number is invariably a reference to the present volume. The index supplies the fullest known forms of names, and, for the Wilson and Axson families, relationships as far down as cousins. Persons referred to in the text by nicknames or shortened forms of names can be identified by reference to entries for these forms of the names.

A sampling of the opinions and comments of Wilson and Ellen Axson Wilson covers their more personal views, while broad, general headings in the main body of the index cover impersonal subjects. Occasionally opinions expressed by a correspondent are indexed where these appear to supplement or to reflect views expressed by Wilson or by Ellen Axson Wilson in documents which are missing.

INDEX

Abbe, Robert, Mrs. (Catherine Amory Palmer), 293,n3
Abbott, Lyman, 172,n1,2
Abridgement of the Debates of Congress from 1789 to 1856 (Benton), 194
Acton, John Emerich Edward Dalberg Acton, 1st Baron, 313,n2
Adams, Charles Francis (1835-1915), 62-63,n3
Adams, Henry, 50-51, 61
Adams, Herbert Baxter, 35n1, 108,n1, 110, 174-75,n2, 485n1; WW estimate of, 264-65
Adams, John, 212
Adams, John Quincy, 263
Ade, George, 228,n1, 234
Aesop's Fables, 269
Aguinaldo, Emilio, 48n2, 217
Ainsworth, William Harrison, 61
Alabama, University of, 106-7,n1,2,3
Alden, Henry Mills, 5-6, 22, 23, 27, 31, 37, 40-41, 60, 60n1, 64n5, 69, 85, 90, 91-92, 94, 112-13, 134, 142
Alderman, Edwin Anderson, 72,n5, 283
Alexander, Charles Beatty, 36n1
Alexander, Edwin Sherlock, 265
Alexander, James Waddel, 30, 74n1, 200n1, 257n2, 319, 321, 341, 342, 346, 347, 354, 356, 383, 421, 430, 474n1
Alexander, John White, 378
Alexander, Samuel, M.D., 455-56,n1
Alexander the Great, 269
Allen, H. J. Gregory, 147n2
Alton, William, 349
Alvey, Richard Henry, 376
American Bar Association, 187
American Historical Association, 194, 229, 284-85
American Nation Series, 229,n1, 230, 231-32, 233, 240, 241n1
American Review, 195
American Revolution (Fiske), 85,n1, 138
American Society for the Extension of University Teaching, 67, 71, 92
Amherst College, 419
anarchism, 185f, 187-88
Ancient Law (Maine), 331, 484-85
Anderson, Leroy Hammond, 384
Andrew, Abram Piatt, Jr., 458,n2
Andros, Sir Edmund, 38
Angell, James Burrill, 281
Annales (Tacitus), 250
Anschütz, Gerhard, 369,n2
Anson, Sir William Reynell, 242
Anthony, Andrew Varick Stout, 439-40,n1
Anthony, Robert Warren, 312n1
Aristotle, 71, 485n1
Armour, George Allison, 5,n4; Mrs.

(Harriette Foote), 75,n5; Armour dinner, 78
Armstrong, John Gassaway, 286
Atlanta *Constitution*, 432,n3,4
Atlantic Monthly, 4n3, 20, 81,n1, 227n
Augusta (Ga.) city bond, 52
Axson, Edward William, brother of EAW, 118n3, 120, 123n3, 126, 128, 129, 130, 148, 153, 393,n3; Mrs. (Florence Choate Leach), 118n3, 126, 129
Axson, Isaac Stockton Keith, paternal grandfather of EAW, 433n4
Axson, Margaret Randolph (Madge), sister of EAW, 117,n3, 118, 126, 127, 228, 391, 392
Axson, Stockton (*full name*: Isaac Stockton Keith Axson II), brother of EAW, 76, 117-18, 118, 119, 120,n3, 122, 126, 128, 286, 304, 315

Babson, William Arthur, 132-33
Bacchylides, 150
Bacon, Nathaniel, 29
Bagehot, Walter, 71, 92, 200, 301, 325, 365, 470
Baker, Ray Stannard, 196n, 359n8
Baldwin, James Mark, 77,n2,3, 326, 327, 329, 331
Ball, Thomas Randolph, 266
Ballantine, P., & Sons, 51n1
Baltimore: Music Hall, 278, 280
Baltimore American, 440n1
Baltimore News, 283n1, 440n1
Baltimore *Sun*, 280n, 283n, 440n1
Bancroft, George, 61, 102
Barker, Albert Smith, 58n3
Barnwell, Charles H., 415
Barringer, Brandon, 451,n2
Barringer, Daniel Moreau, 430-31, 434-35, 451-52, 456; Mrs. (Margaret Bennett), 430, 451
Barringer, Daniel Moreau, Jr., 451,n2
Barringer, Paul Brandon, M.D., 430,n2
Barringer, Sarah Drew, 451,n2
Barron, Alexander Johnston, 99, 286, 312n1
Battle of Princeton, 382
Battle of Trenton, 208-9, 208n1, 216, 217, 463
Bay State Hotel, Worcester, Mass., 192
Beattie, Hamlin, 425,n1
Begges, Adam J., Mrs. (A. Elizabeth Wilson), aunt of WW, 414
Beginnings of New England (Fiske), 85,n1
Benton, Thomas Hart, 194
Berea College, 308
Bergen, Frank, 173n2, 187
Berkeley, Sir William, 29, 104
Berlin, flag-worship in, 260,n1
Berlin, University of, 3, 31-32, 109

Bertha, 123
Beth, *see* Hibben, Elizabeth Grier
Beveridge, Albert Jeremiah, 58n3
Bibliothèque Internationale de Droit Public, 256n
bicycles, 43
Bigelow, John, 171n
Billings, John Shaw, M.D., 281
Bird, William Edgeworth, Mrs. (Sarah Baxter), 59, 66-67, 393, 437
Bird, Wilson Edgeworth, 59,n2
Bismarck, Otto Eduard Leopold von, 252
Blackstone, Sir William, 194n2
Blair, De Witt Clinton, 474n1
Blair, James, 38
Blair, John Albert, 271,n1
Blair, Robert Andrew, 312n1
Blass, Friedrich Wilhelm, 151,n4
"Blessed Damozel" (Rossetti), 354
Board, the, *see* Princeton University. *Trustees*
Böhm, Clara, 130,n1
"Bonheur de ce monde" (Plantin), 65n1
Boston Evening Transcript, 456,n1
Boucard, Max, 81,n2, 241, 256n
Boudinot, Elias, 212
Bowden, George E., 306,n2,3
Bowen, Francis, 39
Bowlby, Harry Laity, 138,n1
Boyer, Clarence Valentine, 459-60
Brackett, Cyrus Fogg, 23, 155, 185, 191, 192, 205, 256, 286, 287, 288,n5, 296,n7, 298, 302, 309, 315, 317, 318, 322, 326, 330, 339, 340, 341, 364, 374, 398
Braddock, Edward, 167
Bradley, Charles, 50-51,n1,2, 51-52, 58-59,n1,2
Bradley, Charles Burnet (Harvard 1904), 50
Bradley, Joseph P., 50-51,n1,2,3, 51-52, 58-59,n1,2
Bragdon, Henry Wilkinson, 200n2, 290n6, 433n, 470n4
Bramble Brae (Bridges), 294,n1
Bridges, Robert, 65,n1,2, 74n1, 139, 141, 206, 239, 294, 416, 436, 462-63, 467-68, 468, 478
Brief Narrative of the Ravages of the British and Hessians at Princeton in 1776-77 (ed. Collins), 5n5
Briggs, Frank Obadiah, 228n1
Brooklyn Daily Eagle, 449,n3
Brooklyn Institute of Arts and Sciences, 301
Brooks, John Hubert, 231
Brougham, Henry Peter, Baron Brougham and Vaux, 470
Brown, Dr. (Baltimore oculist), 463,n2
Brown, David, Mrs. (Susan Dod), 120,n7
Bruce, Philip Alexander, 328n2
Bryan, William Jennings, 79, 357
Bryant, William Cullen, 40,n3

Bryce, James, Viscount Bryce, 242, 471
Bryn Mawr College, 468
Bulkeley, Frances Hazen, 138n
Bulkley, Robert Johns, 286
Bullitt, Alexander.Scott, 405,n1
Burgess, John William, 79,n4
Burke, A. R., Mrs., 384
Burke, Edmund, 45,n1, 46, 71, 84, 86, 87, 211-12,n2,3, 213, 217-18,n4, 221, 470, 477
Burt, Alfred Farmer, 36,n7
Burt, Maxwell Struthers, 36,n6
Burt, Nathaniel, Mrs. (Jane Anna Brooke), 36,n5
Butler, Nicholas Murray, 283, 376, 436; Mrs. I (Susanna Edwards Schuyler), 436
Byles, Axtell Julius, 100, 133

Cadwalader, John Lambert, 3n, 200n1, 383, 398, 399, 455, 474n1
Caesar, Julius, 269
Calhoun, John Caldwell, 194-95
California, University of, 275, 462
Calvert family of Maryland, 95
Cambon, Jules, 144-45, 146,n2
Cambridge Modern History, 313,n2
Cambridge University Press, 313
Camden & Amboy Railroad, 382
Cameron, Arnold Guyot, *10:552,n8; 99, 138, 141, 286, 307, 312, 326, 327
Cameron, Henry Clay, 306,n2, 328, 329
Campbell, Charles, 100
Campbell, John Alexander, 227-28,n1, 463; Mrs. (Fannie Cleveland), 228
Captain Richard Ingle, The Maryland "Pirate and Rebel," 1642-1653 (Ingle), 94,n2, 163, 164
Carnegie, Andrew, 373,n2
Carnegie Institution of Washington, 277,n2
Carolina Tribute to Calhoun (Thomas), 194
Carter, Jesse Benedict, 25,n1, 152, 200n2, 466-67; Mrs. (Kate Benedict Freeman), 467
Catullus, 150
Celebration of the Twenty-Fifth Anniversary of the Founding of the [Johns Hopkins] *University and Inauguration of Ira Remsen, LL.D. as President of the University*, 277n, 347,-n2,3,4
Century Company, 48
Century Dictionary, 267
Century Magazine, 84, 84,n2, 157,n2
Chalmers, Thomas, 55,n4,5
Chapman, George, 328n3
Charge against President Grant and Attorney General Hoar of Packing the Supreme Court of the United States, to Secure the Reversal of the Legal Tender Decision, by the Appointment of Judges Bradley and Strong, Refuted (Hoar), 50,n3
Charlemagne, 269

Charles I, 95
Chatham, William Pitt, 1st Earl of, 211, 218, 470
Chesterfield, Philip Dormer Stanhope, 4th Earl of, 169
Chicago: 312; Chicago Club, 395; University Club, 348
Chicago, University of, 111-12, 145, 239; faculty, 79
Chicago & North Western Railroad, 378,n1
Chicago Tribune, 349n
Childs, Sandy, 415
Cicero, Marcus Tullius, 415
Clark, Edward Perkins, 427
Clemens, Samuel Langhorne, 194n3
Cleveland, Grover, 68-69, 114-15, 116, 122n1, 175n1, 187n1, 288n5, 292n, 295,n4, 297, 298, 309, 315, 316, 324, 330, 339, 341, 346, 357, 366, 367, 368, 382, 422, 441n2, 451n4; Mrs. (Frances Folsom), 78
Clifton, Essex Co., Mass., 464,n4
Clovelly, Devon, 128,n2
Cobden, Richard, 470,n4
Cocke, Lucian Howard, 69-70
Colby, Frank Moore, 87,n1
Coleman, Louis Garfield, 286
Columbia University, football game with Princeton (1900), 35,n2
college men in reform politics, T. Roosevelt plan to involve, 172,n2
Collins, Varnum Lansing, 5,n2,5, 194-95, 196-97, 208
Colonnade Hotel, Philadelphia, 117, 118
Colwell, Percy Robert, 461,n2
Comte, Auguste, 246, 251
Congress at Princeton, 382
Conover, Francis Stevens, 127,n2, 128
constitutional government defined, 178
Contemporary Review, 480
Contrat social (Rousseau), 253,n8
Cooley, Le Roy Clark, 265
Cooley, Thomas McIntyre, 242
Cornbury, Edward Hyde, Viscount, 142
Cornell University, football game with Princeton (1900), 35,n2
Cornwall, Henry Bedinger, 200n2, 257, 327, 329, 331
Cornwallis, Charles, 1st Marquis Cornwallis, 96, 209, 211, 393
Coronado, Francisco Vásquez de, 65,n2
Correspondence of John C. Calhoun (ed. Jameson), 194
Cotton, John, 55
Covington, Harry Franklin, 100,n1, 115, 132
Cox, Henry Bartholomew, 203n, 428n
Craig, Hardin, 461
Craven, Elijah Richardson, 257n2, 394,n1, 400
Critical Study of Nullification in South Carolina (Houston), 196
Critical Period of American History, 1783-1789 (Fiske), 85,n1

Cuba, 211, 217; U.S. policy toward (1901), 79
Curry, Jabez Lamar Monroe, 448,n1
Cutter, John C., Mrs. (Josephine Hunt), 192,n1, 192-93, 264
Cuyler, Cornelius Cuyler, 58, 65, 74n1, 297, 309, 315, 316, 316-17, 317, 318, 319, 322, 323, 323-24, 326, 329-30, 340, 341, 342, 349, 355, 363, 370, 371, 372-73, 374, 377, 378-79, 379, 380, 383, 384, 385, 386, 390, 394-95, 395, 396, 397, 401, 441, 442, 473-74, 474n1, 478, 479
Cuyler, Morgan & Co., 474
Czolgosz, Leon F., 186, 187n1

Dabney, Charles William, 283
Dabney, Richard Heath, 92-93
Dabney, Virginius, 92,n1
Dahlgren, Ulric, 327, 329
Daniels, Winthrop More, 100, 132, 290n6
Danville Sanitarium, 147
Davenport, Frederick Morgan, 442-443,n1,3
Davidson College, 442, 468
Davis, John David (Princeton 1872), 200n1, 203, 295,n5, 297, 309, 315, 400, 422, 474n1
Dean of the Graduate School, *see* West, Andrew Fleming
Death and Funeral Ceremonies of John Caldwell Calhoun (South Carolina General Assembly), 194
Declaration of the Rights of Man and of Citizens: A Contribution to Modern Constitutional History (Jellinek), 161,n1
Delaware & Raritan Canal, 382
democracy, 6f, 175-79
Democracy in America (de Tocqueville), 111,n3
Democratic Review, 195
Dennis, Alfred Lewis, Jr., 403,n1
Denny, George Hutcheson, 306,n1
Denver: Palace Hotel, 340
Dicey, Albert Venn, 242
Dod, Samuel Bayard, 457-58,n1, 464
Dodge, Cleveland Hoadley, 52n2, 66, 434, 445
Dodge, William Earl (1832-1903), 52,-n1, 58
Dodge, William Earl (1858-1884), 52n2
D'Olier, Franklin Woolman, 452-53,n1
Donald, Malcolm, 172n2
Dongan, Thomas, 2d Earl of Limerick, 40,n2
Dorrance, Benjamin Ford, 231
Dreka & Co., 138
Drummond, William, 29, 104
Dubose, McNeely, Mrs. (Rosalie Anderson), 122,n4
Duer, Edith, 409,n1
Duffield, Henry Green, 290n6
Duffield, John Thomas, 120,n5,6, 122,

Duffield, cont.
123, 127, 128,n1; Mrs. (Sarah E. Green), 127
Duguit, Léon, 81n2, 241-56
"Dumb and Formless Scholarship" (Page), 88,n1
Dunning, Henry White, 231
Dunning, William Archibald, 403,n1
Duquesne de Menneville, Ange, Marquis de, 167
Duruy, Victor, 250
Dwight, Timothy (1828-1916), 283

"Early History of the Family" (Lang), 480-85
East Orange (N.J.) High School, 426
Eastman, Anstice Ford, 138
Eaton, Seymour, 179n
Eckels, James Herron, 378
Edmund Burke (Morley), 87
"Educational Uses of Hypnotism" (Quackenbos), 22,n2
Edward I, 62
Elder, William L., 351n1; Mrs. (Laura Bowman), 351,n1, 355
Eliot, Charles William, 281
Elliott, Edward Graham, 3, 26,n3, 31-32, 73-74, 85-86, 109-10, 119, 134, 136-37, 159, 160-61, 162, 194-95, 195, 369, 381-82
Ely, Richard Theodore, 264-65, 402-3, 434
Ely, Robert Erskine, 293,n1
Emerson, Ralph Waldo, 351
Emery, John Runkle, 158
Epochs of American History, 229n2
Espinas, Alfred, 251,n6
Esprit des lois (Montesquieu), 249,n4
"Être ou ne pas être ou du postulat de la sociologie" (Espinas), 251,n6
Evangelical Alliance, 53
Ewing, Robert, 424,n1; Mrs. (Harriet Hoyt), 424n1
"Expulsive Power of a New Affection" (Chalmers), 55,n5

Fables in Slang (Ade), 228,n1, 234
family, the, early history of, 480-85
Farewell Address (Washington), 57
Farrand, Max, 161,n1
Farrand, Wilson, 312
Fentress, David, 438-39,n1, 457; Mrs. (Mabel Kingsbury), 457,n1
Ferris, George Henry, 231
Fielde, Adele Marion, 293,n4
Fine, Henry Burchard, *7:223,n3; 23, 100, 120, 132, 133, 155, 156, 185, 191, 192, 200n2, 205, 256, 257, 286, 287, 288,n5, 295, 296,n7, 297, 298, 302, 305, 309, 314, 315, 317, 318, 322, 327, 330, 339, 340, 341, 363, 364, 366, 373-74, 380, 390, 391n2, 398, 449; Mrs. (Philena Fobes), 120
Finley, John Huston, *7:271,n1; 28,n2, 76,n6, 99, 100, 104, 119, 120, 132,

141, 187n1; Mrs. (Martha Ford Boyden), 76,n6, 120
Fiske, John, 62, 85,n1, 112, 113, 138
Fithian, Philip Vickers, 5,n5
flag-worship, 258f
Flinn, Jean A., 85,n1, 130, 149, 153
Flinn, John William, 86n1
Foley, Maggie, 123,n2
football, 35,n2
Ford, Worthington Chauncey, 218n5
Forman, David, 268
Forsyth, William Holmes, 349
Fort, Franklin William, 100, 133
Fort, John Franklin, 173, 454,n1
Fort Monroe, Va.: Peninsula Twentieth Century Club, 265,n1; WW lecture, 265,n1
Fox, Charles James, 211, 213, 218
Franklin, Benjamin, 164-70, 212, 353, 361
Franklin, Josiah, 170
Franklin, Thomas, 165
Fraser, Abel McIver, 404,n1
Frazer, David Ruddach, 398
Freeman, Edward Augustus, 61, 62, 63
Freeman, Walter Jackson, M.D., 120,-n2, 121, 123, 125, 129, 131
Frelinghuysen, Frederick (Princeton 1770), 268
Freneau, Philip, 5n5
Freund, Ernst, 79,n2, 80
frontier, the U.S., 11, 215
Frost, William Goodell, 308,n1
Froude, James Anthony, 61
Fuller, Henry Amzi, 231
Fuller, Melville Weston, 194n3
fundamentalist controversy, 466n1
Fustel de Coulanges, Numa Denis, 250, 484

Galbraith (surveyor), 73
Garland, M. J. G., Mrs. (Mary Stebbins), 124,n1
Garrett, John Work, *11:113,n2; 5,n4
Gay, Sydney Howard, 40,n3
Gayley, James, 458,n1, 467
Genung, John Franklin, 143,n1
Geographical Distribution of the Vote of the Thirteen States on the Federal Constitution, 1787-8 (Libby), 102,n2
George II, 213
Gibbon, Edward, 61
Gierke, Otto Friedrich von, 32,n2, 109, 136
Gilder, Joseph Benson, 264,n1
Gilder, Richard Watson, 38, 48-49, 67-68, 84, 194n3, 264,n1, 427
Gildersleeve, Basil Lanneau, 194, 271-72, 272
Gilman, Daniel Coit, 35,n1, 87, 108, 110-11, 112, 174-75, 274-83, 447, 458; Mrs. (Elizabeth Dwight Woolsey), 447
Gittings, James, Mrs. (Mary E.), 83,n2, 196, 197-99
Gladstone, William Ewart, 139-40

Gneist, Rudolf von, 15
Godwin, Harold (Pete), *1:249,n3; 404
Gorman, Arthur Pue, 357,n2
Goucher College, 412
Gow, George Coleman, 359
Graham, James Chandler, 120,n3, 122, 126
Grant, Ulysses Simpson, 51n2,3, 269
Gray, John Henry, 483
Green, Elmer Ewing, 463
Green, Henry Woodhull, 5,n2, 401, 474n1
Green, John Richard, 23, 61, 62, 64, 142
Greenville, S.C.: Grand Opera House, 203-4, Greenville Lyceum Association, 204; WW lecture, 203-4
Greenville (S.C.) News, 204n
Gregory, Caspar René, 194
Griffin, Edward Herrick, 347,n1
Guizot, François Pierre Guillaume, 250
Gummere, William Stryker, 376

Hadley, Arthur Twining, 53,n3, 283, 404
Hale, William Gardner, 79-80,n1, 90
Hall, Granville Stanley, *3:73,n1; 281
Hall of Fame of Great Americans, New York University, 27,n1,3
Halle, University of, 26n4, 30,n1, 150-52
Halsey, Abram Woodruff, 193
Hamilton, Alexander, 216, 353, 361
Hammond, A. S., 366
Hampden, John, 218
Hampton Institute, 265,n1
Hancock, John, 212
Hardin, John Ralph, 173n2, 187
Harlan, John Maynard, *8:179,n3; 349
Harlan, Richard Davenport, 313,n1, 348, 372n2
Harper, George McLean, *3:571,n1; 36n1, 108, 141, 185, 290n6, 303, 327, 329, 368
Harper, Joseph Henry, 230, 231, 233-34
Harper, William Rainey, 111-12, 239, 283
Harper & Brothers, 23, 82, 84, 96, 101, 134, 142-43, 146, 155, 158n2, 174, 206, 207-8, 229, 230, 234, 240, 267, 285, 307, 313, 428, 439n1
Harper's Encyclopædia of United States History, 184n
Harper's Magazine, 6n1, 22, 22n2, 38, 38n1, 59, 60,n1, 62, 64n, 65n2, 69, 73, 81,n1, 90, 90n1, 91, 91-92, 94, 98, 104, 115, 134, 141, 142, 143, 174, 472
Harper's Weekly, 449,n2, 452,n3, 464
Harris, Abram Winegardner, 443-44,n1
Harris, Anna, 118n1
Harris, George, 419,n2
Hart, Albert Bushnell, *5:472,n1; 229, 229n1,2, 230, 231-32, 233, 240, 404-5
Harvard University, 145, 147, 148, 149, 150, 151, 152, 458; baseball game with Princeton, June 11, 1902, 420n2; debate with Princeton, May 10, 1901, 132-33,n11, March 26, 1902, 311-12
Harvey, George Brinton McClellan, *11:369,n2; 230, 231, 232-33
Hatschek, Julius, 109,n3
Hawkins, Gaylord Roscoe, 96,n3
Hay, John, 28,n1
Hayden, Horace Edwin, Sr., 231
Haydn, Franz Josef, 280
Hayes, Rutherford Birchard, 4n2
Hazen, Azel Washburn, 128,n2, 129, 132, 137-38, 413-14; Mrs. (Mary Butler Thompson), 128,n2, 129, 132, 137, 413, 414
Hazen, Maynard Thompson, 128, 129, 413
Heath, Daniel Collamore, 419
Hedges, Job Elmer, 96, 97n2, 107, 114
Heffelfinger, Louis, 265
Heidelberg, University of, 3, 85, 109-10, 119, 134, 136-37, 369
Heimera, Rosseau Falls, Ont., 147n2, 179n2
Henderson, Robert Randolph, *1:270,-n1; 144, 412, 431, 433; Mrs. (Louisa S. Patterson), 144
Henneman, John Bell, 425,n1
Henry V of England, 45, 221
Henry, James Addison, 422
Henry, (James) Bayard, 200n1, 257n2, 297, 309, 315, 344, 374, 379-80, 380, 382, 383, 390, 393-94, 398, 401, 474n1
Henry, Patrick, 212, 468
Hepburn, James Curtis, 421
Herbert B. Adams: Tributes of Friends, with a Bibliography of the Department of History, Politics, and Economics of the Johns Hopkins University, 1876-1901, 175n2, 265n1
Hermann, Carl Friedrich, 247
Hibben, Elizabeth Grier (Beth; Mrs. Robert Maxwell Scoon), 36,n4, 77, 163, 394
Hibben, John Grier, *9:125,n1,2; 35-36, 76-77, 108, 132, 163, 290n, 327, 329, 407, 456; Mrs. (Jenny Davidson), 36,n3, 76-77, 163, 290n, 394, 407
Hibben, Paxton Pattison, 368
Hildreth, Richard, 61
Hill, David Bennett, 357,n1
Hill, Edward, 95
Hill, Joseph Hall, 101
Hill School, Pottstown, Pa., 42
Hillard, Miss (of Wilmington, Del.), 21
Hintze, Otto, 32,n4
History of the English People (Green), 142
History of the University of Virginia, 1819-1919 (Bruce), 328n2
Hoar, George Frisbie, 50,n3, 51

Holst, Hermann Eduard von, *2:472,-n3; 102, 195
Homer, 150
Hooker, Thomas, 54-55, 177, 178
Hooper, Franklin William, 301,n1
Hope, Walter Ewing, 99, 100, 101, 133, 266,n1
Hopkins, Edward Washburn, 434,n1
Hopkins, Henry, 406
Hoskins, John Preston, 327
Houghton, Mifflin & Company, 85n, 113, 138, 265
Houston, David Franklin, 196
Howe, Annie, niece of WW, 85, 131,n2, 153
Howe, Edward, 162,n1
Howe, George, Jr., Mrs. (Annie Josephine Wilson), sister of WW, *1:3,-n6; 3,n3, 25, 26, 36, 85, 89,n2, 130-31, 147-49, 149, 150, 153
Howe, George, III, nephew of WW, 3n3, 25-26, 30, 74, 85, 109, 130, 131, 147, 148, 149, 149-54, 160, 431
Howe, James Wilson, nephew of WW, 88-89,n1
Howe, Sir William, 209
Howells, William Dean, 194n3
Howland, Louis, 359n8
Hoyt, Florence Stevens, first cousin of EAW, 112,n1, 123n4, 131,n1, 463-64
Hoyt, James Alfred, *204,n2, 425; Mrs. (Rebecca Caroline Webb), 204-5,n1,2
Hoyt, Jonathan Perkins, great-uncle of EAW, 205n2; Mrs. (Jane Johnson), 205n2
Hoyt, Margaret Bliss, first cousin of EAW, 131,n2
Hoyt, Mary Eloise (Minnie), first cousin of EAW, 120,n2, 120, 122, 123, 125, 126, 127, 128, 393
Hoyt, Nathan, grandfather of EAW, 205n2
Hoyt, Thomas Alexander, maternal uncle of EAW, 59,n1, 67, 129,n2, 131, 444-45; Mrs. (Sadie, or Saidie, Cooper; Aunt Saidie), 129,n2
Hoyt, William Dearing, M.D., maternal uncle of EAW, 131n2
Hübler, Bernhard, 32,n3, 136
Hume, David, 61
Humphreys, Willard Cunningham, 257, 327, 329
Hunt, Theodore Whitefield, *6:528,n1; 114n2, 329
Huntington, William Reed, 53
Hutchinson, Elijah C., 190n3
Hutton, Laurence, 92, 101, 407, 460; Mrs. (Eleanor Varnum Mitchell), 384, 384n1, 460-61
hypnotism, 22,n2
Hypnotism in Mental and Moral Culture (Quackenbos), 22n2

Imbrie, Andrew Clerk, 304
Indianapolis: Benjamin Harrison School, 350, 354; Contemporary Club, 174, 190, 200, 349, 351, 355; WW addresses, 174, 190, 200, 349, 350-54
Indianapolis News, 349n, 354n, 356, 358, 359n8, 391,n4, 472n8
Ingle, Edward, 94-95,n1,2, 102-3, 163, 164, 171, 440
Ingle, Richard, 94-95, 102, 163, 164, 171
Institute of Arts and Letters, see National Institute of Arts and Letters
International Cyclopedia, 87,n2
International Review, 470
Isham, William Burhans, Jr., 65,n3, 205,n1, 407; Isham dinners, 205n1, 206, 407,n1

Jackson, Job H., 39,n2
Jackson & Sharpe Co., 39n2
Jacob Tome Institute, Port Deposit, Md., 443-44n1
Jacobs, Thomas Armstrong, 438,n1
Jacobus, Melancthon Williams (Princeton 1877), *400,n2, 401
James, Abel, 168
James Sprunt Historical Monographs, 75n5
Jameson, Alexander F., Mrs., 206-7
Jameson, James Walker, 99
Jameson, John Franklin, *2:448,n2; 282, 427-28
Jefferson, Joseph, 57
Jefferson, Thomas, 13, 46, 215, 216, 268, 276, 328, 357
Jellinek, Georg, *6:170,n2; 85,n2, 109, 134, 136-37,n1, 161, 162, 369, 382
Jenkins, John Stilwell, 194
Jersey City: Jersey City Club, 267; Lincoln Association, 267, 270; WW speech, 267-71
Jersey Journal (Jersey City), 271n2
Jesup, Morris Ketchum, 373,n2, 376
Jèze, Gaston, 241, 256n
John (King of England, 1199-1216), 47
John C. Calhoun (von Holst), 195
Johns Hopkins Hospital, 277
Johns Hopkins Medical School, 277
Johns Hopkins University, 174-75, 256, 266, 274-83, 453, 468, 471, 472, 485-n1; WW mentioned for president, 35,n1; WW offered professorship, 108, 175, declines, 110-11, 112
Johnson, Robert Underwood, 93,n1, 158, 444
Joline, Adrian Hoffman, *6:683,n1; 409
Jones, David Benton, 200n1, *288,n1,5, 289n, 294-97, 298, 302, 303, 304, 305, 308, 309, 310, 312-13, 314, 315, 316, 317, 317-18, 319, 320, 321, 321-22, 323, 324, 326, 327, 329, 339, 340, 340-43, 343, 344, 346, 347, 348, 349, 354, 355, 356, 359, 363-64, 364, 366, 367, 368, 371,n1,2, 372, 373, 374, 375, 376, 377, 379, 380, 381, 383,

384-85, 386-90, 391n2, 395, 396, 397, 401, 474n1
Jones, John Paul, 103
Jones, Joseph Addison, 101
Jones, Richard Channing, 107n2
Jones, Thomas Davies, *7:614,n4; 322,n1, 322, 326, 349, 474n1
Jordan, David Starr, 283
Journal of the Presbyterian Historical Society, 394,n1
Joy, James Richard, 307,n1
Judd Haven, Muskoka district, Ont., 4n1, 49, 73, 370
Juvenal, 150

Kaiserin Maria Theresia, S.S., 76
Katzenbach, Frank Snowden, 325,n1
Keats, John, 328,n3
Keen, William Williams, M.D., 122,n1, 123, 124
Kellogg, Edwin Henry, 139,n1, 141, 368, 422
Kellogg, Oliver Dimon, 32,n5
Kemper, Frank Hathaway, 409-10,n1
Kennedy, William Blake, nephew of WW, 24-25, 32-33
Kennedy, Wilson Woodrow, nephew of WW, *11:352,n2; 24-25, n1,2, 32-33
Kerr, Alexander James, 433,n1
Kimball, Arthur Reed, 46,n1
Kimbrough (of Mississippi), 153,n8
King Philip (Indian), 29
Kinnicutt, Leonard Parker, 264,n4
Kipling, Rudyard, 361
Knight, Lucian Lamar, 432,n3,4,5
Knox, William White, 422
Kohler, Josef, 85,n5
Küsel, George C., 122,n2, 126, 128

Laband, Paul, 109,n1
Ladd, George Trumbull, 79,n3
Lafayette Hotel, Philadelphia, 81
Lake Forest College, 313,n1, 348, 372, 374, 377-78; WW lecture, 348
Lang, Andrew, 480-85
La Salle, Robert Cavelier, Sieur de, 40,n1
Laughlin, James, Jr., 200n1
Lawrenceville School, 67, 98, 451n4; *Lawrence* (school paper), 99n
Leach, Florence Choate, *see* Axson, Edward William, Mrs.
leadership, WW memorandum on, 365
Leathes, Stanley Mordaunt, 313,n2
Lee, Fitzhugh, 269
Lee, Francis Bazley, 5,n2
Lee, Henry (Light-Horse Harry), 218,-n5, 268
Lee, Robert Edward, 269
Legal Tender Decision of Supreme Court (1870), 50-51,n2,3, 58-59,n1,2
legislation, uniformity of, 173,n2, 187
Lehrbuch der greichischen Rechtsalterthümer (Hermann), 247,n3
Leisler, Jacob, 38

Letters of Theodore Roosevelt (ed. Morison *et al.*), 441n1
Lewis & Hartzog, Greenville, S.C., 204
Libbey, William, *7:176,n1; 158
Libby, Orin Grant, 102,n1, 446,n1
Library of American Biography (ed. Sparks), 39,n1
Life and Memorable Actions of George Washington (Weems), 269-70
Life of John Caldwell Calhoun (Jenkins), 194
"Life of Sir William Phips" (Bowen), 39,n1
Limerick, Thomas Dongan, 2d Earl of, 40,n2
Lincoln, Abraham, 267-70, 350
Lionberger, Isaac Henry, 203,n1
Literary Landmarks of Oxford (Hutton), 92, 101
Littell's Living Age, 195
Little, Henry Stafford, *11:112,n1; 116, 422
Livingston, Robert R., 13, 212
Locke, John, 177, 178, 285
"Log College of Neshaminy and Princeton University" (Craven), 394,n1
Loomis, Elmer Howard, 257, 327, 329
Long, Augustus White, 461,n1
Lord, James Brown, 407,n2
Lord, Lura B., 163
Loudon, James, 282
Louisiana, 4,n3
Lovejoy, Elijah Parish, 26-27,n3
Lovett, Edgar Odell, *10:552,n7; 402; Mrs. (Mary Ellen Hale), 402
Low, Seth, 194n3, 312n1
Lowell, James Russell, 358,n7
Luchaire, Achille, 250
Lyall, Sir Alfred Comyn, 481, 483, 485

McAlpin, Charles Williston, 159-60,n1, 160, 161-62, 370, 375-76, 378, 380
Macaulay, Thomas Babington, 1st Baron Macaulay, 61, 144n1
McCay, Leroy Wiley, 256
McClure, Alfred James, Jr., 410,n2
McClure, Alfred James Pollock, 410,n1
McClure, Jay Cooke, 410,n2
McCook, John James, 383, 396, 437, 474n1
McCormick, Cyrus Hall, Jr. (1859-1936), *5:767,n3; 120,n4, 133, 144-45, 146, 228, 234, 257n2, 288, 288n5, 292n, 295, 296, 297-98, 298, 302, 303, 304, 305, 308-10, 311, 312, 313, 314, 315-16, 317, 318, 319-21, 321, 322, 323, 324, 326, 327, 329, 330, 339, 340-43, 343, 344, 344-45, 346-47, 347, 347-48, 349, 354, 355, 356, 359, 363, 364, 366, 367, 368, 370, 371, 371,n1,2, 372, 373, 374-75, 376, 377, 378, 379, 380, 381, 383, 384, 386, 387, 388, 394, 395, 395-96, 397, 398, 401, 408, 473-74, 474n1, 478-79; Mrs. (Harriet Hammond), 120,n4, 133, 141, 145, 146, 345

McCormick, Stanley, 474n1
McCosh, James, *7:133,n4; 53, 105, 200, 292n, 293n, 420, 468
McCusker, James, 417
MacDonald, Pirie, 417
McElroy, Robert McNutt, 32,n5
McEwan, William Leonard, 461,n3
McFee, Charles Wolf, 413,n1
Machen, Arthur Webster, Sr., Mrs. (Mary Gresham; Minnie), *4:345; *6:538,n1; 465-66
Machen, John Gresham, *465,n1
Machiavelli, Niccolò, 71
McIlwain, Charles Howard, 452,n1,2
McKelway, Alexander J., M.D., 450,n5
McKelway, John Ryan, 450,n5
McKelway, St. Clair, 58n3, 449-50,n1; Mrs. II (Virginia Brooks Thompson), 449
Mackenzie, James Cameron, *8:28,n1; 451n4
McKinley, William, 79, 185-87, 234
McLauchlan, William Henry, 108,n2
McLennan, John Ferguson, 480, 481, 483
Macloskie, George, 36n1, 326, 329, 331
McMaster, Jim, 415
McMaster, John, 415
McMaster, John Bach, 61-62, 102, 115,-n1, 284-85
McMillan, Charles, 105,n2
Macmillan, Kerr Duncan, 32,n5
McPherson, Simon John, 36n1, 200n1, 295,n6, 296, 297, 298, 309, 315, 324-25, 330, 339, 341, 342, 346-47, 347-48, 355-56, 366, 367, 368, 372, 400, 401, 450-51n4
MacVane, Silas Marcus, 79,n4
MacVannel, John Angus, 58n5
McVeagh, Isaac Wayne, 4,n2, 393, 453
Madge, see Axson, Margaret Randolph
Madison, James, 46, 268, 361, 468, 469
Magie, William Francis, *1:360,n6; 36n1, 120, 160, 185, 200n2, 257, 290n6, 291n, 292n, 307, 326, 327, 329, 331, 448-49; Mrs. (Mary Blanchard Hodge), 120, 449
Magie, William Jay, 448,n2
Magna Carta, 44, 47, 219
Maine, Sir Henry James Sumner, 330-31, 480, 481, 482, 485
Mallet, John William, 281-82
Manila Bay, Battle of, 216
Marquand, Allan, *7:51,n2; 327, 329; Mrs. (Eleanor Cross), 384
Maryland, 94-95
Maryland Historical Society, 94, 95n2
Mason, Henry Eager, 348
Mason, Norman Howell, 99,n1
Mathis, John Cass, 288,n1, 303, 349
matriarchal family, 480-83
Maynard, James, Jr., 425
Memorial History of the City of New York (ed. Wilson), 40,n2
Merle-Smith, Wilton, see Smith, Wilton Merle

Merrill, Charles White, 174, 190, 200
Merrill, Elmer Truesdell, 414-15
Meyer, Georg, 109,n1
Meyers, James Cowden, 411,n1
Miles, Nelson Appleton, 58n3
Miller, Hugh Gordon, 268-70,n1, 271,-n2, 306-7
Miller, John Norris, 96-97,n1,2, 107, 114,n2, 154-55
Miller, Samuel Freeman, 50
Minnie, see Hoyt, Mary Eloise
Minor, Mary D., Mrs., 120,n8
Miscellaneous Writings of the Late Hon. Joseph P. Bradley (ed. Bradley), 59n2
Montesquieu, Charles de Secondat, Baron de La Brède et de, 10, 71, 219, 249,n4, 285
Moody, Dwight Lyman, 66n2
Moore, John Bassett, 108,n2
"Moral Value of Hypnotic Suggestion" (Quackenbos), 22,n2
Morgan, Junius Spencer, 5,n3
Morison, Elting Elmore, 441n1
Morley, John, Viscount Morley, 87
Morris, Gouverneur, 212
Mott, John R., 66,n3
Moulton, Arthur Julian, Mrs. (Catharine Lewis), 25,n2
Moulton, Arthur Julian, Jr., 26n2
Munn, Henry Benson, 422
Murphy, Franklin, 326, 454-55,n1
Murray, David, 445
Murray, James Ormsbee, *7:96,n1; 290n; Mrs. (Julia Richards Haughton), 75,n4
Muskoka Lakes, Ont., 4n1, 49-50,n1,2, 73, 89, 91, 370

Napoléon I, 62, 252, 269
Narrative and Critical History of America (ed. Winsor), 40,n1, 41, 49, 194, 229
Nashville American, 440n1
National Institute of Arts and Letters, 93,n2, 158,n1, 465
Neher, Fred, 200n2, 327, 331
Nelson, William, 5,n3, 141-42, 143
New Brunswick Presbytery, 328
New International Encyclopædia, 87,-n1, 4
New Jersey: history, 4-5
New Jersey Commission for the Promotion of Uniformity of Legislation in the United States, 173,n2, 187
New Jersey Historical Society, Woman's Branch, 206-7
New Orleans, 4n2, 13
New York City: Aldine Association, 93, 239,n1; City History Club, 293; Delmonico's, 124n1; Evangelical Alliance, 53; Lawyers' Club, 438; League for Political Education, 293; Lenox Library, 439; New England Society, 52-58, 66, 75,n1; Presbyterian Union, 203; St. Nicholas So-

ciety, 122n1, 124,n1, 125; Waldorf-Astoria Hotel, 58n1, 442; WW speeches, 52-58, 66, 75,n1, 124,n1, 125, 328,n1,2

New York *Evening Post*, 427,n3, 451n4

New-York Historical Society, 40

New York Law School, 472

New York *Sun*, 449,n4, 456n2, 457

New York Times, 35n1, 328n1

New York Tribune, 125n1

New York University, Hall of Fame of Great Americans, 27,n1,3

New-York Weekly Journal, 60

Newcomb, Simon, 282

Ninety-Fifth Anniversary Celebration of the New England Society in the City of New York, 58n1

Nisbet, Charles Richard, 432,n1

Nisbet, James Douglas, M.D., 147,n1, 149, 154

North, Frank Mason, 408,n1; Mrs. (Louise Josephine McCoy), 408

North American Review, 50, 51n2, 195

North Carolina, University of, 75n5, 97-98,n1

Northfield (Mass.) *Echoes*, 478n

Northfield Students' Conference, 66,n2, 474,n1

Norton, Wilbur T., 26,n2

Notman, William Robson, 395,n1

"Ode Recited at the Harvard Commemoration, July 21, 1865" (Lowell), 358,n7

Oertmann, Paul Ernst Wilhelm, 32,n1

"Old-Fashioned Democrat," 356-58, 390-91, 472n8

Old Virginia and Her Neighbors (Fiske), 85,n1

Olney, Richard, 194n3, 357,n4

"On First Looking into Chapman's Homer" (Keats), 328n3

Orange, N.J., 458

Ormond, Alexander Thomas, *6:528,-n2; 200n2, 303, 307, 326, 327, 329, 331, 368, 369

Osborn, Edwin Curtis, 137, 159,n1, 162

Osborn, Henry Fairfield, *7:623n3; 376

Osler, Sir William, M.D., 418,n5

Otis, Elwell Stephen, 48n2

Owen, William Bishop, 152,n6

Pach Brothers, 416

Page, Thomas Nelson, 231-32, 428

Page, Walter Hines, *2:96,n4; 88, 435

Palmer, Benjamin Morgan, 445,n1, 465

Palmer, Edgar, 386n1

Palmer, Stephen Squires, 385,n1, 474n1

Paltsits, Victor Hugo, 439,n3, 440

Park Avenue Hotel, Plainfield, N.J., 312

Parker, Alton Brooks, 357,n3

Parkman, Francis, 61

Parrott, Thomas Marc, 368,n1

Pater, Walter, 354

patriotism, 258-64

Pattee, Fred Lewis, 5n5

Patton, Francis Landey, *3:114,n3; 3n, 20n1, 26-27, 35,n1, 77,n4, 97-98,n1, 116, 119, 145, 156, 158, 159, 185, 194, 200n2, 207, 256-58, 282-83, 285, 286, 288n5; Editorial Note: The Crisis in Presidential Leadership at Princeton, 289-93n; 295-98, 307, 308-10, 311, 313, 314, 315, 316-17, 318, 319, 320, 321, 322, 323, 324, 325, 327, 329, 330, 331, 339, 340, 341, 342, 343, 344, 345, 346, 347, 349, 354, 356, 359, 363, 364, 366, 367, 368, 370, 371, 371,n1,2, 372, 373, 374, 374,n3, 375, 376, 377, 378, 379, 380, 381, 382, 383, 385, 386, 387, 388-90, 394, 395-97, 397n1; resignation presented to Trustees, and accepted, 398-400; 401, 412, 413, 415, 417, 420-21, 422-23, 426, 447, 450-51n4, 455, 456n2, 457,n1, 461, 466, 468, 472, 473-74, 478, 479; F. L. Patton Fund, 473-74, 474n1, 478, 479. *See also* Princeton University, *Retirement of President Patton*

Patton, George Stevenson, *7:528,n1; 374,n3, 385,n2

Peabody, Endicott, 172n2

Peabody Normal Institute, 424

Pearson, John H., 415

Peck, Harry Thurston, 87,n3

Penfield, Edward, 38,n1

Penn, William, 40,n3

Pennsylvania, Historical Society of, 40

Pennsylvania Scotch-Irish Society, 67,-n2

Perry, Bliss, *8:179,n3; 3-4, 20n, 75, 76, 78, 290, 405-6; Mrs. (Annie Bliss), 4, 75, 76, 78, 405-6

Peterson, William, 282

Phi Kappa Psi fraternity, 466,n2

Phidias, 61

Philadelphia: Colonnade Hotel, 117, 118; Lafayette Hotel, 81; Scotch-Irish Society, 67,n2; Witherspoon Hall, 71, 92; WW lectures, 67, 71

Philadelphia Orthopaedic Hospital, 117,n1, 133

Philadelphia *Public Ledger*, 67n2

Philip Vickers Fithian: Journal and Letters (ed. Williams), 5,n5

Philippines and Filipinos, 11, 17, 18, 19, 44, 47-48,n2, 79, 99, 215, 217, 218, 222, 223, 224, 225, 226, 360, 362

Phillips, William Battle, 442,n1

Phinizy, Bowdre, 416,n1

Phips, Sir William, 38, 39

Phraner, Francis Southmayd, 411,n1

Pilgrim's Progress (Bunyan), 269

Pinckney, Charles Cotesworth, 212

Pischel, Richard, 30,n1

Pitcairn, Robert Fulton, 100

Pitt, William (the elder, 1708-1778), 1st Earl of Chatham, 211, 218, 470

Plainfield, N.J.: Park Avenue Hotel, 312; Princeton alumni, 301-2, 312; WW speech, 301-2, 312

Plantin, Christophe, 65n1

Plato, 150

Poems of Philip Freneau, Poet of the American Revolution (ed. Pattee), 5n5

Political Primer of New York City and State: The City Under the Revised Charter of 1902 (Field), 293,-n4

Popular History of the United States (Bryant and Gay), 40,n3

Poughkeepsie Daily Eagle, 363n

Powers, James Knox, 106,n2

"Prayer of Old Age" (Bridges), 65,n2

Prentice, William Kelly, 152,n5

Presbrey, Frank, 74n1

Presbyterian Church in the United States of America [northern]: Assembly's Special Committee on Sustentation, 446,n2; fundamentalist controversy, 466n1; New Brunswick Presbytery, 328

Presbyterian Historical Society, 394,n1

President, the, *see* Patton, Francis Landey

Price, Samuel Britton, 231

Princeton, N.J.: Battle of, 382; Congress at, 382; great ice storm of Feb. 1902, 283-84; history, 4-5; Morven, 382; Potter's Woods, 470; Present Day Club, 76,n7, 78; Second Presbyterian Church, 123,n3; Village Improvement Society, 384,n1

Princeton Alumni Weekly, 71n, 74,n1, 101n, 108n, 116n, 119, 129,n1, 141, 158n, 194n, 200n1, 231n, 265, 304n, 312n, 390,n3, 422, 424n, 451n4, 456,n1

Princeton Club of New York, 200n1

Princeton Historical Association, 4-5,n1

Princeton Inn, 99, 138, 140, 285, 295, 315, 324, 368, 384

Princeton Press, 35n, 173n, 328n, 384-n1, 463n

Princeton Theological Seminary, 375, 432, 466n1

Princeton University: Albert B. Dod Hall, 330; Alexander Hall, *9:215,-n5; 28, 114, 116, 133n1, 158, 187n1, 422; Alumni luncheon, June 10, 1902, news report, 420-24; *Alumni Princetonian*, 74n1; alumni trustees, 200,n1; American Whig Society, 23, 24, 96-97,n2, 100, 107, 108, 114,n2, 154-55, 303-4, 469; charter amended for alumni trustee representation, 200n1; Chemical Laboratory, 307, 326; Cliosophic Society, 23, 24, 96-97,n2, 100, 114,n2; 154-55, 303-4; Commencement exercises, June 11, 1902, news report, 422-24; The Crisis

in Presidential Leadership: Editorial Note, *see Retirement of President Patton*, below; curriculum, 256-58; three-year A.B., 391,n1,2; David Brown Hall, 111,n2; Dickinson Hall, 44; Dodge Hall, 132; elective system, 200n2; executive committee (proposed), *see Retirement of President Patton*, below; football, 35,n2, 66; Halls, *see* American Whig Society, Cliosophic Society; Harvard baseball game, June 11, 1902, 420n2; Harvard-Princeton debate, May 10, 1901, trials, 132-33,n1; debate of March 26, 1902, 311-12; Honor System, 195; inauguration of President Wilson (planned), 441,n2; Library, 4-5; Log College and Princeton, 394,n1; Lynde Debate of 1879, 470; Marquand Chapel, 286, 461; McCosh Hall, 442n4; Monday Night Club, 111,n1, 330; Murray Hall, 33, 34, 100, 132, 139, 273; Nassau Hall, 116,n1, 138, 158; New York *Sun* articles on Patton resignation and Wilson election, 449,n4; Philadelphian Society, *7:61,n1; 33-34, 139; Physics Department, 449; Prospect, 295, 296, 311, 462, 464, 478; representation at U.S. Military Academy Centennial, 1902, 437-38; School of Law proposed by WW (1890f), mentioned, 289n; Sesquicentennial Celebration, 1896, mentioned, 36n1, 194,-n1, 289n; Seventy-Nine Hall, 441,n4; Special convocation following assassination of President McKinley, 187n1; Spencer Trask Prize, 100-1; Stafford Little Lectures, 114-15,n1,2, 116; University Glee Club, 312; University Hall, 92; University Press Club, 138; Yale-Princeton debate, March 30, 1901, 100-1, victory celebration, 115-16

Chicago alumni, 288, 312, 348-49

Class of 1879: "Coronation Committee," 441,n2; Seventy-Nine Hall, 441,n4

Daily Princetonian, 5n, 24n, 33n, 34n, 44n, 51n, 67n, 78, 80n, 92, 99-100, 100n, 104n, 111n, 114n2, 115, 132n, 133, 140n, 141, 273, 285-86, 286n, 331n, 369, 410n2, 470

Faculty committees: On Condition of Scholarship of the Academic Department, 200n2; On Schedule of Studies, 376; On the Graduate School, 36n1, 185, 191, 192, 207, 230, 235-38; To Appear Before and Confer with Trustees, if required, 155, 156, 205,n1, 286, 287, 309, 315, 398; To Confer with Trustee Committee on the Curriculum, 256-58; University Committee on Scholarship, 292n, 307, 326, 327, 329, 363 (text of report, 331-39); School of Science Faculty to confer with Academic Faculty Scholarship Committee, 200n2

Faculty minutes quoted: 23, 155, 185, 191, 200n1, 205, 207, 230, 235-38, 256-58, 286, 307, 326, 326-27, 329, 331-39; Academic Faculty minutes cited, 200n1; School of Science Faculty minutes cited, 200n1

Graduate School: explanatory notes, 36-37,n1, 289n, 291n, 292n; Trustees appoint special committee to confer with faculty committee, June 6, 1900, 36n1; faculty committee appointed, 36n1, 185, terminates existing graduate courses, new courses to be constituted, committee to appear before and confer with Trustees, 191; Trustees approve faculty report, Oct. 19, 1900, 37n1; Graduate School established and Dean West appointed, Dec. 13, 1900, 37n1; faculty committee report on standards of graduate work, 207, 230 (text of report, 235-38), adopted by Trustees, March 13, 1902, 238n1; WW appeals for "a great graduate college," 424

Nassau Literary Magazine, 368-69, 470; banquet, May 6, 1901, 139, 140-41

New York Alumni, 200n1

Northeastern Pennsylvania alumni, 231

Princeton Alumni Weekly, 71n, 74,-n1, 101n, 108n, 116n, 119, 129,n1, 141, 158n, 194n, 200n1, 231n, 265n, 304n, 312n, 390,n3, 422n, 424n, 451n4, 456,n2

Princeton University Bulletin, 28n, 187n, 187n1

Retirement of President Patton: Editorial Note: The Crisis in Presidential Leadership at Princeton, 289-93n; Conference of D. B. Jones and C. H. McCormick with WW, H. B. Fine, and C. F. Brackett on Patton inaction, 288,n5, 295, 298n1, conference of Trustees at Princeton Inn, 295-96, Jones and McCormick confer with Patton, 295-96; proposed executive committee, 288n5, 295, 296, 297-98, 299, 300 (Wilson-Fine-Brackett memorandum, 300-1, 302), 303, 304, 305, 308-10 (McCormick-Jones memorandum, 310), 315, 316, 317, 318, 319, 320, 321, 324-25, 329, 330, 339, 340, 341, 342, 343, 344-45, 346, 347, 354, 356, 364, 367, 389; Jones to WW: speaks of Patton surrender, 312-13; Patton visits C. C. Cuyler, 316-17, writes to J. W. Alexander, 319; McCormick to Cuyler: radical improvements must be made, 319-21; Alexander to McCormick: cannot support revolutionary measure of executive committee without

president, 321; McCormick wishes to keep WW, Brackett, and Fine posted, 322; WW to McCormick: new method ought to be tried, 323; S. J. McPherson dubious about executive committee, 324-25; Patton to McCormick: memorandum involves changes different from what he contemplated, 327; WW to McCormick: Brackett, Fine, and WW approve Patton on executive committee, want Cleveland chairman, McPherson vice-chairman, 330; McCormick to Wilson: agrees with above, he and Jones "appreciate as fully as possible how much Professors Brackett and Fine and you are doing to help in this noble enterprise," 339; McCormick to Jones: "matters are becoming warm with regard to the questions we have started at Princeton"; met WW, Pyne, and Cuyler in New York, Cuyler satisfied Patton was ready to resign at any time, Patton thinks most of criticism comes from West, satisfied with high position taken by WW, 340-43; McCormick to Alexander: hopes to so shape matters that *the president himself* will be willing to make any proposals that are made at the June meeting, 345; Jones to McCormick: doubts support of Cuyler and Pyne, danger of compromise or postponement placing Patton in saddle again, 363; Patton intimates contemplating retirement in interview with Jones, outlines conditions and terms, 371,n1, Jones writes of financial terms, 377, Patton denies proposition, 372, 379; H. B. Fine to Jones: Patton thinking of Henry van Dyke as his successor, 373-74; Jones to McCormick: danger of van Dyke more fancied than real, John A. Stewart, Cuyler, and Bayard Henry all favor WW, Patton got no comfort from Stewart, Pyne, and Cuyler in New York, 380; Jones to McCormick: Pyne has ratted, 384-85, Jones replies strongly to Pyne, 386-88; S. S. Palmer offers to finance Patton retirement, 385; Patton to Jones on retirement and compensation expected, 388-90; Patton conference with Jones and McCormick in Chicago, 395, McCormick informs Pyne of interview, 395-96; McCormick to Cuyler on second Chicago interview, 397,n1; Patton resignation presented and accepted by Trustees, 398

St. Louis alumni, 200n1, 202-3

Trenton alumni, 325-26

Trustees, 5n2, 23, 27, 36n1, 89, 155, 156, 162, 191, 192, 200n1, 205, 238, 256-58, 286, 287, 288n5, 289-93n,

Princeton University, cont.
295, 296, 297, 298, 299, 300, 302, 304, 308, 309, 310, 311, 313, 315, 316, 317, 319, 321, 330, 339, 341, 345, 346, 354, 363, 364, 367, 368, 372, 373, 374, 375, 376, 377, 378, 379, 381, 385, 386, 387, 388, 390, 396, 397n1, 398-402, 411, 413, 422, 423, 435, 437, 448, 455, 457, 461, 464, 472; Committee on the Curriculum, 256-58, 257n2; Committee on Grounds and Buildings, 442; Special Committee on the Affairs of the University (1896-98), mentioned, 289n, 291n; Special Committee on the Curriculum, 257-58n2, 398-99,n1; Special Committee on the Graduate Department, 36n1; Trustees Minutes quoted, 156, 192, 200n1,2, 287, 398-402, 413
   Union County (N.J.) alumni, 301, 312
   Western Association of Princeton Clubs, 200n1
Pritchett, Henry Smith, 283
Problems in Modern Democracy (Eaton and Speirs), 179n
Proceedings of the Annual Conference of Commissioners on Uniform State Laws, 173n2
Prothero, George Walter, 313,n1, 443
Puerto Rico, 17, 225, 226, 362
Puritans, New England, WW on, 53f
Pyle, Howard, *9:316,n1; 5, 29-30, 31, 38, 39-40, 95-96, 97, 103, 103-4, 115, 117
Pym, John, 218
Pyne, Moses Taylor, *5:132,n2; 5, 36n1, 74n1, 122, 125, 200n1, 257n2, 292n, 295, 297, 309, 315, 319, 320, 321,n1, 323, 340, 349, 355, 356, 363, 366, 367, 368, 371, 374-75, 377, 379, 380, 381, 383, 384, 385, 386-88, 395-96, 397, 398, 400, 401, 422, 441, 445n2, 474, 474n1, 479; Mrs. (Margaretta Stockton), 122, 125, 375
Pyne, Percy Rivington (Princeton 1878), 445,n1

Quackenbos, John Duncan, M.D., 22,-n1,2
Queen, John Wahl, 422

Randolph, Charles Brewster, 150,n2, 152
Randolph-Macon College, 305
Rankin, Walter Mead, 200n2
Reading, Pa.: Rajah Temple, 238; WW lecture, 238-39
Reading (Pa.) *Eagle,* 239n
Réalité sociale (Tarde), 252,n7, 254,-n9,10
Recht des modernen Staates (Jellinek), 161,n2

Records of the Governor and Company of the Massachusetts Bay in New England (ed. Shurtleff), 41
Reed, James Hay, 376, 422
Reeves, Alfred Gandy, 312
Reflections on the Revolution in France (Burke), 45,n1, 46, 217-18,n4
Reformation, H.M.S., 94
Reid, Harry Fielding, *8:507,n1; 83, 199n1, 284, 391n1, 397, 453; Mrs. (Edith Gittings), *8:507,n1; 81-83, 196, 197-99, 272-73, 283-84, 391n1, 392, 393, 397, 453-54
Reid, Legh Wilbur, 412,n1; Mrs., 412
Reiter, Howard Roland, 138,n2
Remsen, Ira, 35n1, 256, 278, 280, 447-48
Renick, Edward Ireland, *2:96,n1; 470-71,n5
representative government, 8f
Review of Reviews (New York), 416, 468, 473n
Revue philosophique, 251n6, 252n7
Rhodes, James Ford, 62, 194n3, 465
Rice, Richard Austin, 156-57, 157
Richard (yardman), 127,n1
Richardson, Ernest Cushing, *7:538,-n2; 5, 164n3; Mrs. (Grace Ely), 163,n3
Richardson, Mary Ely, 163,n3
Richmond (Va.) *Times,* 440n1
Ricketts, Henrietta, 163,n2, 228
Ricketts, Louis Davidson, 164n2
Ricketts, Palmer Chamberlaine, Jr., 164n2
Ricketts, Palmer Chamberlaine, Sr., Mrs. (Eliza Getty), 163,n2
Rip Van Winkle (play), 57
Rise of the New West, 1819-1829 (Turner), 241n1
Robbins, Edmund Yard, 200n2
Roberts, William Henry, 446,n1
Robinson, Charles H., 52n1, 71
Robinson, Elizabeth, 391
Robinson, Frederick J., Mrs., 52n1, 72n2
Robinson, Philip Ely, 32,n5
Rockwood, Charles Greene, Jr., 200n2
Rogers, Noah Cornwall, 203
Rood, Henry Edward, 60,n1
Rood, Ogden Nicholas, 194
Roosevelt, Theodore, 164, 172, 194n3, 262, 263, 441, 454
Rosseau Falls, Ont., 147n2, 179n2; Lake Rosseau, 50n1
Rossetti, Dante Gabriel, 354
Rousseau, Jean-Jacques, 178, 181, 244, 251, 253,n8
Royce, Josiah, 282
Royce & Henderson, 370
Runyon, William Nelson, 312
Russell, Archibald Douglas, Mrs. (Albertina Pyne), 474n1
Rutgers College, 445
Rutledge, John, 212

St. Louis: University Club, 202
St. Louis Post-Dispatch, 203n
Satterlee, Henry Yates, 29n1
Saunders, Paul Hill, 152,n6
Saussy, Frederick Tupper, 159,n2, 160
Schmoller, Gustav Friedrich von, 85,-n3, 136
Schouler, James, 102, 281
Schulze, Hermann Johann Friedrich, 109,n1
Scott, Samuel Bryan, 133
Scott, William Berryman, 185, 329
Scribner, Charles, 5,n4, 74n1
Scribner's Magazine, 65, 65n2
Scudder, Horace Elisha, *3:149n1; 265,n2
Sears, Joseph Hamblen, 230, 231, 232
Select Works of Thomas Chalmers, D.D., LL.D., 55,n5
"Session, 1869-70" (Adams), 50-51
Sewickley, Pa.: Woman's Club, 189,n1; WW address, 189,n1
Sewickley Valley (newspaper), 189n1
Shaw, Albert, *3:214,n1; 35n1, 416-17
Shays, Daniel, 115, 117
Shepard, Edward Morse, 357,n5
Shields, Charles Woodruff, 326, 327, 329
Shinn, Charles Howard, *2:661,n1; 437
"Ship That Found Herself" (Kipling), 361
Short History of the English People (Green), 23
Shortz, Edwin, Jr., 231
Sifted Grain and the Grain Sifters: An Address at the Dedication of the Building of the State Historical Society of Wisconsin at Madison, October 19, 1900 (Adams), 63,n3
Sims, John Green, 100
Sloughter, Henry, 38, 39
Smith, Francis Henry, 287,n1
Smith, Francis Hopkinson, 93,n1
Smith, Herbert Stearns Squier, 200n2, 327
Smith, Victor, Mrs. (Saida Bird), 437,-n1
Smith, Wilton Merle, 326,n2
Smith College, 406
Snow, Cecil, 49,n1,2
Snow, Thomas L., 49-50, 73, 146-47, 370
A Soldier of Virginia: A Tale of Colonel Washington and Braddock's Defeat (Stevenson), 113,n2
Sophocles, 61, 151
Sothel, Seth, 38, 39
Southern Quarterly Review, 195
Southern Sidelight: A Picture of Social and Economic Life in the South a Generation Before the War (Ingle), 103,n1
Sparks, Jared, 39,n1

Spartanburg, S.C.: WW lecture, 203,-n1
"Speech on Moving His Resolutions for Conciliation with the Colonies, March 22, 1775" (Burke), 211-12,n2,3
Speirs, Frederick W., 179n
Spencer, Herbert, 246, 480
Sperry, Caroline, 359
Spruance, William Corbit, 422
Sprunt, James, 72,n1, 74,n1,3, 419; Mrs. (Luola Murchison), 74,n3
Sprunt, James Laurence, 419,n2
Sprunt, Marian Murchison, 419,n1
Stacy, William, 269
Standard Dictionary of the English Language, 267
Stanley, Edward Otis, Jr., 426,n2, 440-41
Stanley, Edward Otis, Sr., 426,n1, 440-41
Starr, William G., 305,n1
Steen, Robert Service, 100, 133, 141, 266,n2
Steiner, Bernard Christian, *6:523,n2; 412
Sterling Hotel, Wilkes-Barre, Pa., 231
Steuert, Frederick A., 305,n1, 344, 345, 346, 355, 359, 371, 378, 383
Stevenson, Burton Egbert, *113,n1
Stewart, George Black, 36n1, 435
Stewart, John Aikman (1822-1926), *7:602,n1; 200n1, 342,n1, 356, 370, 371, 373, 379, 380, 383, 386, 396, 398, 399, 400, 401, 474n1
Story, Joseph, 242
Strauch, Hermann, 109-10,n2, 134, 136
Strong, William, 51n3
Stryker, William Scudder, 5,n3
Sullivan, John, 209
Supreme Court: packing by President Grant, 1870, 50-51, 51-52, 58-59
Sutton, Robert Woods, 133
Swoboda, Alois P., 190-91,n1,2
Swofford, Ralph Powell, 141

Tabb, Thomas, 265
Tacitus, Cornelius, 250
Talcott, Charles Andrew, *1:240,n3; 205,n2, 206, 408-9
Tarde, Gabriel, 252,n7, 254,n9,10
Tarkington, Booth, 349
Taylor, James Monroe, 294,n1
Tedcastle, Arthur W., Mrs. (Agnes Vaughn), 117-18,n2, 118, 464,n4
Tennent, Gilbert, 394,n2
Tennent, William, Sr., 394,n2
Thayer, William Sydney, M.D., 418,n5
Thomas, Augustus, 93,n1
Thomas, George Cummins, 312
Thomas, John Peyre, 194
Thomas Joy and His Descendants (Joy), 307,n1
Thompson, Frederick Ferris, Mrs. (Mary Clark), 359,n1
Thompson, Henry Burling, *445,n2

Thompson, Henry Dallas, *7:565,n2; 185, 257
Thucydides, 61
Thwaites, Reuben Gold, 229
Thwing, Charles Franklin, 467
Tocqueville, Alexis Charles Henri Maurice Clérel de, 6, 71, 111,n3, 192
Todd, Alpheus, 242
Tome (Jacob) Institute, Port Deposit, Md., 443-44,n1
Toy, Crawford Howell, 458n1; Mrs. (Nancy Saunders), 458,n1
Trent, William Peterfield, *5:514,n1; 172,n1
Trenton, N.J.: Battle of, 125th anniversary, 208-9, 208n1, 216, 217, 463; Taylor Opera House, 208n, 208n1, 228, 463; Trenton House, 325; WW address, 326
Trenton Times, 326n
Trenton True American, 187, 188n
Triple Cheer, A Parting Song, Dedicated to the Students of Princeton, 402
Trotter, Edward Hough, 430,n1
Trowbridge, Stephen van Rensselaer, 154-55
Truehart, Alice Hoyt (Sal), first cousin of EAW, 129,n1, 131
Tulane University, 357,n6
Turner, Frederick Jackson, *6:58,n1; 102n1, 239-41, 264, 290n, 436, 473; Mrs. (Caroline Mae Sherwood), 436, 473
Tyler, Lyon Gardiner, 68-69

United States Military Academy: Princeton represented at centennial, 437-38
United States Steel Corporation, 458-59, 467

Vail, William Penn, 100
van Dyke, Dorothea, 119,n1
van Dyke, Henry [Jackson, Jr.], *10:9,-n2; 83, 99, 100, 116, 119n1, 125n1, 138, 145, 195, 312, 373, 374, 380, 408, 446, 449, 450-51n4, 456n2
van Dyke, Paul, 200n2, 326, 327, 374
Van Rensselaer, Alexander, 200n1, 474n1
Vanuxem, Louis Clark, 416
Vassar, Matthew, 359,n2
Vassar College, 294; Frederick Ferris Thompson Memorial Library, 359,-n1; WW Founder's Day address, 294, 359-63
Vaughan, Benjamin, 168
Venable, Francis Preston, 97,n1
Venezuelan boundary controversy, Grover Cleveland lectures on, 114-15, 116
Vienna *Neue freie Presse*, 161n
Virginia, University of, 93,n3, 231,n1, 276, 287, 328, 357, 402, 428, 430, 448, 466n2, 468, 470

Voorhees, Foster MacGowan, 158, 173,-n1,2
Vreeland, Williamson Updike, 290n6

Wagner, Adolf Heinrich Gotthilf, 85n4
Waites, Parker, 415
Wake Forest College, 357,n6
Walcott, Charles Doolittle, 282
Waldorf-Astoria Hotel, New York City, 58n1, 442
Wanamaker store, Philadelphia, 80, 128, 129
Ward, Adolphus William, 313,n2
Waring, Antonio Johnston, 368
Washington, George, 57, 67, 95, 96, 115, 117, 209, 211, 212, 217, 218,n5, 268, 273-74, 361, 382, 393; "Washington's Inauguration" (McMaster), 115,n1
Washington, D.C.: Willard's Hotel, 319, 320
Washington and Lee University, 69-70, 306
Waterbury, Conn.: Leavenworth Hall, 46; Women's Club, 46; WW lecture, 22n4, 44-48
Waterbury (Conn.) *American*, 48n
Waterbury (Conn.) *Republican*, 48n2
Webb, James Edward, 106-7
Weeks, William Raymond, 5,n4
Weems, Mason Locke, 270
Welch, Bradley Agard, 141
Welles, Edward Freeman, 417; Mrs. (Harriet Woodrow), 417-18, 462
Welles, Henry Hunter, Jr., 231
Wellford, Beverley Randolph, Jr., 433,-n1, 457
Wellington, Arthur Wellesley, 1st Duke of, 269
Wendell, Barrett, 428,n1
Wesleyan University, 442, 468; Alumni Association, 442,n2; Wesley Bicentennial Commemoration, 314,n1
West, Andrew Fleming, *6:528,n3; 24, 36n1, 152, 163, 200n2, 207, 235, 257, 286, 290n, 290n6, 291n, 292n, 306, 307, 326, 329, 331, 343, 402, 449, 450-51n4
Westcott, John Howell, *7:437,n1; 78, 200n2, 257, 290n6; Mrs. (Edith F. Sampson), 78, 406
Westminster Theological Seminary, 466n1
Weston, Alfred Sewall, 100, 101
Wheaton, Frank Woodruff, 231
Wheeler, Benjamin Ide, 283, 462,n2
Wheeler, Joseph, 270
White, Andrew Dickson, 281, 447
White, William R., Mrs. (Lillian Hoyt), first cousin of EAW, 129,n1, 131
Whitefield, George, 394,n3
Wikoff, James Holmes, M.D., 384
Wilder, William Royal, *1:253,n2; 412,n1, 430, 441-42
Wilhelm, J., 256n

Wilkes-Barre, Pa.: Hotel Sterling, 231; WW talk, 231

Willard's Hotel, Washington, D.C., 319, 320

Williams, Charles Richard, 359n8

Williams, Jesse Lynch, 74n1, 138, 456

Williams, John Rogers, *11:40-41,-n1,3,4; 5n5

Williams College, 156-57, 406; New York alumni dinner, 65

Wilmington, Del.: New Century Club, 21n1,7, 30,n1, 31, 39, 42; WW address, 41-44

Wilmington (Del.) *Every Evening*, 44n

Wilmington, N.C.: WW in, 74-75

Wilmington (N.C.) *Messenger*, 72,n2, 75n

Wilson, Edmund Beecher, 282

Wilson, Ellen Axson, 32, 35, 49, 59, 74-75, 75-76, 77, 78, 80-81, 82, 83, 86, 89, 93, 110, 117-19, 119-24, 125-30, 131, 132, 133, 137, 138, 139, 144, 146-47, 148, 149, 163, 189, 196, 198, 199, 203, 205,n2,3, 241, 273, 284, 314-15, 370, 390-91; Baltimore trip, 391n1, 392-93, 397; 402, 403, 405-6, 407, 408, 411, 412, 414, 416, 417, 418, 425, 428, 432, 433n4, 434, 436, 439, 440, 444-45, 447, 449, 452, 457, 458, 462, 463-64; vacation at Clifton, Mass., with Tedcastles, 464,n4; 465, 478

OPINIONS AND COMMENTS

We must leave our dear home and the sweet, almost ideal life when [WW] was a simple "man of letters" and go and live in that great, stately, troublesome "Prospect" . . . 464

Wilson, Eleanor Randolph (Nellie), daughter of EAW and WW (afterwards Mrs. William Gibbs McAdoo), *6:407,n1; 119, 127, 128, 391

Wilson, James Grant, 40,n2

Wilson, Jessie Woodrow, daughter of WW and EAW (afterwards Mrs. Francis Bowes Sayre), *5:565,n1; 59; operation in Philadelphia Orthopaedic Hospital, 117-24, 125-30, 131, 133, 163

Wilson, John (c. 1591-1667), 55

Wilson, John Glover, 421-22

Wilson, Joseph R., Jr. (Dode, Josie), brother of WW, *1:3,n8; 105-6

Wilson, Joseph Ruggles, father of WW, *1:3,n1; 28n3, 52; illness, 71, 72, 74; 75, 76, 78, 80, 81, 83, 89, 91, 98, 127, 130, 144, 147, 148, 149, 153, 159, 160, 163, 284, 414n1, 418, 419, 457, 464, 465

Wilson, Margaret, daughter of WW and EAW, 123, 127, 128, 391n1, 393,n2, 463,n1

Wilson, William Lyne, 69, 306,n2

WOODROW WILSON

boyhood residence, 440,n3

AND ELLEN AXSON WILSON

My devotion to you, my darling, becomes a deeper and deeper passion with me every day of my life, 75

APPEARANCE

Pirie MacDonald photograph, 1902, 417

fine full-page portrait in *Harper's Weekly*, June 21, 1902, 464

BIOGRAPHY

Robert Bridges article, "President Woodrow Wilson," in *Review of Reviews*, July 1902; text, 468-73

FAMILY LIFE AND DOMESTIC AFFAIRS

Summer vacation at Judd Haven, Muskoka district, Ontario, 1900, 4n1, 89, purchases land there, 49-50,n1,2, 73, 89, 91, 370; proposed sabbatical (1901/02), 27-28, 51, 68, 74, 83, 89, 104, 130; telephone out of order, 78; summer vacation, 1901, at Heimera, Rosseau Falls, Ontario, 147n2

HEALTH

inflamed throat, 44

OPINIONS AND COMMENTS

Ease and prosperity have made us wish the whole world to be as happy and well to do as ourselves; and we have supposed that institutions and principles like our own were the simple prescription for making them so, 12

Methods of electoral choice and administrative organization, which served us admirably well while the nation was homogeneous and rural, serve us oftentimes ill enough now [1900] that the nation is heterogeneous and crowded into cities, 16

government of France, 217-18

government of England, 219f

. . . we have been doing some very ridiculous things in this country. It is becoming a habit in a great many of our public schools to go through the elaborate performance of worshipping the flag of the United States, 260

Practical politics is getting what you can by co-operation, and co-operation is yielding to too many dull fellows, 263

We have bred in this country a race of subtle lawyers, and they read the statutes very subtlely, and you cannot frame a law in American grammar and punctuation, but he can get out of it and drive a coach and six horses through it, and then he

Woodrow Wilson, cont.
will make you believe that was the law which was meant, 263-64
Basil Lanneau Gildersleeve, a radically vain man, 272
It is sentimental to withhold the infliction of the death penalty. Society is of more importance than the individual, and the man that has injured society by a foul murder should hang for it, 353

PRINCETON UNIVERSITY

Chapel Stage Oration, "Richard Cobden—An Historical Lesson," delivered Nov. 2, 1878, mentioned, 470,n4; address at mass meeting in the interest of Whig and Clio Halls, Oct. 12, 1900, notes, 23, news report, 24; proposed sabbatical for 1901/02, 27-28, 51, 68, 74, 83, 89, 104, 130; presentation of John Hay for LL.D. degree at convocation, Oct. 20, 1900, 28,n1,2; "The Principles of Rectitude," address to Philadelphian Society, Nov. 15, 1900, announcement, 33, notes, 33-34, news report, 34; unable to meet classes: inflamed throat, 44; WW classes suspended during absence at the south, 80; member of committee of American Whig Society to abrogate treaty with Cliosophic Society on recruiting, 96-97,n2; response to toast, "Princeton University," at *Daily Princetonian* banquet, Princeton Inn, March 1, 1901, news report, 100; judge of preliminary trials for debate with Yale, March 30, 1901, 100; speech at Whig Hall smoker, March 1901, mentioned, 108; address on de Tocqueville before Monday Night Club, March 18, 1901, news report, 111; introduction of Grover Cleveland as Stafford Little lecturer, Alexander Hall, March 27, 1901, 114-15,n1,2, 116; judge in final trials for Harvard debate of May 10, 1901, 132; response to toast, "The College Man in Journalism," at University Press Club banquet, Princeton Inn, April 30, 1901, news notice, 138, notes, 139; address on Gladstone to Philadelphian Society, May 2, 1901, news report, 139-40; member of faculty committee to appear before and confer with Trustees if required, 155, 156, 205,n1, 286, 287, 309, 315, 398; presents candidates for honorary degrees at Commencement, 1901, 158; appointed to faculty committee on the Graduate School, 185, appears before Trustees, 191, 192; remarks at a special convocation following the assassination of President McKinley, Alexander Hall, Sept. 19,

Woodrow Wilson, cont.
1901, text, 185-87; delegate to 25th anniversary of the founding of Johns Hopkins University and inauguration of President Ira Remsen, 256; "The Christian in Public Life," talk before Philadelphian Society, Feb. 20, 1902, notes, 273, news report, 273-74; "Princeton Men in Public Life," talk at *Daily Princetonian* dinner, Princeton Inn, March 4, 1902, notes, 285, news report, 285-86; conducts vesper service in Marquand Chapel, March 9, 1902, notice, 286, notes, 286-87; addresses nocturnal celebration following debating victory over Harvard, March 26, 1902, mentioned, 312; "A Lawyer with a Style [Sir Henry Maine]" (printed 1898), read to Monday Night Club, April 14, 1902, news report, 330-31; "The Value of *The Nassau Literary Magazine*," remarks at the annual Lit banquet, Princeton Inn, May 12, 1902, mentioned, 369; presents candidates for LL.D. and Hon. A.M. at Commencement, 1902, 370, 375-76, 378, 380; memorandum on proposed changes in the curriculum, 391-92; remarks at alumni luncheon, June 10, 1902, text, 420-21

THE PRINCETON PRESIDENCY

candidacy mentioned, 374n4, 380, 390,-n2
involvement in Patton retirement, 288-89, 297, 302, 304, 305, 310-11, 312-13, 314, 315, 317-18, 320, 321-23, 326, 330, 339, 340, 341, 343, 345, 346, 364
nominated for President, 401
elected 13th President by unanimous vote of Trustees, June 9, 1902, 401; vote mentioned, 457
notification of election, and acceptance, 402
remarks at alumni luncheon, June 10, 420-21
letters of congratulation from Samuel Alexander, 455-56,n1; Daniel Moreau Barringer, 430; A. Elizabeth Wilson Begges, 414,n1; Sarah Baxter Bird, 437; Alexander Scott Bullitt, 405,n1; Jesse Benedict Carter, 466-67; Jabez Lamar Monroe Curry, 448,n1; Frederick Morgan Davenport, 442-43,n1; Alfred Lewis Dennis, Jr., 403; Samuel Bayard Dod, 457-58,n1; Franklin Woolman D'Olier, 452-53,n1; Edith Duer, 409,n1; William Archibald Dunning, 403; Edward Graham Elliott, 431-32; Richard Theodore Ely, 402; Robert Ewing, 424; David Fentress, 438-39,n1; John Franklin Fort, 454; Abel McIver Fraser, 404,-n1; Daniel Coit Gilman, 447; Harold

Woodrow Wilson, cont.
Godwin, 404; Elgin Ralston Lovell
Gould, 430,n1; Albert Bushnell Hart,
404-5; Azel Washburn Hazen, 413-
14; Daniel Collamore Heath, 419;
Robert Randolph Henderson, 431;
John Bell Henneman, 425,n1; James
Alfred Hoyt, 425; Laurence Hutton,
407; William Burhans Isham, Jr.,
407; Thomas Armstrong Jacobs,
438,n1; Adrian Hoffman Joline, 409;
Frank Hathaway Kemper, 409-10,n1;
Edgar Odell Lovett, 402; Alfred
James Pollock McClure, 410,n1,2;
John James McCook, 437-38; Charles
Wolf McFee, 413,n1; Mary Gresham
Machen, 465-66; Charles Howard
McIlwain, 452,n1; St. Clair McKel-
way, 449-50,n1; William Francis
Magie, 448-49; Elmer Truesdell Mer-
rill, 414-15; James Cowden Meyers,
411,n1; Franklin Murphy, 454-55;
Charles Richard Nisbet, 432,n1;
Frank Mason North, 408,n1,2; John
H. Pearson, 415; Mrs. Bliss Perry,
405-6; William Battle Phillips, 442,-
n1; Bowdre Phinizy, 416,n1; Francis
Southmayd Phraner, 411,n1; Percy
Rivington Pyne, 445,n1; Edith Git-
tings Reid, 453-54; Legh Wilbur
Reid, 412,n1; Ira Remsen, 447-48;
James Ford Rhodes, 465; William
Henry Roberts, 446,n1; Theodore
Roosevelt, 454; Albert Shaw, 416-17;
Charles Howard Shinn, 437,n1;
James Sprunt, 419; Edward Otis Stan-
ley, Sr., 426,n1; Bernard Christian
Steiner, 412; George Black Stewart,
435; Charles Andrew Talcott, 408-9;
Nancy Saunders Toy, 458,n1; Henry
van Dyke, 408; Louis Clark Van-
uxem, 416; Harriet Woodrow Welles,
417-18; Beverley Randolph Wellford,
Jr., 433; Helen Sill Woodrow, 418;
James Woodrow, 417; Lawrence
Crane Woods, 420,n1
inauguration plans: "Coronation Com-
mittee" of Class of 1879, 441,n2
WW and New York *Sun* articles on
presidency, 450-51,n4, 456n2

PROFESSIONAL ACTIVITIES AND
CAREER

member of publication committee of
Princeton Historical Association, 5
mentioned for presidency of Johns
Hopkins University, 35,n1
presidency of Washington and Lee
University proposed and declined,
69-70
presidency of University of Alabama
offered and declined, 106-7,n2,3
declines invitation to lecture at University of Chicago in summer of
1901, 111-12

Woodrow Wilson, cont.
sounded out for presidency of Williams College, 156-57
member of New Jersey Commission for
the Promotion of Uniformity of Legislation in the United States, 173,n2,
187
offered professorship at Johns Hopkins,
108,n1; declines, 110-11, 112, 175
declines invitation of Democrats to run
for state senator in Mercer County,
189-90,n2
Litt.D. degree conferred at Yale Bicentennial, Oct. 23, 1901, 193, 194
declines invitation of Albert Bushnell
Hart and Harper & Brothers to contribute to American Nation Series,
229, 230, 231-32, 232-34, 234-35
LL.D. degree conferred by Johns Hopkins at 25th anniversary celebration,
Feb. 22, 1902, 282, 284
suggested for presidency of the U.S.
in letter to *Indianapolis News*, May
5, 1902, 357-58
elected president of Princeton University, June 9, 1902, 401; mentioned,
457
LL.D. degree conferred by Rutgers College, June 18, 1902, 445
declines invitation to teach at University of California in summer of
1902, 462

PUBLIC ADDRESSES AND LECTURES

"Leaders of Men" (1889 and later),
mentioned, 21,n6; text, Vol. 6, 646-
71
"Democracy" (1891 and later), mentioned, 21,n7, text, Vol. 7, 345-68
"Political Liberty" (1895), mentioned,
21,n3. See Index to Vol. 9
"On Being Human" (1897); mentioned, 84; text, Vol. 10, 245-59
"Princeton in the Nation's Service"
(1896); mentioned, 84; text, Vol. 10,
11-31
"A Wit and a Seer [Bagehot]" (1898);
mentioned, 84; text, Vol. 10, 423-42
"A Lawyer with a Style [Sir Henry
Maine]" (1898); mentioned, 84; 330-
31; text, Vol. 10, 443-61
"Nationality," *see* "What It Means to
Be an American" (1900), *below*

"What It Means to Be an American,"
address at the Hill School, Pottstown, Pa., Feb. 22, 1900; mentioned,
21,n5, 42
"Americanism," address at the New-
Century Club, Wilmington, Del.,
Dec. 6, 1900; notes, 41; newspaper
report, 42-44; mentioned, 21,n7
"Self-Government," lecture at Women's
Club, Waterbury, Conn., Dec. 12,
1900; mentioned, 22n4; notes, 44-45;
newspaper report, 46-48

Woodrow Wilson, cont.

After-dinner speech to the New England Society in the City of New York, Dec. 22, 1900; text, 52-58; mentioned, 58, 66, 75,n1

Six lectures on "Great Leaders of Political Thought" [Aristotle, Machiavelli, Montesquieu, Burke, de Tocqueville, and Bagehot], delivered under the auspices of the American Society for the Extension of University Teaching in Witherspoon Hall, Philadelphia, Jan. 9-Feb. 13, 1901; news notices, 67, 71; mentioned, 92,n2, 93, 111,n3. *See Index to Vol. 9*

After-dinner speech before the Pennsylvania Scotch-Irish Society of Philadelphia, Feb. 21, 1901; noticed, 67,n2

"What It Means to Be an American," address at Lawrenceville School, Feb. 22, 1901; mentioned, 67,n3; news report, 98-99

Introduction of Grover Cleveland as Stafford Little Lecturer at Princeton, Alexander Hall, March 27, 1901; text, 114-15,n1,2; news report, 116

After-dinner speech before the St. Nicholas Society, Delmonico's, New York, April 8, 1901; notes, 124,n1, 125

"Americanism," address to the Woman's Club, Sewickley, Pa., Oct. 3, 1901; mentioned, 189,n1

Lecture before Wofford College Lyceum, Spartanburg, S.C., Nov. 28, 1901; mentioned, 203,n1

Lecture on "Patriotism" before the Greenville Lyceum Association at Grand Opera House, Greenville, S.C., Nov. 29, 1901; newspaper notices, 203-4

"The Ideals of America," address at the Literary Exercises commemorating the 125th anniversary of the Battle of Trenton, Taylor Opera House, Trenton, N.J., Dec. 26, 1901; text, 208-27; mentioned, 208, 227-28, 463,n2

"What It Means to Be an American," lecture at Rajah Temple, Reading, Pa., Jan. [16], 1902; newspaper report, 238-39

"What It Means to Be an American," lecture before the Peninsula Twentieth Century Club, Fort Monroe, Va., Jan. 24, 1902; mentioned, 265,n1

Address to the students of Hampton Institute, Hampton, Va., Jan. 25, 1902; mentioned, 265,n1

"Patriotism," address to the Worcester Woman's Club, Association Hall, Worcester, Mass., Jan. 29, 1902; mentioned, 192; news report, 258-64

Speech on Abraham Lincoln before the Lincoln Association of Jersey City,

Woodrow Wilson, cont.

Jersey City Club, Feb. 12, 1902; news report, 267-71; mentioned, 271, 306-7,n1

Address in presenting a testimonial volume from the faculty and alumni to Daniel Coit Gilman upon his retirement as president of The Johns Hopkins University, Music Hall, Baltimore, Feb. 21, 1902; text, 274-77; news report, 278-80; mentioned, 347,n2,3

Speech before the Union County (N.J.) alumni of Princeton, Park Avenue Hotel, Plainfield, N.J., March 20, 1902; notes, 301-2; news report, 312

"The Ideal Princeton Student," remarks at a dinner of Princeton alumni, Trenton House, Trenton, N.J., April 8, 1902; notes, 325; mentioned, 326

Response to toast, "The University of Virginia," at Virginia alumni dinner, New York City, April 12, 1902; notes, 328,n1,2

"The *Man* and the Man of *Letters* (or the *Scholar*)," lecture at Lake Forest College, Illinois, April 24, 1902; notes, 348

Address to Chicago alumni of Princeton, University Club, Chicago, April 24, 1902; news report, 288, 348-49

"What It Means to Be an American," address to the Contemporary Club, Indianapolis, April 25, 1902; news report, 351-54; mentioned, 174, 190, 200, 349

"The Teaching of Patriotism in Schools," address to Indianapolis teachers at Benjamin Harrison School, April 26, 1902; news report, 350-51

"Americanism," Founder's Day address at Vassar College, May 2, 1902; invitation, 294; news report, 359-63

Remarks on the retirement of Mrs. Laurence Hutton at the meeting of the Village Improvement Society, Princeton, May 20, 1902; reported, 384

"Religion and Patriotism," talk delivered at the Northfield Student Conference July 4, 1902; text, 474-78; mentioned, 66n4

"John Wesley's Place in History," mentioned, 314-n1; text in Vol. 14

READING

Authors and works read, cited, alluded to, etc.

Charles Francis Adams (1835-1915), *The Sifted Grain and the Grain Sifters: An Address at the Dedication of the Building of the State His-*

Woodrow Wilson, cont.
torical Society of Wisconsin at Madison, October *19, 1900,* 63,n3
Henry Adams, 61; "The Session, 1869-70," 50-51
George Ade, *Fables in Slang,* 228,n1, 234
Aesop's Fables, 269
William Harrison Ainsworth, 61
Aristotle, 71
Walter Bagehot, 71, 92, 200, 301, 325, 365, 470
George Bancroft, 61
Thomas Hart Benton, *Abridgement of the Debates of Congress from 1789 to 1856,* 194
Francis Bowen, "Life of Sir William Phips," 39,n1
Robert Bridges, *Bramble Brae,* 294,n1; "Prayer of Old Age," 65,n2
William Cullen Bryant and Sydney Howard Gay, *A Popular History of the United States,* 40,n3
John Bunyan, *Pilgrim's Progress,* 269
Edmund Burke, 71, 84,n2, 86, 87, 213, 221, 470, 477; *Reflections on the Revolution in France,* 45,n1, 46, 217-18,n4; "Speech on Moving His Resolution for Conciliation with the Colonies, March 22, 1775," 211-12,n2,3; *Works of the Right Honorable Edmund Burke,* 45,n1, 211-12,n2,3
James Caldwell Calhoun, *The Correspondence of John C. Calhoun* (ed. Jameson), 194; *The Works of John C. Calhoun,* 194
Thomas Chalmers, "The Expulsive Power of a New Affection," 55,n5; *The Select Works of Thomas Chalmers, D.D., LL.D.,* 55,n5
Varnum Lansing Collins, ed., *A Brief Narrative of the Ravages of the British and Hessians at Princeton in 1776-77,* 5n5
Seymour Eaton and Frederic W. Speirs, *Problems in Modern Democracy,* 179n
Ralph Waldo Emerson, 351
Adele Marion Fielde, *Political Primer of New York City and State; The City Under the Revised Charter of 1902,* 293,n4
John Fiske, 62, 112, 113; *The American Revolution,* 85,n1, 138; *The Beginnings of New England,* 85,n1; *The Critical Period of American History, 1783-1789,* 85,n1; *Old Virginia and Her Neighbors,* 85,n1
Philip Vickers Fithian: Journal and Letters (ed. Williams), 5,n5
Edward Augustus Freeman, 61, 62, 63
Philip Freneau, *The Poems of Philip Freneau, Poet of the American Revolution* (ed. Pattee), 5n5
James Anthony Froude, 61
Edward Gibbon, 61

Woodrow Wilson, cont.
John Franklin Genung, *The Working Principles of Rhetoric Examined in Their Literary Relations,* 143,n1
Rudolf von Gneist, 15
John Richard Green, 61, 62, 64
Harper's Encyclopædia of United States History, 184n
Richard Hildreth, 61
George Frisbie Hoar, *The Charge against President Grant and Attorney General Hoar of Packing the Supreme Court of the United States, to Secure the Reversal of the Legal Tender Decision, by the Appointment of Judges Bradley and Strong, Refuted,* 50,n3
Hermann Eduard von Holst, *John C. Calhoun,* 195
Thomas Hooker, 177, 178
David Franklin Houston, *A Critical Study of Nullification in South Carolina,* 196
David Hume, 61
Laurence Hutton, *Literary Landmarks of Oxford,* 92, 101
Edward Ingle, 94-95,n1,2, 102-3, 171, 440; *Captain Richard Ingle, the Maryland "Pirate and Rebel," 1642-1653,* 163, 164; *Southern Sidelights: A Picture of Social and Economic Life in the South a Generation Before the War,* 103,n1
Thomas Jefferson, 13
John Stilwell Jenkins, *The Life of John Caldwell Calhoun,* 194
Johns Hopkins University, *Celebration of the Twenty-Fifth Anniversary of the Founding of the University and Inauguration of Ira Remsen, LL.D. as President of the University,* 277n; *Herbert B. Adams: Tributes of Friends, with a Bibliography of the Department of History, Politics, and Economics of the Johns Hopkins University, 1876-1901,* 175n2, 265n1
James Richard Joy, *Thomas Joy and His Descendants,* 307,n1
John Keats, "On First Looking into Chapman's Homer," 328,n3
Rudyard Kipling, "The Ship That Found Herself," 361
Andrew Lang, "The Early History of the Family," 480-85
Orin Grant Libby, *The Geographical Distribution of the Vote of the Thirteen States on the Federal Constitution, 1787-8,* 102,n2
John Locke, 177, 178
Thomas Babington Macaulay, 1st Baron Macaulay, 61
Niccolò Machiavelli, 71
John Bach McMaster, 61-62
Sir Henry James Sumner Maine, *Ancient Law,* 331, 484-85
Charles de Secondat, Baron de La

Woodrow Wilson, cont.
Brède et de Montesquieu, 10, 71
John Morley, Viscount Morley, *Edmund Burke*, 87
Walter Hines Page, "Dumb and Formless Scholarship," 88,n1
Francis Parkman, 61
Pater, Walter, 354
Christophe Plantin, "Le Bonheur de ce monde," 65n1
John Duncan Quackenbos, "Educational Uses of Hypnotism," 22,n2; "The Moral Value of Hypnotic Suggestion," 22,n2
James Ford Rhodes, 62
Dante Gabriel Rossetti, "The Blessed Damozel," 354
Jean-Jacques Rousseau, 178, 181
Sophocles, 61
South Carolina, General Assembly, *The Death and Funeral Ceremonies of John Caldwell Calhoun*, 194
Jared Sparks, ed., *Library of American Biography*, 39,n1
Burton Egbert Stevenson, *A Soldier of Virginia: A Tale of Colonel Washington and Braddock's Defeat*, 113,n2
John Peyre Thomas, *The Carolina Tribute to Calhoun*, 194
Thucydides, 61
Alexis Charles Henri Maurice Clérel de Tocqueville, 6, 71; *Democracy in America*, 111,n3
George Washington, *Farewell Address*, 57; *The Writings of George Washington* (ed. Ford), 218n5
Mason Locke Weems, *The Life and Memorable Actions of George Washington*, 269-70
James Grant Wilson, ed., *Memorial History of the City of New-York*, 40,n2
Justin Winsor, 62; ed., *Narrative and Critical History of America*, 40,n1, 41, 49, 194, 229

RELIGIOUS LIFE

addresses Class of 1904 prayer meeting in Dodge Hall, Sunday, April 14, 1901, 132; conducts vesper service in Marquand Chapel, March 9, 1902, 286-87; made member of standing committee on the Historical Society by New Brunswick Presbytery, 328; appointed member of the Assembly's Special Committee on Sustentation of the Presbyterian Church, but declined, 446,n2,4; "Religion and Patriotism," talk delivered at the Northfield Student Conference, July 4, 1902, text, 474-78

SELF-ANALYSIS

Plenty of people offer me their friendship; but, partly because I am reserved and shy, and partly because I am fastidious and have a narrow,

Woodrow Wilson, cont.
un-catholic taste in friends, I reject the offer in almost every case . . . 272

WRITINGS

autographed set of WW writings presented to C. H. McCormick, 145
proposed volume of essays (not published), 86,n1; table of contents, 84
use of English spelling-forms given up at request of Harper & Brothers, 267,n1

―――――

"American History and Historians," commentary and critique printed in the Editor's Study, *Harper's Magazine*, Jan. 1901; mentioned, 22, 23; text, 60-64
"Cabinet Government in the United States" (1879); mentioned, 470,n2; text, Vol. 1, 493-510
"Colonies and Nation," *see A History of the American People*
Congressional Government (1885): C. Bradley on error in, 50-51,n2,3, 51-52, 58-59,n1,2; mentioned, 242, 424; sales, 265; text, Vol. 4, 13-179
"Democracy and Efficiency," *Atlantic Monthly* article (written 1900, published March 1901); mentioned, 3, 4, 22n4; text, 6-20; illustration from shorthand draft, 21; proofs, 78,n3
Division and Reunion, 1829-1889 (1893); mentioned, 102, 229,n2, 240, 471
"Edmund Burke and the French Revolution" (written 1897-98, published 1901); mentioned, 84, 84n2, 86; text, Vol. 10, 408-23
George Washington (1897; copyright Dec. 17, 1896); mentioned, 29, 193, 471
A History of the American People (1902); SERIAL PUBLICATION as "Colonies and Nation" in *Harper's Magazine*, Jan.-Dec. 1901: editorial correspondence on installments, 5-6, 23, 27, 37, 49, 60, 85, 90,n1, 91-92, 94; illustrations, 5-6, 22, 23, 29-30, 31, 37, 38, 39, 40-41, 49, 69, 90, 91-92, 95-96, 97, 103, 103-4, 115, 117; mentioned, 38, 62, 65,n2, 66-67, 73, 75, 81, 82-83, 91, 94-95, 98, 134, 135, 141-42, 143, 146, 174, 206, 240, 471-72; BOOK PUBLICATION: title chosen, 206, 207-8; editorial correspondence, 134, 142-43, 146, 155, 206, 207-8, 234, 285, 307, 313; illustrated edition suggested, 23; illustrations, 134, 142, 155, 174, 206, 313, 439-40, 446, 473; mentioned, 65n2, 135, 163, 174-75, 239, 240, 267n1, 391, 428, 429, 471-72, 473, 478; Editorial Note, Vol. 11, 360-365. *See also Index to Vol. 11*
"History of the United States for

Woodrow Wilson, cont.
Schools" (projected and abandoned); mentioned, 83; Editorial Note, Vol. 10, 318-20. *See also Index to Vol. 10*
Introduction to John Bigelow edition of the *Autobiography of Benjamin Franklin* (1901); text, 164-70
"The Making of the Nation" (1897); mentioned (as "The Making of the Union"), 84; text, Vol. 10, 217-36
Memorandum on Leadership, May 5, 1902, 365
Mere Literature and Other Essays (1896); mentioned, 63, 472; sales, 265
"Mr. Cleveland as President" (1897); mentioned, 84; text, Vol. 10, 102-19
An Old Master, and Other Political Essays (1893); mentioned, 472
"On the Writing of History," *see* "The Truth of the Matter"
"The Philosophy of Politics" (projected); mentioned, 27,n1, 49,n1, 67-68, 232,n1, 233, 235, 240
"The Real Idea of Democracy: A Talk," political essay (1901); text, 175-79
"The Reconstruction of the Southern States" (1901); mentioned, 4,n1, 81; text, Vol. 11, 459-79
"Short History of the United States" (projected); mentioned, 48,n1, 49; Editorial Note, Vol. 8, 279-81. *See Index to Vol. 10*
"The Significance of American History," preface to *Harper's Encyclopædia of United States History* (1902); text, 179-84
The State (1889); mentioned, 102, 471; French translation by J. Wilhelm, *L'État: Éléments d'histoire & de pratique politique* (1902), mentioned, 81,n1,2, 256n; preface by Léon Duguit, 241-56
"State Rights (1850-1860)," chapter in *Cambridge Modern History* (written 1899, published 1903); mentioned, 313; proof and bibliography, 443; text, Vol. 11, 303-48
"The Truth of the Matter" (1895), also entitled "On the Writing of History," quoted, 63-64,n4; mentioned, 144n1; text, Vol. 9, 293-305
"When a Man Comes to Himself" (written 1899, published 1901); mentioned, 84, 157, 158; text, Vol. 11, 263-73

Winans, Samuel Ross, 36n1, 78, 200n2, 257, 290n, 307, 326, 327, 329, 331, 369, 373,n1; Mrs. (Sarah E. Macdonald), 78
Winchester, Caleb Thomas, *5:753,n1; 314-15; Mrs. (Alice Goodwin Smith), 314-15
Winn, Mary (May), 123,n1, 129
Winship, George Parker, 65
Winsor, Justin, 40,n1, 41, 49, 62, 194, 229
Wissowa, Georg, 150,n3, 151
Wofford College, Spartanburg, S.C., 203,n1
Wood, Charles, 474n1
Wood, Edward Jenner, M.D., 419,n3
Wood, Thomas, F., M.D., 419n3
Woodrow, Helen, first cousin of WW, 418,n3
Woodrow, James, maternal uncle of WW, *1:41,n1; 88-89, 417; Mrs. (Felexiana Shepherd Baker), 89,n3
Woodrow, James (Princeton 1909), 89n
Woodrow, James Wilson, first cousin of WW, 104-5,n1,3, 159, 160, 171-72, 172-73, 418n4; Mrs. (Nancy Mann Waddel), 171-72,n1, 172-73
Woodrow, Thomas, Jr., maternal uncle of WW, *1:39,n1,11; 104, 105n1; Mrs. (Helen Sill), 105n1, 392,n1, 418,n2, 418, 462
Woodrow, Wilson, Mrs., *see* Woodrow, James Wilson, Mrs.
Woodrow Wilson: Life and Letters (Baker), 196n, 359n8
Woodrow Wilson: The Academic Years (Bragdon), 200n2, 470n4
Woodrow Wilson, the Dreamer and the Dream (Knight), 432n3
Woodruff, Robert Spencer, 189,n1
Woods, Edward Augustus, 157,n1, 189; Mrs. (Gertrude Macrum), 189,n2
Woods, Lawrence Crane, 420,n1
Worcester, Mass.: Association Hall, 258; Worcester Club, 264; Worcester Woman's Club, 192, 258; WW address, 192, 258-64
Worcester (Mass.) Daily Telegram, 264n
Working Principles of Rhetoric Examined in Their Literary Relations (Genung), 143,n1
Works of John C. Calhoun, 194
Works of the Right Honorable Edmund Burke, 45,n1
Wright, Carroll Davidson, 293
Writings of George Washington (ed. Ford), 218n5
Wyckoff, Walter Augustus, 327
Wyman, William Stokes, 107n3

Yale Alumni Weekly, 194n2
Yale University, 275, 458; Bicentennial, Oct. 1901, 193-94; debate with Princeton, March 30, 1901, 100-1, victory celebration, 115-16; football game with Princeton (1900), 35,n2, 66; *Yale Daily News*, 99; *Yale Literary Magazine*, 140-41, 368
Young, Charles Augustus, 290n, 326, 327; Mrs. (Augusta Mixer), 75,-n2,3, 78
Young, Lawrence Andrew, 349
Young, Miss (at Canadian resort), 147